THE OFFICIAL HISTORY OF AUSTRALIA IN THE WAR OF 1914-1918

VOLUME VIII
THE AUSTRALIAN FLYING CORPS

THE
AUSTRALIAN FLYING CORPS
IN THE
WESTERN AND EASTERN
THEATRES OF WAR
1914–1918

BY
F. M. CUTLACK

With 32 maps and 54 illustrations

The Naval & Military Press Ltd

published in association with

**FIREPOWER
The Royal Artillery Museum**
Woolwich

Published by
The Naval & Military Press Ltd
Unit 10 Ridgewood Industrial Park,
Uckfield, East Sussex,
TN22 5QE England
Tel: +44 (0) 1825 749494
Fax: +44 (0) 1825 765701
www.naval-military-press.com

in association with

FIREPOWER
The Royal Artillery Museum, Woolwich
www.firepower.org.uk

In reprinting in facsimile from the original, any imperfections are inevitably reproduced and the quality may fall short of modern type and cartographic standards.

"The heavens are their battlefields. They are the cavalry of the clouds. High above the squalor and the mud . . . . . their struggles there by day and night are like a Miltonic conflict between the winged hosts."—Mr. LLOYD GEORGE on the Vote of Thanks to the Flying Service in House of Commons, November, 1919.

PREFACE

THE main source of information for this war history of the Australian Flying Corps has been the official diaries of the four Australian flying squadrons in the archives of the Australian War Museum. Yet those diaries do not supply an adequate story. The records of the Half-Flight in Mesopotamia, for instance, can hardly be said to exist at all. The author is greatly indebted, as regards that part of his narrative, to the excellent notes written for his guidance by Captain T. W. White, second-in-command of that unit.

For the war-theatre of Egypt and Palestine (No. 1 Squadron), particularly during the early twelve months of the squadron in the desert east of the Suez Canal, the author has had access to the private diaries of Lieutenant-Colonel R. Williams, who served in that unit as flight-commander and squadron-commander. This personal record has proved very helpful. He also owes great thanks to Colonel Williams, the late Lieutenant-Colonel W. O. Watt, and Major A. Murray Jones, sometime flight-commanders in the squadron, and to Major T. F. Rutledge, sometime squadron-commander, who read his manuscript and helped him with their comments.

In the European section, containing the story of Nos. 2, 3, and 4 Squadrons, he is indebted to the late Lieutenant-Colonel Watt, Major Murray Jones, and Lieutenant E. R. Dibbs, of No. 2 Squadron, to Major D. V. J. Blake, of No. 3 Squadron, and to Captain G. F. Malley and Captain A. H. Cobby, of No. 4 Squadron, for reading the manuscript and for their notes, which were of great value, on obscure points. The author had the advantage of personal acquaintance with some of the work of the three squadrons in France during 1918.

Captain Andrew Lang's invaluable notes on types and development of aircraft in the British, French, and German services are published in a special appendix. To Lieutenants H. Johnston and J. J. Malone are due the notes on the development of the use of wireless telegraphy in aircraft.

PREFACE

The books published on the war in the air from the earliest days in 1914 till the beginning of the defeat of the German armies on the western front are already numerous. They are in no sense histories, but, being personal narratives by prominent airmen, British, French, American, and German, they contain some amount of historical material. Among those which the author has consulted he would mention:—*The Royal Flying Corps in the War,* by "Wing Adjutant"; *Aviation in Peace and War,* by Major-General Sir Frederick Sykes, late Chief of the Air Staff; *The Romance of Aircraft,* by Laurence Yard Smith; *Winged Warfare,* by Lieutenant-Colonel W. A. Bishop, V.C., D.S.O., M.C.; *Five Years in the Royal Flying Corps,* by the late Major J. T. McCudden, V.C.; *Guynemer, Knight of the Air,* by Henri Bordeaux; *The Red Air Fighter,* by Baron von Richthofen (edited by C. G. Grey); *With the French Flying Corps,* by Carroll Dana Winslow; *In the Air: Three Years on and above Three Fronts,* by Lieutenant Bert Hall; *Captain Ball, V.C.,* by W. A. Briscoe and H. Stannard; *Tails Up; Everyday Life of Our Airmen,* by Edgar Middleton; and *The German Air Force in the Great War,* compiled by Major Georg Paul Neumann.

F. M. C.

SYDNEY,
 1st January, 1923.

CONTENTS

	INTRODUCTION: THE FLYING ARM IN WAR	xv
I.	MESOPOTAMIA—THE FIRST AUSTRALIAN AIRMEN ON SERVICE	1
II.	MESOPOTAMIA—THE END OF THE FIRST CAMPAIGN	14
III.	THE MIDDLE EAST—ADVENT OF No. 1 SQUADRON	29
IV.	AIR FIGHTING IN THE DESERT	43
V.	INCREASING IMPORTANCE OF AIR WARFARE	56
VI.	THE VICTORY OF GAZA	69
VII.	THE TURKISH RETREAT TO NABLUS	82
VIII.	BEGINNING OF THE AIR OFFENSIVE	92
IX.	THE RAIDS ACROSS THE JORDAN	105
X.	GROWING BRITISH SUPREMACY IN THE AIR	121
XI.	THE ENEMY DRIVEN FROM THE SKY	133
XII.	THE BATTLE OF ARMAGEDDON	151
XIII.	AUSTRALIAN AIRMEN IN FRANCE	172
XIV.	CAMBRAI AND GOUZEAUCOURT	183
XV.	WINTER WORK OVER MESSINES RIDGE	198
XVI.	SPRING FIGHTS NORTH OF THE SCARPE	213
XVII.	MEETING THE GERMAN OFFENSIVE	228
XVIII.	EARLY CIRCUS FIGHTS WITH No. 2 SQUADRON	247
XIX.	No. 3 SQUADRON'S OPERATIONS OVER THE SOMME	260
XX.	EXPLOITS OF No. 4 SQUADRON OVER THE LYS	276
XXI.	HARASSING THE ENEMY ON THE LYS	291
XXII.	THE BRITISH OFFENSIVE ON THE SOMME	305

CONTENTS

XXIII.	THE BATTLES IN THE HINDENBURG LINE	319
XXIV.	THE LILLE AIR RAIDS	337
XXV.	FIGHTS OF THE SWEEP FORMATIONS	352
XXVI.	THE LAST GREAT AIR BATTLES	370
XXVII.	FLIGHTS HOME TO AUSTRALIA	386
	APPENDICES	397
	1 Types of Fighting Aeroplanes	397
	2 Correspondence Relating to Formation of A.F.C.	421
	3 War Flying Instruction in Australia	426
	4 Aircraft Wireless	427
	5 A.F.C. Training in England	430
	6 Organisation of R.A.F. in France	434
	7 Aeroplane Counter-attacks on the German Army, March, 1918	437
	8 Aerodrome Work in the Squadron	440
	9 Use of Incendiary Bullets	443
	GLOSSARY	445
	INDEX	453

LIST OF ILLUSTRATIONS

The Half-Flight in camp at Point Cook, Victoria, March, 1915	4
The Half-Flight at Bombay, May, 1915	5
Kantara, on the Suez Canal, with aircraft park in the foreground	36
Aeroplane view of Nekhl	37
Letter, written 14th July, 1917, from the German aviator Felmy to No. 1 Squadron	72
The "hairpin-bend" road in the hilly country south of El Lubban	86
Jerusalem, from the air, showing the mountainous country around the city	87
Captain Ross Smith and Lieutenant Mustard in their Bristol Fighter, 1918	94
Aerodrome of No. 1 Squadron at El Mejdel, March, 1918	95
Es Salt	106
Jisr ed Damieh Ford across the Jordan, showing the steep valley-sides	107
The Auja Ford, River Jordan	114
Officers of No. 1 Squadron at Ramleh, November, 1918	115
Kerak	122
Amman, showing the aerodrome, village, and railway station, 2nd June, 1918	123
An Australian air-raid on Amman railway station and aerodrome, 4th June, 1918	126
A German aeroplane brought down in the British lines in Palestine by No. 1 Squadron, August, 1918	127
An Australian air-raid on El Kutrani railway station, 15th August, 1918	138
Jenin aerodrome and town, looking east, showing the tracks around the landing ground and the railway to Nazareth	139
A British air-raid on the railway at Deraa, 16th September, 1918	146
A D.H.9 forced to land in the enemy's country	147
Australian aeroplanes with part of Lawrence's Arab force near Azrak, 11th September, 1918	154
Tul Keram railway station, showing material captured on 19th September, 1918	155

ILLUSTRATIONS

An air-photograph of the Tul Keram-Anebta road, showing Turkish transport abandoned under the airmen's bombing attacks on 19th September, 1918	158
An airman's view of the Khurbet Ferweh-Wady Fara road, after the heavy bombing attacks of 21st September, 1918, showing abandoned Turkish transport	159
The Balata-Khurbet Ferweh road, showing enemy transport abandoned after the air-raids of 21st September, 1918	166
Nablus, from the air	167
Officers of No. 3 Squadron at Bertangles, May, 1918	178
R.E.8 (used by No. 3 Squadron)	179
An R.E.8 of No. 3 Squadron detailed for night-bombing	194
An airman's view of the ruins of Ypres, 31st October, 1917	195
A close view of "Augustus Wood," near Passchendaele Ridge, showing the shell-torn ground, 17th October, 1917	206
The German Albatros shot down by Lieutenant Sandy and Sergeant Hughes near Armentières, 17th December, 1917	207
Sopwith Camel (used by No. 4 Squadron)	214
Sopwith Snipe (used by No. 4 Squadron)	214
D.H.5 (used by No. 2 Squadron)	215
S.E.5 (used by No. 2 Squadron)	215
Officers of No. 2 Squadron at Savy, March, 1918	230
Vaulx-Vraucourt, from the air	231
A flight of No. 2 Squadron (S.E.5's) waiting to start from Savy aerodrome, 25th March, 1918	234
A flight of No. 4 Squadron (Camels) preparing to start from Bruay aerodrome, 26th March, 1918	235
Officers of No. 4 Squadron at Clairmarais, June, 1918	270
The Halberstadt two-seater driven down and captured on Flesselles aerodrome by an R.E.8 of No. 3 Squadron on 9th June, 1918	271
An air squadron's contact-patrol accompanying an infantry advance	306
Aeroplane view of the country south of the Somme over which the Australians and Canadians attacked on 8th August, 1918	307
An observation balloon over British heavy artillery, Morcourt, 25th August, 1918	322
An aeroplane photograph of Mont St. Quentin, early in September, 1918 (with key-map)	323
The opening of the bomb-raid by Nos. 2 and 4 Squadrons on Haubourdin aerodrome, Lille, 16th August, 1918 (with key-map)	342
The bomb-raid by Nos. 2 and 4 Squadrons on Lomme aerodrome, Lille, 17th August, 1918 (with key-map)	343

ILLUSTRATIONS

An attack by a British scout-formation through a cloud upon a German formation	374
Aeroplane photograph of a point in the Hindenburg Line, showing systems of trenches and wire	375
A big Handley-Page bomber, of the type used by the Royal Air Force on bombing raids into Germany	382
Skeleton of a large Gotha bomber, at Cologne, December, 1918	383

LIST OF MAPS

1	Mesopotamia (South-eastern portion), showing area in which operations of Australian Half-Flight opened	4
2	Mesopotamia (North-western portion), showing area of later operations of Australian Half-Flight	17
3	Egypt	34
4	Sinai Desert, the scene of the campaign of 1916	42
5	Southern Palestine, showing the position before the Third Battle of Gaza	78
6	The country east of the Dead Sea, showing the Hejaz railway	101
7	Central Palestine, the scene of the Battle of Nablus	137
8	The Wady Fara, in which heavy bombing operations occurred on 21st September, 1918	160
9	Syria, showing the area of the last stages of the campaign against the Turks	170
10	North-eastern France, showing the areas illustrated by maps in this volume	179
11	Cambrai region, showing area of operations of No. 2 Squadron in November and December, 1917, and of No. 2 and No. 4 Squadrons in March, 1918	189
12	Section of a typical artillery map, showing method of ranging by reference to "clock-face"	201
13	Douai region, the "hunting" area of all British scout squadrons	220
14	The Lys region, showing area of operations of No. 3 Squadron, December, 1917-April, 1918, and of No. 2 and No. 4 Squadrons, May-September, 1918	279
15	Villers-Bretonneux region, showing area of operations of No. 3 Squadron, April-August, 1918	311
16	St. Quentin region, showing area of operations of No. 3 Squadron, September and October, 1918	321
17	Lille region, showing area of operations of No. 2 and No. 4 Squadrons, May-October, 1918	355
18	Tournai region, showing area of operations of No. 2 and No. 4 Squadrons, October and November, 1918	374
19	Ath region, showing area of operations of No. 2 and No. 4 Squadrons, October and November, 1918	382

LIST OF SKETCH MAPS

Jaffa-Jordan line, 1/1/18, after enemy retreat from Gaza	89
Messudie Hill Corner	130
Tul Keram Corner	154
The country beyond the Jordan	163
Damascus and approaches	167
Front in Flanders, showing German offensives in 1918	241
Morlancourt Ridge, between the Somme and Ancre Rivers	266
The Lys Valley near Armentières, showing communications by road, rail, and river	286
Sketch illustrating "clock-face" method of checking artillery fire upon enemy batteries	435
Formation flying—V formation, turning manœuvre, and circus formation	448

INTRODUCTION

THE FLYING ARM IN WAR

THE world is now familiar with methods of war vastly more scientific than it ever knew before 1914. In the half-century before the late world war broke out, mankind had already become acquainted with the destructive power of submarine mines and torpedoes, and of artillery firing over ranges of many miles. It was known that a few dozen men with machine-guns could hold at bay many times their number equipped even with the best of rifles. The conflict of 1914–1918, however, was remarkable not only for a tremendous increase of gun-power in battle on land and sea but also for the use of three entirely novel agents—poison-gas, submarine fighting ships, and war in the air.

None of these new forms of warfare was actually unforeseen. All the chief Powers of the world had anticipated their possibilities, and the Hague Peace Conference of 1907 expressly barred the use of poison-gas, attacks by submarines on merchant ships, and bombardment by airships and aeroplanes of open towns. The late struggle afforded a cynical commentary on the binding force of such agreements in the ultimate issue between nations in arms, for not one of these three agencies of destruction was successfully prohibited by the Hague embargo. The use of fighting aeroplanes in the field as distinct from air attack on civilians, was of course a development sufficiently legitimate. In the struggle which closed in 1918, war in the air, for long imagined and described by latter-day prophets with much ingenious detail, became a reality, and thereby a new arm was added to the forces of all nations.

This volume forms but a small contribution to that historical record of military air fighting which is now being carefully compiled in every country. A scientific or technical work it does not pretend to be. No attempt is here made to lay down the proper tactics of fighting in the air. Nevertheless, as the leaders of aeroplane formations steadily sought out some guiding principles, certain proved methods of attack and defence did become recognised, and these will in due course be as far as possible described and explained. At the beginning of the war the existing aeroplanes on either side were but elementary machines. They carried no armament, and were regarded chiefly as auxiliaries to cavalry for purposes of reconnaissance. They were still largely at the mercy of any unfavourable breeze. Their flying speed was not great; their climbing speed, judged by the performances of 1918 types, was ludicrous. At that date there was no sign of any appreciation of distinct and limited duties for this or that type of machine. One pilot, with or without an observer, might be sent out on no special commission at all except to "see what is happening," or with an impossible list of duties, such as to locate guns, discover the enemy's main line of attack, estimate his available fighting strength in half-a-dozen places, and, if it appeared opportune, throw out some handfuls of steel darts upon hostile troops.

Fighting tactics were evolved as pilots grew in experience of air warfare, and, under the influence of accepted tactics, distinctive classes of aeroplanes were developed. Competition enforced improvement of design; special types appeared for special work; and each department of air warfare demanded its peculiar skill. Reconnaissance work became divided into "strategic" reconnaissance—a rapid and constant survey of general dispositions over the enemy's rear areas—and "tactical" reconnaissance, or close scrutiny of the immediate front line and trench works, in which every machine-gun position was located and the strength of every outpost calculated. Photography was introduced to illustrate and confirm intelligence reports thus obtained. Bombing raids from the air were carried out both by day and by night, and in each case evoked special measures for attack and defence. These, again, might be either forward-area bombing attacks or distant raids upon factories and other places far behind the enemy's line; here, too, the types of machine and the special capacity demanded of pilots varied in important particulars.

Above all, the demand was for excellence in the fighting scout. It was improvement in the fighting scout which governed development of tactical ability and fluctuations of the fortunes of warfare in the air towards this side or that.

INTRODUCTION

The battle-patrol pure and simple was the assigned province of single-seater machines of small size, high speed, rapid manœuvring ability, and equipped ultimately with forward armament of double machine-guns. Perhaps the most difficult task of all was that of fitting machine-guns to fire forward through the propellers of aircraft. The Germans succeeded first in producing an " interrupter " mechanism whereby each discharge of the gun was controlled by the revolutions of the propeller. Air fighting included also co-operation of aeroplanes with infantry against hostile forces on the ground. The two chief forms of this co-operation were known as " contact " patrols, assisting an infantry attack, and " counter-attack " patrols, assisting a defence. Both entailed low flying, and low flying against machine-gun fire from the ground was perhaps the most dangerous work demanded of airmen. In this special form of fighting the airmen would often perform lightning evolutions over tree-tops or village house-roofs, or skim the very ground itself while delivering blasts of fire upon the enemy's infantry or guns.

It will be easily realised that this new field of war in the air offered considerable scope to the daring and initiative of the individual. Curiously enough the best pilots were not always physically the most robust. Guynemer, the Frenchman, probably the greatest fighting airman of the whole war, was a young man of delicate health. The supreme qualities demanded of a pilot were youth, sound senses, and good nerves; thus equipped, he might, if he lived, acquire all else needful from flying experience. Both Britain and Germany found that the best raw material for the making of an air pilot was the accomplished horseman. The demand for good heart, good hands, and a quick eye is the same in each case. On the other hand, a safe pilot was not necessarily a good fighting airman. Besides the pilot's ordinary qualifications, there was required for the fighting airman just that little more which may best be described as " devil." It means not so much recklessness as nice judgment of the moment's risks while simultaneously flying and fighting; sustained courage and determination, without hot-headedness; unruffled confidence founded in perfect knowledge of his machine's capacity, estimation of the enemy's ability, and assurance of his own. There was probably no better example of what a fighting pilot should be than the Australian, Ross Smith. Like many of the successful airmen of the Australian Flying Corps, Ross Smith came from the Australian Light Horse.

The air services on each side in the war observed throughout a special chivalry. Air fighting is individual fighting. Combat between formations resolved itself, after initial manœuvres and the opening attack, into a series of duels at close quarters. Each individual engagement was a matter of life or death to either opponent; the one showed the other no mercy, and pursued his foe, if necessary, and where possible, to the ground, shooting at him till the end. But where any flying man was taken prisoner, he was treated by his late adversaries with respect and consideration. The star airmen of the opposing armies regarded each other with a curious mixture of personal esteem and deadly hostility. The Royal Air Force, while thirsting, so to speak, for Richthofen's blood, frequently drank his health at celebration feasts in London. With British men air fighting, though deadly enough, was still in general observance a form of sport. The best German pilots seemed to possess some of the same spirit. But the French airmen, gay and daring as many of them were, fought with no such prepossession. Their gaiety was the ecstasy of soul born of devotion to their country and a high consciousness of the glory of asserting it. They burned with hatred at the very sight of a German machine, and life itself, it seemed, was worthless to many of them if the foe was also to be permitted to live.

The methods of reckoning totals of "hostile aircraft destroyed" in the British, French, and German Armies afford some insight into the human characteristics of their respective flying services. The British, a name which, of course, includes Australians, reckoned no enemy machine destroyed unless the victorious pilot's report were confirmed by at least a second pilot or by some other satisfactory evidence; the British fought always on the enemy's side of the line, and the occasions when German machines were destroyed within the British area—and when the victory could therefore be established beyond any possible doubt—were relatively few. The French command was exceedingly strict, and was for long reluctant to count a defeated enemy as destroyed unless the remains of his machine could be actually recovered; that was one reason why French airmen preferred to engage the enemy over their own army areas, rather than over the German. With the Germans, however, individual claims of hostile aircraft destroyed were admitted often on the flimsiest evidence, and it seems clear that they frequently claimed as victories combats which were no more than successes of the moment. Many a machine fell away " in a spin " from an air-fight not because it was hit or beyond recoverable control, but merely in order to escape from an unequal duel or from a bad manœuvring position. While the line was stationary in trench warfare, the Germans could easily establish the numbers of Allied aircraft shot down, since, on the British front at least, nearly all air fighting took place over German territory—" Hunland," as it was called by British airmen; but during British advances in the late winter of 1917 and the summer of 1918, German reports of British aircraft losses were often based on the wildest guesses.

When war broke out, the equipment of the British Royal Flying Corps and its available numbers of trained men were markedly inferior to those of either France or Germany. By 1918, however, the British flying service, thanks to the principles on which it was trained and developed, led all others. The new arm of war in the new element had to evolve its own fighting tactics, and, for want of corps tradition, its own standard of performance in action. The offensive training of the British air force sought from the first to inculcate the spirit of the British Navy. After all, the tactics of sea and air fighting are not essentially different. It was recognised that the primary duty of an air battle-squadron, as of a battle-fleet at sea, is to seek out the main hostile force and destroy it; and the primary duty of each fighting pilot is to lay himself as speedily as possible alongside the enemy. To this end the enemy's units shall be attacked whenever met, and no victory shall be deemed really complete while a single enemy escapes. This is the Royal Navy's gospel of faith and service, and the Royal Air Force adopted it. The analogue of advantage of steaming power—formerly sailing power—on the sea is, in the air, advantage of flying speed and height; manœuvring ability there, as at sea, is of supreme importance, and its rapid attainment is the finished art in action of the well-built aeroplane and the resolute airman.

It is necessary for the proper perspective of this narrative to introduce a short account of the Royal Flying Corps, later merged with the Royal Naval Air Service into one arm as the Royal Air Force, of which the Australian Flying Corps formed a part. In 1911 what had previously been the Balloon Company, Royal Engineers, was (according to Major-General Sir F. H. Sykes[1]) superseded by the Air Battalion, R.E., consisting of Headquarters, No. 1 Company (airships), and No. 2 Company (aeroplanes). But investigation of the progress of the air arm in other European countries convinced the Committee of Imperial Defence of the necessity of further measures, and in May, 1912, Sykes was instructed " to organise, recruit, train, and command the Military Wing of the Royal Flying Corps." Thus did the Royal Flying Corps come into existence. For the next two years there were two wings, one naval and one military; but on 1st July, 1914, just before the outbreak of the war, the Royal Naval Air Service was formed, and so named, as an organisation separate from the military. The central flying school at Upavon, Wiltshire, continued to be the training institution for both forces.

With the formation of the Royal Flying Corps, flying stations were established at Farnborough, Montrose, Gosport, and Lark Hill, all of which, together with many others, became in course of time well known to Australian airmen. The first British-built military aeroplane was F. S. Cody's—Cody was for long a hero with the British public—while he was in the employment of the British Government. Cody, however—as one authority[2] remarks—did not, until he had left the Government service, succeed in building a machine which could be guaranteed to leave the ground. The early machines were few in number and of what would now be considered very primitive types. Pilots were but infrequently allowed to fly them, for fear the machines might be damaged or destroyed. They were for the most part Caudrons, Farmans, Blériots, and Bristol box-kites. Britain was learning as fast

---
[1] *Aviation in Peace and War*, by Major-General Sir F. H. Sykes.
[2] "Wing Adjutant"; *The Royal Flying Corps in the War*.

INTRODUCTION

as possible from the experience gained by the resolute pioneers of France.

It is unnecessary here to tell in detail the story of that French pioneering, which received its strongest impulse from the demonstrations of the brothers Wright, of the United States. It is an entrancing story, of which some outline is to be found in Laurence Yard Smith's *The Romance of Aircraft*. As early as 1794 the French used balloons in war against the Austrians, and balloons were of considerable assistance to armies on the ground in both the American Civil War and the Franco-Prussian War—when the French even dropped "propaganda literature" on the Germans. Yard Smith describes how the Franco-German competition developed between 1909 and 1911, Germany putting her faith in the dirigible airship, and France putting hers in the more mobile aeroplane. The third great Rheims air meeting in 1911—two had been held in previous years—completely opened Germany's eyes, and incidentally Britain's as well, to the vast progress made by France in the development of the aeroplane. Germany saw that her concentration upon the Zeppelins was narrow and mistaken, and the Germans "at once began a policy of construction by which they hoped soon to outstrip their brainier French neighbours." They standardised their adopted aeroplane design "down to the last bolt," and proceeded to turn out flying machines from their factories in great numbers. It is stated that in August, 1914, Germany possessed over 1,000 trained pilots and 800 military aeroplanes. They were for the most part the famous Taubes of the early days of the war. The French, on the other hand, had at the same date " a motley array of aeroplanes of every size, shape, and make, and this versatility of invention and experiment caused much early confusion. Spare parts of one type of machine would not fit another. The German machines, also, were richer in equipment of speed and climbing gauges and other accessories. But the French airmen had the real *flair* for this new science, and the Germans did not long retain their advantage."

At this stage, the outbreak of war, the Royal Flying Corps consisted of four complete squadrons—each squadron containing three flights, and each flight four machines and two in reserve.[8] Two of these squadrons were equipped with B.E's and two with homogeneous flights of B.E.2's, and Henri- and Maurice-Farmans. The Farman brothers were British subjects, though manufacturers in France, and they had won great success at the Rheims meetings. The B.E. was the best British machine, and there were several types of it in use; it possessed natural stability, mounted either a 70 horse-power Renault or an 80 horse-power Gnome engine, and could fly at about sixty-five miles an hour, if the wind were not adverse. The Farman machines flew at about fifty-five miles an hour, as did also the Caudrons and Shorts among the seaplanes. To climb 3,000 feet in ten minutes was in those days thought to be a wonderful performance, and at that height a machine was considered safe from ground gun-fire. The aeroplane's radius of action was limited to about 130 miles. It is startling to compare these records with those of 1918, when fighting scouts flew at 150 miles an hour or more, could climb 10,000 feet in five minutes, and were sometimes damaged by anti-aircraft gun-fire when flying at a height of 20,000 feet. "Our machines," says Bishop,[4] "were not only called upon to fly faster by far than the swiftest birds, but to do 'stunts' that no birds ever thought of. Whoever heard of a bird flying upside down?"

McCudden[5] tells some quaint stories of the early fighting. The aeroplanes with the first British Expeditionary Force went up loaded with hand-grenades, "as the intention then was to bring a hostile aeroplane down by dropping bombs on it." They were also provided with *fléchettes*, or small steel darts, which were thrown out upon the enemy in handfuls. The observer's seat in the early B.E. machines faced the tail, so that the observer could obtain a good view of the unobscured portion of the ground. McCudden relates how on 22nd August, 1914, at Maubeuge, a Taube appeared, and a Henri-Farman from No. 5 Squadron, Royal Flying Corps, took off to meet it in the air. "Half-an-hour after the

---

[3] *Aviation in Peace and War*. A beginning had also been made to form three more squadrons. Sykes gives the total strength of the Royal Flying Corps (including, presumably, machines and personnel of the naval wing) in 1914 at 150 machines and 1,844 officers and men, and notes that by the end of the war it had expanded to 201 squadrons and 22,000 machines in use, and 300,000 officers and men.

[4] *Winged Warfare*.

[5] *Five Years in the Royal Flying Corps*.

German had departed this machine was still climbing steadily over the aerodrome at about 1,000 feet in a strenuous effort to catch the Boche."

The Farman machines were soon replaced by the Morane Parasol monoplane (a French design), the S.E.4, and the Avro. These types, with the French Nieuport, gave the Allies some temporary air-fighting superiority, and air combats became common. In September, 1915, the Germans brought out the first of the famous Fokkers, an imitation of the Morane, but with wings specially strengthened for the form of attack which the Fokkers used. The Fokker method was to swoop down from the upper air, like a hawk, upon a hostile machine; either the enemy, so tackled, was shot down in the stream of bullets from the forward gun of the Fokker, or, if the attack missed its object, the Fokker continued on in its dive earthward to avoid its opponent's counter-attack, and so sped away to safety. This was the method of attack standardised for German airmen by the renowned Boelcke and Immelmann, and slavishly copied by their immediate disciples. One of these was Richthofen, whose fame in the end eclipsed that of his masters. But undeniably the men who first revealed the possibilities of air fighting, and who created the high *esprit de corps* of the German air service, were Boelcke and Immelmann. Fighting airmen studied their tactics for inspiration, and indeed were compelled so to do. Boelcke's scheme of attack was not only masterly in itself, but demanded high quality in defence, and the requisite defence manœuvre was given to the flying world by Immelmann, with his classic " Immelmann turn."

The 1915 Fokker, as McCudden notes, was slightly faster than the Morane. Both were fitted with machine-guns to fire through the propeller. The Morane, possessing no interrupter-gear to prevent bullets from hitting the propeller, had steel deflectors fitted to the propeller blades. These, however, reduced the efficiency of the propeller by almost 30 per cent. The Fokker, on the other hand, was fitted with a mechanical interrupter-gear. "About the middle of September Lieutenant Immelmann became famous because he appreciated the possibilities of this single-seater firing through the propeller, and also the advantages of a roving commission over localities where enemy machines were known to visit. The enemy was fortunate in finding two such pilots as Boelcke and Immelmann, who apparently were gifted with the necessary foresight and imagination to use these machines to their best advantage on a roving patrol, which gives the skilful and intelligent pilot all the opportunities he desires."

The British withheld their reply to the Fokker for a short time, in order to produce it as a surprise for the Somme offensive of July, 1916. The new British machines were for the time being highly successful. They were the F.E.2.b, which "swept the Germans off the front,"[6] and the D.H.2, a fighting scout which speedily became popular, and "was very nice and light."[7] It was in a fight against a D.H.2 that Immelmann was shot down and killed by a young and newly-trained British pilot named McCubbin.[8]

The Fokker biplanes were further improved in answer to the D.H.2, and there appeared also the Albatros, one of the best designed of German fighting aeroplanes. These were the machines with which Richthofen's "circus" first made its name. It became noticeable in all the armies at this time that, with the rise of star airmen—"aces" the French termed them—types of machines steadily improved. Insistent demands made upon the designers and manufacturers by Richthofen and his comrades brought out better and faster types of Fokker and Albatros, and in 1918 came the small and swift Pfalz scout. So, too, Guynemer, in the French flying service, improved the Nieuport and inspired the creation of the wonderful Spad; and, in the British air force, McCudden, Ball, and Bishop—three crack Royal Flying Corps pilots, who had each a long list of victories—demanded ever better and better machines and constant improvements in technical details. While the French were fashioning the Spad upon the improved Nieuport, the British produced the Martinsyde and the Bristol Fighter two-seater (both used by No. 1 Australian Squadron in Palestine), and, as fighting scouts, the Sopwith Camel (used by No. 4 Australian Squadron) and the S.E.5 (used by No. 2 Australian Squadron). Fokker triplanes and Sopwith triplanes appeared almost simul-

---

[6] *The Royal Flying Corps in the War.*
[7] *Five Years in the Royal Flying Corps.*
[8] Capt. G. R. McCubbin, D.S.O., R.A.F.

taneously in early 1918. The triplane was originally designed by the Sopwith Company in England, but the first two of these machines sent to France alighted by some mischance, behind the German lines, and the enemy thereby received a present of the new design, which was immediately turned to use. Again, one of the earliest constructed giant Handley-Page bombers, being flown across to France, was landed at a German aerodrome near Laon by a pilot who had lost his bearings. Whether or not this prize assisted the enemy in his plans for the big, twin-engined Gotha is not established.

After the coming of the Spad fighting scout, the Allied air forces never lost their supremacy over the Germans; and towards the end of the war, when, subsequently to the Pfalz, there appeared the Roland—known as the German Spad—the British replied with the Sopwith Snipe, whose performances at great heights amazed and dismayed the German airmen.

The present history covers the records of four Australian air squadrons. It should be remembered that these by no means included all the Australian airmen who served in the war. There were many Australian pilots in the Royal Air Force, just as there were New Zealanders, Canadians, and South Africans. The famous airman, Bishop, came from Canada. The percentage of oversea men among the British pilots has never yet been authoritatively stated, but it was remarkably high. It is said that in the earlier part of the war the number of airmen from all oversea dominions amounted to over fifty per cent. in both the Royal Naval Air Service and the Royal Flying Corps. The fortunes of the Australian airmen therein included cannot be followed in a history of the purely Australian Flying Corps.

That history falls at once into three separate and distinct sections. The Australian Flying Corps served in three widely separated theatres of war. The honour of inaugurating the Australian military air service in war belongs to the little half-flight which took part in the first unfortunate expedition up the Tigris valley towards Baghdad in 1915, and which lost three of its four Australian officers engaged in that campaign, together with most of its ground personnel. That portion of the story closes with the besieging of General Townshend in Kut.

INTRODUCTION

The subsequent formation, in early 1916, of the first complete Australian squadron, and its departure for Egypt imparted a distinct fillip to military flying in Australia, and before the close of that year the impulse was felt in the Australian army in Egypt and in France. Light horsemen, weary of the desert sand and flies, and infantrymen in France, who looked eagerly for any relief from the awful Somme mud of the winter of 1916-17, alike turned their eyes aloft and perceived a chance of relief in the air service. They appraised its dangers as highly as did any airman—even exaggerated them, as some airmen thought; but danger they had to meet in any case, and they believed that the realm of the air inspired the needful enthusiasm no longer to be found in the climatic miseries of trenches or desert. Especially to many who had survived the first part of the war in the infantry ranks, the conditions of the flying corps made an irresistible appeal. There, if a man could outlive the chance fate of the day's flying duty, he might look forward to a comfortable and dry bed at night undisturbed by shell-fire. The trenches wore out the hearts of many men; in course of time the infantryman came to count a wound as truly a blessing; and it is easy to imagine the state of mind of the average soldier—British, French, or German—during that seemingly endless stationary warfare, when each day's escape from the visitation of death or wounds meant only continuance of the strain of waiting for the next. There were times when even death seemed better than protracted existence under shell-fire in the trench mud. To volunteer for the flying corps was the happy dream of many an infantryman, as he lay on damp straw in a verminous dug-out, where the sunshine never penetrated.

The first complete Australian squadron, entitled No. 67 Squadron, R.F.C., was committed to service with the British expeditionary force in Egypt, the eastern desert, and Palestine.[9] No. 2 Squadron (originally No. 68, R.F.C.) and No. 4 Squadron (originally No. 71, R.F.C.) were sent from Australia, the former in October, 1916, and the latter in January, 1917, direct to England, where they performed their training in R.F.C. depôts. No. 3 Squadron (originally

---
[9] See Appendix No. 2.

No. 69, R.F.C.) was formed in September, 1916, in Egypt. Its personnel were obtained from No. 1 Squadron and from the light horse in that theatre. That squadron also was trained in England. Nos. 2, 3, and 4 Squadrons all served in France. The active service period of their history began at about the end of 1917, and from that time till the close of the war they fought on the Western Front in the region between Soissons and the North Sea.

Note.—An authoritative and exhaustive account of types of British machines produced during the war, also of leading French and German machines, will be found in Appendix No. 1. It has been written by Captain Andrew Lang, an Australian test-pilot well known on aerodromes in England during the war. The types therein described are referred to by their war-titles in the text of this volume, without further explanation in the course of the narrative.

CHAPTER I

MESOPOTAMIA—THE FIRST AUSTRALIAN AIRMEN ON SERVICE

AT the date of the declaration of the war the air-fighting arm, still a mere infant development in Great Britain, was to all intents and purposes unknown in the oversea dominions. In Australia some efforts were being made in civil and military flying, and, shortly before the war, as one of several important measures adopted for the defence of the Commonwealth, a Central Flying School had been established at Point Cook, near Melbourne. Two airmen, H. A. Petre[1] and E. Harrison,[2] selected in England, had been given honorary commissions as flying instructors, and the Defence Department had acquired five aeroplanes for training purposes at Point Cook. The first course of war-flying instruction, which lasted three months, began on the 17th of August, 1914.[3] It was attended by four officers, who all qualified as pilots—Captain T. W. White,[4] of the 60th Infantry, Australian Military Forces, Lieutenant G. P. Merz,[5] an officer of the Melbourne University Rifles who had just completed his medical course at the University, Lieutenant R. Williams,[6] later squadron-commander and wing-commander in Palestine, and Lieutenant D. T. W. Manwell.[7]

The Australian Flying Corps owes the beginning of its career of service to an inquiry from abroad. On the 8th of February, 1915, the Commonwealth Government received

---

[1] Maj. H. A. Petre, D.S.O., M.C. Aviator; of South Yarra, Melbourne; b. Ingatestone, Essex, Eng., 12 June, 1884.

[2] Maj. E. Harrison; Aust. Flying Corps. Aviator; b. Castlemaine, Vic., 10 Aug., 1886.

[3] See Appendix No. 3.

[4] Capt. T. W. White, D.F.C.; Aust. Flying Corps. Manufacturer; of Melbourne; b. North Melbourne, 26 April, 1888.

[5] Lieut. G. P. Merz; Aust. Flying Corps. Medical practitioner; of Melbourne; b. Prahran, Melbourne, 10 Oct., 1891. Killed in action, 30 July, 1915.

[6] Lt.-Col. R. Williams, D.S.O., O.B.E. Commanded No. 1 Sqn., 1917/18; 40th (Army) Wing, R.A.F., 1918/19. Subsequently Director of Intelligence and Organization, Aust. Air Board. Of Moonta, S. Aust.; b. Moonta, 3 Aug., 1890.

[7] Capt. D. T. W. Manwell, M.B.E.; No. 1 Sqn. Staff Officer for Equipment, A.F.C., London, 1918. Commission agent; b. Queenscliff, Vic., 23 Aug., 1890.

from the Government of India a message asking whether Australia could provide for service in Mesopotamia any trained airmen, flying machines, and motor-transport. Two days later the Australian Government replied that the Commonwealth could furnish some airmen and necessary mechanics and transport, but no aeroplanes.[8]

The available pilots in Australia were the four newly-trained officers above mentioned, the two British instructors, and Lieutenant W. H. Treloar,[9] of the 72nd Infantry, Australian Military Forces, who had learned to fly in England and had returned to Australia just before the outbreak of war. Four were selected to go as pilots with the Mesopotamian Half-Flight (as it was called), namely, Petre (in command), White, Merz, and Treloar.

At that stage of the war the organisation of a flying unit was still undeveloped; the Australian Government suggested (and the Indian Government approved) that mule-transport as well as motor-transport should accompany the force. For personnel, besides the four officers, there were selected forty-one of other ranks, including eighteen air-mechanics.[10] The sergeant-major, staff-sergeant, and sergeant were from the Central Flying School; the quartermaster-sergeant and the farrier-sergeant were from permanent artillery units in New South Wales. The corporals, drivers, and mechanics were obtained from the A.I.F. training camp at Broadmeadows, in Victoria.

A few of the non-commissioned officers only had had any experience of aeroplanes, but the mechanics were carefully chosen from numerous volunteers at Broadmeadows who had worked in motor-engineering shops, and the riggers from those who possessed good credentials as carpenters and joiners. Under the guidance of skilled instructors the motor-mechanics and carpenters were soon able to undertake the repair and maintenance of aeroplanes; later, on active service, these held their own against the best air-mechanics of the Royal Flying Corps. The two repair-shop lorries which accompanied the unit were built on heavy motor-lorry chassis at the

---

[8] See Appendix No. 2.
[9] Lieut. W. H. Treloar; Aust. Flying Corps. Motor mechanic; of Albert Park, Melbourne; b. Fairfield Park, Melbourne, 8 Aug., 1889.
[10] See Appendix No. 2.

Newport Railway Workshops, and were equipped with lathes, drilling-machines, welding-plant benches, and circular saws.

The little force was organised and equipped in haste. Uniforms were with difficulty obtained only two days before departure, and some necessary small stores had to be purchased at Adelaide and Perth *en route* to India. Captain Petre left Melbourne on April 14th for Bombay as advance officer; White then took temporary command and sailed with Treloar and thirty-seven other ranks in the *Morea* for Bombay on April 20th. The quartermaster-sergeant and three mechanics were despatched with the motor-transport in the *Ulysses* on May 3rd, and the horses and mules followed later in another ship. Merz was detained on instruction duties at Point Cook, and did not rejoin the Half-Flight till June 13th at Basra. At Bombay the drivers and the farrier-sergeant were left in barracks to await the arrival of the mules,[11] and the remainder of the force was despatched in the *Bankura* to Basra, where it arrived on May 26th.

At Basra the Australians found two Indian Army airmen (Captains P. W. L. Broke-Smith[12] and H. L. Reilly[13]) and a few mechanics. White, giving his impressions on arrival in the theatre of war, writes:—" These two officers, with about four British and five Indian mechanics, formed the Indian Flying Corps, which was supplemented by an Indian Army reserve lieutenant as engineer officer, and six British motor-transport drivers. They possessed two motor-lorries and a few spare aeroplane parts. With the assistance of Indian pioneers a road of date-palm logs had been made from the Shatt-el-Arab (the canal on which Basra is situated) across a swamp to an Arab cemetery, where tents had been pitched and a small aerodrome was in the making." Another flying officer attached was Lieutenant W. W. A. Burn,[14] a New Zealander sent by the New Zealand Government. There were also present two Maurice-Farman Shorthorn

---

[11] The mule transport was useless in Mesopotamia during the flood season, and remained in India till September. The drivers were there trained with British horse artillery.

[12] Lt.-Col. P. W. L. Broke-Smith, D.S.O., O.B.E., R.E. Officer of British Regular Army; of Cheltenham, Eng.; b. Plymouth, Eng., 27 Aug., 1882.

[13] Maj. H. L. Reilly, D.S.O. Officer of Indian Regular Army; b. 18 Oct., 1886.

[14] Lieut. W. W. A. Burn. Of Christchurch, N.Z.; b. Gippsland, Vic., 17 July, 1890. Killed in action, 30 July, 1915.

Map No. 1

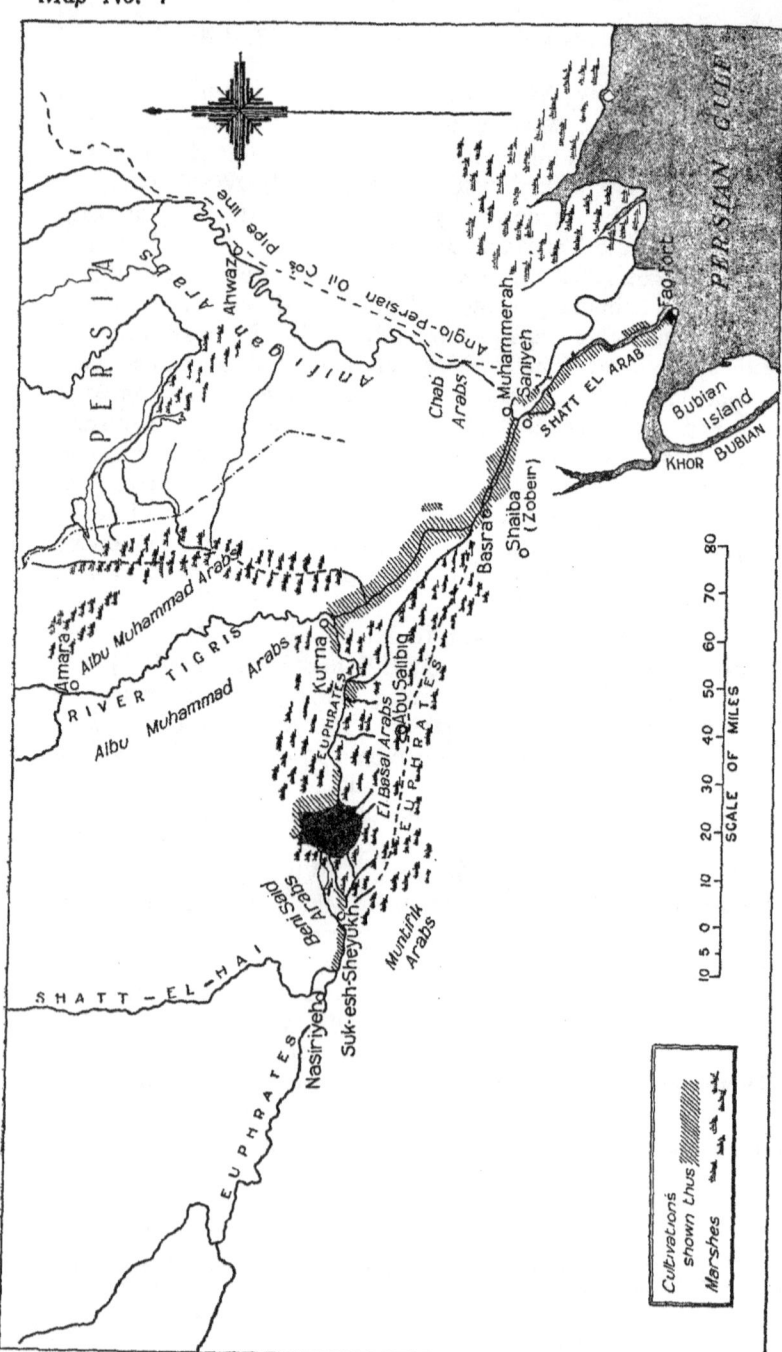

The First Half-Flight of the Australian Flying Corps in camp at Point Cook, Victoria, March, 1915

The officers in the centre are Lieutenant G. P. Merz (on left, holding kitten) and Captain T. W. White (right).

Lent by Capt. T. W. White, Aust. Half-Flight.

THE AUSTRALIAN HALF-FLIGHT AT BOMBAY, MAY, 1915

The officers in centre are Captain T. W. White (left) and Lieutenant W. H. Treloar (right).

Lent by Capt. T. W. White, Aust. Half-Flight.

biplanes—"bought" (says White caustically) "with money given by the Rajah of Gwalior for the purchase of two up-to-date aeroplanes"—and a Maurice-Farman Longhorn, which had seen considerable service in Egypt and subsequently spent most of its time in the workshops. There was not much time to lose, for General Sir John Nixon,[15] the newly-arrived commander of the Tigris Expeditionary Force, had ordered the advance up-river from Kurna for May 31st. In the four days' interval, despite shortage of stores, great heat, and the unsettlement inevitable upon arrival, the joint flying force had finished levelling the tiny aerodrome floor, banked back river flood-waters, and set up the machines and tested them.

The deplorable muddle of the first Tigris campaign involved every department of the army, the flying service as well as units fighting on the ground. Administration on the spot amounted simply to making the best of what there was; administration at distant bases of supply has been heavily castigated by the Royal Commission on Mesopotamia appointed by the War Office. The aeroplanes sent to Mesopotamia were quite unfitted for any sort of war service, least of all for war in such a climate. Their type was primitive. Machines were not provided in sufficient numbers; the supply base did not make proper allowance for casualties. Some machines were defective when they arrived, or were without necessary spare parts and instruments. Some were even second-hand. The engines were a constant source of trouble and anxiety. The machines were not fitted with machine-guns; there were none of the improved types to spare from the main fighting front in France. Such bombs as were dropped upon the enemy were, for a time, 2-lb. infantry hand-bombs thrown out by hand; when 20-lb. aeroplane bombs ultimately arrived, they were frequently found to have been damaged in transit. Bomb-racks supplied from England would not fit, and were unserviceable; these had to be repaired locally; and in some instances the only way in which the bombs could be dropped was through a hole cut out in the floor of the cockpit. In general the sole service to which these machines could be put was reconnaissance, and

---
[15] Gen. Sir John E. Nixon, G.C.M.G., K.C.B. Officer of Indian Regular Army; b. 16 Aug., 1857.

reconnaissance had to be performed in conditions of wind and heat such as no aeroplane designer had hitherto imagined. The flying speed of these aeroplanes on a calm day did not exceed fifty miles an hour; at times when a strong wind blew they simply moved backwards in the face of it.

The Mesopotamian force was officially called "Force 'D'," a short title for "Indian Expeditionary Force 'D'." Turkey was known to be inclined to join in the war on the side of Germany, and the first troops of Force "D"—the 16th Brigade of the 6th (Poona) Division, Indian Army—sailed from India in mid-October. Turkey declared war against Great Britain on October 31st, and a solitary British gunboat, the *Espiègle*, remained in the Shatt-el-Arab below Basra to guard the oil dépôts and other British property at Muhammerah. On November 6th the 16th Brigade arrived off Fao, at the mouth of the Shatt-el-Arab; a Turkish infantry force was driven off, and Fao was captured without loss on the British side. Force "D" then landed, and gunboats entered the river. A week later the whole 6th Division had arrived, and Lieutenant-General Sir A. A. Barrett took over command at Saniyeh, on the right bank opposite Muhammerah. On November 17th the division attacked, and put the Turks to flight from their trenches at Sahil, before Saniyeh. Basra was occupied by the evening of November 21st. River reconnaissance by gunboats disclosed that the enemy had retired to Kurna (the traditionally accredited site of the Garden of Eden), at the junction of the Tigris and Euphrates, and were entrenching there. A rapid advance by a small mobile column up the left bank of the Shatt-el-Arab threatened to cut off Kurna, and the Turks hastily evacuated it, leaving some prisoners and guns in British hands. This happened on December 8th. For the next three months the position of Force "D" was precarious. The Turks greatly outnumbered it, and gradually organised two threatening flank movements— one along the Karun River from the direction of Persia, which, if unchecked, would probably have raised the friendly tribes of the Sheikh of Muhammerah against the British; the other west of Basra, from the direction of Nasiriyeh. This second danger was the more immediate, for by April the Turks were in force at Shaiba, ten miles south-west of Basra. At this juncture the 30th Brigade of the 12th Indian Division arrived at Basra, was sent to attack the Turks at Shaiba, and after a hot fight completely defeated them. The enemy, harassed by Arabs, fled back to Nasiriyeh. A few days later there arrived the remainder of the 12th Division under Major-General G. F. Gorringe, and with it General Nixon, who was to take over the command of the whole force. Simultaneously Major-General C. V. F. Townshend[16] was appointed to command the 6th Division. Towards the end of April the 12th Division supplied a strong column to operate up the Karun River towards Ahwaz and ensure the safety of the oil-pipe line. All was now clear for the projected advance up the Tigris. The Australian Half-Flight, as has been related, arrived just in time to take part in the operations.

The advance began on May 31st with an attack upon the Turks at Kurna. It was a curious battle. Both navy and army participated, and both were afloat. The whole country hereabouts has been flooded in April, May, and June of each year since the days of Noah. The infantry had to attack in Arab war-canoes locally called "bellums," and of these there were over 500 engaged. Mountain batteries were on rafts and the heavier guns on barges and steamers. As the river was mined, two launches swept for mines while the gunboats and the weird·raft-and-canoe fleet conducted the battle. Petre and Burn (observer), and Reilly and Broke-Smith (observer), reconnoitring from a landing-ground south of Kurna, brought in useful intelligence on the first day of the battle, and Reilly and White on the second day (June 1st) discovered the Turkish retreat and dropped news of it to the navy. Soon after midnight of June 2nd the gunboat *Comet* steamed into Amara, carrying General Townshend and Captain W. Nunn, R.N., who, with twenty-two men, bluffed the surprised Amara garrison into surrender. The army was fifty miles in rear down-stream, and did not arrive at Amara till next day. The battle of Kurna was a signal success; two Turkish gunboats were sunk, and seventeen guns, nearly 2,000 prisoners, and much material were captured. The aeroplanes caused consternation among the enemy on the river during the retreat; one launch full of fleeing Turks, which

---
[16] Maj.-Gen. Sir Charles V. F. Townshend, K.C.B., D.S.O. Officer of British Regular Army; elected Member of House of Commons, 1920; b. 21 Feb., 1861.

had narrowly escaped being hit by a small bomb dropped by Reilly and White, construed this misdirected shot as a warning to surrender, and accordingly ran ashore. There it waited quietly, and gave itself up to the first British launch which came up.

The freeing of Kurna from the proximity of the enemy enabled a landing-ground to be made there on an island. From this place the machines returned each evening to Basra dépôt, now styled the aircraft-park, and took with them the Army Commander's reports and despatches to be cabled to India.

Lieutenant Merz arrived from Australia on June 13th. In order that the composite force might work in harmony, the Australasian officer-pilots were granted commissions in the Royal Flying Corps according to their rank, and were temporarily appointed to the Indian Army.[17] Under this arrangement the two Indian Army officers, Broke-Smith and Reilly, took precedence and were promoted temporary majors, the former to be Deputy-Assistant-Director of Aviation, and the latter Flight-Commander. White was appointed adjutant of the half-flight and officer commanding the aircraft-park. At Basra a brick workshop for the overhaul of engines and the manufacture of spare-parts was erected by Arab labour. Tents were replaced by an iron hangar and huts made of rushes. The Australian repair-shop lorries proved invaluable, and supplied all necessary power until stationary power-engines were obtained from India.

The heat in Mesopotamia is intense, and, owing to the swamps and the myriads of mosquitoes, malaria and other tropical diseases soon appeared. Quinine had to be used every second day. Cases of sunstroke were frequent, and all ranks were supplied with spine-pads and dark glasses for protection against the rays of the sun. In Basra during the summer manual work was possible only in the early morning, late afternoon, and night. Parades and work extended from 5 a.m. till 9 a.m., and began again at 4 p.m. The aircraft-park diary and log-book showed that the average temperature

---

[17] Capt. White writes:—"We were merged into the R.F.C., but retained our own uniforms and always wore our 'Australia' shoulder-badges. Our pay and allotments were paid by the Australian Government, the Indian Government reimbursing Australia. When we were captured by the Turks, we automatically reverted to the permanent supernumerary list A.I.F."

during the months June-September, 1915, was 105 degrees in the shade. This heat, together with the fierce and dust-laden northerly "shamal,"[18] caused much trouble to the air-cooled aeroplane engines.

The engines of the three Maurice-Farman machines were 70-h.p. Renaults. One of them had seen considerable service in Egypt before being brought to Mesopotamia, and the others, though fitted to new aeroplane bodies, were second-hand. Engine failures were consequently frequent, and, as predatory Arabs roamed the whole country outside the entrenched camps and line-of-communication posts, the dangers of engine-failure were very real. On July 4th arrived two Caudron machines, with 80-h.p. engines. These were regarded as very frail for active service in such a country, but were gratefully received as an improvement upon the Maurice-Farmans.

After the capture of Amara, General Nixon turned his attention to the Turks in the west at Nasiriyeh. Further advance towards Kut from Amara required that Nasiriyeh should first be cleared, and this work was assigned to Gorringe with a mixed column of troops from the 6th and 12th Divisions. After preliminary reconnaissances over the western end of the long marshes of the Euphrates by Petre and Burn (observer) and by Reilly and Treloar, the Suk-esh-Sheyukh position was captured in an assault by Indian infantry on July 6th. The two Caudron machines, C1 and C2,[19] were then ordered up from Basra. Reilly and Merz made a preliminary reconnaissance in one of them, and Nasiriyeh was captured on July 24th by a decisive attack on both sides of the river. The Turks abandoned all their guns, and their losses in stern hand-to-hand fighting in the trenches were very heavy. The battle was fought "in a shade temperature of 113 degrees, and in an atmosphere of the heaviest and densest humidity," writes Edmund Candler,[20] alluding to the sufferings of the infantry. To the airmen the heat of the marshes was equally

---

[18] "Shamal." Begins about June 15. This is a strong seasonal N.N.W. wind which blows at thirty or forty miles an hour, and "when it blows" (records the Aviation Staff Officer with the I.E.F.) "a machine of the Maurice-Farman type moves backwards when flying at 600 to 1,000 feet."

[19] The machines were numbered after the arrival of the Caudrons, and are referred to by their service titles—C.1, M.F.7, Martinsyde 9—for simplicity. The point of the whole story of their work lies in their frequent break-down and consequently their limited usefulness.

[20] *The Long Road to Baghdad.*

exhausting. Land machines were never meant for operations in this region; yet water-planes there were none.[21]

On the first flight towards Nasiriyeh during the action, Reilly, in one of the Caudrons, was forced by engine-failure to land in the flood waters near Suk-esh-Sheyukh. A small garrison there helped him to save his machine. In reconnaissance patrols before the fighting and during the actual battle the engines of both Caudrons behaved indifferently. On the homeward journey to Basra on July 30th the pilots of the two machines had agreed to keep together, but soon lost touch. Reilly and a sergeant-mechanic flew in one, Merz and Burn in the other. Owing to renewed engine-trouble Reilly landed near a village about twenty-five miles from a refilling station at Abu Salibiq, an island in the southern marshes midway between Basra and Nasiriyeh. Fortunately the Arabs were sufficiently impressed by the recent British victory not to molest him. But Merz and Burn were never seen again. According to reports of Arab eye-witnesses, their machine descended in the desert about twenty miles from the refilling station. They were immediately attacked by a number of well-armed Arabs, and, recognising that they could not defend their machine—which, like all aeroplanes in Mesopotamia at that time, carried no machine-gun—they retreated in the direction of Abu Salibiq. The two airmen had no weapons but revolvers, and after a running fight of about five miles, during which they killed one and wounded five of their adversaries, one of the officers was wounded, and his comrade died fighting beside him. Such was the story told by friendly Arabs. Search parties were sent out from Abu Salibiq and Basra, but no trace of the missing airmen was ever found, though the machine, hacked to matchwood, was discovered by Reilly when on special reconnaissance a few days later.

A punitive expedition, which White accompanied on behalf of the Australian Flying Corps, searched the villages

---

[21] As early as 12 April, 1915, the Deputy-Assistant-Director of Aviation reported:—"Land aeroplanes until August (the end of the flood season) can be used only to a limited extent along the Kurna and Tigris line up to Ezra's Tomb, beyond which point they can be employed more freely. Between Kurna and Suk-esh-Sheyukh (Euphrates marshes) aeroplanes fitted with floats only can be employed, unless the risk of losing a machine by every enforced landing, even though not in the presence of the enemy, is to be faced." It remains to be said that no seaplanes arrived till late in August, and then they were of little use, the flood having subsided, and the seaplanes being confined to the meandering line of the river.

where the Arab murderers were believed to be domiciled.
No signs of the officers' effects were, however, to be found,
and the principal culprits had fled. By way of vengeance the
houses of the Sheikh were burnt. The loss of Burn and
Merz was a severe blow; both were capable pilots, and, as a
medical man, Merz had rendered conspicuous service in the
understaffed hospital at Nasiriyeh on the night before his last
flight. After this experience of the Arabs, long flights
between towns on the line of communications were forbidden
until better aeroplanes should arrive.

The period between the capture of Nasiriyeh and the attack
on Kut (July-September) was occupied by the preparation of
communications up-river for the intended advance. For the
airmen it was a long chronicle of destroyed hangars under the
force of the "shamal," of repairing engines badly overhauled
in England or Egypt, of working desperately to get first one
machine to fly and then another. Tent-hangars were so
frequently blown down that they were soon destroyed. The
material used in their manufacture was of poor quality, and
the tent-sides were soon split into ribbons. For a time the
machines, except at the Basra park, where a corrugated iron
hangar had been built, were simply pegged down in the open.
An effort to convert one Maurice-Farman into a water-plane
proved unsuccessful. Meanwhile, for the coming advance,
the flight fitted out two barges—the one with a broad deck
capable of holding two aeroplanes, the other as a floating
workshop. It also arranged an elaborate scheme of signals
for co-operation with artillery. This was rendered the more
difficult by the fact that, under the peculiar climatic conditions,
Very lights were invisible from the ground when fired at more
than 5,000 feet, and the only possible working signals were
pre-arranged turns of the observing machine and smoke-balls.

In August the flight received reinforcements and became a
squadron—No. 30 Squadron, R.F.C. Four Martinsyde
biplanes (single-seater scouts) were landed at Basra on August
24th, together with the Australian workshop-lorry and stores-
lorry—which eventually proved to be too heavy for the sandy
country—and a number of motor-boats. About the same time
there arrived from East Africa the nucleus of a seaplane
flight, composed of three seaplanes under Major R. Gordon; a

third flight was promised from India. The first Martinsyde was tested by Petre on August 29th, and its performance was very disappointing; it took twenty-five gallons of petrol and twenty-three minutes to climb 7,000 feet, where its best speed was only fifty miles an hour.

During early September the whole of Force "D" was moving up-river and concentrating at Ali Gharbi, more than half-way between Kut and Amara. Ali Gharbi was the base for the Kut attack, and an advanced aeroplane landing-ground was also made at that place. By mid-September Townshend had his advance-posts as far forward as Sanniyat, twenty miles from the Turkish entrenched position at Es-Sinn, and twenty-seven miles down-river from Kut. No. 30 Squadron was greatly crippled by lack of serviceable machines, and possessed at this time at Ali Gharbi only four machines—M.F.1, Caudron 3, and Martinsydes 5 and 6. M.F.1 was smashed by a British pilot in a bad landing on September 11th at Ali Gharbi. Misfortunes with the other machines followed. On September 13th Martinsyde 5 crashed while being tested in a high wind, and three days later Caudron 3, flown by Treloar with Captain B. S. Atkins[22] of the Indian Army as observer, developed engine-trouble while reconnoitring Es-Sinn, and was forced to land behind the Turkish lines. The airmen were roughly handled by mounted Arabs, and finally were taken by the Turks as prisoners to Baghdad. Martinsyde 6 was the only machine now left with Townshend's division, and Petre and White were at once ordered up from Basra with any available machines. Two seaplane barges were already proceeding up-river—one with two seaplanes on board, and the other with the third seaplane and Martinsyde 9 in a case. White flew M.F.7 from Basra up to the first seaplane barge, and Petre flew Martinsyde 8, but smashed it on arrival in landing outside the prepared ground at Sanniyat.

The voyage of the seaplane barges was full of incident. Above Amara a strong wind caught them and blew them into a bank, where M.F.7 was damaged by overhanging trees. The first barge arrived at Sanniyat on September 25th, and M.F.7 was there repaired in time for the battle. The land

---

[22] Capt. B. S. Atkins. Officer of Indian Regular Army; of Lowestoft, Suffolk, Eng.; b. Kimberley, Norfolk, Eng., 4 April, 1885.

machines were then ordered on to Nakhailat, a short distance up-stream from Sanniyat, whither Townshend's force had advanced. Petre's accident left only Martinsyde 6 and M.F.7 available for the attack on Es-Sinn. The seaplanes, working from the river, were attached to the artillery.

Photographs of the Turkish position were taken on September 26th from M.F.7, but these were of little use, for the only available photographic printing-paper was worthless. The ordinary printing-out paper sent from England was old—as most other stores appear to have been—and therefore inferior. The bromide paper obtained at Basra was entirely useless. The reconnoitring airmen had, therefore, to rely on their own eyes alone. Reconnaissance was made next day of the extreme left flank of the enemy's position, and, while this was in progress, the long-prepared attack on the Kut defences began.

CHAPTER II

MESOPOTAMIA—THE END OF THE FIRST CAMPAIGN

Townshend, with the 6th Indian Division, turned the Es-Sinn position and captured Kut by brilliant tactics. The enemy had a division on each side of the river and his reserves on the left bank, behind the entrenched position of Es-Sinn. To delude him into thinking that the attack was coming on the right bank, Townshend on September 27th sent his cavalry to make a feint on that side. Tents were pitched there, and the 16th Infantry Brigade also crossed by a bridge of boats and dug in ostentatiously before the enemy. During the following night almost the whole force was moved back across the river, leaving only a small garrison in a redoubt on the right bank. The cavalry and part of the 17th Infantry Brigade were then sent on a wide encircling movement round and behind the Turkish left flank, where marshy ground had been reported by the aeroplanes as practicable, while an infantry column was to attack at dawn the flank entrenchments. As soon as this left flank should be driven in, a general assault was to begin along the whole Es-Sinn front.

The plan succeeded perfectly. The enemy, though in greatly superior numbers, was completely out-manœuvred; his left flank was rolled up, and a final brilliant bayonet charge drove the retiring Turks into a rout, which also involved reinforcements appearing from the right bank of the river. By evening the victory was complete; the enemy fled from both Es-Sinn and Kut, lost heavily in killed and prisoners, and abandoned fifteen guns.

The two aeroplanes engaged played a useful part in the action by maintaining communication between Townshend's headquarters and Brigadier-General W. S. Delamain's mobile column on the far left flank. Delamain outran the telephone connections, and the airmen kept touch for him all day, reported his movements, and conveyed Townshend's orders. Lieutenant E. J. Fulton, of the R.F.C., flew M.F.7, and Reilly Martinsyde 6. Two of the three seaplanes were attached to the artillery for observation work, but one so engaged early in the day had to descend owing to engine trouble, and between 9.30 a.m. and 5.30 p.m. neither of these seaplanes could rise from the water because of contrary winds in the narrow river reaches. At length, at 6 p.m., they were able to take off and reconnoitre. They might have bombed the retreating enemy, for aëroplane bombs had arrived from India, but the bomb-racks were weak, and promptly became unserviceable. The land machines, however, bombed the Turks to the utmost of their power. The fleeing enemy was pursued by Townshend's division with such rapidity that by October 5th the British were at Aziziyeh, half-way, on an air line, between Kut and Baghdad.

It was not long before the squadron was again in difficulties. A landing-ground had been selected at Kut, and the three land machines, M.F.7 and Martinsydes 8 (now repaired) and 6, flew up at that place on September 30th. One seaplane also flew up; the other was damaged by the wind, and, owing to lack of water-transport, had to remain at Nakhailat. The reaches of the river below Kut are very shallow, and the unfortunate seaplane flight was without adequate transport of its own, and was compelled to supplement what it had by what it could coax from other services. Its second barge was delayed at Ali Gharbi for want of a tug; a flying corps launch, an old and worn vessel, with petrol and other important stores on board, was sunk in collision at Sheikh Saad before the battle of Es-Sinn; and most of the supply steamers were delayed in the shallow reaches below Kut for days after that battle. Nevertheless, by dint of great exertions, the more serviceable seaplane was supplied with spare parts for the remedy of slight defects, and on September 30th it reconnoitred up-river. It found the Turks thirty-six miles above Kut and still retreating, with British gunboats in pursuit. But the delays in transportation were exasperating. On October 4th the aviation staff officer on headquarters of the force recorded:—" No prospect of aeroplane lighter from Amara or seaplane lighter from Ali Gharbi being brought for a long time. Until they come, the flight will be minus a fourth machine (M.F.2) and a reserve Martinsyde (No. 9), and the seaplane flight will be without its shed, in which seaplanes can be conveniently repaired, and without the bulk of its spare parts, and will be unable to repair seaplane 825. Two days ago 600 gallons of petrol was borrowed for the flight from the motor machine-gun section. The flight has used up the greater part of a month's supply in ten days, and 1,800 gallons is delayed in the seaplane lighter at Ali Gharbi (due at the front on September 28th). The flight's land transport is now needed, but the motor vehicles detailed (two light tenders and two heavy) cannot yet be brought up for lack of shipping." It remains to be added that the long-expected mule-transport did not leave Bombay till October 15th. Work was begun on the damaged seaplane on October 6th to convert it into a land machine, and by October 13th a land chassis had been made and attached. The converted machine flew satisfactorily.

Meanwhile on October 2nd Martinsyde 8, piloted by Petre, was smashed on landing at Aziziyeh, through no fault of anyone, unless it be that of the authorities who sent such a type of machine to be used in such a country. The Martinsydes required very smooth ground for landing—"a croquet lawn," says the worried aviation staff officer, in cynical comment. With everything against it, and neglected by distant authorities in most matters of supply and administration, the first Mesopotamian expeditionary force uttered prayers not so much for croquet lawns as for spare parts.

After the capture of Kut, air reconnaissance to discover the enemy's strength was ordered in three directions—towards Nasiriyeh, down the Shatt-el-Hai, an ancient but at times still navigable canal which connects the Tigris and the Euphrates Rivers; northwards from Kut across the marshes towards Persia; and up the Tigris, whither the main body of the enemy was retreating. Reilly, in Martinsyde 6, examined the enemy's position at Ctesiphon, outside Baghdad, on October 5th, and found the Turks strongly entrenched there with an advance-guard occupying Zeur, about half-way between Ctesiphon and Aziziyeh. The northern reconnaissance towards the Persian border was performed by Major Gordon, in the converted seaplane. On October 13th the aeroplane-lighter arrived with M.F.2 from Amara, and in this machine White and Broke-Smith next day examined the Shatt-el-Hai. They found, not a river, but a chain of

Map No. 2

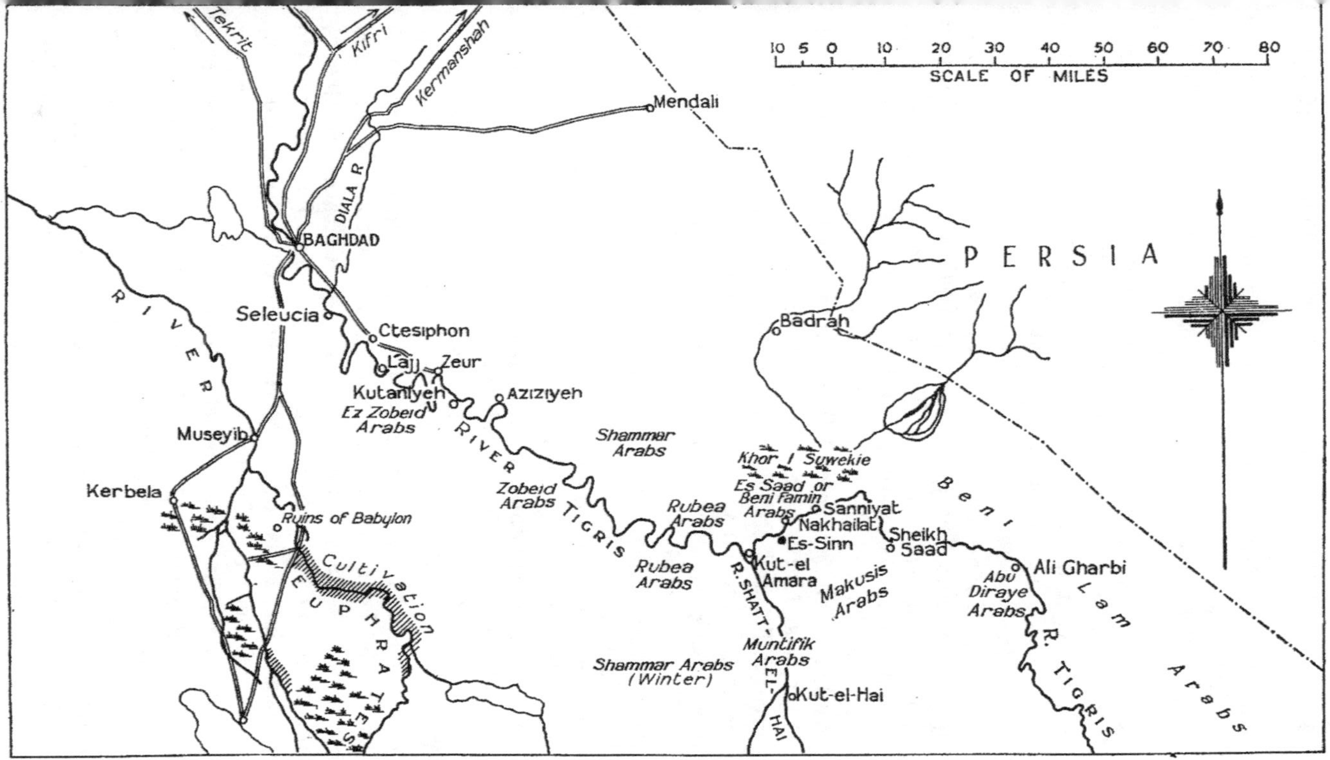

MESOPOTAMIA (NORTH-WESTERN PORTION), SHOWING AREA OF LATER OPERATIONS OF AUSTRALIAN HALF-FLIGHT

water-holes. On October 15th the seaplane-lighter at last reached Kut from Ali Gharbi. "The seaplane flight," records the aviation staff officer, "can now organise properly and become an efficient unit; they have borrowed a lathe from H.M.S. *Comet,* having none of their own at present. Tools have been on order for them for a long time—through the Admiralty, it is understood." Three aeroplane wireless sets were landed at Basra at this time from oversea, but with fittings incomplete.

While Townshend's force was assembling in strength up-stream from Kut, preparatory to farther advance, Gordon's converted seaplane on October 18th reconnoitred as far as Badrah, near the Persian border, forty-five miles north of Kut, and located the camp of an Arab tribe known to be hostile. Four days later White, Fulton, and Reilly in M.F.2, M.F.7, and Martinsyde 6 bombed this camp with two 20-lb., three 30-lb., and sixteen 2-lb. bombs. The raid was entirely successful, and on October 23rd the sheikh of the tribe sent in a message to know if he might tender his submission.

The principal work, however, was up the Tigris. From their main camp before Ctesiphon the Turks had pushed out two forward positions—one ten miles out at Zeur, already mentioned, and the other at Kutaniyeh, only five miles from the British camp at Aziziyeh. The enemy held Kutaniyeh with about 2,000 cavalry and camelry, and the proximity of this force demanded much air reconnaissance. It was thought that the Turks might attack or make raids from Kutaniyeh; and as Aziziyeh was simply a deserted Arab town of mud huts and unsuitable for defence, constant watch had to be kept for reinforcements of the enemy's advanced position. Moreover the enemy's main defences, astride of the river, on the site of the ancient cities of Ctesiphon and Seleucia, had to be carefully reconnoitred and mapped. The brunt of this work fell on White and Fulton, who, during a month spent at Aziziyeh while reinforcements were being brought up, performed about one reconnaissance daily, a duty which White combined with his work as adjutant. These flights were carried out in M.F.2 and M.F.7. They were inadequate machines; one was second-hand from service in Egypt, and had been experimentally converted into a seaplane and reconverted. Most of these reconnaissance patrols, owing to the strong winds and the slow speed of the machines, occupied from two to two and a half hours. Engines were overhauled after every twenty-seven hours' flying, but nevertheless engine failures were frequent, and, as the aeroplanes were not armed with machine-guns, the pilots ran considerable risk in desert landings.

On one occasion White, with Captain F. C. C. Yeats-Brown,[1] of the 17th Cavalry, as observer, was reconnoitring Ctesiphon, when the engine began to miss badly, and a landing had to be made in front of the enemy position of Zeur. There was no time to effect repairs. The engine was running sufficiently well to move the aeroplane, but not to lift it, and as the wind was favourable, the airmen decided to "taxi" along the ground, with the observer standing up to direct the course and ready with a rifle in case of pursuit. In this fashion they ran before the wind for fifteen miles without incident, and drew near to the enemy's position at Kutaniyeh. This was situated on a ridge of sand-hills; the only smooth crossing was by the road which passed over the ridge at some distance from the river. The two airmen dashed for this crossing in their crippled ground-running machine, passed the position safely, and reached Aziziyeh. What the Turks were doing to permit this could only be conjectured.

Such narrow escapes, even in rear of the British lines, were regarded by these airmen as part of the day's work. Owing to the small number of troops engaged in active operations, few could be spared to guard at all points the long river-line of communication. Each town, therefore, from the base to the most advanced position, became an entrenched camp; the territory outside was No-Man's Land, and over it roamed tribes whose custom it has always been to hover, like birds waiting for their prey, on the flanks of invading armies. The outstanding example of the danger from these Arabs is the previously-related disaster to Merz and Burn. The story of their loss might easily have been repeated in November, when an accident happened to a seaplane piloted by Gordon, who carried as passenger Major-General G. V. Kemball, Chief of General Staff in Mesopotamia. The seaplane was forced to

---

[1] Capt. F. C. C. Yeats-Brown, D.F.C.   Officer of Indian Regular Army; b. Genoa, Italy, 15 Aug., 1886.

land through engine failure between Kut and Aziziyeh. Its non-arrival at Aziziyeh caused alarm, and White went in search of it in M.F.2. He found the seaplane aground beside a high bank of the river, close to which was a large Arab camp. While White was flying low above the camp in search of a place to land, the Arabs opened fire on his machine, and their bullets broke an aileron rib and pierced the propeller. White landed on a road about a thousand yards from the river bank. After making a show of force by gesticulating and pretending to point out to a comrade the Arabs who had been shooting, he ran on foot to the river, carrying a spare rifle for the general. He and the general returned to the aeroplane, which the Arabs had meanwhile hesitated to attack, and flew home to Aziziyeh. Gordon was brought in by an Indian cavalry patrol, which had seen the aeroplane descend and had gone over to its help.

The main duty of the air reconnaissances was to supplement existing maps. Owing to the shifting course of the Tigris, the army maps of Mesopotamia were inadequate for tactical purposes, and mapping from the air with primitive appliances was a long and laborious task. Photographs were taken with an ordinary reflex camera, by pilot or observer holding the camera over the side of the machine or pointing its lens through a hole in the floor. Although the photographs showed the formation of trenches and redoubts, they did not locate these with sufficient accuracy for mapping purposes. A night march by compass bearing on the enemy's flank was to be a feature of the attack on Ctesiphon; precision, therefore, was essential. The enemy always concentrated his artillery on aeroplanes; the Maurice-Farman was a slow climber, and reconnaissance was usually at an altitude of from 4,500 to 6,900 feet. Immunity from shell-fire was consequently rare, and machines were compelled repeatedly to turn or zigzag and drop bombs to divert the gunners' aim. Mapping under such conditions was not easy. On one occasion White and Yeats-Brown (observer), ordered to reconnoitre the right bank at Ctesiphon at 1,000 feet to discover the enemy's guns, performed the task by gliding down over Ctesiphon as though hit. At 1,000 feet they saw and located field batteries, and then flew off homeward before the gunners realised the deception.

An implement for accurate mapping was devised by Captain Petre. It was like a small garden rake. A short handle at the side enabled its longer axis to be brought on a level with the eye; the pegs were carefully spaced; and when the implement was held to the forehead, the pegs showed the degrees of distance from the centre. With this crude instrument White mapped and verified the location of the enemy's line, particularly fixing the position known as " V.P." (vital point)—a flank redoubt which was to be used as a pivot of manœuvre in the coming attack. Much of the country in the vicinity of Ctesiphon is scarred with remains of high-level canals of ancient Assyrian and Persian days. The ruined palace of the Persian King Chosroes was a conspicuous landmark in the centre of the Turkish position. The mean of two bearings upon each of several prominent points was taken with the garden rake device from over known points within the British line. Back bearings were then taken in a similar way when the machine was over " V.P." and the ruined palace. The mean of all these bearings was plotted after return to camp on a map marked with a circle of degrees. On the day of battle this map proved accurate.

The battle of Ctesiphon was fought on November 22nd, but before it began one of the two remaining Australian flying officers was lost. General Townshend's intention was to attack an extensive and well-defended Turkish position along the left bank of the Tigris, and with a flanking force endeavour to cut off the enemy's retreat across the Diala River, a few miles behind Ctesiphon. In order to isolate Baghdad from the more distant enemy bases, an aeroplane was to fly out, land behind the town, and cut the wires running west and north to the Euphrates, Constantinople, and Kifri. White and Yeats-Brown volunteered for this task. They set out at dawn on November 13th, the day on which the 6th Division began its forward march. Necklaces of guncotton were carried on the aeroplane, also extra tins of petrol and oil. The distance to be covered was at least sixty miles each way. The airmen did not expect to return if adverse winds should spring up.

In the event they found that the telegraph wires ran westwards from Baghdad along the main road, and not out into the desert, as maps of that region showed. As Turkish troops of all arms were constantly moving along the road, and as there was much bad ground, the choice of a landing place was limited. Finally White chose a plot of ground bounded by canals, where the telegraph lines ran about three hundred yards from the road. It was about eight miles from Baghdad, and in rear of the Turkish position of Seleucia, and the airmen considered that the few individuals in the vicinity could be kept at a distance. However, the narrowness of the ground and the unexpected arrival on the scene of a mounted gendarme led to their colliding with a telegraph pole, which badly smashed a wing and rendered the aeroplane useless. Arabs, soon joined by a party of Turks, attacked the airmen from short range. Nevertheless, Yeats-Brown managed to blow up the wires under fire, while White filled the tanks and kept off the enemy with the rifle. The two then started the engine, buoyed up with the hope of escaping by ground-running as they had done once before at Zeur. But this time there was too much against them. They were seized and roughly handled by the Arabs, until rescued and taken over by the Turks.

The loss to the squadron was severe, and was aggravated on November 21st, when Reilly, in Martinsyde 6, went out on reconnaissance and was shot down by gun-fire. He, too, was taken prisoner. Only one aeroplane and one Australian pilot now remained in A Flight—the old M.F.7 and Captain Petre. They both did useful service during the battle.

Reinforcements for the squadron arrived in the shape of the long-promised new flight of four B.E.2.c machines from England, which reached Basra at the end of October and the fighting front on November 20th, two days before the battle of Ctesiphon began. Some account of their journey up-river from Kut is worth the telling; it is graphic of the worries of the river-line of communication. The aviation staff officer writes:—" On November 14th Tug *T3* (towing the lighter with two B.E.2.c machines) missed the channel twelve miles up and ran aground, then drifting sideways in the current and becoming badly stuck. She was got off at 9 p.m. The *Shirin*, also going up, and one L-class launch spent the night in the same place. On November 15th *T3* grounded sideways again when starting off at 6 a.m. The channel is good enough for this ship, but the pilot had become upset by the *contretemps* of last evening and did not navigate the ship into the proper channel. In the meantime the *Shirin* went on in spite of the order that ships are to render each other assistance, and in spite of lamp signals from *T3* to wait, as we were stuck, which were acknowledged. The hooter of *T3* was also constantly sounded to show that we were stuck.

"A signal was also sent to the *Shirin* (and acknowledged) to send the L-launch down to *T3* as well as to wait. The launch *L6* remained by the bank half-a-mile upstream, and did not come down. The *T3* jolly-boat was sent ashore, and orders were sent to *L6* by messenger along the bank to come down at once. *L6* eventually came at 8 a.m., and then grounded, and did not get off till noon. The mails were sent up in this launch to catch the *Shirin*. The launch stuck three times within four miles and was eventually floated off at 5.30 p.m. When discovered stuck four miles upstream, the crew were told they would remain out the night if they did not get off and come back, and the launch was floated off within ten minutes. Borrowing horses from the local sheikh, self and Captain Murray rode upstream and intercepted the *Shirin* some fifteen miles up-river at 1.30 p.m. The Army Commander's mail-bag, which we took on horseback, was handed over to the officer commanding troops to take up to Aziziyeh. The remainder of the mails could not be sent through on the *Shirin,* as the ship went off without waiting for the *T3* and did not send the *L6* back, and the launch, after great delay in starting, stuck frequently, and did not catch up the *Shirin*.

"The pilot and crew of *T3* were unsuccessful in getting her off till nightfall. Efforts to communicate with Kut by means of the aeroplane wireless set on board failed. The land wireless stations do not receive messages of a less wave length than 600 metres, and the aeroplane set wave length is 300 metres. There was a chance that our message might be picked up, however."[2]

The aeroplanes were then taken out of the lighter, were

---

[2] See note at end of chapter.

erected at Kut, and two of them were flown up-river. Being away from the lighter, they were thus without mechanics, spare parts, and repair shop. In the event only one of them was able to take part in the battle of Ctesiphon.

The attacking force, with Townshend's 6th Division in the van, was assembled at Lajj, before Ctesiphon, on November 21st, and the assault was launched at dawn next morning. The full weight of it was thrown at the enemy's extreme left flank, as at Es-Sinn, and after severe fighting, which lasted all day, the enemy's first and second lines were captured, together with eight guns and 1,300 prisoners. "The Turkish 45th Division," says Candler,[3] "was practically annihilated; but we had no reinforcements to oppose fresh troops that were brought up. The captured trenches changed hands several times, and in the end our line was too thinned to hold the extended position. . . . On the 23rd we were unable to renew the offensive. That night and in the early morning of the 24th we were repelling counter-attacks. On the 24th and 25th our wounded were removed with difficulty to Lajj. On the 25th the Turks received fresh reinforcements." "During the afternoon of November 25th," says General Nixon, in his despatch, "large columns were seen advancing down the left bank, and also inland, as if to turn our right flank, while hostile cavalry threatened our rear. General Townshend was nine miles from his shipping and source of supplies at Lajj, faced by superior forces of fresh troops."

Such is the outline of the sorrowful story. Retreat was inevitable. The force fell back on Lajj, and then upon Kut. This account may not stray from its limits to describe that retreat, or to discuss the criticism afterwards levelled at the local commander and at the distant authority which agreed to the advance on Baghdad with inadequate strength. By December 2nd Townshend's force again reached Kut, thoroughly exhausted. The 6th Division, which actually captured Ctesiphon in this attack, lost in doing so a third of its effectives in killed and wounded. Townshend was invested in Kut with about 3,000 British and 10,000 Indian troops, including followers. The remainder of Force "D" retreated down river to Ali Gharbi. Kut surrendered on the 29th

---

[3] *The Long Road to Baghdad.*

April, 1916, after costly efforts by the British to raise the siege.

The battle of Ctesiphon and the retreat to Kut marked the end of the career of the Australian Half-Flight. At Ctesiphon Fulton, reconnoitring in Martinsyde 8, was shot down by gun-fire and captured, but M.F.7, piloted by Petre, and the converted seaplane carried out important patrols during the first day of the battle, and a second seaplane and one of the new B.E.2.c machines made reconnaissances in the afternoon. They kept headquarters constantly informed of the progress of the attack, and the B.E. effectively bombed a body of 4,000 Turks on a bridge over the Diala River. After the retreat to Kut and the approach of the Turks to invest the town, the remainder of the squadron was ordered to leave Kut by air. The seaplanes had already gone downstream by barge. Two land machines—M.F.7 (Petre) and one of the B.E.'s—left Kut on December 7th; two damaged B.E's and one damaged Martinsyde were left behind, together with several British pilots and observers and most of the non-commissioned officers and mechanics. Among these were nine Australians. There were eight Australian mechanics at the base at Basra, and these were sent to Egypt early in 1916 to join the newly-forming Australian Flying Corps. Captain Petre was also sent to Egypt. He was subsequently transferred to the Royal Flying Corps, and was appointed to command a training squadron in England.

The narrative of the Australians of the Half-Flight who were made prisoners by the Turks may be told in the words of Captain White, who met two of them in captivity in Asia Minor. He writes:—"A reinforcement of thirteen mechanics, under Sergeant Mackinolty,[4] had arrived at Basra from Australia about the 1st September, 1915. Some of them were sent up immediately to Aziziyeh. There were nine Australians among the forty-four non-commissioned officers and men of the squadron besieged in Kut. During the siege the mechanics worked incessantly. Among the Australians Corporal J. McK. Sloss[5] did conspicuous service.

---

[4] Lieut. G. J. W. Mackinolty; Aust. Flying Corps. Air-mechanic; of Korumburra, Vic.; b. Leongatha, Vic., 24 March, 1895.

[5] Flight-Sgt. J. McK. Sloss; (No. 11, Aust. Flying Corps). Motor engineer and proprietor; of Malvern, Melbourne; b. Naring, Vic., 25 Nov., 1878.

Under the command of Captain Winfield Smith, a British pilot, they erected mills for grinding the wheat and barley. The grain was dropped to the garrison from aeroplanes. For excellent work during the siege Corporal Sloss was promoted to flight-sergeant. Captain Petre flew many times from Ali Gharbi over the beleaguered town, and dropped bags of grain and even millstones for the grinding of it. Two Fokker aeroplanes piloted by Germans appeared later on the enemy's side and interfered with this attempt at relief. Nevertheless the British machines dropped at Kut in all about five tons of grain and medical stores.

"After the capitulation of Kut, the 13,000 prisoners were marched over 700 miles to Anatolia. Hundreds died by the way through exposure, fatigue, and starvation. The survivors were set to work in railway construction on the Taurus Mountains, where many more died of typhus, malaria, or dysentery, brought on by mal-nutrition or exposure. Only about 2,000 survived their captivity. Of the forty-four flying corps mechanics, only six survived the march. Of the nine Australian mechanics taken in Kut—one of whom, Air-Mechanic Rayment,[6] was badly wounded during the siege —only two, Sergeant Sloss and Air-Mechanic Hudson,[7] survived their captivity. Corporal Soley[8] and Air-Mechanic Curran[9] died at Nisibin, and Air-Mechanics Williams,[10] Rayment, Adams,[11] Lord,[12] and Munro[13] in the vicinity of the Taurus Mountains.

"During 1916, Sloss, in company with two British prisoners, attempted to escape from a working camp in the

---

[6] Air-Mechanic W. C. Rayment (No. 49, Aust. Flying Corps). Heating engineer; of Surrey Hills, Melbourne; b. Jan Juc, Vic., 22 Jan., 1892. Died while prisoner of war, 11 Nov., 1916.

[7] Air-Mechanic K. L. Hudson (No. 12, Aust. Flying Corps). Motor mechanic; b. Launceston, Tas., 1892.

[8] Cpl. T. Soley (No. 10, Aust. Flying Corps). Motor mechanic; b. Eltham, Eng., 1891. Died while prisoner of war, June–July, 1916.

[9] Air-Mechanic D. Curran (No. 45, Aust. Flying Corps). Carpenter; b. The Mallard, Raholp, Downpatrick, Ireland, 1879. Died while prisoner of war, 16 June, 1917.

[10] Air-Mechanic L. T. Williams (No. 16, Aust. Flying Corps). Carpenter and joiner; b. Fitzroy, Melbourne, 1892. Died while prisoner of war.

[11] Air-Mechanic F. L. Adams (No. 44, Aust. Flying Corps). Carpenter; of Spreydon, Christchurch, N.Z.; b. Sydenham, Christchurch, 8 Oct., 1892. Died while prisoner of war, Aug.–Nov., 1916.

[12] Air-Mechanic W. H. Lord (No. 23, Aust. Flying Corps). Moulder; b. Fitzroy, Melbourne, 1894. Died while prisoner of war.

[13] Air-Mechanic J. Munro (No. 47, Aust. Flying Corps). Chauffeur; b. Darlinghurst, Sydney, 24 Dec., 1892. Died while prisoner of war, 13 Oct., 1916.

Taurus Mountains, situated about thirty miles from the Gulf of Alexandretta. They succeeded in reaching the coast, but could not find a boat in which to get away, and, after their food had run out, had to give themselves up again. For this Sloss was imprisoned for three months, during which time he contracted typhus. During 1917 and 1918, in company with other prisoners, Sloss constructed a·collapsible boat of canvas and iron, in which five of them hoped to reach Cyprus, but on Sloss being sent to another working camp, the attempt had to be abandoned."

White himself and Yeats-Brown, after being captured before the Ctesiphon battle began, were taken from Baghdad by cart to Mosul. There they found Atkins and Treloar. For two and a half months they were closely confined in barracks, and received very bad treatment at the hands of the prison authorities. A space about twenty-five yards by six, in a filthy balcony overlooking a courtyard, was their sole exercise ground. Neither furniture nor food was supplied by the Turks, but all necessaries had to be purchased out of their daily pay of 4s. 6d., paid by the Turks and debited to the British Government. Reilly and Fulton were also sent to the Mosul prison-camp. Later the prisoners were taken to Afion Kara Hissar,[14] in the interior of Asia Minor.

In March, 1917, Treloar and four British officers were sent to Constantinople. There they were imprisoned in an underground cell, as a reprisal against alleged ill-treatment of Turkish officer prisoners in Egypt. One of these British officers died of typhus in that cell.

White was sent to Constantinople in July, 1918, and succeeded in escaping from custody during a railway collision in the suburbs of that city. Disguised as a Turk, he stowed away on a Ukranian steamer in company with Captain A. J. Bott,[15] of the Royal Air Force, who had also escaped from custody. The vessel remained thirty-three days at anchor in the harbour at Constantinople, and the officers spent an uncomfortable time below, sometimes hidden in the ship's ballast

---

[14] The prison-camp concerning which Lieut. Jones wrote, in *The Road to En-dor*, the graphic story of the experiences of himself and Lieut. Hill (an Australian in the Royal Flying Corps).

[15] The detailed account of the remarkable escape of these two officers is told in *Eastern Nights and Flights*, by Alan Bott (" Contact "). (Capt. A. J. Bott, M.C. Journalist; b. Stoke-on-Trent, Eng., 14 Jan., 1893.)

tanks by the engineers, whom they bribed with cheques cashed surreptitiously before their escape. Eventually they reached Odessa, which had just been wrested from the Bolsheviks by an Austro-German army. False passports describing them as Russians enabled them to remain a month in Odessa, and they had made arrangements to join the anti-Bolshevik army, when they heard of the impending armistice with Bulgaria. With the help of an interned Englishman and a Russian merchant-service captain, they stowed away in a Ukranian hospital-ship, sailed to Varna in Bulgaria, there regained touch with the Allied forces, and eventually arrived at Salonika a week before the armistice with Germany.

Note.—The reader will find in a number of books written on the Mesopotamian campaign many graphic references to the difficulties of navigation on the Tigris and the inefficiencies of the craft supplied for the work. The fleet of hundreds of Arab "bellums," in which the British infantry attacked in the battle of Kurna, has already been briefly described; in that respect it was one of the most remarkable battles ever fought by the British Army. Of the river fleet which was used subsequently for transport of supplies up the Tigris, Edmund Candler writes in his story of the campaign, *The Long Road to Baghdad*:—
"To supplement the self-respecting paddle-steamers of the Tigris the most heterogeneous collection of scrap-iron and remnants of river-traffic were gathered in, taxing the resources of India's inland navigation from Bhamo to Sind. How this craft ever found its way over the ocean the Providence which watches over the improvident alone knows. Beyond question the boat of the most catholic ancestry on the Tigris in those early days was the *Aerial*, half houseboat, half aeroplane. Its hull was from the Brahmaputra, and it was fitted with an air-propeller and a 50-horse-power semi-Diesel-type engine, and it made more noise than a minor battle. It once plied as a *shikar*-boat in Assam, but its owner and navigator had a happy inspiration, and this miracle of private improvisation became the officially-recognised hospital ferry, plying hourly between the field ambulance on the river bank and the hospital camp. For months it ran the gauntlet of shot and shell and mine, and the adventures of its navigator between Ctesiphon and Sheikh Saad alone would provide material for a bulky volume. Another boat, indigenous to the Tigris, is the cauldron-like *gufar* of Baghdad, probably the oldest vessel in the world. A *gufar* moored alongside the *Aerial* offers a striking picture in the evolution of craft. It is a reed basket with wooden uprights, plastered over with pitch from the bitumen wells of Hitt. Herodotus describes *gufars* as being "round as bucklers," spinning downstream with merchandise from Nineveh to Babylon. Each *gufar* carried a donkey, and was navigated by two men. Arrived in Babylon, and the merchandise disposed of, it was dismembered and the parts carried back overland by the passenger ass. We first met with these craft at Amara. Their most northerly limit upstream is Tekrit."

CHAPTER III

THE MIDDLE EAST—ADVENT OF No. 1 SQUADRON

It became the custom of the people, and even of the authorities, in Britain to refer to all operations in which British troops were engaged, in theatres of war other than France and Belgium, as "side-shows." In a sense they were such, and certainly they were for the greater part of the war treated as of secondary importance in the matter of equipment and reinforcements. The Germans also regarded the Turkish theatre in much the same light. Both sides believed, and rightly, that the decision on the Western Front in France would settle the issues on all other fields. At least on the British side the lot of the troops who were engaged in "the side-shows" was probably harder than that of those on the main front—harder, because supplies and equipment were generally inferior or insufficient, because soldiers' home leave was almost unknown, and because, as the war lengthened out, commanders on minor fronts were liable to be hampered and thwarted indefinitely by the demands of "the general strategical situation."

The Palestine campaign—perhaps the most important of all the Allies' minor-front campaigns—was carried to its brilliantly successful conclusion after bitter experience of muddle, wasted energy, false moves, and inefficient support of earlier operations in the Near East. In 1915 the British Army learned its hard lesson in the Gallipoli Peninsula and in Mesopotamia. By early 1916 the only relief in the sombre disillusion of the nation was the splendid heart of the men who fought and suffered and died and in part somehow survived in those badly organised ventures. The British Government seemed in the beginning to believe that Britain's prestige in the Near East was as good as an army already fighting for her there. So to some extent it was. The bombardment of the Dardanelles forts and the military landing in Gallipoli on one side of Turkey, and Townshend's advance upon Baghdad on the other, were each, in the enthusiasm of this belief credited beforehand with assured success. They were dramatic blows, and both movements were expected to march swiftly to the desired and perfect *dénoûment*.

The strategy of the simultaneous attack upon Turkey from two sides was sound, but the plans were ill-considered. Turkey was "the ramshackle Empire," and the British attacked her, if not with ramshackle, at least with careless, tactics. The scheme of operations was left too much to fortunes of the moment; its authors seemed to leap over every stage between the launching of the plan and its conclusion. No military force, however daring, can, if left unsupported, perform a task which depends on constant reinforcement of men and supplies, the clearance of wounded to adequate hospitals, and the establishment of efficient communications along the line of advance. These lessons had been learned in former wars by the British Army, but apparently not by Government departments in Whitehall. The eastern campaigns of 1915 flickered out with Townshend's surrender in Kut and the evacuation of Gallipoli. Those efforts made the military reputation of the Australians, and added laurels to the name of both British and Indian soldiers. Not to them belongs any disgrace of defeat. The War Office subsequently explained that these operations served an important purpose in holding down and crippling the Turkish military strength. This also is true; but it was not the designed objective, nor did it assuage the soldiers' bitter memories of lost opportunity in Gallipoli, or of the awful scenes among the neglected wounded who died in agony along the Tigris.

The year 1916 brought to Britain disillusion, but not yet her darkest hour. In the early part of that year the great German blow against Verdun failed. In July the first full-weight attack by the Allies on the Western Front, the offensive on the Somme, failed also in its local objective, though it relieved German pressure on Verdun. As the immensity of the task of beating Germany gradually became realised in Britain, the British people were roused to supreme endeavour. Conscription for the Army replaced voluntary enlistment; the tide of recruiting in all the Dominions reached its highest mark. The whole Empire now recognised that the Germans meant to fight to the death. Roumania joined the Allies.

The United States seemed to be turning steadily against Germany. The Allies prepared an immense effort for the campaign of 1917 against the Western Front. In the early months of that year the minor British fronts in the Near East were also awakened to new life with the advance of the Egyptian Expeditionary Force from the Suez Canal towards Palestine and the arrival of a new Mesopotamian army under Lieutenant-General Sir Stanley Maude at Baghdad.

In these great efforts Australia played her full part. The Australian infantry force, withdrawn to Egypt from the fierce schooling of Gallipoli, was early in 1916 expanded into four divisions, which were sent to France as soon as they were formed. The Australian Light Horse, in combination with the New Zealand Mounted Rifles, having been increased in strength to two cavalry divisions, remained in Egypt. The Camel Corps, later converted into cavalry, was also largely Australian. The Australian Flying Corps was founded in fact as well as in name, and 1916 saw also the first complete Australian flying squadron on service in the desert between the Suez Canal and El Arish. By the end of the year the establishment of a squadron had swollen to a scheme for four service squadrons. This in due course led to the formation of an Australian wing of four training squadrons in England for the supply of reinforcements to the fighting fronts.

Australia alone among the oversea dominions of the Empire established a flying corps of her own for service in the war. It was a portion of the Australian Imperial Force, though its squadrons for the most part served separately from each other and under the orders, as in the case of all British air squadrons, of the Royal Air Force. The first proposal for such oversea units came from the Army Council at the end of 1915, in a suggestion that the Dominions might wish to raise complete squadrons for service with the Royal Flying Corps[1] instead of continuing to encourage individual enlistments in the British flying arm. The Australian Government, perceiving the value of an air force for future training as well as for the present emergency, promptly adopted the suggestion.[2]

---

[1] The Royal Flying Corps was then the title of the military air arm. Australia was invited to form military air squadrons only, not naval. The re-amalgamation of the R.F.C. and the R.N.A.S., under the name of the Royal Air Force (as has been explained in the Introduction) was not brought about till 1 April, 1918.

[2] See Appendix No. 2.

Accordingly the first complete Australian flying unit, No. 1 Squadron, Australian Flying Corps, together with first reinforcements for the same—a total of twenty-eight officers and 195 other ranks—embarked from Port Melbourne in the transport *Orsova* on the 16th March, 1916, under the command of Lieutenant-Colonel E. H. Reynolds.[3] The squadron was a twelve-aeroplane squadron, with three flights —" A ", " B ", and " C "—each of four machines. " C " Flight also bore the wireless equipment and personnel. At a later time, in Egypt, the wireless section was transferred to squadron headquarters, and each flight was equipped, as were R.F.C. squadrons, with six machines, making eighteen in all. On embarkation the several flights were commanded —" A " by Captain W. Sheldon,[4] " B " by Lieutenant Manwell, and " C " by Captain Williams. The squadron took with it from Australia no technical equipment of any sort except two motor-cars and seven motor-bicycles, all presented by members of the unit who owned them. Its machines and technical outfit were supplied in Egypt by the R.F.C. The original intention was that Australia should pay for such material, and that, on the conclusion of the war, the squadron should take back to the Commonwealth what was left. The war, however, lasted longer than was generally expected, and at the Armistice any machines and stores held by Australian squadrons were returned to the Royal Air Force as equivalent to the original issue of equipment, no money passing between the British and Australian Governments on account of any technical material used. In other respects, the Australian Flying Corps was equipped and maintained in the field under the same arrangement as that applying to other Australian units. Many expenses were in the first place met by the British Government, the Commonwealth afterwards repaying them on a *per capita* basis in calculating which the British Government showed an invariable liberality.

The personnel of the squadron was raised in Australia from pilots and observers who had completed courses at the Australian flying school, from suitable volunteers already in

---

[3] Lt.-Col. E. H. Reynolds, O.B.E. Staff Officer for Aviation, A.I.F., London, 1917/18. Officer of Aust. Permanent Forces; b. Paddington, Sydney, 20 Oct., 1878.

[4] Maj. W. Sheldon. Commanded No. 4 Sqn., 1916/17, No. 2 Sqn., 1918. Officer of Aust. Permanent Forces; of Melbourne; b. Singapore, 20 Aug., 1889.

ADVENT OF No. 1 SQUADRON

A.I.F. camps, and from civilians with special qualifications. Artisans enlisted from special trades were required to be skilled in those trades, and their training in Australia was practically confined to drill and the first principles of soldiering. They received in Australia little aircraft training, except for some practice in the swinging of propellers. Nor were the pilots and observers instructed at Point Cook in gunnery, armament, photography, or bombing. On arrival in Egypt most of them were sent to England for further training. When, on April 14th, the squadron arrived at Suez, it was split up within a week into parties for training with local British squadrons.

The military position in Egypt was then one of desultory warfare on at least two fronts. In Upper (or southern) Egypt the Senussi were as yet unsuppressed. In the east the desert beyond the Suez Canal was either in Turkish hands or a No-Man's Land. In the previous winter Kitchener had visited Cairo and passed his famous criticism that "the troops were supposed to defend the Canal and not the Canal the troops," and more aggressive tactics were beginning. There were in Egypt two R.F.C. squadrons—forming the 5th Wing, R.F.C.—one on the Canal at Kantara and Ismailia, and one at Heliopolis for service in Upper Egypt. The enemy had one German flying squadron operating against the Canal. British aircraft factories could not yet supply improved machines for other fronts than the French, and in Egypt at this date the British machines were of ancient type—B.E.2.c two-seaters (90 h.p. R.A.F. engine). The Germans possessed single-seater Fokker scouts and two-seater Aviatiks, machines superior in speed, climbing, manœuvring, and fighting power. Lieutenant-Colonel (then Captain) Williams writes:—"At that time we had no guns firing through the propeller, and could not fire straight ahead. Our observers were in front of the pilots. The Aviatik observer was in rear of the pilot and the pilot could fire straight ahead. We really had very little chance with him. When bombing, we had to go without observers, and although we carried a machine-gun, it was quite impossible to fly the machine and use the gun too. We depended mainly on luck. These old machines, however, did much good work."

Map No. 3

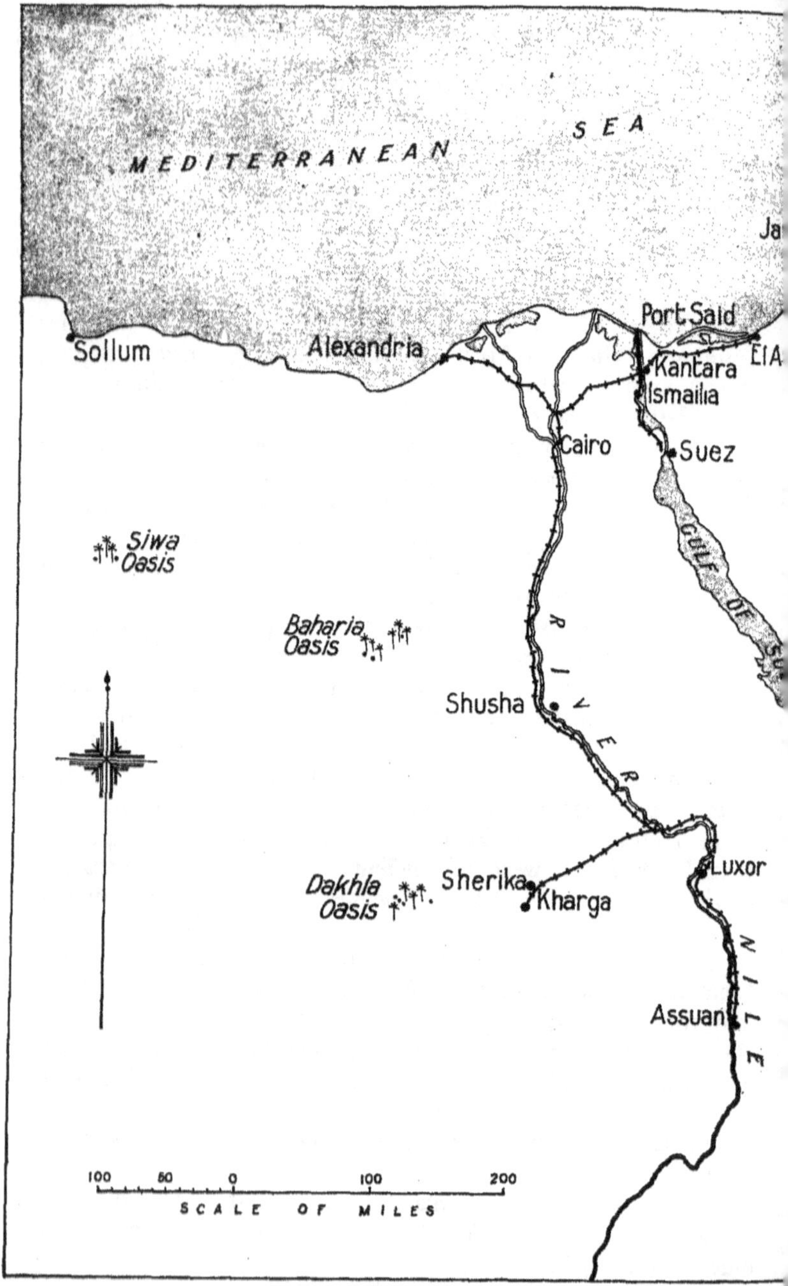

EGYPT

During its first six weeks in Egypt the Australian squadron was without machines. Most of the flying officers were sent to England for training; and the mechanics, whose instruction was equally important, were split up into parties, and attached with flight-commanders to the two British squadrons in order to learn their work. One party under Captain D. V. J. Blake[5] and one under Captain Williams went to stations of No. 14 Squadron, R.F.C., at Kantara and Ismailia respectively; two other parties, under Captain Sheldon and Captain W. H. Anderson,[6] to No. 17 Squadron, R.F.C., at Heliopolis; and a fifth under Lieutenant R. Ross[7] to "X" Aircraft Park, R.F.C., at Abbassia. In such training the squadron spent the remainder of April and all of May. A general uncertainty hung over its future, rumour assigning it in turn to France, Salonica, and the Canal Zone. Its commanding officers were constantly being changed. Colonel Reynolds left it at Suez, and eventually became Staff Officer for Aviation at A.I.F. Headquarters, London; Major H. D. K. Macartney[8] succeeded him, but shortly afterwards went to England and was transferred to artillery; Major A. A. J. Broun[9] followed him in command, but on June 1st gave place to Major T. F. Rutledge.[10] Rutledge arrived from England in company with an Australian who had been flying for nearly two years in the French Flying Corps, Captain Oswald Watt.[11]

By June 12th the fate of the squadron was known. No. 17 Squadron, R.F.C., was ordered to Salonica, while No. 1 Australian Squadron took over its machines and its Canal stations, with headquarters at Heliopolis. For some months the squadron was split up, with its several flights at stations

[5] Maj. D. V. J. Blake. Commanded No. 3 Sqn., 1918. Officer of Aust. Permanent Forces; of Parramatta, N.S.W.; b. Harris Park, Parramatta, 10 Nov., 1887.

[6] Maj. W. H. Anderson, D.F.C. Commanded No. 3 Sqn., 1918/19. Subsequently Director of Personnel and Training, Aust. Air Board. Of Melbourne; b. Kew, Melbourne, 30 Dec., 1891.

[7] Capt. R. Ross; No. 3 Sqn. Engineer; of Toorak, Melbourne; b. Carnegie, Melbourne, 23 Sept., 1891.

[8] Lt.-Col. H. D. K. Macartney, C.M.G., D.S.O. Commanded 7th A.F.A. Bde., 1916/18. Officer of Aust. Permanent Forces; of Brisbane; b. Waverley Station, Q'land, 1 Feb., 1880.

[9] Maj. A. A. J. Broun; No. 1 Sqn. Orchardist; of Spreyton, Tas.; b. Orchard House, Orchard, near Lanark, Scotland, 21 Feb., 1876.

[10] Maj. T. F. Rutledge, R.A.F. Sharebroker; of Melbourne; b. Warrnambool, Vic., 21 March, 1887.

[11] Lt.-Col. W. O. Watt, O.B.E. Commanded No. 2 Sqn., 1916/17 and 1917/18. Merchant and grazier; of Sydney; b. Bournemouth, Eng., 11 Feb., 1878. Drowned in Australia, 21 May, 1921.

widely separated. "B" Flight under Watt was the first to be equipped with machines and technical stores, and on June 14th it relieved at the Suez station a detachment of No. 17 Squadron. Here "A" Flight under Sheldon joined "B" Flight for a few days on June 25th, but on July 9th was transferred to Sherika in Upper Egypt. "C" Flight under Williams remained for a time with squadron headquarters at Heliopolis; in July part of the flight worked with No. 14 Squadron at Kantara, and on August 16th the whole flight took over from a detachment of that same squadron the Port Said station. No. 1 Squadron headquarters relieved No. 14's command at Kantara on September 20th; there "C" Flight from Port Said joined it on September 27th, and "A" Flight from Sherika on November 8th. The squadron did not come together on one aerodrome until December 17th, by which time the Egyptian Expeditionary Force had advanced nearly to El Arish, the last position held by the enemy within the Turco-Egyptian frontier.

The period between June and December was, therefore, one of isolated air operations. Till mid-August many Australian pilots, both for the sake of experience and because material equipment was a slow and gradual process, worked with No. 14 Squadron along the Canal and used that squadron's machines. The first six months of No. 1 Squadron's active service falls, therefore, into two natural divisions. During the first half of that period the flights were working far apart, as has been explained. During the second three months the flights, still not collected to one squadron centre, were all working east of the Canal—"B" Flight from Mahemdia, east of Port Said, and "A" and "C" from Kantara.

The Suez operations were without special incident. They consisted of frequent reconnaissances over the desert within a radius of twenty-five or thirty miles of Suez, occasionally marked by the dropping of a few bombs to impress Arab parties.

From Sherika reconnaissances of the Senussi district covered all the western desert a hundred miles or more west of the Nile from the Baharia Oasis in the north to the Dakhla Oasis, west of Kharga, in the south. A notable flight was that of Captain Murray Jones,[12] of "A" Flight, on September 7th

---

[12] Maj. A. Murray Jones, M.C., D.F.C.; No. 2 Sqn. Pharmacist; b. Caulfield, Melbourne, 25 Feb., 1895.

KANTARA, ON THE SUEZ CANAL, WITH AIRCRAFT PARK IN THE FOREGROUND

Lent by Lieut.-Col. R. Williams, No. 1 Sqn., A.F.C.
Aust. War Museum Collection No. A647.
Taken in January, 1919.

To face p. 36.

Aeroplane view of Nekhl, in the Sinai Desert, between Suez and Akaba

Lent by Capt. A. T. Cole, No. 1 Sqn., A.F.C.
Taken in 1917.

and 8th. A British camel patrol had gone out to examine the Baharia Oasis and had failed to return. Jones flew from Sherika to Shusha on September 7th, and next day reconnoitred the Baharia region for eight hours, but found no trace of the missing patrol. He flew through the heat of the day, a considerable performance for both man and machine, and one hitherto not attempted in the desert. Engine failure would almost certainly have meant death. Some months later, when British troops occupied the oasis, they learned that the lost patrol had been captured and killed by the Senussi. On October 12th, upon news that the Senussi were abandoning the Dakhla Oasis, farther south, Williams arrived at Shusha with two officers from Kantara on a special mission to co-operate with " A " Flight in reconnoitring Dakhla and Baharia. Murray Jones and Lieutenant A. G. Adams[13] (observer), and Lieutenants L. J. Wackett[14] and V. P. Turner[15] found these oases empty of the enemy. They flew far along the track towards Siwa without seeing anything except evidences that the Senussi had departed. The return flights by Williams and Wackett from Shusha to the Canal with one stop at Cairo—flights lasting five hours and a half and six hours respectively—were in those days a fine achievement.

In the Port Said area, while " C " Flight was still attached to No. 14 Squadron, R.F.C., at Kantara, information was received of enemy movement advancing towards the British position at Romani. At this time the Turco-Germans held the valuable hod[16]-country east of Oghratina, and their main positions stretched from Mageibra northwards to Oghratina, then eastwards to Bir el Abd, Salmana, and Bir el Mazar. In this coastal sector they seemed to be nervous of naval operations on their flanks, and British monitors, co-operating with Australian airmen who directed their fire, sought to encourage this apprehension. By the end of July the German airmen became distinctly aggressive, and frequently bombed Port Said,

---

[13] Lieut. A. G. Adams; No. 1 Sqn. Clerk; b. South Yarra, Melbourne, 18 May, 1894. Died as result of aeroplane accident, 19 Feb., 1917.

[14] Maj. L. J. Wackett, D.F.C., A.F.C.; No. 3 Sqn. Duntroon graduate; of Townsville, Q'land; b. Elphinstone, Townsville, 2 Jan., 1896.

[15] Lieut. V. P. Turner; No. 1 Sqn. Surveyor; b. Digby, Gunnedah, N.S.W., 9 Aug., 1890.

[16] Hods are small oases in the desert, generally scattered clumps of palm trees. They mark the location of wells or of water near the surface.

Kantara, Cairo, and British military camps in the desert. The B.E.2.c's constantly took the air to intercept the raiders, but, owing to inferior speed, could rarely catch them. The British and Australian pilots carried out retaliatory bombing raids on the enemy's camps as far east as Bir el Mazar, though well aware that, should the German machines go up to meet them in the air, the B.E's had small hope of beating them off. In such risky adventures the lack of initiative in the Germans was no less remarkable than the daring of the B.E. pilots. In spite of the enemy's superiority, the B.E's regularly made at least one daily reconnaissance of the Turkish positions—flights sometimes of over two hours. Some D.H.1's began to arrive in Egypt at this time, but they were few and far between, though extremely useful for escorting the defenceless old B.E's. There were several brief and indecisive fights at the end of July between these reconnaissance machines and German scouts. El Arish was the enemy's main aerodrome, and Bir el Abd his advanced landing-ground. On the way to Mazar the B.E's had to fly over the Bir el Abd ground. No. 14 Squadron sometimes flew an early Bristol scout, which, however, was useless against the German aircraft, for it was slow—having only an 80-h.p. Gnome engine—and could not fire straight ahead. The Germans who bombed the Canal towns always flew at an altitude which it was quite impossible for British machines, starting from the ground, to attain in any useful time.

On July 31st the Germans began to drop bombs on Romani and Mahemdia, and on British outposts thereabout. For some days it had been reported that the enemy was concentrating east of Katia, and his bombing of British forward areas marked a definite advance of the Turks against the northern end of the Canal. Lieutenants A. W. L. Ellis[17] and Wackett on August 1st took part in a raid of seven machines on the Turkish concentration, and Williams directed the fire of the British monitor from the sea on the hods about Oghratina. An Aviatik, which attacked this monitor next day, was engaged by a D.H.1 from No. 14 Squadron and was forced to land near Salmana. That night the Turks advanced closer to

---

[17] Maj. A. W. L. Ellis, M.C. Commanded No. 4 Sqn., 1918. Engineer; of Malvern, Melbourne; b. Steiglitz, Vic., 14 Oct., 1894.

Romani and brought up anti-aircraft guns to Katia. Outpost fighting on August 3rd was accompanied by several air-bombing attacks on each side, Lieutenants Ellis, Wackett, and Edwards (a pilot of 'No. 14 Squadron) bombing the Turkish front line, while Williams escorted them in a Bristol scout.[18] This work was done without casualty, though Edwards' machine was hit by anti-aircraft fire. On the following day the Battle of Romani was in full swing, and the Romani landing-ground was under a smart artillery fire.

During April the enemy in his advance to the outskirts of Romani had driven in small British yeomanry outposts holding the hods around Oghratina and Katia. Airmen confirmed the yeomanry reports of the Turkish attack on a wide desert front and in considerable strength. At this time the newly-formed Anzac Mounted Division, commanded by Major-General H. G. Chauvel,[19] was being trained west of the Canal. Its 2nd Brigade was promptly moved to Romani, the remainder of the division soon followed, and British infantry was also sent to strengthen that important position. The Turks were plainly preparing a big attack, and by the beginning of August the British had a line of infantry strong-posts extending from Romani to the sea and flanking the position on the south. On the night of August 3rd the Turks, having driven in all eastern outposts, moved a force of about 18,000 men to outflank the position on the south-west. It was a shrewd blow, but had been foreseen by Chauvel, who had placed the 1st Light Horse Brigade at the desert end of the infantry line. Attacked here at midnight, the 1st, Brigade fought against greatly superior numbers till morning; it lost ground, but its line was unbroken, and at dawn the 2nd Brigade arrived in support. The two brigades and some infantry fought all day cn August 4th, yielding ground foot by foot but exacting a heavy price for it from the enemy. At the end of the day the New Zealand Mounted Rifles Brigade and a brigade of yeomanry,

---

[18] At this time bombing raids were generally made during daylight. The machines sent out to drop the bombs required the protection of fighting scouts, because, when descending to bomb their targets, the bombers would expose themselves to hostile air attack. The B.E's, slow fliers at all times, flew slower still when carrying the extra weight of bombs, and, as German aircraft were active, the B.E's had to be protected throughout such duty.

[19] Lt.-Gen. Sir Harry G. Chauvel, G.C.M.G., K.C.B. Commanded Des. Mtd. Corps, 1917/19, and G.O.C. A.I.F. troops in Egypt, 1916/19; subsequently Inspector-General of the Aust. Military Forces., Of Clarence River District, N.S.W.; b. Tabulam, Clarence River, 16 Apr., 1865.

supported by an infantry force, fell on the Turkish left flank, and the tide of battle turned. At dawn next morning, August 5th, the enemy broke and fled under a bayonet attack all along the line. The Turks stood for a day at Katia, where the light horse were again involved in severe fighting. A few days later these rear-guards were forced out of their last position in the hod-country at Bir el Abd. The light horse were not equipped for far pursuit in the desert and lost touch with the retreating enemy. The airmen, however, followed the Turks past Salmana to Bir el Mazar and the region of El Arish, bombing them repeatedly.

The air work during the Romani operations was performed by No. 14 Squadron at Kantara and Ismailia, to which were attached pilots of No. 1 Australian Squadron. On August 10th the Australian airmen left the British squadron and re-joined their own flights, for which machines were now available. "C" Flight took over Port Said on August 16th and worked also from an advanced landing-ground at Mahemdia. From these bases it conducted reconnaissances to Salmana and beyond, ahead of the advancing light horse, alternating daily in this duty with No. 14 Squadron at Kantara. By August 22nd the rearmost Turkish post firing anti-aircraft guns was located at Bir el Mazar.

The German airmen gave vent to the enemy's anger at the defeat by bombing Port Said. Their raid on that place on September 1st led to sharp retaliation by "C" Flight on the Turks at Bir el Mazar, three days later. Here Lieutenant S. K. Muir[20] dropped twelve bombs with great effect, silenced the anti-aircraft guns with two bombs, and blew several tents to pieces. Two machines, led by Muir, again bombed Bir el Mazar on September 7th. "B" Flight, from Suez, moved to Mahemdia on September 18th, and "C" Flight to Kantara on September 27th. Meanwhile the light horse had been concentrating about Salmana and Ganadil, and on September 16th reconnoitred Bir el Mazar in force. Under cover of "C" and "B" Flights in the air—Ellis patrolling as far as Maghara to the south—the light horse on September 17th pressed their reconnaissance to a sharp engagement with the

---

[20] Capt. S. K. Muir, M.C. R.A.F. (previously Australian Light Horse). Station overseer; of Mathoura, N.S.W.; b. Elsternwick, Melbourne, 6 April, 1892. Killed in action, 12 Sept., 1917.

enemy's outpost at Bir el Mazar. In fact they tried the defence so hard that the Turks turned their anti-aircraft guns upon the light horse rather than upon the aeroplanes above. The Australian force withdrew from Bir el Mazar at 11 a.m. with a few prisoners, while the airmen of No. 1 and No. 14 Squadrons, who had reconnoitred tracks well to the eastward, covered their retirement and dropped messages on divisional headquarters at Salmana reporting the situation. Four days later Bir el Mazar was found to be clear of the enemy. The Turks had withdrawn to the line of the Wady El Arish, with garrisons at El Arish, Lahfan, and Magdhaba.

At this stage orders were published for the despatch from Australia to England of another Australian air squadron—No. 2 Squadron. Captain Watt, of "B" Flight, was recommended for the command of the new unit.

Notes.—Lieutenant-Colonel (then Captain) Walter Oswald Watt began flying in England in 1911, when he qualified for his pilot's certificate in a Bristol biplane. In 1913 he spent several months flying in a Blériot monoplane in Egypt, where he met several of the noted French airmen of the day. Leaving Egypt, he took his machine to France, and from May, 1914, until the outbreak of the war he was flying at Blériot's aerodrome at Buc, near Paris. On the eve of war, when it was widely believed in France that Great Britain would remain neutral, Watt enlisted as a pilot in the *Aviation Militaire* section of the Foreign Legion as "*soldat de deuxième,*" which was equivalent to third-class air-mechanic. He was posted to the Blériot Squadron No. 30 as a *poilu* (soldier in the ranks), but was always called "*Capitaine,*" in acknowledgment of his rank as honorary captain in the 5th Scottish Rifles in Australia in pre-war days. In April, 1915, Watt was transferred to the Maurice-Farman Squadron No. 44 at Toul, which became one of the most famous in the French Army. For valuable and courageous work done in this squadron until February, 1916, Watt received the *Legion d'Honneur* and the *Croix de Guerre,* and won the brevet rank of captain in the French service. During his service as pilot in No. 44 Squadron he earned the admiration and esteem of all his comrades—many of whom were renowned airmen—for his daring, devotion to duty, and good-fellowship. He had many narrow escapes, including one forced landing in No-Man's Land and subsequent adventurous escape under heavy fire.

Being a foreigner in the French service, Watt could not be given a position of command, and in 1916 he transferred to the Australian Flying Corps with the rank of captain and flight-commander, and was sent in May of that year to Egypt to No. 1 Squadron. In October, 1916, he was promoted major to command No. 2 Australian Squadron, which was formed in Egypt and sent to England for training. Watt took this squadron to France and commanded it for several months in the field. In February, 1918, he became lieutenant-colonel with command of the Australian training wing in England. He had an exceptional ability to instil his own high ideal of service into all who served under him and, after his death by drowning in Australia in May, 1921, an Australian pilot who had long served under him wrote: "That he was the best commanding officer we had ever served under was the opinion of every officer and man in the Australian Flying Corps. He had every quality to make him a great leader of men—courage, determination, and an immense capacity for work, a stern and just man of discipline, unfailing courtesy to and thoughtfulness for his subordinates, and above all, the greatest factor in leadership, a genius for endearing himself (without conscious effort) to all who served under him."

When No. 1 Squadron arrived in Egypt in April, 1916, many of the personnel had never seen an aeroplane or an aeroplane-engine. Some of the officers had flown machines to a limited extent, whilst others had never flown at all. They arrived without equipment or machines.

The training carried out was as follows: the squadron was divided into detachments and these were attached to the two R.F.C. squadrons on service in Egypt. Each man and officer understudied a corresponding man and officer in those British squadrons. At the end of each week reports upon the training were furnished under three headings, (a), (b), and (c), representing different standards of efficiency—

> (a) good workmen, efficient; can work without supervision;
> (b) promising, but requires supervision;
> (c) requires training.

Under these conditions the squadron worked for six weeks, and its progress was remarkable. At the end of that time practically 80 per cent. of the men had attained (a) standard of efficiency. The squadron was then concentrated at Heliopolis. The first flight was mobilised for active service, and on 14th June, 1916, was despatched to Suez. In a very short time the whole squadron was on active service. Major-General W. G. H. Salmond, commanding the Royal Air Force in the Middle East, recorded officially: "The rapid training and mobilisation of the squadron reflected great credit on the industry, keenness, and discipline of officers and all ranks."

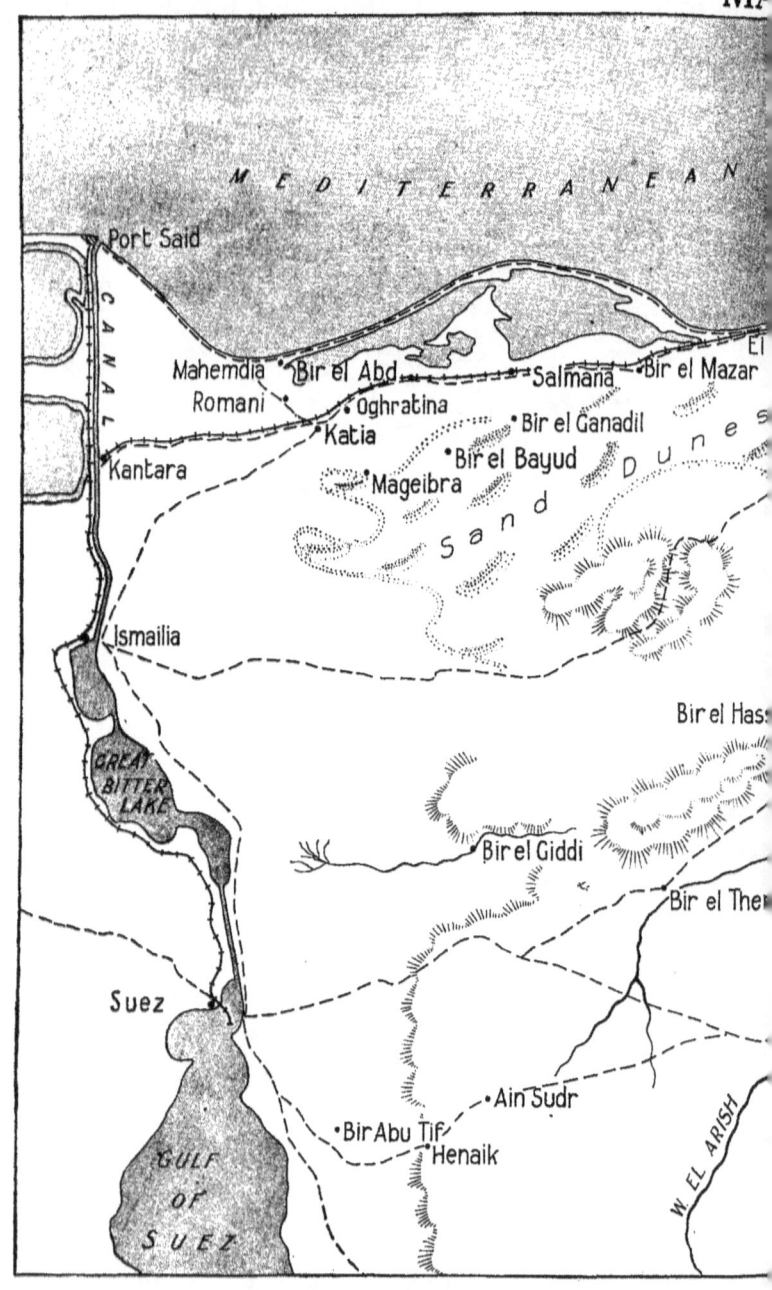

SINAI DESERT,

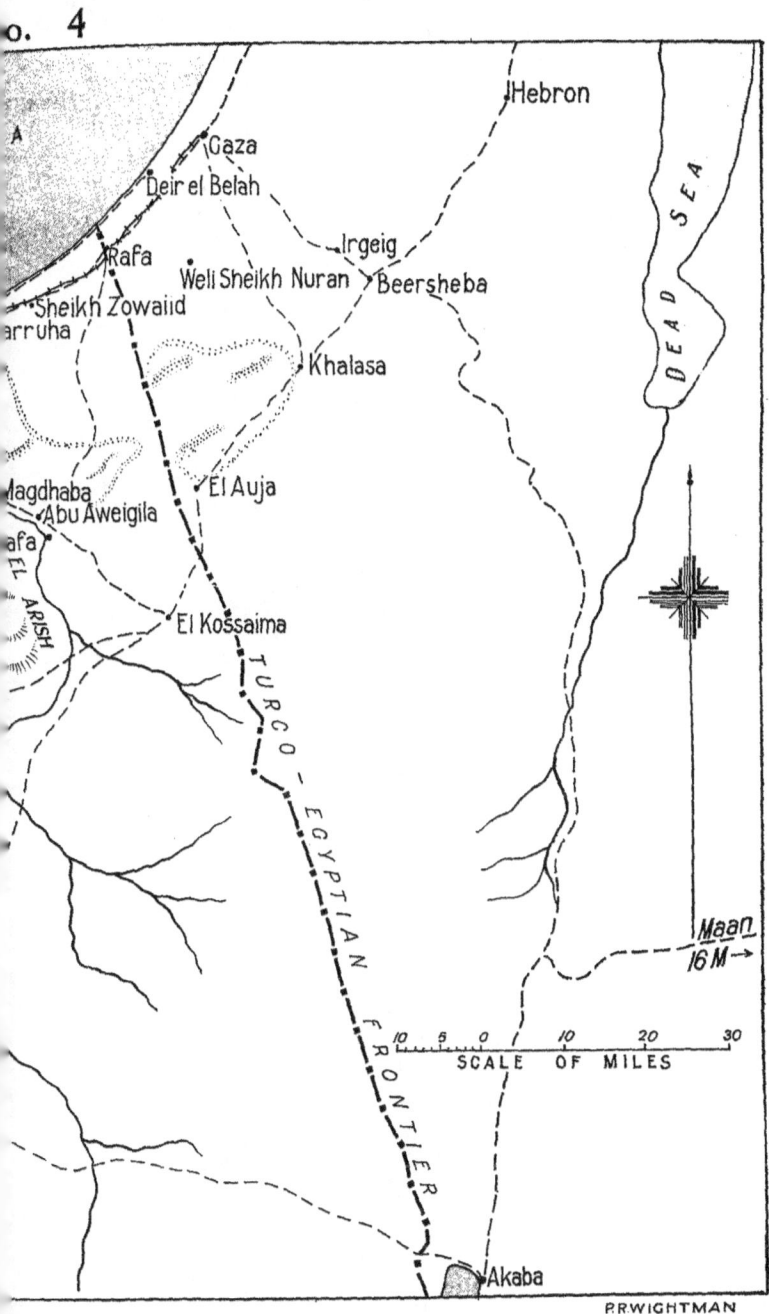

CAMPAIGN OF 1916

CHAPTER IV

AIR FIGHTING IN THE DESERT

BIR EL MAZAR lies nearly half-way between Salmana and El Arish, and, while the crossing of the intervening desert was fairly easy for a mounted raiding party, it was a much more serious undertaking for a main force of all arms which had to consolidate its position as it advanced, make road, railway, and telegraph communications where none existed, and bring artillery and vast quantities of supplies in its train. While the army was moving up, the airmen constantly reconnoitred the El Arish region. On September 28th Lieutenants Wackett and J. Bell,[1] and two British machines from Ismailia, bombed and photographed El Arish, but the clouds prevented good photography. Another patrol to El Arish by Lieutenants E. G. Roberts,[2] A. D. Badgery,[3] and Muir on October 2nd disclosed the fact that the German hangars at that place had disappeared. Following this, air raids on El Arish became frequent. An advance-party of troops temporarily occupied Bir el Mazar on October 5th and removed hand-pumps from the wells. On the same day both Masaid and El Arish were bombed, Masaid by No. 1 Squadron and El Arish by No. 14.

A flank position in the Maghara hills, across the desert to the south, had not been cleared of the enemy. There had been some previous fighting with the Maghara Turks shortly after the Romani battle. A mixed body of light horse, yeomanry, and camelry made a reconnaissance of this position in force on October 15th, and all available Australian machines, though much hindered by fog, co-operated by patrolling or bombing ahead of the troops. After a short engagement these withdrew, as in the affair at Bir el Mazar.

An important patrol by Lieutenants Roberts, R. M. Drummond,[4] and W. J. Y. Guilfoyle[5] on October 25th en-

---

[1] Capt. J. Bell; No. 3 Sqn. Grazier; of Rokewood, Vic.; b. Melbourne, 7 Oct., 1885. Died of wounds in France, 27 Dec., 1917.

[2] Lieut. E. G. Roberts; No. 1 Sqn. Accountant; of Canterbury, Melbourne; b. Camberwell, Melbourne, 8 Jan., 1894.

[3] Capt. A. D. Badgery; No. 1 Sqn. Aviator; b. Sutton Forest, N.S.W., 19 Nov., 1888.

[4] Capt. R. M. Drummond, D.S.O., O.B.E., M.C. R.A.F. (previously A.A.M.C.). Of Cottesloe, W. Aust.; b. Perth, W. Aust., 2 June, 1894.

[5] Lieut. W. J. Y. Guilfoyle, M.C. R.A.F.

countered no anti-aircraft fire over El Arish, and discovered signs of diminished strength in the Turkish force there. This observation was confirmed by another reconnaissance report two days later, and there quickly ran round the army the rumour of a coming new advance. The uneasiness of the enemy was only one ground for this report; another, far surer, was the rapid progress of the railway from Kantara, which the Egyptian construction gang had by now taken well forward of Salmana. Aerodrome hangars were arriving at the new Salmana landing-ground, and No. 1 Squadron was searching for a ground as far forward as Bir el Mazar. Australian pilots were returning from courses finished in England. "A" Flight arrived at Kantara from Upper Egypt on November 8th, and No. 1 Squadron was now working as one unit—an immense tactical advantage. A new note of confidence was discernible in the squadrons; they still had inferior machines, but pilots coming from training in England brought news of great development in the home factories, both in production of aeroplanes and in improvement of design. The Egyptian Expeditionary Force was looking ahead towards Palestine. A few months ago El Arish had seemed an ambitious goal; it was now but an obstacle between the desert and the Land of Promise. New strength, new eagerness, in No. 1 Squadron demanded a wider sphere of work; within a fortnight a series of important raids began upon points far behind the enemy's lines; and by the end of November an Australian machine had flown beyond the Dead Sea.

On October 30th Captain Williams and Lieutenant Turner (observer), and Lieutenants Muir and P. Ainsworth,[6] escorted by Guilfoyle in a Martinsyde, took twenty photographs of Masaid. Wackett photographed the whole line El Arish-Magdhaba on November 4th; two days later Muir and Guilfoyle visited this line again, and No. 14 Squadron reconnoitred Rafa. While these preliminary patrols spied out the land, the squadron worked hard to overhaul and refit every available machine for a raid on Beersheba. That town was at this time the Turkish army headquarters and the site of the

---

[6] Lieut. P. Ainsworth, 126th M.G. Coy. (42nd Div.).

Germans' chief aerodrome, and the raid by No. 1 Squadron on November 11th was on the largest scale yet undertaken by the Australians or by any other air squadron in the East. One Martinsyde and nine B.E.'s, loaded with bombs and petrol, left the Kantara and Mahemdia aerodromes at dawn and assembled at Mustabig, just west of Bir el Mazar. There a raiding force of five B.E.'s and the Martinsyde filled up with petrol and bombs and set off in formation towards Beersheba. When over El Arish they saw one German machine on the ground; a bomb was dropped near it, but the German could not be persuaded to take the air. Over Beersheba the anti-aircraft guns engaged them with high explosive and shrapnel, and the raiders flew through a flurry of white, black, and green bursts The Martinsyde dropped a 100-lb. bomb fair in the centre of the aerodrome; two 20-lb. bombs hit tents; others made direct hits on the railway line and the station. Only two of the Australian machines were capable of defending themselves against air attack—a structural defect of the B.E.2.c as a fighter has already been described—and those two were the Martinsyde (Guilfoyle) and one B.E. (Wackett and Turner), in which Wackett had fitted to the top centre-section a gun-mounting contrived by himself. A Fokker and an Aviatik ascended from the ground to fight, and, as luck had it, they attacked only these two Australian machines. The Germans were decisively beaten off and decamped. After photographing Beersheba and the damage caused by the bombs, the airmen turned homeward, and on the way back Wackett and Turner reconnoitred Khan Yunis and Rafa. All machines arrived safely, after having spent seven hours in flight. Two days later a German aeroplane retaliated by bombing Cairo. Australian machines which took the air to intercept it on its return journey lost the enemy in consequence of his superior speed.

The next British advance, against the Wady El Arish line, was to be made by a cavalry movement round the enemy's left flank, south-east of Magdhaba. Reconnaissance patrols over the El Arish line were a daily duty of No. 1 and No. 14 Squadrons, and, in preparation for the further offensive, the Australians photographed an extensive triangular region on the flank of Magdhaba—the area between El Kossaima, El Auja, and Abu Aweigila. This was done on November 15th in the course of a four hours' flight by Williams and Turner (observer), escorted by Guilfoyle in the Martinsyde; they photographed all camps and dumps in that area with twenty-four exposures. The value of such work at this time, and later in Palestine, was inestimable; the available maps were inaccurate and incomplete, and had to be supplemented and revised in the field primarily by means of air-photography.

The non-interference by German airmen during this and other daily enterprises was remarkable. The Germans had the advantage in fighting aeroplanes; and till December, 1916, there were no British anti-aircraft guns in the field against them. With a little enterprise the enemy could have enormously crippled General Murray's[7] offensive, for the British force was still weak—a third infantry division, the 53rd, was only beginning to arrive—and relied greatly on the ability of its two air squadrons to furnish intelligence and to demoralise the enemy in his defences. The opportunity to attack and harass the British advance was surely to be found at this time and place, when Murray's army was on the point of emerging from the long stretch of desert. Across this desert the advancing force and much of its supplies could as yet pass only upon a track of wire-netting laid over the sand. The railway from Kantara was being carried forward with all speed, but was still far behind the head of Murray's force. Yet after Romani the enemy refrained from any strong offensive measures, even from the air, against these communications; his bombing of forward camps was of the slightest; to attain the air superiority which seemed well within his reach he made, until it was too late, no effort worth mentioning. Unquestionably his reluctance owed something to the daring of the airmen he had to meet. The British and Australian pilots compensated by their individual courage, determination, and initiative for the inferiority of the machines they flew; and though they never claimed, until the arrival of the S.E.5's and improved Bristol Fighters in late 1917, to hold the supremacy, yet the student of their long struggle in the older

---
[7] Gen. Sir Archibald J. Murray, G.C.M.G., K.C.B., C.V.O., D.S.O. Commanded E.E.F., 1916/17. Officer of British Regular Army; b. Sutton, Surrey, Eng., 21 April, 1860.

machines will be persuaded that virtually they ruled the air from the outset of the campaign, and ruled it solely by their own boldness and skill. Theoretically they should not have had the supremacy, which was nevertheless certainly theirs. Good luck alone will not suffice to explain why no attempt was made to interrupt the raid on Beersheba or the daring venture on November 24th of two Martinsydes, one from No. 1 Squadron piloted by Muir and the other by Freeman of No. 14 Squadron. These flew from the Mustabig advanced landing-ground across a long stretch of enemy's country and over the Dead Sea, bombed the important Hejaz railway, and returned unchallenged. There was also the gallant exploit of Freeman and Minchin of No. 14 Squadron on December 2nd. While they were reconnoitring Gaza and Beersheba, two Fokkers and an Aviatik, which were waiting for them, attacked and shot holes in both of Minchin's tanks. Minchin landed perforce at Rafa in enemy country, and burnt his damaged machine; Freeman then landed alongside him, picked him up, and brought him home. Next day Muir, in an Australian Martinsyde, engaged an Aviatik near the British outpost line, and drove the enemy home to Masaid.

By mid-December the railway was well forward in the vicinity of Bir él Mazar, and No. 1 Squadron moved on to a new aerodrome at Mustabig, immediately west of Mazar oasis. About this time began the first changes in its equipment. Hitherto its machines had been B.E.2.c's, with one Martinsyde attached to each flight. In December the squadron acquired three Clerget-engined Bristol scouts, one for each flight, but in the course of the next three months these machines, inadequately engined, were found to be too slow in climbing power and flying speed, and were returned. Meanwhile B.E.2.e's arrived and gradually replaced the old 2.c's, and by March, 1917, each flight had two Martinsydes attached instead of one. A few weeks later B.E.12.a's began to replace the 2.e's. Yet in France the very name of these obsolete B.E. machines had been forgotten and their place long since taken by the R.E.8's,[8] which did not appear in Palestine till October, 1917. Not till the day of improved Bristol Fighters, with powerful Rolls-Royce

---

[8] R.E.8—see Appendix No. 1—a useful all-round working machine and capable of effective defence against attack, as the pilots of No. 3 Australian Squadron often showed in France.

engines, was No. 1 Squadron adequately equipped to seek out and attack the German airmen. That day—the end of 1917—was, however, as yet twelve months ahead.

The Egyptian Expeditionary Force was by mid-December assembling before the line of the Wady El Arish (the Biblical "River of Egypt"), and on December 14th, preparatory to further attack, grand manœuvres of three divisions were carried out, with aeroplanes co-operating. The spectacle obviously excited the enemy. At dawn on December 15th German aeroplanes were over on patrol, and two days later six machines, from No. 1 and No. 14 Squadrons, sent up in the afternoon to wait for the enemy, met an Aviatik. With this Muir, in a Martinsyde, fought an engagement for as long as the enemy was inclined to fight. The Australian put the German observer out of action and chased the Aviatik twenty miles beyond El Arish. The restlessness of the enemy was patent to air patrols. Reconnaissance of Maghara, on the desert flank, revealed in the wadys a concentration of tribesmen and goats, which generally betokened abandonment of a district, and on December 20th both Maghara and El Arish villages were reported by Australian airmen to have been evacuated by the enemy. The light horse occupied El Arish the same night. That the Turks had side-stepped as well as retreated was made clear next day by No. 1 Squadron's reports, for an increased Turkish force was noted at Magdhaba, farther south along the Wady El Arish. Wackett patrolled over Gaza and Rafa; in a coastal village west of Rafa the inhabitants assembled and displayed a large white flag for the edification of the machine overhead. In the following night, December 22nd, the light horse moved out to attack Magdhaba.

To distract the Turk's attention from this flank, the two air squadrons on December 22nd sent five Martinsydes to bomb the important railway bridge at Irgeig, north-west of Beersheba. The bombs hit, but did not greatly damage, the bridge, which, like most solid bridges, was not very susceptible to that form of attack. Two Fokkers and an Aviatik gave battle over Beersheba, and one of the Fokkers was chased down. The same afternoon one British and ten Australian machines dropped over a hundred bombs on Magdhaba, where the Turks were strongly entrenched. The Anzac Mounted Division marched that night across the desert on Magdhaba, surrounded it, and attacked from all sides next morning. It was a long fight, for the Turkish strong-posts could not be rushed at once, and had to be subdued in detail. There were a few guns on each side, but the action was mainly one of rifle and bayonet. Australian airmen were over Magdhaba all day, dropped a few bombs, and attempted to assist the dismounted light horsemen by machine-gunning the enemy, but the targets were well concealed. Towards the end of the day it became increasingly urgent to finish the fight, for the horses were suffering from thirst, the nearest water was at El Arish, and a second day before Magdhaba was unthinkable. The Australians succeeded dramatically as dark was setting in; a few strong-points fell suddenly, and the position was rushed in a final charge from three sides at once. The surviving garrison, 1,250 strong, was captured, and the Anzac Division, after setting fire to the village, retired again during the night to El Arish, whole squadrons fast asleep on their horses as they trekked across the desert. Next day No. 1 Squadron's patrols up the wady beyond Magdhaba found the village a blackened ruin, and El Ruafa and Abu Aweigila also deserted by the enemy. El Auja and El Kossaima, farther east and south-east, were seen, however, to be still strongly held.

At this time No. 1 Squadron was using the old German aerodrome site of Fageira, at El Arish, as an advanced landing-ground. By mid-January the railway had gone ahead of El Arish, and the squadron moved its aerodrome from Mustabig to Kilo. 143, just west of Masaid, and five miles west of El Arish. The weather of early January was wild with sandstorms and rain squalls, and more than one pilot crashed in desert landings during these winds. On only the worst days, however, was flying stopped. The army was working hard to advance its services a few more miles so as to be clear of the desert, and was relying more and more on air reconnaissance to keep touch with the enemy and to ascertain the extent of his retreat. After El Arish and Magdhaba he elected—and was observed by the airmen on December 28th—to fall back to a main position on the Gaza–Beersheba line, and this entailed the withdrawal of his headquarters from Beersheba. The weather cleared up on January 5th, and No. 1 Squadron's patrol observed 2,000 or 3,000 Turks digging an advanced position at Rafa. General Murray decided upon an immediate attack on this place. Air patrols on January 7th reported the Turks still at El Auja and El Kossaima on the extreme southern flank and the garrison at El Auja apparently slightly increased; but these places caused little anxiety. German airmen bombed El Arish during the morning and evening of this day, taking advantage of the British concentration there. On January 8th No. 1 Squadron's patrols were in the air all day covering the assembly of the light horse for an attack on Rafa. That evening the force—comprising the same brigades which had reduced Magdhaba—set out from El Arish on its night march to Rafa.

The plan of action at Rafa next morning, January 9th, was a repetition of the Magdhaba fight. The light horse surrounded the village, galloped up under fire as before, and then engaged dismounted in an all-day struggle against strongly defended field-works. The position was a treble system of trenches around an earthwork redoubt on a knoll. The light horse cordon slowly drew closer under a hot fire over the bare, gently-sloping ground. As at Magdhaba, with the thirsty horses a supreme consideration, the Australians made a final effort at sundown and captured the village in a series of determined assaults. Aeroplanes fitted with wireless hovered over the fight during the afternoon, reporting its progress constantly to the light horse headquarters, and at intervals dropped bombs about the solitary tree on top of the knoll which was given out as the objective of the attack. Rafa was captured, with about 1,500 prisoners and some guns, in the nick of time. Four machines bombed Beersheba in the afternoon and threw the German aerodrome there into confusion; on its return journey this patrol sighted at evening a considerable force of enemy infantry about Weli Sheikh Nuran, marching to the relief of Rafa. The village fell, however, before this force arrived, and after dark nothing more was heard of it. The light horse withdrew by night and retired to Sheikh Zowaiid, some ten miles south-west along the coast. Williams and Muir, flying over the place next day, saw in

Rafa only plundering Bedouin parties hunting for rifles and cartridges. Muir landed there with temporary engine-trouble, and found piles of Turkish dead in the trenches.

Vigorous reconnaissance work continued over the area as far forward as Gaza and Beersheba. The enemy evidently did not intend to abandon these places until forced to do so. The line Rafa–Auja is the boundary between Turkey and Egypt; it is also very nearly the boundary between the sandy desert and a new, relatively pleasant land of brilliant winter flowers. Lieutenant L. W. Heathcote[9] reconnoitred El Auja on January 11th, and Lieutenant F. H. McNamara[10] photographed Weli Sheikh Nuran, which the enemy was entrenching. Anti-aircraft guns also appeared at Weli Sheikh Nuran next day. Between January 14th and 19th Beersheba was several times bombed by No. 1 Squadron in day and night raids, and on one of these raids Murray Jones, in a B.E., dropped twelve 20-lb. bombs direct upon the biggest German hangar. After these raids the German airmen evacuated Beersheba and moved their aerodrome to Ramleh. Its position there was identified by Lieutenants Roberts and Ross Smith[11] (observer) a few days later. Patrols over the right flank on January 19th reported that the enemy had evacuated El Kossaima and were in decreased strength at El Auja.

That day was also notable for the first reconnaissance of the distant rear of the Turkish army—the towns of Beit Jibrin, Bethlehem, Jerusalem, and Jericho—performed by Roberts and Ross Smith, escorted by Murray Jones and Ellis in Martinsydes. Their exploit fired the whole squadron with the romance of sailing the air over Palestine and its tumbled floor of great hills and steep-banked wadys, famous old sacred towns, and alluring green patches of cultivation. Here were enemy railways and troop movements to be bombed, and somewhere here was the German aerodrome removed from Beersheba. One patrol, out hunting for it on January 27th,

---

[9] Lieut. L. W. Heathcote; No. 1 Sqn. Air mechanic; b. Collingwood, Melbourne, 4 Sept., 1893.

[10] Capt. F. H. McNamara, V.C.; No. 1 Sqn. School teacher; b. Waranga, Rushworth, Vic., 4 April, 1894.

[11] Capt. Sir Ross M. Smith, K.B.E., M.C., D.F.C., A.F.C.; No. 1 Sqn. (previously Light Horse). Warehouseman; b. Adelaide, 4 Dec., 1892. Killed in aeroplane accident, 14 April, 1922.

was turned back from near Junction Station by bad weather. Next day Roberts's patrol, better favoured, found it, as was expected, at Ramleh. Williams, also out on patrol, dropped propaganda leaflets for the benefit of the Bedouin; "I'll bet not one of them can read any of it," is his laconic note in his diary.

Air bombing was heavy on both sides at the end of January. The Germans regularly visited El Arish, now becoming a great British store dépôt, and No. 1 and No. 14 Squadrons as regularly retaliated on Beersheba, Weli Sheikh Nuran, and Ramleh. On February 3rd definite orders were received from General Chauvel, of the Desert Column, that the bombing of the enemy must cease, as German retaliation on the Egyptian Labour Corps was upsetting the railway gangs, and the British command had ordered that the railway should be carried forward to Rafa with all speed. The railhead was now near El Burj, half-way between El Arish and Rafa, and the wire-road had nearly reached Sheikh Zowaiid. The enemy, also working hard upon his communications, was engaged upon a light railway from Tel el Sheria, midway along the Gaza-Beersheba defence line, to Shellal, near Weli Sheikh Nuran; and Lieutenants A. T. Cole[12] and J. M. Glen,[13] reconnoitring this vicinity on February 5th, were attacked by two German scouts and obliged to return. Moreover, anti-aircraft fire was becoming increasingly heavy in the Gaza area, and the enemy was clearly sensitive of inspection on a front which he was actively fortifying. By the progress of the British line towards Rafa the Turks could calculate the length of time allowed them to elaborate their own defences. Murray was faced by the necessity of a pitched battle for Gaza which would demand infantry and artillery in considerable force. These, in turn, required a railhead at least as far forward as Rafa to ensure supplies.

While the remainder of February passed in this preparation, and the attacking army and its supplies were being assembled, the British command determined to clear up the situation in the desert west of Suez, where Turkish posts had never been dislodged since the attack on the Canal in 1915.

---

[12] Capt. A. T. Cole, M.C., D.F.C.; No. 2 Sqn. Student; of Melbourne; b. Malvern, Melbourne, 19 June, 1896.

[13] Lieut. J. M. Glen; 4th Royal Scots. Attached No. 1 Sqn., 4 Oct., 1916/10 June, 1917.

This part of the Sinai desert was a region where, beyond the fierce raiding of lonely parties which Arab warfare has made familiar, fighting was impossible. It is mostly inhospitable desert, made the more hideous by great sand-hills heaped up by scorching winds—a vast waste of land whose dangers and loneliness are to the unsophisticated European as terrible as any sea. The tracks which reach out over it are routes which must often be followed rather by compass or stars than by landmarks or tracks of the latest traffic. The waves of the desert obliterate, as surely as the waves of the sea, the traces of its nomads' passages. The wadys receive indifferently the flush of rainstorms or the burden of overwhelming sand-clouds. No army could ever dream of operating here.[14] The organisation of even a small mobile column was an exacting business. There may be mentioned, as an example, the excursion in October, 1916, of a British mounted column sent out over the northern fringe of this desert from Bir el Bayud, near Salmana, to attack the Turkish position on the Gebel Maghara. The distance of the march was only thirty-five miles, the strength of the column only 1,100 rifles, and the duration of the expedition less than a week; yet to supply this column in food and water entailed the employment of 7,000 camels, 2,300 horses, and 5,000 extra men (including natives).

The Turks still occupied all the Sinai desert south of the sand-hills which reach across it from near El Kossaima, on the Turkish frontier, to the vicinity of Suez—Gebel Helal, Gebel Yelleg, and Gebel el Heitan. Some sixty miles east of Suez the desert tracks converge at the large village of Nekhl, and about forty miles due north of Nekhl is the village of Bir el Hassana, in the gap between the Gebel Helal and the Gebel Yelleg. From Nekhl and these desert hills came the enemy's half-hearted attacks towards Suez in 1915. The enemy occupation of this wild country on Murray's flank was not dangerous, for where the light horse and the camelry found sustained warfare an impossible task the enemy was not much happier. The Turks remained here chiefly in order to assert what control was possible over the Arabs. The growing hostility

---

[14] Djemal Pasha's army, which marched towards the Suez Canal in 1915, included a special force of 4,000 of all arms to march on Suez across this desert, from Maan *via* Akaba, but it apparently suffered here severely.

to the Turks on the part of these uncertain desert tribes—especially those under the King of the Hejaz—and the Arabs' designs against the Mecca railway, made it clear by the beginning of 1917 that the Turks would not remain for much longer in the Sinai desert. The advance in February, 1917, from the Canal defences was meant to test the strength of the Turks at Nekhl.

The raid was made by two mounted columns—one consisting of 11th Light Horse Regiment from Serapeum, near Ismailia, and one of British yeomanry and Indian infantry from Suez. Three machines left No. 1 Squadron at El Arish and co-operated with the columns, working from the aerodrome of No. 57 Reserve Squadron at Ismailia. The pilots were Captain Williams and Lieutenants Drummond and Cole, and the observers Lieutenants Ross Smith, Turner, and A. J. Morgan.[15] The duty of the aeroplanes was to keep contact with the progress of the two columns by daily patrols, to drop messages from headquarters for them, and to scout ahead of them if necessary. There was, in the event, no fighting at all, but the expedition is interesting for the insight it provides into modern organisation of desert campaigning. It was arranged that Turner and two mechanics should go out with the light horse column to choose advanced landing-grounds and carry petrol, oil, and small spares in case of any aeroplane breakdown. The columns set out on February 13th, and were reported to each other by aeroplane on February 15th at Bir el Giddi and Henaik respectively. Next day they had reached Bir el Themada and Ain Sudr. On February 17th all three machines landed at Bir el Themada, where the light horse had to dig for water, and the little air force spent the night there. It was bitterly cold, and the airmen burnt petrol in lamps for warmth. The reconnaissance of the day disclosed that the Turks had abandoned Nekhl, about which the two columns were preparing to close, and early next morning, February 18th, Cole and Ross Smith went out at dawn to hunt for any signs of the enemy. No enemy was seen, though two machines searched seventeen miles beyond Nekhl; "consequently," reports Williams, "our bombs have to be brought back again

---

[15] Lieut. A. J. Morgan; 9th Shropshire Light Infantry. Attached No. 1 Sqn., 9 Oct., 1916. Killed in action, 30 May, 1917.

by camel." One officer and forty-five men of the enemy garrison had, it was discovered, fled only the day before.

"Went back to Nekhl," Williams writes, after the last reconnaissance, "and had a look round. There were no inhabitants—those who were loyal to the British left when the war broke out and went to Ismailia. There are about fifty houses of mud and stone, a mosque, and an old fort. The fort seems to have been a really good one when it was built, but it is some hundreds of years old. We took a few photographs around the place and some men got a few old Bedouin guns. The southern column got in about 10 o'clock (February 18th) and left again at 11. The light horse (northern column) didn't like coming all that distance and nothing to fight at the end. They left again when their patrols came in. We flew back to Themada and packed up and came on to Ismailia."

CHAPTER V

INCREASING IMPORTANCE OF AIR WARFARE

For a time the Turks seemed disposed to fortify the outposts of the Gaza–Beersheba line. The garrisons at Weli Sheikh Nuran, Shellal, and El Auja were increased. Meanwhile the airmen of No. 1 and No. 14 Squadrons continued raiding behind the enemy's front. Murray Jones bombed Beersheba in mid-February and destroyed three German machines. Jaffa was shelled by a French battleship at dawn on February 25th, while Cole and Glen (observer), in a B.E., directed the fire by wireless. Simultaneously Williams and Lieutenants Drummond and R. F. Baillieu,[1] after a flight in the dark, bombed the German aerodrome at Ramleh. The British force was steadily concentrating about El Arish, and a visit of General Murray to the forward areas at the end of the month emphasised the fact. The enemy obviously smelt trouble coming; El Auja was found to be abandoned on February 27th, and on the night of March 4th the light horse patrols harried the Turks, who were discovered in the act of evacuating Weli Sheikh Nuran and Shellal. Shortly before midnight the airmen were aroused by news of this withdrawal, and at dawn, in a fog, six machines bombed the railhead at Tel el Sheria, whither the Turks from Weli Sheikh Nuran were withdrawing. This bombing force was drawn from both squadrons and met with a warm reception. The anti-aircraft fire was unexpectedly heavy. Cole had his petrol tank shot through and was compelled to land on his way home; and a D.H.1 of No. 14 Squadron was shot down, and both pilot and observer were captured. Williams, too, was nearly lost, through a curious accident which may be told in his own words.

"When I arrived at Sheria," he records, "I throttled down to lose height and bomb the railway station. I was just getting ready and was about 2,000 feet up when I got archies[2] all

---

[1] Capt. R. F. Baillieu, M.C.; No. 1 Sqn. Of Melbourne; b. Queenscliff, Vic., 1896.

[2] "Archie." See Glossary.

round me—by Jove they did stick, too! I went in and dropped my two 112-lb. bombs and the engine stopped. I am for Constantinople now, all right, I thought. I thought an archie had got my engine, for they were going off all round me the whole time. I tried all the petrol taps and could get no result; then undid my belt and stood up to see if anything was wrong in front, but saw nothing. During all this time I was being peppered with archies and I said to myself, 'Well, you might see I am coming down.' I dropped two smoke balls as distress signals to our other machines, but they seemed an awful way off and a long way above me. By this time I was nearly on the ground and was picking out a spot to land on, when I looked at my switch on the outside of the machine. It was *off*. I switched on and, thank Heaven! the engine started firing. She choked a bit at first, so I throttled back and then gradually opened up. The engine picked up and I was going again. By this time I was under 500 feet and was making for the Turks. They must have opened fully six or eight machine-guns at me, so I turned to get out of that." Williams's principal anxiety while coming down, he adds, was that there was an Australian mail due to arrive, and he would miss his letters. He escaped with his machine badly holed.

During March 6th all available machines bombed the busy Turkish railway running into Tel el Sheria from Arak el Menshiye, but the damage done was not great. The Turkish retirement from Weli Sheikh Nuran enlivened the whole front, and air operations were continuous from this time till the first attack on Gaza. The anti-aircraft fire over Tel el Sheria hit Lieutenant J. V. Tunbridge's[3] machine during a patrol on March 7th; he was forced to land at Rafa, and set out to make his way home on foot through a country still considerably unsettled, over which Arabs of doubtful friendship were hunting for loot. He was rescued in an exhausted state by Lieutenants P. W. Snell[4] and Morgan in a B.E., who saw him and landed to pick him up. Tel el Sheira[5] was bombed by relays of raiders in the moonlight throughout

---

[3] Lieut. J. V. Tunbridge, M.C.; No. 1 Sqn. Warehouseman; b. Ballarat, Vic., March, 1894.

[4] Lieut. P. W. Snell, A.F.C., R.A.F. Attached No. 1 Sqn., 17 Feb.-24 May, 1917.

[5] Sheria was till June headquarters of the enemy force in the Gaza-Beersheba line. In consequence of the British air bombing it was moved in July to Huj.

the evening of March 7th. Next morning six bombing machines attacked Junction Station, north of Arak el Menshiye. While these raiders were out, considerable excitement was caused at the El Arish aerodrome by the appearance of a Fokker, which, at 4,000 feet, dived direct over the landing-ground. The watching Australians expected bombs; the German dropped merely a message bag[6] and made off home again. Before his purpose was perceived, two Australian machines had left the ground to attack, but they failed to catch him. The message-bag was found to contain two letters from officers of No. 14 Squadron who had been captured a few days before, and one addressed to a German prisoner with the British. No. 14 Squadron promptly sent off two machines to Beersheba with a reply message, which thanked the Germans for the letters, and, on behalf of the Australians, apologised for having in the circumstances sent up two machines to attack the message-carrier. Then No. 1 Squadron sent out another patrol to drop bombs on Tel el Sheria.

With the day of the Gaza attack now approaching, attacks on Junction Station, a vital Turkish supply point, became increasingly important. During a raid of eight machines from the combined squadrons in the afternoon of March 9th, Heathcote from No. 1 Squadron was taken prisoner. He landed with engine-trouble in the sand-dunes north of Gaza, and Snell, who stood by for a time to pick him up, was unable to find a landing patch in the sand to permit of it. Arabs later brought in a message from the Turkish commander at Gaza saying that Heathcote was a prisoner. For a few days strong sandstorms prevented flying. The wind-driven sand, indeed, caused six train derailments on the desert railway in one space of twenty-four hours. In an interval between storms, Junction Station was again bombed on March 13th; on the way the raiders met a German scout near Gaza, but it fled on sight. As soon as the sandstorms were over, both squadrons resumed the bombing of the railway from Junction Station to Tel el Sheria. In one of these raids, on March 19th, a machine of No. 14 Squadron was shot down and had to land in sight

---

[6] This method of correspondence between opposing airmen was a feature of war in the air on all fronts.

of the enemy. Baillieu and Ross Smith (observer) descended and picked up the pilot after he had burnt his machine. On the following day, coming home from another attack on the railway, McNamara repeated and surpassed this performance under most difficult circumstances. The enemy's anti-aircraft fire had been severe. Captain D. W. Rutherford's[7] machine was hit, and the pilot landed in the presence of Turkish troops near the railway. McNamara, in a Martinsyde, though badly wounded in the leg, flew down at once to Rutherford's assistance and alighted close beside him. Rutherford climbed into the Martinsyde, but McNamara had not sufficient strength in his injured leg to control the machine on re-starting, and it crashed badly. They set fire to the Martinsyde and both then returned to Rutherford's machine—by this time in great danger of being captured by the Turks, who were running up—and started the engine. In spite of some damage to struts and fuselage, McNamara flew the aeroplane home, a distance of seventy miles, with Rutherford as passenger. It was a brilliant escape in the very nick of time and under hot fire.[8]

Murray's advance began on March 23rd with the occupation of Khan Yunis and Deir el Belah, immediately in front of Gaza. During the next two days the infantry moved up for the assault, with the light horse on the right flank; and at dawn on March 26th the attack on Gaza was launched. No. 1 Squadron had moved forward to a new landing-ground at Rafa, and was to have assisted the opening attack, but fog was so heavy that all machines had to turn back, and nothing of the ground could be seen from the air before 9 o'clock. The plan of attack was the same as at Magdhaba and Rafa, but on a larger scale; Gaza was to be surrounded and stormed before the enemy could bring up reinforcements. Infantry attacked on the south and east; then on the north of the town came yeomanry, New Zealanders, and, next the sea, Brigadier-General Ryrie's light horse brigade. The assault was gallantly pressed, especially on the north,[9] and nearly

---

[7] Capt. D. W. Rutherford; No. 1 Sqn. (previously Light Horse). Salesman; of Rockhampton, Q'land; b. Rockhampton, 29 Sept., 1890.

[8] For this performance McNamara received the Victoria Cross.

[9] The Light Horse attack was so hotly pressed that the Australians and New Zealanders captured 800 prisoners in the north of Gaza town, including the general commanding the Turkish 53rd Division, and also several guns.

succeeded; but the Turks, though driven from the outskirts of the town, clung desperately to the main part of it, and the attacking forces were eventually withdrawn before the threat of strong enemy reinforcements which appeared from north and east. By March 29th the infantry had retired to a line on the Wady Ghuzze and were digging in there.

The airmen played an important part in this fight. Their patrols constantly reported the progress of the attack. The throwing of cavalry so far ahead around Gaza was a daring operation and could never have been undertaken without the aid of the air squadrons. When the Turkish relieving columns from Mejdel, Huj, Tel el Sheria, and Beersheba came upon the scene in the late afternoon, it was the air-watch which calculated and reported the strength and dispositions of those columns and superintended the withdrawal of the cavalry. The position on March 27th was doubtful. Murray's infantry were on the Sheikh Abbas ridge, with their desert flank thrown back, and the enemy apparently intended a threat against this flank. Constant air reconnaissance cleared up the situation, and by evening established the fact that a large force of Turkish cavalry, with guns, was marching around the rear of the camel corps on the British extreme right. Light horse were sent out to counter this threat, and while the British line was withdrawn that night to the Wady Ghuzze, the Turks also fell back to the Gaza–Hareira road. Next morning the artillery aeroplanes[10] reported no enemy within range of the British guns. Rutherford and Lieutenant W. R. Hyam[11] (observer), in one of these artillery machines, were attacked from below by an Aviatik; both pilot and observer were wounded, and Hyam later died of his wounds. Murray Jones flew to their assistance and chased off the enemy, who had the speed of the Australian machines and could escape at will. This was the first serious air combat fought by No. 1 Squadron, and was the beginning of a long contest which ended in the driving of the Germans absolutely from the air. But that victory was not yet in sight, and many months of difficulty with inferior

---

[10] An aeroplane observing for artillery signalled back the fall of each shell until the battery was on the target. "Artillery machines" were specially detailed for this duty, and generally did nothing else.

[11] Lieut. W. R. Hyam; No. 1 Sqn. (previously Light Horse). Farmer; of Bairnsdale, Vic.; b. Thirsk, Yorkshire, Eng., 20 Jan., 1891. Died of wounds, 30 March, 1917.

machines still lay ahead. With the hot weather now beginning
the engines were over-heating, particularly the Beardmore
engines in the Martinsydes. One of No. 14's machines
descended in the sea on March 28th in consequence of this
trouble, and Ellis came in that day from patrol with the white
metal on his engine running liquid.

It became clear after a few days' doubt that the enemy was
determined to hold the Gaza–Beersheba position, and that he
was being strongly reinforced there. His air strength also
was increased by many new machines, an event which he
signalised by reconnoitring the British lines with hitherto
unprecedented enterprise. Lieutenants Turner and C. de C.
Matulich[12] (observer), escorted by Murray Jones, were setting
out on patrol on April 6th, when they encountered over Weli
Sheikh Nuran five Germans making towards Rafa. Jones
fought all five of the enemy till his machine was damaged
and he was forced to land near Weli Sheikh Nuran. The
Germans machine-gunned and bombed his aeroplane while
it lay on the ground, but Jones himself escaped unhurt.
Turner flew back to Rafa and warned the aerodrome. Three
more Martinsydes then went out and engaged this German
formation between Weli Sheikh Nuran and Tel el Sheria;
there were several duels, but none of them decisive, and the
enemy made off. During the fighting two other hostile aircraft
bombed Bir el Mazar. The fact was that each army
could see the other plainly preparing to renew the battle for
Gaza—the British tanks and heavy howitzers coming up from
the desert must have been easily evident—and bombing by
each side was maintained strenuously. In reply to the attack
on Bir el Mazar, four Australian machines and several from
No. 14 Squadron set out in the night of April 7th to raid the
Ramleh aerodrome. Lieutenant N. L. Steele[13] smashed two
hangars with his bombs, and Drummond, Murray Jones, and
one British pilot also hit the aerodrome; the others failed
to find it, and bombed Gaza instead.

The Germans replied on April 12th by attacking the Rafa
aerodrome at dawn with three machines. In quick retaliation
seventeen machines from the combined squadrons left the

---

[12] Lieut. C. de C. Matulich; No. 1 Sqn. Electrical engineer; of Adelaide; b. Peterborough, S. Aust., 6 May, 1894.

[13] Lieut. N. L. Steele, No. 1 Sqn. Student; b. Kew, Melbourne, 6 Dec., 1895. Died of wounds, 20 April, 1917.

aerodrome at 9 o'clock and heavily bombed the Turkish positions in the Beersheba line. Another German raid on Rafa and a second raid by No. 1 Squadron on the Beersheba positions followed in rapid succession before midday. Similar raids and counter-raids marked the three subsequent days while Murray's troops were moving up on Gaza, and the fire of heavy artillery on each side increased notably. Bombing attacks were not the only demand on the airmen; the Turkish position was daily reconnoitred, and by April 18th all British heavy guns had been registered upon allotted targets. The Turkish guns were cunningly hidden, and to locate them the artillery machines would fly up and down the line marking down every flash; the enemy's field batteries in some places were obliging enough to open fire upon the observing airmen and remove all doubt about a concealed position. Nevertheless, some of the enemy's guns in Gaza were not discovered before the battle.

The advance began in the night of April 16th. The infantry occupied the Sheikh Abbas ridge and at daylight the tanks—used here for the first time on the Eastern Front—worked round the ridge to mop up Turkish posts. There followed two more days of preparation, searching for hostile batteries, and ranging of artillery and ships' guns on the Gaza–Hareira positions, and then, after a two hours' preliminary bombardment came, with dawn on April 19th, the second assault on Gaza.

It was again a failure—a failure far worse than the former attempt, which nearly succeeded. This time there was no attempt at envelopment, but a frontal attack in force along the ten or twelve miles of entrenched defences. The infantry's effort made little impression; the enemy's guns were not only well concealed but also numerous and exceedingly well served. The fight was not marked by any special incidents in the air. Murray Jones and Steele, on patrol at one time after noon, met five German machines and engaged them with a few bursts of machine-gun fire; though both the Australians' guns jammed badly, the two reached home without hurt. The patent failure of the attack on the first day encouraged the enemy to counter-attack, and an intercepted wireless message warned Murray's troops of bomb raids and a hostile flank movement timed for next morning. At the expected hour German airmen duly attacked the British camps, and Turkish cavalry was massed at Hareira for some action, but this did not seriously develop. Williams, leading a patrol of three B.E's and two Martinsydes, found this cavalry assembling and bombed it severely; thereafter it did not make its thrust. That the bombing drove the heart out of the Turkish horse was confirmed by later intelligence. Steele was lost on this adventure; his Martinsyde was shot down by gun-fire, and the pilot died of his wounds soon afterwards.

The enemy's anti-aircraft artillery was particularly well served, as is manifest from the number of aeroplanes shot down or damaged by this means. On April 21st, the day following Steele's death, Williams and Lieutenant E. S. Headlam[14] (observer) were reconnoitring Tel el Sheria, with Cole and Tunbridge escorting in Martinsydes, when Cole's machine was hit by a piece of shell and forced to land. Williams went down after him and picked him up after he had burnt his machine.[15] Lieutenants G. C. Stones[16] and Morgan, in an artillery machine, were shot down by gun-fire over Gaza on May 30th; they fell within the British lines, but both were killed.

Eight months had brought the Egyptian Expeditionary Force under Murray from the Suez Canal Defences to the entrance into Syria. In the eighth month Murray had twice failed to take Gaza, which blocked his advance into Palestine, and his army now sat down for a spell of six months of trench warfare, to await reinforcements of artillery and infantry and a new leader. That leader was found in General Sir Edmund Allenby,[17] who came from the command of the British Third Army in France. He arrived in Egypt in June and took over the command from Murray at the end of that month. In August the so-called "Eastern Force" and the Desert Column ceased to exist as such. With large reinforcements now received, the Eastern Force was converted into two army corps —the XX (Chetwode) and the XXI (Bulfin)—while the Desert

---

[14] Lieut. E. S. Headlam; No. 1 Sqn. (previously Camel Corps). Law student; b. Bothwell, Tas., 1892.

[15] Cole had also previously been shot down by anti-aircraft fire on March 5th.

[16] Lieut. G. C. Stones; No. 1 Sqn. (previously Light Horse). Orchardist; of Matlock, Derbyshire, Eng.; b. Wisbech, Cambridge, Eng., 31 July, 1882. Killed in action, 30 May, 1917.

[17] Field-Marshal Lord Allenby, G.C.B., G.C.M.G., p.s.c. High Commissioner for Egypt. Of Felixstowe, Suffolk, Eng.; b. Brackenhurst, Southwell, Notts, Eng., 23 April, 1861.

Column became the Desert Mounted Corps (Chauvel), including the Australian Mounted Division and the Anzac Mounted Division.[18] The enemy also was greatly reinforced. The period April–October, 1917, was one of strenuous preparation for a pitched battle for the gate to Palestine. Both British and Turks laid railways and water pipe-lines and brought up troops, guns, and vast quantities of ammunition. Active operations during this period were confined almost entirely to the air. On the British side the air force was increased in order to equip the growing army with an aircraft service on European lines. Each corps required its corps flying squadron for strictly local reconnaissance work and other multifarious duties. The army wing had to be strengthened with a squadron of fighting scouts. Most important of all, improved types of machines were necessary, so that British and Australian airmen might combat the enemy's technical superiority. As the air force grew, it had to be re-organised, and in April, 1917, orders were published that British flying officers attached to No. 1 Squadron must leave that unit, and that Australians must take their places. One effect of this order was that in May Rutledge returned to the Royal Flying Corps and Williams took command of the squadron. It was not till October 5th that, in pursuance of this re-organisation, No. 1 Squadron was formally incorporated in the 40th (Army) Wing of the Palestine Brigade, R.F.C.

From April, 1917, onwards, therefore, the air work on the fighting front became steadily more arduous and important. Existing maps had to be corrected and new ones made, and in this task the survey companies of Royal Engineers at Army Headquarters depended chiefly upon the airmen's photographs of vast stretches of country. The progress of the Turks' defensive work, and of their organisation far back along rear communications, had daily to be watched and recorded, and, while for the time being the artillery battle diminished, bombing raids correspondingly increased. In the desert in 1916, during operations of smaller forces, aeroplane patrols had for the most part been conducted without air fighting. Now the concentration of growing forces upon a smaller and definite front, the accumulation of supply dumps and communications services, and the necessity which each

---

[18] See note at end of chapter.

command felt for daily information concerning the other's preparations and intentions, awoke intense rivalry in the air. Reconnaissances hitherto unmolested were challenged, and had to be pressed against the opposition of hostile aircraft. Bombing raids were not merely repaid in kind—and No. 1 Squadron henceforth dropped four bombs for every one from the enemy—but, as far as possible, were forestalled and prevented. In short, air fighting began to assume the aspect to which pilots in France had long become accustomed. Upon special patrols, and later upon special squadrons, was imposed the duty of seeking out and destroying the enemy's aircraft wherever they might be found—in the air or on their aerodromes—in order that other British machines might perform with the least possible interruption the essential daily work of detailed reconnaissance, photography, and artillery observation.

Till better machines arrived the British airmen almost invariably had the worst of air combats. On May 11th Tunbridge fought a duel with a Fokker; a bullet exploded a Very-light cartridge in the Australian machine, and Tunbridge had to descend with his clothing on fire. He landed successfully, but so badly burnt about the body that he was discharged invalided to Australia. Five days later Murray Jones fought another engagement with a German scout, and was forced to land, wounded in the leg. Against the handicap of inferior equipment the British airmen, however, never gave in, and where they could not take revenge upon the enemy in the sky they bombed his camps and aerodromes. They assisted the cavalry in tearing up sections of the Turks' El Auja–Asluj railway in the desert on May 23rd, and Cole and Drummond bombed Abu Hareira on May 30th. Under the redoubtable Felmy[19] a German air raid was organised on May 25th against

---

[19] There were two brothers of this name associated with the German air service in Palestine. Felmy the elder was in command of the first German squadron to proceed to that front early in 1916. It consisted of fourteen C.1 Rumplers (150-h.p. Mercedes engines). When other units joined the original squadron, Captain Felmy was raised to the command of the whole air service on the enemy's Mediterranean front. He apparently did little flying over the lines, and returned to Germany in March, 1917. The Felmy here concerned was the younger Felmy, who began his service as pilot in the early squadron commanded by his brother. He was an expert airman, and Colonel Williams in his diary speaks of him as "easily our most formidable opponent." Lieutenant Felmy was responsible for the two attacks upon the desert pipe-line from Kantara to the front, which supplied the British Palestine army with water. With the arrival of a squadron of Pfalz scouts for the German service, Felmy the younger was given command of it. Shortly before Allenby's September offensive, Felmy, according to a report by an Australian officer then a prisoner in German hands, was killed at Damascus aerodrome in an accident during a test flight.

the British railway communication from Kantara. Three of the enemy landed in an Aviatik near Salmana and tried to blow up the railway, but they were surprised and driven off by the British West Indian guard, and left behind several articles and a note from Felmy asking for information about lost enemy airmen. Felmy was a stout and enterprising opponent, and under him the German airmen became distinctly more aggressive. In June they flew almost daily over the lines, and the slower Martinsydes rarely managed to prevent them. It was an unsatisfactory and unequal contest. The need for improved British aircraft was made clear again in the disaster to Lieutenant J. S. Brasell[20] on June 25th. He was flying the only B.E.12.a (a newly-arrived machine) in the squadron, in escort of a reconnaissance patrol near Tel el Sheria, when he was attacked by three Fokker scouts, shot through the head, and fell inside the enemy's lines.

Failing to come to terms with the enemy in the air, No. 1 and No. 14 Squadrons organised further raids on his aerodromes. In the early morning of June 23rd, before dawn, seven Australian machines bombed Ramleh, while a formation from an R.N.A.S. squadron attacked from the sea the Turkish railway centre at Tul Keram. The Ramleh raiders smashed two German aeroplanes on the ground, but otherwise effected no important damages. A more exciting raid was one by eight machines on June 26th on the Turkish Fourth Army headquarters at the Mount of Olives, Jerusalem. The attack considerably annoyed the Turks, who immediately afterwards placed six anti-aircraft guns on the Mount.

But on the way home the raiding formation met with an extraordinary series of accidents. Near Beersheba the engine of one B.E. seized, and the pilot, Lieutenant C. le B. Brown,[21] was forced to land. Cole, in a Martinsyde, and Lieutenant R. A. Austin,[22] in a B.E., landed alongside Brown and burnt his machine, and Austin picked him up. The formation then resumed its flight homeward, but about five miles south-east of Beersheba Austin's engine also seized, and he had to land

---

[20] Lieut. J. S. Brasell; No. 1 Sqn. Electrical engineer; of Melbourne; b. Wanstead, Essex, Eng., 1889. Killed in action, 25 June, 1917.

[21] Lieut. C. le B. Brown, M.C.; No. 2 Sqn. (previously Light Horse). Station overseer; of Inverell, N.S.W.; b. Paterson, N.S.W., 14 Sept., 1892.

[22] Capt. R. A. Austin, M.C.; No. 1 Sqn. (previously Light Horse). Station manager; of Lake Bolac, Vic.; b. Eilyer, Vic., 21 June, 1893.

with his passenger. The ground was bad; Cole landed and first tried to take off both Austin and Brown, and then one of them alone, but could not achieve either effort in the Martinsyde. Finally his engine stopped, and the machine landed badly from a drop of ten feet and broke its undercarriage. The three airmen buried a camera and their guns, and started to walk in through a dangerous stretch of No-Man's Land. They were rescued by the light horse outposts. Meanwhile, hovering about to give assistance in case of possible attack, two more pilots, Lieutenants J. H. Butler[23] and L. M. Potts,[24] exhausted petrol and oil and both had to land near Khalasa; they were picked up by the remainder of the formation and left their machines unburnt, in the hope of salving them. Later pilots went out in a tender with petrol and oil to bring in the abandoned B.E.'s, but the Turks and Arabs had meanwhile hacked the fabric of them to pieces and only the engines were worth carrying back.

Note.—In March, 1917, the order of battle of the E.E.F. was:—

CAVALRY.

Anzac Mounted Division.
Imperial (later Australian) Mounted Division.
5th, 6th, and 22nd Yeomanry Brigades.

INFANTRY.

52nd (Lowland) Division.
53rd (Welsh) Division.
54th (E. Anglian) Division.

Reinforcements swelled this force, and under the re-organisation it appeared thus:—

CAVALRY.

Desert Mounted Corps.

Anzac Mounted Division.
Australian Mounted Division.
4th Cavalry Division.
5th Cavalry Division (arrived March, 1918).
Imperial Camel Corps Brigade, re-organised as cavalry, June, 1918.

---

[23] Lieut. J. H. Butler; No. 1 Sqn. (previously Light Horse). Jackeroo; of Hobart, Tas., and Darling Downs, Q'land; b. Bellerive, Hobart, 19 Jan., 1894.
[24] Lieut. L. M. Potts; No. 1 Sqn. (previously Light Horse). Bank clerk; b. Karori, Wellington, N.Z., 1893.

INFANTRY.

XX Corps.

10th (Irish) Division (arrived September, 1917).
53rd Division.
60th (London) Division (arrived June, 1917).
74th (Yeomanry) Division (formed January, 1917, left for France, May, 1918).

XXI Corps.

3rd (Lahore) Division (arrived April, 1918).
7th (Meerut) Division (arrived January, 1918).
52nd Division (left for France, April, 1918).
54th Division.
75th (Territorial and Indian) Division (arrived October, 1917).

The 42nd Division, which served in the desert advance, left for France early in March, 1917.

AIR FORCE.

Till near the end of 1917 No. 1 Squadron, A.F.C., and No. 14 Squadron, R.F.C., were the sole flying units with the Palestine army. At the end of 1917 or during the summer of 1918 the Palestine Brigade, R.A.F., was organised and the air strength was increased to these proportions:—

5th (Corps) Wing.

No. 14 Squadron, R.A.F.
No. 113 Squadron, R.A.F.
No. 142 Squadron, R.A.F.

40th (Army) Wing.

No. 111 Squadron, R.A.F.
No. 144 Squadron, R.A.F.
No. 145 Squadron, R.A.F.
No. 1 Squadron, A.F.C.
No. 21 Balloon Company—Nos. 49, 50, and 57 Balloon Sections.

CHAPTER VI

THE VICTORY OF GAZA

INFERIOR technical equipment was not the only hindrance to air work by No. 1 Squadron in the four months prior to the Third Battle of Gaza. Three new Australian service squadrons were being trained in England for the French war theatre, and behind them had to be built up training squadrons for the supply of reinforcements in pilots and mechanics. The natural result was that A.I.F. Headquarters called upon No. 1 Squadron to provide experienced pilots for the new units. Captain Watt had gone away in October, 1916, to command No. 2 Squadron; Captain Sheldon departed in March, 1917, and subsequently succeeded to that same command when Watt left it to take charge of the Training Wing in England. Many attached British flying officers left No. 1 Squadron in June and July under the new order for re-organising with A.F.C. officers.[1] Captains Ellis and A. L. Macnaughton,[2] both flight-commanders, and Lieutenant Baillieu, all left No. 1 Squadron in September. Before the end of the year Captain S. I. Winter-Irving,[3] another flight-commander, went to Australia on leave, and in December Murray Jones and Cole were sent to the new squadrons in England—Cole to become a flight-commander in No. 2 Squadron, and Jones eventually to command that squadron in succession to Sheldon. The loss of so many tried and valuable pilots would have been severely felt by any flying unit, and No. 1 Squadron at the time could ill-afford to spare them.

The local recruiting field, however, was all that could be desired. Since the beginning the squadron had enlisted volunteers from the light horse, and horsemen were the finest possible material for the work required. As the attached British officers, both pilots and observers, quitted the squadron, their places were filled by Australians, the majority of them being selected candidates from the light horse. As has already

---

[1] See page 64, Chapter V.
[2] Capt. A. L. Macnaughton, Aust. Flying Corps. Law student; of Brisbane; b. Townsville, Q'land, 11 Oct., 1894.
[3] Capt. S. I. Winter-Irving, M.C.; No. 1 Sqn. Grazier; b. Melbourne, 1891.

been explained, other things being equal, the good horseman has all the qualities of the good airman. The head and hands required of him in horse-mastery are precisely what the skilful pilot must needs possess. The cavalryman must have a good eye for country; so must the airman. It seemed natural, too, that, while the traditional scouting duties of the mounted arm were being transferred to the air, the horsemen themselves should turn spontaneously in the same direction.

The ground personnel of No. 1 Squadron was also severely taxed. Good mechanics are precious, and the squadron had to give up some of its best men to be training instructors in England. In this respect also the loss was only temporary, for both in Australia and at the new flying school in Egypt mechanics could then be trained more easily than flying officers. As the supply of mechanics increased, the squadron-commander could afford to invite his experienced non-commissioned officers and mechanics to volunteer for commissions as pilots and observers, and when in July he called for a few such applications, half the squadron responded. Needless to say, nothing like so many could be spared.

The daily work of reconnaissance and photography on the fighting front also took its toll of Australian airmen. Between July and October—when the third and final battle for Gaza took place—No. 1 Squadron performed the whole of the strategical reconnaissance on the front, some of the tactical reconnaissance,[4] and much of the photography. Artillery observation was the duty chiefly of No. 14 Squadron, but Australian machines occasionally took part in this work as well. Photography demanded almost a daily patrol; the machines flew in pairs, and their objective was the photographing of the Turkish line for the purpose of map-making. The maps of the area from Gaza to Beersheba were drawn almost entirely from air-photographs taken by No. 1 Squadron. The airmen thus became the true precursors of the army's movements. They carried their cameras ever farther and

---

[4] Reconnaissance was divided into forward-area patrolling and distant patrolling far over the enemy's rear communications. The former, called "tactical" reconnaissance, required detailed examination of trench works, gun positions, strength of wire, and the like; the latter, called "strategical" reconnaissance, aimed at keeping a continuous record of railway activity, the state of the enemy's supplies, the size of his reserve camps, and all movements of troops behind the lines. Tactical reconnaissance became recognised as the duty of the corps air squadron; strategical reconnaissance was carried out by high-flying scouts of the army wing which sometimes ranged over hundreds of air miles a day.

farther afield. The maps made from their photographs enabled the artillery to shatter the enemy's defence positions at Gaza and later on in the Nablus hills, and by their maps, too, the light horse rode at last on their triumphant sweep through the Esdraelon plain.

For a long time the technical superiority of the enemy's aircraft made this photography trying and dangerous. Such air fighting as took place in the summer of 1917 revealed the Germans still as the aggressors. Reconnaissance patrols at this time had to reckon upon constant attack from German scouts. For this reason air escort of all photography and artillery machines was a regular order. The British squadrons were still on the defensive. The time when the possession of fighting scouts would permit of true tactics—the seeking out of the enemy and destroying him—was not yet come.

The dangers awaiting the slower British machines were well illustrated on July 8th. On that day a patrol of three went out from No. 1 Squadron—Captain C. A. Brookes[5] in a Martinsyde, Lieutenant C. H. Vautin[6] in a B.E.12.a, and Lieutenants T. Taylor[7] and F. W. F. Lukis[8] (observer) in a B.E.2.e. Taylor and Lukis were to make the reconnaissance; the other two were escorting. Near Gaza two German scouts attacked the escorts. One dived at Brookes, who spun away to avoid the attack; but the wings of his Martinsyde were seen to fold up and the tail to fall off, and the broken machine went down like a stone. The Germans then made for Taylor and Vautin. Taylor met the challenge with two well-directed bursts of fire, from which the German sheered off and joined his comrade in attacking Vautin. Taylor and Lukis reached home, but Vautin was driven down by the superior manœuvring power of his opponents, forced to land, and taken prisoner. The amiable Felmy sent a letter by aeroplane messenger two days later to say that Brookes was killed and was buried with military honours. " Felmy wrote that Vautin was quite well, and hoped we

---

[5] Capt. C. A. Brookes; Wiltshire Regt. and R.A.F. Attached to No. 1 Sqn., 26 June, 1917. Masonry contractor; of Bradford-on-Avon, Wilts., Eng.; b. Winsley, Eng., 11 Dec., 1887. Killed in action, 8 July, 1917.

[6] Lieut. C. H. Vautin; No. 1 Sqn. (previously Light Horse). Commercial traveller; of Perth, W. Aust.; b. Warracknabeal, Vic., 5 March, 1890.

[7] Lieut. T. Taylor; No. 1 Sqn. (previously Light Horse). School teacher; b. Lucknow, Vic., 1895.

[8] Capt. F. W. F. Lukis; No. 1 Sqn. (previously Light Horse). Farmer; b. Balingup, W. Aust., 1896.

would send him some kit. Vautin, he said, was a very kindly man and a gentleman. Felmy enclosed two photographs of Vautin and himself, taken together. He said he had shown Vautin Jerusalem. Two letters from Vautin were in the dropped bag—one to me and one to his father. He wrote that he was safe and sound and being well treated, that he had been flown back in a German aeroplane, and that, when he started out from here the other morning, he did not expect to be in a German aeroplane that afternoon."[9] Following the receipt of these interesting messages from the element wherein war was carried on with such old-fashioned chivalry, Murray Jones flew over the lines with Vautin's clothes, small kit, and home letters. Felmy and other German airmen were waiting for him on their aerodrome at Huj. Jones descended as low as fifty feet and dropped the parcel among them, then circled the ground, returned the enemy's hand-waving, and flew home again. No shots were fired at him. The incident affords a pleasing picture of the knightly fashion in which airmen frequently treated each other between determined duels.

Further misfortune for the squadron followed on July 13th. Two B.E.2.e's went out that morning on photography-patrol over the Beersheba area. By some mistake the escort, which was to have been provided by No. 14 Squadron, failed to appear over Esani, the meeting place, at the time arranged, and the two B.E's—Lieutenants A. H. Searle[10] and G. L. Paget[11] (observer) in one, and Baillieu and A. E. Barbe[12] in the other—went on without escort. They were taken by surprise almost at once by an enemy scout, which attacked them from the sun.[13] Searle and Paget were shot down and fell in the Turkish lines, killed. Baillieu and Barbe managed to escape with injury to their machine, and landed safely in the British lines. They, too, narrowly missed being shot down, and the

---

[9] Note by Williams in his diary.

[10] Lieut. A. H. Searle; No. 1 Sqn. (previously A.A. Pay Corps). Clerk; of Hampton, Melbourne; b. Bendigo, Vic., 27 Dec., 1887. Killed in action 13 July, 1917.

[11] Lieut. G. L. Paget; 7th Northumberland Fusiliers. Attached No. 1 Sqn., 17 March, 1917. Killed in action, 13 July, 1917.

[12] Lieut. A. E. Barbe; 5th Highland Light Infantry. Attached No. 1 Sqn., 24 June, 1917.

[13] The best possible position of advantage in the air was to have the height of the enemy in direct line between the sun and the hostile machine. In such a position it was quite impossible for the lower machine to see an attacker.

to Germany 14.7.18
Please send the His letter and to send Bag
westphalia

All dear sport!,

My joy was very dull to receive your many letters. Tomorrow Vautin comes, to take all the things and all the letters (with photo), which were dropped. He is a such well educated and gentle boy, that we make with pleasure all! What is pleasant for him.

But when if you write

for us, you must write more distinctly, because our English is not so perfectly, that we can read all. The most legible machine finely has your writing=machine! Vautin has – Murray Jones. Vautin has told very much of him. I hope to fight with this sport more oftener. I thank him for his kind letter. – I thank also for the decoration of the "Rising sun" from Mr. Lex Macnaughton (?). Perhaps I can see the sun later in Australia

LETTER, WRITTEN 14TH JULY, 1917, FROM THE GERMAN AVIATOR FELMY TO NO. 1 SQUADRON, A.F.C.

Enclosed in a message bag, it was dropped by a German machine over the Australian aerodrome. The envelope was addressed to Captain Murray Jones.

Lent by Capt. A. T. Cole, No. 1 Sqn., A.F.C.

For my best thanks for the photo of Mr. Brown and for the kind letter and many photos of R.F. Baillieu.

In order to answer your questions: 1) 2nd Lt. Steele is unfortunately dead. He expired soon after his imprisonment, he was shot down by our airties. 2) Mstr. Heathcote is in captivity and well, I think in the same place as Mstr. Palmer and Floyer. Murray Jones is a very courageous man, we have feeled it in flying and when he came

to drop the things for Austin so down. (perhaps 100 feet)!! I would like to have his address in Australia, to write him what a photo of him and the ship, but — I beg — a little more bigger the photos, because I could scarcely perceive "your sport = eyesights! — "Ramadan" is not practical for a visite at you! we must fast all the day. — For souvenir I have exchanged my watch with Austin, and we havet engraved our names. — Where can I dispense more our aqueduct? Flying! our petrol condition is continuing long time. With best wishes for all, who have written to me us! With hearty respects your G. Felmÿ Oblt.

whole episode showed that for photographing machines to go out unescorted into enemy country was to offer themselves an easy prey to the speedier fighting scouts of the other side. The Australian aerodrome was not surprised when Felmy—recognised by the machine which he always flew—appeared next morning. He looped the loop in friendly gymnastic over the landing-ground, dropped a message bag, and departed. One letter therein related the last particulars concerning the unfortunate airmen; Searle, it stated, had been shot through the head, and both were found dead in the wreck of the machine. This extraordinary correspondent also sent a packet to Murray Jones—whose fighting qualities he greatly admired—containing a letter, a packet of cigarettes, and some photographs. One of these pictures showed a group of German flying officers; another was an enlarged presentation of Felmy and Vautin. The letter related some news of Steele, acknowledged to have been omitted previously by some oversight. It gave the definite information that Steele, who was lost on April 20th, had been shot down by anti-aircraft fire and had died soon after landing.

The Germans, however aggressive against undefended patrols, were not over-keen in attacking reconnaissance machines under escort, even though the escorting De Havillands or Martinsydes were of inferior manœuvring speed. As a rule they would not attack unless they could be sure of some tactical advantage; their daring was generally tempered with much discretion. A German scout, on July 16th, sheered off from an attack when an escort prepared to meet him. Next day an artillery machine was directing fire on German anti-aircraft batteries with such good results that the gunners wirelessed in distress to Ramleh—No. 1 Squadron's station intercepted their signals—and in response a hostile scout appeared on the scene. This scout attacked, but the Australian machine met it with a full drum from its Lewis gun, and the German went down and landed, evidently damaged, on the Beersheba road.

On the ground there was infantry raiding by each side in the latter part of July, and, following the successful capture of a strong enemy post near Irgeig, Turkish cavalry made a strong demonstration from Beersheba. The light horse moved out in strength in the night of July 19th to try to cut them off, but air reconnaissance by daylight next morning showed that the Turks had retired. A second and weaker attempt north of Esani, on July 28th, similarly died away. The air was markedly quiet, and the Australian photography-patrols covered large areas of unmapped ground about Beersheba.

The long-mooted expansion of the British air force on this Eastern Front was now plainly becoming fact. New machines, Bristol Fighters, were dribbling up in ones and twos for the recently-arrived No. 111 Squadron, R.F.C. No. 113 Squadron, R.F.C., was reported to be shortly following, to operate as a corps unit, which would relieve No. 1 Squadron of much trench-reconnaissance duty. No. 1 Squadron, under the new arrangement, was to be made a special bombing squadron. All this news presaged increased strength and more detailed organisation of duties, which, in turn, meant better equipment. New Australian pilots and observers, fresh from the training school, were reporting to the squadron, and further applications were invited for cadet flying-officers from the ranks of the aerodrome and from the light horse. The responses were overwhelming, and selection was of the strictest kind. In August, No. 1 Squadron was authorised by A.I.F. Headquarters to hold a reserve of fifty per cent. of flying officers above establishment—a licence granted by reason of heavy work in the squadron and the drain upon its trained members from oversea. The full value of this useful provision became evident in the heavy fighting of 1918.

On August 3rd, the enemy laid an artful trap. A reconnaissance patrol from No. 1 Squadron reported a hostile machine abandoned on the ground near Beersheba, and it was still there next morning. Four machines were sent out to bomb it, and two others to guard against a surprise attack. When the bombers descended to attack the object on the ground, they saw that the supposed aeroplane was a dummy. The Australians grasped the truth in a flash and promptly zoomed up again to meet the expected squall. It burst without loss of time. Two German scouts darted down from the sun, where they had been hovering unseen, and in a moment the fight was joined. The enemy did not enjoy the advantage he expected, for the Australian escorting machines were also watching cautiously, and after some hot exchanges the Germans broke away for home.

August passed almost without fighting incident. On August 5th a German aeroplane again landed in the desert near Bir el Abd and attempted to blow up the rear railway communication, but was again foiled by the guard.[14] A night raid by a demolition party of light horse against the Turkish railway near Irgeig was likewise unsuccessful. At the end of the month an enemy formation bombed a yeomanry camp; No. 1 Squadron immediately replied with an air-raid on Abu Hareira. Ross Smith and Ellis, in Martinsydes, reconnoitring on September 1st, attacked a German scout over Beersheba and put it to flight. Smith was slightly wounded in the head, but the German did not escape scot-free, for the wireless caught an enemy message stating that " Lieutenant Schmarje[15] has crashed, and another escort is required in his place," and that " one machine is not enough to get through the English blockade." Thereafter the Australian daily patrols worked for some days unmolested.

The railway was now pushing out rapidly on the desert flank towards Karm, in a straight air-line between Rafa and Beersheba. No. 1 Squadron, which had already gone forward to Deir el Belah, was preparing to move on again to Weli Sheikh Nuran. The new aerodrome at that place was finished and occupied in mid-September. No. 111 Squadron, with its coveted Bristol Fighters, was established at Deir el Belah. A few days later—September 28th—No. 1 Squadron was joined at Weli Sheikh Nuran aerodrome by the new No. 113 Squadron. In the areas behind the front all was restless; reserves, supply-dumps, and all arms auxiliary to the infantry moved up constantly with the advancing railhead, and by the end of September No. 1 Squadron was reconnoitring a new advanced landing ground among the light horse forward camps north of Esani.

The Bristol Fighters of No. 111 Squadron soon demonstrated their powers, and the enemy formally made their acquaintance on October 8th. Several Bristol Fighters were sent out that day to wait for the usual German reconnaissance,

---
[14] See page 66, Chapter V.
[15] The name cannot be confirmed from available German records.

and soon sighted two Albatros scouts. One of these was caught without chance of escape from the new and swifter British machines, and was shot down in the light horse lines. The pilot was unwounded, and the Albatros, little damaged, was repaired by the Australian squadron's mechanics. The perfect running of its engine was greatly admired. The enemy's curiosity was aroused by the loss of this machine, and on October 15th three more Albatroses crossed the lines. British anti-aircraft gunners, a few minutes after opening fire on the enemy formation, observed it to be in violent commotion. A waiting Bristol Fighter, whose attention had been attracted by the anti-aircraft bursts, had attacked from the upper air. The German nearest to it was apparently thrown into convulsions. It looped and spun and performed a variety of manœuvres to elude the Bristol Fighter; finally it went into a prolonged spin, one wing fell off, and it crashed into the ground. The victorious pilot proved to be the same airman, a Lieutenant Steele, from No. 111 Squadron, who had shot down an Albatros a week earlier. He told an interesting story of the fight. He put the German's engine out of action in his first attack. The enemy pilot signalled the Bristol Fighter off and glided down as though to land. Steele stopped firing and flew earthwards alongside the Albatros, but noticed that the enemy was gliding towards the Turkish lines, and signalled him to turn back. The German declined to turn. Steele's observer accordingly re-opened fire and shot off one of the Albatros's wings, which finished the dispute.

Two days later, No. 1 Squadron received from Kantara the first of its new equipment of R.E.8's. The remainder followed quickly, and the squadron was warned to prepare for heavy bombing operations to accompany the coming attack on the Gaza line. The R.E.8's were not the only improvement in the squadron's technical outfit; new Martinsydes, fitted with 160-h.p. engines, arrived to replace the older type (120-h.p. Beardmore's).

The attack on the Turkish positions was to begin with operations for the capture of Beersheba, which would lay open the flank of the stronger defences between Abu Hareira and the sea. The date, fixed by the progress of the railway towards Karm, was to be October 31st. The air preparation entered its intense stage on October 28th. From that date onwards No. 1 Squadron carried out daily two strategical reconnaissances of the whole Turkish front, escorted by the Bristol Fighters of No. 111 Squadron. This work included the photographing of the Turkish defences each day for the revision of maps, and copies of these photographs were supplied every evening to the troops which were to make the assault. The artillery bombardment of Gaza opened on October 27th. The observation for this was performed by No. 14 Squadron, also under escort, No. 1 Squadron's R.E.8's and B.E.12.a's escorting on the first day, and No. 111's Bristol Fighters later. No. 1 Squadron also was busy fitting out for bombing operations as soon as the attack should begin. Another bombing unit (known as "X" Squadron, R.F.C.) arrived at Weli Sheikh Nuran on October 30th. The enemy was distinctly apprehensive, and German aeroplanes, though constantly in the air, avoided all risk of encounter.[16]

The battle opened on October 31st with the attack of the 60th Division, the 74th (Yeomanry) Division, and the Camel Corps on the works between Khalasa and the Wady Saba, south of Beersheba. These defences were captured by 1 p.m. During the preceding night the Anzac Mounted Division and yeomanry had moved out across the desert and round to the east of Beersheba. The Australians and New Zealanders arrived at Khashm Zanna, five miles from Beersheba, in the early morning, and shortly afterwards attacked. While the infantry were assaulting the defences south-west of the town, the light horse had deployed to the north-east. The New Zealand Mounted Rifles in the centre went for Tel el Saba, a fortified hill; the 1st Light Horse Brigade advanced on their left; the 2nd Light Horse Brigade dashed across on the right to occupy Sakati on the Hebron road. Till afternoon there was hard fighting for these positions; they were ultimately captured late in the day, and about the same time other light horse detachments and yeomanry charged into Beersheba from the east, on the left of the New Zealanders. The Turks were thrown out of the town in great disorder, leaving 2,000 prisoners and thirteen guns; over 500 of their dead were buried on the field. The objective at Beersheba, apart from

---

[16] See note at end of chapter.

Map No. 5

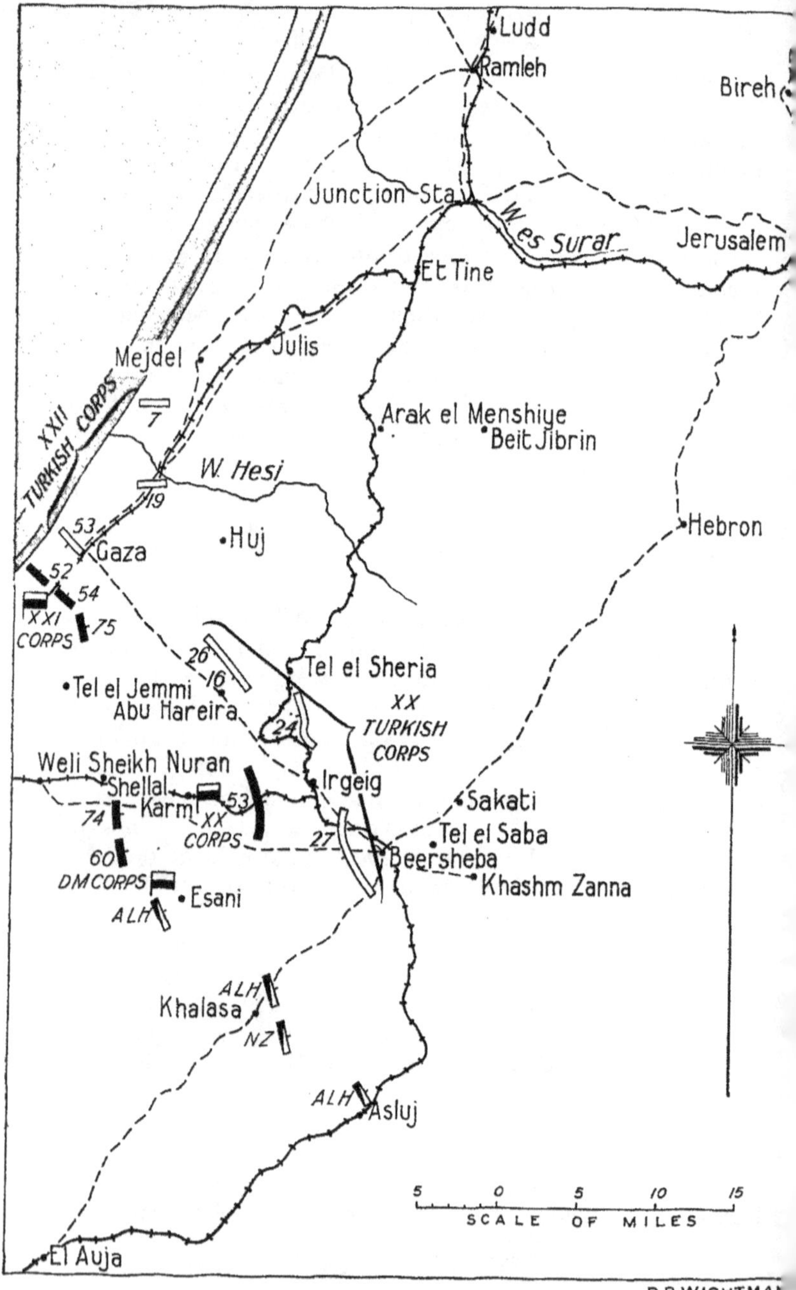

SOUTHERN PALESTINE, SHOWING THE POSITION BEFORE THE THIRD BATTLE OF GAZA

the facilitating of the coming assault on Gaza, was water—still the most pressing necessity of all. In the event the supply at Beersheba was disappointing. The requirements of four actively-engaged divisions (two of them cavalry) overtaxed the Beersheba wells, and on November 4th the yeomanry had to go back for water as far as Karm.

In the evening of the day following the capture of Beersheba, the 52nd Division advanced on the sea flank of the line, and captured Umbrella Hill, an important position 2,000 yards south-west of Gaza. This was the immediate preliminary to a strong attack, delivered at dawn on November 2nd, by the 52nd and 54th Divisions, assisted by men-of-war which shelled the coast defences from Umbrella Hill to Sheikh Hasan (north-west of Gaza). Nearly all the desired objectives were taken, and the enemy was compelled to commit to this fight reserves which might otherwise have turned the scale on the Beersheba flank. As it was, the Australian and New Zealand cavalry were heavily engaged for five days in hill fighting north of Beersheba which drew in all local Turkish reserves. Then, on November 6th, the 10th, 60th, and 74th Divisions conducted the second stage of the attack, overran the Sheria defences, and made a gap in the enemy's line. By early afternoon the Desert Mounted Corps was pushed forward here and penetrated as far as Huj, ten miles east of Gaza. Gaza had meanwhile been under heavy bombardment. At midnight on November 6th, infantry patrols south of Gaza found the place evacuated. A general advance at dawn next morning passed through the town, and advance-guards, hastening up the coast, crossed the Wady Hesi that same evening. Huj was taken by the yeomanry on November 8th, and the enemy fell back in full retreat. By dawn on November 10th the British had occupied Mejdel and Arak el Menshiye.

Throughout this fighting the airmen constantly patrolled the whole battlefield. Bombing began on the night of November 1st, when Williams, in a B.E.12.a, dropped twelve bombs on Gaza. During daylight hours of November 3rd and 4th machines of No. 1 Squadron accompanied the operations in the hills north of Beersheba. The work of all hands in the squadron was increased through overheating of the engines. On November 6th, the airmen perceived an early sign of a general retreat by the enemy, the moving back of his hospitals; next morning, after Gaza had been taken, No. 1 Squadron's patrols reported the Turks retreating on the whole front and Allenby's troops in pursuit. Large numbers of the enemy were seen making for Mejdel. Thirty machines—twelve from No. 1 Squadron—were sent out promptly to bomb them, and this raid hustled the enemy out of Mejdel ahead of the advancing cavalry.

German aircraft were rarely met during the fighting for the Gaza lines. Not till November 6th did they attempt to interfere with the Australian machines. In the afternoon of that day two R.E.8's, patrolling, and two B.E.12.a's, photographing, from No. 1 Squadron, were attacked by four Albatroses and badly mauled. Although the German air force did not suffer in the battle, it sustained severe losses during the subsequent pursuit. The morning reconnaissance of November 8th found that, while the enemy was everywhere moving back, his air squadrons were apparently delayed, and that on aerodromes at Julis (just beyond Mejdel), Arak el Menshiye, and Et Tine, machines were waiting on the ground and many hangars were not dismantled. Another bombing raid of thirty machines—nine of them Australian—was promptly organised to attack the largest of these aerodromes at Arak el Menshiye. A further raid upon the same place followed in the afternoon. The bombs wrought considerable havoc, several hangars were seen to be set on fire or damaged, and aeroplanes on the ground were disabled. The Germans then abandoned Arak el Menshiye in haste. Serviceable aircraft which escaped from this place and from Julis were bombed again twice next day at Et Tine, and the German airmen burnt and left that aerodrome also. When the cavalry advance-guards reached Arak el Menshiye and Et Tine, on November 10th and 11th, they found the charred remains of eight aeroplanes and both the aerodromes and Arak el Menshiye railway station in ruins.

Note.—An illuminating document, captured at Nazareth in September, 1918, may be quoted here. It is unsigned, but was apparently a report from General Kress von Kressenstein (G.O.C. of the enemy's Sinai front) to "Yilderim" (the official name of German Headquarters with the Turkish army in Palestine). It is dated from Huleikat (north of Huj), 29th September, 1917. It reads—

"The mastery of the air has unfortunately for some weeks completely passed over to the English. Apart from the withdrawal of some particularly efficient officers from Squadron 300, and apart from numerous cases of sickness in this squadron, frequent damage to material, and the irregular supply of working material, the reason for this sudden change is to be sought in the great numerical superiority of the English, and in the appearance of a new type of machine which is far superior to our one-seater."

(Here occurs a firm-pencilled note in the margin: "This cannot be the case. The English in Flanders certainly have not bad aircraft, yet we have the superiority there.")

The report proceeds—

"Our aviators estimate the number of the enemy aircraft at from thirty to forty. Against this we have at present two two-seaters and two one-seaters fit for use.

"I have, therefore, already proposed to the Headquarters, Fourth Army, an increase of our air-fighting strength, to be accelerated as far as possible. I further hold an increase of the anti-aircraft sections, and in particular a speedy and considerable increase of anti-aircraft ammunition, to be necessary."

It remains to be noted that during October, 1917, fifty-six aeroplanes, belonging to Nos. 301, 302, 303, and 304 Squadrons of the German flying corps, arrived in Palestine from Germany. There was also a No. 14 (Turkish) Squadron (which was about the strength of a flight) stationed at Kutrani; its machines were A.E.G. two-seaters.

CHAPTER VII

THE TURKISH RETREAT TO NABLUS

THE victory of Gaza gave the British Jerusalem. For more than a month after that decisive battle the enemy was retreating to the Nablus hills, the nearest natural defence position in his rear. The Turks' immediate object was the removal of vast quantities of supplies collected around Junction Station, and here on November 10th No. 1 Squadron heavily bombed a number of loading trains. The light horse and infantry advance-guards soon afterwards occupied Junction Station and Ramleh, while the airmen, still bombing and reconnoitring ahead of them, found the enemy falling back on Jaffa, Ludd, and Jerusalem. The roads of retreat were littered with abandoned ammunition, exploded railway trucks, smashed waggons, and dead animals. One highly satisfactory feature of the advance was the enemy's serious loss of flying material, and the destruction of machines and stores, at his several aerodromes on the way up to Jaffa.

German documents subsequently captured afforded evidence of the serious demoralisation of the enemy in this retreat from Gaza. One of these, a report of the evacuation of the Bavarian Flying Squadron No. 304[1] from the aerodrome at Arak el Menshiye, is worth recording in some detail, both for its own story and because of the picture it draws of the disorganisation which accompanies a hasty retreat. At a conference on November 4th with Felmy (Commander of the German air force) it was decided that No. 304 Squadron (and presumably the others also) should move to a new aerodrome in rear of the Wady es Surar, near Junction Station. For three days this move was postponed " owing to urgent need of pilots." " On November 7th the moving of material and preparing of a new aerodrome at Wady es Surar was ordered by the squadron-commander, reported to headquarters, and their sanction obtained. Loan of transport from No. 301 and No. 302 Squadrons was asked for," but

---

[1] This was one of the new German squadrons. See note at end of Chapter VI.

was not available, as it was wanted for those squadrons themselves. That same day, November 7th, the excitement began. At 10 o'clock that morning (according to No. 304 Squadron's report) British cavalry was said to have broken through at Tel el Sheria and to be advancing northward, and an officer with a water column declared that he had been shot at by hostile cavalry two kilometres south of the Arak el Menshiye aerodrome. Machine-guns were placed ready on the aerodrome; aeroplanes were even drawn up at the squadron place of assembly, so that their armament also might be used from the ground in defence of the camp. At 11 o'clock the report that British cavalry were near by was stated to be false. At noon lorries borrowed from No. 303 Squadron arrived, were loaded, and began the trek towards Wady es Surar. Then came urgent orders to "start moving back at once," and panic revived. There was only one empty railway waggon at Arak el Menshiye station. For the past day and a half loaded trains had been standing waiting there. Then two machines went off to reconnoitre. One of them soon came back—with its observer shot in the stomach—from a machine-gun attack on British infantry camps.

Next day, November 8th, transport lorries returned from the first journey to Wady es Surar, and were again loaded and sent off. No. 303 Squadron at Et Tine promised to send its transport again to No. 304 Squadron, but it was held back because Et Tine also was threatened and the squadron there had itself to move. These squadrons seem to have been greatly impeded by the amount of baggage they possessed, for No. 304 Squadron is stated to have had on its strength fourteen three-ton motor-lorries. At 8 o'clock British cavalry were seen south of the aerodrome, and Felmy soon afterwards wired that yesterday's alarming reports were now confirmed. Nobody had any news of the Beersheba–Jerusalem front, or of any other front, except that the British were heavily attacking on the Wady Hesi, on the coast. At 10 o'clock British airmen were over Et Tine and Arak el Menshiye, and alarm gongs were sounded, but no bombs fell. These, however, came later from raids before and after noon, as has been already related. The first raid, according to No. 304 Squadron's report, wrecked two machines and ruined a precious motor-lorry. The second destroyed one machine, slightly damaged several others, and wounded a number of Turkish soldiers. All telephone communications from the aerodrome were destroyed. No. 301 Squadron was again asked for transport, but without success. In the growing anxiety a staff officer of the Turkish Eighth Army drove up at 6 p.m. in a car and communicated orders for immediate retreat, since by 11 o'clock that night the rear-guard was required to be in position five miles north of Arak el Menshiye. No. 304 Squadron's report proceeds, in desperate tone: "A complete move was only possible if railway waggons could be placed at our disposal. . . . . The request (to Arak el Menshiye station) that waggons loaded with corn should be set free for valuable flying material was met by the reply that the Army Group had ordered that it was of the utmost importance to send back provisions. Lieutenant Berthold thereupon threatened the military commissioner that the squadron would place the railway station under fire with machine-guns if waggons were not handed over. Without listening to any further contradiction, the squadron had a corn-waggon emptied, and loaded with flying material. The only lorry we had left, on account of this night loading, went into a trench; the axle broke, and the lorry became unserviceable. Thereupon the men had to carry to the railway heavy material and clothing cases. We held up the departure of the train by seizing the engine until the waggon was loaded."

During that night (November 8th) the situation became more threatening. To make the confusion worse, the squadron-commander, after landing in the Wady es Surar, was convinced that that place was useless for an aerodrome, and he selected a new site near Ramleh. The new orders were that machines should assemble at Et Tine and transport at Wady es Surar. But the lorries due to return to Arak el Menshiye for the last load of stores did not arrive; they were diverted to Et Tine by someone who said that the British had occupied Arak el Menshiye. After sitting up all night beside their machine-guns on the Arak el Menshiye aerodrome for the lorries which never came, the disconsolate officers and men were informed at 6 a.m. on November 9th that the British were in the hills close to Arak el Menshiye, that the Arak el

Menshiye station had been mined and was ready for blowing up, and everyone was ordered to make a speedy retreat. The officers of No. 304 Squadron accordingly began to set on fire their remaining material, and Arak el Menshiye station was blown up. The squadron marched to Et Tine. At 4.30 p.m. they had reached a well on the road south of that village and there halted, as they had had nothing to drink all day. "During this halt suddenly there occurred a flight of Turks in the direction of Et Tine, for which hardly any reason could be seen. To the question of the squadron-commander to Turkish officers galloping past, mostly no reply was given; only one officer shouted back, '*Nous ne serons pas.*' On receiving this enlightening answer concerning the situation, the squadron continued getting water, until suddenly some shells, coming from the direction of Et Tine, whistled close over the waggons, and burst a hundred metres behind." The further march was delayed, as it was feared that the dust raised by the lorries on the road would bring them under fire again. About dusk they resumed the trek, and the wreckage of overturned vehicles along the road "bore witness," says the German report, "to the destruction which had ensued." Meanwhile, the machines assembled at Et Tine aerodrome had been again raided by the British and Australian airmen and had suffered serious damage.

Between 8 and 9 p.m. on November 9th some four air-force lorries and one car moved off northward again towards the Wady es Surar. At a railway crossing north-east of Et Tine the road was blocked by eight lorries, the foremost on fire and most of the others abandoned with engines running. The airmen salved some of these lorries, partly cleared the road, and resumed their journey towards the Wady es Surar. "'The road to Wady es Surar," says the German report, "offered a sad spectacle with material strewn along the whole road, stationary lorries, broken-up carts, dead horses, camels, bullocks, and sheep lying around, with fugitives and wounded here and there." Soon after the German airmen on this wretched retreat had reached Ramleh "the order was received that we should go back to El Afule." Some of No. 303's waggons went off by the northern route, but became stuck in the sand, and those of No. 304 accordingly retired *viâ*

Jerusalem. Its men had to convey flying material by lorry with them, because at Ramleh a railway collision damaged two trucks and no new ones could be obtained. Such material as was worth salving from this new mishap was accordingly put on to lorries, and set on the round-about road for El Afule. On November 12th the unfortunate little column had reached El Lubban, south of Nablus, at 3 p.m., and was being collected for the descent of the steep hairpin bends, when the last lorry, "driving rather fast, went over the side of the road." It was completely wrecked and most of the men riding in it were killed. Finally the hard-tried remnant reached El Afule, the new aerodrome, on November 20th. Five machines only of No. 304 Squadron reached that place. They flew from Ramleh.

The disorganisation of the enemy's air scouting and fighting force was plainly perceptible in the absence of patrols or any opposition from the air to Allenby's advance. The British and the Australian scouting machines flew out into the blue towards Nablus and Tul Keram, and each fresh rear-guard which they reported was dislodged and thrown back by the advancing cavalry. On November 17th, the day after Jaffa was occupied, the Australian airmen found on the main road from Jerusalem to Nablus the first signs that the enemy was abandoning the Holy City. The road was crowded with transport all going northward.

The cavalry pushed forward towards this road about Bireh, and No. 1 Squadron bombed that village ahead of them on November 22nd and 24th. On November 28th a combined force from No. 1 and No. 111 Squadrons attacked the enemy aerodrome at Tul Keram, and here at last again met the German airmen. One S.E.5.a from the British squadron was missing after the action, and a B.E. and an R.E.8 from No. 1 Squadron were forced to land behind the British lines on the way home. The German machines, while not venturesome in the daytime, had at evening been bombing and machine-gunning British camps near Ramleh. On both sides air bombing suddenly revived. Tul Keram was again attacked by a combined force of eleven machines on the morning of November 29th, and about the same time a British pilot in a

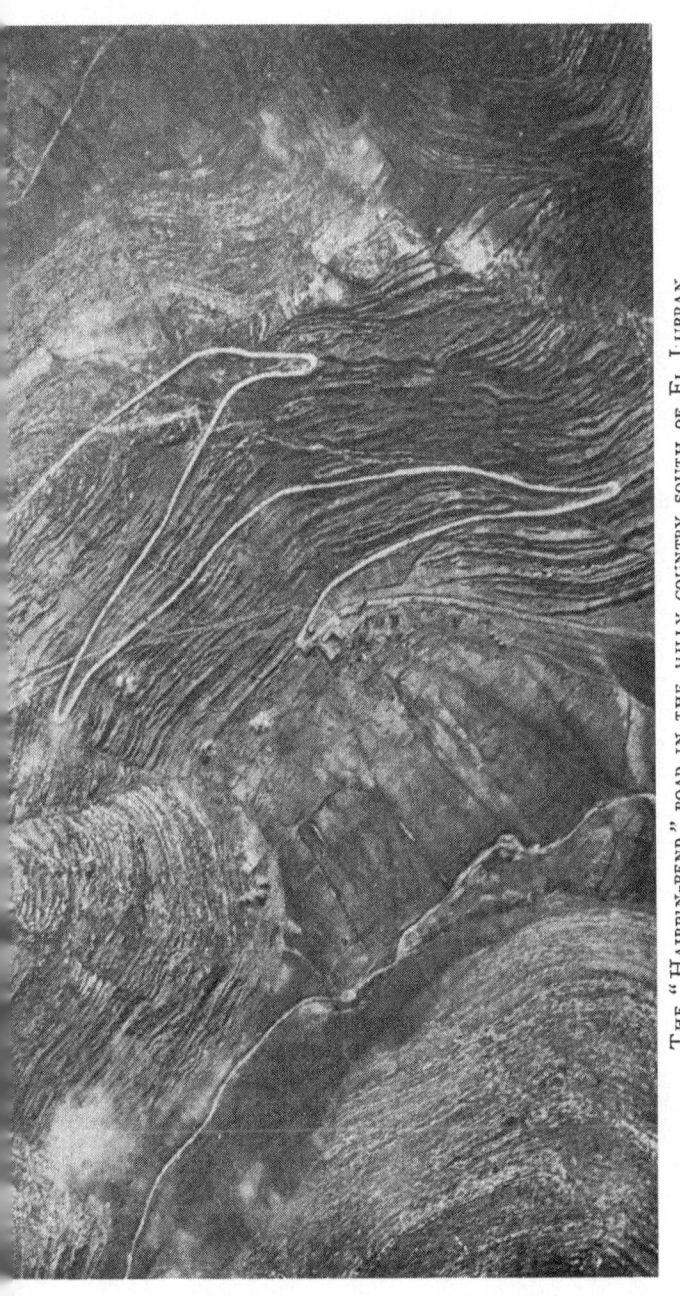

THE "HAIRPIN-BEND" ROAD IN THE HILLY COUNTRY SOUTH OF EL LUBBAN

Several bombs can be seen bursting to the left of the village.

Aust. War Museum Official Photo. No. B3320.
Taken 9th March, 1918.

JERUSALEM, FROM THE AIR, SHOWING THE MOUNTAINOUS COUNTRY AROUND THE CITY

Lent by Capt. A. T. Cole, No. 1 Sqn., A.F.C.

To face p. 87.

Bristol Fighter and Lieutenants Austin and G. Finlay[2] (observer) in an R.E.8 met six German scouts and shot down two of them out of control. The Germans that day were also bombing; they raided Julis aerodrome and hit No. 113 Squadron's orderly room. Tul Keram, in reprisal, was promptly attacked again in a night-raid.

Tul Keram presently became famous and was a favourite landmark of Australian airmen.[3] It is notable especially in the record of one of them, Captain Drummond, a Western Australian boy, who, after enlisting in the A.I.F. straight from school, had joined the Royal Flying Corps and qualified as a pilot early in 1916. Thence he was attached to No. 1 Australian Squadron in its early days, and about this time (the end of 1917) was transferred as a flight-commander to No. 111 Squadron, and subsequently to No. 145 as squadron-commander. On December 12th Drummond was flying a Bristol Fighter of No. 111 Squadron, with an air-mechanic as observer, in escort of an Australian patrol of two slow two-seater machines. Near Tul Keram three German Albatros scouts suddenly appeared over them and prepared to attack. Drummond at once flew over alone to meet the enemy, regardless of the odds against him. He shot down one Albatros, which crashed, and chased the other two; one of these, severely damaged by Drummond's fire, broke up in the air while manœuvring to escape, and the other, chased down very low and seeking to land in a hurry, flew into the side of a hill and was smashed to pieces. Drummond thus destroyed all three single-handed.[4]

This was an example of what British and Australian airmen, when once they were adequately equipped, could do against hostile aircraft. The arrival of the Bristol Fighter and the S.E.5.a in Palestine marked the end of the German airman's reign of superiority in the sky. His new squadrons[5] were equipped with Albatros D.3 single-seater scouts and A.E.G. two-seaters. But, as has been previously explained, when the enemy technically held the superiority, he never

---

[2] Lieut. G. Finlay, D.F.C.; No. 1 Sqn. (previously Light Horse). Labourer; b. Sydney, 1893.
[3] See note at end of chapter.
[4] See note at end of chapter.
[5] See note at end of Chapter VI.

fully asserted it, and by the time his numbers were reinforced modern British machines had arrived and his opportunity had disappeared. From January, 1918, onwards he was gradually driven out of the air, until finally he was almost afraid to show himself in the sky at all.

In No. 1 Squadron the change from the mixed collection of R.E.8's, venerable B.E's, and Martinsydes was made gradually. Nieuports and S.E.5's arrived for No. 111 Squadron in ones and twos, and for each fighting scout thus acquired that squadron transferred a Bristol Fighter to No. 1 Squadron. The Australians in turn handed over their replaced R.E.8's to the corps squadrons of the 5th Wing, and the B.E's and Martinsydes to the new No. 142 Squadron. There was some difficulty with the Nieuports—French machines—which arrived without certain fittings and with the technical directions for assembling the machines written in French. Ultimately these were all replaced by S.E.5's. The R.E.8's were quite serviceable for tactical reconnaissance on the front line with the corps squadrons, but were unfitted for long strategical patrols over the enemy's rear areas. This was in future to be the work of the Army Wing. It was safer and more economical to use Bristol Fighters for distant reconnaissance than to send out older and slower machines escorted by the Bristols. The wisdom of this policy was amply justified.

Thus by the end of January, 1918, No. 1 Australian Squadron was equipped with nine Bristol Fighters, two R.E.8's, five Martinsydes, and five B.E's. By the end of March all older types had disappeared and the squadron comprised eighteen Bristol Fighters. The Mark I Bristol Fighters (190-h.p. Rolls-Royce engines) were gradually replaced during 1918 by Mark III type (260-h.p. Rolls-Royce). Thenceforth No. 1 Squadron, with these machines, carried out most of the Army's distant reconnaissances and all the photography for map-making purposes; it furnished frequent bombing patrols and special escorts, and its pilots sought out the enemy for combat as regularly as did the single-seater fighting scouts of No. 111 Squadron. Month by month the Australians' record of "number of hours' flying" always exceeded that of any other squadron. They made and kept this proud position largely by virtue of their extra strength in flying officers.[6]

Jerusalem had been occupied on December 9th, after a strong attack by the XX Corps on the Jerusalem–Nablus road had forced the Turks to evacuate the city. The enemy was pushed rapidly out of the hills on the north and east. The weather was stormy and wet, and the airmen were able to afford little assistance to the operations on the ground. In a sunny two-days' interval No. 1 Squadron bombed the supply

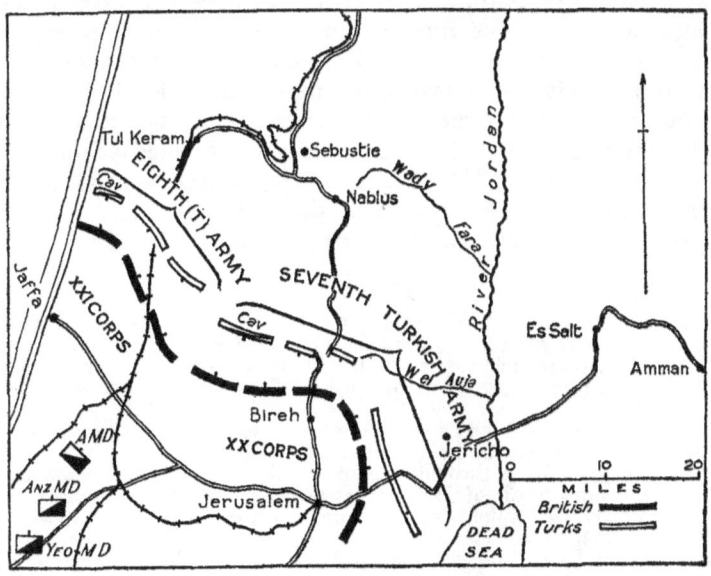

dump and boats at Rujm el Bahr at the northern end of the Dead Sea. Then the rain-storms returned. Flying being mostly impossible, No. 1 Squadron devoted its energies to moving up from Weli Sheikh Nuran aerodrome to Julis, where No. 111 Squadron was already located. The heavy rains almost immediately revealed the worst features of the clay landing-ground, and No. 1 Squadron changed over to a better-drained site closer to Mejdel.

Meanwhile, in continued rain, the XXI Corps on the Mediterranean flank attacked again, crossed the Wady el

---

[6] See page 74, Chapter VI.

Auja north of Jaffa, and drove the Turks to further retreat. Despite rough weather, all four air squadrons on the front bombed these retiring Turks. The enemy made several serious attempts to retake Jerusalem. His loss of it was also a grave loss of prestige; indeed, captured documents described it as a political calamity. But all his counter-attacks were beaten off; their result was only the pressing forward of the British line nearer to Jericho.

The end of the year 1917 marked also the end of the drive forward from Gaza. The Turkish armies had been broken into two parts; one force of about five wasted divisions had halted in the plain north of Jaffa and Ludd, and another, of approximately six divisions, on the eastern side of the mountains of Judæa in the region of the Jordan Valley. By degrees the enemy's line of battle was adjusted so that the Turks had their XXII Corps occupying the coastal sector, their XX Corps at the head of the Dead Sea,[7] and their III Corps in the hilly centre before Nablus.

Note.—Not long afterwards, on 27th March, 1918, Drummond fought a most gallant engagement with six German scouts over Tul Keram. Drummond has told the story in Australian newspapers. "We were just sitting down to breakfast," he said, "when news came of a German machine over the lines, wirelessing. Two pilots were ordered out to deal with him. One could not get his engine to start, so I took his place and went out in my machine, a Nieuport. It had only one gun, firing through the roof. We chased the German back from the lines north of Jaffa to his aerodrome at Tul Keram, where I got a good burst into his tail, and his observer dropped down hit into the machine. The other pilot was chasing him down to the ground, but I stood off, as I had just seen six enemy machines coming in from the north. My mate did not see them, followed the first German machine down, and went off in ignorance of the danger. I had a stiff fight with the six new enemy scouts, shot down one for certain, and sent another down in a spin. But the remaining four were making the fight too hot, and attacking me from underneath, where I could not get at them with my gun. They forced me down lower and lower, my engine was not working too well, and I was nearly done. I had had no breakfast—it is a bad thing to go up without breakfast. I dropped towards the enemy aerodrome in a spin, thinking I was beaten, and it was better to be captured than killed.

"I landed there on their aerodrome, and some men came rushing out. Suddenly I found my engine picking up, and determined to give

---

[7] It is a curious point that two of the Turkish Corps, and also several of the divisions within those Corps, had the same numerical titles as British Corps and divisions opposed to them.

them another run for it. I took off from the ground and got about half-a-mile's start from the four Germans above, who had also concluded that the fight was over. I skimmed the hangars, and made for our lines. Here and there infantry tried to shoot at me. I was flying very low, only a few feet above the ground, and simply went straight at any men on the ground, and forced them to lie down. I landed four times altogether in Turkish territory—whenever my engine failed or a hill appeared—once in the middle of a cavalry·camp at Mulebbis. Here they came up to take me again, and one fat man actually laid a hand on one of my wings, but again my engine picked up, and I fired a few more frantic shots and flew on skimming over their heads. I carried away a line full of washing with my undercarriage as I left this camp. The four German machines kept on behind and above me, but at last only one was left in the chase, and he, we found afterwards, was Felmy. I finally got home and landed just inside the Australian lines on the side of a hill. I fell unconscious when I got out of the machine—an evil effect of no breakfast."

CHAPTER VIII

BEGINNING OF THE AIR OFFENSIVE

THE first intention of the British High Command was to prosecute the campaign in Palestine with all vigour and to continue the attack towards Damascus. In view of the threat of the Germans against the Allies' front in France, however, it was decided that no further reinforcements could be sent to Allenby for some time; and Allenby, on his part, was determined not to continue his offensive until he was assured an adequate support. Meanwhile he resolved to seize Jericho and the crossings of the Jordan near Ghoraniye. Study of the map and of the enemy's situation makes clear the reasons for this move. It would interrupt the nearer communications of the Turks between Nablus and the east of Jordan, set free Jerusalem from the close presence of the enemy on the northeast, and improve the British line on that flank; more important still, it would facilitate co-operation with the Arabs under the King of the Hejaz, whose forces were working northward through the desert and were beginning to appear in strength south-east of the Dead Sea. Early in January these Arabs raided and captured Turkish posts north of Maan, and on January 13th they entered Et Tafile, fifteen miles southeast of the lower end of the Dead Sea. A fortnight later the Turks attacked the Arab advance-guards between Et Tafile and Kerak (twenty-five miles north of Et Tafile), but were completely repulsed with the loss of 400 killed and 300 prisoners (including the Turkish commander), together with guns, machine-guns, and other material. Across the desert to the south of the Dead Sea Allenby was without communication with the Hejaz Arabs. It was necessary for him to have command of a passage of the Jordan, looking towards Amman, in order to be able to effect a junction with them as soon as that might become possible.

While preparations for further immediate fighting on the ground were thus limited, the work demanded of the airmen was vastly increased and expanded. With the improved machines regular reconnaissance was possible far in rear of the enemy's lines. The whole disposition of the Turkish armies from the front lines back to Jenin and the Esdraelon plain, along the valley of the Jordan, across to Es Salt and Amman, and over the desert along the railway to El Kutrani, had to be recorded and watched from day to day, the strength at each important point estimated, and the tactical condition of the country ascertained. Daylight bombing raids were to be made upon selected points, in order that the moral effect of the defeat at Gaza might be maintained. While the general offensive on the ground below had to be postponed, it was to be continued in the air and from the air. Railways, roads, and camps were open to severe punishment under bombing raids and machine-gun attacks. It was calculated that this form of harassing warfare would not only make the enemy himself uneasy, but would also influence against him the inconstant Bedouin. Such was the general scheme of the part which the British and Australian airmen were now called upon to play in opening the final stage of the Palestine campaign. Moreover, a new and vitally important duty became apparent. The air reports showed that all existing army maps, always recognised as deficient in detail, were so inaccurate that they would have to be drawn afresh. The positions of important roads and villages in the enemy's front areas were wrongly given; points of military significance located by aeroplane observers were not shown on the maps at all. It was resolved that most of the front-line region must be re-mapped, and for this purpose a complete overlapping series of air-photographs was required. This entailed the photographing of a strip of country thirty-two miles deep from the Turkish front lines rearwards, comprising an area of about 624 square miles. The task was allotted to No. 1 Australian Squadron, was begun on January 15th, and, despite unfavourable weather on several days, was accomplished in a fortnight.

It was a splendid achievement, and the brunt of the work was borne by five pilots—Lieutenants A. R. Brown,[1] H. L. Fraser,[2] E. P. Kenny,[3] L. T. E. Taplin,[4] and L. W. Rogers.[5]

[1] Capt. A. R. Brown, D.F.C.; No. 1 Sqn. (previously Artillery). Draper; of Launceston, Tas.; b. Launceston, 24 April, 1895.

[2] Lieut. H. L. Fraser, M.C.; No. 1 Sqn. (previously Light Horse). Station overseer; b. Rockhampton, Q'land, 1891.

[3] Lieut. E. P. Kenny, D.F.C.; No. 1 Sqn. (previously Light Horse). Accountant; b. Trafalgar, Vic., Jan., 1888.

[4] Lieut. L. T. E. Taplin, D.F.C.; No. 4 Sqn. (previously Engineers). Electrical engineer; of Parramatta, Sydney; b. Unley, Adelaide, 16 Dec., 1895.

[5] Lieut. L. W. Rogers; No. 1 Sqn. (previously Light Horse). Station manager; b. 28 Sept., 1886.

The method was for five machines, Martinsydes and B.E.12.a's, to fly in line 1,000 yards apart at a height of 12,000 feet, thus ensuring an overlap of the exposures of each camera. Day after day this patrol worked devotedly, under the escort of three Bristol Fighters—two of them from No. 1 Squadron, manned by Captain S. W. Addison[6] and Lieutenant H. Fysh[7] (observer) and Captain Ross Smith and Lieutenant E. A. Mustard[8] (observer), and the other from No. 111 Squadron. One day the work had to be done in a gale, with the wind blowing at sixty-five miles an hour at 5,000 feet. At other times parts of the area would be obscured by clouds; such localities were faithfully revisited by the pilots responsible for them. This work was not performed without interference by the enemy's scouts and anti-aircraft. In the afternoon of January 17th, Fraser, in a Martinsyde, while photographing with the patrol south-east of Jenin, was attacked by one of a formation of five Germans, but the escorting Bristol Fighter from No. 111 Squadron, attracted by Very-light signal,[9] drove it down towards Jenin. That same morning Taplin, in a B.E.12.a, was photographing at about 12,000 feet over the Nablus hills, when his camera jammed. Working the flying control-stick with his knees, he dismantled the camera to re-adjust it, and, while thus engaged, he was attacked from behind by an Albatros scout. Taplin at once turned to engage it. His Vickers gun, being cold, jammed after the first shot. While Taplin cleared the stoppage, the Albatros dived to get underneath him. The Australian promptly turned upon the enemy's tail, fired a burst of twenty rounds into him at close range, and the Albatros went down in a vertical dive. Taplin then mended his camera and resumed his place in the photographing formation.

Apart from these engagements the chief opposition was from anti-aircraft fire and the weather. The completion of the task in fourteen days was a record for such work in

---

[6] Maj. S. W. Addison, O.B.E. Commanded No. 1 Sqn., 1918. Journalist; b. Huon, Tas., 31 Jan., 1887.

[7] Lieut. H. Fysh, D.F.C.; No. 1 Sqn. (previously Light Horse). Wool classer; of St. Leonards, Tas.; b. Launceston, Tas., 7 Jan., 1895.

[8] Lieut. E. A. Mustard, D.F.C.; No. 1 Sqn. (previously Signal Services). Vic. Govt. Railways employee; of North Fitzroy, Melbourne; b. Oakleigh, Melbourne, 21 Sept., 1893.

[9] An escorting machine leaving course to attack hostile aircraft, or any machine desiring to attract assistance, fired a red Very light as signal to companion machines.

Captain Ross Smith (left) and Lieutenant E. A. Mustard in their Bristol Fighter, 1918

Lent by Lieut.-Col. R. Williams, No. 1 Sqn., A.F.C.
Aust. War Museum Collection No. A658.

To face p. 94.

AERODROME OF No. 1 SQUADRON, A.F.C., AT EL MEJDEL, MARCH, 1918

The trenches beside the tents in the foreground are for protection of the men in camp during bomb raids

Aust. War Museum Official Photo. No. B1550.

Palestine; it entailed thirty-nine patrols and the exposure of 1,616 plates. From the negatives the Survey Section produced a new series of maps of the whole region, accurate to the smallest detail. Brigadier-General A. E. Borton[10] (commander of the Palestine Brigade, R.A.F.) said in congratulating No. 1 Squadron:—" The photographs are a very fine achievement, and probably mark the highest point which has yet been reached in map-making photography."

Other reconnaissance patrols swept the country well beyond the area which was being photographed, and penetrated as far as sixty miles behind the enemy's lines. From this time onward the airmen continued to report new aerodromes, important railway centres, new railway and road works, dumps, parks of transport, and troop camps. Constant observation enabled several suspected enemy headquarters to be certainly located. The importance to the enemy of the Nablus–Tul Keram road and the road along the Wady Fara[11] to the Jisr ed Damieh ford across Jordan was early perceived. Amman was reconnoitred for the first time on the 31st of December, 1917, and was found to be an active supply centre; the patrol on that day reported 300 rolling-stock, several hundred tents and shelters, much horse- and motor-transport, and over 1,000 troops, besides cavalry. Along the road from Ghoraniye bridge over the Jordan towards Es Salt were other camps comprising several hundreds of tents and long transport lines. On January 3rd Lieutenants A. R. Brown and O. M. Lee[12] (observer) brought in a graphic report of two aerodromes at El Afule, one of nine and the other of six hangars. The larger of them, judging by the absence of machines or " skid-marks," was only newly erected. The other had several machines on the ground and showed every sign of considerable activity. There were also 200 rolling-stock in the station, 200 tents, apart from the aerodromes, and forty-five dumps of ammunition and stores. Both aerodromes were south-east of the station. On the west were fifteen ammunition dumps

---

[10] Brig.-Gen. A. E. Borton, C.M.G., D.S.O., A.F.C. Commanded Palestine Brigade, R.A.F.; b. 28 Sept., 1886.

[11] There are two Wady Faras, both running into the Jordan on the right bank—one, called also the El Kelt, passing through Jericho, and the other flowing from north of Nablus to Jisr ed Damieh. The Wady Fara here mentioned, and frequently referred to later in this narrative, is the more northerly stream.

[12] Lieut. O. M. Lee, M.C.; No. 1 Sqn. (previously Light Horse). Storekeeper; b. Mole Creek, Tas., 1886.

"three times the size of those at Tul Keram." At Jenin also they observed two aerodromes, a large camp of tents, forty dumps, and much infantry movement; Jenin was a "good bomb target, as all camps are concentrated."

The airmen who brought back this information were in an R.E.8, which accompanied a combined raid of sixteen machines (eight of them from No. 1 Squadron) upon El Afule aerodrome. In all 1,200 lbs. of bombs were dropped, with excellent effect, among the hangars; one two-seater in the open was destroyed by a direct hit, and an ammunition store was exploded. It was learned later than forty Turks were killed. On the way home two Albatros scouts attacked the formation, but Lieutenants Austin and L. W. Sutherland,[13] in an escorting Bristol Fighter, climbed above the enemy, attacked, and shot down one, which was seen to crash near the railway between El Afule and Jenin. This was the first enemy destroyed in air combat by No. 1 Squadron. The other Albatros attacked Brown and Lee, in the R.E.8, from behind and above, but that quarter is not one from which to engage a two-seater. Lee met the enemy with sustained and accurate fire,[14] from which the Albatros dropped in a vertical dive and was lost to sight near the ground. Next day, January 4th, No. 1 Squadron sent ten machines in another joint raid, this time against Jenin aerodrome. Again enemy scouts attacked the patrol on the way home. On this occasion the Albatros scouts had the advantage of broken clouds, which permitted a surprise attack. One Albatros suddenly dived from a cloud upon an R.E.8 from No. 113 Squadron, and as this machine span away it collided with an Australian R.E.8 (Lieutenants J. D. S. Potts[15] and V. J. Parkinson[16]), and both machines fell and crashed. Of the Australians, Potts was killed instantly, and Parkinson was injured. The information was conveyed to the squadron by a message dropped from a German aeroplane.

Though bad weather in mid-January prevented long-distance flights, front-line patrols went on as usual. January

---

[13] Lieut. L. W. Sutherland, M.C., D.C.M.; No. 1 Sqn. (previously Signal Services). Carpenter; of Murrumbeena, Melbourne; b. Murrumbeena, 17 Dec., 1892.

[14] The direction of fire could generally be distinguished by the trail of the tracer bullets. See Glossary (Incendiary Bullets), and Appendix No. 9.

[15] Lieut. J. D. S. Potts; No. 1 Sqn. (previously Light Horse). Jackeroo; of Sydney; b. Malden, London, Eng., 2 April, 1897. Killed in action, 4 Jan., 1918.

[16] Lieut. V. J. Parkinson; No. 1 Sqn. Wireless operator; of Sydney; b. Auckland, N.Z., 8 July, 1892.

17th broke fine, and, while two Australian Bristol Fighters were reconnoitring south of Nablus, at 11,000 feet, they fell in with two hostile formations—one of five Albatros scouts 500 feet below them, and the other of three about 1,000 feet above. The enemy above did not seem anxious to attack. Leaving the escort machine (Lieutenants F. W. Haig[17] and C. J. Vyner[18]) to watch that quarter, Lieutenants L. M. Potts and F. Hancock[19] (observer) dived at the rearmost machine of the lower enemy formation, fired thirty rounds into it, and saw it turn on its back and go down out of control. They were prevented from pursuing it by the presence of other enemy aircraft, which, however, soon broke off the engagement and fled. This incident, otherwise not specially noteworthy, marks the beginning of a new phase; the enemy, even in a position of advantage and with greatly superior numbers, was shy of tackling the Bristol Fighters, and henceforth Australian pilots engaged and defeated the German airmen in whatever strength and circumstances they were encountered. Captain Addison, subsequently commander of No. 1 Squadron, records:—
" The enemy was not long in realising the futility of relying upon his flying service to drive off our inquisitive machines, and accordingly resorted to other means in an endeavour to obtain some protection against this persistent observation. This took the form of increased anti-aircraft guns. Several new batteries were brought to the front in January and February, 1918, while batteries that were already covering places of importance were noticeably strengthened. In addition, a number of mobile anti-aircraft guns, mounted on motor-lorries, made their appearance. It was their special duty to patrol the main roads. They were meant to protect troops on the move against air attack; but subsequent events showed that the crews of these mobile guns were no better able to withstand the determined onslaught of our machines. Frequently they were observed to abandon their guns and join the other forces attacked in search for cover."

---

[17] Lieut. F. W. Haig; No. 1 Sqn. Engineer; of Kew, Melbourne; b. South Melbourne, 29 July, 1895.

[18] Lieut. C. J. Vyner; No. 1 Sqn. (previously Light Horse). Grazier; of Walcha, N.S.W.; b. Harrogate. Yorks., Eng., 14 Sept., 1888.

[19] Lieut. F. Hancock; No. 1 Sqn. (previously Light Horse). Clerk; b. Prahran, Melbourne, May, 1890.

Nevertheless, the enemy's anti-aircraft crews, mostly German or Austrian, were good gunners, and their shooting was uncomfortably accurate. Their chief nests were among the earliest places marked down by the Australian airmen—Amman, Jericho, Huwara (south of Nablus), Messudie Junction (a hot railway corner in the hills at Sebustie), Tul Keram (the great supply centre and army headquarters), and Kalkilieh (on the railway south from Tul Keram). Tul Keram and Kalkilieh were renowned among the British airmen as the "hottest corner" of all, and many a machine grew wary of its anti-aircraft barrage. Fraser's machine was hit at this place in three successive flights in January, and once it was seriously damaged. A number of others were hit at least once or twice. Lieutenants A. V. Tonkin[20] and Finlay (observer) were heavily shelled here on January 10th. Finlay was wounded by shell-splinters twice on the same patrol. A few days later, on January 20th, Lieutenants A. A. Poole[21] and Hancock (observer), patrolling near the coast, were forced to land. A shell from the Tul Keram or Kalkilieh guns hit their engine. They had to glide down, and failed by only a few hundred yards to reach the British lines. Lieutenants A. R. Brown and Finlay (observer) flew down in the hope of picking them up, but the enemy was too close. Poole and Hancock burned their machine, and were last seen holding up their hands to an approaching party of Turks.

On this flight Brown and Finlay found a number of large transport lines at Huwara holding fully 450 horses. Ross Smith and Mustard (observer) next day observed sixteen lines there, averaging forty horses on each line. Huwara, apparently a refilling point, was deemed too good a target to be left in peace, and shortly before noon on January 25th six Australian machines dropped half-a-ton of bombs upon it. By an unfortunate chance for the enemy, a body of about 2,000 troops in two columns had halted on the road just to the north of Huwara. Of the bombs dropped, twenty made direct hits upon these men; the force was dispersed in panic,

---

[20] Lieut. A. V. Tonkin, D.F.C.; No. 1 Sqn. Grocer; of Glenferrie, Melbourne, b. Avenel, Vic., 16 Dec., 1886.

[21] Lieut. A. A. Poole; No. 1 Sqn. Marine engineer; b. Surry Hills, Sydney, May, 1893.

leaving the road strewn with dead and injured. The airmen then passed on to the horses, and stampeded them with the remainder of their bombs.

The enemy's anti-aircraft nests indicated tender spots in his defence. The Messudie railway corner in the hills was no exception. In the tangle of steep gullies about which the railway winds, there were, within a radius of a mile and a half from one point, at least four railway stations or sidings, and many bridges. Here was the site of dumps, camps, transport parks, and the meeting-place of all the neighbouring roads. No. 1 Squadron raided it on January 18th, 20th, and 22nd, and destroyed a number of the dumps, besides causing other damage.

The attention of the Australian airmen, however, had by no means been confined to the coastal sector of the front. Early in January the reports of Arab operations beyond the Dead Sea, and the activity of the enemy between the Jordan and Amman, attracted special interest. The British Command also was planning operations against Jericho. On January 3rd an Australian air patrol discovered a traffic of small boats, many of them motor-driven, on the Dead Sea between Ghor el Hadite (behind Point Costigan) and Rujm el Bahr, at the northern end of the sea. These boats carried corn and hay from the plains east and south-east of the Dead Sea to Rujm el Bahr, for distribution to the forces at Amman and along the Jordan Valley. Ghor el Hadite was a busy little port, with small sailing-vessels—" like Nile boats," said the observers —and supply-dumps. Motor-lorries were occasionally to be seen on the broad white road to Kerak. A special reconnaissance by Lieutenants Mills (of No. 111 Squadron) and W. A. Kirk[22] (observer) on January 19th produced an interesting report on the modern land of Moab. " The towns between the Seil el Kerahi (a stream running into the southern end of the Dead Sea) and Kerak are well built, and surrounded by much ploughed land. Kerak appears to be situated in a position of great natural strength. There are several well-built three-storied yellow houses in the town, and a good reservoir with water. The Plateau of Moab is an

---

[22] Lieut. W. A. Kirk, D.F.C.; No. 1 Sqn. (previously Light Horse). Engineer; of Lismore, N.S.W.; b. Belfast, Ireland, 6 Aug., 1887.

open tableland, with many cattle grazing and much plough. The road running east to the station at El Kutrani is in good condition, and the northern road also appears excellent. Large flocks and many Bedouin shelters seen on the Seil el Buksase (running through Kerak to the Dead Sea). From the mouth of this stream northward the cliffs run straight into the sea, and the only apparent landing-places are the mouths of the wadys, where there are small beaches. One or two small boats were seen at the mouths of most of these streams along the eastern coast." Such was a modern wartime bird's-eye view of the land through which Moses led his Israelites.

A small raid on January 3rd first disturbed the Dead Sea boat-traffic. A few bombs were dropped, and the two Australian machines concerned caused a panic on board the small craft by swooping down and spraying them with bullets. Air attacks were continued until the boat service was closed down. On each occasion when Australian patrols flew over this region and sighted the little craft moored or in passage, they fired drums of ammunition into them and drove them shorewards in panic.

The next object of No. 1 Squadron's attention was Amman and its railway station, the railhead of the Jordan defences. On January 10th six machines, under Addison, dropped forty-eight bombs on Amman and Kissir (a station six miles south), and made several direct hits on rolling-stock, station buildings, and troops. For the remainder of January, and through early February, in view of coming operations, patrols were directed particularly to the Jordan Valley between Jericho and Shunet Nimrin, and tactical details were registered with the utmost accuracy. The number of tents and shelters at all camps was tallied and checked on each flight, and the state of supply dumps, the movement on the railway at Amman, and the condition of roads and tracks were closely watched. The sectors west and east of Jordan were reconnoitred thus on alternate days.

While plans for the attack on Jericho were being made, a patrol on February 2nd reported a heavy increase in camps at Miske, immediately behind the Turkish lines near the

Map No. 6

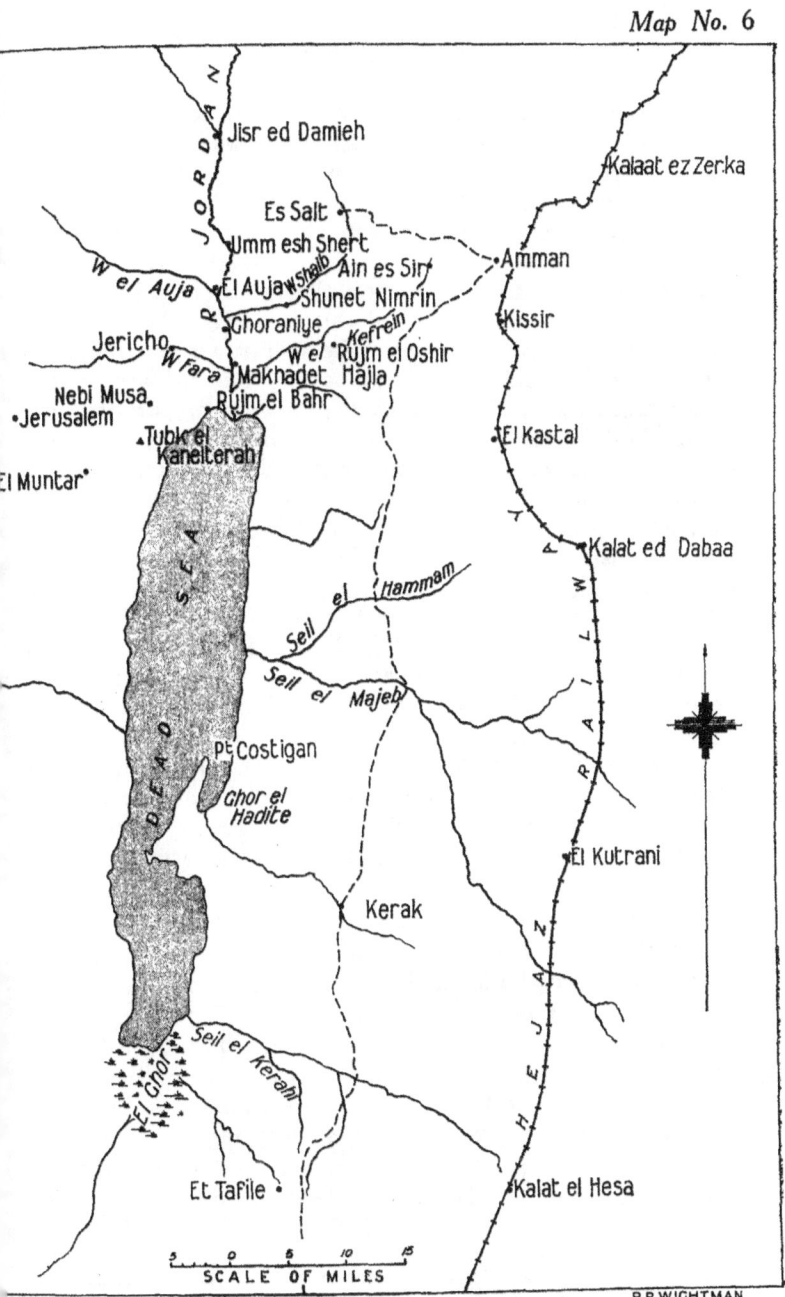

THE COUNTRY EAST OF THE DEAD SEA, SHOWING THE HEJAZ RAILWAY

Mediterranean coast. On that day a compact mass of 400 tents was noticed, and next morning it was raided by five machines from No. 1 Squadron, which dropped sixty bombs on the target and made thirty-two direct hits. The attack was repeated next morning, though nearly half the camp had been moved after the first raid. Another diversion was a double raid on El Kutrani, on the desert railway east of Kerak. Two reconnaissances of this area showed little movement, but light earthworks were being thrown up around El Kutrani station, and fairly large cavalry and infantry camps were noticed there. Judging by the enemy's preparations, the Hejaz Arabs were evidently not far off. Accordingly six machines from No. 1 Squadron bombed the place on February 12th with good results—fourteen direct hits on camps, buildings, and railway. In a second raid, on the following day, only two machines reached the objective—the others dropped out with engine-trouble—but those two again caused panic and damage. On February 25th Kerak also was attacked from the air, Lieutenants Haig and D. R. Dowling[28] bombing it in two Martinsydes. Haig dropped one 112-lb. bomb fairly in the centre of the citadel; numbers of Turks rushed into the big square adjoining, and Dowling then released a shower of 20-lb. bombs upon the crowd. Photographs taken afterwards showed that a pagoda-like tower which had ornamented the middle of the ancient edifice had entirely disappeared, and Arab agents reported that the Turkish casualties were very heavy.

The advance on Jericho was ordered for February 19th. During the week before the attack No. 1 Squadron reconnoitred the Jordan Valley daily, but found no sign of alteration in the enemy's numbers and dispositions. The attack was made by the 60th Division towards Jericho, by the 53rd Division on the left towards the Wady el Auja, and by the Anzac Mounted Division on the right towards Rujm el Bahr. For two days the fighting was against stout defenders in rugged hills, "a surpassingly malignant terrain," as the army commander described it. The enemy held in force a series of precipitous heights from Tubk el Kaneiterah (near the Dead

---

[28] Lieut. D. R. Dowling; No. 1 Sqn. (previously Light Horse). Engineer; b. Condong, Murwillumbah, N.S.W., 1894.

Sea), through Talat ed Dumm (on the Jericho road), to beyond the Wady Fara; deep and sinuous valleys divide these hills, whose rocky faces provided admirable natural facilities for the concealment of bodies of troops. Most tracks ran along the beds of the ravine, passable only by mounted troops, and then only in single file. Sometimes men in the attacking parties had to haul each other in turn over a cliff and fight the enemy hand-to-hand at the top. Cavalry can rarely have fought in more impossible country. Indeed the operations could scarcely have succeeded without the co-operation of the airmen. Throughout the three days' operations No. 1 Squadron's machines followed the attack from above, bombed or machine-gunned Turkish parties to assist the advance, and reported to headquarters both progress made and estimates of the enemy's dispositions and strength. Messages were dropped on troops in the line wherever urgent reports would assist them. In this fashion the advancing line was warned of groups of the enemy lurking on reverse slopes or in the beds of the wadys, and frequently such parties were scattered and disorganised under air attack. That the German airmen made no effort whatever to interfere with this highly effectual support was remarkable. By noon on February 20th, the second day of the attack, the enemy's opposition was broken with the storming of Talat ed Dumm and the heights which look down immediately upon Jericho, and by evening the hills overlooking the Wady Fara were also taken. That afternoon it became clear that considerable Turkish reinforcements had arrived at Shunet Nimrin (east of the Ghoraniye bridge), and a raiding formation from No. 1 Squadron there bombed a large new collection of troop tents, marquees, and supply-dumps. Next morning the Turks had evidently accepted defeat; Jericho was entered early by the Australian Light Horse, and soon afterwards the enemy was in full retreat across the Jordan.

For the next three days low-lying clouds prevented the airmen from harassing the enemy's retreat. On February 25th, however, it was observed that he had removed guns and a pontoon bridge from Ghoraniye, and that there were no Turks left west of the river. Shunet Nimrin was held in strong force, and was being rapidly entrenched.

The description of the fight in the Turkish *communiqué* of February 21st was satisfactory admission from a quarter which reluctantly admitted any defeat: " The enemy renewed his attacks against our left flank. As we were not able to repulse these attacks everywhere, we withdrew our troops to positions previously prepared."

CHAPTER IX

THE RAIDS ACROSS THE JORDAN

THE capture of Jericho and the west bank of the Jordan was only the first stage of operations of the utmost importance. The Jordan position was more than a good defensive flank; it offered an opening for attack, with good prospects of success, against the Turkish communications along the Hejaz railway. The Sherifian Arabs were still raiding the enemy south of El Kutrani, and in early March were present in some force about Et Tafile. Turkish columns from Kerak, to the north, and from the railway, on the east, drove them out of Et Tafile on March 11th, but a week later had withdrawn again to their camps on the railway. It was deemed to be of the highest importance to interrupt the communications of these Turkish troops by cutting the railway about Amman, and especially by destroying a railway viaduct at the south of that town. Moreover, the Bedouin tribes about Madeba were inclined to hostility against the Turks, and it was held that any successful operations against Amman might count to some extent on their co-operation. Hence the great raids of March and April against Amman, Es Salt, and the Turkish garrisons east of the Jordan had a direct importance, evidenced in the event by the enemy's sensitiveness. They had also an indirect result of the greatest possible value, as subsequently appeared. In these spring operations Allenby probably builded better than he knew. When the time came for the final assault which destroyed the Turkish armies, the enemy was still inclined to suspect that the British intended to attack across the Jordan rather than along the Mediterranean coast. The expectation was manifestly inspired by the earlier operations now to be described.

The British advance to the western bank of the Jordan produced an immediate effect of its own. The enemy promptly reinforced his eastern section from other parts of the front. At Amman large new camps sprang up to support the lower Jordan defences. Es Salt fed increased garrisons at Shunet Nimrin, and was itself the eastern end of an increasingly busy route from Nablus and the Jenin railway by way of the road down the Wady Fara to the Jisr ed Damieh ford. Jisr ed Damieh (more shortly called Damieh) took the place hitherto held by Ghoraniye bridge in the Turkish defence scheme, and became the enemy's main link between his eastern and western sectors. A pontoon bridge was built here immediately after that at Ghoraniye had been withdrawn.

Soon after the Jericho fight, movement on the railway east of the Dead Sea attracted the attention of No. 1 Squadron. Austin and Finlay (observer) reconnoitred El Kutrani on March 1st and reported a camp of 150 tents there, fourteen large dumps, 150 rolling-stock (including three made-up trains), and seven gun-positions south-west of the station. Near by were a new aerodrome with six hangars, a number of tents and marquees, and two large two-seater aeroplanes on the ground. A combined raid of five machines from No. 1 and No. 142 Squadrons dropped forty-five bombs on this aerodrome on March 4th, but without marked effect. Better success attended a second raid next day at Kalat el Hesa station, farther south on the railway, and due east of Et Tafile; of forty-eight bombs dropped, thirteen hit a small Turkish camp and two damaged the reservoir, an important target. Meanwhile No. 1 Squadron covered the whole front, and particularly that beyond the Jordan, in several exhaustive patrols, which noted down the condition of every camp and supply centre, and the state of all main roads. The whole of the Shunet Nimrin area was examined in this way on March 3rd by Ross Smith and Mustard, who reported a considerably increased collection of tents at Shunet Nimrin, with a headquarters' camp and twenty-eight dumps, a good target for bombs. Bombed this place accordingly was on March 6th by five machines (three of them Australian), and with excellent results; troops rushing from the camps were attacked and scattered by the airmen's machine-gun fire.

Patrols on the Mediterranean flank were at this time mostly without incident. On March 5th, while reconnoitring over Jiljulieh, Lieutenants Headlam and E. B. S. Beaton[1] (observer) and C. N. Watt[2] and T. C. Macaulay[3] fought an

---

[1] Lieut. E. B. S. Beaton, D.F.C.; No. 1 Sqn. (previously Light Horse). Motor driver; b. Durban, S. Africa, Jan., 1894.

[2] Lieut. C. N. Watt; No. 1 Sqn. Commercial traveller; of St. Kilda, Melbourne; b. Melbourne, 6 Sept., 1891.

[3] Capt. T. C. Macaulay, M.C., R.A.F.

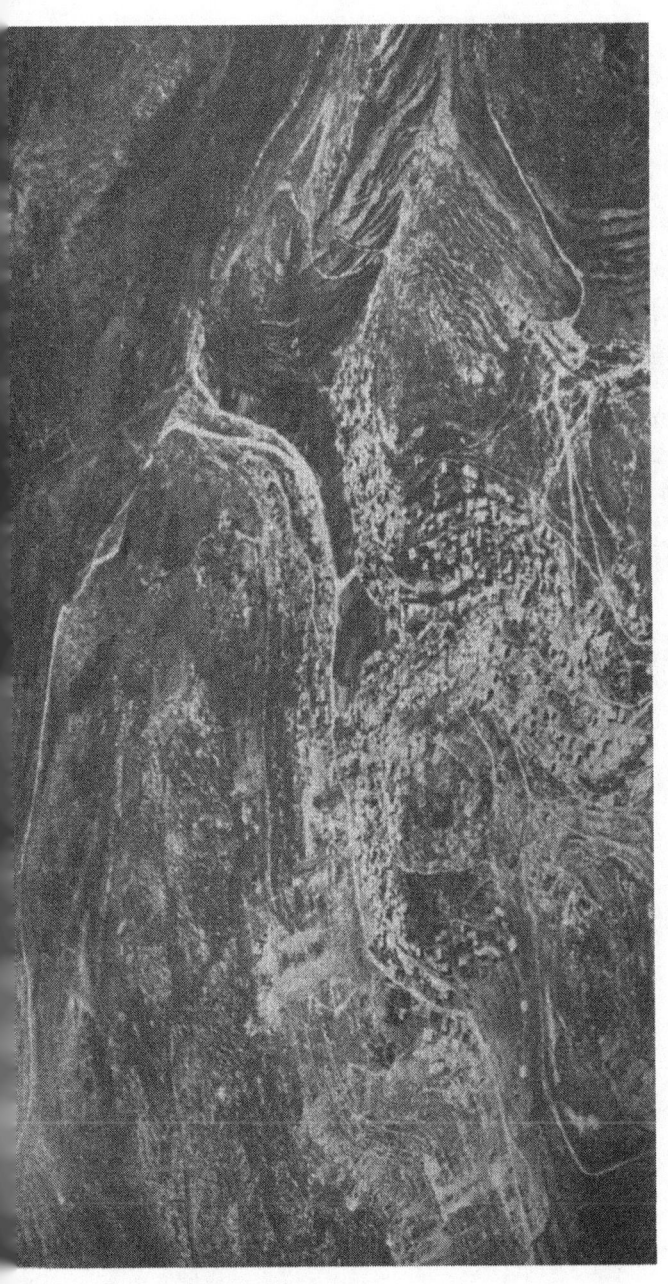

Es Salt, lying in the hills east of Jordan
The view is from the north-west.

*Aust. War Museum Official Photo. No. B3328.
Taken 21st March, 1918.*

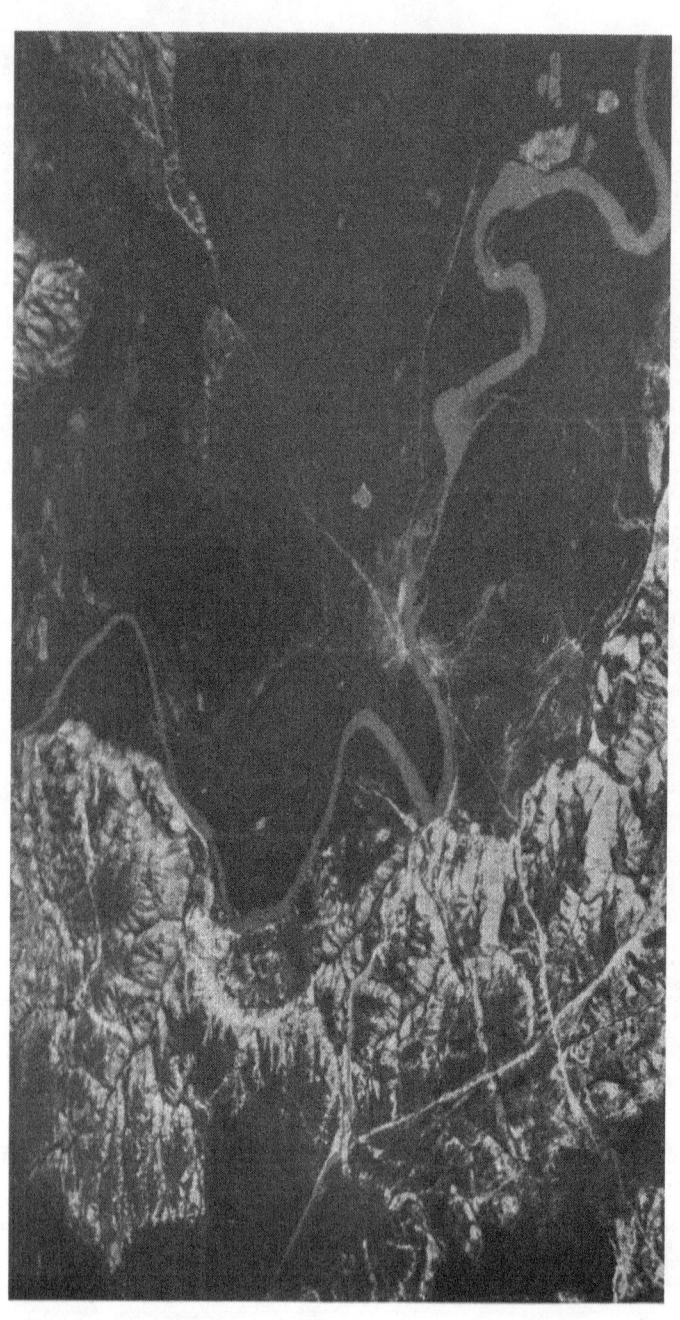

JISR ED DAMIEH FORD ACROSS THE JORDAN, SHOWING THE STEEP VALLEY-SIDES

*Aust. War Museum Official Photo. No. B3326.
Taken 20th March, 1918.*

engagement against five Albatros scouts, which attacked, but were beaten off, two of them being driven down out of control.

The enemy was very active on the roads between Nablus and Es Salt, and constant watch had to be kept on the camps along the Wady Fara track. The Lubban–Nablus road also was remarkable for movement, new gun-positions, and increased size of its camps; the enemy seemed to be expecting an attack there, and this surmise was confirmed by the statement of a Turkish officer taken prisoner towards the end of the month. Three machines from No. 1 Squadron and three from No. 142 bombed these Lubban-road camps on March 9th, and twice again on the following day. The raids were completely successful; the Australian airmen dropped nearly 150 bombs, causing the enemy many casualties and much destruction of material. Six bombs fell fairly among a party of 150 infantry; others wrecked transport parks, stampeded horses, and fired a petrol-dump. The airmen calculated upon increasing, by means of these raids, the enemy's fears of an infantry attack to follow in the same sector.

Having spread alarm and confusion south of Nablus, No. 1 and No. 142 Squadrons next attacked the Damieh bridge and camp with six bombs weighing one hundredweight each. They were meant for the bridge, but bridges are not easy targets, and all six bombs missed. One, however, fell in the middle of a camp of tents, and was, therefore, not entirely wasted. The four machines concerned flew low and fired over 1,000 rounds from their machine-guns into fleeing parties of the garrison. Between March 19th and 24th, the Australians made seven more attempts to hit this bridge with bombs (some weighing as much as 230 lbs.), but without causing any important damage.

A raid of four Martinsydes (three of them from No. 1 Squadron) visited El Kutrani on March 19th. Heavy clouds obscured the town, and the main event of the raid, the dropping by Haig of a 230-lb. bomb on the station, could not be clearly observed. The formation met with bad luck on the way home. Major A. J. Evans, in the Martinsyde from No. 142 Squadron, had to land with engine-trouble near Kerak. Austin and Lee, in an escorting Bristol Fighter, went down to pick

him up, but in landing broke a wheel. The three officers had
no alternative but to burn their machines and give themselves
up to Arabs, who quickly came up and subsequently handed
them over to the Turks.[4] Two Bristol Fighters, sent out after
the raiders had returned, failed to find any trace of the missing
airmen or machines,[5] but reported three railway trucks burnt
out and a large bomb-crater at the edge of the railway track
at the northern end of El Kutrani station.

The attack on Amman across the Jordan was launched on
March 21st. The strong British raiding force included the
Anzac Mounted Division. Only two fording places were
available—at Ghoraniye and Makhadet Hajla—and each was
covered by heavy Turkish musketry and machine-gun fire.
That night all attempts to put rafts across at Ghoraniye were
defeated, but at Makhadet Hajla a few men from the 60th
(London) Division and Australian Engineers swam the river
with a rope and then pulled over the first raft. By 8 a.m.
next day an infantry battalion was established on the eastern
bank without heavy casualties. Not till the following morning
(March 23rd) was any useful progress made, but Ghoraniye
bridge-head also was cleared that day by the cavalry, and
thereafter bridges were thrown across at each place. An air
raid, in which one Australian Martinsyde took part, bombed
Shunet Nimrin camp ahead of the Londoners, who shortly
afterwards captured it and the hills overlooking it. That
night, pursuit of the enemy began in two directions—up the
Es Salt road and towards Rujm el Oshir. Heavy rain fell
all through March 24th and 25th; most tracks became
impassable for wheeled traffic, and supplies had to be sent
up to the advancing troops by camel and pack-horse. Es Salt
was occupied at midnight of March 25th–26th by the light
horse and handed over to the infantry. By March 26th, the
cavalry were beyond the Es Salt–Amman road. That night
they blew up a section of the railway south of Amman, but
could not reach the desired viaduct. A two-arched bridge on
the railway north of Amman was also destroyed. All efforts,
however, failed to dislodge the Turks from Amman station.
Amman village, two miles west of the station, was actually

---

[4] See note at end of chapter.
[5] The story of the capture of these three airmen will be found in *The Escaping Club*, by A. J. Evans (late Major R.A.F.).

entered by the New Zealand Mounted Rifles after desperate and protracted fighting, which culminated in a determined night attack at 2 a.m. on March 30th. But the Turkish machine-gun positions in the hills beyond were too strong, and the enemy, seriously alarmed, was reinforcing his troops near Es Salt from Nablus and threatening a second counter-attack from the Nahr ez Zerka on the north. The raider's flank here had to be strengthened at the expense of the Amman attack, and on the night of March 31st the withdrawal from Amman was ordered. The retirement was by way of Es Salt, was well carried out, and by evening of April 2nd all troops were again across the Jordan, except those holding bridge-heads at Ghoraniye and Makhadet Hajla. One cause of anxiety had been the rising of the river after the rains of March 24th and 25th and the consequent danger to the bridges.

The airmen were out continuously over the scene of operations. Their reports from the battlefield were invaluable. They had assisted preparations for the action by photographing the Jordan front and the Amman position, and by reporting closely the details of all camps and defence positions; thereafter during the attack they roamed the air to observe and assist the fighting over ground which they had learned by heart. The Wady Fara region was seen astir on March 22nd and 24th, when the first reports of the Jordan crossing reached the enemy. Nablus camp was on parade. Many small bodies of infantry and transport were on the march towards Khurbet Ferweh and the Damieh crossing. On March 24th A. R. Brown and Kirk (observer) noted a large troop-train in Leban station making north towards Amman. They attacked it with their machine-guns, halted it, and fired 700 rounds into its troops, who fled in panic. By March 27th, Huwara camp had increased to three times its previous size, cavalry and infantry were marching north, and other forces were on the road out from Nablus, all heading for the battle. Camps were swelling along the Wady Fara. On the same day three troop-trains were seen to enter Amman from the north and one from the south, and strong bodies of troops held the hilly positions about the village and the station. Addison and Fysh (observer), at noon on March 27th, found at El Kutrani and Kerak cavalry assembled and preparing to march north; these airmen carried a bomb, which they dropped in the middle of one unlucky cavalry group; they then pursued the horsemen over the plains with machine-gun fire. Small Turkish parties were moving north from every station on the Amman–Kutrani line. During the afternoon of March 27th and all day of March 28th every air patrol reported bodies of cavalry, infantry, and transport marching along the Wady Fara road towards Damieh. Bomb raids on Damieh on March 26th and 27th again failed to destroy the bridge, but inflicted heavy damage on troops and camps. All patrols machine-gunned enemy camps and parties wherever seen. Another raiding patrol, on March 27th, attacked Amman; the British machines from No. 142 Squadron bombed the station with excellent results, but the Australian machines by some mistake dropped their explosives on El Kastal station instead. Lastly, in the days immediately before the retirement from Amman, the enemy's threatening concentration about the Nahr ez Zerka, north of the Es Salt–Amman road, was reported and promptly bombed. To complete his mental picture of the scene from the air, the reader must imagine no clear sunny air above, but bright intervals in a generally cloudy sky, sometimes rain storms, and an untidy and often mountainous floor below; he must imagine, too, a low-lying bulk of cloud frequently hiding some point to be reconnoitred, and the air scout diving beneath it to keep a view of the ground or to identify troops discerned, and often narrowly skimming some misty hilltop in pursuit of his quarry.

The enemy's airmen were active, but rarely venturesome, though thirteen German machines bombed the attacking force at Shunet Nimrin at dusk on March 28th. For the most part they avoided any risk of air combat. Lieutenants C. C. Cameron[6] and Kirk (observer) fought a short and indecisive engagement on the way home from a raid on Damieh on March 19th. Headlam and Kirk, reconnoitring Amman in the early morning of March 27th, met two A.E.G. two-seaters at 5,000 feet and drove them both to ground; one of them (Headlam records) flew around in dazed circles at 1,000 feet, then landed, and Kirk fired into it on the ground. Several men

---
[6] Lieut. C. C. Cameron; No. 1 Sqn. (previously Light Horse). Stock and station agent; of Jamestown, S. Aust.; b. Jamestown, 30 April, 1890. Died of illness, 18 Nov., 1918.

came to help the pilot, but were driven off by the Australians' fire. " Tracer " bullets were manifestly hitting the crippled two-seater, and " neither pilot nor observer were seen to leave the machine." During this combat Lieutenants J. M. Walker[7] and Finlay (observer) and Rutherford and Lieutenant J. McElligott[8] were reconnoitring Kissir, south of Amman They fought another A.E.G., drove it down, and destroyed it on the ground in much the same fashion as that described by Headlam. These were the only encounters between No. 1 Squadron and enemy airmen on all the battle-front during these operations. The fighting scouts of No. 111 Squadron elsewhere reported a number of air combats; they met the enemy rather more often than did the Australians. Nevertheless, it must be held that on the whole the Germans avoided their duty in the air.

Such was the Australian airmen's verdict at the time. The enemy admitted the truth in documents which were captured at a later date. An official diary found at Nablus in September records, under date of April 4th:—" The situation in the air is still unfavourable to us; the A.E.G. and Rumpler C.4 do not satisfy demands any longer." A little later the diary notes:— " Our machines are no longer a match for the English," and it proceeds, by a reference to the activity and fighting power of the Bristol Fighters, to indicate the particular foe whom the enemy dreaded. Towards the end of June, for instance, the German staff opinion was:—" The enemy, who possesses in his Bristol Fighter an exceptionally fine machine, has made himself lately very redoubtable. Nearly always flying in twos, the Bristol Fighters present an extraordinary fighting force, and their harassing of our activities becomes more and more felt." Another complaint is that of " the aggravated shortage of reinforcements, especially pilots." An entry in the diary of May 6th reads:—" No. 302 Squadron had to discontinue its flights, all pilots being either wounded or sick." Three weeks later there is mentioned a report, furnished to the Turkish Command, which may be regarded as intended to break gently the news that the German airmen were feeling unable to

---

[7] Lieut. J. M. Walker; No. 1 Sqn. (previously A.A.M.C.). Chemist; b. Grenville, Ballarat, Vic., 1888. Killed in action, 22 Aug., 1918.

[8] Lieut. J. McElligott; No. 1 Sqn. (previously Light Horse). Telegraphist; b. Bundaberg, Q'land, 7 Jan., 1893.

promise much improvement. "As long as the English use two-seaters which are superior to our machines in climbing capacity," says this report, "successful activity on our part is very much in question, owing to the impossibility of the single-seater even attempting to make an attack on higher-flying and better-climbing two-seaters, and owing to our inability during the attack of the enemy to take over the attack ourselves." Yet the Germans' own two-seaters were speedy enough, as was frequently proved. The enemy squadrons, besides single-seater Albatros D.5.a scouts and A.E.G. two-seaters, contained Rumplers (260-h.p. Mercedes), L.V.G's (260-h.p. Benz), and Halberstadts—all serviceable two-seaters—which were the equal in flying-speed of the Bristol Fighters. In many a running fight the Germans made a long stern chase of it, and often escaped. Where they failed was in the manœuvring skill, daring, and morale of pilots. The German airmen, as a corps, ignored the fighting maxim, " Never show tail to the enemy," and therein, as nearly as a single phrase will express it, lay the difference between the two flying services.

The first (Amman) raid across the Jordan had as its immediate tactical objective the destruction of the Amman viaduct. The second (Es Salt) raid was planned to envelop and capture the Turkish garrison at Shunet Nimrin, opposite the Ghoraniye bridge-head. From Es Salt ran the only metalled road which served the Nimrin position. A second road to Shunet Nimrin, no more than a fair-weather track, ran along the Wady Es Sir from Amman. The Beni Sakr tribe of Arabs, who lived along the wady, promised to assist if the British would attack before the first week in May, at which time (the tribe represented) it would have to move to fresh grazing-grounds. For the new venture a slight re-arrangement was made in the duties of the two air squadrons of the army wing. It was found necessary to increase what were called "hostile-aircraft patrols" (or, colloquially, "hopping-off patrols"), since, on several chance occasions when the Amman raiding force was concentrating in the Jordan Valley, enemy airmen had taken advantage of the absence of British machines, dashed across the line, and bombed the light horse camps. To oppose any repetition of these attacks, a watching patrol was stationed over the concentration area throughout the hours of daylight. No. 1 Squadron performed its share of this duty. Moreover, the old work of constant strategic reconnaissance over the enemy's rear area had to be repeated, and revised maps were wanted of the Amman–Es Salt district. Reconnaissance was especially the department of No. 1 Squadron. Consequently the carrying out of bombing raids was now assigned to No. 142 Squadron (Martinsydes and B.E.12.a's). No. 111 Squadron (S.E.5.a fighting scouts) pursued its own task of roaming the whole front with destroyer-patrols. In preparation for the Es Salt raid, No. 1 Squadron made about twenty special photography-patrols over the eastern Jordan region, and exposed 609 plates. These supplied the basis for a new set of maps, showing all local roads, tracks, and caravan routes.

The enemy soon repaired the railway bridge north of Amman. On April 3rd a train was seen to leave Kalaat ez Zerka and arrive at Amman. Another train, carrying a crane in one truck and rails in three others, was on the same day observed to move out northward from Kissir towards the other break in the line. Repairing of this section went on till April 10th, when it was completed. Amman station was bombed on April 3rd, 4th, and 5th by No. 142 Squadron. A. R. Brown and Finlay (observer) on April 3rd made an exhaustive reconnaissance of "the horse-shoe road"—the road up to Tul Keram and round by Nablus to El Lubban. Trenches were being dug near Kakon, north-west of Tul Keram. Ross Smith and Mustard subsequently confirmed this report, and farther over, at Jenin, they observed the double aerodrome to have greatly increased in size; it now had seventeen hangars, and fourteen machines were counted on the ground. There was also a hospital south of the station. A few days later, large enemy camps were seen on the coast, near Mukhalid. Till April 15th the Australian machines found no Germans in the air, though in the interval the scouts of No. 111 Squadron fought a dozen combats. On that day, however, Lieutenants R. S. Adair[9] and R. A. Camm[10] (observer), returning at noon

---

[9] Lieut. R. S. Adair; No. 1 Sqn. Engineer; b. Maryborough, Q'land, June, 1894.
[10] Lieut. R. A. Camm; No. 1 Sqn. (previously Camel Corps). Farmer; of Scottsdale, Tas.; b. Zeehan, Tas., 1893.

from patrol over Et Taiyibeh (south of Tul Keram), saw three Albatros scouts flying towards them from the south-east, and slightly above. Adair fired a light to warn Lieutenants G. C. Peters[11] and J. H. Traill[12] (observer), whom he was escorting, and climbed to meet the enemy. The fight began at 9,000 feet, when, as the enemy dived to attack, Adair turned, closed on the centre Albatros of the formation, and fired 100 rounds into it. This Albatros tried to spin away, failed, and then dived steeply, with Adair still following and firing. It landed ultimately near Kalkilieh in rough country and tilted over on one wing. Meanwhile, Peters attacked a second Albatros, shot that down into a steep dive earthward, and then engaged the third Albatros until his gun jammed. Adair picked up this opponent at about 5,000 feet, but it span away earthward and was lost to view in the shadows of the hills. Two other Bristol Fighters—Lieutenants Kenny and F. C. Hawley[13] (observer) and E. C. Stooke[14] and H. B. Fletcher[15] (observer) —fought a similar engagement with four Albatros scouts south of Nablus on April 28th, and drove down three of them.

By April 19th, when the British concentration for the Es Salt raid was beginning, the enemy camps at Shunet Nimrin were likewise reported to have considerably increased. The number of tents seen was not always a sure indication, for it was usual to furl tents in the daytime. Better tokens of enemy strength were probably the heavy traffic on the Es Salt–Amman road and the great activity at Amman station.[16] All airmen flying over the plains about Madeba saw the unimpressionable Bedouin—large numbers of them—ploughing and grazing flocks as though no war were anywhere near. They decamped across the railway as soon as the second battle began at Shunet Nimrin.

---

[11] Capt. G. C. Peters, D.F.C.; No. 1 Sqn. (previously Engineers). School teacher; b. Adelaide, 1893.

[12] Lieut. J. H. Traill, D.F.C.; No. 1 Sqn. (previously Signal Services). Station hand; b. Bligh, Cassilis, N.S.W., 1895.

[13] Lieut. F. C. Hawley, D.F.C.; No. 1 Sqn. (previously Light Horse). Commercial traveller; of Sydney; b. Wellington, N.Z., 26 July, 1890.

[14] Lieut. E. C. Stooke, D.C.M.; No. 1 Sqn. (previously Camel Corps). Station hand; b. Hawthorn, Melbourne, 1895. Killed in action, 19 Aug., 1918.

[15] Lieut. H. B. Fletcher, D.F.C.; No. 1 Sqn. (previously Light Horse). Auctioneer; of Stanthorpe, Q'land; b. Newcastle, N.S.W., 22 Nov., 1890.

[16] At Shunet Nimrin the Turkish garrison of 3,000 was increased by reinforcements to 8,000 to meet this attack. This was learned subsequently.

THE AUJA FORD, RIVER JORDAN

Aust. War Museum Official Photo. No. B3570.

OFFICERS OF No. 1 SQUADRON, A.F.C., AT RAMLEH, NOVEMBER, 1918

Aust. War Museum Official Photo. No. B1238.

The attack was opened on April 30th by two brigades of the 60th Division, but the Shunet Nimrin position was strong, and no real success was gained before it. Moreover the Beni Sakr Arabs gave no assistance; the tribes were always cautious allies. The cavalry crossed at Ghoraniye in the evening of April 29th, and the 4th Light Horse Brigade marched all night up the track to Damieh and arrived at that place early the next morning. While this force held the enemy at the crossing, two other mounted brigades marched on Es Salt, fought an action north-west of the town, and entered it amid great enemy confusion at 4.30 p.m. on April 30th. They just missed capturing the headquarters of the Turkish Fourth Army. The 4th Brigade was unable to seize the Turkish bridge-head at Damieh, and on May 1st the enemy, here heavily reinforced, attacked and gradually pushed this brigade back towards the Umm esh Shert crossing of the Jordan. It was imperative to hold Umm esh Shert at all costs as a line of retreat for the brigades at Es Salt, since to this point ran the only available track across the hills from the Es Salt direction. The Anzac Mounted Division was to have taken Shunet Nimrin in flank from the north, but could not direct all its strength to this purpose; in response to Turkish pressure the greater part of two of its brigades were sent to reinforce the light horse near Damieh and around Es Salt. The threat from these two points by early morning of May 3rd compelled the abandonment of the whole venture, the object of which—as has been described—was not the forcing of the enemy out of Shunet Nimrin, but rather the surrounding and capture of his garrison there. The light horsemen on the exposed flank to the north narrowly escaped being hoist by their own petard and themselves cut off. By evening of May 4th the attacking force had recrossed the Jordan and the original bridge-head at Ghoraniye was re-established. Bridge-heads were also held at El Auja ford, to the north of Ghoraniye, and at Makhadet Hajla to the south of it.

The successful withdrawal of the light horse owed much to the co-operation of the Australian airmen. No. 1 Squadron's pilots watched and recorded the advance on Es Salt, and on May 1st they reported the enemy's threat from north-west of

Damieh. A strong south wind blowing over the Amman area made the day unfavourable for flying. Two Australian machines, sent out on the dawn reconnaissance—Rutherford and McElligott (observer) and Lieutenants Haig and R. T. Challinor[17] (observer)—were to drop leaflets on the Beni Sakr Arabs. Near Amman machine-gun fire from the ground perforated both of Rutherford's petrol tanks.[18] He was forced to land, and burned his machine. Haig and Challinor alighted alongside to pick up Rutherford and McElligott, and Haig tried to take off again with all three passengers; but one wheel collapsed as they were starting, and the aeroplane toppled over on its nose. The Australians set fire to it, and then surrendered to Circassian cavalry which had ridden up to them. They were handed over to the German flying corps, and German airmen later dropped on the Australian aerodrome letters from the four officers describing their mishap.

That evening, May 1st, at least 800 cavalry and 400 infantry were reported on the road south-east of Damieh by the Australian escort of a bombing raid upon Damieh undertaken by No. 142 Squadron. The Bristol Fighters flew low after the bombs had been dropped, and fired 700 rounds into the scattering cavalry. Guns also were seen coming into action at Damieh against the light horse beyond the river. On May 2nd the position was an anxious one, and No. 1 Squadron reconnoitred the Es Salt area three times in the morning of that day. On the first reconnaissance, at 6 a.m., Lieutenants P. J. McGinness[19] and Hawley (observer), escorting Lukis and Beaton, sighted a German two-seater at about 9,000 feet between Jericho and Damieh. The enemy was well above, and McGinness, after warning the reconnaissance machine, climbed to the combat. On arriving near the German's level, the Australian machine attacked from below, and both pilot and observer fired bursts from this position

---

[17] Lieut. R. T. Challinor; No. 1 Sqn. (previously Light Horse). Clerk; of Brisbane; b. Beenleigh, Q'land, 13 Nov., 1889.

[18] Besides the main petrol tank, fighting machines carried above the centre section a small reserve tank for emergency. This was meant to enable the airman to fly home if his main tank were shot through and his petrol supply exhausted.

[19] Lieut. P. J. McGinness, D.F.C., D.C.M.; No. 1 Sqn. (previously Light Horse). Farmer; b. Framlingham East, Vic., March, 1896.

into the enemy until he stalled, rocked unhappily from side to side, and then went down in a slow spin. McGinness had to swerve sharply aside to avoid collision as his opponent fell; the Bristol Fighter's engine cut-out at this moment, and the German was not seen again. Lukis and Beaton reported enemy reinforcements still arriving at Damieh, and Lieutenants E. L. Spragg[20] and Vyner (observer) half-an-hour later brought in news of large enemy cavalry forces about Ain es Sir (south-east of Es Salt). By noon the Turks were hurrying reinforcements and ammunition from Nablus to Mejdel Beni Fadl, foreshadowing pressure down the western bank of the Jordan. The lower Wady Fara road was full of transport, cavalry, and guns. The Damieh–Es Salt road was littered with Turkish cavalry. Amman showed at least 500 infantry and 100 rolling-stock in the station, and another large troop-train was entering from the north. Towards Es Salt, at Ain es Sir, were strong bodies of cavalry and infantry. a fairly large new hospital, and 200 horse-waggons. This picture of the field situation derives its military interest from the fact that the details of it were not collected from reports after the action, but were seen and recorded from the air at the time.

Lieutenants H. S. R. Maughan[21] and Fysh, who brought in this noon report, and their escort, Lieutenants A. W. Murphy[22] and Camm, fought three Albatros scouts while over Amman. The Australians were at 6,000 feet when they saw the enemy machines leave the Amman aerodrome, and flew to 10,000 feet to await them. As soon as the Germans had made 8,000 feet, the Australians dived at them together. Murphy attacked the centre machine and split the formation. The Albatros on the left promptly attacked from below, but Camm fired into him. The Albatros swung back and came again from the right, flying level. Camm again fired a burst into him, so that he stalled and disappeared into a cloud. Next

---

[20] Lieut. E. L. Spragg; No. 1 Sqn. (previously Light Horse). Station bookkeeper; of Morven, Q'land; b. Sydney, 29 March, 1889.

[21] Lieut. H. S. R. Maughan, D.F.C.; No. 1 Sqn. (previously Artillery). Printer; of Ipswich, Q'land; b. Brisbane, 27 May, 1893.

[22] Lieut. A. W. Murphy, D.F.C., A.F.C.; No. 1 Sqn. Air mechanic; b. Kew, Melbourne, Jan., 1892.

moment Murphy was engaged in a hot duel with his first opponent. The two attacked each other head on in a dead line, both firing hard, and the Australian had to zoom sharply to avoid collision.[23] The Albatros simultaneously dived, but attacked again from the left. It received a fierce sixty rounds at close quarters from Camm, and then it, too, fell into a cloud. Meanwhile, Maughan had engaged and driven down the rightmost Albatros of the formation. He then met Murphy's second opponent and fired more shots into that as it span away. Diving through the clouds from the scene which the enemy had left, the Australians saw all three Albatroses gliding down to their aerodrome again. In the evening Captain A. R. Brown and Lieutenant Finlay (observer) and R. Burton[24] and Fletcher, escorting a British bomb raid on Amman, chased a German two-seater to earth near Suweile (on the Amman-Es Salt road); they fired into this machine as it lay on the ground, at others on Amman aerodrome, and into every party of infantry and cavalry around the town for as long as their ammunition lasted.

The days of the withdrawal (May 3rd and 4th) saw every available machine from No. 1 Squadron over the east-Jordan area. The knowledge that the light horse were involved in a difficult retreat was the keenest spur to the Australian airmen, most of whom had aforetime been light horsemen. May 3rd was marred by an accident to Lieutenant J. K. Curwen-Walker[25] and Corporal N. P. B. Jensen[26] in a Bristol Fighter which got into a spin and crashed as it was leaving the aerodrome at dawn. Brown and Finlay (observer) and G. V. Oxenham[27] and H. A. Letch[28] set out at the same

---

[23] An exciting situation which sometimes occurred when opposing airmen were keen fighters. It was a good test of nerve. Pilots appear to have received no distinct instruction in training as to the proper manœuvre for avoiding collision in such circumstances. Ordinarily one machine would pass another on the right, as with ships at sea. Fighting tactics of two-seaters were generally a matter of arrangement between pilot and observer, especially where these were experienced comrades.

[24] Lieut. R. Burton; No. 1 Sqn. Engine-fitter; of Kalgoorlie, W. Aust.; b. Payneham, Adelaide, 7 April, 1892.

[25] Lieut. J. K. Curwen-Walker; No. 1 Sqn. Salesman; of Prahran, Melbourne; b. Windsor, Melbourne, 18 March, 1888. Killed in action, 3 May, 1918.

[26] Cpl. N. P. B. Jensen (No. 506, No. 1 Sqn.). Sailor; b. Bornholm, Denmark, 6 March, 1892. Killed in action, 3 May, 1918.

[27] Lieut. G. V. Oxenham; No. 1 Sqn. Grazier; of Boggabri, N.S.W.; b. Randwick, Sydney, 26 March, 1893. Killed in action, 27 June, 1918.

[28] Lieut. H. A. Letch, M.C.; No. 1 Sqn. (previously Light Horse). Clerk; of Hampton, Melbourne; b. Donnybrook, Vic., 3 May, 1894. Killed in action, 22 Aug., 1918.

hour and found that enemy strength at the Wady Fara and Damieh camps had increased overnight. Turks were crossing at Damieh in a punt. Holding on their flight past Es Salt, the two Australian machines at 7 a.m. chased down an enemy two-seater at Suweile and riddled it on the ground with bullets. Other patrols during the day watched the retirement from Es Salt. The enemy was evidently glad to see the light horse go at their own pace. Next day, May 4th, every Australian machine sent out on reconnaissance carried four 20-lb. bombs to harass Turkish reinforcements. At dawn the light horse rear-guards were about half-way between Es Salt and Umm esh Shert. Amman station was crowded with tents, transport, and stores, and two Bristol Fighters on the dawn patrol dropped their eight bombs in the middle of the traffic. Two others repeated this performance at 10 o'clock upon a collection of cavalry at Amman, and fired 400 rounds into other cavalry advancing from Ain es Sir. The afternoon patrols bombed Es Salt and Amman, and, when the bombs were expended, the steady stream of cavalry marching through Ain es Sir provided a constant target for machine-gun fire. To the best of the airmen's ability every sort of reinforcement making forward to worry the light horse retreat was impeded and exhausted long before it reached the scene of the fighting. The enemy made few attempts to imitate this example of co-operation with troops on the ground. The special hostile-aircraft patrols on the British side kept guard against any such venture. Two German machines did attack British infantry withdrawing west of Shunet Nimrin on May 4th, but were both shot down by that infantry.

Note.—Turkish documents captured in September disclosed the following scale of rewards offered by the enemy:—
   For every Arab or Indian prisoner, 40 piastres.
   British private, T£1 (coin).
   Colonial or Indian officer, T£2.
   British officer, T£5.
   Documents containing strengths or movement orders, T£1.
   Official orders of units, 20 piastres.
   Letter or map, 5 piastres.
      (Captured order of 158th Regiment, dated 15/12/17.)

Rewards for bringing down a British aeroplane were:—
  To an airman, T£40.
  To a company of infantry, T£30.
  To an anti-aircraft gun crew (including T£15 for the gunner), T£30.

(Captured order, dated 1/3/18.)

The Bedouins were not slow to perceive the possibilities of this trade. Even friendly tribes required money payment for returning to British Headquarters, on one occasion, two captured Australian airmen, Lieutenants Tonkin and Vyner. The price was £50 each.

CHAPTER X

GROWING BRITISH SUPREMACY IN THE AIR

FOR some time after the attacks of March and April east of the Jordan Allenby's operations were necessarily restricted. The 52nd and 74th Divisions, together with ten British battalions drawn from other divisions, nine yeomanry regiments, and a number of heavy siege-batteries and machine-gun companies, were sent to France to reinforce the Western Front against Ludendorff's formidable offensive. These troops were replaced by Indian divisions. Not till August was the re-organisation of Allenby's army completely effected.[1] Nevertheless several successful attacks were carried out during the early summer. An advance made in April by the British XXI Corps on a twelve-mile front between the Nablus road and the coast railway was followed by a further slight advance in June on the coast sector with the same general objective—to secure from the enemy certain high ground immediately overlooking the British line. In turn, the Turks on July 14th seized the hill Abu Tellul, near the Jordan, but were promptly ejected by the light horse, and a simultaneous attempt against El Hemu ford, below the Ghoraniye bridge, was shattered by Indian lancers before it could be delivered. The enemy remained convinced that the next British general attack, when it came, would be delivered across the Jordan. This induced him to keep considerable forces concentrated in the Amman–Es Salt area, a disposition which weakened his detachments engaged with the Arabs in the south along the Hejaz railway.

During these months of re-organisation, preparation, and waiting for the army's full opportunity, the British and Australian airmen steadily asserted a rising supremacy over their own particular foe. The confidence they felt is reflected in their daring distant reconnaissances and in the increasing list of their victims in combat. It is impossible to avoid the impression that, in making the army acquainted with the enemy's dispositions and with the character of the ground he held through the hills up to the plain of Armageddon, the

---

[1] See Allenby's despatches, dated 18 Sept., 1918.

airmen infused into the troops whom they served some of their own sense of triumph. The army below had also its own reasons for confidence.

With the end of the east-Jordan operations, No 1 Squadron again devoted close attention to the Nablus area. It moved forward in the last week of April from Mejdel to a new aerodrome outside Ramleh. In the afternoon of May 7th Ross Smith and Mustard (observer) and Tonkin and Camm reconnoitred the horse-shoe road and made a careful count of all camps. Beyond the hills they found the western of the two aerodromes at Jenin increased by seven more hangars. While approaching this place at 11,000 feet they sighted a Rumpler at the same height. Tonkin climbed above the enemy, then discovered that it was a two-seater, and dived at once under its tail to attack.[2] The two Bristols chased the Rumpler down for 9,000 feet, flying in alternately to close quarters and firing into it, until at length the German dived for the last time, crashed into the side of a hill near Jenin, and burst into flames. On the way home over Tul Keram they engaged and drove down two Albatros scouts. A British formation of nine machines dropped nearly a ton of bombs at Jenin on May 9th, pitted the landing-ground and the railway station with holes, and burned several hangars. Most of the machines of the German No. 305 Squadron were damaged in this raid. Peters and Finlay, who escorted the bombers, drove down a Rumpler after a fight over Jenin aerodrome, from which other enemy airmen would not be enticed to more decisive combat.

Photography for mapping purposes was steadily continued. No. 1 Squadron had already furnished material for the east-Jordan maps. On May 13th four machines in a systematic sweep took nearly 200 negatives, which enabled a new map to be drawn of the Damieh region—" a large and difficult

---

[2] The tactics of a two-seater differ radically from those of a single-seater. The pilot of a single-seater, in attacking a machine of his own class, seeks the advantage of height, so that he may dive upon his enemy, for to aim his gun he must aim the nose of his aeroplane. If, however, he is fighting a two-seater, he will as a rule attack from below the two-seater's tail, the "blind-spot" which the observer's gun of the upper machine cannot reach. This principle holds good in such case whether the attacker be of the same class—that is, a two-seater—or a single-seater. To attack a two-seater from above is to expose the attacking machine to the fire of the other's observer. A two-seater, attacking from below, would secure full use of the observer's armament, which in the Bristol Fighter consisted of two Lewis guns.

KERAK, ON A RIDGE BETWEEN TWO DEEP GULLIES (EACH INDICATED BY A SHADOW)

"Kerak is built on a pinnacle of rock which rises abruptly from the bottom of a deep gorge. To reach the town from any side it is necessary to descend nearly 400 feet into the gorge down a most precipitous path of loose stones, and then climb by a path even steeper and stonier in which there are seven zig-zags to the citadel, which is almost on a level with the rim of the gorge." (Major A. J. Evans, R.A.F.: *The Escaping Club*.) The citadel is on the neck of the ridge, about the middle of the photograph.

Aust. War Museum Official Photo. No. B3379.

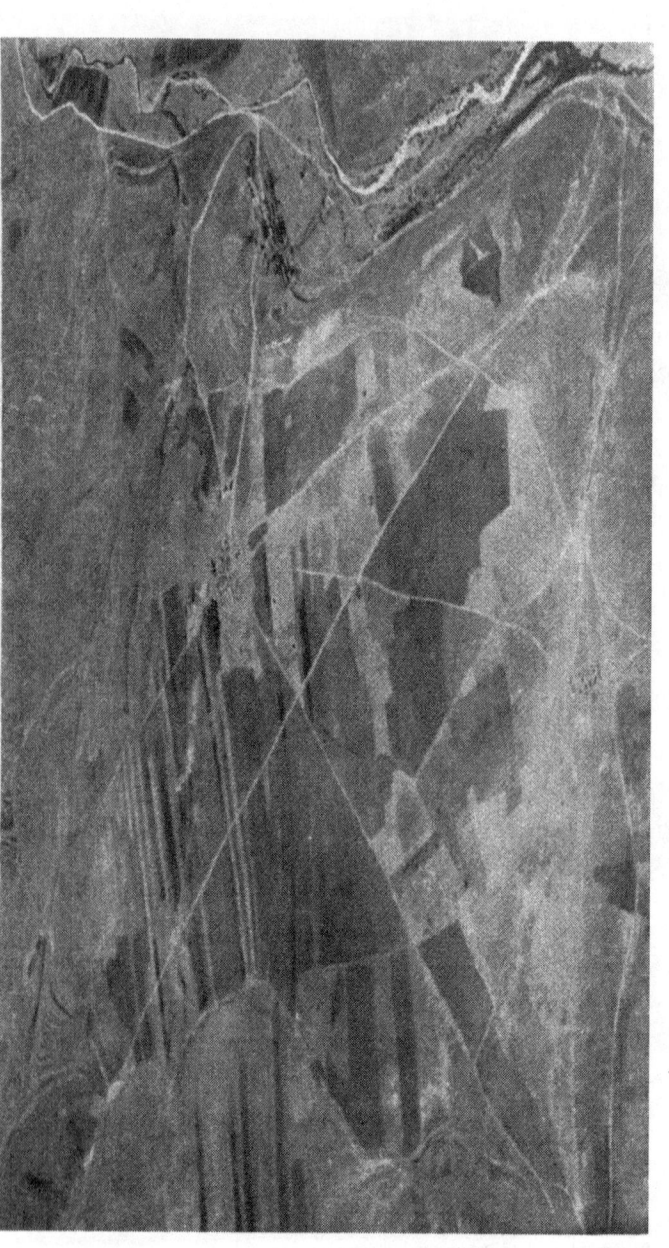

AMMAN, SHOWING THE AERODROME, VILLAGE, AND RAILWAY STATION, 2ND JUNE, 1918

A line of bursting bombs can be seen across and to the left of the aerodrome.

Aust. War Museum Official Photo. No. B3348.

area," as General. Borton described it in an official letter of appreciation. A few days later attention was again attracted to the Mediterranean seaboard. At Mukhalid, Kakon, and Kulunsawe, large gangs of men were collected for the harvesting of crops. On the dawn patrol of May 22nd Ross Smith and Kirk (observer) and Kenny and W. J. A. Weir[3] fought two Albatros scouts at 11,000 feet over Nablus. The Bristol Fighters, relying solely upon their observers' guns, attacked from below. Neither of the Albatros scouts fired a shot, and both fell away into clouds, badly out of control. Lieutenants C. S. Paul[4] and Weir (observer) and Tonkin and Camm, patrolling south of Nablus about the same time, met four more Albatros machines flying south, and attacked them near Huwara at 12,000 feet. Each shot down one German out of control at the first encounter; Paul and Weir then carried on a long fight with a third, which, spinning away from each burst of fire, flattened out again, only to find Paul at its tail, still shooting. This duel continued until the German was very near the ground at Nablus. In a final dive the Australian pilot overflew his opponent, turned to recover position, and saw the Albatros land heavily and turn on its back. The Australians waited till the pilot crawled out of the wreckage, and then chased him to cover with sprays of bullets. Stooke and Weir (observer) and Peters and Traill shot down a two-seater in flames near the same place on May 29th.

No. 1 Squadron's patrols had for a fortnight watched the accumulation of supplies at Amman, and especially an increase of hangars on the Amman aerodrome. The new hangars doubtless came from El Kutrani aerodrome, which had for some time been little used. The Turks in that southern region were growing anxious concerning Arab movements. Maan, on the railway eighty miles south of El Kutrani, was practically invested by Prince Feisal's[5] Hejaz Arabs; the hilly forest country south of the Dead Sea, from Maan to Et

---

[3] Lieut. W. J. A. Weir, D.F.C.; No. 1 Sqn. (previously Light Horse). Plantation overseer; b. Leichhardt, Sydney, 1890.

[4] Lieut. C. S. Paul, D.F.C.; No. 1 Sqn. (previously Light Horse). Surveyor's assistant; b. Thanis, N.Z., 1893. Drowned at sea, 22 Jan., 1919.

[5] Son and representative in the field of the Sherif Hussein, King of Mecca and the Arabs of the Hejaz.

Tafile, was occupied by the tribes under the Sherif Nazir, and the neighbourhood of Et Tafile and El Kutrani was becoming highly unsafe for the Turks. On May 16th Ross Smith flew to this desert and from his Bristol Fighter landed Lieutenant-Colonel T. E. Lawrence,[6] the British adviser to the Arab leader, who had visited Allenby's headquarters to discuss Arab co-operation. Lawrence made his way through Nazir's tribal camps to Abu Lesal, south-west of Maan, the Arab headquarters, from which place was to start the Arab expedition to Azrak for the autumn operations.

Throughout the month of June much reconnaissance east of Jordan and the Dead Sea was demanded of No. 1 Squadron's patrols. The immediate activity of both Turks and Arabs around El Kutrani was concerned with the harvesting of the local crops. Between that station and El Kastal the number of white men's tents and Bedouin shelters steadily increased through June, and small trains were busy on the railways. The concentration, however, was not all of labourers, for cavalry and gun-limbers were frequently seen on the Kerak road.

Amman, too, became busier than ever. The traffic of the harvest accounted for much of it, but the British Command suspected some other business afoot, not unconnected with bigger camps at Es Salt and in the Wady Fara, and with a growing curiosity of German airmen concerning the Jordan Valley. Peters and Traill on May 23rd chased away a prying Rumpler two-seater in the lower Jordan Valley. On June 3rd and 4th German reconnaissance machines were again found over the neighbourhood of Jericho. McGinness and Fysh on June 3rd exhausted their ammunition in an engagement with a Rumpler near Jericho, and had to break off the fight. The following day's combat was more serious. Tonkin and Camm were returning about 8 a.m. from patrol near Damieh at 12,000 feet, when shell-bursts over Jerusalem attracted their attention. Flying towards this spot they discovered a Rumpler just above their level. The Australian machine approached in the face of the morning sun; the Rumpler had its guns pointing upward, and was apparently blissfully ignorant of Tonkin's presence. Tonkin flew

---

[6] Lt.-Col. T. E. Lawrence, C.B., D.S.O. Historian; b. Wales, 1888.

directly underneath it, turned, and gave Camm position for a close delivery from both guns into the Rumpler's belly. Then Camm's right gun jammed. Tonkin manœuvred to use his own front gun, but found it would not respond to the control. The Rumpler then counter-attacked, and its observer fired into the Bristol Fighter a burst which hit the engine. Water sprayed over Tonkin, and, not knowing the extent of the damage, he turned for home. The Rumpler made no effort to intercept him, but a final shot from its observer wounded Camm in the wrist, and Tonkin landed at the nearest hospital. Camm's wounds were serious enough to cause him to be invalided to Australia.

At Amman anti-aircraft guns—the result of an effective raid by No. 142 Squadron a few days previously—were noticed for the first time on June 2nd. A second British raid bombed Amman on June 3rd, and the next day three machines from No. 1 Squadron attacked the aerodrome, damaged the hangars, and scattered troops in the neighbouring wady. They then swooped upon the anti-aircraft battery, silenced it with machine-gun fire, and dispersed the crews. A. R. Brown and Letch repeated this performance during another British raid a week later. The same two airmen, patrolling northward from El Kutrani on June 8th, chased down to the ground near Amman a Rumpler into which they fired 400 rounds after its occupants had run away from it.

Mid-June was selected by the British air force for a general enlivening of the enemy's harvest operations. On that day British squadrons, escorted by the Bristol Fighters, made three bomb raids on the El Kutrani fields—raids with incendiary bombs as well as the ordinary explosive kind. This visitation caused much panic among Bedouin reapers and Turkish cavalry. After parties of these had been scattered, the escorting Australians lashed with machine-gun fire the unusually busy El Kutrani railway station and a train which, under the attack, "stopped and then ran in the opposite direction." While British squadrons were harassing the Moabite harvest gangs, bombing raids from No. 1 Squadron were directed against the grain fields in the Mediterranean sector. On June 16th—the day of the El Kutrani raid—the squadron sent three raids, each of two machines, with incendiary bombs against the crops about Kakon, Anebta, and Mukhalid. One of the most successful efforts was that of Peters and Maughan, who dropped sixteen fire-bombs in fields and among haystacks, set them alight for a time, and machine-gunned gangs who rushed up to extinguish the flames.

These were useful operations, but were regarded by No. 1 Squadron rather as diversions from ordinary routine work. The demands for photographs and detailed reconnaissance of camps were unending; the day's work, however heavy, never diminished the volume of the same work to be done on the morrow. While some Bristol Fighters were bombing Amman and El Kutrani or chasing home Rumplers from Jaffa or the Jordan, other patrols steadily pursued their mapping-photography. The series for the new Es Salt sheet were no sooner finished than photographs were ordered for a map of the Samaria–Nablus region. On June 8th Ross Smith and Kirk made the first British reconnaissance of Haifa, examined the whole coast up to that point, and came home with photographs of Haifa port.

Nablus and Messudie railway stations and the Lubban-road camps were unusually active on June 11th and 12th. Lieutenants Stooke and L. P. Kreig,[7] escorting Ross Smith, chased a Rumpler down to a hasty landing north of Tul Keram during an early morning patrol on June 11th. Two mornings later, just after dawn, Paul and Weir met with better success. While they were waiting for hostile aircraft near the front line at Bireh, anti-aircraft shelling gave notice of a German machine at about 16,000 feet, and the Bristol Fighter at once began to make height. The enemy, a Rumpler, turned homeward as soon as he saw the Australian. Just as Paul was reaching its level, the Rumpler, being then about over Nablus, put its nose down in a straight dive towards Jenin. This manœuvre gave the Bristol Fighter the opportunity to come within range, and the Rumpler opened the action with its rear guns at 300 yards. Paul replied with his forward Vickers, and then flew underneath the enemy and gave his observer

---

[7] Lieut. L. P. Kreig; No. 1 Sqn. (previously Light Horse). Farmer; of Toowoomba; Q'land; b. Dimboola, Vic., 24 Oct., 1892. Killed in action, 19 Aug. 1918.

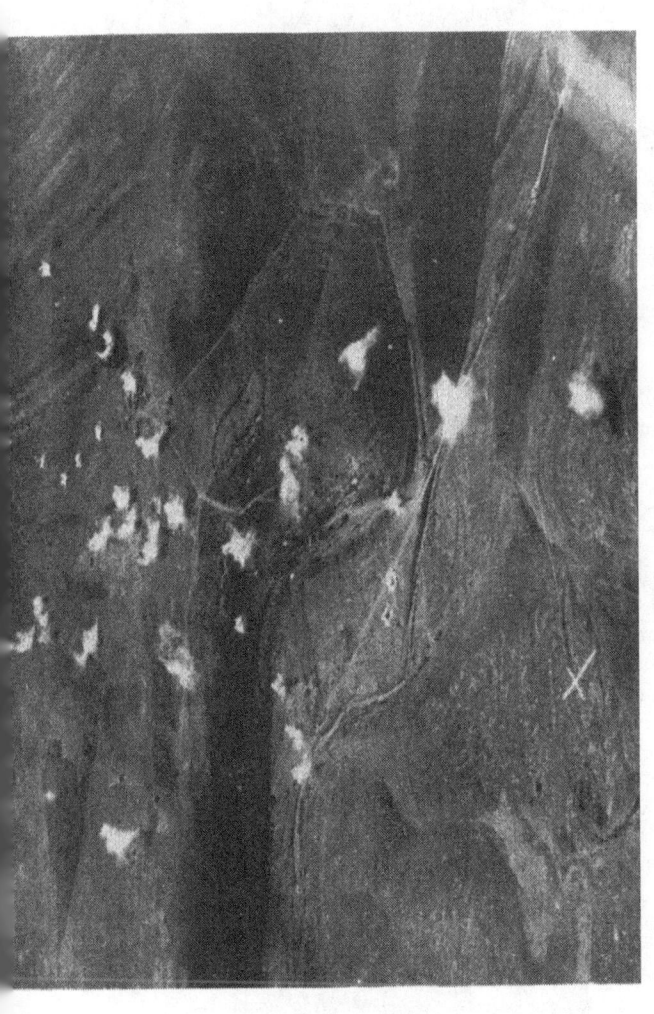

AN AUSTRALIAN AIR-RAID ON AMMAN RAILWAY STATION AND AERODROME, 4TH JUNE, 1918
(The white cross or arrow is a conventional sign inserted in most military air-photographs, pointing towards the north.)

*Lent by Lieut.-Col. R. Williams, No. 1 Sqn., A.F.C.
Aust. War Museum Collection No. A628.*

A GERMAN AEROPLANE BROUGHT DOWN IN THE BRITISH LINES IN PALESTINE BY NO. 1 SQUADRON, A.F.C., AUGUST, 1918

Aust. War Museum Official Photo. No. B3565.

the target. A running fight ensued for twenty minutes. Each machine manœuvred skilfully, and each several times secured the desired position of advantage on the underside of its opponent. At length the enemy's observer was put out of action, and Paul finished the engagement with his front gun. From a spin near the ground to escape a head-on attack, the Rumpler flattened out, met a final and decisive burst from the Bristol's forward armament, and crashed, nose first, into the side of a hill.

The German airmen were certainly making an effort to do the duty required of them, if not exactly to challenge the growing supremacy of their adversaries. Their favourite time for visiting the British line was at the first light of day. Their inquisitiveness concerning the Jericho and lower Jordan area has been mentioned, and it was persistent. Ross Smith and Kirk on June 9th drove off from the river-line a high-flying Rumpler, which was forced to land near Damieh, but only after fighting a remarkably good fight and striving for five minutes of close combat at 16,000 feet to get the advantage of the Australians. During this time, records the Australian pilot, " we flew around in circles, the E.A. (enemy aircraft) doing numerous Immelmann turns,[8] apparently with the object of getting on my tail. I remained under E.A's tail, and my observer kept up a steady stream of short bursts, but accurate shooting was difficult, owing to the rate of manœuvre. E.A's observer returned a large volume of fire, but his shooting was very wide, and he appeared to have numerous stoppages. He finally disappeared in his cockpit altogether." While the Jordan area remained apparently of particular interest to the enemy—possibly in preparation for his July attack in that region—his dawn patrols also visited the Lubban-road sector of the front and the coast sector. Over the coast he generally appeared from a wide *détour* seaward. Addison and Fysh (observer) and Stooke and Sutherland caught a formation of four Albatros scouts southeast of Bireh on June 23rd, split them up, and chased them from 10,000 feet to near the ground before the fight was abandoned in low clouds. According to documents found later, one of these machines broke up in the air and crashed.

---

[8] See Glossary.

On June 26th, Lieutenants Murphy and A. W. K. Farquhar[9] engaged over Ramleh an Albatros two-seater which came in from the sea at nearly 18,000 feet, and the two machines fought an exciting combat. At 5,000 feet the Albatros, its observer being by then out of action, made as if to land on the Australian aerodrome, when Murphy noticed that Farquhar also had sunk into his cockpit. Murphy had a stoppage in his own gun, and by grace of this delay the enemy escaped. When the Bristol Fighter landed, Farquhar was found to be dead from bullet wounds.

On such ventures over the lines the German airmen almost invariably flew at a great altitude, and it was to be presumed that their observation of the ground lacked detail. The Australian airmen frequently reported that reconnaissance even at 10,000 feet was difficult, owing to heat haze. The efforts which the enemy was now making in the air were his last on this front, and they lacked the real aggressive spirit. They were prompted by a sort of desperation, by the reproaches of the Turkish Command, and by the growing animosity between German and Turkish officers. The earlier morale of the enemy air force under Felmy had vanished. Its intelligence-patrol reports were now as a rule vague or incorrect. Its pilots were disheartened; they must have counted a reconnaissance successful if all machines returned safe from the flight, a combat satisfactory if they survived with a whole skin. Such close scouting as the Australian airmen counted a daily duty was, on the side of the enemy, utterly impossible. The pilots of the British squadrons made straight at enemy formations whenever sighted. The instinct on the other side was, as a rule, to fight only if escape seemed otherwise impracticable. A new indication of the enemy's helplessness in the air now began to appear.

Machine-gun attacks upon Turkish ground-troops were first practised to any notable extent during the east-Jordan operations of March and April. They offered excellent fun for the airmen and wrought demoralising damage upon infantry, cavalry, and transport alike. As disinclination on

---

[9] Lieut. A. W. K. Farquhar; No. 1 Sqn. (previously Light Horse). Jackeroo; of Sydney; b. Ingham, North Q'land, 15 Aug., 1894. Killed in action, 26 June, 1918.

the part of German airmen to keep the air became more and more marked, British and Australian pilots sought out such other enemy as they could find to fight, and with their machine-guns "shot-up" rest camps and road-transport far in rear of the Turkish lines. Their air supremacy carried no sharper sting than this. Bombing formations began the practice; machines upon ordinary reconnaissance followed suit. This galling form of attack may be said to date from a notable reconnaissance made on June 21st by two Bristol Fighters, manned respectively by Ross Smith and Kirk (observer) and by Paul and Weir.

These machines were that day over the Nablus–Tul Keram area on the morning patrol between 6 and 9 o'clock. They flew up the Lubban–Nablus road, counting camps, road-transport, and parties of troops, saw breakfasts being prepared at camps north of Nablus, and flew on up the road and railway to Jenin. The aerodrome there was peaceful, and no German machines disputed the detailed survey of it. This was all as usual. They then flew back again on their course, and, when about Burka (north of Samaria), they saw at a siding on the railway line an engine and light rolling-stock with infantry entraining. The Australians promptly dived at this target, and at 1,000 feet fired several furious bursts into it. Within a few seconds the peace of a calm summer morning was dissipated in a mad local panic. This initial success sent the Australian airmen on a joyous career of destruction along the line from Burka to en Nakurah (south of Samaria). The best description of it is their own. Ross Smith reported:—

"We descended to 1,000 feet and machine-gunned train and troops in station. Panic ensued, and troops ran everywhere. Train started north, and we flew alongside it firing at close range with apparently good result. Both machines concentrated fire on locomotive and varnished coach with white roof. We then turned south and attacked Messudie station from 1,000 feet, causing panic amongst troops. We flew along road to en Nakurah station, firing at motor-transport and other targets on the road. We attacked the M.T. park, a large camp, and the station at en Nakurah, from 1,000 feet. Troops ran from tents and dumps seeking cover in all directions, apparently very demoralised. One two-horse limber bolted—last seen going south. Considerable machine-gun and rifle fire experienced at all railway stations."

Paul's story was equally exciting. "Weir fired 200 rounds," he says in his report, "from 1,000 feet at train while stationary, and another 200 after it had pulled out on its way to Jenin. Dived on and fired a burst of fifty rounds from front gun at engine. We then proceeded to Messudie station at the same height, where I fired fifty and Weir 100 rounds at troops in station buildings, with apparently demoralising

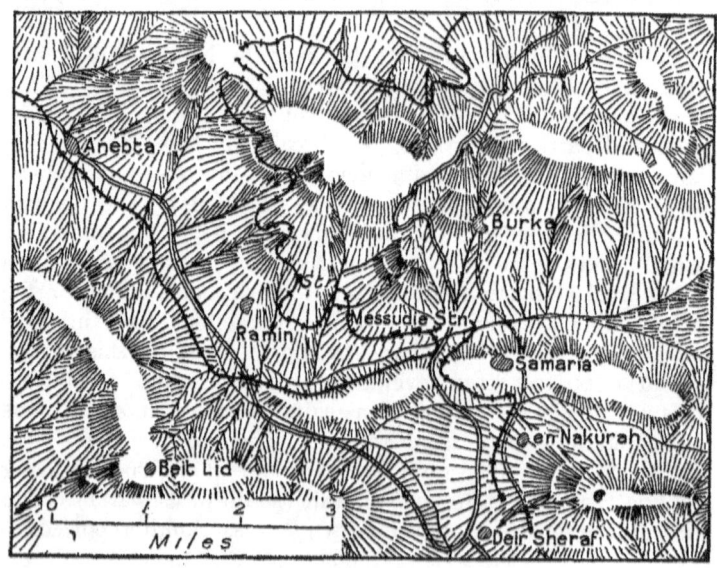

effect. I next fired 200 rounds in en Nakurah from the same height at station buildings and motor-transport on road. Troops scattered in all directions. We experienced considerable machine-gun fire and rifle-fire at all stations, especially at en Nakurah, where smoke-tracer ammunition was used." Between them they expended 2,000 rounds in this fashion. They then finished their reconnaissance *viâ* Tul Keram and Kulunsawe.

Thereafter such attacks became the rule with every patrol sent to El Kutrani and Kerak; and in that more open region cavalry and infantry parties were wont to scatter as soon as they sighted an aeroplane. During June the Bristol Fighters constantly visited this district, where, after the rush of the harvest was over, road-making and railway gangs maintained the number of the camps. German aeroplanes were rarely seen thereabout, but in the early morning of June 27th two Bristol Fighters unexpectedly sighted two heavily-armed A.E.G. two-seaters making north from El Kutrani and 4,000 feet above them. The Australians—A. R. Brown and Finlay (observer) and Oxenham and L. H. Smith[10]—at once gave chase. The Germans held northwards for a few miles while the Australians climbed, but eventually turned south again, and Brown at length overhauled one of them and engaged it from below. At Brown's second attack this German went down in a straight dive, belching out much smoke, landed hurriedly, and fell on one wing. Meanwhile, well away in the distance, Oxenham was fighting a duel with the other A.E.G. Brown flew to rejoin, and arrived just as this second German machine also landed. Both its occupants ran into a wady, and the Australians fired destructive bursts into the abandoned two-seater. While so engaged, Oxenham was fatally hit by a bullet fired from the ground, and his machine crashed. Later a letter was received from Smith, wounded and a prisoner, describing the disaster.

Oxenham's loss was avenged next morning by two Australian machines at Amman. Lieutenants S. A. Nunan[11] and Finlay (observer) and Adair and Vyner were making a close reconnaissance of east-Jordan camps. As they were nearing Amman at 10,000 feet, six Albatros scouts came up on their left front, 500 feet above and slightly in the sun. Adair, escorting, at once fired a red light to warn Nunan, and flew upward straight towards the enemy. At 300-yards' range he opened fire, and the enemy formation divided as though to envelop the two Bristols. Adair clung, firing, to the machine he had first engaged, until it heeled over and fell in a vertical side-slip; he followed it down, still firing at it, till another Albatros dived at him in turn. A rapid climbing turn by Adair avoided this attack and placed him on the German's

---

[10] Lieut. L. H. Smith; No. 1 Sqn. (previously Light Horse). Salesman; of Hurstville, N.S.W.; b. Cardiff, Wales, 7 July, 1896.

[11] Lieut. S. A. Nunan; No. 1 Sqn. (previously Engineers). Motor salesman; of Parkville, Melbourne; b. Malvern, Melbourne, 9 July, 1892. Died in Australia, 10 Dec., 1921.

tail. Vyner, his observer, put in one hot burst at the top of Adair's climb, and this was followed by a delivery from the pilot's own gun at the finish of the manœuvre. This Albatros also then span away out of control. At this point Adair had to pull out of action to clear a stoppage, and, while doing this, he saw his first opponent crash behind a sand-hill east of Amman station. His gun stoppage cleared, Adair was about to rejoin Nunan, when he caught sight of two Albatroses, which had evidently retired from the fight, gliding towards Amman aerodrome. He dived at these, fired into them, and gave Vyner a close shot at them. The Germans seemed quite demoralised, and fluttered down aimlessly with Vyner shooting into them at every chance. Seeing Nunan still engaged above with two of the enemy, Adair decided to lose no more altitude, and flew to join his comrades.

Meanwhile Nunan had fought a duel with two of the enemy whom, at the opening of the combat, he had chased northward. He fastened on to one Albatros and punished it heavily during its dive for safety. It hit the ground in an orchard and burst into flames. The second Albatros had not been inclined to venture too close to Nunan, and after the destruction of its companion it flew away north with another Albatros, the last of the six. These were the two machines Nunan was pursuing when Adair rejoined. The two Bristols between them had fired 1,700 rounds, Adair's gun was out of action, and they had scarcely any ammunition left. They therefore gave up the chase over the Nahr ez Zerka, and turned for home. The enemy made no attempt to re-engage.

CHAPTER XI

THE ENEMY DRIVEN FROM THE SKY

OF the demoralisation of the enemy's airmen prior to Allenby's offensive, British and Turkish evidence furnishes conclusive proof. That demoralisation contributed as much as any other factor to the Turkish disaster, and it was due entirely to the superb performances of the British and Australian air squadrons. The records of No. 1 Squadron are themselves illuminating documents; they are more than a story, almost a song of triumph. The papers seized in September at the Turkish headquarters at Nazareth offer ample confirmation of the Australian airmen's every claim.

The air supremacy wrested from the enemy in May and June was used to the full throughout the weeks up to the day of the attack. "During one week in June" (records the commander of No. 1 Squadron[1]) "hostile aeroplanes crossed our lines one hundred times—mainly on the tip-and-run principle. They came over at altitudes (16,000 to 18,000 feet) from which accurate observation was impossible." Still, that they came at all showed that they were at least in the air. In the last week in August the number of enemy visitations had dropped to eighteen. During the three following weeks of September it was reduced to four. For several vitally important days immediately before the attack no German machines whatever were seen near the line.

What did the enemy learn, even when his airmen did appear during July and August, of the vast preparations in progress behind the British lines? Nothing. "That the enemy expected an offensive on my part about this date (September 19th)," writes General Allenby, " is probable; that he remained in ignorance of my intention to attack in the coastal plain with overwhelming numbers is certain." Indeed, the Turks were persuaded that the attack was to come across the Jordan. The patrol reports of the German airmen—those who were fought down all through the summer and denied the air altogether in the autumn—are pitiable. Major Addison, in his official summary of the situation, declares

---

[1] Major Addison. On 28 June Major Williams, then commanding the squadron, was promoted to command the 40th (Army) Wing, and Captain Addison succeeded him as squadron-commander.

bluntly that they relied upon imagination rather than any other faculty. Between September 1st and 16th, when Allenby was gathering his striking force in the groves of Ramleh, Ludd, and Jaffa, the German airmen could furnish only this sort of intelligence report:—" The total camp capacity of the enemy has remained as before"; "no changes of importance have occurred"; "traffic on roads and railways in the long-distant reconnaissance centre were small"; "only unimportant re-grouping of troops without change of strength."

The truth of the matter is plain, and is set down beyond all doubt in the captured diary of the German flying service. This record states, under date of August 31st, that, owing to the activity of the Bristol Fighters far behind the Turkish lines, the short-distance reconnaissance work of the German machines was rendered "extraordinarily difficult." The Bristol Fighters, it proceeds, were continually over German aerodromes, and on August 27th even the men's tents on the Jenin aerodrome were attacked with machine-gun fire. "The loss of two machines of No. 301 Squadron compelled the suspension of all flying of other machines in front of the Eighth Army. The carrying on of flights on the rest of the front will be attempted occasionally." Further (the diary proceeds), the shortage of machines is soon to be overcome by the arrival of replacements. But pilots were scarce, "owing to sickness and other causes." On September 15th, four days before Allenby's attack, occurs this entry:—" Owing to the extraordinary lack of pilots, limited flying only can be carried out, in spite of the arrival of twenty new D.F.W's." The Australian airmen may well take pride in this confession of German impotence. During the two months prior to the attack all enemy machines destroyed on the whole British front —fifteen absolutely destroyed and twenty-seven driven down— fell to the airmen of No. 1 Australian Squadron. Many of those forced down were so damaged by their assailants' machine-gun fire after landing that they were abandoned.[2]

---

[2] From the beginning of July to the date of the Turkish armistice (October 31) No. 1 Squadron's record was—2,862 hours' flying, 157 strategic and 77 photography reconnaissances, 604 square miles of enemy territory photographed, 150 bomb raids, 21 tons of bombs dropped, 241,000 rounds of machine-gun ammunition fired in air combat or against troops on the ground, 17 German machines destroyed in combat and 33 others driven down. "This work," wrote the commander of the Palestine Brigade, R.A.F., "has been carried out with a gallantry and determination beyond all praise."

Before the special work began of blinding the enemy to Allenby's concentration, there were some long flights down the Hejaz railway. Ross Smith and Kirk disturbed El Kutrani camp and aerodrome with machine-gun fire on July 1st. On July 6th Kenny and Sutherland reconnoitred Jauf ed Derwish station, north of Maan, using the old German aerodrome at Beersheba as an advance landing-ground. The garrison at El Kutrani was putting that place in a state of defence; south of it the railway communication was interrupted by the Arabs' destruction of bridges over the Wady es Sultane. Kalat el Hesa and Jauf ed Derwish were surrounded by trench-systems; at the last-named place gangs of men were repairing railway culverts. Arabs in force were seen along the Wady Esal, between the Dead Sea and the railway south of El Kutrani. Two days later Jauf ed Derwish was bombed by a British formation escorted by Lieutenants H. A. Blake[3] and E. A. Mulford[4] (observer) and Adair and Sutherland, who flew over Maan and found it strongly garrisoned. The Turks east of the Dead Sea were distinctly nervous, and with good reason, for the Arab army was appearing in strength. No. 1 Squadron's patrols watched the whole length of the railway assiduously during the first fortnight of July. An interesting operation which provided excitement for several days was the attack on a convoy of about 2,000 camels south of Amman. On July 13th Lieutenants McGinness and Fysh (observer) and G. W. Sheppard[5] and Kreig found the convoy, escorted by 500 cavalry, moving south towards Kissir; they machine-gunned it severely and scattered horses and camels over the plain. That same afternoon three more Bristol Fighters routed the caravan near Kissir. Then Dowling and Mulford found it several days later at Amman, and worried it again. Other camel-transport parties were attacked at El Kutrani on July 15th and 16th by patrols from British squadrons.

On the main front A. R. Brown and Finlay on July 3rd chased a German two-seater near Lubban, drove it down from 10,000 to 200 feet, and would probably have destroyed it but

---

[3] Lieut. H. A. Blake; No. 1 Sqn. Electrical engineer; of West Perth, W. Aust.; b. Brisbane, 6 Dec., 1890.

[4] Lieut. E. A. Mulford, D.C.M.; No. 1 Sqn. (previously Light Horse). Electrician; b. Sydney, Jan., 1891.

[5] Lieut. G. W. Sheppard; No. 1 Sqn. (previously Artillery). b. Murrumbeena, Melbourne, 1893.

for heavy machine-gun fire from the Turkish infantry at close range. On July 6th patrols photographed the Et Tire area near the sea for the map-draughtsmen. About mid-July the British Command issued to the air squadrons orders for offensive measures against all hostile reconnaissance, orders which suggested preparations for advance on a grand scale. The airmen construed them in only one light—to attack everything they saw, in the air or on the ground, in any conditions of weather, and no matter what the odds. Sometimes a machine would take a few bombs, but the favourite plan was to carry as much machine-gun and Lewis gun ammunition as possible for ground-shooting. In the airman's eyes no other form of attack quite equalled this for excitement or for challenge of his nerve and skill; the effect was always certain and the damage done unmistakable. Ross Smith and Kirk (observer) and Paul and Weir, the four who had previously "shot up" the Nablus railway, were out on road patrol on July 9th, and flew as far as Jenin to photograph the aerodrome. They noted down the state of its camps and dumps. Then some ground machine-guns opened fire at them. If this was a challenge, it was unwise. The two Bristol Fighters descended to 2,000 feet and circled the aerodrome, Ross Smith taking photographs, and, behind him, the escorting machine blazing off ammunition into the hangars. Then a motor-car appeared at the aerodrome, ran along one line of hangars, and, as though obeying some order, five enemy scouts were suddenly wheeled out with engines running. Kirk fired 100 rounds into them impartially. The motor-car rushed out to them; orders were apparently countermanded; the engines of the machines were stopped. The Australians remained over the place for twenty minutes, waiting for the Germans to rise, and shooting off a short burst at every man who showed himself. Two days later the same four airmen repeated the performance near Nablus. The Balata aerodrome was small and sparsely populated; consequently, after firing only a few hundred rounds at its hangars, "we flew round in circles," reported Ross Smith, "attacking, in turn, transport parked at Balata, and horse-lines and small camps on the east side of Nablus. About fifty men were in the courtyard of barracks at Nablus shooting at us. Kirk fired 100 rounds at them, and

Map No. 7

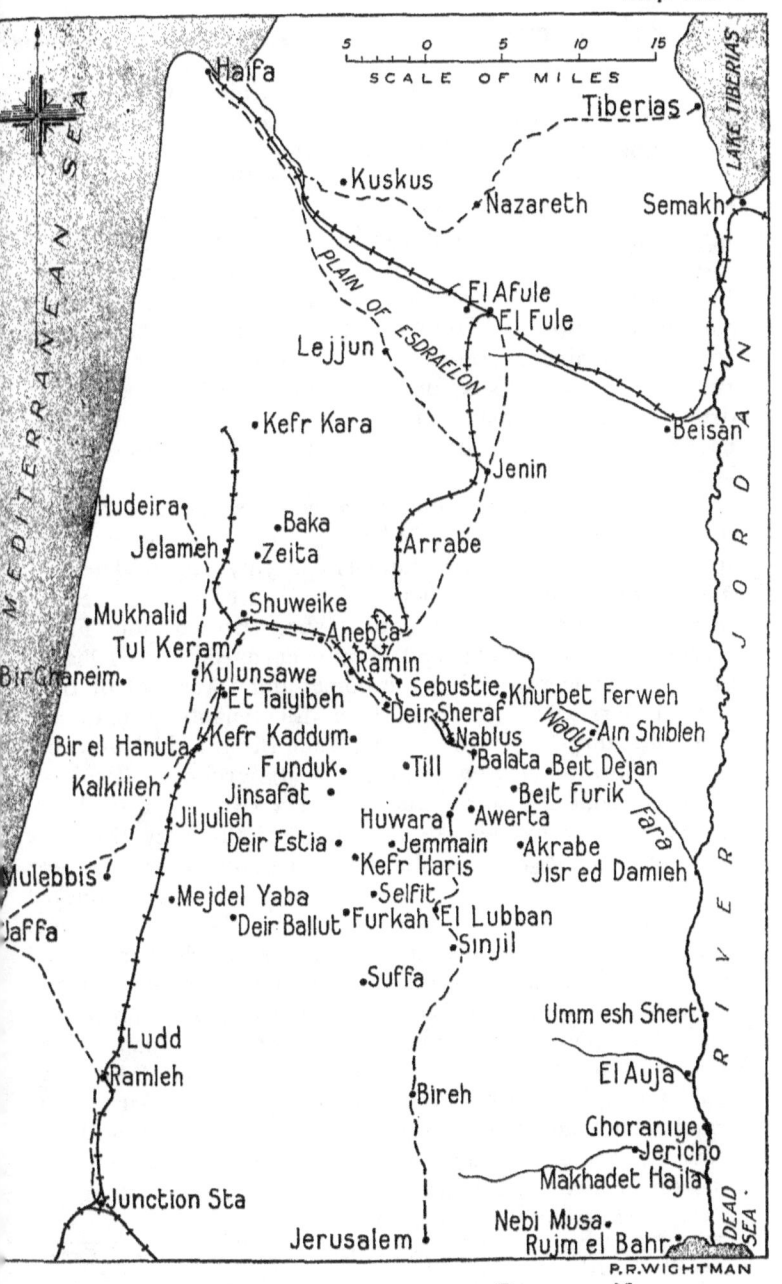

CENTRAL PALESTINE, THE SCENE OF THE BATTLE OF NABLUS

they all ran inside. Troops in this vicinity appeared panic-stricken, and ran in all directions." The two Bristols then flew home along the Lubban road, stampeding horse-teams and men on motor-lorries, and throwing traffic on the road into the utmost confusion. Nunan and Mulford that same morning found 200 horses and 300 camels on lines in the Wady Fara and many parties of horse-waggons on the road. They flew back and forth over this collection, and fired 600 Lewis gun rounds into it. " Horses on the lines and in the waggons fell; the remainder either bolted or rushed together and were further shot up. Men in the bivouacs rushed about quite demoralised." Nunan took the news home, and two other machines went out and machine-gunned this transport park in the afternoon.

The German airmen must have been exasperated by these contemptuous ravages. Whatever the incentive, they appeared in the air in some numbers on July 16th. The Australians were waiting for them. The first encounter occurred near Tul Keram at 7.30 a.m., when Brown and Finlay (observer) and Peters and Traill engaged four Albatros scouts which were making for home, and forced all of them to land hurriedly. An hour later Lieutenants Tonkin and A. V. McCann[6] fought three more from Bireh to Nablus, drove them all down, and fired into them on the ground. Paul and Weir at about the same time chased a two-seater to Jenin, but were unable to overtake it; baulked of this prey, they flew low and fired heavy fusilades into a column of camels near Arrabe and into a train north of Ramin, and finally attacked three Albatros scouts on the ground at Balata aerodrome. These were probably the same machines which Tonkin and McCann had already engaged. Next morning Dowling and Mulford (observer) and Sheppard and Kreig made an indecisive attack upon two unwilling Rumplers near Amman. They killed the observer in one German machine, but the enemy would not fight, and desired only to land. The Australians turned their machine-guns upon 200 cavalry massed near the aerodrome and 2,000 camels on transport-lines, apparently the same unfortunate beasts which had been harassed along the railway during the preceding days.

---

[6] Lieut. A. V. McCann, D.F.C.; No. 1 Sqn. (previously Light Horse). Farmer; b. Yea, Vic., 4 July, 1893.

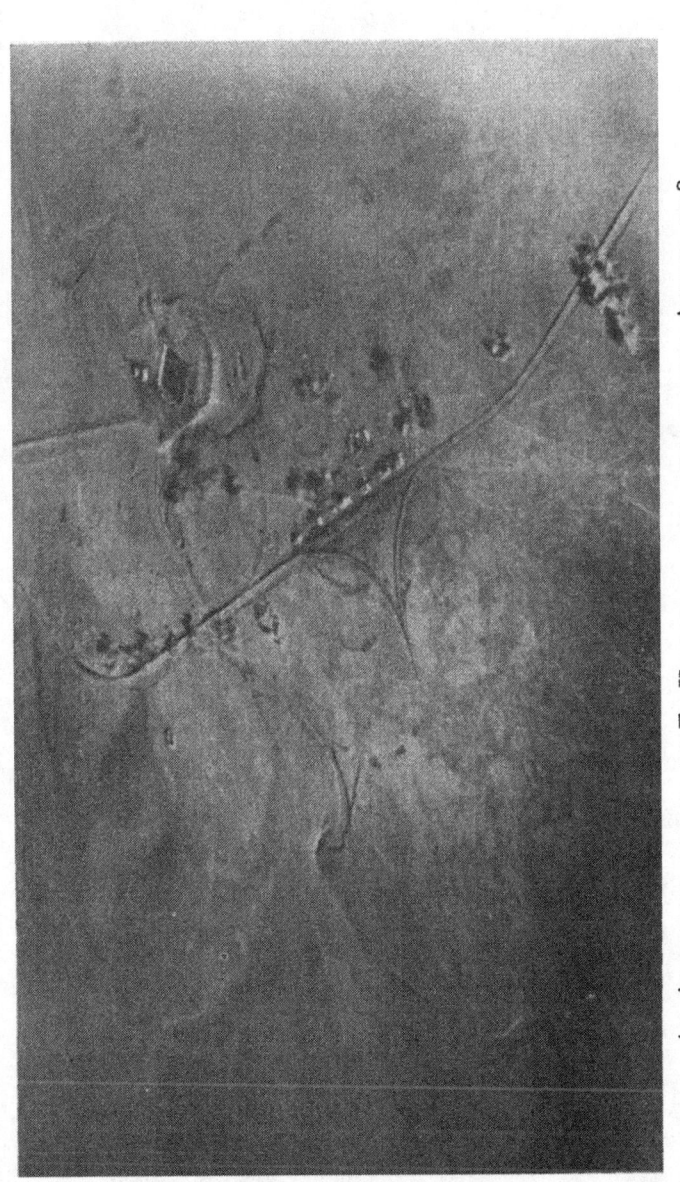

AN AUSTRALIAN AIR-RAID ON EL KUTRANI RAILWAY STATION, 15TH AUGUST, 1918

Aust. War Museum Official Photo. No. B3416.

JENIN AERODROME AND TOWN, LOOKING EAST, SHOWING THE TRACKS AROUND THE LANDING GROUND AND THE RAILWAY TO NAZARETH (WINDING ACROSS THE PICTURE)

Aust. War Museum Official Photo. No. B3386.
Taken 9th July, 1918.

While this engagement was taking place over Amman, Ross Smith and Kirk, on dawn hostile-aircraft patrol,[7] destroyed two Albatros scouts after a thrilling fight at 11,000 feet over the Wady el Auja. The enemy turned tail at once and dived straight for earth, with the Bristol after them like a flash. At only 50 feet from the ground Ross Smith fired a short burst into one from over its tail, and that Albatros promptly fell and crashed. Then ensued an exciting chase after the other along a little wady towards the Nablus road. The two machines skimmed the ground, flashed past rocky corners or over tree tops, until at last " over a yellow tent," reported the Australian pilot, " I fired at close range, and the enemy dived into the ground and smashed up on the Nablus road." Kirk photographed both victims, and the Bristol Fighter then resumed patrol. Lukis and Beaton subsequently joined it in pursuit of a Rumpler two-seater over the Jordan, but the German made good his escape.

On July 22nd Tonkin and McCann destroyed a Rumpler after a fight much like that of Ross Smith's. They also were on dawn patrol, south-west of Lubban. At first view the enemy had the advantage of height, but he sought only to escape. Tonkin cut him off from Balata aerodrome, for which he was making, and turned him south-west, both losing height steadily. Every few seconds the Australian fired a burst into the German's tail, the scared enemy pilot meanwhile kicking his rudder[8] from side to side in the effort to shake off his pursuer. At last the Rumpler, apparently hit, flattened out near the ground. With no more than a few feet of clearance, he flitted desperately along a wady, the Bristol Fighter still pursuing him. After a few moments of this course, the German crashed badly, and one wounded man crawled out of the wreckage.

Soon after dawn on July 24th Peters and Traill (observer) and Walker and Letch destroyed a patrolling enemy two-seater north of Mejdel Yaba. This German kept up a hot

---

[7] To ensure to air squadrons rapid warning of hostile aircraft over the lines, the system was for special wireless stations in the forward areas to send back warning to the aerodrome. No. 1 Squadron had a Klaxon horn fitted in a central position, and this horn bellowed out the wirelessed warnings to the hangars.

[8] The rudder of an aeroplane connects with a bar in the pilot's cockpit worked by the feet.

duel against odds until his observer was put out of action. Another, a Rumpler, which crossed the lines near Jericho at noon on July 28th, carried two plucky airmen who fought two Bristol Fighters—Brown and Finlay (observer) and Paul and Weir—in determined fashion from near Jerusalem to the upper Wady Fara. In this combat the Australian machines expended over 1,700 rounds—a sufficient indication of the efforts demanded of them. The German observer gave them shot for shot all the way, and the Rumpler landed safely in the wady; but Paul shot down pilot and observer as they ran from it, and both Bristols fired into the abandoned machine on the ground. Kenny and Sutherland drove down another Rumpler in this vicinity in the morning of July 30th and killed the observer.

The situation demanded daily observation of the regions around Nablus on the one side and Amman on the other, and the keenest watch on the enemy's troop movements. The building of an embankment for a railway from Tarbane, on the Afule–Haifa line, south-westward to the Kakon supply railway had been carefully noted for some days, and in mid-July the traffic on the roads over all this district was considerable. Though this denoted increased defensive preparations in the coast sector, on the other hand the trench-system about Kakon was reported to be in a badly neglected state. The Australian pilots brought in photographs of all Turkish activity in this important region as well as their own bird's-eye reports. Special patrols procured the smallest details of roads and tracks immediately opposite the British front and crossings of the important Nahr Iskanderuneh. This river— one of the many geographical features in Asia Minor which owe their names to the renowned Alexander of Macedon— runs west and north-west of Tul Keram, and Allenby's projected cavalry attack would have to cross it. The Australian patrol reports at this time are models of air scouting. No examination of the ground by cavalry scouts could have furnished better intelligence. Kenny and Sutherland on July 23rd flew up the coast to the Esdraelon Plain and over to Nazareth (the Turkish General Headquarters), and confirmed an agent's report of a new aerodrome at Kuskus (between Nazareth and Haifa). One Albatros scout was on the aerodrome ground, but did not rise; the Australians fired 200 rounds into the hangars, and also at a large new supply camp at Beit Lahm, near by. If, however, the Nablus region showed the enemy to be alert and busy, it was yet too soon to deduce special uneasiness, for the east-Jordan area was no less active. Sheppard and Kreig on July 24th found the Amman camp bigger than ever, and reported particularly massed concentration of tents in one wady, which British and Australian machines bombed twice during the following days.

Another reconnaissance of great value—that of the roads running east and north-east from Nablus and over the rough country from the Wady Fara to Beisan—was made on July 31st by McGinness and Fysh (observer) and Walker and Fletcher. Here the retreating Turks were to suffer disastrous bombing attacks by the Australian airmen after the Battle of Nablus. The reports returned by McGinness and Walker left hardly a detail unrecorded of the main routes across that difficult terrain. After finishing the road reconnaissance they had what they called "a day in the country." At Beisan they found a train entering from the west; they machine-gunned it and the transport park alongside the station. Leaving panic and confusion there, they next put a force of 200 cavalry into a mad stampede. They flew on north to Semakh, where there was a busy station with six sidings, and a small aerodrome a few hundred yards away from it. With bursts of fire they chased several hundred troops about station yard and aerodrome. Men sprawled on the ground, fired rifles, threw themselves into ditches, and made for any available cover. A dump of flares exploded and started a local fire. Men jumped out of a train; horses bolted in all directions. The Australians had no ammunition left for the sailing vessels on the Tiberian lake, or for two passive German aeroplanes on the floor of Jenin aerodrome, examined in passage on the way home. During the following weeks other pilots, on almost daily patrols, photographed in overlapping series all the roads and tracks from Nablus and the Wady Fara up to Beisan, and from Tul Keram northwards; and from the negatives which they furnished—nearly 1,000 in all—new maps were issued for Allenby's offensive, covering nearly 400 square miles of country.

The practice of "shooting-up" enemy troops, roads, and traffic-centres became general with all British and Australian machines. Even photography-patrols, when they had finished their assigned duty, would regularly fly low homeward and fire into any target which offered. In this practice the airmen found a new method of countering the enemy's anti-aircraft artillery. Thus during a British bombing raid against Amman on August 8th, Lieutenants Nunan and F. C. Conrick,[9] escorting, flew down and drove off the gun-crews engaging the bombers, and by hovering over the battery kept it silent throughout the raid. Brown and Finlay (observer) and Maughan and Letch performed the same effective service on August 21st, while six Australian machines bombed Amman station and aerodrome, and wrecked several German aeroplanes in the hangars.

With the decline of the German air service the enemy failed to fend off these demoralising attacks. Anti-aircraft artillery and machine-guns seemed unable alone to check the wholesale terrorising of the countryside. Kenny and Sutherland (observer) and McGinness and Fysh, on special reconnaissance on August 2nd, sighted between Kuskus and El Afule four Albatros two-seaters. Kenny chased one down to a landing near Lejjun, and then climbed again to 3,000 feet to attack another; he was himself attacked by a third, but Sutherland fired a burst of 100 rounds into this last at close range, and it fell completely out of control. By this time McGinness had joined the combat. He flew straight at the second Albatros, which had been fighting a clever duel with Kenny, and both he and Fysh fired heavily into it at the top of a wonderful loop which the German machine was performing over the other Bristol Fighter. From this attack the Albatros did not recover; it flew straight to the ground and crashed in a heap. The fourth enemy escaped while opportunity offered. The Australians then fired 700 rounds into the hangars in El Afule aerodrome and at rolling-stock and troops in the railway station.

On August 5th Adair and Mulford (observer) and Nunan and Conrick counted the camps along the Wady Fara and reported small cavalry movement over Ain es Sir, near

---
[9] Lieut. F. C. Conrick, A.F.C.; No. 1 Sqn. (previously Camel Corps). Grazier; b. Cooper's Creek, Vic., Oct., 1891.

Amman. They then fell in with an Albatros scout and chased it down to Amman aerodrome. Returning over the Wady Fara again, they machine-gunned a column of infantry and 200 camels; the men in charge of the camels fled for cover, and the convoy was scattered in bunches. Other machines again harried the camps at this place a few days later. Tonkin and Vyner on August 9th pursued a two-seater for fifty miles, from north of Nablus to far up Lake Tiberias, without being able to overhaul it. Cameron and Fletcher, in a low-flying attack on the same day, threw a large transport park at Nablus into panic. Next morning, McGinness and Fysh (observer) and Lieutenants Headlam and W. H. Lilly[10] found on a road in the hills west of Nablus a column of 200 horses, motor-transport, and infantry; they shot 850 rounds into this mass, blocked the road, and stampeded the horses into a mad gallop northward. Brown and Finlay on August 14th reported a large cavalry camp carefully camouflaged at Mukhalid on the coast. They fired into it with good effect, and at the end of the afternoon returned with Paul and Weir to attack it again. They first shot the horse-lines and men's camps into utter confusion, and then flew to the beach, where at least 300 men and many horses were bathing, and machine-gunned this party from a height of a few hundred feet. Despite much counter-fire from the cliffs, the airmen darted up and down the beach, pursued the bathers into the water or out of it into crevices in the cliff-side, and stampeded the horses along the shore. They fired in all 2,350 rounds in this attack. Paul returned to the aerodrome with twenty-seven bullet-holes in his machine.

The German airmen failed everywhere to meet the challenge offered them. They received new machines—Pfalz scouts—and still were beaten. McGinness and Fysh (observer) and Lieutenants W. C. Thompson[11] and M. D. Lees[12] first encountered these new aircraft over Jenin aerodrome on August 14th. They were a formation of six, having the advantage of height by 2,000 feet. A climbing race promptly

---

[10] Lieut. W. H. Lilly; No. 1 Sqn. (previously Light Horse). Clerk; of Kalgoorlie, W. Aust.; b. North Melbourne, 12 July, 1892.

[11] Lieut. W. C. Thompson; No. 1 Sqn. Mechanical engineer; of Abbotsford, Melbourne; b. Abbotsford, 9 Oct., 1894.

[12] Lieut. M. D. Lees; No. 1 Sqn. (previously Light Horse). Bank clerk; of Goulburn, N.S.W.; b. Goulburn, 3 May, 1895.

began, and when the enemy discovered that they were being outclimbed, they dived in formation at the two Bristols. McGinness deftly avoided, counter-attacked, and split the formation. Clouds interfered with the fight, but all six Pfalzes were engaged and forced to land. The following days were remarkable for German efforts to cross the lines. Paul and Weir, responding to an enemy-aircraft alarm at breakfast-time on August 16th, picked up a Rumpler making homeward at 10,000 feet, and shot it to pieces in the air. Headlam and Lilly on August 21st drove down a Rumpler which had been over the Jordan Valley, and shot its observer. During the action Lilly's Norman compensating fore-sight[13] was shot off by a piece of anti-aircraft shell, and to that mishap, which made further accurate shooting impossible, the Rumpler probably owes its escape. An L.V.G. two-seater was shot down near Ramleh next day by Brown and Finlay, and its occupants taken prisoner, but the fight was marred by the loss of Walker and Letch, who were patrolling with Brown. The enemy crossed the lines at a great height, and the Australians climbed to cut him off. The whole squadron saw the fight from the aerodrome floor. The L.V.G. turned for home, and Walker took the grave risk of attacking from above and behind in full sight of the German's rear gun.[14] In a few seconds Walker's machine was seen to fall and burst into flames. Brown, who had manœuvred in front of the L.V.G., gave Finlay the shooting. Finlay's guns, however, fell out of their mounting, and Brown then attacked the L.V.G. head-on and drove it down to a bad landing near the Ramleh aerodrome.

The determined efforts of the enemy to penetrate the British air screen were well demonstrated in a great fight between Tul Keram and Kalkilieh on August 24th, when two Bristol Fighters defeated eight German machines and destroyed four of them. An early hostile-aircraft alarm that morning brought out Peters and Traill (observer) and McGinness and Fletcher, to whom British anti-aircraft fire indicated an L.V.G. two-seater over Jelil (on the coast) at 9,000 feet. Peters flew towards it, and the German, turning

---

[13] See Glossary.
[14] See foot-note 2, page 122.

north, fired several lights. Suddenly six hostile scouts in formation, obviously waiting for the signal, appeared from the north-west, and the L.V.G. turned to pass beneath them. There was no more than an instant for the decision; Peters made it, and dashed after the L.V.G. McGinness just as promptly turned in between him and the scouts and met their attack. The scout-leader, with the other five behind him, dived straight at McGinness, but Fletcher received him with a steady fire. From this the leader sheered off and dived on towards Peters below. Two more scouts followed, attacking McGinness; again Fletcher's fire deflected the attack, and the two passed on, each turning outward. The remaining three scouts dived below McGinness, and, with the last of the upper enemy gone, McGinness, in turn, put his nose down and struck straight for the centre machine of those three. He opened fire behind this scout's tail at fifty-yards' range, and the German went down in a trail of smoke and burst into flames as he hit the ground.

Meanwhile Peters pursued the original two-seater, while Traill, his observer, kept the attacking scout-leader at a distance. Two close, blazing rattles of fire, one from Peters and one from Traill as the enemy turned, shook the two-seater, and then Peters swooped below it, came up again under its belly, and delivered a burst of eighty more rounds into it. The L.V.G. went down like a leaf and crashed near Bir el Hanuta. By this time the last three scouts were coming down under McGinness's attack, and the whole fight was drifting north at a low height. Two of these scouts dropped to attack Peters, but Traill shot both in turn into bad spins. One was lost to sight, manifestly hit; the other Peters turned and pursued, and, after receiving two straight bursts of fire, this second scout plunged into the ground and fell on its back. Peters, now very near the ground, drove straight at a section of anti-aircraft guns and put the crews to flight. McGinness chased north-westward the one Pfalz remaining in sight, drove it down to 200 feet, and a last fusillade from Fletcher sent it crashing into a motor-lorry on the Nablus–Messudie road. As the pilot tried to get out of the wreck Fletcher shot him dead. Peters, flying homeward while this was taking place, saw another L.V.G. two-seater near the lines at 10,000 feet, and chased it to Nablus, but then had to give up the pursuit owing to lack of ammunition. Enemy records later showed that of the seven machines engaged in the first combat only one scout got back to its aerodrome. The victorious Australian airmen received personal congratulations from the Middle East Air Force commander and a special telegram from General Allenby.

The compliments which No. 1 Squadron received from the highest quarters on its work during these important weeks[15] were ratified in significant fashion. On August 29th General Borton arrived at Ramleh with a giant new Handley-Page bomber, which he had flown from England. This machine, the only one of its type in the East, was put on the strength of the Australian Squadron.

The enemy's aircraft losses steadily mounted. Nunan and Conrick on August 27th circled over Jenin aerodrome for an hour, challenging seven scouts and a two-seater on the ground there to come up and fight them, but the enemy was not willing. Nunan then flew low, and he and his observer fired 500 rounds into the line of machines and hangars, and drove the mechanics into a wild scurry for cover. Next morning two Bristol Fighters broke off from a photography-patrol north-west of Nablus to attack two L.V.G's. These promptly made for the Jenin landing-ground. Dowling and Mulford (observer) and McGinness and Fysh intercepted a patrol of two L.V.G's west of Mulebbis in the afternoon of August 31st, and Fysh destroyed both of them; one crashed in the British lines, and one near Kalkilieh. This action was an outstanding example of proper fighting tactics against a two-seater. McGinness laid his machine alongside one of the enemy for close action by putting his observer in position under the L.V.G's tail. Dowling engaged the other L.V.G. from above and in front, but (to quote his report) "the

---

[15] Major-General Salmond, commanding R.A.F. in the Middle East, inspected No. 1 Australian Squadron at Ramleh in July, 1918, and then declared that it ranked as "one of the best squadrons in the Royal Air Force. Its interior economy, workshops, and discipline are excellent. The turn-out of its mechanical transport, and, above all, of its aeroplanes, are models of their kind. On this squadron has always fallen a large portion of the work which has had to be performed by the Royal Air Force in Palestine since the day that the Egyptian Expeditionary Force left the Canal. The results that have been achieved by the Royal Air Force have been, to a very marked degree, due to the fine work of No. 1 Squadron, Australian Flying Corps. It is a matter of pride to me to have had this squadron under my command since the days of its formation."

A British air-raid on the railway at Deraa, 16th September, 1918

The smoke and dust of bombs in the foreground. A hospital can be seen on the far edge of the town.

Aust. War Museum Official Photo. No. B3551.

A D.H.9 FORCED TO LAND IN THE ENEMY'S COUNTRY

The incident here shown occurred after the air-raid on Deraa on 16th September, 1918. The crew of the lost aeroplane have put out strips (of cloth) to indicate to an accompanying machine that the ground is too bad to permit of a successful landing.

enemy aeroplane was so well handled that I found it extremely difficult to maintain position, and so decided to attack from below." Before he could do this his engine failed, and he had to turn away. McGinness, having seen his own opponent destroyed, took up the combat with the second German, and Fysh shot down this also from position below.

The Germans never really took the air again over this part of the front. One or two of their machines were seen in the far distance, and there is record of one German scout who on September 15th flew in quickly from the sea, south of Jaffa, and turned north at once. Nor did the British airmen find much evidence of the enemy's flying even over his own lines. No. 111 Squadron saw one distant two-seater just before the offensive began, and Dowling and Mulford (observer) and McGinness and Fysh on September 14th destroyed a Rumpler two-seater near Jenin. Otherwise, for the eighteen days prior to Allenby's attack, there were no German airmen seen abroad.

This of itself would be a proud record for an air service charged with preventing the enemy from learning the secret of the planned offensive. But it was by no means all. Reconnaissance machines swept the entire Turkish front and rear areas in daily revision of accumulated scouting intelligence. Photography-patrols produced a new set of pictures of the front-line defences and coastal obstacles in order to bring maps up-to-date in the last available details. All machines punished enemy troops and transport wherever they made a sufficiently good target for machine-gun attack. The Turkish cavalry camp at Mukhalid was frequently disturbed by these airmen's lightning strokes. The cavalry camps between the Wady Fara and Es Salt and at Ain es Sir were also favourite targets. Amman aerodrome and railway station were bombed by five several raids on August 21st— one of them an attack by six Australian machines. The aerodrome and its material were badly damaged, and the enemy was so disheartened by this pounding that he shortly afterwards abandoned it and was not observed to use it again. Three Bristol Fighters, raiding Kissir that same day, fired 1,300 rounds into an armoured train at the station there, and drove troops from it into the shelter of neighbouring wadys.

On September 14th a German camp, discovered at El Howeij on the Es Salt–Nimrin road, was severely bombed and machine-gunned by four Bristol Fighters. Such were the low-flying ground-attacks made in the last two or three weeks of the British preparations. That there were not more of them was due not to want of opportunity, but to the fact that machines of all squadrons had to be nursed for the utmost effort in the grand attack to come.

Before describing the part played by No. 1 Squadron in the battle on the field of Armageddon—officially called the Battle of Nablus—it is necessary to follow shortly those Arab operations in the desert beyond the Amman railway, wherein No. 1 Squadron was intimately concerned. This is not the place to tell the interesting story of the party of British officers under Colonel Lawrence who accompanied the Arab Northern Army from south of Maan across the desert to Azrak, and thence in the attack made upon the Turks at Deraa in conjunction with Allenby's sweep around the sea-flank. No. 1 Squadron first became interested in these operations on May 16th, when Ross Smith flew Colonel Lawrence from Allenby's headquarters to the plains near El Kutrani and there landed him. At Cairo a special air detachment, called " 'X' Flight, R.A.F.," was formed to work in the desert with Lawrence. With this flight were a number of Australian mechanics and two B.E.12.a machines, which, with two or three specially selected British officers, landed at Akaba, at the head of the north-eastern arm of the Red Sea, and thence trekked to the headquarters of the Arab Prince Feisal near Maan. The B.E. machines, when they arrived from Akaba, proved to be of no practical use, though possibly they served to impress the Arabs. On August 12th a Bristol Fighter—Murphy and Hawley (observer)—flew from Ramleh to join Lawrence in the desert.

The Arabs were to operate in two armies—one, the Northern Army, to strike across the desert to Azrak (fifty miles east of Amman and about eighty from Deraa), thence to attack the important Deraa railway centre; the other, the Southern Army, to harass the probable retreat of the Turks from Maan and south of that place. The region between El Kutrani and Maan was frequently reconnoitred during August by patrols from No. 1 Squadron, the object being to watch for developments among the Bedouin, to worry the Turkish railway garrisons, and to confirm Arab faith in British air supremacy. The Bedouin tribes had learned from the attentions of airmen on both sides at various times a great respect for aeroplanes—"Tiyaras" (*i.e.*, "female flying things") they called them—and the frequent sight of British machines was calculated to encourage the Anglo-Arab *entente*.

An accident to Tonkin and Vyner on August 13th assisted this design. They were reconnoitring about Maan that morning, and were forced by engine-trouble to land near El Shobek. They burned their machine and endeavoured to make their way towards Beersheba. The Bristol Fighter escorting them reported their mishap, and three machines, sent out next day to rescue them, found Tonkin and Vyner in the hands of Arabs who were friendly and much impressed. The two Australians were treated with all hospitality, and were handed over to a British camel-patrol a few days later at a reward-price of fifty sovereigns each.

Lawrence's party and the air-mechanics moved across the desert to Azrak on August 31st and September 1st, and a fortnight later demolition parties—composed of Englishmen, Frenchmen, Indians, and Arabs, in weird assortment—trekked westward towards the railways.[16] The force, called "the Arab Northern Army under Brigadier-General Nuri Said," was not yet fully collected, and the allegiance of Bedouin tribes was nearly upset by several German air raids from Deraa. Murphy and Hawley destroyed one of these hostile machines on September 16th, but had to fly back to the squadron at Ramleh for repair of a slight defect. On September 16th and 17th Lawrence's detachments succeeded in blowing up sections of railway north and south of Deraa, and a special detachment of Gurkhas (serving under Lawrence's orders) temporarily captured and destroyed the station and bridges at Mezerib Junction, north-west of Deraa. This work was an essential part of Allenby's plans. To assist it, No. 144 Squadron, with its large new D.H.9 bombers, raided

---

[16] Some of these particulars are taken from an interesting account of Lawrence's expedition, written by a British officer who took part in it, and published in *Blackwood's Magazine* of May and June, 1920.

Deraa station on both those days; they dropped a ton and a quarter of explosives on the station, including six bombs of a hundredweight each. One D.H.9 was forced to descend with engine-trouble on the way home from the first raid, and was captured by the enemy. However, Lieutenants Blake and E. Sullivan[17] (observer) and Dowling and Mulford, sent out next day specially for that purpose, found it where it had landed, covered by the enemy with branches of trees. They set it on fire with incendiary bullets.

Note.—With reference to the shooting down of Lieutenant J. M. Walker in flames, and the loss of several German machines in the same fashion, some observation on the use of incendiary bullets will be found in Appendix No. 9.

---

[17] Lieut. E. Sullivan; No. 1 Sqn. (previously A.A.M.C.). Farrier; b. Carlton, Melbourne, 1894.

CHAPTER XII

THE BATTLE OF ARMAGEDDON

THE plan of Allenby's attack is already a classic. It was to burst the enemy's line by a hurricane infantry attack on the extreme coast flank, to throw nearly the whole of his cavalry force through the breach, and to direct it at full speed towards Nazareth and the upper Jordan, in order to cut off the northern line of retreat of the Seventh and Eighth Turkish Armies about Nablus. This cavalry force was to make touch as soon as possible with the Arabs at Deraa, and thus close the enemy's retreat by the eastern railway also. The fighting, which ended in the annihilation of three Turkish armies—for the enemy's Fourth Army, about Amman, was also cut to pieces—will be described here as the airmen saw it. The victory could not have been complete without them. They prepared it during the weeks beforehand. They consummated it in the critical days. The worst scenes of destruction were their work. Many thousands of Turks believed the Bristol Fighter to be a direct instrument of Allah.

The 40th (Army) Wing had been strengthened for this battle by two more squadrons—No. 144 of D.H.9's (bombers) and No. 145 of S.E.5.a's (fighting scouts). This wing was the British striking force in the air. The plan of action for September 19th was as follows:—

S.E.5.a's (Nos. 111 and 145 Squadrons), to patrol over Jenin aerodrome all day, prevent any attempted enemy air action from that quarter, and to attack with bombs and machine-guns all targets in the vicinity.

D.H.9's (No. 144 Squadron), to maintain bombing of El Afule railway station and Turkish headquarters at Nablus.

Bristol Fighters (No. 1 Australian Squadron), strategical reconnaissance and bombing.

This meant that No. 1 Squadron was to have the general oversight of the battle-area and report all developments. It was the place of honour in the air attack. Moreover, the squadron had the privilege of opening Allenby's offensive with the big Handley-Page machine before-mentioned. El Afule and Nablus had for long been closely reconnoitred; the locations of Turkish headquarters, and especially of the main telephone exchanges, had been precisely observed; and at 1.15 a.m. on September 19th, Ross Smith set off in the Handley-Page with Mulford, Lees, and McCann as observers, and carrying sixteen 112-lb. bombs. With these the Australians smashed the central telephone exchange at El Afule and temporarily wrecked the railway junction. During the day the D.H.9's wrought further havoc both here and at Nablus, where also the telephone exchange was destroyed. As a result of the wreckage of these nerve-centres, the Turks east of Nablus remained in complete ignorance of Allenby's triumphant attack during at least the first two days of the battle.

At 4.30 a.m. the artillery bombardment began, and a quarter of an hour later the XXI Corps assaulted with five infantry divisions. The Turkish front was shattered at once. By 7.30 a.m. two divisions of cavalry were advancing up the coast. By midday the 5th Cavalry Division was well across the Nahr Iskanderuneh, still going north; and in the afternoon the 4th Cavalry Division struck eastward for Tul Keram, and the Australian Mounted Division north-eastward towards El Afule.

Among the first Bristol Fighters out (5.20 a.m.) were those of McGinness and Fysh (observer) and Headlam and Lilly. They saw a large working party repairing the wreckage at El Afule station and all Turkish camps quiet between El Afule and Tul Keram, but farther south the alarm was beginning. From Bir el Hanuta a full infantry battalion was doubling southward towards the firing, and cavalry were alarmed and collecting in groups. West of the railway line enemy movement northward was beginning about Bir Ghaneim, but British cavalry were also pushing north along the sea-edge, and were already ahead of the local Turkish retreat. At 6 a.m. Maughan and Sutherland escorted a bomb raid by D.H.9's to El Afule. One D.H.9 had to land in enemy country; Maughan followed, picked up both its occupants, and brought them back.

Then came the first great news of success. Cameron and

Fletcher (observer), accompanied by two other Bristols, returned from an hour's patrol and reported Turkish guns, cavalry, and transport retiring at a gallop and in disorder about Et Tire. The numbers were estimated at 2,000 cavalry, 5,000 infantry, and 600 wheeled vehicles. The three Australian machines dropped their twenty odd small bombs upon masses which it was impossible to miss, and fired over 2,000 machine-gun rounds into disorganised mobs of men and animals. At 10 a.m. A. R. Brown and Finlay (observer) and Peters and Traill found the enemy south of Nablus all quiet, and apparently unaware of what was happening. They flew on to Jenin, bombed it, and came home by the coast. British cavalry, they reported, were at 11.30 advancing on Liktera. Turks at Kakon, well on the cavalry's right rear, were alarmed and beginning to pack up, and southward to Kulunsawe all roads were alive with retreating traffic. Meanwhile, acting on Cameron's earlier news, bombing relays had begun. The first bombing formation—five Bristol Fighters—took off at 11.40 a.m.; each dropped eight bombs along the retreating column between Et Tire and Tul Keram, and each fired hundreds of machine-gun rounds into bunches of mounted men and transport. This attack drove loose parties of disordered men and animals in two directions—one towards Kakon and one into Tul Keram. The enemy was, however, not yet too demoralised to attempt defence; the ground machine-gun fire was fairly heavy, and of this formation Dowling and Mulford were wounded, obliged to land, and taken prisoners. The light horse recaptured them a few hours later. At 12.30 p.m. a second formation of three machines repeated the attack on the same retreating mass at the Tul Keram road-corner.

Two Bristol Fighters reconnoitred east of Jordan and found all the camps peaceful. They attacked and put to flight a large body of cavalry exercising at Ain es Sir; then, flying homeward, they observed a column of fifty motor-lorries moving south along the Wady Fara road, dropped their remaining bombs on it, and blocked the road with a direct hit on one lorry. In the late afternoon a second pair of roaming Bristol Fighters attacked this transport, which was then parked on the roadside by the wady.

Meanwhile in the west six machines opened the afternoon raiding series. Two of them pursued the mixed crowd fleeing north of Kakon towards Baka; this multitude, however, was already lost, and could be left to fall into the hands of the cavalry. The other four machines found a congested mass of men, carts, guns, horses, and camels making from Tul

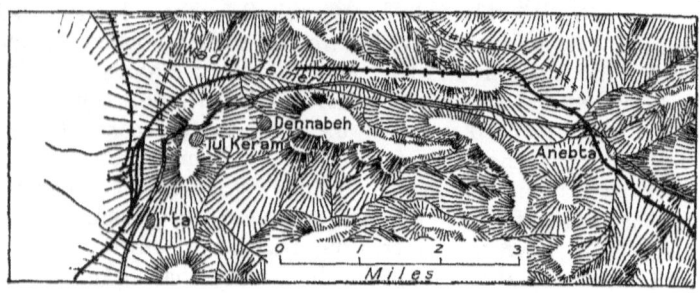

Keram towards Anebta. The road they had to take runs with the little Wady Zeimer through a defile; steep hills look down on either side; and the routed enemy was caught there in a trap, of which the airmen took full advantage. Lieutenants Tonkin and L. S. Climie,[1] flying low to "shoot-up" the rear of this mass, came to grief—hit by bullets from the ground —but landed unhurt. They were taken by the Turks, but pursuing cavalry recovered them. Before the Turks issued from this bloody defile, another raiding formation of seven Bristol Fighters cut them up at about 5 p.m. west of Anebta.

The evening air patrols, roaming the sky from El Afule south-westward, brought in graphic stories of the enemy's plight in the north. The Turkish Seventh Army Headquarters was still at Nablus, after being bombed all day by British squadrons, and was judged to be quite ignorant of what had happened. The entire force of the Turkish Eighth Army was in flight, and Tul Keram, its headquarters, was in the hands of British infantry. The roads here for miles north were occupied by British cavalry and the light horse. Sumrah, a small village situated where the coast road branches off across the hills towards El Afule, had been a Turkish supply

---

[1] Lieut. L. S. Climie; No. 1 Sqn. (previously Engineers). Assistant surveyor; b. Albany, W. Aust., 1893.

AUSTRALIAN AEROPLANES WITH PART OF LAWRENCE'S ARAB FORCE NEAR AZRAK, 11TH SEPTEMBER, 1918

Aust. War Museum Official Photo. No. B3456.

To face p. 154.

TUL KERAM RAILWAY STATION, SHOWING MATERIAL CAPTURED ON 19TH SEPTEMBER, 1918

Aust. War Museum Official Photo. No. B3502.
Taken 24th September, 1918.

To face p. 155.

centre. That evening its camps and grain dumps were all in flames, the hospital was gone, and a confused rabble of troops was halted in the hills beyond it.

In the evening, and again in the small hours of the following morning, Ross Smith, in the Handley-Page, delivered heavy loads of bombs on Jenin aerodrome and railway station. The scene at daylight on September 20th was extraordinarily interesting. Lieutenants Nunan and L. W. Gregory[2] (observer), with Brown and Finlay, saw all camps on the horseshoe road between Anebta and Deir Sheraf either burnt or abandoned, and from Deir Sheraf northward the enemy was evacuating by road and rail towards Jenin. At Messudie station Turkish working parties were industriously loading two trains facing north. From Burka northward, as far as the eye could see, the road was littered with carts, camels, and a rabble of soldiery. Jenin aerodrome was a rubbish-heap; only a wrecked German two-seater and a few abandoned hangars were left of the former two large aerodromes. El Afule was blackened and wrecked from the previous twenty-four hours' bombing. Four trains without engines lay in the station yard, not a tent or a hangar was left unburnt on the aerodrome, and on the ground were four aeroplanes and some men busy around them. The Australians dropped their bombs about these and the rolling-stock, and flew westward to meet the cavalry and light horse. These troops had marched through most of the night to fulfil Allenby's timetable. The airmen saw the British advance-guard of three armoured cars half-way across the Esdraelon Plain, moving rapidly upon El Afule, and a large crowd of prisoners walking in the opposite direction. Three cavalry brigades were entering the plain behind the cars—one at Lejjun and the other two slightly in rear, all advancing towards El Afule on a broad front.

A second dawn patrol—Paul and Weir (observer) and Maughan and L. H. Smith—ranged the Jordan Valley. Damieh bridge and Es Salt were apparently blissfully unconscious of the ruin beyond the central hills. The important Damieh–Beisan road was tranquil and empty. From Beisan

---

[2] Lieut. L. W. Gregory; No. 1 Sqn. (previously Machine-Gun Corps). Sawmiller; b. Kogarah, Sydney, 1892.

south-westward towards Nablus the cross-country route was still quiet as far as Tubas, but farther on, between Khurbet Ferweh (at the Wady Fara elbow) and Nablus, a new flight was beginning. Here, for over about five miles of road, was spread a loose column of about 200 vehicles, all making away from Nablus. The Bristol Fighters swooped down upon it. They had only eight bombs, but three of them made direct hits on transport and blocked the road, and the effect of the others was equally destructive. Frightened by the explosions, and by bursts of machine-gun fire delivered from close overhead, many horses bolted over the precipice on one side of the road, and, on the other, men ran in panic to shelter in the hillside. Several motor-lorries, either deserted by their drivers while still running, or colliding with bolting horse-transport, likewise fell over the precipice. Yet this was no more than a hint of what was to come later. The two Australian machines fired all the ammunition they had, and then flew homeward. The transport parks at Nablus and Huwara appeared deserted, and a great crater had been blown in the road south of Huwara.

This day's Australian air attack was upon the Samaria–El Afule road, and was opened about 9 a.m., shortly after the return of A. R. Brown's dawn patrol. Between Burka and Jenin five machines dropped forty bombs and fired 4,000 machine-gun rounds into several retreating columns. The object of the attack was to delay these Turks, in order to allow the cavalry to arrive at El Afule in ample time before them. Congested bodies of troops at Burka and Jenin suffered terrible casualties. They were closely packed, and nearly every bomb fell plumb among them. When the airmen had exhausted their ammunition, they returned to the aerodrome, filled up again, and repeated the attack at noon in the vicinity of the village of Arrabe. Not a man or a beast in this road escaped; those who survived the air attack and finished their march, delivered themselves up gratefully to the light horse in the hills on the southern fringe of the plain of Armageddon.

The troops who fled along this road were mostly from the Turkish Eighth Army overthrown on the previous day. British and Indian infantry were engaged throughout September 20th in fighting resolute rear-guards of that army for the possession of the hills overlooking the road and railway about Messudie. By the end of the day the 60th Division held Anebta, the 7th (Meerut) Division had taken the village of Beit Lid on the hills commanding the road-junction at Deir Sheraf, and the 5th Australian Light Horse Brigade had cut the Jenin railway by occupying Ajjeh, south of Arrabe. These operations sealed the Jenin line of retreat to the Turkish Seventh Army (south of Nablus), which could thereafter escape only by the north-east towards Beisan. The column which Paul and Maughan had discovered at dawn retreating from Nablus in that direction was not, as was at first supposed, the head of the Seventh Army's retreat, but probably reserves from near Nablus. To hold the Seventh Army in its positions, the British XX Corps attacked, with special weight on its left flank, all day of September 20th. Meanwhile detachments of the Desert Mounted Corps pushed on from El Afule and Jenin, northward for Nazareth and eastward for Beisan. By evening of September 20th the cavalry reached Beisan, and closed that road of retreat also to the Turks between Nablus and the Jordan.

The airmen watched from above the convulsions of the entire body of the enemy's army. Throughout September 20th the pulse of this body was the Nablus–Ferweh road, and No. 1 Squadron felt that pulse with the closest attention. About noon Paul and Maughan again patrolled from Huwara to Beisan, and dropped a message to the British cavalry at El Afule reporting the road still clear. Some horse-transport was parked about Ferweh, and a few small groups were on the road—and were duly bombed—but the retreat here had not yet begun. Returning to Ramleh after a four hours' flight, these airmen brought the good news that the rabble on the Jenin road was being captured as fast as it reached the British cavalry outposts near Jenin. Near the front line the enemy, Germans and Turks, under the attack of the 3rd (Lahore) and 10th (Irish) Divisions, were sending back much transport on the Azzun-Funduk road north-eastward towards Nablus. It was clear from this noon reconnaissance that the British victory would fulfil the most sanguine hopes, and that the doom of the Turkish Seventh Army was assured. The enemy still seemed to be unconscious of the fate awaiting him, and his intelligence service and communications were completely stunned. Under the thorough precautions of the S.E.5's, not a German aeroplane was able to take the air from Jenin or El Afule during the whole course of the battle. All evidence pointed to the same conclusion, that the paralysis of the Turco-German Command was complete.[3] One German machine did appear on September 20th. It was a D.F.W., came from the north, and landed at El Afule with two bags of German mail for headquarters. Only after it had reached the ground did its occupants recognise that the aerodrome was in British hands. It tried to take off again, but an armoured car opened fire, wounded its pilot and observer, and they were obliged to stop and give themselves up. At noon on this second day of the battle, the enemy holding the eastern half of the Nablus front was still ignorant of the fact that Allenby's cavalry had completely cut its rear communications.

As for the Turkish Fourth Army, east of Jordan, an Australian patrol at midday found it quietly basking in the sun. From Amman to the Damieh crossing the whole area was placidly asleep, utterly unaware of its danger. The Wady Fara road showed no commotion whatever. The airmen saw some more of the small dribble north-eastward, reported by Paul also, between Nablus and Khurbet Ferweh, and they attacked it as Paul's patrol had done.

The last reconnaissance that day of the region around Nablus discovered the first signs of distress. Three large fires were burning at Nablus railway station, the Balata dumps were also alight, and this great glare under heavy evening clouds formed an alarm signal to the whole Turkish line from El Lubban to the Jordan. During the night that line decamped *en masse;* but too late. The Australian evening patrol which reported the Nablus fires, observed also a brigade of British cavalry from El Afule entering Beisan at the trot. This left no room for doubt. The retreat of the Turkish Seventh Army was closed.

---

[3] On September 21 (notes Williams in his diary) Ross Smith landed at Jenin and El Afule. He found vast quantities of material of all sorts and many aeroplanes burnt. A German officer captured there told him that the Jenin road was bombed every few minutes on September 20, and that he had never imagined that an air force could play such havoc among troops. The columns on the road were completely demoralised. A motor-lorry driver, sent from Nablus to Jenin, said that nobody at Nablus knew the British were at Jenin and El Afule, and that Nablus headquarters suffered severely from the bombing in the morning of September 19.

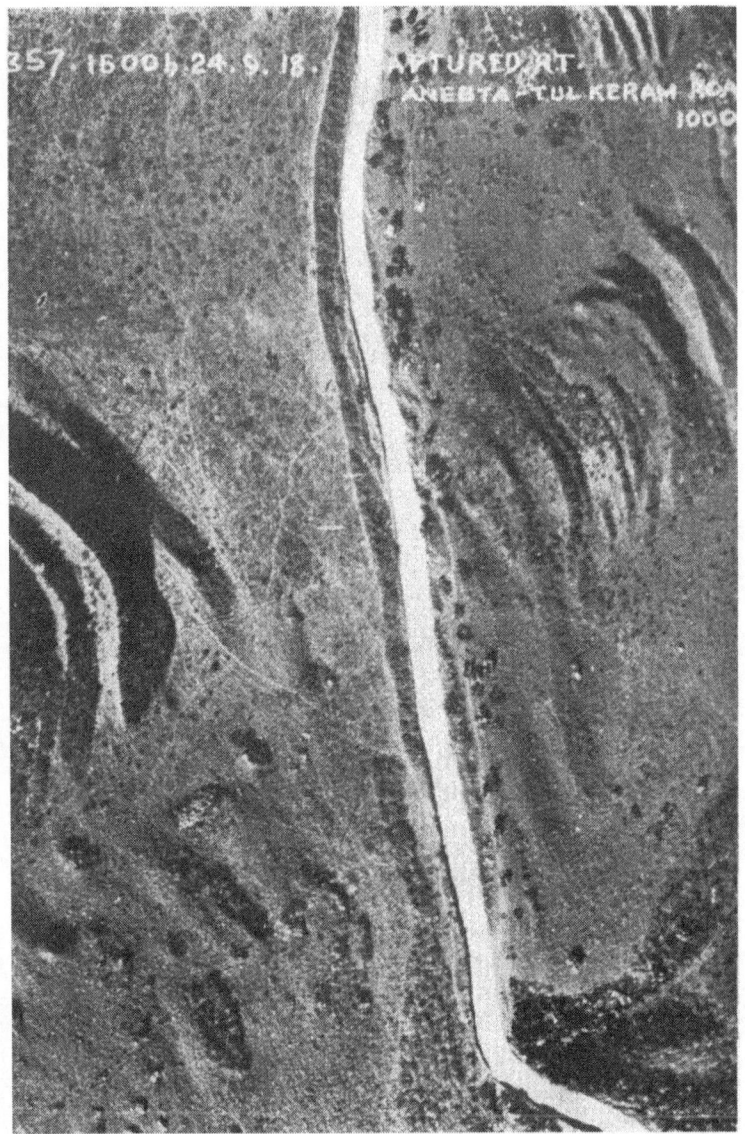

AN AIR-PHOTOGRAPH OF THE TUL KERAM-ANEBTA ROAD SHOWING TURKISH TRANSPORT ABANDONED UNDER THE AIRMEN'S BOMBING ATTACKS ON 19TH SEPTEMBER, 1918

Aust. War Museum Official Photo. No. B3484.
Taken 24th September, 1918.

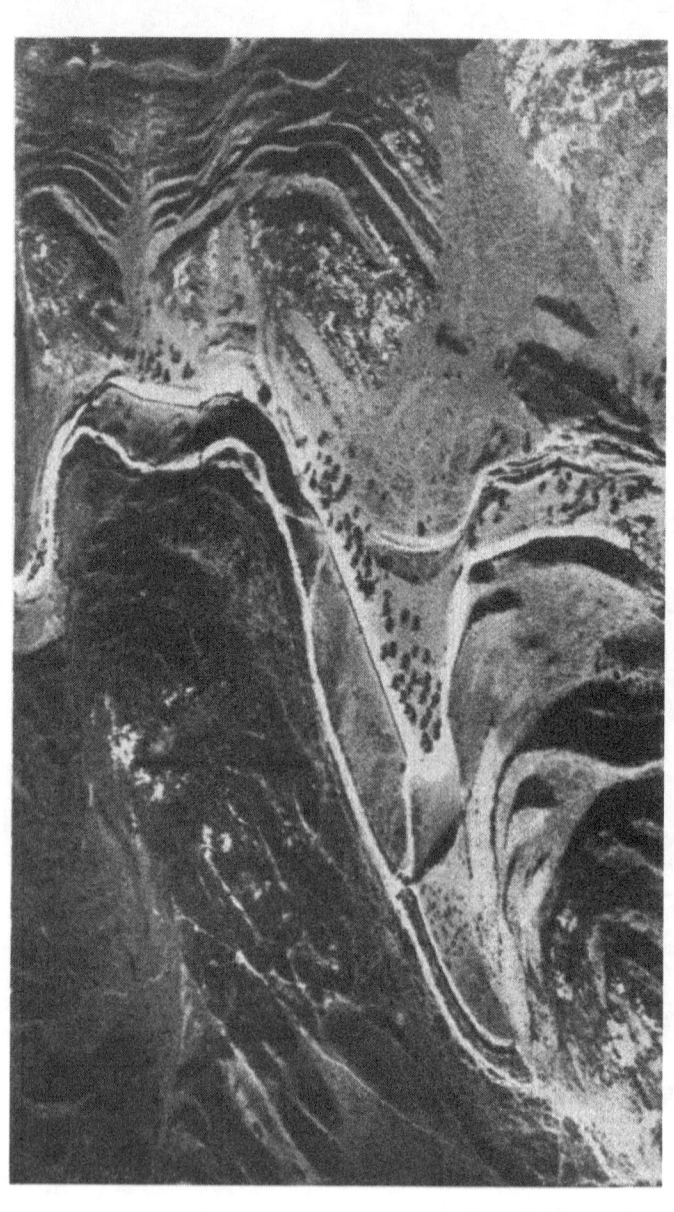

An airman's view of the Khurbet Ferweh–Wady Fara road, after the heavy bombing attacks of 21st September, 1918, showing abandoned Turkish transport

Aust. War Museum Official Photo. No. B3492.
Taken 24th September, 1918.

The advance of the cavalry towards Lake Tiberias, and of the infantry towards Nablus, continued all night, and by dawn on September 21st nearly the whole of Allenby's army was moving northward. In the first pale of sunrise Brown and Finlay (observer) and Nunan and Conrick set off on patrol of the upper Wady Fara. The scene which met their eyes at break of day was unforgettable. Shortly before 6 a.m. Brown sent a message back to the aerodrome by wireless—specially fitted to his machine[4]—reporting that all enemy transport was attempting to escape by way of the Balata–Ferweh–Shibleh–Jordan road. This road, an old Roman highway, runs north-east from Balata along the Wady Beidan, with steep hills on the left hand and a sheer precipice into the wady on the right. At Khurbet Ferweh it crosses the upper Wady Fara and wheels, first east with the wady, and then south-east under the Jebel Tammun ridge, to Ain Shibleh; there it leaves the wady and strikes sharply north-eastward towards the Jordan. On the Jordan cliffs it junctions with the Damieh–Beisan road, and at first is much shut in by hills—still on the left hand—but later enters a broad lowland run into Beisan, crossing innumerable small streams. From Balata towards the Jordan, the important section, the road forms a big S.

Brown and Nunan saw the Turkish Seventh Army transport pouring into Balata from south and south-east, and counted from Balata to Khurbet Ferweh about 600 horse-waggons and guns, which filled the whole length of the road. In Khurbet Ferweh, and for a mile or two beyond it, were over 200 more horse-transport, and approaching Ain Shibleh from either end of the Wady Fara other long columns. From Ain Shibleh, heading north-east, was a mass of cavalry and transport which had passed the worst stage of road. The two Australian machines attacked the troops on the precipice-road between Balata and Khurbet Ferweh, made five direct hits with their bombs on transport, and fired 600 machine-gun rounds into the confusion. That was the beginning of a massacre. By 6.30 a.m. the first three Australian bombing machines, sent out in response to Brown's wireless message, arrived, bombed the column, and raked it from end to end.

---

[4] See Appendix No. 4.

Map No. 8

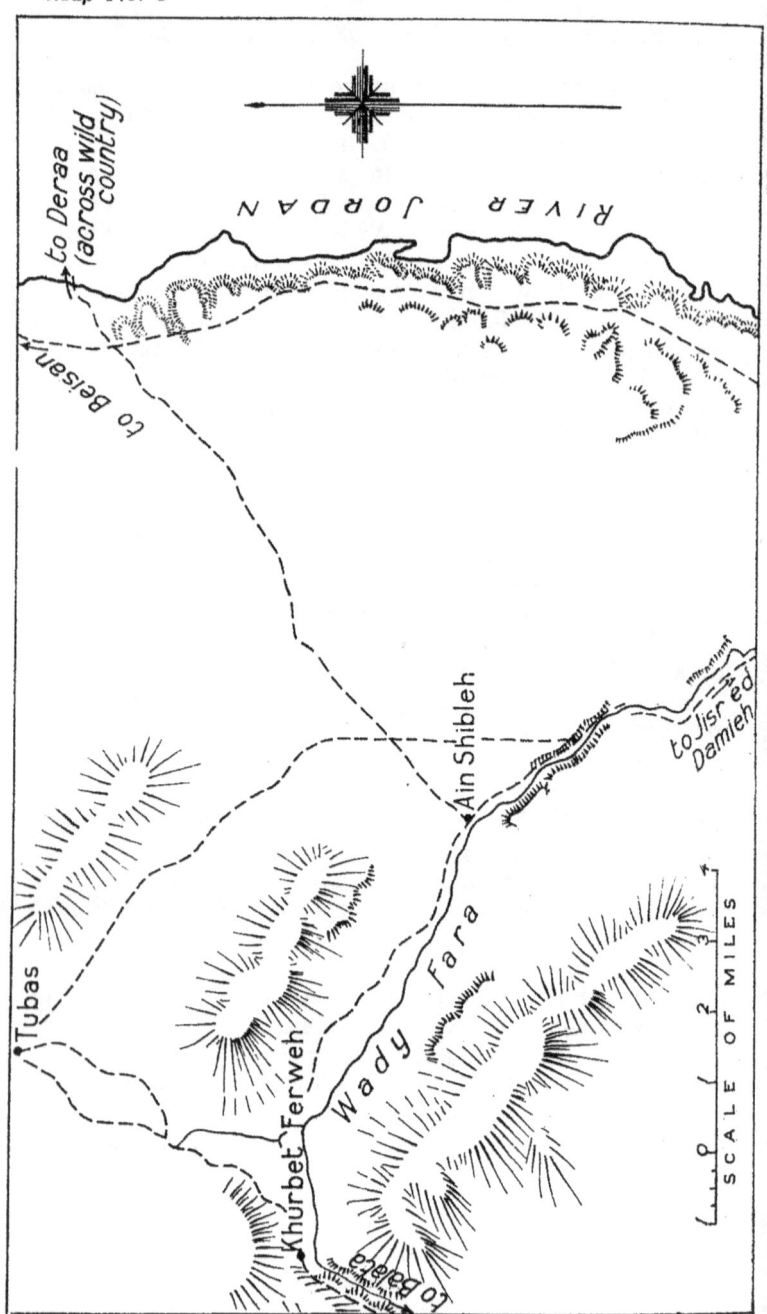

A British formation followed and repeated the attack. All day long air raids were maintained along this S-road by available machines from all squadrons. Towards noon the columns under punishment at that place included thousands of infantry and cavalry as well as transport. No. 1 Squadron made six heavy raids during the day, dropped three tons of bombs, and fired nearly 24,000 machine-gun rounds into the struggling parties in those terrible valleys. Yet this was only half the total ammunition expended, for the British squadrons attacked this same road with another three tons of bombs and 20,000 machine-gun rounds. The panic and the slaughter beggared all description. The long, winding, hopeless column of traffic was so broken and wrecked, so utterly unable to escape from the barriers of hill and precipice, that the bombing machines gave up all attempt to estimate the losses under the attack, and were sickened of the slaughter. In all the history of war there can be few more striking records of wholesale destruction. The passes were completely blocked ahead and behind by overturned motor-lorries and horse-waggons; men deserted their vehicles in a wild scramble to seek cover; many were dragged by the maddened animals over the side of the precipice. Those who were able cut horses from the waggons and rode in panic down the road to Damieh. When British cavalry two days later passed along this road they found abandoned or wrecked 87 guns, 55 motor-lorries, 4 motor-cars, 75 carts, 837 four-wheeled waggons, and scores of water-carts and field-kitchens.

The Turkish Seventh Army as a fighting force was destroyed. In the morning of September 22nd broken parties of that army were again attacked from the air along the Shibleh–Beisan road, near the Jordan, and under this further attack a column of several thousand troops first scattered in panic, and then later were seen marching back towards the Wady Fara under a large white flag. Some fugitive parties crossed the Jordan and wandered across country towards Deraa. There they were met by British cavalry and the Arabs, and very few escaped death or capture. Allenby was now free to devote himself to the advance on Damascus. By the evening of September 25th the 5th Cavalry Division and the Australian Light Horse, followed by infantry, began a forced march from Haifa and Acre and the western shores of Lake Tiberias along the straight road to the capital city of Syria.

During the three days of fighting west of Jordan, the Turkish Fourth Army, between Amman and Shunet Nimrin, did not move. In the evening of September 21st the Shunet Nimrin position was still strongly garrisoned, and the roads and tracks running west from Amman were busy with the usual supply-traffic back and forth. As late as the morning of September 22nd No. 1 Squadron's patrols found Shunet Nimrin undisturbed, though the camp at Rujm el Oshir was broken up and fires were burning west of Amman station. Ain es Sir camp was full of troops. The fugitives who had fled down the Wady Fara to Damieh in the previous afternoon probably carried the alarm to Es Salt, which packed up in haste about midday of the 22nd. Between 3 and 6 p.m. that day Australian airmen saw the whole area stirring and troops and transport steadily making for Amman. Two Bristol Fighters bombed a massed body of traffic at Suweile, half-way between Es Salt and Amman, and fired nearly 1,000 machine-gun rounds into it.

Meanwhile the Deraa railway in the desert had been wrecked at important points. The Arab Northern Army had been collecting in order to join in Allenby's enveloping attack as soon as the cavalry sweep by the coast should succeed. While these Arabs were gathering, Lawrence's mixed force left Azrak and pitched camp at El Umtaiye and Um es Surab, five miles east of the railway between Mafrak and Deraa. It was a daring move, for the Turks were very close, and could have overwhelmed them without difficulty. As it was, the enemy attempted nothing beyond machine-gun defence of the railway stations, when attacked, and air raids from Deraa aerodrome. Lawrence's demolition parties proved more than a match for the railway guard-posts. The German airmen from Deraa, however, badly scared the Arab auxiliaries until machines from No. 1 Squadron arrived upon the scene. From their new raiding centres near the railway, Lawrence's force on September 17th captured Tel Arar station (north of Deraa), blew up the railway bridge over the neighbouring wady, and systematically destroyed ten miles of railway between Deraa and Ghazale. While one detachment was so employed, another, consisting of some Indian infantry and a mountain battery, marched on Mezerib junction (north-west of Deraa), captured it, killed or took prisoners the entire Turkish garrison, burnt the station and rolling-stock, and cut the telegraph line to Nablus.

That night (September 17th) the raiders continued their destruction of the railway from Mezerib in three directions, including nearly ten miles of most effective demolition on the hilly section westward, between Mezerib and Tel esh Shebab. This was on the enemy's main Nablus railway, the supply-line for his entire force west of the Jordan. The first-mentioned raiding party evacuated Ghazale station early on September 18th, and in the afternoon attacked and took Nasib station (south of Deraa), blew up an important viaduct north of Nasib, and destroyed several miles of railway with "tulip" bombs.[5] Similar demolition was continued north and south of Mafrak during September 19th, the day of the British attack.

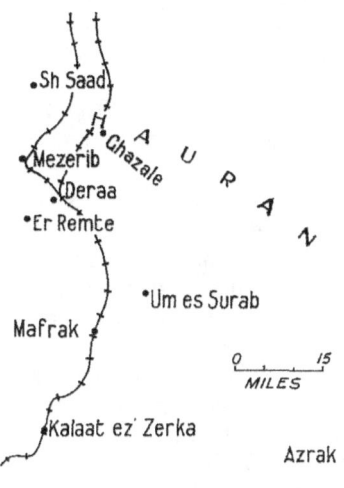

The German airmen at Deraa discovered Lawrence's camp at El Umtaiye, and bombed it several times during September 18th and 19th. The two B.E.12.a's brought from Akaba with the expedition were quite unequal to a combat with these Deraa machines, and both were put out of action—one in an air-fight, one by German bombs.[6] Lawrence decided to represent the situation personally at Allenby's headquarters. Peters and Traill flew from Ramleh to Azrak on September 21st, and there Peters left Traill and returned with Lawrence. Meanwhile Lawrence's raiders retired from El Umtaiye to

---

[5] These bombs were planted under the rails and sleepers and were fired in series. The raiders facetiously styled this effort "tulip-planting," and the name stuck.

[6] Murphy and Hawley, who had a Bristol Fighter with Lawrence's force (see p. 149) were away at this time. They apparently flew a British officer back to Akaba on some mission.

Um es Surab, a place whose only perceptible merit was that it was farther away from the hornet's nest at Deraa. On September 22nd Lawrence, on his return journey, reached Um es Surab in the observer's seat of Peters' machine. Ross Smith and Mustard (observer) and Headlam and Lilly were sent with Peters in order to attack the German machines at Deraa. The news which the airmen brought of the events on the coast greatly excited the force in the desert. The Arabs received the Bristol Fighters with acclamation, but when next day the giant Handley-Page machine arrived at Um es Surab the tribes were moved to the wildest enthusiasm. They sang, danced, and cheered around it, firing volleys into the air in an ecstasy of delight.

The German air force at Deraa, which consisted of three Pfalz scouts and a number of D.F.W. two-seaters, soon received a rude shock. The three Bristol Fighters arrived at Um es Surab in the early forenoon of September 22nd. The airmen were sitting at breakfast at 10 o'clock when enemy aircraft were reported to be approaching. Ross Smith and Headlam at once took off and sighted two Pfalz scouts and one D.F.W. two-seater. The enemy turned for home as soon as they saw the Bristol Fighters, but the Australians shot down the two-seater near Mafrak, killing one German, and set the machine alight on the ground They then returned to resume their breakfast—their porridge, according to one account, was kept hot for them the while—but at 10.30 a.m. three more Pfalz scouts were reported in sight. Ross Smith and Mustard again flew out and drove down all three. Two landed near the railway and ran along the ground to Turkish outposts; the third returned hurriedly to Deraa. The Australians, after the chase to Deraa, visited the other two machines and fired fifty rounds into each on the ground at close quarters. In the afternoon a D.F.W. bombed Um es Surab camp, but was pursued by Peters and Traill and driven down smoking near its aerodrome. Peters flew low over it as it lay on the ground, and Traill destroyed it with Lewis gun-fire and killed its pilot and observer. Early next morning Kenny and Maughan from Ramleh dropped sixteen bombs on the Deraa aerodrome, set one hangar on fire, and destroyed or damaged several two-seaters. That night the Handley-

Page completed the wreck and shattered the railway station with nearly a ton of bombs, dropped from 1,000 feet with excellent effect. From this time onward nothing more was heard of the Deraa air force until British troops occupied the place and found the burnt remains of machines and stores. The Bristol Fighters remained at Um es Surab until September 27th, bombing Turkish working parties on the railway. Their presence attracted numbers of wavering tribes to the Arab army, and henceforth throughout the Hauran hills Bedouin co-operation against the Turks was assured.

At Amman the Turks were now in full flight, with Deraa, their goal, already devastated, and the railway, their one hope, wrecked beyond present repair. They may have consoled themselves with the fact that they were at least in better case than their comrades farther south about Maan. Brown and Finlay, reconnoitring at dawn on September 23rd, observed a column of fairly orderly traffic of all arms streaming down the road from Es Salt to Amman, and other bodies making towards the same place from the hills to the south-west. They bombed and machine-gunned this column, and flew off to Ramleh with the news. Kenny and Sutherland (observer) and Maughan and McCann about the same time saw the Turks at Semakh and Deraa fleeing for their lives. Semakh camps were seen to be burnt, and a long train with steam up was facing east. It would never arrive anywhere, for ahead of it were the Arabs and a destroyed track. At Deraa the airmen saw a few abandoned machines on the landing-ground, and one, a D.F.W., in the air. Kenny and Sutherland promptly shot down this German and bombed it on the ground. In Deraa station were a couple of trains pointing northward towards a plain already littered with Bedouin parties; frenzied men were scrambling on to the roofs of some of the carriages. Ragged parties of Turks were approaching from the hill-fringed plain in the south-west, survivors of the unhappy flight from Nablus. And this was the refuge towards which the Fourth Army from Amman was making in headlong retreat!

That morning (September 23rd) the first bombing formation of six Bristol Fighters fell upon the retreating columns on the Es Salt–Amman road soon after 7 a.m. The retreat, begun in good order, was soon converted into a rout like that around Nablus, and by the same means. The raiders dropped forty-eight bombs into the traffic, aiming especially at any thickly-grouped transport in order to block the road. Eight direct hits on waggons or lorries achieved the purpose. Men fled into wadys for cover; under a withering fire of 7,000 machine-gun rounds every man and beast who could leave the road did so. Thereafter the day's air attacks were directed upon Amman, where traffic was converging from all quarters. No. 1 Squadron's machines expended here during the day nearly three tons of bombs and 15,000 machine-gun rounds, and British bombing formations half as much again.

By afternoon of September 24th nearly all the area west of Amman was clear of the enemy, and General Chaytor's force— the Anzac Mounted Division and some odd infantry units— was east of Ain es Sir and was advancing on Amman from two directions. On September 25th a new bombing target appeared. The head of a mixed column from Amman was seen in the early morning at Mafrak and to the south of that place—300 horse-transport and guns, 600 camels, and 3,000 infantry and cavalry. Between 6 and 8 o'clock ten Australian machines attacked and utterly demoralised this force. The wreckage which they caused at Mafrak station was enormous; several dumps were blown to pieces, and a long train, which 500 infantry were entering, was shattered. The obstruction of the railway resulting from this attack was fatal. A number of trains reached Mafrak during the day from Amman, and, as each one arrived, it was attacked by a fresh air formation. No. 1 Squadron bombed the place three times with all available machines; the British squadrons alternated in relays with them. The airmen in all dropped here four tons of bombs and fired nearly 20,000 machine-gun rounds. The losses of the Turks were awful. The fate of many survivors—men and beasts— was worse than the fate of those destroyed under the airmen's scourge. Many horses were found later starving or dying of thirst and covered with wounds, sores, and galls. Many Turks fled into the desert. The Arabs found some mad for want of water; others were never seen again. Still, despite the destruction wrought upon the retreat at Mafrak, some thousands of men on foot or horse, having abandoned the wheeled-transport, managed to escape from the slaughter and

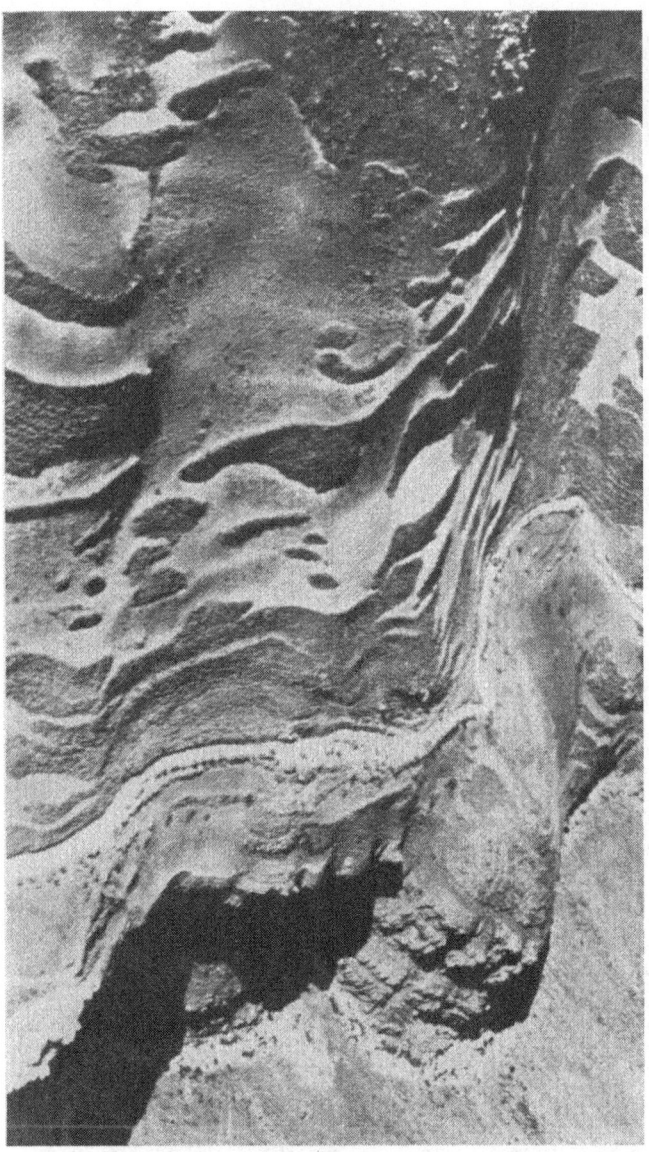

THE BALATA-KHURBET FERWEH ROAD—WITH MOUNTAINSIDE (ABOVE) AND A PRECIPITOUS VALLEY (BELOW)—SHOWING ENEMY TRANSPORT ABANDONED AFTER THE AIR-RAIDS OF 21ST SEPTEMBER, 1918

Aust. War Museum Official Photo. No. B3494.
Taken 24th September, 1918.

NABLUS, FROM THE AIR

Aust. War Museum Official Photo. No. B3486.
Taken 24th September, 1918.

To face p. 167.

plodded on towards Deraa and Damascus. Two British airmen of No. 144 Squadron, captured by the Turks on September 17th, marched with their captors in the retreat from Es Salt. They were found later near Deraa with a wounded light horseman, whom they had carried or pushed in a cart from Mafrak to Deraa. They described the ghastly terror of the retreat under constant bomb-attacks from Es Salt to Mafrak; they had no food rations issued to them after leaving Amman, where the Turks, they said, abandoned all stores and all further desire to fight. They left Deraa in a Turkish train; at a destroyed part of the line the train ahead of them ran off the rails, and their own train collided with it. Only one of the airmen had strength enough to escape. He walked back to Deraa to get help, and there found the British cavalry.

In all some 6,000 or 7,000 fugitives, mostly from the Fourth Turkish Army, escaped by way of Deraa or the Lake Tiberias road towards Damascus. There was little serious rear-guard fighting, though the cavalry and the Australian Light Horse were held up for some hours by a broken bridge, and by some opposition beyond it, at Jisr Benat Yakub (Bridge of the Daughters of Jacob) on the upper Jordan, north of Lake Tiberias. Ahead of the cavalry the Australian airmen reconnoitred Damascus 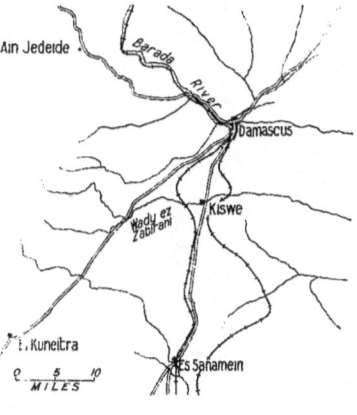 for the first time on September 27th. The railway station was filled with hundreds of rolling-stock. On the roads southward from both Deraa and the Jordan were parties of troops and transport in full flight. In the afternoon of September 28th four Bristol Fighters raided Damascus aerodrome, where eight D.F.W.'s had been seen by the morning patrol. Next morning Brown and Finlay reported the aerodrome burnt, no machines to be seen there, and Damascus plainly being evacuated in haste.

The remnant of the Turkish II Corps, previously in the Maan region, surrendered to Chaytor's Force at Amman on September 28th. Of the Turkish Fourth, Seventh, and Eighth Armies there remained, therefore, on September 29th still at large only about 6,000 men fleeing from the Arabs in a bee-line for Damascus. Brown, on that morning's patrol already-mentioned, saw practically the full strength of these survivors on the road about twenty miles south of the city. They were in several parties and had only about 150 horse-transport and 300 camels. At the outskirts of Damascus were a few hundred more infantry with pack-camels. Five Australian machines bombed these columns at noon, smashed numbers of waggons, and inflicted losses on the troops. The Turks everywhere fled from the road. This attack occurred just south of Kiswe, on the Wady Zabirani. Maughan and Weir saw the last of this unhappy retreat on September 30th; about 4,000 infantry and cavalry were scattered along the north bank of the Zabirani, under the hill Jebel Aswad. Maughan dived at them, but the Turks remained sitting resignedly on the ground, too exhausted to move. They had run to a finish. The Australians, in pity, abstained from firing on them. In the afternoon Nunan and Conrick broke up a small machine-gun defence-post on the road at the south-west entrance to Damascus, which was holding up the British cavalry, and attacked some Turks fleeing along the Beirut road. Next morning, October 1st, the cavalry and light horse entered the city.[7]

Little more remains to be told. While some of the British mounted troops occupied Damascus, other columns with armoured cars had skirted it and were pursuing the late Damascus garrison up the roads to Beirut and Homs. During the following days No. 1 Squadron moved from Ramleh to an aerodrome at Haifa, and in mid-October one flight was detached for advance-guard work and operated in turn from Homs and Hama. The enemy's rapid retreat made it necessary for the Bristol Fighters to patrol an exceptionally wide area of country. Reconnaissance flights were demanded over vast distances, sometimes as great as 500 or 600 miles, and advanced landing-grounds were selected far ahead of Allenby's main

---

[7] Major Addison writes:—"After our entry into Damascus on October 1, it was found that the remnant of the Turkish armies in Palestine and Syria, numbering about 17,000, of whom only 4,000 were effective rifles, had fled northward in a disorganised mob without transport or equipment."

army. In assistance of the cavalry and armoured cars the Australian airmen reconnoitred Rayak, Homs, Beirut, Tripoli, Hama, and Aleppo, as the pursuit drove ever northward. Towards the end of October they roamed the air as far north as Killis and Alexandretta. They met with little opposition, but some bombing still continued, chiefly against the last of the German aerodromes. One of these, at Rayak, was raided on October 2nd, and another, at Muslimie (junction of the Baghdad railway), north of Aleppo, on October 23rd. When the British advance-guard subsequently reached these places it found good evidence of damage wrought by the air raids. At Rayak thirty-two German machines, including some of the latest type, had been either abandoned or burnt by the enemy.

The pace of the pursuit was governed entirely by the supply service and the capacity of the cavalry horses. Cavalry and armoured cars kept touch as far as possible with the Turks under the guidance of the scouting airmen. There was no more fighting except from the air. On October 9th five Bristol Fighters attacked with bombs and machine-gun fire troops entraining at Homs station, and trains at Hama station were likewise raided on October 16th. Three days later Ross Smith and McCann (observer) and Headlam and Lilly met the first German seen in the air since the fights over the desert at Deraa. It was a D.F.W. two-seater. They forced it to land, and the German pilot and observer left the machine and stood away on the ground with hands up. The Australians landed near by, fired a Very light into the D.F.W., and set it ablaze. They were obliged to leave their airmen-prisoners behind, because the ground was so soft that the Bristol Fighter would not have been able to take off with the extra weight. It started away just as a group of excited Bedouin horsemen galloped up to the burning machine.

The attack on Muslimie junction was noteworthy for the daring enterprise of Lieutenants S. H. Harper[8] and Lilly, who on early morning patrol met two D.F.W's and chased them down to the aerodrome. There were four more two-seaters just about to take off, and these six machines were apparently all that was left of the German flying corps in Syria. Harper

---

[8] Lieut. S. H. Harper; No. 1 Sqn. Fitter and turner; b. Armidale, N.S.W., 1895.

Map No. 9

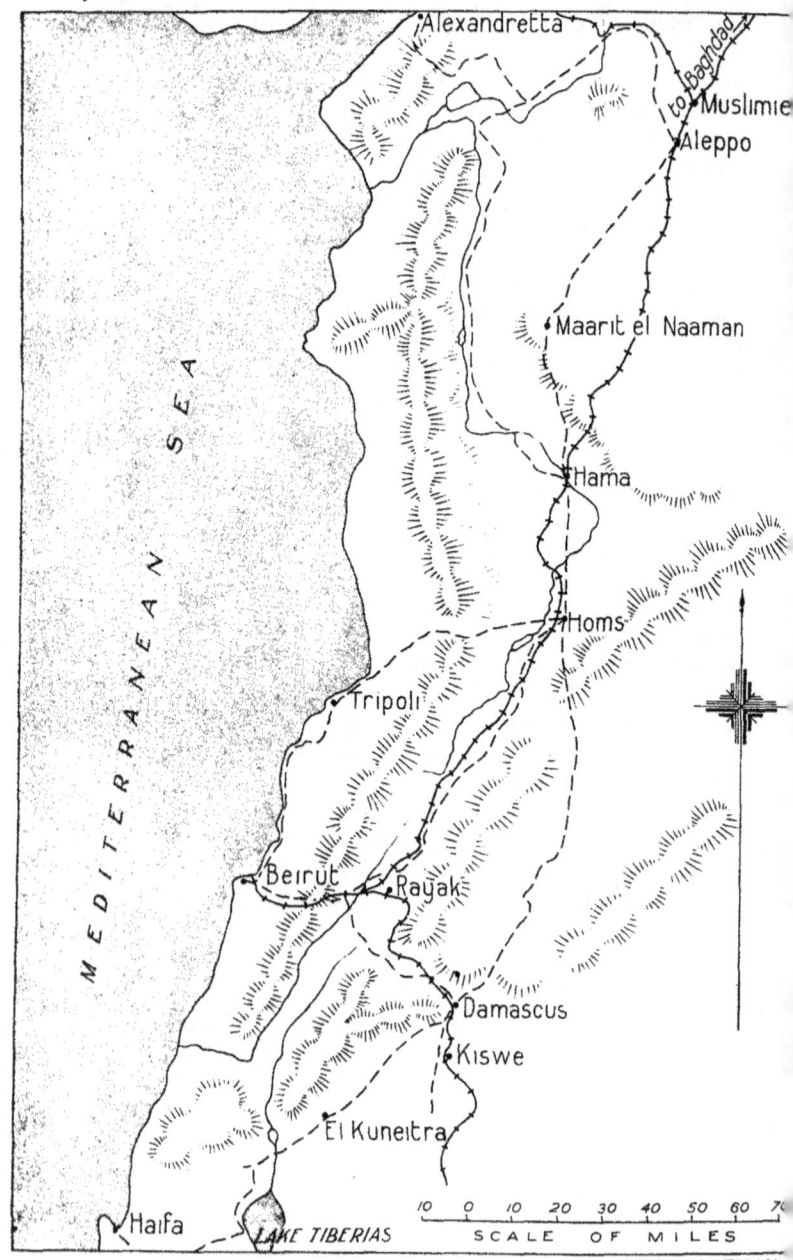

SYRIA, SHOWING THE AREA OF THE LAST STAGES OF THE CAMPAIGN AGAINST THE TURKS

attacked all six with bombs, and he and Lilly flew low overhead, back and forth, firing into them; but not one of the Germans rose to the challenge. Three hours later two other Bristol Fighters found the aerodrome deserted and burnt, and at noon five more Australian machines bombed Aleppo station and severely damaged buildings and railway. On October 26th armoured cars and the Hejaz Arabs occupied Aleppo, and British cavalry were north-west of the town riding towards Alexandretta.

An armistice on October 31st ended the war with Turkey. No. 1 Squadron moved back to Ramleh in December and to Kantara in February, 1919. There, at one of its last parades, on February 19th, General Allenby, who travelled from Haifa to Kantara for this special purpose, addressed the officers and men of the squadron in a farewell speech. It was a fitting *finale* to their splendid service career. General Allenby said:—

"Major Addison, officers, and men: It gives me considerable pleasure to have this opportunity of addressing you prior to your return to Australia. We have just reached the end of the greatest war known to history. The operations in this theatre of the war have been an important factor in bringing about the victorious result. The victory gained in Palestine and Syria has been one of the greatest in the war, and undoubtedly hastened the collapse that followed in other theatres. This squadron played an important part in making this achievement possible. You gained for us absolute supremacy of the air, thereby enabling my cavalry, artillery, and infantry to carry out their work on the ground practically unmolested by hostile aircraft. This undoubtedly was a factor of paramount importance in the success of our arms here. I desire therefore personally to congratulate you on your splendid work. I congratulate you, not only the flying officers, but also your mechanics, for although the officers did the work in the air, it was good work on the part of your mechanics that kept a high percentage of your machines serviceable. I wish you all *bon voyage,* and trust that the peace now attained will mean for you all future happiness and prosperity. Thank you, and good-bye."

CHAPTER XIII

AUSTRALIAN AIRMEN IN FRANCE

IN both Mesopotamia and Egypt the Australian airmen were among the pioneers of the aerial arm of war, and bore their share in the experimental stages and development of the flying service. On the Western Front, in France and Belgium, they were late arrivals. To this front were sent three squadrons of the four which Australia maintained in the field. There the Australian airmen found air warfare already a highly-developed science, and they were plunged from the outset into an experienced system of fighting, not so much of individual combats, as of strong formations.

The expectations of a short and lively war, prevalent in 1914, had by the spring of 1915 given place to the certainty of a grim and protracted struggle between immense and increasing armies entrenched against each other from the North Sea to the Swiss mountains. While the armies on this front swelled in numbers and accumulated vast quantities of artillery and other engines of war, each side for two years of fluctuating campaigns strove to win on the Russian front the decisive victory which might bring a solution of the deadlock in the west. The breaking of the fortified lines in France would plainly be a costly effort to either army. The serried rows of barbed-wire entanglements, the array of artillery and machine-guns, dismayed the infantry trench-garrisons, both of the Allies and of the Germans. On this Western Front during these earlier campaigns the Germans attempted twice to break through—once at Ypres in April, 1915, before the northern flank of the Allied line was firmly entrenched, and again at Verdun in the spring of 1916. Each attempt failed, although each nearly succeeded. The strategy of the Allies at those dates was governed largely by the policy of assisting the operations of the Russians. The French attack in Champagne, the weak British efforts at Neuve Chapelle and Loos, in 1915, were impressive in their failure to dislodge the confident German line. It became clear that an offensive against that line, wherever delivered, would demand the concentrated force of all reserves in the Allied armies. Nothing less could succeed.

In 1916 each side attempted such an offensive. The British and French Commands prepared a blow at the point of junction of their armies on the Somme, and this attack was to synchronise with one by the Russians in Galicia. The necessity of waiting for the snows to melt on the Russian front compelled the Allies to delay the operations in the west until the spring was far advanced. The advantage of initiative thus lay with the Germans. They seized it at the earliest possible moment, and in February attacked with great force the French at Verdun. The artillery fire brought to bear on the French forts and trenches was terrific beyond any bombardment yet experienced in war. After a swaying battle of several months Verdun held firm, but the conflict exhausted much of the French strength, and when at length, on July 1st, the Anglo-French offensive began on the Somme, the Allies acknowledged an objective over and above the original plan—the necessity of relieving the pressure on Verdun. Therein the Somme offensive, in which the Australian divisions played a renowned part, met with success; the penetration of the German lines between Bapaume and Péronne, together with the drain of men towards the Russian front, compelled the enemy to relinquish his assault on Verdun. For a time the Somme offensive progressed hopefully, but was then itself brought to a dead halt, partly through the exhaustion of the Allies, but even more through the impossibility of carrying the army forward over a terrain ruined by artillery-fire and swamped by the autumn rains. The effort died away in the early winter.

On the Western Front the offensive in 1917 lay with the Allies. The German plans for that year were to stand on the defensive in France and to attack in Russia. The strategy of the British and French Commands devised a double blow on the German line south of Arras (weakened by the 1916 Somme offensive)—the British to attack at Arras and the French in Champagne. The enemy to a large extent deranged this scheme by withdrawing in the early spring—again before the snows had melted—from Bapaume to the strongly-fortified Hindenburg Line which ran from south-east of Lens to St.

Quentin. The British attack at Arras in April recovered the Vimy Ridge; the French companion-attack in Champagne was stopped after the opening stage by political interference with the French military command and by local but serious mutinies in certain French divisions. Thereafter the British Army alone continued the offensive on the Western Front, and the British Army exhausted itself in four months of bloody fighting at Ypres for the Passchendaele Ridge. When this campaign opened on July 31st, the hope was that the thrust might roll up the enemy's right flank to the line of the Scheldt and win back the Belgian coast. Any such hope was shattered by the wet summer, and from early August till late November the attacking divisions, constantly replaced and retried, floundered in a morass of mud in the blighted countryside east of Ypres. The German Army suffered equal, if not worse, torture in that soul-devastating struggle. The artillery-fire and the rain storms made effective movement on either side impossible.

Then, at the end of November, came General Byng's surprise attack on the Hindenburg Line before Cambrai. He broke down the German wire, not with artillery-fire, but with a great line of tanks. The effort nearly succeeded; perhaps, if sufficient reserves had been available, its success would have been complete. It introduced new tactics of assault upon fortified trench-lines. It alarmed the enemy, who had affected to despise the tanks. It gave new hope to an army which had been enslaved to nerve-shattering preliminary artillery bombardments. Henceforth disappeared the old plan of blowing to bits the surface of an area which infantry were to assault, and over which subsequently it was generally impossible to move up the necessary guns and stores.

The Battle of Cambrai marked the advent on the Western Front of No. 2, No. 3, and No. 4 Squadrons of the Australian Flying Corps.[1] In the final campaign of 1918 those squadrons played their full part, both in defeating the terrific German offensive in March and April towards Amiens, Hazebrouck, and Noyon, and in the grand counter-offensive of all the Allies, which began under Foch in July between Soissons and

---

[1] Originally numbered respectively Nos. 68, 69, and 71 Squadrons, R.F.C., and so known on service until Jan., 1918. The squadrons, for sake of simplicity, are referred to throughout this record by their later (Australian) numbers.

the Marne, and in a few weeks extended northwards towards Flanders and eastwards through Champagne.

The three Australian air squadrons—untrained, unequipped, and incompletely formed—arrived in England in the winter of 1916-17, at a time when the British were straining every nerve to beat the Germans in the air. The era when the Fokker had had all its own way was over; on the Allied side improved machines—Nieuports, Spads, S.E.5's, Sopwiths, and Bristol Fighters—were coming forward to challenge the German designers. The race was for manœuvring and climbing speed, and for superiority in the power-unit. Of the Australian squadrons, No. 3, under the command of Major Blake, landed in England on the 28th December, 1916; No. 2, under the command of Major Watt, on the 30th January, 1917; No. 4, under Captain A. Lang,[2] on the 27th March, 1917. All three squadrons were strengthened by the attachment from No. 1 Squadron of experienced flying officers and aerodrome personnel. No. 3 Squadron was sent for training to South Carlton, Lincolnshire (23rd Training Wing, R.F.C.), No. 2 to Harlaxton, Grantham, Lincolnshire (24th Training Wing, R.F.C.), and No. 4 to Castle Bromwich, near Birmingham (25th Training Wing, R.F.C.).[3] Soon after the arrival of No. 4 Squadron in England Major Sheldon took over the command from Captain Lang. The training lasted in each case for about eight months, and was carried out so as to familiarise pilots and mechanics with every possible type of aeroplane which they might have to use in France. The time had arrived when pilots and observers were really taught the new science, and were not, as in the earlier days, sent abroad to pick it up as best they could over the battle-lines. Besides the technique of the aeroplane, they were called upon to learn intimately the construction of machine-guns and Lewis guns, shooting from the air, navigation by compass, observation of country and the tricks of distinguishing ground objects from the new angle, the practice of photography from the air, and the artillery-officer's work of battery-ranging and "spotting" for fire-effect. In addition, pilots and observers

---

[2] Capt. A. Lang; No. 4 Sqn. (afterwards well known as a test-pilot of new fighting-types in England). Motor engineer; of Melbourne, Vic.; b. Corowa, N.S.W., 25 Aug., 1888.

[3] The squadrons' training in England is sketched in Appendix No. 5.

received from experienced pilots regular lectures upon local conditions on the Western Front, and upon the latest tactics in the science of air fighting.

McCudden in his book describes what highly important advantages in this matter the later-trained pilots possessed over those who had fought in the early part of the war. Writing of a period which he spent as a training officer with the home establishment early in 1917, he says:—" I often explained how much better off they (the later pilots) were in their training than were the pilots who had gone out to fight in the air a year previously, for at this time the pilots were receiving very good training indeed, and were quite competent to go into their first fight with a good chance of downing their opponent. At the time I went to France to fly a fighter-aeroplane I had not even flown the type which I was to fly over the lines next morning, let alone not having received any fighting instruction. I must admit that even after I had flown for five weeks over the lines as a pilot, when I went on to De Havilland scouts I did not even appreciate the necessity of turning at once when an opponent got behind me, and I only just realised that I had to get directly behind him to get a shot at him."[4]

Several Australian pilots, in the two fighting-scout squadrons which were being trained in England, obtained their first experience of war in the air before their squadrons did. They were pilots who early revealed marked proficiency during the home training, and it was obviously to the advantage of a raw unit that it should include as many experienced men as possible. As has already been explained, there were distributed among all three service squadrons in England both flying officers and mechanics who had seen service with No. 1 Squadron in Egypt. This was especially the case with No. 2 Squadron.[5] Air fighting in France, however, was considerably more severe and made far heavier demands upon the scout pilot than air fighting in the East. Of the two Australian scout squadrons in England, No. 2 was two months ahead of No. 4 in general training, and was therefore due earlier for

---

[4] *Five Years in the Royal Flying Corps* (pp. 175-6).
[5] The late Colonel Watt stated that No. 2 Squadron was composed (except for ten of its ground personnel) entirely of men who had been on service in Egypt with the light horse or with No. 1 Squadron, or with both.

despatch to the front. In July and August, 1917, several pilots of No. 2 Squadron were sent to France for a period of three or four weeks' battle-flying experience with British fighting-scout squadrons on service at Ypres. Among these were Lieutenants V. A. Norvill[6] (attached to No. 29 Squadron), and Lieutenants G. C. Matthews,[7] G. C. Wilson,[8] H. G. Forrest,[9] and Captain R. C. Phillipps[10] (attached to No. 32 Squadron). Four of the five returned from this service and shortly became flight-commanders in their own squadron.[11] Norvill flew several times with British fighting patrols during the reconnaissances preliminary to the Third Battle of Ypres. He was shot down, wounded, and taken prisoner on July 29th after a sharp fight over the lines between seven British machines and twenty-five German scouts.

The honour of being the first Australian flying unit to arrive in France belongs to No. 3 Squadron. Leaving observers, transport personnel, and other details to go by water, the three flights (each of six machines) left South Carlton by air on the 24th August, 1917, under Major Blake and flew to Lympne in Kent, the first stage. Each pilot carried an air-mechanic in the observer's seat. One machine, which was forced to land in Kent before reaching Lympne, crashed on taking off again, and both occupants, Lieutenant F. C. Shapira[12] and Air-Mechanic W. D. Sloane,[13] were killed. The other machines were detained at Lympne for some days by orders from France and by bad weather, but finally, on September 9th, flew across to St. Omer, and thence next day to their appointed aerodrome at Savy, half-way between St. Pol and Arras. Here the squadron was posted to 1st (Corps) Wing,

---

[6] Lieut. V. A. Norvill; No. 2 Sqn. Mechanical engineer; b. Melbourne, 31 May, 1895.

[7] Capt. G. C. Matthews, A.F.C.; No. 4 Sqn. (previously Light Horse). Master mariner; b. Stranraer, Scotland, 25 July, 1883.

[8] Capt. G. C. Wilson, M.C., A.F.C., D.C.M.; No. 2 Sqn. (previously Engineers). Pattern maker; b. Minnie, Northumberland, Eng., Aug., 1895.

[9] Capt. H. G. Forrest, D.F.C.; No. 2 Sqn. (previously Infantry). Clerk; b. Brunswick, Melbourne, 5 Dec., 1895.

[10] Maj. R. C. Phillipps, M.C., D.F.C.; No. 2 Sqn. (previously Infantry). Accountant; of Perth, W. Aust.; b. North Sydney, 1 March, 1892.

[11] See note at end of chapter.

[12] Lieut. F. C. Shapira; No. 3 Sqn. (previously Infantry). Accountant; of Sydney; b. Stepney, London, Eng., 30 July, 1889. Killed in aeroplane accident, 24 Aug., 1917.

[13] Air-Mechanic W. D. Sloane; No. 3 Sqn. Motor engineer; b. Mulwala, N.S.W., 1890. Killed in aeroplane accident, 24 Aug., 1917.

R.F.C.[14] For purposes of initiation into active service it was ordered to act as supporting squadron to the British corps squadrons[15] on duty with the two army corps in the line—No. 5 Squadron, R.F.C. (with the Canadian Corps), and No. 16 Squadron, R.F.C. (with the XIII Corps). The Australian pilots and observers, who were at first given but minor tasks, in order to "learn the line," settled down promptly to the duty of watching for enemy gun-flashes, observing movement in the German forward areas, and conducting some of the counter-battery work of the two British corps squadrons.

No. 2 Squadron followed twelve days later under Major Watt. All its machines flew on September 21st from Harlaxton to St. Omer in the one day—a record in the British service—and next day to Warloy, close to Baizieux, the site of their appointed aerodrome. In Baizieux, fated in the following year to become still more closely connected with the Australian forces, the squadron installed its D.H.5's in its first service hangars. There it was attached to the 13th (Army) Wing, R.F.C., operating with the British Third Army.

In the course of their early reconnaissances several machines of No. 3 Squadron fired their first shots at the enemy at close quarters, though without serious combat. No. 2 Squadron—naturally perhaps, being scouts—fought the first Australian air combat. A patrol of four D.H.5's led by Captain W. A. McCloughry,[16] when coming back from over St. Quentin at 10,000 feet just before noon on October 2nd, saw an enemy two-seater below, and the leader immediately dived towards it. The German made for the ground, and the D.H.5's had to abandon the chase, the German having the speed of them. A quarter of an hour later they met another two-seater, which Lieutenants L. H. Holden[17] and R. W. Howard[18] attacked; but this too escaped by superior speed.

---

[14] In consequence of the amalgamation of the Royal Flying Corps and the Royal Naval Air Service on 1 April, 1918, under the new title of the Royal Air Force, the initials R.F.C. in the description of British squadrons became changed to R.A.F.

[15] For organisation and duties of the British air service in the field see Appendix No. 6.

[16] Maj. W. A. McCloughry, D.S.O., M.C., D.F.C.; commanded No. 4 Sqn., 1917/18. Law student; of Adelaide; b. Knightsbridge, S. Aust., 26 Nov., 1894.

[17] Capt. L. H. Holden, M.C., A.F.C.; No. 2 Sqn. (previously Infantry). Assistant-manager; of Turramurra, Sydney; b. East Adelaide, 6 March, 1895.

[18] Capt. R. W. Howard, M.C.; No. 2 Sqn. (previously Engineers). Engineering student; of Hamilton, N.S.W.; b. Sydney, 9 Oct., 1896. Died of wounds, 22 March, 1918.

OFFICERS OF NO. 3 SQUADRON, A.F.C., BERTANGLES, MAY, 1918

Aust. War Museum Official Photo. No. E2765.

To face p. 178.

R.E.8 (USED BY No. 3 SQUADRON, A.F.C., FROM SEPTEMBER, 1917, ONWARDS)

Aust. War Museum Official Photo. No. E4320.

To face p. 179.

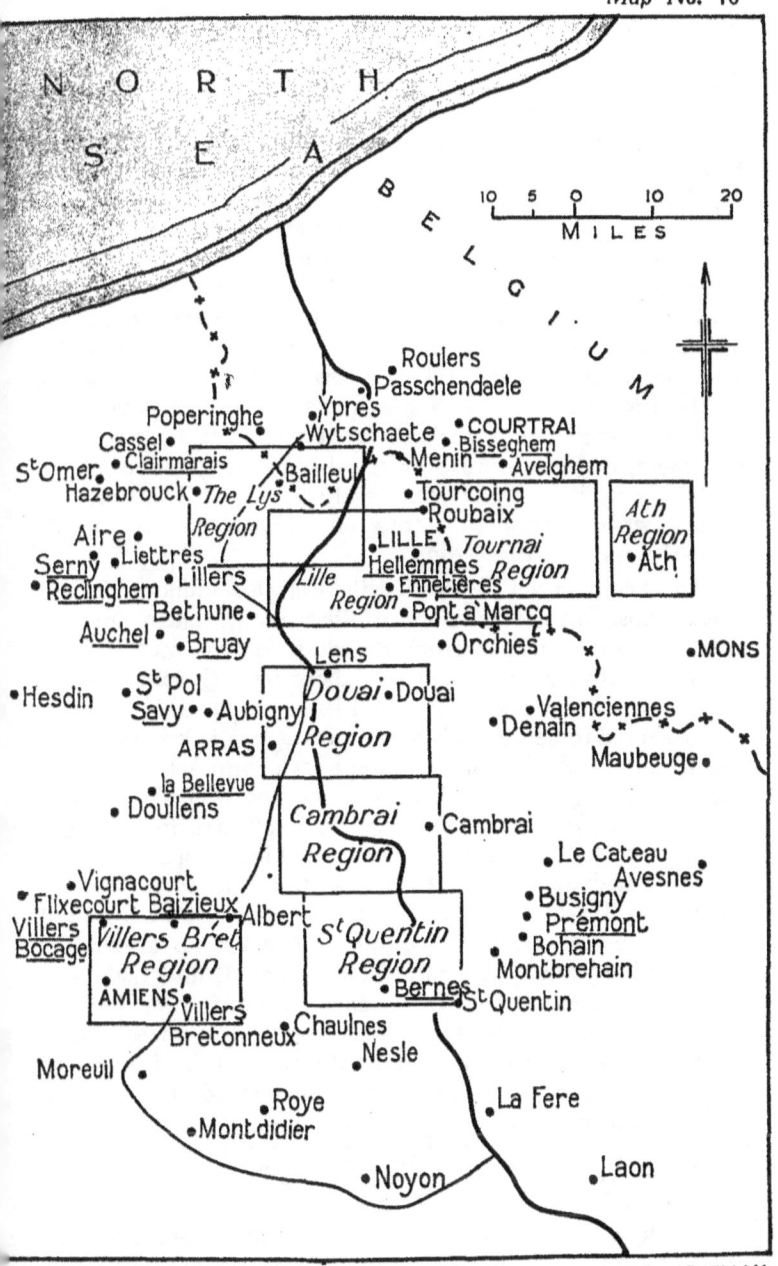

Map No. 10

P.R.WIGHTMAN

NORTH-EASTERN FRANCE, SHOWING THE AREAS ILLUSTRATED BY OTHER MAPS IN THIS VOLUME. THE DARK LINE MARKED SHOWS THE FRONT HELD BY THE ALLIES IN OCTOBER, 1917, AT THE BEGINNING OF THE A.F.C. OPERATIONS IN FRANCE. THE THIN LINE SHOWS THE LIMITS OF THE GERMAN ADVANCE IN 1918. THE NAMES OF AERODROMES OCCUPIED AT ANY TIME BY AUSTRALIAN SQUADRONS ARE UNDERLINED

The Australian formation flew home, missing Lieutenant I. C. F. Agnew,[19] who had been present at both engagements. Later the squadron received news that he had been forced to land in enemy territory and was a prisoner of war. He was the first battle-casualty among the Australian flying squadrons in France. The same squadron's patrols fought several other indecisive engagements during October, notably on the 16th, when McCloughry's patrol of four beat off an attack by eight Albatroses of the "black-tailed circus." These encounters depended, as a rule, on the enemy's willingness to stay, his machines being the faster. The members of the squadron looked forward to the newer and faster scouts known to be coming to them; they realized what the British airmen had told them, that battle in the air had not merely to be offered to the enemy but offered without alternative. The time was coming when Australian scouts on offensive patrol would scour the entire British front.

An encounter on October 13th was also unlucky for the Australians. In the forenoon of that day a patrol of five D.H.5's was returning from the duty known as "C.O.P." (close offensive patrol), and was about over Quéant at 8,000 feet, when one machine, piloted by Lieutenant D. G. Morrison,[20] was observed to be some distance in rear. His fighting partner, Lieutenant R. W. McKenzie,[21] went back to pick him up. At this moment four fast Albatros scouts approached from the north and pounced upon the straggler. McKenzie flew straight at the enemy leader and fired a burst into him at long range, but almost immediately developed engine-trouble and had to make for home. He had no time to observe effect of his fire, but although he was crippled the Germans made no attempt to prevent his escape. The next news heard of Morrison was that he had been shot down by enemy aircraft near Quéant, and had fallen in No-Man's Land wounded in three places. He was rescued by men of the 13th London Regiment, but died soon afterwards. The Germans shelled his crashed machine to pieces as it lay between the lines.

---

[19] Lieut. I. C. F. Agnew; No. 2 Sqn. (previously Artillery). Pastoralist; of Epping Forest, Tas.; b. Oatlands, Tas., 17 Feb., 1893.

[20] Lieut. D. G. Morrison; No. 2 Sqn. Orchardist; b. Kilmore, Vic., 8 May, 1895. Died of wounds, 29 Oct., 1917.

[21] Lieut. R. W. McKenzie, M.C.; No. 2 Sqn. (previously A.A.M.C.). Chemist; b. Adelaide, June, 1895.

No. 3 Squadron, at Savy, with its R.E.8's, was in different case, as has already been explained; its duty was intelligence work over the front line, and not the seeking of combat. Nevertheless, the R.E.8's found much fighting in the course of that duty, even though British scouts of the army wing were generally out to protect them. The squadron's first scene of action was the area between Arras and La Bassée. On October 21st, Captain Anderson and Lieutenant J. R. Bell[22] (observer), flying near Lens while observing a bombardment for a 4.5-inch howitzer battery, were attacked by four Albatros scouts. Anderson maintained a gallant and skilful fight until two other R.E.8's came to his assistance, when the Germans retired. Ten days later a similar combat occurred during the ranging of a battery near Neuville St. Vaast. Anderson and Lieutenant K. C. Hodgson,[23] escorted by Lieutenants E. J. Jones[24] and E. R. Dibbs[25] in another R.E.8, beat off four fast Albatros scouts. These encounters, and the squadron's participation on October 31st in a great daylight bombing raid on the enemy's lines about Oppy and Neuvireuil, east of Arras, were the principal excitement during the learning weeks at Savy. Those weeks provided valuable experience in every department of the varied work of a corps squadron, and on November 9th No. 3 Squadron was moved to responsible charge of an area of its own—the Messines sector held by the I Anzac Corps (later the Australian Corps). Here the squadron's headquarters were at the well-known aerodrome beside the cemetery at Bailleul. It was natural that the Australian airmen should be vastly pleased to be serving with their own countrymen.

Note.—Among the pilots of the Australian squadrons training in England Phillipps acquired a notable place. He had been a captain in the 28th Australian Infantry Battalion, was wounded in the first Australian infantry raid in France, and was invalided to Australia with a leg partly paralysed. He returned to England with No. 2

[22] Lieut. J. R. Bell; No. 3 Sqn. Accountant; b. Scottsdale, Tas., 1889.

[23] Lieut. K. C. Hodgson; No. 3 Sqn. (previously Engineers). Metallurgist; b. Camberwell, Melbourne, 1892.

[24] Capt. E. J. Jones, M.C., D.F.C.; No. 3 Sqn. (previously Engineers). Railway surveyor and draughtsman; of South Yarra, Melbourne; b. Abbotsford, Melbourne, 1 June, 1892.

[25] Lieut. E. R. Dibbs; No. 2 Sqn. (previously Infantry). Bank official; of Mosman, Sydney; b. North Sydney, 9 March, 1894.

Squadron as adjutant, and during training in England, after several flights as a passenger, he secured permission to train as a pilot. Before the conclusion of his term of war-flying experience in France Phillipps was actually patrol-leading with the British squadron to which he was attached.

Before the formation of the Australian squadrons, large numbers of Australians enlisted in the British flying service. In April, 1917, in response to a call for volunteers for the air service, seven officers and twenty-five other ranks were selected from applications among the A.I.F. and were sent to England, understanding that they were to be trained as observers for the Australian Flying Corps. "There, for some unfathomable reason," writes Lieutenant Dibbs, one of the seven officers, "the officers were trained as army-squadron observers, and the twenty-five others as corps-squadron observers. The only Australian two-seater squadron training in England, as we knew, was No. 3 Squadron —a corps squadron. With No. 3 Squadron the twenty-five cadets went to France, but the other seven were sent to France to British squadrons." Of these Lieutenants K. W. Holmes[26] and C. R. Edson[27] lost their lives. Lieutenant A. G. Bill[28] was seriously wounded, and his pilot killed, in an action from which the Australian observer, with great difficulty, landed the machine. On recovery from his wounds Bill was transferred to kite-balloons. A fourth, Lieutenant Dibbs, met Major Blake in London just before No. 3 Squadron went to France, and told him that these Australian observers, meant for the Australian Flying Corps, were in British units. A few weeks later Lieutenants Dibbs, V. P. Barbat,[29] and S. J. Moir[30] were ordered to leave their British squadrons and join No. 3 Squadron at Savy, which they did. The seventh man, Lieutenant B. J. Blackett,[31] remained with the R.F.C. on intelligence work.

---

[26] Lieut. K. W. Holmes; R.A.F. (previously Australian Infantry). Civil engineer; b. Prahran, Melbourne, Aug., 1889. Died while prisoner of war, 11 Aug., 1917.

[27] Lieut. C. R. Edson; 22nd Sqn., R.A.F. (previously A.A.S.C.). Customs officer; of Port Adelaide; b. York, S. Aust., 3 Nov., 1893. Died of wounds, 17 Aug., 1917.

[28] Lieut. A. G. Bill; Aust. Flying Corps (previously Infantry). Surveyor and engineer; of Melbourne; b. Armadale, Melbourne, 16 Nov., 1892.

[29] Lieut. V. P. Barbat; No. 3 Sqn. (previously Engineers). Draughtsman and engineer; of Newtown, Sydney; b. Ipswich, Q'land, 23 Nov., 1892.

[30] Lieut. S. J. Moir, A.F.C.; No. 3 Sqn. (previously Infantry). Tailor's cutter; b. Paddington, Sydney, Aug., 1896.

[31] Lieut. B. J. Blackett; R.A.F. (previously Australian Infantry). Civil engineer and tea and rubber planter; b. Potters Bar, London, 23 June, 1886.

CHAPTER XIV
CAMBRAI AND GOUZEAUCOURT

During August, September, and October of 1917 the British Army had been continuously on the offensive in the Ypres area. What was left of the old Ypres Salient after the Battle of Messines and Wytschaete in the previous June developed during the later fighting around Ypres itself into a far more dreadful region of mud and misery. The artillery-fire on both sides was the most devastating of the whole war. The British offensive consisted of a series of attacks, each of which aimed at taking a definite bite out of the German positions. " Positions " they were still called, though shell-fire had torn up the terrain past all recognition and littered it with the débris of houses, trees, trench material, and military transport, while continual rain, accompanying the destruction wrought by the guns, filled the shell-craters with water and made a mud-morass of the entire battlefield. The offensive eventually stopped at the end of the autumn, and at nearly the end also of the endurance of the infantry. The British won the famous Passchendaele Ridge, or what remained of it, but at enormous cost of life and material.

About this time—November, 1917—the German strength being concentrated in Flanders, a blow was suddenly delivered by the British in a distant sector. In this attack very different methods were employed. The system in use at Ypres—that of blowing to pieces by gun-fire the front of the assault—resulted in the destruction quite as much of the attackers' prospects of advancing as of the enemy's defences. At Ypres the roads were destroyed, and not even the lightest wheeled-transport could pass forward over the ground taken. Pack-mules and walking infantry could reach the line only with the utmost labour. The interest of General Headquarters was attracted by a proposal of General Byng, commanding the British Third Army, that he should be allowed to put to the test a plan of breaking the German defences ahead of an assault with a massed force of tanks in place of the customary pounding by artillery. The

Third Army was at that time on the Cambrai front. The Hindenburg Line, the obstacle immediately opposite, was a tough nut to crack, but there appeared to exist an opportunity for a successful surprise attack. At this juncture the heavy reverse suffered by the Italians on the Isonzo front made a counterstroke advisable. Byng's suggestion was therefore approved. His tanks were assembled with all secrecy and launched at the enemy's line immediately north and south of Flesquières in the misty morning of November 20th.

No. 2 Australian Squadron, being in the Third Army, was closely concerned in this battle, and for ten days or so before the attack its pilots practised assiduously at low-flying in couples, machine-gunning ground targets, and bomb-dropping. Despite foggy weather and the dangerous nature of the work even at practice, there was only one accident; through engine-failure one pilot flew into a haystack and broke his machine to pieces, though he escaped personal injury.

The morning of November 20th was misty, as most others had been. Six machines in formation under Captain J. Bell[1] took off soon after the hour of dawn, flew over the advancing tanks and infantry across the Hindenburg Line, and dropped bombs on the best obtainable targets. Selection of such targets was limited; the fog was so thick that low-flying in flight-formation was impossible, and machines, therefore, hunted in pairs instead. The bombs having been released, the pilots flew up and down roads and trenches and over batteries, emptying their machine-guns at every pocket of Germans. It was risky work, for the heavy fog meant that the flying had often to be done at only twenty or thirty feet off the ground; but the rewards were great. These attacks dismayed the German artillery, and McKenzie drove the gunners in panic from one battery near Cambrai. Bell, who was flying in company with McKenzie, was shot through the chest by rifle-fire from the ground, and subsequently died in hospital. Before the first patrol was back at the aerodrome, two more flights, each of six machines, had started out under Wilson and Phillipps on the same errand, and these also hunted in couples over the battle-line. Only one enemy

---

[1] Capt. J. Bell, formerly of No. 1 Sqn.

aeroplane was seen, and that flew away immediately into the fog. Lieutenant A. J. Pratt[2] delivered his bombs upon two heavy machine-gun emplacements, and then "shot up" a considerable stretch of the main Cambrai road, during which enterprise, to his delight, he attacked a staff motor-car and drove it into a ditch. Lieutenant F. G. Huxley[3] dropped one bomb plumb upon a gun moving out of action, machine-gunned the men around it, and shot three of the horses dead. Having next blocked the road into Cambrai by smashing in similar manner a supply-waggon, he flew on through the mist, and suddenly saw a body of 300 enemy infantry drawn up in fours as if waiting for him. "This parade," he related afterwards, "was dismissed quicker than parade ever was before." Lieutenants Holden and R. L. Clark[4] made direct hits with bombs on a communication trench full of troops, and then fired into the resulting confusion, until such men as were able left the trench and fled. Holden returned to an advanced landing-ground behind Havrincourt Wood, with his machine a flying wreck. Every part of it was shot full of holes, including petrol-tank, tail-plane, both longerons, and part of the undercarriage, while the elevator control was shot clean away. Lieutenant L. N. Ward's[5] machine being disabled by groundfire, he was forced to land behind the German lines, broke his leg in so doing, and was taken prisoner.

Probably the most extraordinary adventure of the day was Lieutenant H. Taylor's.[6] His machine was shot down, like Ward's, inside the enemy's lines, where it crashed badly. As the occurrence was officially described, he "attacked parties of the enemy with a German rifle, joined an advanced British infantry patrol, led it forward, and brought in a wounded man. He found Captain Bell's machine and tried to fly it, but without success. He then rejoined the squadron at the advanced landing-ground." His flying partner of that

---

[2] Lieut. A. J. Pratt; No. 2 Sqn. (previously Engineers). Engineer; b. Ascot Vale, Melbourne, 1893.

[3] Lieut. F. G. Huxley, M.C.; No. 2 Sqn. (previously Infantry). Shop-keeper; b. King Island, Tas., 1892.

[4] Lieut. R. L. Clark; No. 2 Sqn. Mining engineer; of Annandale, Sydney; b. Glebe, Sydney, 4 Sept., 1889.

[5] Lieut. L. N. Ward; No. 2 Sqn. (previously Light Horse). Clerk; b. Walkerville, S. Aust., Jan., 1893.

[6] Lieut. H. Taylor, M.C., M.M.; No. 2 Sqn. (previously A.A.S.C.). Mechanic; b. Birmingham, Eng., 1889. Killed in aeroplane accident, 18 Aug., 1918.

morning, Wilson, relates the glowing detail of Taylor's story. "Taylor and I found the enemy," he says, "being massed to repel the attack—confused and dazed by surprise. Close together we dived down and opened our machine-guns on the Germans, pulling up to the level of the fog again (about thirty feet off the ground), and letting a bomb drop as we rose. For a few moments we continued this, scattering and demoralising troops, and preventing them from concentrating their fire on our own men.

"Then, as I zoomed up after a burst of machine-gun fire and turned to dive again, I missed Taylor. I was half enveloped in the mist, and for a moment thought he must have pulled up into the fog to clear a machine-gun stoppage. The next second the red light of a pilot-rocket showed up beside me. I guessed that it was fired by Taylor, and that it meant he was in distress. Another red light followed rapidly, and then I saw him down on the ground wrecked and among the enemy. That he was sufficiently alive to fire his rockets was amazing. His machine was just a heap of wreckage. One wing lay twenty yards away from the rest of the heap, from which Taylor had scrambled and was now firing his rockets to attract my attention.

"Fifty yards or so away from him were scattered groups of the enemy, who had stood off as his machine came down, uncertain whether it was really falling, or whether the pilot was just diving at them and waiting till the last second to let loose his bullets. I saw them turn as they realised that Taylor had crashed, and lift their rifles to fire. I dived at them immediately and scattered them again. It showed Taylor that I had seen his signals.

"Crouching behind a slight mound, he pulled out his automatic and fired at some Germans who rushed towards him as I pulled up ready for another dive. Then, as I dived and scattered the Germans again, he dashed back a few yards, dropped to the ground, and fired again. He repeated this until he had got back maybe sixty yards from his machine and nearer to our own men, and then I saw him surrounded by a small band of British soldiers. He picked up the gun of a fallen man, and he and his little party lay firing at the enemy, who were gradually creeping up and spreading out fan-shape to surround them. For a while I saw snapshots of the unequal contest as I dived down and zoomed up repeatedly to try and scatter these groups of Germans. Then there was a crashing sound against my head and I was blinded.

"Two bullets had pierced the wind-screen in front of my eyes, and dust from the triplex glass had been flung into my eyes. Pulling back the 'joy-stick'[1] and giving the engine full throttle, I climbed up into the fog away from hostile fire, to wait until my eyes cleared. For a while I flew about anywhere, certain of one thing only, that I was climbing up clear of enemy fire. Gradually the glass-dust got washed from my eyes, and I was able to see again.

"Descending through the fog bank, I picked up my bearings and sought the spot where I had last seen Taylor fighting with a handful of infantry against odds that seemed to give them no chance. Neither he nor his party were to be seen. Here and there a German jumped up from behind cover and dashed forward between the mud-splashes of falling shells, and little rips in the canvas of my aeroplane wings told me that others unseen were firing at me. It seemed certain that Taylor and his party had been captured or killed—that the ground was in possession of the Germans.

"I returned to the forward landing-ground, which had been arranged for the day just behind the lines, and alongside which French and British cavalrymen were waiting to ride forward if the surprise attack should break a hole in the German line. There I reported what I had seen of Taylor, and we gave him up for lost.

"The rest of the story comes from Taylor himself—or, rather, from the people who brought him back, for whenever Taylor was asked about his own work he just grinned and said something which had nothing to do with the case. The party of men he had found had lost their officer. He had stayed with them till they battled their way, edging back yard by yard, to the main body of troops from whom they had advanced too far. Here he left them to try to get back to the advanced landing-ground for another machine. On the way he found the damaged aeroplane of Captain Bell, who had been shot down earlier. With the help of some troops

---

[1] "Joy-stick"—see Glossary, under Control-stick.

he tried to start the engine, but it refused to work, and he continued back to the aerodrome, which he reached in time for dinner."

Out of eighteen machines which took part in the low-flying battle on that day, No. 2 Squadron lost in all one missing and six shot down, and of pilots one missing, one dead of wounds, and one wounded. The entire operation was a splendid performance for a new and untried squadron, under conditions of risk which portended, if not general disaster, at least considerable sacrifice. Whether the Battle of Cambrai would have finished differently if the cavalry had been more adventurously used is a debatable question, but the fact remains that the cavalry were hardly used at all that day, and for what success the army had, after the first piercing of the line by the tanks, it owed its thanks mainly to the "cavalry of the air." General H. M. Trenchard, commanding the Royal Flying Corps in the field, visited No. 2 Squadron on November 22nd, and, on his return, he wrote to General Birdwood—

> "I have just been to see the Australian fighting Squadron No. 68 (*i.e.* No. 2) for the second time in the last week, and I have talked to some of the pilots who carried out the great work on November 20th, 21st, and to-day. Their work was really magnificent. . . . . These pilots came down low and fairly strafed the Hun. They bombed him and attacked him with machine-gun fire from fifty feet, flying among treetops; they apparently revelled in this work, which was of great value. You might like to let some of your people know that I think them really great men, and I am certain that in the summer next year they will all give a very fine account of themselves. They are splendid."

No. 2 Squadron, it should be remarked, was only one of a number of British aeroplane squadrons engaged in the low-flying operations.

On the evening of November 20th notions of the magnitude of the British success were rather inflated, but by the evening of the following day it became clear that Byng had failed to break through the German front. Cambrai, the fall of which was to be the signal of strategic success, remained in

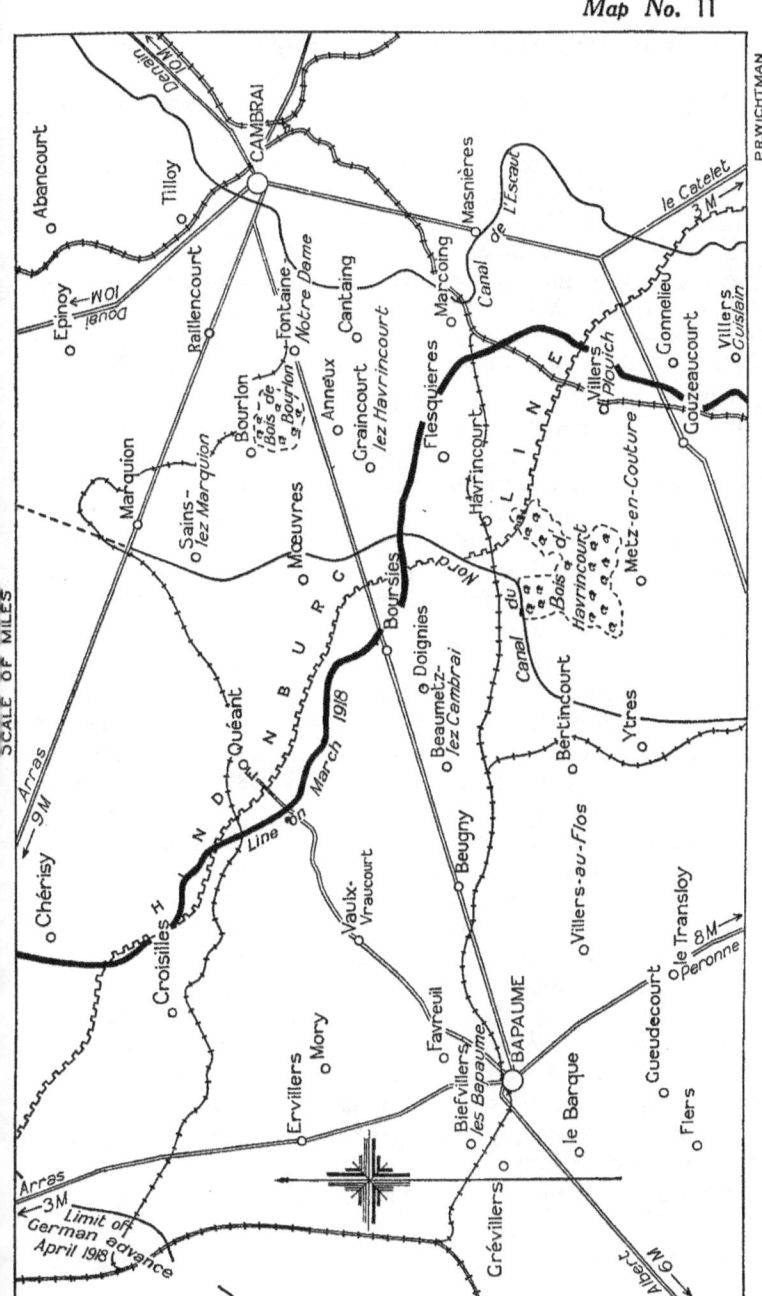

Cambrai Region, showing area of operations of No. 2 Australian Squadron in November and December, 1917, and of No. 2 and No. 4 Australian Squadrons in March, 1918, during the German offensive

German hands, and even Bourlon Wood, which was taken, was held only by a desperate defence. The battle was at its fiercest on November 22nd and 23rd, when strong German reinforcements of guns and infantry came up. The British holding on to Bourlon Wood were especially hard pressed. On these days again No. 2 Squadron, among others, had all available machines out low-flying and bombing, or escorting other patrols. While they were engaged upon this work in the forenoon of the 22nd, the first enemy aeroplane to be destroyed by the squadron fell to Huxley. Huxley had bombed and " shot-up " a column of infantry marching on the road running south-west from Raillencourt—an effort which completely cleared the road, except for two large holes and two heaps of dead—and had risen to turn away, when he saw an Albatros scout flying below and in front of him. " It was a gift," he said. Huxley dived straight on to the German's tail, and at fifty feet fired thirty rounds into him. The German hovered for a moment and then nose-dived into the ground.

Between 11 o'clock and noon that same morning, R. W. Howard, having dropped his two bombs upon troops on the roadway in Raillencourt village, skimmed low along a German trench near Marcoing, and machine-gunned troops assembling there. He then climbed, and, finding himself alone, joined a British formation of S.E.5's. One of these machines, straggling from its formation, was attacked by an Albatros scout. Howard turned, drove off that assailant, and a few minutes later, having dived with the S.E.5's to 1,000 feet, met a D.F.W. two-seater. The Australian fired the opening shots, and the German immediately began to glide down. Two S.E.5's joined in the attack, and the D.F.W. was driven down to a landing in the British lines. Phillipps, who, also out bombing and machine-gunning enemy posts beyond Bourlon Wood, saw Howard's combats, was himself attacked by an enemy scout from above. Phillipps eluded this adversary by a sharp turn, dived back upon the German, and fired 150 rounds into him. The enemy, avoiding further fight, continued his dive to the ground and landed.

The low-flying work could not be done without casualties. Pratt was wounded by anti-aircraft fire on November 22nd, and, in trying to land, crashed in the front-line trenches. The German anti-aircraft batteries, always efficient, were now being brought up in increasing numbers. Pratt was rescued, but before being taken to hospital he reported the location of a German battalion headquarters at the north-west corner of Bourlon Wood, which he had bombed and attacked with his machine-gun. Two more pilots were lost that day— Lieutenants A. Griggs[8] and D. G. Clark,[9] who were both shot down and mortally wounded by ground-fire over Bourlon Wood; and a third, Lieutenant S. W. Ayers,[10] met with a like fate next morning in the same locality. Griggs on the 22nd had already carried out one successful and daring low-flying attack on the trenches and strong-posts beyond the wood, and he was on a second mission when he was brought down. Holden again brought his machine in wrecked, almost every part holed or broken—clear evidence of the dangers of the work and of his own good luck.

An instance of the value of such air fighting in close contact with the infantry was reported on the morning of November 23rd, by Huxley. The infantry were still striving to wrest Bourlon Wood from the enemy. Huxley went out with three others on the usual low-flying patrol, and saw three British tanks held up in the wood by a German battery. He flew over to the battery and, from a hundred feet, dropped four bombs, one by one, on the guns, silenced them, and enabled the tanks to advance. The other machines wrought havoc among parties of German troops retiring along the road from Bourlon and Fontaine towards Cambrai. Victory seemed within grasp that afternoon, when Fontaine and Bourlon Wood were reported taken and the airmen had seen the tanks advancing from Fontaine towards Cambrai.

But since Byng was without reserves, the prize of Cambrai was beyond his reach. The fighting subsided during the next two or three days; the airmen reported that there was hardly any movement of troops before Cambrai, and the whole front-line area was very quiet. Taylor, patrolling over

---

[8] Lieut. A. Griggs; No. 2 Sqn. Civil Engineer; b. Meridian, Miss., U.S.A., 23 Sept., 1887. Died of wounds, 23 Nov., 1917.
[9] Lieut. D. G. Clark; No. 2 Sqn. Grazier; of Killara, Sydney; b. Picton, N.S.W. Killed in action, 22 Nov., 1917.
[10] Lieut. S. W. Ayers; No. 2 Sqn. Mechanic; b. Cootamundra, N.S.W., 1893. Died of wounds, 24 Nov., 1917.

Bourlon Wood at 1,500 feet on November 26th, met a D.F.W. two-seater at the same height. When 500 yards separated them, the German turned away, nose down. Taylor immediately dived upon it, and opened fire at 200 yards. The D.F.W. continued its flight straight into the ground, "where it stopped dead," reported the humorous Taylor, "without any run and with no signs of life." On November 29th R. W. Howard had a spirited fight with a fast German two-seater at 400 feet near Cambrai. After some manœuvring he put out of action the D.F.W's observer, and the machine then made for the ground and landed. On that day German aircraft were out in force, a fact which, considering what subsequently happened, might have been deemed significant by the British Intelligence Staff. In the forenoon a bombing patrol of four D.H.5's under Wilson was resolutely opposed by eight Albatros scouts over Bourlon Wood and Fontaine. The Germans made no effort to attack so long as the Australian machines did not cross the lines, but at every attempt to do so the enemy patrol would dive at them. The D.H.5's were handicapped for manœuvring by the extra weight of four 20-lbs. bombs each. Finally they dropped the bombs, and, thus unencumbered, climbed to meet their opponents. The enemy, however, did not wait, and, having the speed of the D.H.5's, they made off east.

The morning of November 30th came, foggy as all mornings were at this season in those downland valleys, and with it an unheralded German counter-attack on the southern side of the newly-won ground, towards Gouzeaucourt. It was the morning when, outside that village, the general commanding a British division was surprised in his pyjamas, and cooks and batmen had to be lined up with rifles to cover the rescue of staff papers. The Germans had broken, without trouble and with no artillery warning, through the thin British line—a foolishly thin line it was deemed after the event— and in the thick shrouding mist no co-operation between the defenders was possible. The Germans were, in fact, replying in kind to the British surprise attack, and with the great advantage of not having to cross heavily-fortified trenches of the sort which had confronted Byng's infantry. They brought out their aeroplanes also, meaning to retaliate upon the British with the same scourge from the air. No. 2 Squadron, with all other units, received the alarm just after breakfast, and two flights went off promptly into the fog. They found gun-fire very heavy on the whole front, but on the northern side of the battle-area the hard-won Bourlon Wood was still held by British infantry. Great numbers of German aeroplanes were seen, but were flying so low that air fighting in such conditions of the weather was almost impossible. Only four of the Australian airmen carried bombs. They dropped them on parties of Germans wherever found, and also used their machine-guns on the same troops; but for a time No. 2 Squadron's chief duty was to smash the enemy's air attack upon the infantry. This task was rendered the more difficult by the hazy atmosphere. Here and there a pilot would see some vague form flicker past him in the haze, chase it, and lose it again immediately in a new belt of fog. Lieutenant H. G. Cornell[11] was shot down near the line, and spent twenty-four hours in a shell-hole under hot fire before he escaped and got home again.

The first air patrols came in at 10.30 a.m. At 11 o'clock, Wilson led out another formation of four machines, which met with exciting adventures. They dropped their bombs immediately on the foremost German troops. "There was no chance of using machine-guns on ground-troops," reported Wilson, "owing to the presence of numerous enemy aeroplanes." Taylor met four enemy two-seaters at 2,000 feet flying towards him. He faced them, and flew directly at the leader. Under the threat of a head-on collision, Taylor held his course till he had the German pilot filling his Aldis sight,[12] and then at point-blank range delivered a burst of fire into his opponent. The enemy turned sharply away to the right, and Taylor wheeled swiftly after him, but seeing the other three Germans about to attack, he zoomed into the clouds, and there lost them. Wilson had his petrol tank shot through by a splinter of anti-aircraft shell, was forced to turn back, and landed at Bapaume. On his return towards the battle-area, when near Gonnelieu village—by that time in German hands—he met a D.F.W. two-seater at 1,600 feet with

---

[11] Lieut. H. G. Cornell; No. 2 Sqn. Electrical engineer; of Ballarat, Vic.; b. Richmond, Melbourne, 10 Aug., 1891. Killed in action, 11 Dec., 1917.

[12] *Aldis sight*—see Glossary.

only its rear gun in use. The two machines opened fire at the same moment, and at Wilson's first burst the German observer fell down into his cockpit and his gun stuck up in the air. Wilson pursued this enemy as far as Bantouzelle village, firing without visible further effect, and then was attacked by a second D.F.W. He made a sharp turn, got directly underneath the German, and firéd forty rounds into him. The D.F.W. fell steeply, recovered control, and tried to land, but in doing so turned completely on its back. Wilson had one bomb left in his racks. He flew down to the D.F.W., dropped this bomb on it, and blew it to pieces. He had now no more ammunition left, and made for home, but was intercepted by a third two-seater, which opened fire at long range. Bluff was Wilson's only remaining chance. He flew straight at the German, feigning attack. This settled the matter; the enemy turned away and flew east, and Wilson made a bee-line for home.

Again, in the afternoon, ten machines were out from No. 2 Squadron, and most of them made two sorties over the German lines, bombing and machine-gunning. They recorded thirty direct hits with bombs on bodies of enemy troops and 4,000 rounds fired into them from machine-guns. To the British artillery—whose observers were still blinded by the mist—the reports of the Australian pilots were invaluable, enabling the guns to concentrate their shelling upon the enemy's assembling infantry.

The German thrust on the Gouzeaucourt side, continued on December 1st, was held, but the gain of ground by the enemy on the southern side of the salient seriously weakened the British hold on the whole position, and next day it became clear that Bourlon Wood and Fontaine would have to be abandoned. On both these days the infantry fighting in this region was intense and of uncertain advantage to either side, and the duty of the British air squadrons was to arrest enemy pressure while the line was re-formed. On December 1st, the early morning patrol of four Australian machines found the mist as heavy and deceptive as ever. A fog-bank, seemingly impenetrable to the pilot flying through it at a few hundred feet, would suddenly end with a clear view down to the ground. Then the mist would drift over again. But the

Aust. War Museum Official Photo. No. E1176.

AN R.E.8 OF NO. 3 SQUADRON, A.F.C., DETAILED FOR NIGHT-BOMBING

Taken at Savy aerodrome, October, 1917. Upper photograph—loading the bomb-rack; lower—ready to start.

Aust. War Museum Official Photo. No. E1178. *To face p. 194.*

AN AIRMAN'S VIEW OF THE RUINS OF YPRES, 31ST OCTOBER, 1917

Aust. War Museum Official Photo. No. E1257.

same interval would be marked by a spasm of furious anti-aircraft fire directed at the disclosed machines. In one such interval, Huxley, suddenly emerging from the fog, saw an Aviatik two-seater only a hundred yards away on his right and just below his level. He made a diving turn at the German, whose observer opened fire from underneath. The Australian pilot turned rapidly aside, and fired a hot burst into the enemy. Before the Aviatik's observer could switch his gun over to meet Huxley's manœuvre, he was hit, and collapsed into his machine. After receiving a further hundred rounds, the Aviatik went into a nose-dive, hit the ground, and turned over on to its back. Two hours later, when on a second bombing mission, Huxley saw it there surrounded by a group of Germans. He dropped a bomb into the middle of the group, and blew off the tail of the wrecked machine.

During this same patrol Taylor had two short indecisive encounters with enemy machines, which flickered into sight and vanished again in the mist. His own machine was much damaged by ground-fire, and he was forced to land away from home. Lieutenants L. Benjamin[13] and W. A. Robertson,[14] patrolling at noon beyond Gouzeaucourt, were also compelled to land with machines badly holed. Nevertheless their shooting and bombing worried the Germans, who retaliated by sending over, under escort of five scouts, a large three-seater machine, looking like a Gotha bomber, to fly low and fire into the British trenches. Forrest and McKenzie with the noon patrol, encountered this enemy formation in the mist near Villers–Guislain. Forrest immediately rose, drove a scout into the clouds, dived again, zoomed up under the three-seater, and fired into it from below until it turned away homeward. Meanwhile McKenzie, zooming up behind Forrest, fired a fierce stalling[15] burst into a revealed Albatros scout. This immediately dived for the ground. McKenzie saw it land badly and pitch on to its nose in a shell-hole.

All efforts of the enemy against Mœuvres, at the northern

---

[13] Lieut. L. Benjamin; No. 2 Sqn. (previously A.A.M.C.). Student; of St. Kilda, Melbourne; b. St. Kilda, 23 Aug., 1896.

[14] Capt. W. A. Robertson; No. 2 Sqn. (previously Engineers). Engineering student; b. Albert Park, Melbourne, 1896.

[15] Stalling—see Glossary.

end of the salient, were beaten back. By the morning of December 4th the British line had been withdrawn to south and west of Bourlon Wood, and the Cambrai battle was over. With No. 2 Squadron the intense low-flying attacks gave place to the more normal duties of reconnaissance and close offensive patrols. On the afternoon of December 5th, a formation of seven machines from No. 2, under Wilson, crossing the line to attack the German aerodrome at Awoingt, ran into twelve Albatros scouts and four two-seaters. A hot fight seemed certain, and the D.H.5's dropped their bombs to clear for action, but Wilson had a bad stoppage in his machine-gun as soon as he opened the attack, and was obliged to fall out to remedy it. While preliminary firing was still in progress, two other D.H.5's were compelled to break off—McKenzie with gun jammed, and Robertson with engine-trouble. The Germans, however, did not press the engagement, and as the Australian machines, by now scattered over a wide area, flew to rejoin formation, the Germans made off east. The Australians wondered at the enemy's reluctance, until they perceived overhead a strong patrol of S.E.5.a scouts from a British squadron. They watched the new arrivals with interest; they themselves were in a few days' time to change to S.E.5's, which were superior to the D.H.5's in both speed and fighting efficiency.

The Germans attacked again at Fontaine in the late afternoon of December 6th. It was too dark to observe the progress of this attack clearly from the air, but two Australian patrols were out, each of four machines—one led by Wilson and one by Howard—and they thoroughly bombed the main reserves of the attack. Howard's patrol, finding the roads east of Bantouzelle village congested with German troops and traffic, dropped its load of bombs right among the closely-packed masses. Wilson's formation dispersed in the failing light an enemy concentration in a bleak quarry by Lateau Wood. These events occurred before the Germans were fully deployed for their assault, and they must have had much of the heart taken out of them. Huxley, in Wilson's patrol, having launched his bombs, made out two D.F.W. two-seaters below him in the half-light, dived at them, and sent one to the ground in flames with his first burst, delivered at fifty-feet range.

The other attempted to attack Huxley from behind, but, seeing his companion drop, made off eastward.

This was the last fighting of No. 2 Squadron with the D.H.5 machines, and during the next few days the Australians were busied in exchanging them for S.E.5's.[16]

---

[16] For the sake of brevity, these machines are styled " S.E.5's " throughout this narrative. They were strictly of the type S.E.5.a, an improved model.

CHAPTER XV

WINTER WORK OVER MESSINES RIDGE

MEANWHILE No. 3 Squadron, on the Messines front, found during November hardly one good day for photography or artillery observation. The weather was constantly either dull or raining, verging on the condition called in airmen's language "dud." Nevertheless the Ypres offensive was still proceeding, though in point of fact that excellent military word (indicating effective movement) is but poorly expressive of the struggle going on in the mud about the Passchendaele Ridge. The British Army fought on through the late autumn in evil conditions of climate which, though well-known of old to armies in Flanders, can surely never before have been defied by a military offensive pressed to exhaustion. No human mind uninformed with actual experience of the mud and beastliness of the Ypres battlefield at the end of 1917 can form adequate conception of the sufferings of the unhappy infantry there on either side. The mud became so deep and continuous that men not only could not fight; they could not even move to run away. At length it came to pass that the men of a battalion ordered to the assault in the battle for Passchendaele regarded that order as sentence of death, and prayed that the end would come soon and quickly.

While this was what the wretched weather at Ypres meant to the men on the ground, the airmen overhead thanked their stars that they belonged to the flying corps and not to the "foot-sloggers." They took the air, whatever the weather was like, so long as there was a chance of working, of seeing anything of the ground, of flash-spotting, or of helping the infantry in any fashion at all. The operations of No. 3 Squadron over the Messines Ridge were immediately south of the main conflict. Day after day its machines coming in from reconnaissance reported: "Patrol unsatisfactory. Visibility bad during entire flight." On every possible evening the R.E.8's would take their own revenge of the enemy in what was called "retaliation and offensive patrol." This meant that a couple of machines would stay out as late as possible, and, dropping low just at dark over the German front lines with bombs which they carried for the purpose, would release them upon the roof of some concrete fort or other strong-point in the enemy's outpost defence system. The spectacle cheered the heart of many an infantryman, and encouraged him in the belief that the air force was doing its best.

In December the weather grew worse, and visibility was very bad. But more than ever at this time of the year, when observers either on the ground or in stationary balloons could see very little, it was necessary for the corps squadrons, serving as the eyes of the artillery, to go up, find the enemy batteries, and range the guns on them. Colonel Bishop, in his book, says truly: " It is no child's play to circle above a German battery observing for half-an-hour or more, with your machine tossing about in the air, tortured by exploding shells and black shrapnel puff-balls coming nearer and nearer to you like the ever-extending finger tips of some giant hand of death. But it is just a part of the never-ceasing war. In the air service this work is never finished. Everywhere along the line the big guns wait daily for the wireless touch of the aeroplanes to set them booming at targets carefully selected from previous observation. Big shells cannot be wasted. The human effort involved in creating them and placing them beside the well-screened guns at the front is far too great for that." The rain squalls and cold winds which froze the marrow in a man's bones on those Flanders' flats in winter-time made work in the air only a degree less unpleasant.

Considering the danger and the strain, No. 3 Squadron lost astonishingly few men and machines. Captain H. H. Storrer[1] and Lieutenant W. N. E. Scott[2] (observer) were killed near the aerodrome on December 2nd in a sudden squall, which carried them into the brick wall of the Bailleul cemetery as they were starting out on an artillery-patrol. Another machine immediately set off on that duty. Any lull in a storm, any interval of weak sunshine which lifted the haze, was the signal for artillery-observation machines to hum out to the

---

[1] Capt. H. H. Storrer; No. 3 Sqn. Accountant; of Geelong, Vic.; b. Geelong, 3 Sept., 1888. Killed in action, 2 Dec., 1917.

[2] Lieut. W. N. E. Scott; No. 3 Sqn. (previously Artillery). Electrical engineer; of Elsternwick, Melbourne; b. Elsternwick, 15 Aug., 1894. Killed in action, 2 Dec., 1917.

lines, locate some sentenced enemy battery, call up—by wireless buzzing—British heavy artillery detailed for the work, and proceed to pound the German gun-position. Sometimes the bombardment had to be abandoned because of bad weather or other causes, but generally the Australian airmen stuck to their task, until they had seen the German gun-pits blotted out in craters, or the ammunition beside the pieces exploded, or our own guns so well ranged on the target that they could demolish it without further observation.

Artillery ranging by aeroplane is work of a high order. An instance from the squadron record book under date of December 6th is a good illustration—

"R.E.8 A3815 Capt. W. H. Anderson, Lt. J. R. Bell (O); Art. Obs. with 155 S.B. 6-inch How.; Pilot. Start, 9.25 a.m.; return, 12.25 p.m. Remarks: S. K'out. EB PZ 19. Called up 9.37 a.m. First G sent at 9.55 a.m.; 35 RRO obtg. 2 Ys, 3 Zs, 17 As, 8 Bs, 4 Cs, 1 D. Bty. put out V at 10.50 a.m. Obs. during fire for effect 5 MOKs, 1 MA, 1 MZ. Damage to target uncertain, but one small explosion OK in pit at 11.20 a.m. First half-hour of fire for effect good, after that inclined to be scattered occasionally, especially one gun. CI sent at 12.19 p.m. T out."

Which report, being interpreted, means: "R.E.8, number of machine, pilot's and observer's names; duty, artillery observation with No. 155 Siege Battery of 6-inch howitzers; pilot observing. Left aerodrome 9.25 a.m., returned 12.25 p.m. Remarks: Satisfactory 'knock-out.' Engaged enemy battery numbered PZ 19 (a zone number). Called up our battery at 9.37 a.m. First signal to fire sent at 9.55 a.m. Observed thirty-five rounds obtaining two hits ten yards from centre of target, three twenty-five yards out, seventeen fifty yards out, eight 100 yards out, four 200 yards out, and one 300 yards out.[3] Our battery put out a V ground-strip signifying ranging considered complete at 10.50 a.m. Observed during battery fire for effect five rounds mostly direct hits and two others slightly out. One small explosion in centre of enemy gun-pit at 11.20 a.m. Signal 'coming in' sent to

---

[3] Reckoned by means of "clock-face" diagram upon a map. See Appendix No. 6.

Map No. 12

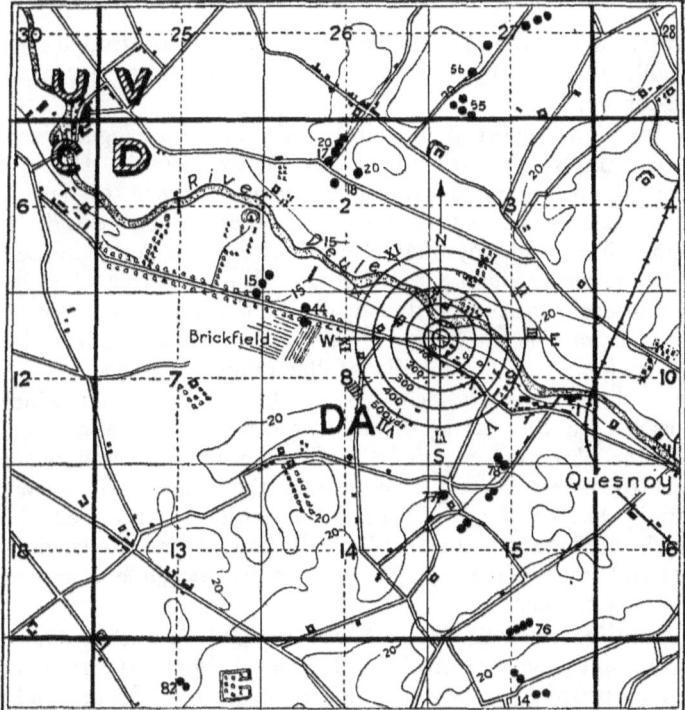

SECTION OF A TYPICAL ARTILLERY MAP, SHOWING METHOD OF RANGING BY REFERENCE TO "CLOCK-FACE." THIS SECTION SHOWS AN AREA IN REGION NORTH-WEST OF LILLE.

● ● ● ENEMY BATTERY POSITIONS

The clock-face diagram is placed, from actual example in the field, with its centre at an enemy battery position. The whole map illustrates the British Army system of placing—or "pin-pointing"—by means of map-squares any position. Military maps were in contiguous sheets, divided into 1,000-yard squares. The main divisions were lettered with capital letters, A, B, C, D, &c., and represented areas measuring 6,000 yards x 6,000 yards, or in some cases for convenience 6,000 x 5,000. The full square D in this example, for instance, contained 36 squares each 1,000 x 1,000, marked from 1 to 36, beginning at the left-hand top corner and ending at the right-hand bottom corner. These 1,000-yard squares, again, were divided into four 500-yard squares, labelled in the same sequence a, b, c, and d. To take an example, the small square farm south-west of the Brickfield is in D7d. To "pin-point" this farm precisely, the method was to imagine each side of the small d square to be divided into ten equal sections. The further calculation by means of these was first horizontally, then vertically—i.e., first east, then north from the left-hand bottom corner of each small square. Thus the farm in the example would be at D7d29. Where it was required to define the point even more precisely these tooth-comb scales were measured to one decimal place; thus the centre of the farm would be set down as D7d2095.

The larger square DA, one quarter of the map square D, was a more general subdivision used by artillery only. One or more British batteries might be allotted the task of dealing with all hostile movement, or guns, in the square DA, that is, in a zone measuring 3,000 yards x 3,000. The targets (enemy batteries) in every such square were numbered as soon as located. Artillery fire could then be called down upon any of them by simply mentioning the letters of the square and the number of the target—*e.g.*, DA76 (which in the map here shown was an enemy battery in the S.E. corner of square DA).

battery at 12.19 p.m. as battery had out T ground-strip signalling 'Go home (no longer requiring aeroplane assistance).'"

The above report of the wireless shorthand intelligence sent to the guns is not the end of the pilot's report. He also included times and locations by map-reference of enemy gun-flashes, movement of trains or other things behind the enemy lines, and anything else of interest seen by himself or his observer during the flight. While waiting for his guns to begin the bombardment, the pilot dropped two twenty-pound bombs on an enemy trench strong-point and recorded its location. In the middle of the ranging (at 10.10 a.m.) the said R.E.8 was attacked by a D.F.W. two-seater which appeared on the scene from the direction of Warneton. Bell, the observer, engaged the German machine and put a burst of ninety rounds into it, and the enemy fell steeply without having fired a shot. An artillery officer on the Messines Ridge saw the D.F.W. fall straight into the enemy's lines and crash. This was the first German machine destroyed by No. 3 Squadron.

Occasionally, when a pilot was engaged on such duty, he might observe activity on the part of some enemy battery other than that which he was detailed to engage. Or he might be seriously inconvenienced in his work by the fire of anti-aircraft guns. He then signalled back to artillery headquarters "N.F." (neutralising fire), together with the location of the active battery, which would bring the British guns into action against it. There were other calls pre-arranged to indicate the relative importance of enemy artillery activity observed. When the desired effect had been produced, and the enemy guns silenced, the aeroplane signalled "N.T.," to convey that information. "G.F.," with location, was the call for fire on transport or bodies of troops moving, and "L.L." the call for all available guns to open fire when a serious hostile attack was apparently assembling.

The varied duties of a corps squadron have been explained elsewhere.[4] Specially detailed machines would occasionally fly low over the lines for a close inspection of the German defences—as, for instance, when an infantry raid was being

---

[4] See Appendix No. 6.

prepared. This work also will best be explained by example. Lieutenants W. V. Herbert[5] and F. J. Rae[6] (observer) reconnoitred 2,000 yards of German outposts and trenches for a raid by Australian infantry below the Wytschaete Ridge on December 6th. Their report reveals both the daring and the value of the work. It read—

"Patrol satisfactory. Visibility over trenches fairly good. German outposts at (map-reference) O17b93, Bang Farm, strongly protected and occupied. Also outposts at O18a24 and at O17d89 occupied and apparently strongly reinforced with concrete and sandbags. At Whiz Farm no barbed-wire visible. Fly Buildings at O23b6095 reinforced with sandbags and earthworks (concrete) and occupied. Bee Farm apparently occupied. All tracks to above-mentioned outposts appear to be well worn. New works not evident. Whiz Farm and Fly Buildings appear to be strongly held. Ridge Farm at O24a6510 strongly reinforced and occupied. *Barbed-wire:* Three rows plainly visible apparently in good order. No openings through wire to outposts visible in front of enemy trenches through (map-squares) O24c, O24a, O24b, O18d, O18b. Enemy trenches appear to be in good order and strongly held. The Twins do not appear to be strongly held. One hundred and fifty rounds fired by observer through the flight into various outposts. Two twenty-pound bombs dropped at Bang Farm, one at O11d9025, and one at Whiz Farm between 12.15 and 12.45 p.m."

Several machines went out in the afternoon of December 17th in a spell of unusually fine weather. One of them met with perhaps the most extraordinary adventure recorded on the Western Front. Lieutenant J. L. Sandy,[7] with Sergeant H. F. Hughes[8] as observer, while ranging an 8-inch howitzer battery, was attacked by six Albatros D.5.a scouts. Sandy was

---

[5] Capt. W. V. Herbert, A.F.C.; No. 3 Sqn. (previously Light Horse). Station overseer; b. Ocean Grove, Vic., 28 July, 1893.

[6] Lieut. F. J. Rae; No. 3 Sqn. (previously Artillery). School teacher; of Yea, Vic.; b. Blackwood, Vic., 20 May, 1883.

[7] Lieut. J. L. Sandy; No. 3 Sqn. (previously Artillery). Company secretary; of Burwood, Sydney; b. Ashfield, Sydney, 4 Feb., 1886. Killed in action, 17 Dec., 1917.

[8] Sgt. H. F. Hughes; No. 3 Sqn. Civil servant; b. Prahran, Melbourne, 1890. Killed in action, 17 Dec., 1917.

hard-pressed, but fought vigorously and finally shot down one of the German machines to a forced landing in the lines of the 21st Australian Infantry Battalion, where the wounded pilot was taken prisoner. This was reported by British anti-aircraft gunners, who witnessed the whole action. Sandy fought an unequal fight for several minutes before assistance arrived, and one of the artillery officers watching from the ground described it as the most gallant action he had seen. Then E. J. Jones and Hodgson came up in another R.E.8 and the two fought the five German scouts for nearly ten minutes before the enemy, seeing yet a third R.E.8 approaching, broke off the combat. Jones reported that after the action he flew close to Sandy's machine, still cruising normally on its "beat," recognised it by its number, and then, concluding that its pilot and observer were unhurt and continuing their artillery work, made back to the aerodrome for more ammunition. But Sandy's wireless messages had ceased. By the time Jones had returned to the line, Sandy's machine was not in sight either in the air or on the ground. That night the squadron sent out telephone messages far and wide enquiring for the missing airmen, but not till the following evening was any news received. Then from a stationary hospital near St. Pol came a telegram to the effect that the dead bodies of Sandy and Hughes had been found in a wrecked R.E.8 in a neighbouring field. The report of a subsequent examination by officers of the squadron states: "From a post-mortem on the bodies at the hospital, and an examination of the scene of the crash, it would appear that both pilot and observer were killed in the aerial combat, and that the machine flew itself in wide left-hand circles until the petrol supply ran out. An armour-piercing bullet had passed through the observer's left lung and thence into the base of the pilot's skull. Medical opinion was that the pilot had been killed instantly. It was apparent that the observer had made no attempt to ship the auxiliary joy-stick, and that the throttle was open when the machine crashed. The theory that the machine flew itself in wide circles is supported by the fact that the wind that day was north-east, which would cause a south-west drift. The place where the machine was found is on an air-line distant fifty miles south-west from the scene of the combat. The bodies of neither pilot nor observer were further injured in the crash." While still missing, Sandy had been recommended for immediate award of the Military Cross in recognition of his gallant fight, and Sergeant Hughes for the Distinguished Conduct Medal.

Heavy snow fell at the close of the year, and the first bright interval while snow lay on the ground was a summons to No. 3 Squadron to photograph the enemy lines opposite the corps front. Snow concealed all defence works for so long as the garrisons made no movement. But the first man who went out to walk about in the snow left the plainest of tracks behind him. Tracks to camouflaged gun-pits, tracks to camouflaged battalion headquarters, to ammunition- or other supply-dumps, tracks to and from the line, which revealed a route taken by fatigue parties marching up at night—all these were zealously recorded by the local branches, at division and corps headquarters, of the widespread army intelligence service. A doubtful active battery-position would be made certain by the new-made tracks leading into it. Consequently, with the first sunshine after snowfall, while the snow still lay, the photographing aeroplanes were out to collect this valuable material for the revision of the artillery maps.

Such a day was the 1st January, 1918, and at noon an extensive photography-reconnaissance was carried out in formation by three machines of No. 3 Squadron. Under special arrangements for protection by scouting aeroplanes and for neutralising fire by our artillery upon all known enemy anti-aircraft batteries, the Australian machines covered with their cameras the entire Australian Corps front. The work was highly successful, and the squadron was congratulated next day by the army commander.

Such photography-patrols, it may be necessary to repeat, were not restricted simply to days when snow lay on the ground. The enemy lines were photographed at constant intervals, and the distribution of negative-prints, especially to the infantry, became ever wider and wider. Earlier in the war, before the value of photography-reconnaissance was properly appreciated, the pictures made were but scantily distributed to divisions in the line—in numbers of perhaps two or three or half-a-dozen; if one copy were occasionally sent on to an infantry battalion in the line, it was an act of grace and goodwill. The value of a constant flow of intelligence from rear to front of the army, as from front to rear, did not easily win recognition. The photographs of German front-line defences were regarded as things which would amuse the general of the division, or even perhaps the brigade-commander, rather than as vitally important information for the fighting men in the line, whose work was to harass the enemy in those defences, or, upon occasion, to turn him out of them. Staff officers would collect aeroplane-photographs as souvenirs of " sections of the front where we have been engaged." Those were the days of half-serious hopelessness at ever " beating the old Boche." The infantry themselves were not much quicker in the beginning to perceive the value of aeroplane-photographs. The science of ferreting out what was called " hostile intelligence " in the front line was not in 1915 and early 1916 the enthusiastic and unending work which it became later. Among the first to perceive the advantages of the new aid were the company-commanders, who used to be held responsible for the regular drawing of little sketch-maps of their own and the enemy's forward positions—thereby recording officially the fact that the battalion knew its muddy area, and facilitating " handing over the line " to relieving units. In those early days, moreover, when infantry raids were only beginning, the line battalions rarely possessed any system for the interrogation of prisoners, or felt any great faith in the value of information so obtained now and then from " higher up." The taking of any prisoners at all was a matter of sheer luck; the raids were designed, not to procure intelligence, but to " buck up the troops," and to take revenge at close quarters upon the hated *minenwerfer*-crews.

As soon as the army had grown to accept the view that fighting the Germans was a problem as much of science and intelligence as of rude force, these old notions underwent a change. If the date of such a change must be named at all precisely, it would probably be the spring of 1916. Towards the close of that year front-line intelligence of the enemy had become almost a fetish with staffs of army corps, and a new officer had appeared on the staff of the division—the

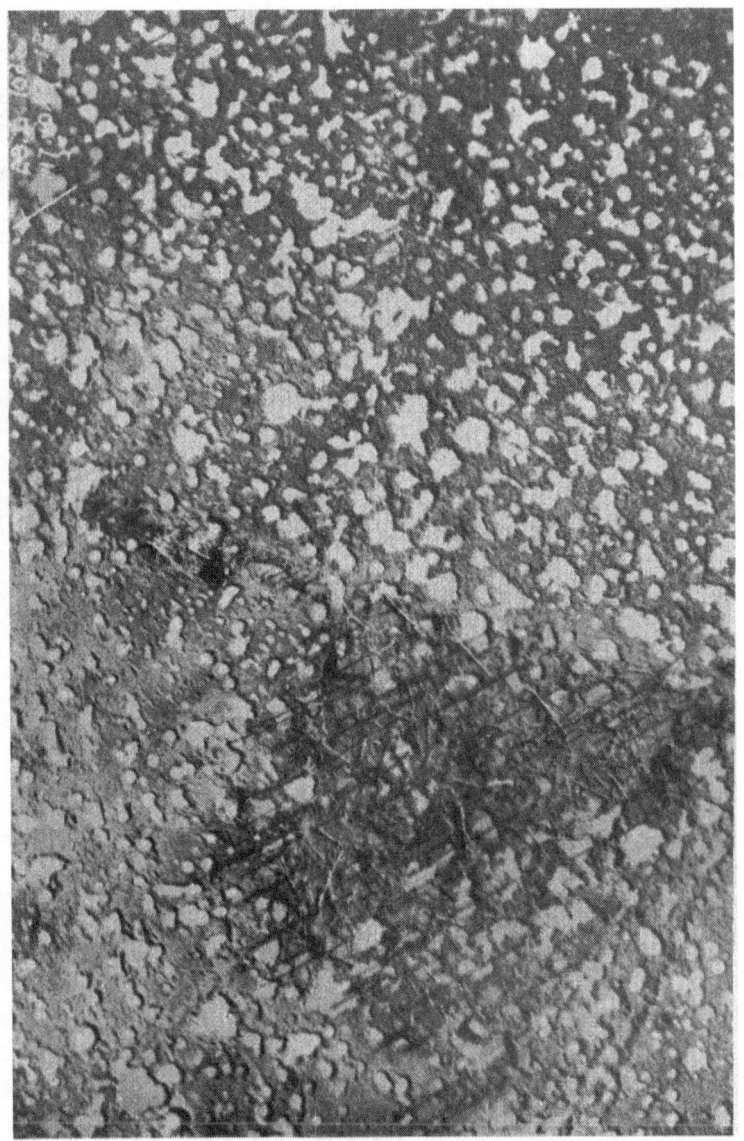

A CLOSE VIEW OF "AUGUSTUS WOOD," NEAR PASSCHENDAELE RIDGE (YPRES), SHOWING THE SHELL-TORN GROUND, 17TH OCTOBER, 1917

German concrete forts ("pillboxes") can be seen on each edge of the wood, slightly below its two upper corners.

British Air Force Photograph.
Aust. War Museum Collection No. J388.

The German Albatros shot down by Lieutenant J. L. Sandy and Sergeant H. F. Hughes (observer) near Armentières, 17th December, 1917
(This machine is now in the Australian War Museum.)

WINTER OVER MESSINES RIDGE

Division Intelligence Officer. Part of his special training was the interpretation of the evidence of aeroplane photographs, and divisions thereupon came to demand these photographs at more and more frequent intervals and in greater numbers for distribution. For a time the map-making sections of corps and army staffs absorbed most of the newly-taken photographs, and the information gleaned was then issued to the line in the form of new editions of trench maps. A strictly limited number of copies of the photographs themselves reached the infantry closest to the scene, and even yet infantry officers seldom read them with full intelligence. The reading of what were called " vertical photographs " was a matter mainly of constant practice guided by a few elementary principles. But by the latter part of 1917 (the date at which No. 3 Australian Squadron began its service career) no doubt remained about the supreme importance of photographs to the infantry in the line. Raids would not be planned without them. For a grand attack copies would be issued for close study, not merely to platoon-officers, but also to non-commissioned officers and men. By their help the attacking force could be made almost as intimate with the main features of enemy country to be captured and fortified as they were with their own lines from which they issued to the attack.

As the winter passed, and as in early 1918 it became clear that a grand German offensive had to be faced at some part of the Western Front, No. 3 Squadron—among others—photographed the enemy's lines on every possible day, with a view to searching out any changes or signs of preparation. The eyes of the scouting squadrons saw the ammunition dumps increasing, new gun-positions being made, and the growing signs of heavy transport in the enemy's rear, and at every opportunity photographic-reconnaissances were made by other squadrons, charged with that duty, to confirm the more fleeting observation of the eye. February and early March were a succession of bad spells of weather lasting several days, with here and there a fine day between. Each of these fine days was a day for photographic-reconnaissance, as well as for artillery-shoots, flash-spotting patrols, and patrols of German trench-defences, bomb-dropping and machine-gunning of ground targets. Corps squadrons are maids-of-all-work. Frequently they would drop into the German trenches "propaganda" as well as bombs; and sometimes, when the wind would carry a little roll of paper into the British lines instead of those of the enemy, the infantry would pick it up and pore over it and wonder what it meant. Its precise effect on the German soldier was never definitely ascertained, but it was a cunning scheme. Back in some prisoners' cage or prison-labour camp, captured Germans would be asked whether they would like to send a postcard home to say they were in good health and well treated. There was never any dearth of such messages. The prisoners would write their postcard and address it—they were not allowed to write of anything except their health and general treatment—and of these cards multiple copies would be made from a jelly-pad, sorted into bundles of a dozen or so of selected cards, and each bundle wrapped up in a fly-sheet with a notice in German printed on it in bold type. This notice was stereotyped, and read:—

"Soldaten! In dem Schützengraben erfriert man. Heraus aus dem Schützengraben! Hinein ins warme Bett! Täglich drei heisse Mahlzeiten! Wo? Warme Kleidung! Wo? Bezahlte Arbeit! Wo? Bei den Engländern! Darum ergebt Euch ihnen. Die Engländer töten keine Gefangenen. Im Lager der Engländer dürft Ihr Euren Civilberuf aufnehmen. Für Eure Arbeit werdet Ihr gut bezahlt. Im Lager der Engländer dürft Ihr an Eure Freunde und Verwandte schreiben, und Ihr erhaltet sämmtliche Briefe und Postpackete welche sie Euch zusenden. Es ist nicht unpatriotisch sich ehrenhaft dem Feind zu ergeben um später in die Heimat zurückkehren zu können. Darum ergebt Euch und erfriert nicht in dem Schützengraben."

["Soldiers! One freezes in the trenches. Come out of them! Come into a warm bed! Three hot meals a day! Where? Warm clothing! Where? Work for which you can receive pay! Where? With the English! Therefore surrender yourselves to them! The English do not kill their prisoners. In the camps of the English you may take up again your civilian employment. You will be well paid for the work you do. In the camps of the English you may write to your friends and relatives, and you will faithfully receive every letter and parcel which they send to you by post. It is not unpatriotic to give yourselves up honourably to the enemy in order to be able later to return to your own homes. Therefore come over and surrender, and do not go on freezing in the fire-trenches!"]

Not very many Germans came over as deserters in answer to this appeal, but it must have made the mouths of some of them water, even though its composition was not exactly classical.

The squadron's maid-of-all-work duties continued steadily through the winter. Patrols were rarely without incident. As the spring came nearer, the enemy machines—sent out to prevent the constant British reconnaissance—took the air in increasing numbers, and it became almost the daily rule for No. 3 Squadron's patrols to be attacked by scout formations. Escorting British scouts were generally there to defend the slower R.E.8's, but the R.E.8's were quite able to defend themselves on occasion, and Sandy's last fight was a magnificent demonstration of the fact. On January 25th Lieutenants C. C. Matheson[9] and C. T. Brown[10] (observer) on patrol met the attack of two German two-seaters and shot down one of them in flames. The squadron-commander, reporting on this, grimly commented: "It is interesting to note that Lieutenant Brown had just previously been declared the winner of the 2nd Brigade, Royal Air Force, machine-gun competition." The enemy's anti-aircraft action also increased in volume with his efforts to prevent observation of his plans. Lieutenants C. Donahay[11] and J. R. Blair[12] had their machine badly damaged by anti-aircraft fire on January 26th and crashed fatally at Dranoutre on their way home; three weeks later another of No. 3's machines, with Lieutenants H.

---

[9] Capt. C. C. Matheson; No. 3 Sqn. Motor mechanic; b. Trafalgar, Vic., 1898.

[10] Lieut. C. T. Brown; No. 3 Sqn. (previously Infantry). Fitter and turner; b. Charters Towers, Q'land, 1896.

[11] Lieut. C. Donahay; No. 3 Sqn. (previously A.A.M.C.). Optician; of Hawthorn, Melbourne; b. Camberwell, Melbourne, 14 Feb., 1892. Killed in action, 26 Jan., 1918.

[12] Lieut. J. R. Blair; No. 3 Sqn. (previously Infantry). Pastoralist; b. Rockhampton, Q'land, 1892. Killed in action, 26 Jan., 1918.

Streeter[13] and F. J. Tarrant,[14] while ranging a heavy battery, suddenly fell to pieces in the air over the lines near Wytschaete. There was no anti-aircraft fire at the time, and no hostile aeroplane to be seen, and the presumption was that the R.E.8 was hit by a British shell in flight. But in return for such losses the squadron took heavy toll of the enemy on the ground. Its pilots, besides their other work, assisted the artillery to put out of action sixty-one enemy batteries in January, fifty-one in February, and sixty-seven in March. These figures do not include the batteries upon which bombardment did not lead to some satisfactory result.

In March No. 3 Squadron had to leave its aerodrome at Bailleul. Throughout the winter on favourable nights, especially those about the full moon, the Germans had sent over bombing squadrons of Gothas, their chief target being always Bailleul town and aerodrome. A heavy night raid on December 4th was followed eight days later by a determined attack in the early afternoon from a formation of fifteen Gothas. If the fleet of these giant machines, with their sonorous double-hum, made a spectacle terrifying to the average civilian, the troops did not like them much better. On the day in question they dropped six enormous bombs of about 230 pounds each, but their aim was hampered by the attack of British scouts and their bombs missed the aerodrome, with the exception of one, which fell between two hangars and failed to explode. On the way home one of the monsters was brought down on fire by a British scout and fell in No-Man's Land. Again on February 2nd Gothas attempted two daylight raids upon the aerodrome, but each was driven away by anti-aircraft fire. That night the Gothas returned twice. No. 3 Squadron's habitation was clearly their target, but the raiders still failed to hit it. The full moon of mid-February saw a succession of enemy night air raids; Bailleul railway station was severely damaged, but the aerodrome escaped. In March it became clear that the Germans had marked down Bailleul for destruction. Besides the intermittent night bombing, shelling began on March 12th from

---

[13] Lieut. H. Streeter; No. 3 Sqn. (previously Infantry). Building contractor; b. Brunswick, Melbourne, 1894. Killed in action, 17 Feb., 1918.

[14] Lieut. F. J. Tarrant; No. 3 Sqn. (previously Artillery). Tailor's cutter; of Clifton Hill, Melbourne; b. Carlton, Melbourne, 12 Oct., 1895. Killed in action, 17 Feb., 1918.

long-range guns and produced deadly effect. By March 22nd the aerodrome became untenable. Many streets of the town were littered with the débris of broken houses, almost all the civilian population had gone—though these people did not customarily leave their homes while any hope remained—and that day the town was declared out of bounds to all troops. No. 3 Squadron had to leave also—the shelling was too dangerously close to their hangars—and that same day a move was made to Abeele, though without interruption of the squadron's patrols over the line. Next morning the enemy's long-range guns at last hit the abandoned aerodrome huts. The squadron did not entirely escape loss, for the shelling killed an air-mechanic and wounded an officer and a corporal, who had been left behind to clear up the aerodrome and salve remaining stores.

The long-range shelling of Bailleul was accompanied by shelling of other important towns which were road and railway centres—Hazebrouck, Lillers, St. Pol, Doullens—all normally reckoned beyond the danger zone. This proceeding was part of the wide programme of the great German offensive, which began on March 21st against the British line near St. Quentin, and which was preceded by great activity against the whole Allied front in order to mask the actual point of assault. The Allies had accurately forecasted the location, and even the date, of the attack, but warnings were issued that the enemy offensive might also come at more places than one along the line. The area between La Bassée and Ypres was accounted one such danger-place by every division in that area. The awaited offensive did not begin in that quarter, although an important thrust was made there not long afterwards. The issued warnings made No. 3's reconnoitring patrols all the keener, and, for increased preparedness, special counter-attack patrol machines were maintained over the German lines at about dawn and dusk on every day from March 11th onwards. In its work through the winter, and especially during March, the squadron, by record of results achieved, won itself pride of place in the 2nd (Corps) Wing.

Early in April No. 3 Squadron moved again. The Australian Corps had gone south to the Somme to meet the German advance on Amiens, and thither the corps squadron followed it. By April 8th it was established in the aerodrome at Poulainville, alongside Australian Corps Headquarters at Bertangles. The last notable event in the north before it left Abeele was a brilliant fight about noon on April 1st, when Lieutenants R. G. D. Francis[15] and R. Hainsworth[16] (observer), while ranging a heavy battery, were attacked by a D.F.W. two-seater. The German dived down on them and missed, and the R.E.8 instantly turned to counter-attack. Francis cut the German off from his own side of the lines, and then by skilful manœuvring began driving him steadly westward. He out-flew and out-fought the D.F.W. for several exciting minutes. The enemy could not break back, and every turn he made found the R.E.8 ready for him with another burst of fire. After Francis had fired about 350 rounds, his opponent went down in a steep dive and crashed. The fight was witnessed throughout from Francis's own aerodrome.

---

[15] Capt. R. G. D. Francis, D.F.C.; No. 3 Sqn. Chemist; of Kew, Melbourne; b. Corio, Vic., 22 Dec., 1889.

[16] Lieut. R. Hainsworth; No. 3 Sqn. Electrical fitter; b. Willoughby, N.S.W., Nov., 1892.

CHAPTER XVI

SPRING FIGHTS NORTH OF THE SCARPE

CHRISTMAS-TIME 1917 saw the appearance in France of the last-formed Australian flying squadron, No. 4. From the training-ground near Birmingham its three flights flew across the Channel on December 18th and landed at the base aerodrome at St. Omer that same day. The squadron entered the field under the command of Major W. A. McCloughry. At this beginning of its service, two of the three flight-commanders—Captains A. H. O'Hara Wood[1] and R. E. A. W. Hughes-Chamberlain[2]—were R.F.C. officers. The third was Captain Matthews, who had previously gone to the front for a few weeks with No. 2 Squadron, and then, like McCloughry, had been ordered back to join No. 4.

No. 4 Squadron flew Sopwith Camels, which among British aircraft rivalled the S.E.5's for speed and fighting efficiency. Four days after arrival in France the squadron was ordered to the aerodrome at Bruay, where it came under the command of the 10th (Army) Wing, operating with the British First Army. To this same wing in the following month was also posted No. 2 Squadron, which moved on January 7th from Baizieux to Auchel, and a fortnight later from Auchel to Savy, the aerodrome at which No. 3 Squadron had been quartered on its first arrival in France. Between mid-December and mid-January not only No. 4 Squadron but also No. 2 was engaged mainly in fighting and flying practice, for No. 2 had to break in its pilots to their new S.E.5's.

The first fortnight of No. 4 Squadron at Bruay passed in various war-flying practice and in learning the country. "C" Flight began its career with extraordinarily bad luck. On the morning of the 6th of January, 1918, five of the six pilots of that flight were practising formation-flying, when, in crossing during a turn, Lieutenants A. M. Anderson[3] and R.

---

[1] Capt. A. H. O'Hara Wood, R.A.F. Attached No. 4 Sqn., Nov., 1917, to Feb., 1918.

[2] Maj. R. E. A. W. Hughes-Chamberlain, R.A.F. Attached No. 4 Sqn., Nov., 1917, to Feb., 1918.

[3] Lieut. A. M. Anderson; No. 4 Sqn. b. Melbourne, 1892. Killed in action, 6 Jan., 1918.

H. Curtis[4] collided, and, as they fell, a portion of the wreckage struck the machine of Lieutenant J. N. Cash[5] flying below them, and brought him down also. All three pilots were killed. Before the month was out—on January 28th—another pilot of the same flight, Lieutenant E. B. Nelson,[6] also crashed fatally on the aerodrome after returning from an offensive patrol.

The squadron made its first sortie into "Hunland"[7] on January 9th, when two patrols went out, one to escort photography-machines and one on offensive-patrol. For two or three days this work continued uneventfully. Then, on January 13th, occurred the squadron's first air combat. Lieutenant F. B. Willmott,[8] straggling in behind his formation from a patrol, was cut off by three German scouts, forced to land, and taken prisoner. O'Hara Wood, leading a battle-formation on January 24th, avenged Willmott by shooting down the squadron's first German victim, a D.F.W. two-seater, which crashed near La Bassée.

The weather in January and early February was almost constantly bad, and flying, when not actually impossible, was frequently rendered useless by obscuring clouds. The two Australian squadrons spent this mid-winter period in low reconnaissances, offensive-patrols, escorting photography-machines and bombing formations over the German lines, and, seeking excitement to relieve monotony, in machine-gunning villages in the nearer German areas between Lille and the River Scarpe. The front upon which they were thus operating was one of the classic hunting-grounds of British airmen. It contained many German aerodromes, especially about Lille and Douai, and was studded with anti-aircraft

---

[4] Lieut. R. H. Curtis; No. 4 Sqn. (previously A.A.M.C.). Grazier; of Glen Innes, N.S.W.; b. Glen Innes, 1 March, 1894. Killed in action, 6 Jan., 1918.

[5] Lieut. J. N. Cash; No. 4 Sqn. (previously Artillery). Stockman; b. Newcastle, Eng., 1896. Killed in action, 6 Jan., 1918.

[6] Lieut. E. B. Nelson; No. 4 Sqn. Electrical engineer; of North Sydney; b. St. Leonard's, Sydney, 7 Jan., 1892. Died of wounds, 29 Jan., 1918.

[7] "Hunland" was the name used throughout the British air service to designate the territory beyond the German front lines. The Royal Air Force developed a language of its own, as distinctive as that of the Royal Navy. As a short title for "territory under enemy occupation," "Hunland" has particular merits. Other valuable words in the airmen's vocabulary were "stunt," "strafe," and "dog-fight." "Strafe" was a general army term for any enterprise meant to punish or harass the enemy, and was borrowed from the famous German invective, "Gott strafe England!" "Dog-fight" was the universal name among British airman for the savage mêlée of a willing fight between opposing air formations.

[8] Lieut. F. B. Willmott; No. 4 Sqn. Motor mechanic; b. Adelaide, Jan., 1895.

SOPWITH CAMEL (USED BY NO. 4 SQUADRON, A.F.C., FROM DECEMBER, 1917, TILL OCTOBER, 1918)

Aust. War Museum Official Photo. No. D129.

SOPWITH SNIPE (USED BY NO. 4 SQUADRON, A.F.C., FROM OCTOBER, 1918, ONWARDS)

Lent by Lieut. T. A. Swinbourne, R.A.A.F. (then of No. 2 Sqn., A.F.C.).

To face p. 214.

D.H.5 (USED BY NO. 2 SQUADRON, A.F.C., OCTOBER-DECEMBER, 1917)
Aust. War Museum Official Photo. No. E1445.

S.E.5 (USED BY NO. 2 SQUADRON, A.F.C., FROM JANUARY, 1918, ONWARDS)
Aust. War Museum Official Photo. No. E1446.

To face p. 215.

batteries. Over Douai, as the weather improved, roving pilots, out to increase their lists of victims, never failed to find enemy aircraft, and some found more of them than they desired. Hither came the crack British pilots on the full summer days when the sky was empty elsewhere, for when the famous Richthofen Circus[9] was on the British front, it was generally located at Douai. The scotching of Richthofen was the great ambition of every fighting pilot who had begun his ascent of the glorious ladder of " aces "[10] in the list of " number of enemy machines destroyed." By the time the Australian scouting squadrons appeared in France, the days of the earlier crack German airmen, Immelmann, Boelcke, Wolff, Voss, had ended. Richthofen, the successor of Boelcke in command of the destroying " circus," the star of stars in the German Air Force, was now in the zenith of his fame. First in the Fokker, and later in the improved Albatros, he carried on the tactics inculcated by the admired Boelcke, and would ride the higher air in leadership of his formation, waiting until a hostile formation were met and a fight begun. He rarely fought alone. When battle was joined, and a " dog-fight " was on, his own tactics were to remain hovering high above it until his chance came to dive upon some straggler on its fringe, or upon some opponent who happened to be at a temporary disadvantage. At this moment Richthofen would descend like a hawk upon the selected victim. " Everything that is in the air beneath me," he boasted, " is lost." The machines of his circus were painted red from nose to tail; its pilots were all crack airmen, and they did no other work but hunt for British and French machines to destroy. They were not for reconnaissance, nor for any sort of escort work, save when they escorted those decoy machines which our own men learned to treat with much wariness. An unfrightened lumbering old German two-seater, or a couple of them, in the offing and low down, gave to British aerial huntsmen a direct warning of danger lurking in the sun or the clouds above.

Every airman—and Richthofen must be included among them—had now and then some bowels of mercy for an opponent hopelessly outclassed. Richthofen relates of one

---

[9] Circus—see Chapter XVIII, pp. 247-8, and Glossary.
[10] Ace—see Glossary.

fight against a photographing-machine, that he perceived the pilot to be wounded and his aeroplane to be showing signs of catching fire; he manœuvred to compel his adversary to land in the German lines, not wishing to shoot him down. Such consideration was, however, not usual with Richthofen, who was out to beat records in the list of aces. The large account of victims with which he was credited in his own service would, it is said, have required heavy pruning in that of the British. Richthofen's accredited total of eighty victims was widely declared to include some shot down by his squadron in combined attack, where the destruction of a victim was the work of several machines. Australian airmen had at least three brushes with the Richthofen Circus.

Meanwhile, during the last stages of the winter, the two scouting squadrons—No. 4, engaged in low-flying attacks upon the ground, and No. 2, flying at a " ceiling "[11] of 15,000 feet or more—ranged the whole First Army front, searching every day for the first spring Fokkers to appear. No. 2 Squadron especially was itching to try its new S.E.5's upon them. O'Hara Wood, flying with Lieutenants A. H. Cobby[12] and E. F. Pflaum,[13] fought several indecisive combats with enemy machines low over Brebières (south-west of Douai) on February 3rd, and drove one two-seater down out of control. On the three succeeding days—days of wind and cloud—No. 4's patrols sighted occasional and distant enemy machines, which remained well in the rear of their own lines. Only once did they see one on the British side of the line, and that at tremendous height over Arras; a patrol led by Captain D. P. Flockart[14] climbed hard to reach it, but at 14,000 feet lost sight of it, still high overhead. Each day the patrols, failing to bring any hostile machines to action, emptied their gun-belts into villages occupied by German troops. On February 5th, after patiently patrolling round about Douai for many days, a patrol of five from No. 2 Squadron, led by Forrest, found four Albatros scouts going home from the direction of Lille.

---

[11] Ceiling—see Glossary.

[12] Capt. A. H. Cobby, D.S.O., D.F.C.; No. 4 Sqn. Bank clerk; of Glenhuntly, Melbourne; b. Prahran, Melbourne, 26 Aug., 1894.

[13] Capt. E. F. Pflaum; No. 2 Sqn. (previously Light Horse). Auctioneer; of Loxton, S. Aust.; b. Birdwood, S. Aust., 5 Jan., 1892.

[14] Capt. D. P. Flockart; No. 4 Sqn. Electrical engineer; of Melbourne; b. Casterton, Vic., 3 Sept., 1894.

It was hardly a fight, for the enemy, though they had the height of Forrest, avoided engagement; the only Australian machine to climb near enough for a shot was R. W. Howard's, and from him the enemy span away at once into a cloud. Nevertheless the climbing powers of the S.E.5 thoroughly pleased the Australians.

The weather of the days between February 7th and 15th made flying impossible. Then came two or three fine days, which brought out the German machines as well as the British. On February 17th patrols from No. 4 Squadron, led by O'Hara Wood and Flockart, met small enemy formations near Lille in short fights. In the engagement of Flockart's formation Lieutenant F. S. Woolhouse[15] fired a hundred rounds from both his guns at point-blank range into a German two-seater, which went down out of control.[16] Lieutenant C. H. Martin[17] of the same patrol was lost; his machine, while flying unmolested, was seen suddenly to break in pieces in the air, probably hit full by a shell. Such a mishap was sufficiently rare to mark as extraordinary the fact that, not two hours previously in the same afternoon, a similar fate befell a machine of No. 3 Squadron over the Messines Ridge.[18]

The Germans were in the air in strength on February 18th, and in the forenoon Lieutenants Huxley and A. L. Paxton[19] from No. 2 Squadron, flying at 15,000 feet between Loos and Lille, met four fantastically-coloured Albatros scouts. The Australians had the height of them, and Huxley dived on the enemy leader, while Paxton stayed aloft to protect him. Huxley fired fifty rounds into his opponent at 150 yards, and saw the German turn on his wing-tip and go down out of control. Another Albatros darted upon Huxley, but as soon

---

[15] Lieut. F. S. Woolhouse; No. 4 Sqn. (previously Infantry). Signwriter and decorator; of Perth, W. Aust.; b. Roeburne, W. Aust., 21 Feb., 1896. Killed in action, 10 Apr., 1918.

[16] That a machine "fell out of control" did not always mean that it was destroyed. A pilot attacked from above would often "put his machine into a spin," which meant that it fell away rapidly, whirling in a corkscrew course; and while in a "spin" an aeroplane is not under its pilot's control. While this was a common method of escape from attack, it was also frequently a sign that either the pilot or the machine had been put out of action. In such case a crash frequently ensued, especially when the fight occurred near the ground. The attacker, when he was able, would follow his spinning adversary down and continue firing into him. See Glossary.

[17] Lieut. C. H. Martin; No. 4 Sqn. (previously Infantry). Building foreman; of Port Melbourne, Vic.; b. Port Melbourne, 1 April, 1894. Killed in action, 17 Feb., 1918.

[18] See Chapter XV, p. 210.

[19] Lieut. A. L. Paxton, R.A.F. Attached No. 2 Sqn., 10 Jan. to 26 July, 1918

as Paxton dived in turn to thwart him, the remaining Germans broke off and flew away east. As they came home, the pair chased a two-seater to a forced landing from over Festubert. At 12.30 on the same day R. W. Howard and Holden, looking for prey between Lens and Douai at 16,500 feet, saw beneath them six red-tailed Albatros scouts in two flights of three, pursuing an R.E.8. They at once dived on the nearer group, and a hot burst from Howard sent the leader down in a vertical nose-dive with a slow spin from which he was not seen to recover. The other Germans hastily turned and made for the ground near Lille. By the time the Australians had again made height over Douai they met five more German scouts, but, just as the fight was beginning, six Bristol Fighters appeared overhead and the Germans turned tail for home. On the same day the Camels[20] also were engaged in several indecisive encounters at lower altitudes with enemy two-seaters, which they drove in from artillery-ranging.

Next day visibility was very bad for all except those who continued the war at 17,000 feet. While rifts in the haze and clouds showed them Pont-à-Vendin on the floor below, McKenzie and Benjamin of No. 2 Squadron had a short, sharp fight with three green Albatros scouts, from which engagement one German fell away in a spin. A little later, in the same vicinity, Lieutenants Huxley and A. G. Clark,[21] meeting two obvious decoys and refusing to be drawn towards them under a cloud, stood off, to see six German scouts suddenly dash out of it as though expecting to entrap them. Having thus exposed their plan, the enemy, though in force of eight to two, had no heart to wait for the attack which the Australians then prepared to deliver, and turned away home.

In a burst of spring weather on February 21st Lieutenants A. G. Clark, Benjamin, R. Lang,[22] and W. Q. Adams,[23] from No. 2 Squadron, encountered over Brebières ten Albatros scouts with silver bodies and red noses, in two formations, six

---

[20] "Camels"—Here and elsewhere in this narrative used as a short term for "Sopwith Camels." See Appendix No. 1.

[21] Lieut. A. G. Clark; No. 2 Sqn. (previously Light Horse). Grazier; b. Ashfield, Sydney, Aug., 1896.

[22] Lieut. R. Lang, M.M.; R.A.F. Attached No. 2 Sqn., 10 Jan. to 21 Feb., 1918.

[23] Lieut. W. Q. Adams; R.A.F. Attached No. 2 Sqn., 10 Jan. to 22 July, 1918.

and four. Clark, the leader of the Australian four, said: "One hostile machine dived at me. I fired both guns, Lewis and Vickers, into the nose of this machine, getting a burst of fifty rounds into it at a range of forty yards. The machine fell over on its left wing and dropped vertically into an uncontrolled spin." He then led his formation into a climb in order to get height before attacking again. Meanwhile Benjamin, as he said later, suddenly saw a silver-fish dive straight across his front not more than thirty yards off. "I had nothing to do," he reported, "but put my finger on my trigger and keep it there, and the enemy got it fair in the middle." In the climb to continue the fight they all lost sight of these victims for a few seconds, but, as the remainder of the German formation broke away for home, Lang, diving, saw one Albatros crash on the ground and another going down completely out of control. A quarter of an hour later a patrol of four from No. 4 Squadron —Lieutenants J. C. Courtney,[24] G. Jones,[25] A. W. Adams,[26] and A. Couston[27]—engaged six enemy scouts which were escorting four two-seaters near the line between Lens and Arras. Jones shot an Albatros to pieces in the air, and Adams, chasing another from the *mêlée*, followed it with bursts of fire till he saw it crash near Haubourdin, twenty miles north of the first encounter. Couston, in a duel with a third German, was carried away during the fight nearly to Douai, and was finally shot down by his opponent, but made a landing near that place and was taken prisoner. This engagement was scarcely over when Phillipps and Holden from No. 2 Squadron appeared on the scene at 16,000 feet, and found six red-nosed Albatros scouts over Esquerchin, near where Couston's duel had finished. The two attacked this formation and broke it up. Two of the Germans span away into clouds; the remainder sheered off. It remains to be said that during the rest of the day no German formation was observed in the sky by either of the Australian squadrons.

---

[24] Lieut. J. C. Courtney; No. 4 Sqn. Fitter and turner; of Manly, Sydney; b. Auckland, N.Z., 14 April, 1893. Killed in action, 7 April, 1918.

[25] Capt. G. Jones, D.F.C.; No. 4 Sqn. (previously Light Horse). Motor mechanic; b. Rushworth, Vic., Oct., 1896.

[26] Lieut. A. W. Adams; No. 4 Sqn. Rubber worker; b. Woodend, Vic., Apr., 1894.

[27] Lieut. A. Couston; No. 4 Sqn. (previously Machine-Gun Corps). Telephone mechanic; b. Launceston, Tas., July, 1893.

Map No. 13

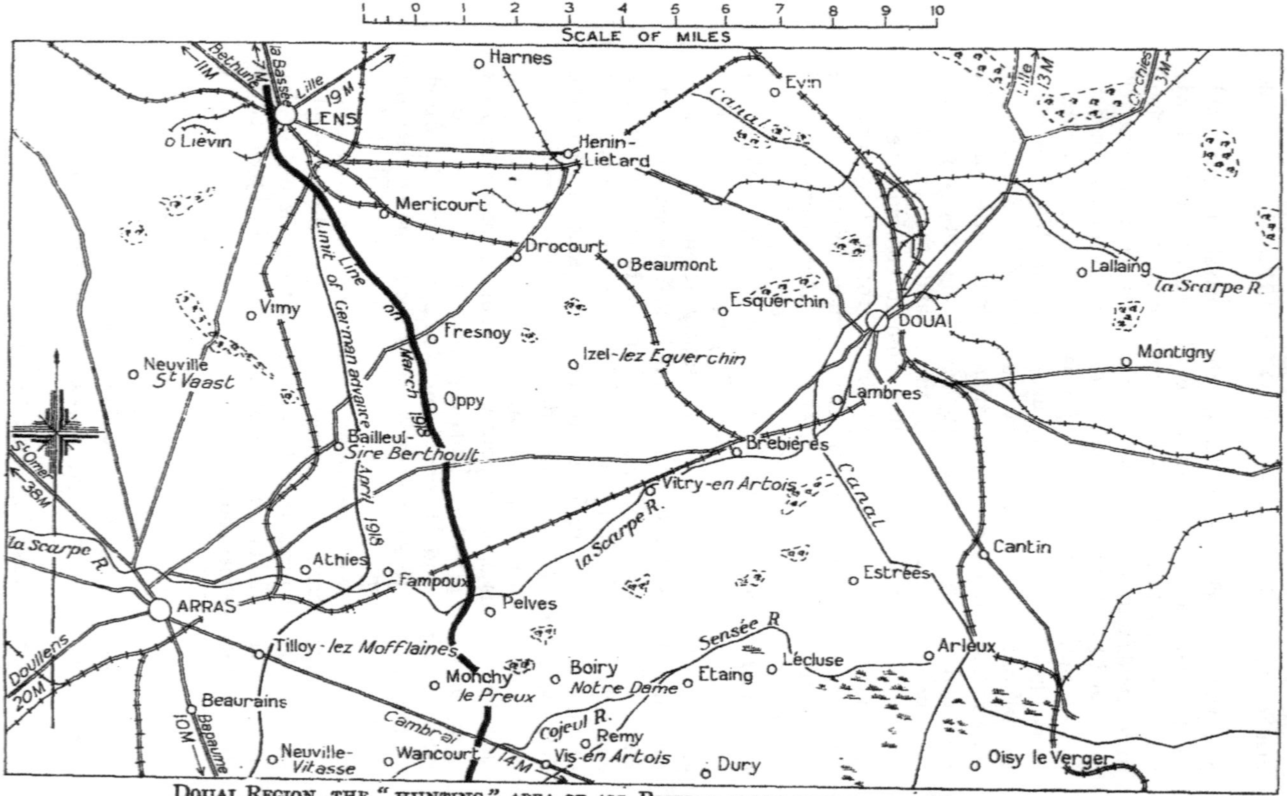

Douai Region, the "hunting" area of all British scout squadrons. Many aerodromes of German scout squadrons were situated in the vicinity of Douai.

Hitherto No. 4 Squadron had been seriously handicapped, as compared with other fighting squadrons, by reason of having only eighteen machines on its strength. Towards the end of February it received six more machines, making up its full complement, and from that time the efficiency of the squadron in offensive-patrols and in the extent of its operations was greatly enhanced. A further mark of the squadron's progress was its proved capacity to provide its own flight-commanders, and on February 18th O'Hara Wood and Hughes-Chamberlain, who had been lent from the British service, returned to their own corps, and Australian pilots took their places as flight-commanders.

For nearly a fortnight air fighting died down during stormy weather. Australian patrols continued on every possible occasion their bombing and machine-gunning of enemy villages and road transport. In this work Lieutenant W. B. Randell,[28] of No. 4 Squadron, and Lieutenant G. C. Logan,[29] a newly-arrived pilot in No. 2, were shot down by anti-aircraft fire over German lines and taken prisoners. The German battle-squadrons were nursing their strength for the great offensive, which every man on the Allied front knew to be in preparation. By March 11th all British airmen were ordered to hold themselves specially on the alert.

The enemy's preparations were multiplying. Pilots from distant reconnaissance daily brought reports of new field-hospitals springing up behind the German lines, of the growth in numbers and sizes of ammunition-dumps, and of an immense increase in artillery. The German plan—as has already been explained—was to prepare everywhere at once, in order to set the British Intelligence Staff the problem of guessing the precise point of the intended offensive. Many of the new battery-positions were dummies; many more were real enough, but unoccupied. In some places, as on the Champagne front, German artillerymen were set to driving waggons up and down and round about false battery-positions in order to distract observation from the real points of concentration.

The bad weather broke at the end of the first week of March, and German aircraft at once appeared upon

---

[28] Lieut. W. B. Randell; No. 4 Sqn. (previously Artillery). Electoral inspector; b. Mt. Pleasant, S. Aust., 1892.

[29] Lieut. G. C. Logan, R.A.F. Attached No. 2 Sqn., 10 Jan. to 21 Feb., 1918.

reconnaissance and to range the German guns upon British batteries. On the morning of March 6th seven machines from No. 4 Squadron observed several Rumpler two-seaters, escorted by six Albatros scouts, over the British lines at Arras. Flockart's patrol of four machines climbed to meet the escort, while the other three dispersed the two-seaters. The Albatros formation turned for home, but was brought by Flockart to action, in which he and Woolhouse shot down one, which crashed near the River Scarpe. Lieutenant F. J. Scott[30] chased a Rumpler as far as Lens and destroyed it. March 8th was a glorious flying day. Every available Australian machine was in the air; the sky over the Douai area was filled with these winged huntsmen waiting for the enemy to break cover from his aerodromes. An early patrol of four S.E.5's under Lieutenant R. L. Manuel[31] sighted near Lens twenty-six German scouts in two formations. Two of the Australian machines had given signs of engine-trouble, and Manuel accordingly avoided engagement. News of the enemy was reported to the aerodromes, and at 10 a.m. twelve Camels left Bruay, while four more S.E.5's took off from Savy aerodrome. They spent no time in looking for the reported German armada, but made for the vicinity of the enemy's aerodromes in order to meet him there. Just west of Douai Flockart's formation attacked a bunch of German scouts, presumably some of the earlier fleet returning; Flockart and Woolhouse shot one of them down in flames, and Lieutenant G. Nowland[32] sent another down out of control. A little to the north of them four S.E.5's under R. W. Howard attacked two two-seaters and forced one to land in a hurry. Returning a quarter of an hour later from scouring this area for traces of the enemy, they drove down out of control another two-seater. An Albatros scout which then appeared from the direction of Douai met with the same fate. The S.E.5's were turning towards home, when they saw a black two-seater flying over Henin-Liètard. They dived on this too eagerly, for, as the two-seater put his nose down

---

[30] Lieut. F. J. Scott, M.C.; No. 4 Sqn. Grazier; b. Korumburra, Vic., 1895.

[31] Capt. R. L. Manuel, D.F.C.; No. 2 Sqn (previously Infantry). Farmer; of Kerang, Vic.; b. Kerang, 7 Oct., 1895.

[32] Lieut. G. Nowland; No. 4 Sqn. Tent-maker; of Clifton Hill and North Fitzroy, Melbourne; b. Fitzroy, 23 March, 1892. Killed in action, 22 May, 1918.

eastward, the Australian patrol was suddenly attacked by eight Albatros scouts from the sun.[33] Howard perceived them in time to avert disaster, and turned towards the British lines, making a left bank and climbing sharply in order to gain height. The Germans did not press the attack, and the Australians, having been out for over an hour and a half and running a risk of petrol shortage, courted no further action, but made for home.

From March 11th onwards German airmen became increasingly active. Though the Australians were constantly meeting them and exchanging shots, such encounters amounted as a rule to no more than sparring matches. The Germans were waiting for the day of Ludendorff's offensive. Machines on both sides now flew in large formations. The manœuvring by a formation on either side would be for advantage of height; if such a manœuvre succeeded, the opposing formation would dive away in order to avoid attack, and then either seek to climb again for a counter-attack or else break off the engagement. All depended on advantage of position. On neither side had the scouts the speed of their opponents in any considerable measure, except that the S.E.5 and the Camel could usually beat the Albatros on the climb. The bringing on of a "dog-fight"—where both sides were willing and where they met on fairly equal terms of position—depended for a time either on the enemy formation being so cornered by the British scouts that it had no other hope, or upon that formation being one of the aggressive circuses whose members were known by their machines, and whose prestige was such that they always fought as a matter of principle.

Ten S.E.5's under R. W. Howard cornered some of the enemy on March 12th over Wingles, just north of Lens. Flying in a wide spread, the Australians found themselves well over six Albatros scouts escorting a two-seater. Howard, being in the sun, and evidently unseen, dived on the escort. The enemy scattered in all directions, and one, turning desperately to escape Lieutenant A. R. Rackett,[34] who was fast on its tail, suddenly gave Holden an excellent target. Holden zoomed up and fired into it a stalling burst of fifty rounds.

---
[33] See note 13, Chapter VI, p. 72.
[34] Lieut. A. R. Rackett; No. 2 Sqn. (previously Signal Services). b. Port Adelaide, S. Aust., 1896.

The Albatros forthwith fell out of control and was seen to hit the earth in flames. McKenzie dived clean through the enemy scouts upon the two-seater below, fired ninety rounds into it, and that also fell in flames. Another Albatros was destroyed next morning by the same pilot—again over Wingles —when nine Australian machines cut off from home two German scouts, well separated. These were not days for scouts to fly alone, and one of the Germans paid the penalty for his foolishness.

The tactics of this waiting period were further demonstrated by the experience of No. 4 Squadron. Soon after sun-up on March 13th a patrol of eleven Camels under Courtney found large numbers of German two-seaters at work between Lens and La Bassée, but could not attack them, for the reason that enemy scouts were waiting in the sun well overhead. But two days later Courtney, leading a patrol of ten, routed a number of German two-seaters observed to be without escort south of the Scarpe, and shot down four, two of them out of control. These fights were only preliminary air skirmishing. The German airmen, as has been explained, were avoiding battle until the desired moment; the plan of the British squadrons was to draw them on to engagement, and offensive-patrols swept the enemy's front, searching for his strength, bombing his aerodromes, taunting him to fight, probing unceasingly to discover the main secret—the selected moment of his onslaught. It was expected that the first shock would be felt in the air. The patrols sought for that shock, for the first touch of the enemy's battle-fleet. It might appear at any part of the front and at any moment. Each day after March 11th increased the strain. British battle-patrols multiplied their efforts.

Suddenly No. 4 Australian Squadron made the desired touch. In the morning of March 16th two flights, of five machines each, under Captain N. L. Petschler[35] and Lieutenant G. F. Malley,[36] set out to bomb Douai railway junction, Malley escorting. Petschler and two others were compelled to turn back by engine-trouble. Seven Camels

---

[35] Capt. N. L. Petschler; No. 4 Sqn. Indentor; of St. George District, N.S.W.; b. Rockdale, Sydney, 22 Nov., 1892.

[36] Capt. G. F. Malley, M.C., A.F.C.; No. 4 Sqn. (previously Artillery). Mechanic; b. Mosman, Sydney, Nov., 1892.

reached Douai, and had just climbed to about 16,000 feet after dropping their bombs, when they were attacked from above by sixteen enemy scouts. It was Richthofen's Red Circus, renowned as stormy petrels. The Germans dived upon the Australians in twos and threes and at once broke up Malley's formation. In all twelve attacked in this fashion; the other four remained hovering above the fight, in order to prevent any recovery by the Camels for counter-attack. Lieutenants Malley and C. M. Feez,[37] avoiding the first onset, fastened upon two red Albatros scouts which were diving together, and shot both of them down in flames. Lieutenant A. W. Adams, who was flying 2,000 feet below Malley when the action began, fought a fierce duel with a couple of the enemy and sank one, which was believed to have crashed. On the Australian side the fight was a desperate effort to escape, which barely succeeded. Lieutenant W. H. Nicholls,[38] a newly-joined pilot, was chased down to the ground and just failed to reach home. He was forced to land in the German front line, and was taken prisoner. Lieutenant P. K. Schafer[39] received the full force of the enemy's opening fire; he dropped 10,000 feet in a spin earthward, followed by three red scouts, all shooting at him, and was saved chiefly by the Germans' reluctance to continue the struggle at low height over the British lines. Schafer reached Bruay aerodrome with sixty-two bullet-holes in his machine, including several through the wind-screen in front of his face.

The report of Richthofen's Circus in action over the Scarpe sector sent a thrill through local British air squadrons. For the next two days no further important events happened. Large Australian offensive patrols north of the Scarpe failed to pick up Richthofen or any other enemy, but fired some thousands of machine-gun rounds into the German trenches near Lens and La Bassée. R. W. Howard, leading a flight of S.E.5's destroyed a solitary Rumpler two-seater near Lille on March 18th. Then fog shut down on the front for three days.

---

[37] Lieut. C. M. Feez; No. 4 Sqn. (previously Aritllery). Grazier; of Yeronga, Brisbane; b. Brisbane, 14 Dec., 1897.

[38] Lieut. W. H. Nicholls; No. 4 Sqn. (previously Light Horse). Auctioneer; b. Adelaide, 1895.

[39] Lieut. P. K. Schafer, M.M.; No. 4 Sqn. (previously Infantry). Clerk; b. Ascot Vale, Melbourne, 1897.

and through this fog, on March 21st, Ludendorff's mighty offensive burst upon the British lines at St. Quentin.

The probable region of the assault had been deduced by the British High Command from a variety of evidence. Divisions in the line there had been warned, and on March 20th No. 4 Australian Squadron received orders to extend its patrols south of the Scarpe to cover the region of Bapaume. At 8 o'clock in the morning of March 21st, in a dense mist, ten machines left Bruay in two formations, under Courtney and Cobby, to search the new area. Cobby with his five scouts led, while Courtney flew above and behind him to watch the tails of the leading flight. The mist made flying in good formation almost impossible. "The country was obscured by mist," reported Cobby, "and after about forty minutes' flying I confess that I, the leader of the whole patrol, had but a vague idea of where I was. Every now and then we would see a captive balloon peeping through the mist. Finally I determined to follow this line north until near home, then strike across towards Bruay and endeavour to locate the aerodrome.

"At 9 a.m. we were flying north at about 4,000 feet, just above the balloons and fog, when three Albatros scouts came through the fog just below and to the left of us. They were followed by a straggling line of Pfalz and other scouts, and were flying on a line parallel to our own. Apparently they did not see us, for they made no attempt either to fight or avoid us. Rocking my machine fore and aft—the usual signal to follow the leader into action—I dived into the centre of the enemy formation. Courtney came down from above and joined in, and for about four minutes an all-in dog-fight ensued.

"It was Richthofen's Circus again; all were red machines, except one yellow-and-black Albatros. The leaders first seen did not join the fight; they were ahead in the fog." Cobby destroyed two of the enemy. Lieutenants Pflaum and A. E. Robertson[40] each shot down a selected opponent, pursued him through the ground-mist, and saw him crash. Lieutenant G.

---

[40] Lieut. A. E. Robertson, M.C.; No. 4 Sqn. Electrical engineer; b. Prahran, Melbourne, Apr., 1892.

M. Elwyn[41] fought a strenuous duel with one red scout, and then, his own engine being badly damaged by bullets, had to land behind the British lines near Bapaume.

By evening of that day the attention of both the Australian scout squadrons was turned to the northern area of the battle, the right front of the British Third Army, in the Bapaume sector.

---

[41] Lieut. G. M. Elwyn; No. 4 Sqn. (previously Light Horse). Stock and station agent; b. Texas, Q'land, 1894.

CHAPTER XVII

MEETING THE GERMAN OFFENSIVE

UNTIL the opening of Ludendorff's offensive on March 21st, the strain of expectation in the Allied Armies was intense. The news of the definite event brought a notable relief. There was never any doubt about the seriousness of the German effort. It was promised as a fight to the death. The British Army knew that it had its back to the wall; the Germans proclaimed this to be their last grand attack. Action, when it came at last, though tremendous the issue, brought new vigour to men haunted by weeks of anxiety. If it were to be its last fight, the British Army had resolved it should be a good one; and—despite many ill-informed stories during those latter days of March concerning the broken Fifth Army opposite St. Quentin—a good fight it was.

In the main, and especially among those troops who had not to bear the first overwhelming shock, the feeling in the crisis was one of exultation. Airmen came back to the British aerodromes that morning thrilled with amazement at the mighty drama which had been unfolded before their eyes on the ground below. The terrific artillery bombardment by the enemy guns at dawn had aroused to the alert the whole neighbourhood behind the British lines. Soon after dawn, a pilot landed at a British aerodrome, white-faced and shaking with excitement at what he had seen through the mist. "There are thousands of them—thousands and thousands," was all he could say. "The whole countryside is alive with them, all advancing." Every aeroplane in the vicinity took the air, loaded with every kind of bomb, emptied the explosives on to the nearest body of enemy infantry, blazed off its machine-gun ammunition into grey masses at close range, and then returned home for supplies to repeat the attack. The work done by the heavy bombers far behind the German lines was enormous. But still the masses of the enemy pressed forward, along lanes which had been shot clean through the British position by the fire of heavy artillery, filtering through at any weak point where resistance had been destroyed, outflanking dazed and gasping rear-guards caught in the fumes of gas-shells. One British airman, killed on the following day, wrote home on the evening of that twenty-first of March a letter describing what he had seen:[1]

"Since an early hour in the afternoon rolling clouds of picric smoke smothered the surface of the earth, almost obscuring it from reconnaissance. The effect was most startling. At one moment the smoke would roll back like a coverlet; the stretch of road and railway, village and field, below would be almost bare of movement. At another, through a rift could be caught a fleeting glimpse of indescribable masses of grey, which at first against the greyer shadow of the earth would appear motionless, then develop animation at various points; a great human snake that writhed this way and that, endeavouring to free itself from its own voluminous coils. I dived lower, and rapidly fired off a tray and a half of cartridges from my machine-gun, encountering little or no defensive fire and certainly causing casualties.

"A broad, straight highway running directly north and south indicated Le V—— (Le Verguier), where a great mass of British infantry (the 24th Division) was lying. Gradually, very gradually, it was dwindling away in long ceaseless tendrils from the main body to a more expansive mass in the rear ground. Tiny shoots of flame stabbed the smoke cloud from all directions. It was denser here, and difficult to distinguish friend from foe. The hurl and shock and recoil of the infantry battle were here plainly visible. By this time I had run out of ammunition."

The climax of the Allied counter-attack from the air was yet to come. Meanwhile, the two Australian squadrons were also engaged in meeting the German attack. The first to enter the fight was No. 2 Squadron, on March 22nd, when a double formation of ten machines, under Phillipps and Forrest, started at 2 p.m. for their old fighting-ground around Cambrai and St. Quentin, now the scene of the right of the German attack. Two of them had to turn back immediately in consequence of engine-trouble, but the other eight drove on for St. Quentin, and there met five enemy two-seaters and a number of scouts with them. Forrest dived on a two-seater,

---

[1] This description of an eye-witness of the great scene is quoted in Middleton's *Tails Up*.

which fell in flames from a hot burst at forty-yards' range. Simultaneously McKenzie engaged an Albatros scout and sent it down out of control. These fights took place at 18,000 feet. The formation turned north along the German front, and five minutes later was over Bourlon Wood. There they saw five German triplanes below them. Singling out the leader, Phillipps attacked and chased it downward for 2,000 feet, firing into it at close range. It rolled over on to its back, went spinning down slowly, and was last seen only a thousand feet from the ground, and still spinning. The remainder of the enemy scattered into the haze. Passing on, the Australian formation attacked more Albatros scouts over Bullecourt, and Forrest shot down two of these out of control, and Holden a third, in rapid succession. Shortly after this patrol came in, another went out under R. W. Howard. In a general engagement at 9,000 feet, Rackett drove down an enemy scout north of St. Quentin, but the fight was remarkable chiefly for being the last fought by Howard, the gallant leader of the formation, who was shot down near Epehy and mortally wounded.

At 8 o'clock next morning, March 23rd, Phillipps and Forrest again led out a combined patrol. They began operations with a sweep north of the Scarpe, but found in this region only one two-seater over Brebières at 10,000 feet, which McKenzie shot down in flames. Farther south, over Bourlon Wood, the S.E.5's fell in with eight Albatros scouts. Phillipps shot down one out of control at close range, and the remainder dived into clouds to escape. But the chief excitement in the air was with No. 4 Squadron. This day, the third of the German onslaught, was one of grave anxiety on the Third Army front, whose right flank was compelled to fall back in accordance with the retreat of the Fifth Army. Through March 23rd and 24th the engrossing question was: "Will the Third Army hold?" The fate of the whole British line depended on it, and in the event that line was saved by the magnificent defence of the British divisions at the centre of the Third Army's front south-east of Arras. The right, however, was exceedingly hard pressed, and on the Saturday, March 23rd, was fighting a desperate rear-guard action around Bapaume. That morning the battle was very heavy about

OFFICERS OF No. 2 SQUADRON, A.F.C., SAVY, MARCH, 1918

Aust. War Museum Official Photo. No. E1883.

To face p. 230.

VAULX-VRAUCOURT, FROM THE AIR

It was on the main road, which can be seen running from left to right through this village, that the advancing German transport and reserves were in March, 1918, heavily bombed by British and Australian aeroplane squadrons.

From the collection of the late Lieut.-Col. W. O. Watt, No. 2 Sqn., A.F.C.
Taken 1st September, 1918.

Vaulx-Vraucourt and along the Bapaume–Cambrai road, and No. 4 Squadron was among those detailed to harass the attacking Germans at this place.

The first machines left the aerodrome at a few minutes after 10 o'clock. They were in two formations, under Courtney and Malley respectively, and each consisted of six machines. Courtney, flying at under 500 feet, led his formation in a bombing and machine-gun attack on Vaulx-Vraucourt village and the fields around it. There was no lack of targets for the airmen; the ground was swarming with German troops, and the roads were packed with other marching bodies and their transport. The five machines which first attacked spread dismay and confusion between Vaulx-Vraucourt and Lagnicourt, each firing between 500 and 600 rounds. Meanwhile, Malley's formation, flying slightly above Courtney's, intercepted an attack on Courtney from low-flying Albatros scouts. Malley himself shot down two of these Germans, both of which immediately crashed, and Scott defeated another whose fate was not seen. There was no height for a machine to manoeuvre or to save itself from a bad spin. The effect on the infantry may be imagined—the rush down from the misty air of a flight of aeroplanes; the ear-splitting din of the propellers as the machines dived and wheeled and zoomed and dived again above the crowded road and over the village streets; the rush into ditches and holes to escape the searing sprays of bullets; the little broken-legged heaps of men and horses on the road; the collisions of bolting waggons; the new roar of more machines above, as aerial battle was joined over the heads of the low-shooting scouts; here and there the terror of a machine falling to wreck and death, perhaps in the narrow village street, perhaps in the field outside, but anywhere likely to crash upon some part of the crowd below; then the second rush, as the flight escorting the first attackers came down, in its turn to repeat the first deadly whirlwind.

As the Australian machines finished their attack and flew away for further supplies to renew it, formations from other British squadrons succeeded them. Now bombing began as well. The machines from No. 4 Squadron also brought bombs in their second attack. Bapaume was in the hands of the advancing enemy, and the first bombs dropped were aimed to fire the British dumps there, which, for want of explosives at the proper moment, had not been destroyed in the retreat. The Germans were crowding into Bapaume by every road from east and south—crowding there because the roads all led to that centre and the wheeled traffic was obliged by the boggy state of the fields to keep to the roads. There was little artillery fire, but against the enemy the aeroplane bombs took the place of shells. Into that packed road-centre nine Australian machines, each in orderly succession, dropped two 25-lb. bombs from so low a height that to miss was impossible; then they spread out to smash up the road-traffic outside with machine-gun fire. German scouts again attacked them while at this work, but with no other effect than loss to themselves. Lieutenant A. E. Robertson, having dropped his bombs on Bapaume dump, rose to meet a formation of enemy scouts, destroyed one Fokker triplane, and shot down two others out of control. Cobby, who was flying with him, drove off another, an Albatros. No. 4 Squadron's scourge had barely vanished when five S.E.5's from No. 2 Squadron, flying at 17,000 feet over Bapaume, shot down two German two-seaters in succession. Phillipps, attacking one of them at short range, shot dead the observer, whose gun fell out of the machine; the jamming of his own guns then forced him to leave this enemy spinning earthward. Forrest destroyed the other in flames a few minutes later.

In the afternoon of Sunday, March 24th, a critical day, a gap appeared in the British line at Delville Wood, on the old Somme battlefield, and for some hours disaster was feared. The gap was filled by the throwing in of the British 35th Division and some hard-worked cavalry reserves; but the enemy pressure was maintained very heavily around Bapaume also, while on the other side of the Fifth Army the French left was in retreat, with rear-guards greatly outnumbered. Both Australian squadrons had patrols over the Third Army front all that Sunday, and an early flight from No. 4 Squadron, under Courtney, while visiting the Vimy Ridge front before starting for the south, observed German concentration beginning there as well. Two pilots dived and fired some hundreds of rounds into crowded billets and trenches near

Lens. Then the formation of six flew on to Vaulx-Vraucourt and Mory, out-lying villages near Bapaume, to continue there the work of the previous day. The other two flights of the squadron, under Malley and Captain W. B. Tunbridge,[2] also appeared here about noon. All machines from No. 4 again bombed and machine-gunned the roads behind the advancing German front—roads which were vital for its supplies and artillery, if the advance was to be maintained—and especially the main Bapaume–Cambrai road, which was packed with transport endeavouring to get forward. Throughout the afternoon the airmen flew up and down that road, scattering every large party of infantry and holding up the wheeled-traffic. Since time was vital to the Allied Command, the demoralisation of enemy reserves, however temporary, was good work done. Every machine, when it had dropped its bombs and fired all its ammunition, flew home for more, and as soon as each formation was re-assembled and ready on the aerodrome, it started out again to repeat the attack.

Malley has described the excitement of this work and the scenes revealed to the airmen over the battlefield. "Owing to the Germans' rapid advance towards the Somme, numbers of squadrons from the northern sectors (Arras, Armentières, Ypres, and Belgian fronts) had to carry south petrol, bombs, and ammunition, and fly to the hard-pressed right front of the British Third Army about Bapaume. The British squadrons already in that sector were more or less disorganised. They had orders to pack up equipment or stand-by to leave their aerodromes at a moment's notice. So quickly did these evacuation orders come, that many British pilots who flew out on a patrol in the morning would return a few hours later to find the whole of their squadrons' personnel gone to some unknown destination—in some cases without their stores and equipment—and the aerodrome being shelled by the enemy. This naturally disorganised those squadrons. The pilot would avoid landing if the aerodrome were being shelled, and would fly on to some place of safety —perhaps choosing, as he thought, a flat quiet field. He was often handicapped by shortage of petrol, and in some cases he had to remain with his machine for several days before he

---

[2] Capt. W. B. Tunbridge; No. 4 Sqn. (previously Light Horse). Farmer; b. Ballarat, Vic., 7 June, 1893.

could get petrol or make communication with his squadron again. This made it necessary to call in assistance from squadrons in other sectors.

"No. 4 Australian Squadron devoted many days entirely to this sort of relief work. Flights would leave Bruay for Bapaume, and begin bombing and 'shooting-up' enemy transport and infantry along the roads, around Vaulx-Vraucourt, Bapaume, and farther south. The weather at the beginning of the advance was indifferent for flying, being very misty, and heavy ground clouds made it difficult for pilots to gauge with accuracy the position of the German skirmishing line, especially while advancing so fast. Pilots would often fly for ten miles without seeing ground, and then would dive through dense clouds to try and pick up bearings, only to find themselves from fifty to a hundred feet above dense formations of Germans, who would hear a machine long before it appeared beneath the cloud, and would be ready to open fire on it directly it emerged from the mist. If the pilot were lucky, and were not vitally hit, he would immediately ascend into the cloud again and fly west, very often too far, and would have to feel his way back again to the moving line. Each day pilots had to judge for themselves the local situation.

"After the first few days, the weather began to clear a little. Australian pilots who had fought in the infantry through the battles of the Somme, in 1916, felt outraged on finding the Germans not only again in possession of Bapaume, but advancing also on Pozières, Albert, and the River Ancre.

"The Bruay aerodrome was a busy spot. Sometimes five squadrons of aeroplanes were lined out on the green—loading bombs and ammunition, checking sights, filling up with petrol, and overhauling machines. Pilots, chafing to get off to the line again, were all working with the mechanics and testing ammunition, which was of vital importance so that faulty rounds might not jam the guns in action. Each pilot arriving from the line would invariably have exciting news to impart to his comrades.

"After dropping bombs, and using up their ammunition, pilots always made a point of lingering for a while to survey the spectacle of the one army advancing against the other.

A FLIGHT OF No. 2 SQUADRON, A.F.C. (S.E.5's), WAITING TO START FROM SAVY AERODROME, 25TH MARCH, 1918

Aust. War Museum Official Photo. No. E1879.

To face p. 234.

A FLIGHT OF No. 4 SQUADRON, A.F.C. (CAMELS), PREPARING TO START FROM BRUAY AERODROME, 26TH MARCH, 1918

Aust. War Museum Official Photo. No. E1878.

To face p. 235.

Details of this colossal movement visible from the air held one spellbound: villages for miles around all on fire; the smoke climbing from each blaze, and uniting at a great height to form a dense haze, pierced here and there by gun-flashes; roads teeming with transport; aerodromes, ammunition-dumps, Nissen[3]-huts, and engineers'-dumps being dismantled, burnt, or shelled. One incident of six British tanks in retreat made a queer spectacle. Artillery, horse-transport, and motor-transport, a little farther back from the line, crowded the roads. Infantry were stolidly tramping the shell-riddled fields.

" Much to our relief, German anti-aircraft batteries were not a great deal in evidence, apparently owing to field-guns having preference on the crowded roads. German aircraft, although seen flying at a great height and well over their own side, seemed indifferent about attacking, or attempting to approach our line. The great numbers of British machines evidently made them feel uncomfortable. Occasionally one of them would sneak through the mist and shoot at the British infantry. Often it was his last shot. Others merely fired a few rounds and raced away back to safety."

The German airmen—at all events in the experience of the Australian squadrons—were, in the main, unable to interfere. Such hostile scouts as at times appeared were either driven off by protective British battle-formations or intimidated by the sight of them. On March 24th, nine Australian S.E.5's encountered eight Albatros scouts and three two-seaters over Bapaume. In this engagement A. G. Clark shot down a scout out of control, and Phillipps shot away the wings from a two-seater, which then fell like a stone. The chief danger, as always, for the low-flying aeroplanes was from ground-fire, and though none of the Australians was lost this day, their machines came back full of bullet-holes, and G. Jones returned from the last bombing attack of the evening wounded in the back.

During the next two days, March 25th and 26th, the bombing of the Germans' communication routes increased in intensity. Till now the chief targets had been infantry reserves. On the Monday every road leading to Bapaume, and all the other main roads south of that place behind the

---

[3] Semi-circular army huts of corrugated iron, so named after the designer.

German front, were crowded afresh with transport. The German drive had so far proceeded mainly on the strength of such food and ammunition as the infantry could carry with them. Now supplies were wanted forward, and guns had to be brought up. The enemy's wheeled-transport was obliged in most places to keep to the roads, for the fields alongside were wet and holed and boggy. The Bapaume–Cambrai road was one of the main arteries for the supply of the advancing German front in this region. Over that road the machines of No. 4 Squadron made a sort of ant-trail in the sky. Pilot after pilot recorded that his bombs burst in the middle of troops or transport, and so thick was the traffic that any block in it must prove serious. The airmen blew craters in the road-surface with their bombs, and then concentrated their attack on the traffic, which became bunched at such craters in the effort to make the narrow passage round them. With machine-gun fire the airmen ditched motor-lorries, blocked the road with broken waggons and maimed horses, set field-gun teams into panic-gallops away from their route, and played all possible havoc with the German rear-services. A bomb from W. B. Tunbridge blew up a dump on the main road just north of Bapaume and caused a big fire. Parked vehicles and guns in Vaulx-Vraucourt were badly damaged by the fire of one machine after another. Marching infantry were scattered in all directions into temporarily panic-stricken bunches of men, who either fell or fled and were chased over the fields. Courtney dropped one bomb fair on to one of the hated "flaming-onion"[4] batteries which had come into action against the aeroplanes, and thereafter there was no more shooting from it. No. 4 Squadron fired in all 15,000 machine-gun rounds that day. The attack was interrupted once—at noon—by German scouts. The Australians were ready for them with watching machines, and A. E. Robertson shot down two triplanes and an Albatros—one triplane being seen to crash—while Scott destroyed a Rumpler two-seater.

The story was the same next day, March 26th, on the roads and villages a little nearer west. The Germans were pushing out westward and northward from Bapaume, and were

---

[4] "Flaming-onions"—These were fired from a revolver-gun similar to a howitzer; six or seven white or green balls of fire, apparently chained together, leaving a like number of black smoke-streams. The fire-balls rose to above 5,000 feet.

beginning to extend the attack along the front before Arras. Relays of patrols from No. 4 bombed all the length of the roads from Bapaume to Ervillers on the north, to Achiet-le-Grand on the north-west, and to Miraumont on the west and south-west. The bombs rarely missed their targets, and heavy casualties were plainly inflicted upon the German reserves.[5] It was known later that the aeroplane attacks affected severely, and perhaps decisively, the success of the German offensive against the Third Army. Neither gain of ground nor the breaking of Gough's Fifth Army was the enemy's objective. He meant to reach Amiens at least, and, if he had taken Amiens, Abbeville should reasonably have fallen soon afterwards, and the Anglo-French Armies have been forced apart. That, and nothing short of it, was his plan: the rolling up of the British lines on the one flank and of the French on the other, a situation from which, in the bad morale resulting from so stunning a defeat, the troops of each command might not have been able to recover. A thorough examination of the action of the Allied air forces at this critical time before Amiens, in the closing days of March, makes it almost certain that, while it was the heroic infantry of outnumbered British and French divisions which held up the enemy advance—and the Australian divisions played a glorious part in the later stages—it was principally the untiring exertions of the airmen in delaying, damaging, and disheartening the enemy's reserves, and throwing his whole transport system out of gear, which enabled the Allied infantry to succeed.

The work of the Australian squadrons was only a fraction of what was happening along the whole front of the German assault, and the bombing of trains, supply-centres, and the enemy's traffic system went on by day and night right back to the big busy railway centres on the borders of France and Belgium. "Our hat was in the ring," as the Americans said, and the air force was ordered to count no cost whatever in machines, pilots, anything, but to fling itself at the mass of the German divisions behind the skirmishing line, to smash it, and to go on smashing it, night and day. If this was to be our final defeat, the air force would be the first to sacrifice

---

[5] See Appendix No. 7.

itself; if it was to be the beginning of the Allied victory, it lay first with the airmen to turn the tide. The fight was to save the morale of the Allied Armies.

Sunday, Monday, and Tuesday were the critical days. Farther south, General Petain, the Commander-in-Chief of the French Armies, ordered every flying squadron within striking distance of Ham to take the air and attack the German reserves. "Within half-an-hour of that order," says Middleton,[6] "the air was black with machines from French aerodromes making for this immediate strategic centre." At one point of the advance Reuter's special correspondent on the French front reported on March 27th that, south of the Somme, two entire German divisions advancing towards the battle-front were disorganised, before they were able to fire a single shot, by machine-gun fire and bombs from over a hundred French aeroplanes. This incident is also mentioned in an airman's letter from the front quoted by Middleton:—

"On Tuesday morning," writes this airman, "I saw a pretty bit of work. Fully 25,000 Germans were advancing below—under our very eyes, from 10,000 feet above—when from the direction of Chauny there swung round seven French fighting squadrons, 105 machines, glinting in the sun. They manœuvred beautifully. Fancy, Jim! a hundred 'planes in a vertical turn at once! They sprang a lovely E-flat note, and 50,000 German ears heard it. It was laughable and tragic. Down swooped the Frenchmen with a whiz. They spread fanwise. A mighty crescent of 100-lb. bombs fell, then another, then small stuff. Hundreds upon hundreds were killed. I saw 5,000 men flat on their faces at once trying to escape. It was just awful."

On the British side of the German drive the air work was just as intense, and the severity of it may be judged by the British and German official reports of losses. During the five days, March 21st–25th, the enemy claimed to have shot down ninety-three Allied machines and six balloons. During the same period the British pilots alone destroyed or captured 137 German machines, drove down eighty-three more out of control, and burned three balloons. Many of the machines on each side were shot down from the ground while flying low.

---

[6] *Tails Up*, p. 248.

There was not an aeroplane in the Australian scouting squadrons which was not riddled with bullets; yet, during this hot period of fighting low near the ground against infantry, they lost only two pilots—Lieutenants T. Hosking,[7] killed, and O. T. Flight,[8] shot down and taken prisoner. Three were wounded and evacuated to hospital—Lieutenants G. Jones (as already related), A. W. Adams, and J. W. Wright.[9] Of these, Jones and Wright returned to the front in July.

No. 4 Squadron continued the same work on March 27th around Bray and in front of Albert—where the German advance was now slowing down before the reinforced British line—and on March 28th immediately east and south-east of Arras, where the enemy was attacking in force the centre and left of the Third Army front. On the former day, before Albert, the Germans were definitely stopped, partly by combined artillery and aeroplane attack on the roads entering that town, partly by determined infantry resistance from the British line, which was ordered to stand at Albert and was reinforced by part of the 4th Australian Division. That afternoon, just in front of this infantry, in an encounter between formations of low-flying Australian and German scouts, Lieutenant E. R. Jeffree,[10] of No. 4 Squadron, destroyed two Fokker triplanes which were harassing the British trenches. Scott and Feez, of the same squadron, when low down, were attacked by a two-seater; after manœuvring from a bad position Scott destroyed the German. Next morning, Feez, when on patrol, was forced by engine-trouble to land south-east of Arras, and was captured. The German attack at Arras on March 28th was so decisively repulsed by the British that for the next three days No. 4 Squadron's scouts were relieved from "ground-strafing," and resumed on the Flanders front the higher offensive patrols of their normal duty.

It has already been explained that the chief work of No. 2 Squadron during this period was offensive patrolling to

---

[7] Lieut. T. Hosking; No. 4 Sqn. (previously Infantry). Electrician; b. Brockley, London, Eng., 1893. Killed in action, 28 March, 1918.

[8] Lieut. O. T. Flight; No. 2 Sqn. (previously Engineers). Student; b. Bendigo, Vic., 1895.

[9] Capt. J. W. Wright, D.F.C.; No. 4 Sqn. (previously Light Horse). Factory manager; of Wahroonga, Sydney; b. Quirindi, N.S.W., 4 Jan., 1893.

[10] Lieut. E. R. Jeffree; No. 4 Sqn. (previously A.A.M.C.). Clerk; of Sydney; b. Sydney, 29 June, 1895.

protect No. 4 Squadron's formations flying below them. Some of the escorting S.E.5's occasionally joined in the low-flying attacks on the roads. Benjamin, one of Manuel's patrol on the morning of March 26th, destroyed an attacking Albatros scout over Bapaume, and Holden's patrol the same morning chased away a two-seater and shot its observer dead. A formation of four machines under Phillipps next day reported an excellent example of the responsibility of an air escort. The weather was still misty, though the hour was noon, and, flying in the haze at 2,000 feet near Albert, the S.E.5's suddenly caught a glimpse of eight German triplanes above them. Phillipps promptly fired a warning light and zoomed up into the mist. He emerged into clear air over Pozières on the tail of a triplane, chased it southwards to Suzanne, and there put fifty rounds into it at close range. The German went down in flames. Meanwhile the other three Australians failed in the haze to find the rest of the enemy formation; but none of the triplanes, as it happened, attacked the bombing formation from No. 4 below. Twenty minutes later, Phillipps destroyed another German scout at Méaulte. That same morning Forrest and Manuel, flying south of the Somme, destroyed a German two-seater over the French lines at Démuin.

In the last days of March the German advance on the Somme front was definitely brought to a halt about Albert (just held by the enemy), Corbie, and Villers-Bretonneux, the line occupied by the newly-arrived Australian Corps. To the immediate north the Third Army decisively repulsed the attempted widening of the German assault—the attack on Arras. To the immediate south of the Australian area, Petain's French reserves stayed the progress of the drive south-westwards. The Germans, however, were staking everything on their offensive, and were obliged to continue it; their scheme had not yet succeeded. The failure to reach Amiens meant that the British and French Armies had not been forced apart. Had the enemy continued to attack straight along the Somme, there were now reserves at hand ready to meet him there. With the idea of attracting these reserves to other parts of the front, the Germans next began to press upon each distant flank of this central position—upon the British line in Flanders between Bethune and Ypres, and upon the French towards the Chemin-des-Dames and Soissons. The attack on the British began in April, and that upon the French in June.

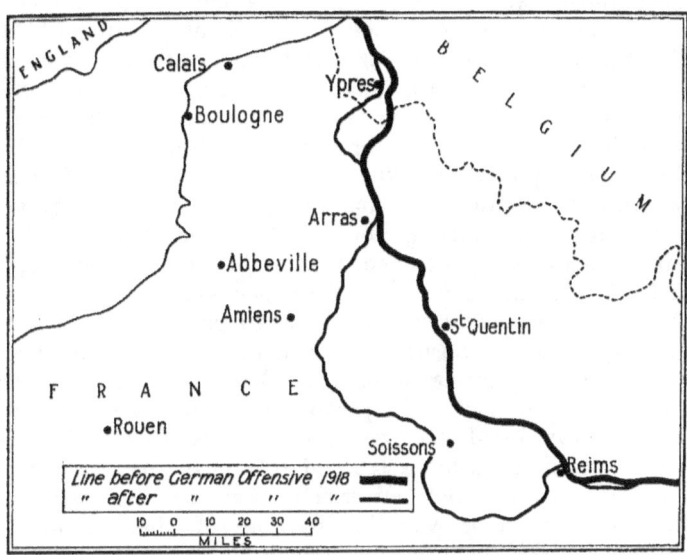

Of the Australian air squadrons, No. 3 was now with the Australian Corps in the Somme Valley; No. 2 was in the same vicinity, and, after one or two moves, was stationed at Bellevue, east-north-east of Doullens, as part of a British circus wing; No. 4 was operating in Flanders on the front of the First Army. Before describing the new activities of the No. 2 and No. 3 Squadrons, it will be best, for the sake of the continuity of the story, to follow No. 4 Squadron in its work against the German drive through the Portuguese Division on the Lys, about Laventie.

If the failure to capture Amiens was not a warning to Ludendorff that his plans were breaking down, the failure even to dent the British line at Arras must have been so. Throughout the first week of April the patrols of No. 4 Squadron, roaming the air between Lens and the Scarpe River witnessed the recoil of the discomfited enemy in that quarter, and from the reserve, or Hindenburg, line at Drocourt to the front lines in the chalky plain before Arras they worried with bombs and machine-gun fire the thickly-held villages and trenches and the crowded battery-positions. Concealment was gone; gun-pits were mostly open to view, and billets of reserve troops were plainly distinguishable. For the first three days of April the Australian squadron shared with other British squadrons the ceaseless duty of thus hammering home upon the German storm-troops the penalty of failure. Then came three days of bad weather, when flying was impossible. When the machines took the air again on April 7th it was clear that the enemy's centre of gravity hereabouts was shifting northward. The dawn bombing patrols that morning attacked as usual the trenches about Oppy and Lens, but in the forenoon the attack was concentrated for the first time on unmistakable German preparations between La Bassée and Armentières. The new German spearhead seemed to be pointing straight at Bethune along the Lille-La Bassée road, a fact of especial interest to No. 4 Squadron, since its own aerodrome was at Bruay, just behind Bethune. The Australian machines bombed that busy road, as far as Fournes, heavily and effectively, but in the operation Courtney's machine was hit by one of the much-hated "flaming-onion" batteries and fell in flames.

On April 9th the storm broke on the Portuguese before Fleurbaix and Laventie—the old "nursery sector"[11] of the line—and smashed through it at once. The assault was just north of the allotted area of No. 4 Squadron, and the Australian airmen entered the fight there on the evening of that day. The Germans had then reached the Lys at Sailly and the little creek called the Loisne about Lacouture and Vieille Chapelle. Then began another season of the same work which the squadron had been doing in the theatre of the enemy's southern offensive around Bapaume. Morning, noon, and evening the Camels of No. 4 Squadron attacked the reserves and transport behind the enemy attack, of which the foremost wave was pouring on over the wet flats towards Bethune and Hazebrouck. British reserves could not arrive

---

[11] It had long been a quiet sector into which new divisions were sent in order to obtain their first experience of trench-warfare.

for some days, and meanwhile the holding of the enemy on the ground had to be done by scattered and weak rear-guards, for with every yard of retreat the line extended and the men available to hold it grew fewer. The Scots of the 51st Division fought magnificently to save Bethune, and were assisted in that effort by the 12th (Army) Brigade of Australian Field Artillery, which was sent up hurriedly from a position on the Vimy Ridge. Farther north, before Merville, a British colonial cavalry regiment, King Edward's Horse, fought the finest day of its varied war service by holding up all day long on April 10th most of a full German division. North of them again the 29th and 31st Divisions maintained a gallant rear-guard action against heavy odds from the Lys right back to the outskirts of Hazebrouck, where they were joined at length on April 13th by the 1st Australian Division, newly-arrived from the Somme.

The first bombing formation out from No. 4 Squadron on the morning of April 10th caught large bodies of enemy infantry at the Rouge Croix cross-roads between Neuve Chapelle and Estaires, and also parks and moving columns of guns and transport on many roads between Laventie and Richebourg–St. Vaast. The splendid targets for aeroplane attack in this region were but a short distance from the Australian squadron's aerodrome, and in an average time of thirty or forty minutes a formation could start out, drop its bombs, empty its machine-guns into the enemy, and return to the aerodrome. No. 4 Squadron's bombing relays were therefore considerably more rapid than at Bapaume in the previous month. From dawn till early afternoon every available machine was engaged in the work. Even when weather permitted, it was rarely that this strenuous duty could be maintained all day long, since pilots required rest, and machines, inevitably much shot about by fire from the ground, had to be patched and mended. Within the limits of the capacity of men and machines, No. 4 Squadron carried on to its utmost the counter-attack from the air. The first attacking formation on April 10th left the aerodrome at 6 o'clock, the next at 8, and five others followed during the forenoon. Heavy punishment was inflicted on struggling transport columns and bodies of men marching towards the Loisne about

Vieille Chapelle. Roads were blocked by fallen horses and broken waggons; other waggons were ditched in the effort to make détours across fields round the obstacles; bodies of infantry scattered in panic or by order, re-formed after the blast from above had passed over them, and scattered again before another hosing of bullets. This sort of treatment takes much heart out of troops, and—what is of more immediate importance—saves precious time for the defence. The defence was here hard-pressed, and above all things required time to allow supplies and reinforcements to be brought up, sundered companies and battalions to be re-formed, and guns to be saved. In the event the Germans were unable to pass Merville for several days, and one agent in holding them up and harassing every effort to send forward men and guns and supplies was again the air force.

The wonder is that the losses were so slight, for there was no time to count any risk. No. 4 Squadron lost two more pilots in the morning of April 10th, both shot down by ground-fire near Laventie. Woolhouse was apparently hit, his machine crashed out of control, and he himself was killed in the wreck. Almost at the same time Lieutenant H. K. Love[12] also had to land in enemy territory, either wounded or with his machine damaged, and was taken prisoner. He was seen to land under control, but hit a fence, and his machine went over on its back. An hour later Cobby destroyed near Estaires an Albatros scout which came up to interfere with the bomb-dropping.

Weather grew worse on April 11th, but the air attack continued with little interruption. Some German batteries were now beginning to come into action hereabouts, near the stream of the Loisne—a sure sign of a stiffening British defence against the skirmishing line farther forward. Most of the airmen made direct hits with bombs on machine-gun and field-gun positions behind the Loisne. By April 12th the Germans were definitely held around Bethune, and the airmen began to transfer their attentions to the Estaires–Merville road, farther north. On that day the enemy was in Merville, and the main road running east from the town was crowded

---

[12] Lieut. H. K. Love; No. 4 Sqn. (previously Infantry). Electrical engineer; of East Malvern, Melbourne; b. Brighton, Melbourne, 9 Oct., 1895.

with his traffic. By evening No. 4 Squadron was concentrating its attacks on Merville and the roads south-west from it towards Robecque and St. Venant, and during the next two days this vicinity was one of the chief points of danger. Robecque was in the direct road for Lillers, and any further break in the defence at that point would have meant the loss of Bethune by out-flanking from the north-west. The efforts of the British infantry, seconded by the fierce assaults of the airmen on the road junctions of Calonne and Pacaut, stayed the enemy's thrust. Pacaut village was full of German batteries in position, and the German losses here in men and material must have been very heavy, for throughout the morning of April 14th No. 4 Squadron put its full force into the bombing of that nest. The road through Paradis, a village just behind Pacaut, was filled during the afternoon by a large column of troops marching north to Merville. Shortly after 3 o'clock, one patrol from No. 4 flew straight along the road, and the six machines dropped twenty-four bombs along that column, almost all fair among the troops. Two hours later another six machines repeated the performance. The results of such an attack are far greater than the actual casualties caused; the effect was undoubtedly to render quite useless for offensive purposes that night the entire enemy force concerned.

During April 15th and 16th the enemy was held north of Merville in the direction of Hazebrouck, where reinforcements (including the 1st Australian Division) had now arrived, and by the 17th the airmen of No. 4 Squadron withdrew from the bombing of the Merville neighbourhood and resumed their attack on the thickly-held German positions before Bethune. The enemy was suspected of designing further assault on that town, but, if he did so, the attack never developed. April 18th, 19th, and 20th were days of steady bombing of the enemy's central position between Merville and Bethune, a centre containing many batteries and supply-dumps; and the morning of April 21st was devoted to the devastation of new German supply-dépôts at Lestrem and La Gorgue, on the south-west side of Estaires. By the 22nd the end of the immediate crisis on the Lys was indicated by the resumption by No. 4 Squadron of its ordinary duty of offensive-patrols.

Meanwhile the enemy airmen had been bombing as strenuously as the British, though more by night than by day. Night after night the Gothas hovered over Bethune—among other places—to drop the big bombs, whose explosions could be heard miles away. Among the night-bombers were several which would pass Bethune and fly on to Bruay to attack No. 4 Squadron's aerodrome. Bruay, too, was now under fire from the German heavy guns. These circumstances compelled the squadron to move at the end of April to an aerodrome at Clairmarais North, north-east of St. Omer. Here it received improved long-stroke Clerget engines for its machines in place of the short-stroke Clergets hitherto employed; here also. it entered upon a new career of offensive air fighting, which endured until the signing of the Armistice.

CHAPTER XVIII
EARLY CIRCUS FIGHTS WITH No. 2 SQUADRON

"CIRCUS" was the name given, jocularly in the beginning, to a specially selected fighting squadron which travelled from one part of the front to another, wherever offensive air strength was required. It was a fleet of air-destroyers, or fast air-cruisers. In the German circuses its pilots were crack airmen drafted from all squadrons; the British circuses were composed rather of crack squadrons, not necessarily of selected airmen, though expert airmen, returned to the front from home instructional courses or from convalescence, were frequently sent to a circus squadron instead of to the squadron to which they had formerly belonged.

The circus system inevitably accompanied the development of various duties of fighting aeroplanes. The early war pilots performed all and any sort of work—one day reconnoitring, another ranging artillery, another photographing, another going out simply on the chance of a fight—all with the same class, or any class, of machine. The airmen of those days were not specialists within their arm. Specialised training was introduced as the air service developed. Machines improved also, and at length were designed for various purposes—some for weight-carrying, some for stability, some for speed, some for rapid climbing and manœuvring. Thus they were classified for special duties, and pilots likewise with them. The temperaments and physical capacities of airmen differ in important respects. The airman with a quick eye at his gun was often less useful as an observer of ground features for reconnaissance. Some men were naturally gifted with the cool head for the instantaneous decision in the fierce racket of a "dog-fight." Therefore, as squadrons, by reason of types of machines allotted to them and the training of their pilots, became marked down as bombing squadrons, artillery co-operation squadrons, photographers, fighting scouts, and so forth, the "circus" also was in due time bound to come. A circus was an offensive formation first and last; it attacked wherever it found the enemy, and moved constantly about the front. The first circus appeared on the German side.

The name was appropriate, and any derision which may have originally suggested it speedily disappeared. Circus, because it was always travelling about the front; circus, because its star airmen, esteeming themselves the *élite* of the air service (and they were), painted their aeroplanes with all manner of fantastic and brilliant colour-schemes. Richthofen's circus could for long be distinguished on sight by the brilliant red of its machines. Another red Albatros squadron, whose speciality was black tails, was known as "the black-tailed circus." But a whole circus was not necessarily of uniform colour, and some airmen would paint their machines entirely after their own fancy. Boelcke flew a black Fokker with white crosses. Voss flew a "silver-fish." Others were remarkable for patchworks of colour, meant to deceive, like the camouflage-paint of ships at sea.

During April No. 2 Squadron from Bellevue aerodrome, a central position on the British front, began to operate in a British circus with No. 43 and No. 80 British Squadrons. On its southern flank it was occasionally over the French area about Montdidier, both bombing and fighting. Towards Villers-Bretonneux and Montdidier the enemy was still pushing in the first days of April, though gaining little ground; if the concentration of his air scouts in the vicinity meant anything, he attributed some importance to this part of the line. Here, in a dawn patrol on April 2nd, Forrest and Manuel, escorting low-flying machines of their own squadron, attacked a D.F.W. two-seater, shot the observer dead, and then crashed the machine near Démuin. On the afternoon of the same day, while ten machines of No. 2 Squadron were returning from an offensive patrol south of the Somme, they sighted an enemy formation between Amiens and Corbie. Lieutenants A. G. Clark and G. H. Blaxland[1] dived and cut off the rearmost German machine, fired several bursts into it, and saw it go down on fire near Corbie. The squadron was occupied on April 4th and 5th in moving to its new aerodrome, and the only patrol performed on these two

---

[1] Capt. G. H. Blaxland; No. 2 Sqn. (previously Light Horse). Electrical engineering student; of Fremantle, W. Aust.; b. Broken Hill, N.S.W., 10 March, 1896.

days was on the 4th by Lieutenants L. J. Primrose[2] and G. R. Brettingham-Moore,[3] when Primrose caught and destroyed an Albatros scout over Villers-Bretonneux. This was the day of the first attack on that town by the Germans, and of their repulse, after heavy fighting, by the British cavalry and the 9th Australian Infantry Brigade. The weather remained bad, and, while there was important fighting on the ground at Albert and Villers-Bretonneux, there was little opportunity for circus operations in the air. No. 2 Squadron sent out its own small offensive patrols on all possible occasions. Four S.E.5's under Clark destroyed a black German two-seater over La Motte, just east of Amiens, on the afternoon of April 6th. Every patrol which went out on these days lost some of its numbers through forced landings due to mists and storms.

A bright interval occurred on April 21st, an eventful day in the story of air fighting at this time. On that day Richthofen, whose circus had been tempted out over the Somme area by the fair flying-day, was killed over the Australian lines. No. 2 Squadron patrols were engaged elsewhere at the time of Richthofen's last fight, and did not hear of it till it was all over. But No. 3 Squadron played a part in it, although a small one. The honour of shooting down the redoubtable German air-leader was much disputed, but the evidence of the time clearly indicated that it belonged to Australian Lewis gunners on the ground, though a British squadron of Camels has never abandoned its claim to him as its own victim.

The fight began at about 10.40 a.m. Two photographing machines of No. 3 Australian Squadron, flown by Lieutenants S. G. Garrett[4] and A. V. Barrow[5] (observer) and T. L. Simpson[6] and E. C. Banks,[7] were starting out on reconnaissance of the German lines near Hamel, when at 7,000

---

[2] Lieut. L. J. Primrose; No. 2 Sqn. Lecturer in science and mathematics; of Ballarat, Vic.; b. Ballarat, 14 May, 1890. Killed in action, 4 June, 1918.

[3] Lieut. G. R. Brettingham-Moore; No. 2 Sqn. (previously Infantry). Metallurgical chemist; of Hobart; b. St. Servan, France, 27 Jan., 1894.

[4] Lieut. S. G. Garrett; No. 3 Sqn. Architect; of Box Hill, Melbourne; b. Bendigo, Vic., 30 Sept., 1894.

[5] Lieut. A. V. Barrow; No. 3 Sqn. (previously Infantry). Salesman; b. Harrogate, Yorks., Eng., 3 July, 1889.

[6] Lieut. T. L. Simpson, D.F.C.; No. 3 Sqn. (previously A.A.M.C.). Electrical engineer; of Hamilton, Vic.; b. Hamilton, 19 May, 1895.

[7] Lieut. E. C. Banks; No. 3 Sqn. (previously Engineers). Surveyor; of Mosman, Sydney; b. Paddington, Sydney, 13 July, 1895

feet over that village they saw a flight of enemy triplanes approaching. The weather was hazy and visibility very poor, and the Australian machines were attacked at short warning of the enemy's presence. Four triplanes dived almost at once on Simpson and Banks in the nearer machine. Banks fought them off to the best of his ability, and fired in all 200 rounds; this fire, combined with the pilot's skilful manœuvring of the machine, served its purpose. Simpson eluded the attack in the clouds, and two of the enemy passed on to attack Garrett and Barrow. Barrow met the enemy with equal resolution, and beat them off with several effective bursts of fire. One triplane was plainly hit and began to go down; the other then hauled off. The Germans had sighted a formation of British scouts in the offing and abandoned the attack on the two-seaters. The R.E.8's emerging from the action unpursued, continued their reconnaissance. On returning at the end of it an hour later, and when about to cross the line at 8,000 feet in the same vicinity, Simpson and Banks were again attacked by a large formation of Albatros scouts. The enemy was now savage and out for vengeance, for in the interim Richthofen had been defeated and had gone to his death. Simpson dodged the attackers and dived for the ground, with his observer keeping up a hot fire on the pursuers. At 2,000 feet he escaped from them and reached home safely.

Meanwhile, at about 10.45 a.m., the red circus, having passed the lines after the first escape of the two R.E.8's, immediately encountered a formation of Camels from a British naval air squadron operating as fighting scouts in the Amiens sector. These scouts had witnessed the approach of the enemy, and it was evidently their presence which had saved the Australian photographic machines in the first attack. The two formations flew straight at each other, and in a few seconds the infantry on the great natural grandstand of the Morlancourt Ridge were spectators of a first-class air battle. They could not see the whole fight, for the mist hid much of it. But the extent of the firing told all they could not actually see. Bishop, in his story of his own career, has described vividly the tremendous moments of a willing airfight. " You fly round and round in cyclonic circles. Here a flash of the Hun machines, then a flash of silver as my squadron-commander would whizz by. All the time I would be in the same mix-up myself, every now and then finding a red machine in front of me and getting in a round or two of quick shots. There was no need to hesitate about firing when the right colour flitted by your nose. Firing one moment, you would have to concentrate all your mind and muscle the next in doing a quick turn to avoid a collision. Then your gun jams, and you have to zoom up and fuss with it to put it right."[8]

Suddenly the watching gunners of the 53rd Australian Field Artillery Battery, 5th Division, near the crest of the ridge, saw two whirling and twisting forms emerge from the haze where the popping of the machine-guns had been heaviest. Then one machine dived for the ground with the other on its tail. They darted about wildly for a few seconds. Suddenly the pursued aeroplane, evidently in desperate straits, made straight for the crest of the ridge near the battery. The gunners saw that it was a British machine and its pursuer a red triplane. The Lewis gun on the nearer flank of the battery made ready to fire, but at first could not, for the machines were flying so low and close that the fleeing Camel blocked the gunner's sight of the German. The German was firing rapid short bursts at the Camel just beyond his nose, and the hunted British machine was making no attempt to turn and fire. The pilot afterwards explained his hopeless position by saying that he had his guns jammed, had no room to manœuvre so near to the ridge, and was making a dash for a landing as his only hope.

The machines flew on right overhead, careless of everything else except their own duel, and at this point, at about a hundred yards' range, the artillery Lewis gunners and a machine-gun from another Australian camp behind the crest of the ridge opened fire on the German. Splinters of wood were seen to fly off immediately from near his engine. The triplane wobbled, side-banked up, swerved across to the left in a half-circle, obviously crippled, then dived straight into the ground about 400 yards away and was smashed to pieces.

---

[8] *Winged Warfare*, p. 151.

The Australians into whose territory it fell discovered from the watch and papers on the dead pilot that he was Richthofen. No. 3 Squadron salved his body and the remains of his machine that evening, and buried him a couple of days later. The British Camel Squadron which vanquished the Richthofen circus in this flight stated that there were about fifteen machines engaged on each side, and that four enemy triplanes were driven down without loss to the victors.

The experiences of No. 2 Squadron as part of a circus were for a time disappointing. On the circus patrols three formations flew together—one of S.E.5's from No. 2 Squadron at 16,000 feet and two of Camels (Nos. 43 and 80 British Squadrons) at 14,000 and 12,000 feet respectively. The Camels were the more-easily manœuvred machines, the S.E.5's the stronger for long diving and zooming. Constant flying at 16,000 and 17,000 feet, especially when the enemy will not come out to relieve the monotony, is a strain on pilots, for the air is considerably thinner at that height. The strategy of the circus was only too successful; and, as the commander of No. 2 Squadron[9] pointed out, "on the approach of our formation" (the treble-decked circus formation) "the enemy's aircraft, unless surprised, invariably dived east, thus avoiding combat. Whereas this has the desired effect of restricting the work of his air force, it does not do very much towards the primary objective of a scout squadron, that is, the destruction of all enemy machines."

For the first few weeks of the life of the circus its success was judged, in the same report of the No. 2 Squadron commander, to be "not as great in actual results as might have been expected." During this period the front was, from the circus point of view, quiet. The German Air Force was being husbanded for a further offensive, or was engaged on the French front between Noyon and Rheims and eastwards over the Champagne, then the principal region of enemy infantry pressure. "It has been experienced," continues the report, "that on quiet fronts greater numbers of enemy aircraft are destroyed by sending out comparatively smaller formations and thus encouraging the enemy to fight.

---

[9] Major A. Murray Jones, M.C., D.F.C., formerly of No. 1 Sqn.

"There are two methods of working scouts, namely:—
   (a) In large organised formations capable of dealing with similar formations of the enemy; and
   (b) in small patrols of anything up to five machines, whose primary object is to destroy two-seaters, balloons, and small enemy scout patrols which are liable to molest our artillery machines.

"The advantages of these methods are:—
   (a) Pilots are encouraged to work with one another and to sacrifice individual results for those of the patrols.
   (b) Much more scope is given to the individual pilot, so that he may take advantage of the fleeting chance which often offers itself.

"The disadvantages are:—
   (a) The initiative of the pilot is apt to be cramped.
   (b) No experience is gained of the organised methods of aerial warfare which become so necessary during offensive operations.

"It is intended by the foregoing to point out that during this month (May), when no offensive operations were being carried out, better results would most probably have been obtained, both as regards the squadron personnel and as regards the number of enemy aircraft destroyed, by the use of smaller formations."

The squadron-commander, keen on obtaining the best results, is in these comments recording complaints of a new system which at times fell short of expectations. No. 4 Australian Squadron, not being at this date in a circus, was meeting enemy scouts far more frequently than No. 2. It should here be mentioned, moreover, that No. 4 Squadron was openly trying to beat No. 2 in records of enemy machines destroyed. It had come upon the scene a little later than No. 2 Squadron; the handicap—if it may be so regarded—was itself a challenge; and rivalry was quickly aroused.

Thus eagerly seeking out the enemy, No. 2 Squadron's patrols in the circus fleets roamed the British front from Amiens to Bailleul. In the forenoon of May 3rd Forrest led one formation from his squadron in a circus-cruise northward, and Phillipps another southward. Only the northern circus met the enemy, who attacked fifteen strong, but after a few shots fled east. In this patrol Lieutenant E. D. Cummings[10] was flying at 10,000 feet near Meteren after the encounter, and was about to dive on a lone German two-seater below him, when he observed a camouflaged white-and-grey triplane on his own level. Flying towards it, he made an Immelmann turn[11] and came out in a dive on the triplane, firing a burst from both guns. The triplane went down in a spin, Cummings following and firing at it; at 5,000 feet it turned on its back, and a minute afterwards crashed near Meteren. Meanwhile, just as Cummings had put the finishing burst into his victim, four more triplanes fell on him from above, and their opening fire shot away the Australian's elevator controls, instrument board, and petrol and oil pipes. After a long spin, Cummings just managed to regain control as he neared the ground, but crashed in No-Man's Land near Meteren. Luckily his safety-belt broke, and he was thrown clear of the wreckage into a shell-hole. He was rescued by infantry of the 1st Australian Division, who had watched the fight.

The circus did not meet the enemy again till May 8th, over Armentières, and then the Germans numbered only six triplanes and promptly turned tail. Lieutenant J. A. Adam,[12] leading No. 2's patrol, caught up one triplane and drove it down out of control, but, in the urgency of trying to cut off the other five, could not follow it. Three other patrols out that day found no enemy in the sky. In the following afternoon, after further vain sweeping operations through the morning, the circus attacked fifteen German scouts east of Bapaume; the S.E.5's dived and cut off one Pfalz scout at 14,000 feet, and Adam and Lieutenant F. R. Smith[13] between them destroyed it. It fell near Marcoing. The enemy was out in strength in the same vicinity that evening; the circus chased eastward a body of twenty enemy scouts, and Forrest drove down out of control a two-seater flying over Ervillers under-

---

[10] Capt. E. D. Cummings, D.F.C.; No. 2 Sqn. (previously A.A.S.C.). b. Franklin, Tas., 1896.

[11] See introductory chapter, p. xxiii, and Glossary.

[12] Lieut. J. A. Adam; Canadian officer in R.A.F. Attached No. 2 Sqn., 10 Jan. to 26 July, 1918.

[13] Capt. F. R. Smith, M.C., D.F.C.; No. 2 Sqn. (previously Infantry). Clerk; b. Brisbane, 1896.

neath the protecting scouts. The solitary result of a sweep on May 10th was the stern chase of a formation of four two-seaters on the Somme. Blaxland shot down one, which fell from 13,000 feet to 5,000 feet in a helpless spin and was then lost to sight.

Bad weather prevented flying for four days, and then, on May 15th, the enemy airmen returned to the Somme region in some strength. At noon the circus had a short indecisive skirmish with a German circus formation of nine Pfalz scouts and six triplanes east of Albert, and drove them home; and as many as forty or fifty of the enemy were seen by the evening patrol, but at a distance. A strong dawn patrol of thirteen Australian S.E.5's on May 16 attacked six Pfalz scouts at a great height near Bapaume, and Phillipps destroyed one after chasing it down for 4,000 feet. Again in the next two days small enemy formations were frequently in the air east of Albert, but avoided combat. Major Murray Jones shot down a triplane out of control from 16,000 feet in one of these fleeting engagements in the evening of May 17th. The circus roamed northward again in the evening of May 19th and fired 600 rounds in an indecisive combat with eighteen of the enemy over Armentières. Then for twelve days the weather was so bad that, except for brief intervals, only practice-flying could be done. The circus ranged the Somme area for two hours in the afternoon of May 30th and found six Pfalz scouts at 17,000 feet over Bapaume, of which Lieutenant G. Cox[14] destroyed one in flames.

At the beginning of June the airmen of No. 2 Squadron began to find the circus justified, and to feel rewarded for their four or five weeks of mostly vain sky-sweeping. The German machines had for a time been deliberately kept in leash in preparation for a renewed offensive. The Germans, in fact, always used their air force strictly as a part of their whole war-machine, and though Richthofen's squadron may be regarded as an exception, their airmen were not adventurers of the air so much as an inseparable body of one great organisation. While concentrating troops for an offensive, the enemy left the air to his opponents; then he released his

---

[14] Lieut. G. Cox; No. 2 Sqn. Cabinet maker; b. Carlton, Melbourne, Aug., 1894.

fighting scouts in full force at the calculated moment, much as he released his massed-artillery bombardments and finally his massed infantry. While the British also observed a similar air-strategy on the eve of an offensive, yet they never left the air undisputed to the Germans, even for the shortest season. When a British offensive was preparing, those aeroplane squadrons which were not being nursed for the attack were ordered to chase off at any cost all enemy airmen who appeared over the line. The Germans, on the other hand, when concentrating for a great attack, preferred to rely, for protection against hostile observation from the air, upon anti-aircraft fire, carefully-planned schemes for concealment, and night movements of all troops.

Hence when the Germans on June 6th renewed their grand offensive against the French in the Montdidier–Noyon region, the British airmen recognised the reason for the comparative absence of enemy machines in the sky on the British front during the latter half of May. On the morning of June 1st, six days before the date of the renewed enemy attack, re-awakening air activity was obvious over the Somme. Next day the sky in that quarter was alive with German scouts. The pilots of No. 2 Squadron shot down fifteen of them on those two days alone, and British and French airmen accounted for many others.

On June 1st, an early patrol, a circus formation including eight machines from No. 2 Squadron under Phillipps and W. Q. Adams, found the first signs of new enemy tactics about 8 o'clock, when it encountered six Pfalz scouts over the Somme near Cappy. The German formation was at 16,000 feet—1,500 feet above the top flight of the circus—and promptly attacked. Three Pfalzes dived on the S.E.5's, while the other three stayed up aloft. Adams's flight was higher than the others, and, as the Germans dived past him, Adams followed them and fired a burst of a hundred rounds into one of them at close range. This German slipped sideways, and broke up in the air. The others sheered off. The circus moved on eastward at increased height, and at 9 o'clock the S.E.5's were at 18,500 feet over Pozières. Here they saw below them an enemy formation of three Pfalzes and three triplanes; one Pfalz broke away from that formation and dived down on the Camels, which were as usual flying below the S.E.5's. Straightway Phillipps and Cummings darted down upon it in pursuit; Cummings followed it down for 7,000 feet, and there fired a final burst, from which the Pfalz crashed.

That evening there was again hot fighting over the German aerodrome at Bray. Twelve machines from No. 2 Squadron were out with the circus, and at 7.30 p.m. met eight Pfalz and triplane scouts five miles east of the line. The Germans turned away for home, but the S.E.5's had the height of them, and either destroyed or shot down out of control five of the eight. Cole[15] and Primrose dived together upon the rearmost German machine. After chasing it down for 1,000 feet Primrose zoomed up at a second Pfalz, fired 200 rounds into it at close range, and saw it fall like a leaf. Cole, who had pursued the first Pfalz, was obliged with his gun jammed to turn away, but the Pfalz was damaged beyond recovery and fell to the ground near Estrées-en-Chaussée. Meanwhile Forrest fastened on to a triplane which had climbed above another S.E.5. Forrest zoomed above this German, fired seventy rounds into him at only thirty-yards' range, and saw the triplane tumble to the ground beside a Red Cross station at Chuignes. Cox, who had dived on a Pfalz, followed it down, shooting into it, to 6,000 feet, and there left it, still falling out of control. Manuel did the like with another, but could not see it in consequence of engine-trouble, which compelled him to break off and return home. The patrol lost Rackett during this fight, shot down in combat and taken prisoner.

Next morning, near Bray, the locality of the action of the previous evening, nine machines from No. 2 Squadron at 14,000 feet met six Pfalz scouts. The enemy turned away, and Manuel, diving on the nearest, sent it down rolling, spinning, and side-slipping, completely out of control. His own machine also fell into a spin during the strain of the dive; then, regaining control at 11,000 feet, Manuel saw another Pfalz on his left front and slightly below. He flew at this machine and engaged it; the enemy fell over on his back and a wing broke off. While Manuel was thus occupied,

---

[15] Capt. A. T. Cole, M.C., D.F.C., formerly of No. 1 Sqn.

a third Pfalz had been manœuvring to attack him, but Forrest, watching, dived with the enemy, punished him heavily at short range, and watched him fall in a series of stalls and side-slips until he passed beyond sight. The remaining Germans had fled, and the Australians were flying home to breakfast in loose array, when three of them encountered eight Pfalz scouts near Albert on a level. Forrest promptly manœuvred into position and attacked from the sun. He shot down out of control one German, which was firing into Lieutenant C. H. Copp,[16] and W. Q. Adams similarly disposed of another, but the fight was so fierce that neither could watch the fate of these victims. The three, though outnumbered, fought on for a few minutes, until, having drifted over the British lines, the enemy broke off the combat.

After June 2nd No. 2 Squadron and the others of the circus moved to Foquorolles, in the Noyon–Soissons sector, where the threatened German attack on the French left was expected. That attack began on June 6th, but gained little ground, and, after three days of unexciting offensive patrolling, the squadron assisted the French airmen in low-flying counter-attacks against the advancing Germans. This work, here as on the Lys in April, was a repetition in kind of the operations in March, though on smaller scale. It was performed in the usual fashion by a constant sequence of small patrols, and greatly assisted the infantry in checking the enemy. That done, the S.E.5's resumed offensive scouting. In the afternoon of June 11th five machines under Forrest brought six enemy two-seaters to an engagement over Cuvilly. Lieutenant T. J. Hammond[17] destroyed one of them. Soon after dawn next morning Hammond was himself shot down and killed near Noyon in a fight with the circus against eight Pfalz scouts and four Fokker triplanes. Two Pfalzes having dived on a Camel of the second deck of the circus, Manuel, leading the S.E.5's, promptly attacked one and set it on fire. In the general engagement which followed Hammond was killed, but three enemy machines were shot down by the Camels, two of them in flames.

---

[16] Capt. C. H. Copp; No. 2 Sqn. (previously Infantry). Consulting optician; of Middle Park, Melbourne; b. Middle Park, 29 March, 1893.

[17] Lieut. T. J. Hammond; No. 2 Sqn. (previously Light Horse). Grazier; b. Sydney, 1893. Killed in action, 12 June, 1918.

At noon that day (June 12th) followed more heavy air-fighting, remarkable for the success of Phillipps, who led the S.E.5's at top height in the circus. Over Ribecourt, at 13,000 feet, six Fokker triplanes were tempted to attack the lower (Camel) formation. Phillipps dived from the clouds above on the leader of the Fokkers, who appeared not to see him, and fired fifty rounds into the enemy at point-blank range. The Fokker side-slipped, fell over, and crashed near Gury. Phillipps zoomed up into the fight again and attacked another triplane head on; a sustained burst of fire vanquished this German also; it turned over on its back and fell like a stone. Before the circus regained height from this encounter, Phillipps saw two L.V.G. two-seaters a little below him at 6,000 feet. He attacked these, firing into first one and then the other, and the second crashed in the French lines south of Marquéglise. The circus climbed again to resume sweeping the sky, for enemy machines in sight were still numerous. At noon they were chasing some two-seaters, when ten Fokker scouts appeared and dived at the Camels. The S.E.5's immediately flew to the rescue. Phillipps selected the nearest as his opponent, and shot it down into a spin, but being attacked by other Fokkers, could not follow it. The falling Fokker was, however, seen by the Camels to be wrecked on the ground.

The weather was bad for most of the week following, but by June 20th immediate danger in the Montdidier–Noyon area was past, and the circus moved north again to Liettres, south-west of Aire. Shortly afterwards it was broken up, and No. 2 Squadron was transferred from the 9th Brigade, R.A.F., to the 10th Brigade, and was embodied in a new wing (80th Wing) with No. 4 Australian Squadron and two British Squadrons —Nos. 46 (Camels) and 103 (D.H.9's). No. 2 and No. 4 Australian Squadrons thus came together on July 1st, when they took up their quarters in one aerodrome at Reclinghem, on the upper Lys, south-west of Thérouanne.

CHAPTER XIX

No. 3 SQUADRON'S OPERATIONS OVER THE SOMME

No. 3 SQUADRON had been operating over the Somme Valley, with the Australian Corps, for a fortnight before Richthofen's death. It arrived on the scene at about the same time as Australian Corps Headquarters Staff, that is to say, at the end of the first week in April. To meet the situation of a still unsettled line, only lightly dug-in, where " active and continuous operations " (the official name for open warfare) might be resumed at any moment, the duties of the corps squadron were for a time re-arranged. The artillery-patrols located enemy batteries as they appeared, and called down counter-battery fire upon their guns whenever they were observed to be in action. For some weeks after the squadron's arrival in the Somme area, it carried out bombing and machine-gunning of the German positions on a much larger scale than it had done in Belgium. The fairly constant presence during April of low-flying German scouts showed that the enemy had not yet given up his offensive designs in this region, and on April 11th three R.E.8's, out learning the line at 4,000 feet, were attacked by six Albatros scouts over Hénencourt. After some ticklish manœuvring, in which the enemy were driven off from two of the Australian machines, the third was seen to go down badly out of control. Both pilot and observer (Lieutenants A. W. Rees[1] and G. A. Paul[2]) were wounded, but by skilful handling of the machine the pilot managed to land within the British lines. On the following day two accidents occurred on the aerodrome through machines crashing in taking off; Lieutenants G. W. Best[3] and O. G. Lewis[4] (observer) were killed, and Lieutenants L. Fryberg[5] and O. H. Suess[6] were injured. The

---

[1] Lieut. A. W. Rees; No. 3 Sqn. Engineer; b. Junee, N.S.W., 1895.

[2] Lieut. G. A. Paul; No. 3 Sqn. (previously Infantry). Electrician; of North Adelaide; b. Beechworth, Vic., 7 Nov., 1893.

[3] Lieut. G. W. Best; No. 3 Sqn. Draper; of Hobart; b. Hobart, 1 Feb., 1896. Killed in action, 12 April, 1918.

[4] Lieut. O. G. Lewis; No. 3 Sqn. (previously Engineers). Engineering student; of Armadale, Melbourne; b. Elsternwick, Melbourne, 19 July, 1896. Killed in action, 12 April, 1918.

[5] Lieut. L. Fryberg, M.M.; No. 3 Sqn. (previously Infantry). Metal dealer; b. Bendigo, Vic., 1896.

[6] Lieut. O. H. Suess; No. 3 Sqn. Fitter and turner; b. Brisbane, 1894.

bad weather, which interfered with No. 2 Squadron's air fighting, also greatly hindered reconnaissance by No. 3, but E. J. Jones and Hodgson (observer), diving through low clouds on April 13th along the Bapaume–Albert road, attacked and dispersed two small columns of infantry and transport. Lieutenants Herbert and F. A. Sewell,[7] while bomb-dropping on a similar target on the Somme road west of Etinehem in the evening of April 19th, were attacked by six Pfalz scouts, but made a skilful running fight back to Hamel. In the course of it, they shot down one of the enemy out of control, and near Hamel four British scouts, in answer to their signals, came to their assistance. A two-seater, well managed, had the advantage over a single-seater in fore and aft armament. The weak quarter, the blind spot, of a two-seater was the rear and underneath, since the observer could not bring his gun to bear in that direction; but, unless an enemy could manage to approach unseen and manœuvre into this position, he always found a two-seater an awkward opponent to tackle. The fight by Herbert and Sewell provided a good example of this. Two days later, April 21st, E. J. Jones and Lieutenant A. L. D. Taylor[8] fought two Pfalz scouts over Albert for five minutes, and destroyed one. It was a curious engagement in several respects. Jones was on early morning line-patrol, and for three-quarters of an hour had noticed six enemy scouts cruising just over the German lines between Albert and Thiepval. Two of these finally separated and flew towards Albert, and Jones at once attacked them. He manœuvred so as to give his observer close shooting at the Germans, who after a few minutes' firing turned away towards home. Almost immediately afterwards an explosion occurred in one of them, and it fell and burst into flames on the ground.

Counter-battery work gradually increased in intensity as the line hardened in this region, and during the three days April 21st-23rd the Australian artillery-patrol machines located fifty batteries by flashes, sent calls for fire upon

---

[7] Lieut. F. A. Sewell, D.F.C.; No. 3 Sqn. (previously Artillery). Student; of Kew, Melbourne; b. Caulfield, Melbourne, 7 May, 1898.

[8] Lieut. A. L. D. Taylor; No. 3 Sqn. (previously 2nd Pioneer Bn.). Engineering draughtsman; b. Williamstown, Melbourne, 1896. Killed in action, 20 May, 1918.

twenty-nine, and of these nine were put out of action. The generally bad visibility in many cases prevented observation of fire effect. Most of this new enemy activity was noticed in the flats south of the Somme, and was counted a sign of impending attack in that quarter. The sequel was the assault in the early morning of April 24th on the British position at Villers-Bretonneux by a Prussian Guards Division. On the 22nd Captain J. R. Duigan[9] and Lieutenant A. S. Patterson[10] (observer) first detected, firing near Harbonnières, the big railway-gun which was subsequently captured during the offensive of August 8th, and which is now in Australia.

An illustration of the difficulties of the April fogs and clouds about the Somme is afforded by the exciting adventure of Herbert and Sewell when on a special counter-attack patrol in an R.E.8 at dawn on April 24th. The mist was not very thick near Corbie, and they patrolled thence northward along the corps front at about 500 feet. Finding that sector quiet, the pilot turned back to examine also the southern line beyond the Somme. Near Vaire Wood the machine ran into a heavy fog, which shrouded all the high ground about Villers-Bretonneux. The Germans were by that hour in occupation of the town. The fog was unexpectedly thick, and the airmen lost sight of the ground. In a few seconds the only thing of which they could be sure was that they were losing height and were dropping in a steep spiral. The pilot shut off his engine to recover, fell into a side slip, and suddenly saw ground close below him. The danger was immediate. He re-started his engine, flattened out, and thereafter for about twenty minutes flew at about thirty feet from the ground—the fog was then right down to earth—trying to get his bearings. Several times he just skimmed over trees and houses. He could give no attention to his compass, for the reason that he had to use all his wits to dodge looming obstacles. The airmen were completely lost, and knew only that they were over the enemy's lines, for now and again they saw groups of German artillerymen at their guns. Occasionally they could see heavy batteries well camouflaged and out of

---

[9] Capt. J. R. Duigan, M.C.; No. 3 Sqn. Electrical engineer; of Melbourne; b. Terang, Vic., 31 May, 1882. Built, in 1910, first Australian aeroplane to fly.

[10] Lieut. A. S. Patterson, R.A.F. Attached No. 3 Sqn. from 5 March, 1918. Killed in action, 9 May, 1918.

action. Realising that at any moment they might be obliged to land, Sewell, determined to do what damage he could, fired bursts from his Lewis gun into every new group of Germans. Herbert was, in fact, casting about for a favourable landing-spot, when suddenly a rift in the fog showed him a battery, limbered up, below his right wing-tip. Sewell fired three times into one group of men beside a limber, and all were either hit or dropped to the ground for cover. Judging, reasonably enough, that to alight and surrender alongside that battery was no longer wise, Herbert zoomed up through some trees—so close a shave that he caught a piece of branch in his right aileron and jammed it. This seemed to declare disaster certain; nevertheless Sewell climbed out and sat on the top wing of the machine to compensate for the jammed aileron, and thereby enabled the pilot to continue climbing. The R.E.8 eventually emerged from the fog bank into sunlight at 1,800 feet. The time was 6.12 a.m.—sixty-seven minutes since they had left the aerodrome—and for nearly half of that time they must have been lost in the fog. By working the control-stick Herbert managed to free the aileron, and the observer then resumed his normal seat. He flew west by compass, but the fog still hid all sight of the ground for the next quarter of an hour. Unable to identify the country at length disclosed, he kept on westward until he caught sight of a British field hospital, and at 7.30 they landed—to discover that they had made Trouville, beyond Rouen. After repairing bullet-holes in the machine and a badly punctured tyre, the two airmen returned to their aerodrome in the evening, after a two hours' flight.

By the end of April the opposing lines on the Somme were hardening again into strong trench-systems. The enemy's last offensive stroke in this quarter was at Villers-Bretonneux and Hangard on April 24th; after the Australians re-took the town in the night following, the Germans made no more attacks on the Somme, and definitely gave up the plan of seizing Amiens. The British construed this at the time as failure of Ludendorff's main plan. The deduction was correct. The Germans continued, it is true, to push their attack against the French on the Roye–Noyon front and, later, towards the Marne and Paris. But their drive at last petered out on the

Marne at Chateau-Thierry; here Foch's counter-offensive in mid-July stopped it dead, and began immediately to roll it back.

On the Somme, as in other parts of the British line, the period May-June-July was a waiting period—waiting for a grand counter-attack by Foch's reserve divisions, reinforced by American divisions now arriving. Nevertheless the Australians allowed the Germans no peace. Constant small attacks by the Australian Corps along the Morlancourt Ridge, and by the 1st Australian Division in Flanders opposite Merris, steadily corroded the German line as fast as it was made. Raids by night and by day were the fashion, and at intervals one brigade after another attacked and extended its position between the Ancre and the Somme. This infantry fighting proved the superior mettle of the Australians; it kept them in good training for any greater attack in which they might be called on to take part;[11] and it wore down a series of German divisions in a fashion which the enemy found alarming.

The renewal of trench warfare on the Somme demanded heavy work of the airmen of No. 3 Squadron, who had now to resume the placing of all enemy batteries for regular counter-battery bombardment, the constant photographing of the corps front, close reconnaissance of trenches, tracks, and transport routes, and all the old trench duty made familiar at Messines in the winter. That duty became the more strenuous by demands upon the squadron for special assistance in the infantry's "minor operations." Bombing and machine-gunning of the enemy defences also steadily increased.

Captain H. D. E. Ralfe[12] and Lieutenant W. A. J. Buckland[13] (observer) were killed on patrol at dawn on May 6th. They were attacked by five German machines over the Morlancourt Ridge and were shot down in flames. Several

---

[11] The Allies' general counter-offensive, which, during the spring of 1918, was conceived as possible in 1919 at the earliest, developed in August, 1918, as the result of the unexpected success of (1) Foch's blow on the Soissons flank in July and (2) the Australian and Canadian attack south of the Somme on August 8.

[12] Capt. H. D. E. Ralfe; No. 3 Sqn. (previously Artillery). Officer of Aust. Permanent Forces; of Brisbane; b. Sydney, 29 May, 1890. Killed in action, 6 May, 1918.

[13] Lieut. W. A. J. Buckland; No. 3 Sqn. (previously Engineers). Engineer; of Mirboo North, Vic.; b. Moe, Vic., 1894. Killed in action, 6 May, 1918.

indecisive fights occurred on succeeding days, and on May 9th Lieutenants T. L. Baillieu[14] and E. F. Rowntree[15] (observer) fought three combats during one patrol. Duigan and Patterson were compelled to interrupt a photography-patrol at noon the same day under attack by four German triplanes over Villers-Bretonneux. The R.E.8 made a splendid fight against overwhelming odds, managed to escape after both pilot and observer had been wounded, and landed in the French lines on the flats around Cachy village. The pilot refused to have his wounds attended to until his camera-plates were extracted and sent off to the squadron aerodrome. Every day the same danger was waiting for the relatively slow low-reconnaissance machines. Fighting scouts rode above to protect them, but the sky was rarely clear of clouds, and clouds gave the enemy his opportunity. E. J. Jones and Hainsworth (observer), photographing over Morlancourt on May 16th, suffered Duigan's and Patterson's experience, but with better success. Six Fokker triplanes fell on them. The first two, which dived at the tail of the R.E.8, one on each side, were met by the observer with steady fire; one Fokker turned away, but the other held on, and after a burst from Hainsworth at point-blank range a small flame licked out from under the Fokker pilot's seat, and he went down in a spin. The remaining four Fokkers were shaping to continue the attack, when British scouts appeared on the scene. The enemy thereupon decamped. Jones was again attacked by six triplanes while on duty on May 20th; A. L. D. Taylor, his usual observer, was this time with him. The R.E.8 had ranged a 6-inch howitzer battery on some enemy guns, and was about to watch " fire for effect," when the triplanes appeared. Taylor was shot dead in the fight; Jones was wounded, but managed to fly his machine home. By that time Jones had, while on reconnaissance, engaged the enemy six times in less than three weeks, being on five of those occasions accompanied by Taylor. The R.E.8's, though slower than the German scouting machines, and generally at a disadvantage in the matter

---

[14] Lieut. T. L. Baillieu, D.F.C.; No. 3 Sqn. (previously Artillery). Student; of Toorak, Melbourne; b. Canterbury, Melbourne, 7 April, 1898.

[15] Lieut. E. F. Rowntree, D.F.C.; No. 3 Sqn. (previously Infantry). Engineer; of Hobart; b. Hobart, 23 Jan., 1894.

of height, were, when well-handled, no mean antagonists, as will appear from the combats above-mentioned. Moreover the enemy scouts, brave enough against a solitary two-seater, were always wary of the R.E.8's in company. When, on the evening of May 28th, eight Pfalz scouts attacked two R.E.8's near Hamel, and were driven off by answering fire, they made haste to withdraw as soon as a third R.E.8 appeared on the scene. The exacting duties which devolved upon No. 3 Squadron at this time resulted in all three of its flight-commanders becoming casualties in one fortnight—Ralfe killed, and Duigan and Jones wounded and sent to hospital.

The success of the 6th Australian Infantry Brigade's attack at Ville-sur-Ancre on May 19th was greatly assisted by No. 3 Squadron in the air. Some description of what that assistance amounted to will illustrate the general work of the squadron at that time. The capture of Ville greatly annoyed the enemy, for it entailed the loss of a local observation position. The corps front had been thoroughly photographed by No. 3 Squadron in preparation for the infantry operations. In the early morning of May 18th patrolling R.E.8's noted every feature in the threatened sector, and then passed on to drop bombs and empty their magazines upon Hamel. These machines had hardly left duty, when two more R.E.8's appeared; one flew low along the front line on close reconnaissance; the

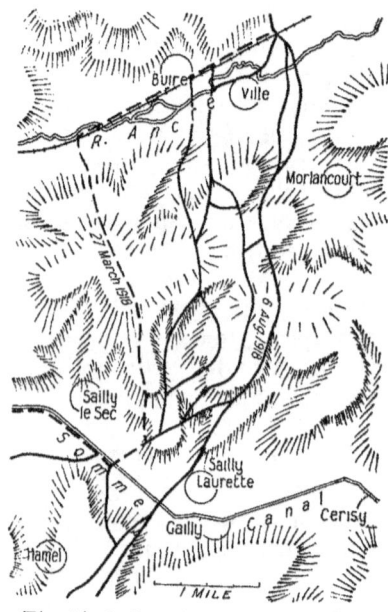

The black lines indicate successive minor advances made between 27th March and 6th August, 1918.

other directed 9.2-inch howitzers on to an enemy battery near Morlancourt, and destroyed several gun-pits. Hostile scouts appeared in the offing, but were met by British scouts and French Spads, which shot down one German. Then a fresh R.E.8 arrived and began a bombardment by 6-inch howitzers of another Morlancourt battery. Visibility deteriorated, and, damage to the target being uncertain, the airmen dropped bombs into Morlancourt village and went home. All this before breakfast-time.

The counter-artillery work continued through the forenoon. Two more German batteries were put out of action in the early afternoon, and several explosions, the result of British field-gun fire, were seen in Albert, Hamel, and Sailly Laurette. If the enemy suspected an attack, he was being puzzled as much as possible as to the point at which it would come. In the afternoon the Ville-sur-Ancre front was photographed again for evidence of damage by artillery-fire, and three enemy batteries on the Hamel flats were silenced and damaged by bombardment. In the early evening two more R.E.8's patrolled the front, looking for gun-flashes and dropping bombs into Hamel and Morlancourt. Ville was by this time on fire. Another machine practised message-dropping with a reserve infantry brigade in rehearsal of the next morning's task. A German battery at Morlancourt was bombarded under air-observation till daylight failed.

After this heavy day's work in preparation, contact-patrols were over the line before 4 o'clock next morning (May 19th) to accompany the attack of the infantry on the Ville position. As the assault progressed, the airmen called with Klaxon horns[16] for flares, and, from the answering lights of the Australian infantry below, located the new line beyond Ville. Messages containing this information were then dropped at brigade and division headquarters. Three more R.E.8's were out at 4.30 a.m.—two to observe enemy artillery action, and one specially to observe counter-action by the enemy's infantry. Every possible detail of the aftermath of the fight was recorded by these airmen by message to headquarters. The examination was repeated at 6 o'clock and again about 10, while another R.E.8, taking up the duty of watching for active enemy guns, directed the corps artillery on to four batteries in succession. The German reply to the Australian attack

---

[16] See Appendix No. 6.

was confined mainly to artillery bombardment of the new line, and this provided further work for No. 3 Squadron in directing[17] counter-battery fire. On May 20th, for example, eight batteries were located by flashes, and six others were put out of action by bombardments; on the following day seventeen were located from flashes, and five were silenced.

Between the occasions of these minor offensive operations, photographing and counter-battery work from the air never ceased. On every day of favourable visibility, five or six such batteries would be "successfully engaged"—sometimes twice that number. While watching the rounds of the British guns, the recording airmen would drop bombs on other targets in order to distract the enemy's attention from the main work in hand. The front opposite the Australian Corps was one of the most thoroughly photographed enemy sectors on the British front. German aircraft constantly sought to interfere, and the R.E.8's often had to defend themselves, but help from escorting scouts was rarely far distant. There were, however, occasions when they were obliged to fight without such assistance. One such occasion was a dawn patrol on June 3rd; T. L. Baillieu and Sewell (observer) were attacked three times between 4.20 and 4.30 by two Albatros scouts over Hamel. The enemy were twice beaten off, but a third attempt brought on a close combat. At this moment Lieutenants R. C. Armstrong[18] and J. H. Jeffery[19] (observer) appeared, and just as they were making to cross the lines near Vaire Wood, the two enemy scouts dived on them. Baillieu promptly joined the fight. The nearer of the Germans received the fire of both Australian observers simultaneously and at close range; he fell steeply, and burst into flames on the ground beside the wood. Ten minutes later the other Albatros attempted again to interfere with Baillieu over the Somme, but finally gave up and

---

[17] It will be understood that this term, used for the sake of brevity, means, as it did in the air force on service, that the aeroplane observed for the heavy-artillery battery which engaged the hostile guns. That a German battery was silenced under bombardment indicated as a rule little more than that the British fire was accurate and the enemy's gunners had left their guns. A battery was by no means necessarily destroyed even when its position was seen to be more or less demolished. But accurate shooting against it generally meant that it would have to move position.

[18] Lieut. R. C. Armstrong, D.F.C.; No. 3 Sqn. (previously Infantry). Engineer; b. Footscray, Melbourne, Apr., 1894.

[19] Lieut. J. H. Jeffery; No. 3 Sqn. (previously A.A.S.C.). Draper; of Brighton, Melbourne; b. Armadale, Melbourne, 28 Oct., 1890.

retired. Meanwhile Armstrong and Jeffery flew over Vaire Wood near the destroyed Albatros. They dropped four bombs and fired 100 rounds into the dugouts and defences of the wood in order to emphasise the victory of which the German infantry had been spectators.

The woods along the Somme between Sailly Laurette and Etinehem and on the ridges south of Hamel were becoming active enemy artillery areas, and eight batteries were silenced in that region on June 6th. On the following day nine more gun-positions thereabout were engaged and damaged. Gun-pits were plainly seen to be wrecked by direct hits, and in some cases 150 or 160 rounds were fired at one position under airmen's observation. This work proceeded with the constant bombing of woods, villages, and important trenches; it was, in part, preparation for an attack projected by the 7th Australian Infantry Brigade above Sailly Laurette.

Lieutenants Armstrong and F. J. Mart[20] (observer) were on artillery-patrol in the forenoon of June 9th. The front was all quiet, and little fire of any sort had been observed. The R.E.8 had dived and machine-gunned Morlancourt for the edification of the Australian trench-garrison opposite, and was returning to the aerodrome, when, over Querrieu (well behind the British lines), the airmen noticed anti-aircraft fire. This could mean only one thing, and the pilot steered for the shell-bursts. There at 2,000 feet he came upon a Halberstadt two-seater, making eastward for home. It appeared later that this German machine had been engaged with others in low-flying patrol during an attack on the French lines near Montdidier, and that its pilot had lost his bearings. He and his observer betrayed some lack of experience—afterwards admitted—by their faulty knowledge of the country and by the panic they betrayed as soon as the R.E.8 cut them off from home. They made no attempt to shoot, and, after one or two feeble efforts to escape, consented to be driven west like a sheep. No other simile will fit the case; Armstrong shepherded the Halberstadt towards Flesselles aerodrome like a dog working a lone wether. Once he had set the Halberstadt on the desired course, the Australian pilot maintained position about 300 feet away behind it and slightly above, and forced

---

[20] Lieut. F. J. Mart; No. 3 Sqn. (previously 5th Tunnelling Coy.). Station overseer; b. Semaphore, S. Aust., Apr., 1889.

it steadily down. The forward Vickers gun of the R.E.8 was trained on the enemy. Now and again Mart would shout to his pilot—" Give him a burst to make sure," but Armstrong would look back, grin, and shake his head. He meant, as he said afterwards, to " take him home." Eventually the Halberstadt landed with all docility on No. 3 Squadron's aerodrome.[21] The captured Halberstadt, quite intact, was claimed as a war trophy, and was subsequently presented to the Australian Government. Maps and papers giving the details of the German forces employed against the French on the Noyon front were found on the captured airmen.

The attack by the 7th Brigade was over the southern side of the Morlancourt Ridge, where it goes down in a broad and bare slope, with a deep, long gully on either side, to the Somme above Sailly Laurette. It was another nicely calculated bite into the German lines. The brigade carried out the operation after dusk in the evening of June 10th, dug itself into the new position during the night, and at dawn next morning contact-patrols from No. 3 Squadron made record of the new line from flares, as on previous occasions. The visibility in the morning was poor, and, to counter the heavy enemy shelling of the ridge, the Australian artillery was compelled to fire without air-observation. During clearer light in the evening of June 11th the airmen enabled the guns to silence two batteries behind Morlancourt and four behind Hamel, which were concentrating fire on the new line. Nevertheless the German guns exceedingly distressed the forward infantry, for the newly-won ground, besides being open to view, was open also to a galling enfilade fire from the woods around Hamel beyond the Somme and eastward in the Somme Valley. The reader may picture himself standing in the infantry's trenches on the bare Sailly slope, with German earthworks visible in front on a similarly bare patch of the main ridge; over his right shoulder, and almost indeed behind his back, on the lower and gentler slopes across the river, lay the German position about Hamel. He may then translate himself in imagination to the German batteries there hidden, and recognise the splendid target offered to them at about 4,000 yards' range by a series of new and shallow trenches

---

[21] See note at end of chapter.

Officers of No. 4 Squadron, A.F.C., Clairmarais, June, 1918

Aust. War Museum Official Photo. No. E2543.

To face p. 270.

The Halberstadt two-seater driven down and captured on Flesselles aerodrome by an R.E.8 of No. 3 Squadron, A.F.C., on 9th June, 1918

Lent by Lieut. T. A. Swinbourne, R.A.A.F. (then of No. 2 Sqn., A.F.C.).

running up and over the ridge, in full view and beyond all hope of camouflage. The said batteries had simply to shoot straight up those trenches over open sights, and this they did, with great discomfort, and no inconsiderable loss, to the infantry garrison. Though the 7th Brigade's attack did not entirely create this situation—which had existed in some degree since the Australians took up their position in April—it enlarged the German gunners' opportunity and advertised it to all their batteries on the south bank of the river. The situation has been thus described in order to make clear one excellent reason for that attack on Hamel which was shortly afterwards made by the Australians, and which was at this time being prepared.

Meanwhile Australian air-reconnaissance was directed specially to those positions on the Morlancourt Ridge itself and along the Ancre towards Albert, against which a series of night-raids was being planned by the Australian 5th Division in the Ancre-Somme sector. Every useful point on the enemy's side was bombed, a few more batteries were found and bombarded, and, as a matter of course, a new series of photographs was taken specially of the areas marked down for the raids. The precision with which every detail was worked out—the allotment of targets to the artillery, trench-mortars, and machine-guns, the organisation of each infantry group in numbers not too many and not too few for each act of the raid—made these operations as certain of success as human ingenuity could do. It was good training for fighting; it was excellent training for junior staff officers and battalion and company commanders. The airmen oversaw them all, and fed them constantly with intelligence. Between June 18th and 25th several battalions of the 15th and 8th Brigades thus raided the German trenches on the Morlancourt Ridge for prisoners and for the sake of moral effect.

There now began the work of close reconnaissance from the air of the Hamel position—the location of enemy batteries, dumps, assembly-points, and approach-march tracks, in preparation for the intended assault. Long reconnaissance-patrols every day closely observed the whole area along the Somme as far east as Bray. No. 3 Squadron also rehearsed an extensive programme in assistance of the infantry—the ordinary contact-patrol work of sketching an advancing line from flares, of marking down hostile batteries in action, and of bombing and machine-gunning in advance of the infantry line to co-operate in the reduction of hostile strong-points. Further there was practice in a device for dropping boxes of small-arm ammunition on the captured position, thus saving the infantry carriers extra labour and danger. The dropping was done by parachute from bomb-racks underneath the fuselage, and experiments on the aerodrome convinced the corps and the army staffs that the idea was good.[22]

In the evening of June 26th Francis and Lieutenant H. A. J. Sturgeon[23] directed fire upon four batteries behind Hamel. These gun-positions were demolished. Lieutenants F. N. McKenna[24] and W. S. J. P. Heslop,[25] while engaging another battery between Hamel and Cerisy next morning, were surrounded by twelve Albatros scouts, which hovered over the R.E.8 and fired long-range bursts at it. The R.E.8 withdrew by skilful manœuvring, but was forced to land, damaged, behind Corbie. On that day, June 27th, the whole Hamel position was photographed on an extensive series of overlapping negatives. Nine more hostile batteries were engaged in the evening, and either damaged or put out of action; but this work cost the squadron further loss, for Lieutenants P. H. Kerr[26] and A. O'C. Brook,[27] while returning from that duty at about 9 p.m., were shot down by a Pfalz scout. The observer was killed in the air and the pilot wounded; the machine was wrecked in landing at Pont Noyelles. During June 28th there were eleven long

---

[22] Major Blake (No. 3 Squadron commander) has stated that "this device for dropping ammunition from aeroplanes was first obtained from a captured German document. General Rawlinson (Fourth Army commander) asked whether it could not be copied. The job was handed over to No. 3 Squadron and the preliminary details were worked out. Captain Wackett was the pilot chosen to make the early trials; he had a gift for mechanical invention. The apparatus used was the ordinary bomb-rack and release-gear adapted to hold two boxes of ammunition attached to parachutes. Much credit is due to the squadron's workshop mechanics under Sergeant Nicholson, whose skill made the success of the gear eventually produced. It was adopted throughout the R.A.F. for this purpose." (Sgt. W. H. Nicholson, motor mechanic; of Cronulla, N.S.W.; b. Parramatta, N.S.W., 15 Aug., 1894.)

[23] Lieut. H. A. J. Sturgeon; No. 3 Sqn. Clerk; b. Brighton, Eng., 1895.

[24] Lieut. F. N. McKenna; No. 3 Sqn. Public accountant and auditor; of Taradale, Vic.; b. Bendigo, Vic., 15 Jan., 1890.

[25] Lieut. W. S. J. P. Heslop; No. 3 Sqn. Grazier; b. Preston, Melbourne, 6 July, 1894.

[26] Lieut. P. H. Kerr; No. 3 Sqn. (previously Light Horse). Station manager; b. Melbourne, 3 Jan., 1880.

[27] Lieut. A. O'C. Brook; No. 3 Sqn. Telegraphist; of Tallangatta and Benalla, Vic.; b. Dederang, Vic., 6 Aug., 1893. Killed in action, 27 June, 1918.

reconnaissances of the back areas, and six more batteries were bombarded. Twice R.E.8's were attacked, but each time beat off their opponents. The days following were equally strenuous. On the 30th the Hamel front was again photographed, and throughout the heat, haze, and dust of the first three days of July long reconnaissances were made over the enemy's front and reserve positions.

The details of the squadron's part in the battle were arranged with the same meticulous care which marked the infantry plan on the ground below. The theatre of the attack was divided into areas, and the important hours between 3 and 10.45 a.m. were similarly divided into patrol periods. In accordance with this table, two flights maintained artillery-patrols on the line until the battle was over; thereafter two machines in reliefs constantly watched the enemy till dusk, meanwhile photographing the new line as it was dug in. The third flight provided both a counter-attack patrol of one machine over the line throughout the day—an aeroplane sentry, regularly relieved—and also contact-patrols during the battle to follow the infantry and report by dropped messages to Australian Corps Headquarters. Except these contact-patrols, every machine carried bombs, with instructions to drop them either on specially allotted targets or, failing the urgency there, upon the best hostile living targets wherever found. A detailed scheme was worked out under which every pilot, when desiring to call for neutralising artillery-fire, had certain field and heavy guns waiting ready for his signals.

Just before the launching of the infantry attack at dawn, in order to distract the enemy's attention from the sound of the tanks approaching over the last few hundred yards to the line, aeroplanes flew low over Hamel, making as much noise as possible and dropping bombs into the village. The result was that, till the moment of the opening artillery bombardment, the enemy knew nothing of the fate about to fall upon him. The whole operation moved by the clock in the smoothest fashion, and was completed at remarkably light cost in casualties to the attacking troops. By a few minutes after 5 a.m. the first airmen on contact-patrol had returned messages showing the new line at the desired position beyond Hamel. They saw little but the locating flares, here and there the lumbering tanks crawling over German posts, small fires of burning houses, a rain of shell-bursts sweeping the enemy area, and only a few vain reply-shots from the German guns; vague knots of men in the half-light, and little columns of pioneers going up to dig in; over all a haze of mist and smoke undispersed by the first shafts of the rising sun. No. 9 British Squadron (also R.E.8's), operating from the Australian aerodrome, performed the work of dropping ammunition on the new line, and delivered nearly 12,000 rounds by this means. All enemy batteries seemed to be smothered in the counter-fire of the British guns. The airmen's reports through the day told of complete success throughout the battle-plan. No. 3 Squadron's machines had their own victories also. Lieutenants A. E. Grigson[28] and H. B. James[29] (observer), on artillery patrol near Accroche Wood, were twice attacked by enemy scouts. Two dived on them in the first combat, and the R.E.8 destroyed one; three more attacked it a few minutes later, but were beaten off, losing one driven down out of control. Lieutenants D. F. Dimsey[30] and Mart, on counter-attack patrol, also had two flights at about the same time and place, and shot down a Pfalz scout from a formation of three which was attacking another R.E.8. During the afternoon three machines photographed on 108 negatives the whole of the new front line.

In all the war the Australians fought no more finished and successful fight than the attack at Hamel. The Corps Command gave much of the credit for that success to the airmen. It is not too much to say that Hamel first showed many soldiers a vision of the days to come, when battles might be directed chiefly from the skies.

Note.—The squadron-commander (Major Blake) thus described the arrival at the aerodrome:—" The Germans landed with their engine still ticking over, and appeared to be on the point of taking off again, when the situation was saved by the corporal of the guard, the only armed man in the vicinity, who ran up with his revolver and presented it at the head of the pilot with the order, 'Hands up!' They did.

[28] Lieut. A. E. Grigson, D.F.C.; No. 3 Sqn. (previously Artillery). Jackeroo; of Sydney; b. Sydney, 9 Nov., 1896.
[29] Lieut. H. B. James; No. 3 Sqn. (previously A.A.S.C.). Draughtsman; b. Harden, N.S.W., 1896.
[30] Lieut. D. F. Dimsey, D.F.C.; No. 3 Sqn. Customs officer; of Albert Park, Melbourne, and Mildura, Victoria; b. Dimboola, Vic., 2 July, 1891.

"The German had ample ammunition for both front and rear guns. About this time complaints had been made by both sides as to the use of explosive and incendiary bullets. In common with other squadron-commanders, I had received orders, in the event of a German machine being captured, to seal up any ammunition remaining in trays, drums, magazines, and forward it to A.H.Q. for expert examination. This was to be done in the presence of the enemy pilot and observer, if still physically competent to understand our action. As luck would have it, this machine fell into our hands immediately after the receipt of the orders. I sealed the ammunition of pilot and observer separately in empty ammunition boxes with paper seals, which I directed the two Germans to sign. The observer complied, but the pilot, with visions of a wall behind his back and a firing-party in front, refused volubly, explaining in French that British pilots were never treated that way when captured. He persisted in this refusal after explanations, but finally, on production of sealing wax, the temptation to use a very ornate seal he carried overcame his scruples and he sealed the box. The box contained both explosive and incendiary bullets."

Comment on the use of incendiary bullets will be found in Appendix No. 9.

CHAPTER XX
EXPLOITS OF No. 4 SQUADRON OVER THE LYS.

THE situation created by the holding up before Amiens of the Germans' main drive against the junction of the Allied Armies has already been explained. Beyond question the most fatal dilemma in which the enemy could have placed the British Command in the spring of 1918 was that which alarmed Kitchener in 1914—the alternative of retreating on the Channel ports and separating from the French, or of retreating with the French towards the south and thus abandoning the bases on the northern coast. The seizure of Amiens in 1918 would have meant no less than that to the British. General Birdwood in April, 1918, deemed Villers-Bretonneux the key to Amiens. Yet probably the denial of Villers-Bretonneux did not disturb the Germans more than the failure of their attempt on Arras, for Arras was a chief bastion in the northern line.

Having been thwarted, then, at Arras and Amiens, the enemy, as has been explained, pushed out his flanks on either side—in the north towards Hazebrouck, in the south towards Noyon, Soissons, and the Marne. Apart from the local objectives of these attacks, a strategic aim was possibly to draw away the Allied reserves (said at the time to amount to twenty or twenty-five divisions, including some trained American divisions) in order to weaken the central position. The drive towards the Marne ended in July with a sharp recoil under Foch's counter-attack at Soissons. The drive in the north across the Lys ended at the outskirts of Hazebrouck, leaving the enemy on the flats there in a position which can have been of no great use to him except as a jumping-off place for a renewed attempt. After the Allies' counter-offensive had caused him to retreat from this district, there was discovered ample evidence, in the shape of ammunition-dumps and other preliminaries, to convince the British staff that he had planned to continue his attack.[1] The participation of No. 2 Squadron

---

[1] Ludendorff states in his book, *My War Memories*, quite clearly the German intention. "Again and again," he says, they thought of attacking in Flanders, but the English reserves were strong and the problem (during most of the summer) too difficult. They therefore decided to attack first at Rheims in the middle of July, and then "possibly a fortnight later in Flanders." They were going (after the Rheims offensive) "to concentrate artillery, trench-mortars, and flying squadrons on the Flanders Front." The notion of the Flanders offensive was discarded after July 18.

in the attempt in the Montdidier-Noyon area has been described. It remains now to follow the work of No. 4 Squadron in the northern, Flanders, sector. It may be added that the enemy's activity in the air on this front was at the time proof to the British of the seriousness of his intentions.

From its new aerodrome No. 4 Squadron, together with other British squadrons, continued during May the bombing and machine-gunning of the German infantry which was consolidating a line in the Lys flats, around Bailleul and the higher ground towards Mont-des-Cats, around Kemmel Hill, and on the southern part of the old Ypres Salient. The Germans also were never out of the air in this region. Their duty was to register their artillery, to procure intelligence of the arrival of the Allied reserves, and to bomb British supply-dumps and bases between Cassel and the coast; and this demanded fighting squadrons to protect the working formations. The air fighting was consequently heavy and incessant. The Australian airmen early established their superiority, and in the hunt for enemy victims began the renown of crack Australian pilots in the list of British aces.

In bad visibility during the early days of May German artillery machines rarely attempted to work. W. B. Tunbridge's patrol in the afternoon of May 1st drove off a two-seater east of Ypres and another near Locre, and Jeffree, one of a formation under Malley, destroyed a solitary Albatros over Bailleul in the afternoon of May 2nd and another early in the next forenoon. The squadron steadily bombed and machine-gunned the Bailleul-Armentières and Merville-Armentières main roads on those cloudy days. The Bailleul main road was a famous target, for its broad tree-lined space was the main resting-place (as it had been with the British before) for supply-lorry parks, and the fields on either side were mostly too wet for traffic. What our guns could not see on this road, the low-flying airmen could, and they bombed and shot at everything they saw. Another favourite target was the thickly-housed road running parallel behind the enemy's new front from La Bassée northwards to the Hazebrouck railway, especially that section of it around Neuf Berquin and Vieux Berquin. While shooting-up this road in the afternoon of

May 4th, Tunbridge and Lieutenant J. H. Weingarth[2] each forced down an Albatros out of control; Weingarth watched his opponent to a landing at Vieux Berquin and dropped bombs about it. The Australian patrol, however, paid a penalty here, for in beating off a sudden attack from seven enemy scouts, Lieutenant B. W. Wright,[3] a British pilot attached to No. 4 Squadron, was shot down in flames.

During the following days the German scouts came out in greater numbers, mostly flying high. The full force of the squadron was on patrol on May 7th and 8th, and fought several indecisive encounters with German scouts in the low clouds. The latter were mostly well behind the German lines, and were guarding hostile artillery machines. By May 10th the Germans showed signs of annoyance at the constant presence of British airmen over their lines, and that evening five Camels from No. 4 Squadron near Wytschaete were attacked from above by nine Pfalz scouts, of which Malley shot one to pieces in the air.

A great joint bombing attack by No. 4 Australian Squadron and No. 110 (Naval) Squadron, R.A.F., was planned for the evening of May 11th on the ammunition-dumps at Armentières. Malley and Petschler, each leading flights of five, were the escorts. Shortly after 7 o'clock the bombers blew up a big dump and started an extensive fire. As the airmen were about to turn homeward, a cloud of German scouts—about thirty in all—attacked from the east. In Petschler's formation Lieutenant H. G. Watson[4] destroyed one Pfalz, and Petschler shot down an Albatros out of control, but the flight lost Lieutenant O. C. Barry,[5] whose machine fell in flames from a fierce duel. Malley's formation also drove down an Albatros. It was the longest air battle Australian airmen had hitherto fought. In the light of the evening sun it was often difficult to tell friend from foe. Inevitably formations were completely

---

[2] Lieut. J. H. Weingarth; No. 4 Sqn. Licensed surveyor; of Darling Point, Sydney; b. Marrickville, Sydney, 17 May, 1892. Killed in aeroplane accident, 4 Feb., 1919.

[3] Lieut. B. W. Wright; R.A.F. Attached No. 4 Sqn. from 17 April, 1918. Killed in action, 4 May, 1918.

[4] Capt. H. G. Watson, D.F.C.; No. 4 Sqn. (previously A.A.S.C.). Dépôt manager; of Sydney; b. Caversham, Dunedin, N.Z., 30 March, 1890.

[5] Lieut. O. C. Barry; No. 4 Sqn. (previously Machine-Gun Corps). Sugar-cane inspector; b. Harwood Island, N.S.W., 1892. Killed in action, 11 May, 1918.

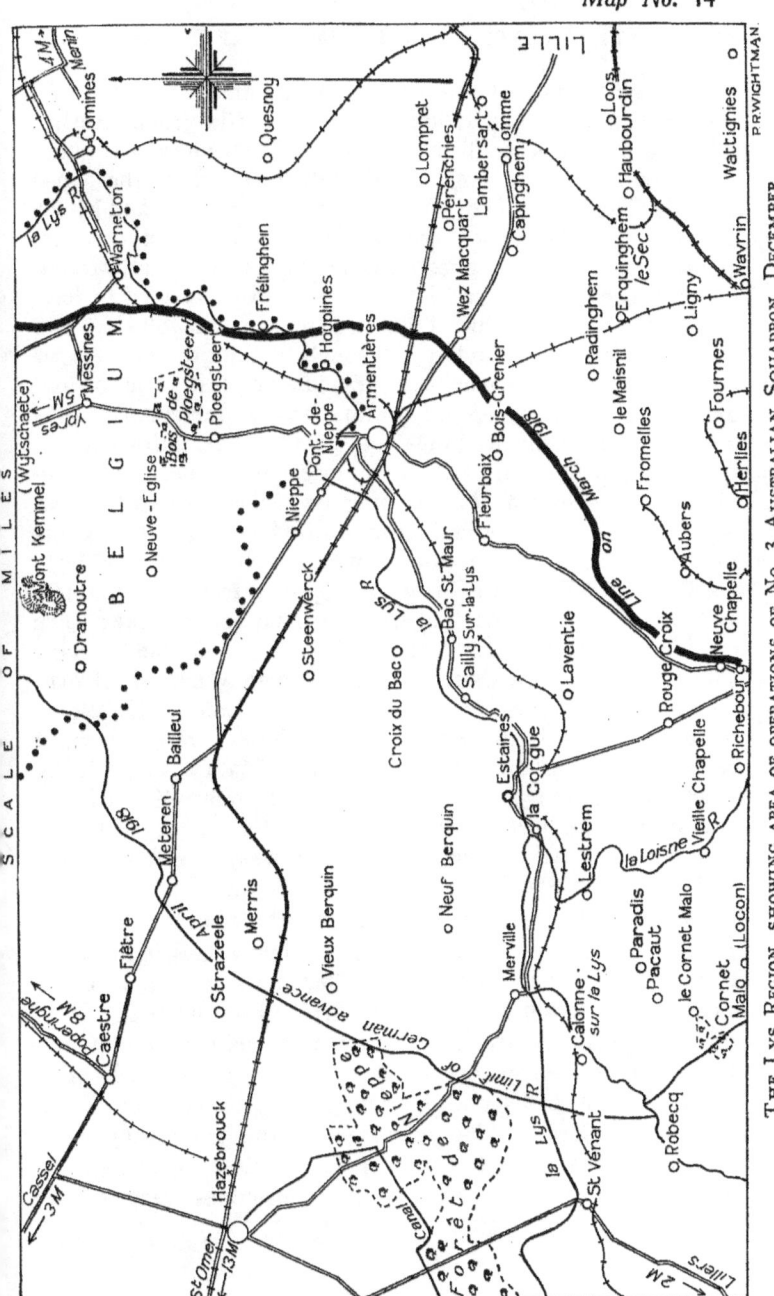

Map No. 14

The Lys Region, showing area of operations of No. 3 Australian Squadron, December, 1917–April, 1918, and of No. 2 and No. 4 Australian Squadrons, May–September, 1918

broken up and scattered over a wide area of sky. As eventually the raiders, individually or in little groups, turned homeward, they were dismayed to find everywhere a smother of white fog below them. Setting their course by the sun—still visible above the horizon at their great height—and by the distant fire of the Armentières dumps, they flew west, descending slowly. "We just guessed where home was," said Malley, "and as we finally dived into the cloud we expected to have to penetrate only a film of haze. Instead, we found it was thick fog for a thousand feet through to the ground. As we entered the fog, all machines immediately lost sight of one another. The first sign of ground was a blurred mass only a few feet under the machine—too late for some, unfortunately, to pull out of their dive. It was impossible to select a landing-place, and night was fast coming on. Some did not know whether they were descending to sea or land. The only thing to do was to slow the machine down, shut your eyes, and hope for the best. In my case I hit the top of a tree, somersaulted, and landed upside down, but whole and no bones broken. The machine in the fog and darkness looked a pitiable wreck." The British and Australian airmen ultimately landed all over the country, not one of them at his aerodrome. Of No. 4 Squadron's contingent alone, six machines were damaged beyond repair in the emergency which Malley has vividly described; it was remarkable that only one pilot of the squadron was injured. He was Lieutenant F. W. Webster,[6] an attached R.A.F. officer, whose foot was broken in a bad spill. No. 110 Squadron's force was less lucky, and lost two pilots killed through bad landings in the same fog.

The Germans had been thwarted for many days in the work of registering their batteries. They now began bringing balloons into action to assist their artillery aeroplanes. Their reconnaissance for artillery work was so persistent that the British Second Army on this front instituted a special air-patrol, the "stand-by patrol," over the region between Ypres and Nieppe Forest. The squadrons in the army wing were detailed in daily turns to stand by for wireless signals, and to be prepared to chase any German machines reported as

---

[6] Lieut. F. W. Webster; R.A.F. Attached No. 4 Sqn., 27 April to 12 May, 1918.

working in this sector in co-operation with the German artillery.

This patrol was controlled from R.A.F. brigade headquarters. The sector was divided into three, with a wireless swinging arm (known technically as a " loop antenna ")[7] in the centre of each division. These wireless stations were in direct communication with one another by telephone, and also with R.A.F. brigade headquarters. The sole duty of the stations was to " listen in." " Listening in " meant that the operator sat with his ear-pieces on, picking out the different aerial sounds of wireless sent by the German aeroplanes to the batteries for which they were spotting. Any one of these stations, or perhaps all three, on picking up a wireless call from a German machine would swing the aerial arm round until the sound on the instrument was loudest, when the arm would be pointing in the direction of the enemy machine sending. The wireless operator would then ring up a neighbouring station and obtain the direction of its aerial arm. Thus the triangle would be marked on a map. This operation would take only about five minutes. The stations promptly informed the squadron " standing by " for the day, and two pilots, waiting for the call, would be allowed seven minutes to leave the ground. Flying over the station which had sent the message, they would find there a white arrow on the ground pointing in the direction of the enemy machine heard working. This arrow would, if possible, be marked off by black lines in thousands of feet to indicate the estimated height of the German. The pilots would then proceed to stalk him; their main object was to keep out of sight until they could descend behind him and cut off his retreat. Keeping out of sight was difficult, as the enemy anti-aircraft batteries would warn their machine by firing a smoke-shell as close to it as possible and salvos of shrapnel and high explosive at the attackers. Usually the German artillery machines took the safe course of keeping well over their own side of the line. At the first suspicion of any interference by British aircraft

---

[7] Such an aerial arm, or loop antenna, serves the same purpose as the more familiar overhead aerial wires for collecting wireless waves. It consists of a coil of wire wound on a rectangular frame. It has a marked effect in establishing direction; it will pick up only waves originating from a station (*e.g.*, a wireless-fitted aeroplane) whose direction is in the plane of the loop.

they would snap on their wireless to their working batteries to report "hostile chasers." Often the opposing machines would play hide-and-seek with each other about a handy cloud.

The wireless listening-stations generally caught news of the combat thus taking place. Messages such as these—picked up from the enemy ranging machine—were often learned after a pilot's arrival home:—" British chasers approaching, wait five minutes"; "Chasers driven off, go on with shoot"; "Numbers of chasers about, send out protection"; "Attacked by British chasers, wait .... wait .... wait ten minutes, am going home pursued by .... "—message unfinished, clearly showing the plight of the enemy. This work was regarded by the Intelligence Department as some of the most valuable performed by the flying service.

Several times during May 14th No. 4 Squadron, having received signals (intercepted and sent on by wireless) that the Germans were registering guns between Ypres and Bailleul, sent out "stand-by patrols" to attack aeroplanes or balloons engaged in that work. Malley and Lieutenant R. King,[8] sent out in response to these calls for counter-action, each shot down a two-seater, but were unable to watch the fate of the Germans below the clouds. Lieutenants K. L. Sinclair[9] and R. G. Smallwood,[10] who engaged another German artillery machine late in the same day, were attacked by three Albatros scouts, which forced Sinclair to land, damaged, south of Zillebeke. He was taken prisoner. Throughout the next day messages reporting similar German activity were constantly received at the Australian aerodrome. Three machines on "stand-by patrol" destroyed in flames one two-seater near Neuf Berquin at 7 a.m., and drove away several others near Bailleul. Half an hour later another small patrol again chased away a two-seater from this vicinity. Simultaneously two strong formations under Cobby and Watson heavily bombed field-batteries in action near Bailleul. Five times more during the day enemy

---

[8] Capt. R. King, D.S.O., D.F.C.; No. 4 Sqn. (previously Light Horse). Motor salesman; of Forbes, N.S.W.; b. Bathurst, N.S.W., 13 May, 1894.

[9] Lieut. K. L. Sinclair; R.A.F. Attached No. 4 Sqn., 17 April to 14 May, 1918.

[10] Lieut. R. G. Smallwood; No. 4 Sqn. Mechanical engineer; b. Ballina, N.S.W., 4 June, 1893.

airmen returned to the Merris-Bailleul area and were driven off. Next morning, May 16th, eleven Camels from No. 4 Squadron put to flight five Albatros scouts near Armentières, and then, coming home, bombed the new La Gorgue aerodrome near Estaires, believed to be a nest of the persistent two-seaters. If it was, the bombing had no effect, for the two-seaters were out constantly all the forenoon, and, as they were strongly escorted, the Australian scouts found difficulty in dispersing them. Again on May 17th Malley with a strong force bombed La Gorgue aerodrome and four balloons were hurriedly pulled down under the attack. No enemy artillery-ranging ensued on that day, though bad visibility was probably one reason for the fact. On May 18th eleven machines repeated the bombing of La Gorgue, while Lieutenants W. S. Martin[11] and R. C. Nelson[12] left the formation to attack four triplanes near Bailleul and shot down two of them, one seen to be destroyed. Other strong fighting patrols from No. 4 Squadron scoured the German battery-areas without meeting opposition, and bombed the La Gorgue aerodrome and dumps and gun-positions between Armentières and Estaires. The enemy returned the compliment at night—the big Gotha bombers came with the full moon every month—and for an exciting hour after 10.15 p.m. Major W. A. McCloughry waged a duel with two Gothas in succession in the beams of the searchlights over Clairmarais Wood, but without visible result.[13] He repeated this performance, also unsuccessfully, on the night of May 30th. The British heavy night-bombing squadrons more than retaliated for the Gotha expeditions, and No. 4 Squadron, like many others, bombed the battle areas continually during the daylight hours. The German infantry and artillery who heard the night-traffic of the bombers overhead, must have listened to their Gothas with mixed feelings, for they knew that the smaller British aeroplanes would visit retaliation upon

---

[11] Lieut. W. S. Martin; No. 4 Sqn. (previously A.A.S.C.). Motor mechanic; of Geelong, Vic.; b. Geelong, 5 Aug., 1893. Killed in action, 12 June, 1918.

[12] Lieut. R. C. Nelson; No. 4 Sqn. Student; of Jamberoo, N.S.W.; b. Jamberoo, 9 June, 1896.

[13] The squadron reported:—"Towards the end of May, and repeatedly in June, enemy night bombing machines persisted in their attempts to bomb the squadron from Clairmarais North aerodrome. So persistent were these bomb raids (sometimes three or four each night) that orders were given for the squadron personnel to leave the aerodrome at night, and sleeping accommodation had to be sought in fields four or five miles distant."

their heads in daylight. And it came daily with the dawn patrols.

One such patrol, under Cobby, nine strong, ranged the whole area between Kemmel and Merville before breakfast on May 20th, and shot down between them six machines—three Pfalzes and three two-seaters. This experience seemed to damp the enemy's flying spirits for the day. Again next morning Cobby led twelve machines like destroying angels over this region; they bombed and started a fire at La Gorgue, drove two two-seaters to ground, and, after attacking everything to be seen on the roads, fired 1,000 rounds into barges on the Lys near Bac St. Maur. Cobby finally set a German balloon in flames near Neuve Eglise. This was the squadron's first balloon victim. "Balloon-strafing," as it was called, was an attractive but highly dangerous enterprise on either side, more dangerous perhaps for British airmen on account of the superior efficiency of German anti-aircraft batteries. These balloons were the stationary "sausage-balloons," and were used especially to assist artillery observation. As they hung anchored in the air at 3,000 or 4,000 feet, they could be seen for miles. As a target they were in themselves vulnerable enough to the special incendiary bullets[14] used against them, but they were nearly always guarded by a line-patrol of fighting aeroplanes, and were protected by well-placed anti-aircraft artillery and machine-guns. At the first approach of British airmen the German balloons would as a rule be pulled down on their ground-windlasses, while their observers would leave nothing to chance, but would jump out with parachutes. The attacking machine, if it persisted against the balloon, had to run the gauntlet of fierce ground-fire, and often risked a surprise attack from the air as well. A balloon fight, therefore, was at times highly dangerous, and to shoot down a balloon was, as a rule, an achievement no less creditable than spectacular. The attacking airman would sometimes fire a few rounds at the unfortunate observer who had jumped and was swinging and dangling from his parachute *en route* earthwards. The Germans were the first to indulge in this merciless practice; the Royal Air Force paid them back in their own coin. Watson, for instance, in a balloon attack on June 1st

---

[14] See Appendix No. 9 and Glossary.

with Cobby's patrol, shot through the rope of a descending observer's parachute.

Cobby's balloon success started a new popularity of balloon-hunting in No. 4 Squadron. The dawn patrol under his leadership on May 22nd found three more balloons, but the attack upon them was frustrated; Lieutenant A. D. Pate,[15] however, destroyed a two-seater north of Wytschaete. On the same day balloons brought two of Malley's noon patrol to grief near Neuf Berquin. Lieutenants Nowland and A. Finnie,[16] two accomplished airmen, dived at one balloon together, collided in the air, and both crashed and were killed. The Australians were not, however, daunted by the dangers of the game; indeed the extra danger urged them on. They got no further chance at balloons till May 30th—the intervening days were mostly days of bad weather, clouds, and rain[17]—but on that afternoon sixteen machines, in two flights under Malley and Cobby, swept the region of the Lys above Armentières. After the whole force had bombed the Bac St. Maur dump, it flew on south and westward, and at Estaires the two leaders destroyed a balloon each within five minutes, while two more balloons were hurriedly pulled down. Zooming up again from his burning balloon victim, amid a fury of ground-fire, Cobby met and attacked a protecting Albatros scout and destroyed that too. Watson shot down another, which fell out of control. In this attack the Australians, with premeditated cunning, appeared from the German side of the balloons, and the watching balloon-hands apparently mistook them at first for friendly machines. Two more attempts in the same vicinity next day failed to catch the enemy napping. Then, on June 1st, after eleven Camels had again bombed Bac St. Maur, Cobby and Watson rose high above the Estaires balloon-pitch,

---

[15] Lieut. A. D. Pate; R.A.F. Attached No. 4 Sqn., 27 April to 1 June, 1918.

[16] Lieut. A. Finnie; No. 4 Sqn. (previously Engineers). Sheet-metal worker; b. Botany, Sydney, 1893. Killed in action, 22 May, 1918.

[17] Although for a week at this time, with the exception of a few bright intervals, the weather was very unfavourable for flying—so bad that enemy machines rarely appeared in the sky—No. 4 Squadron was daily over the German lines, bombing and machine-gunning the only enemy to be seen, the infantry on the ground. A laconic report of operations on May 25, for instance, reads—" Weather bad. Visibility very bad. Impossible for patrols to get above 700 feet over the line. Twenty-two 20-lb. bombs dropped on Bac St. Maur." Next day—" Low clouds and mist. Visibility too bad to observe any ground movement. Twenty-four 20-lb. bombs dropped on Estaires." On May 27 and 28, under some temporary improvement in the weather (which brought a few enemy scouts out also) dumps were bombed and set burning at Bac St. Maur and south-east of Armentières. On May 29 No. 4 bombed Bac St. Maur again in the rain.

and at a well-timed moment Cobby dived. One balloon was late in descending; Cobby followed it, firing, and at 2,000 feet it burst into flames. Watson, as has already been related, shot the rope away from the parachute of the observer who had jumped. A few minutes later the formation, flying westward towards St. Venant, sighted an Albatros scout pursuing an evidently unsuspecting Camel. Just as the German was about to drop upon his intended victim, Cobby fired at long range to distract his attention. The Albatros immediately turned for home, and Cobby flew up into the sun. The air being apparently clear, the Albatros turned again towards Merville. Unseen in the sun the Australian pilot renewed his attack, this time at close quarters. The German pilot was evidently badly hit; his machine staggered and turned towards Estaires, Cobby pursuing and firing, then side-slipped, lost its left wings, and crashed.

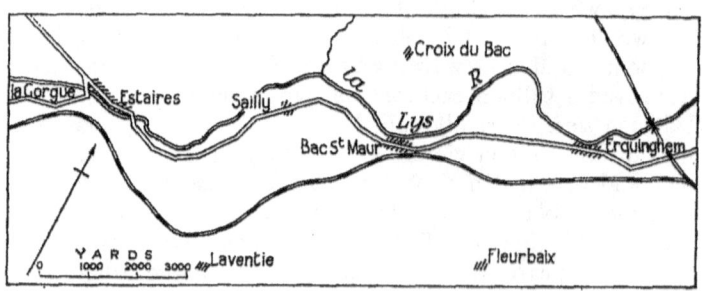

In the afternoon Malley's formation lost a pilot in circumstances which showed the importance of maintaining formation on an offensive-patrol. At 14,000 feet over Bac St. Maur, Malley noticed, as the formation turned, that Lieutenant A. Rintoul[18] had either strayed from his station or fallen out with temporary engine-trouble. Two Pfalz scouts to the eastward had also noticed it, and were quick to attack him. Malley promptly dived to help him. Rintoul having by this time manœuvred on to the tail of one Pfalz, Malley went for the other, and destroyed it by shooting off one of its wings in the air. But Rintoul was not seen again, and was later reported a prisoner of war.

---

[18] Lieut. A. Rintoul; No. 4 Sqn. (previously Infantry). Invoice clerk; b. Melbourne, 1897.

The special objective of the Australian airmen's attacks in this region will be clearly perceived from the map. That objective was the River Lys, the main road, and the railway, which ran almost alongside each other from Merville to Armentières; and the favourite points of attack on this triple line of supply were the dépôts at Bac St. Maur and Estaires. Between Sailly and Estaires was a line of German balloons, upon which the enemy depended for much of his artillery observation. After dropping their bombs at Bac St. Maur, the Camels would dash along the Lys on the chance of catching the balloon-line napping, or roam the district for early hostile scouts, or, failing these excitements, would dive down on the forward trenches on the way home and shoot-up the infantry resting after the night's duty and alarms. The faithful repetition of this simple strategy day after day should have notified the Germans that the sound of dull explosions about the lock-gates of Bac St. Maur was a warning to get ready to pull down the balloons at Estaires. Yet they many times failed to work the balloon-windlasses fast enough. These patrols rarely missed some sort of good hunting. The daily average of bombs dropped on the Lys dumps was from forty to fifty. On June 7th Watson set fire to another balloon over Sailly. Captain E. J. K. McCloughry,[19] leading a patrol in the forenoon of June 12th over the daily tracks of No. 4's marauding formations, destroyed another Estaires balloon, and Martin just missed setting a second on fire as it was drawn down. The patrol was promptly attacked in turn by nine Albatros and Pfalz scouts. McCloughry turned upon one Pfalz, which was diving at him, fired a burst into the enemy's side at thirty yards' range, and the Pfalz went down out of control. It was seen by anti-aircraft observers to crash. Martin was not so fortunate; a Pfalz shot him down from above, and he fell in No-Man's Land near Meteren, and was killed.

In the evening of June 17th fifteen machines flew out from No. 4's aerodrome. They reached Bac St. Maur a little before sunset and each dropped two 20-lb. bombs on that much-punished little village; they then returned up the Lys

---

[19] Capt. E. J. K. McCloughry, D.S.O., D.F.C.; No. 4 Sqn. (previously Engineers). Student; of North Adelaide; b. Hindmarsh, Adelaide, 10 Sept., 1896.

to Merville, machine-gunning ground targets as they went. Cobby and Watson, flying apart from the others, observed four Pfalz scouts and one Albatros near Laventie on the same level—about 4,000 feet. They flew towards the Germans and by concerted arrangement dived together, Cobby on the right- and Watson on the left-rear machines. Cobby shot the right wings off his victim; Watson set his in flames. Each of them immediately attacked the next two. Watson zoomed up, arrived over the tail of the Pfalz, fired a long burst at close range, and the German dropped and crashed east of Laventie. Cobby chased his second German, which was badly hit, nearly to the ground; the enemy tried to land, but, taking a hedge in a hurry, crashed in the field beyond. Cobby dived three times at the wrecked Pfalz, firing in all 400 rounds at it from close quarters. "I shot the pilot's cockpit and the centre section to pieces," he records; "the pilot did not move after crashing."

Coming from the bombing of Bac St. Maur again next morning, June 18th, E. J. K. McCloughry, with sixteen other machines, shot down out of control a triplane which was attacking an R.E.8. Again in the evening sixteen more machines dropped two bombs each on Bac St. Maur, and while the formation, seeing nothing in the sky, was emptying its machine-guns along the Lys on the return journey, Major F. I. Tanner,[20] one of the patrol, found an Albatros low down near Merville and destroyed it. King, with the evening bombing-patrol on June 20th, burned a balloon at Estaires. Cobby and McCloughry, who had returned early from the bombing in consequence of faults in their guns, went out again towards the Nieppe Forest and there found four Pfalz scouts attacking British balloons. Three of them saw the Camels and turned back; the fourth was chased by Cobby, was shot down, and fell into the forest.

Mist, clouds, and rain interrupted air fighting for a few days after June 20th, but the bombing of Bac St. Maur and the machine-gunning of enemy trenches did not cease. During a bombing-patrol in the evening of June 25th, Cobby and Watson destroyed two more enemy machines near Estaires. They dived at three Pfalz scouts at 9,000 feet, and Cobby

---

[20] Maj. F. I. Tanner; R.A.F. Attached No. 4 Sqn., 25 May to July, 1918.

shot one to pieces in the air. Watson missed his opponent in his first dive, left it, and, continuing his dive, joined Cobby in attacking an A.G.O. two-seater flying at 5,000 feet near Bac St. Maur. The German dodged Cobby, who overshot it, but Watson, keeping behind, fired several heavy bursts at it from underneath, and the two-seater span into the ground near Estaires. Next evening a similar patrol, after the customary visitation of "evening hate"[21] on Bac St. Maur, which set a large fire going there, flew on over Lille. The Australians found no enemy in the air till, on the return journey, they observed five yellow Pfalz scouts, also flying west, in front of them near Armentières. Cobby, Watson, and King dived together on this formation, and Watson and King set their victims on fire in the air at about 10,000 feet. Cobby then made for two which were trying to escape east, and followed down to 5,000 feet one Pfalz which was dropping completely out of control and emitting much smoke. Beyond that height the mist shut it off from his view.

Although the Germans had not yet finally abandoned their plans for a further offensive in Flanders, the re-appearance at this time of the enemy's reconnaissance machines on the front may have been prompted chiefly by anxiety concerning British intentions. At dawn on June 28th the British 5th Division assaulted the enemy's lines before Nieppe Forest, and drove him out of his positions west of the Vieux Berquin high-road, while simultaneously infantry parties of the 1st Australian Division, to the left of the attack, raided with great audacity in broad daylight and captured almost the entire garrison of the German trenches in front of Merris. Patrols from No. 4 Squadron were out to watch the attack as soon as daylight permitted, and the pilots came back during the morning grinning with delight at the work which they had seen the Australian infantry performing at Merris. A low-flying Albatros two-seater, attacking the British near Vieux Berquin, was shot down by Lieutenant G. S. Jones-Evans[22] at 11.30 a.m., after a short fight at 250 feet. Cobby

---

[21] The "morning hate" and the "evening hate" were expressions which lived with the British Army as long as trench-warfare lasted. They covered artillery bombardments and aeroplane bombing alike. The British Army in 1915 received the famous *Hymn of Hate* (composed by the German poet Lissauer) as an enormous joke, and them, at any rate, its shaft never pierced.

[22] Lieut. G. S. Jones-Evans; R.A.F. Attached No. 4 Sqn., 1 June to 28 July, 1918.

and King went out in the afternoon to combat other Germans reported to be flying over the same locality. They found about twelve enemy machines in scattered groups in the sky, and flew at once to attack five two-seaters making towards Vieux Berquin. Cobby destroyed one of them, an L.V.G., over Oultersteene, and then zoomed up to engage one of a number of approaching scouts. This machine also went down, burning. The others decamped. Malley, out alone on what was officially designated "practice," bemoaned his lot in arriving just too late to join in this hunting, for he and Cobby were in close rivalry for the record of highest number of enemy aircraft destroyed. Shortly afterwards a larger patrol of Camels, chasing six more German machines away from Merville, was robbed of one intended victim by a British anti-aircraft shell, which blew it to pieces in the air. The mist was heavy over the battle area in the evening, and the line-patrols saw nothing more there, but German two-seaters were active near Wytschaete, farther north, where the visibility was better, and Cobby and King went off at 6 o'clock to that region in answer to wireless calls. As they emerged from a cloud over the Messines Ridge, they dropped upon three two-seaters, one L.V.G. making east and two Halberstadts crossing the ridge towards the lines. King appeared from the cloud in position to shoot straight into the L.V.G.; he promptly seized the opportunity, and the two-seater span away and fell into the ground among the German batteries. Cobby dived below one of the Halberstadts, of which he laconically recorded "speed and armament unknown," zoomed up under its belly, and fired into it at deadly close range, until it fell on its back and crashed on the hill near the ruins of Messines. The same two airmen led a formation of thirteen over this area next evening, swept it far and wide, and dropped 500 lbs. of bombs on Comines, the site of an aerodrome and a big supply-dump.

CHAPTER XXI

HARASSING THE ENEMY ON THE LYS

By mid-July the fortunes of the enemy, having reached high-water mark, began to recede. July also found both of the Australian scouting squadrons located at the same aerodrome at Reclinghem (south-west of Aire), and during the summer both sides seemed to concentrate air fighting strength on the Flanders front. This flank of the battle-line was a tender spot for the enemy. He had to withdraw from about Lille more and more divisions to stay the central Allied attack south of Arras; if his right flank were turned, disaster might ensue to his whole army. Hence, as the main battle swelled, the increasing importance of the northern operations, the essential need for good air-reconnaissance, and therefore the accumulating strength of the air forces on both sides. July and August were months of poor weather for flying, attended, as summer months in the Low Countries frequently are, by rain storms and bad visibility. Nevertheless each side kept the air in great force, and August and September, when the critical fighting came, were remarkable for great battles in the skies over the area around Lille.

No. 2 and No. 4 Squadrons were by now frankly engaged in a keen, though friendly, competition for the largest number of enemy aircraft destroyed. The fact of their sharing the same aerodrome naturally increased this rivalry. The first fight from the new aerodrome was that of a patrol under Captain E. J. K. McCloughry, of No. 4 Squadron, in the afternoon of July 1st. He was one of a formation of ten which dropped 400 lbs. of bombs on Estaires. Three Pfalz scouts dived out of the upper air upon him, but almost at once two of them collided, and one, losing a wing torn off, fell to the ground. The third Pfalz opened fire on him, but was outmanœuvred, and flew away east. McCloughry then attacked the second Pfalz of the colliding pair, fired 100 rounds into it, and it fell in flames.

Next morning No. 4 Squadron again bombed Estaires with two successive formations, while accompanying patrols from No. 2 roamed the sky at 18,000 feet. Many triplanes and Fokker biplanes were seen south-east of Merville and west of Armentières, but too far off to engage. In the early afternoon three machines from No. 4 Squadron were out on special missions after German airmen engaged in reconnaissance. Cobby, in one of them, flew to the Lys balloon-line in quest of prey, attacked a balloon from directly above, and set it on fire. While regaining height from this effort, he perceived four Fokker triplanes flying towards Merville from La Bassée. Three of them were at 10,000 feet; the fourth was about 1,500 feet lower. Cobby was one of the most daring spirits in the Australian air service. He made straight for the four Fokkers, flying under clouds in order to get east of them unseen. With nice judgment he at length emerged from the clouds in position slightly above the lower and under the three upper machines, and at the same moment another friendly cloud cut him off from the sight of those three. He fell like a hawk on the lower triplane, and fired 150 rounds into it at about fifty-feet range. The triplane fell into a carpet of cloud completely out of control. Cobby went down after it to observe its fate, despite the fact that the other three had seen him, and were coming down to attack. They chased him back across the lines, but, after they had turned away again, Cobby flew back to La Bassée and there saw his victim lying in a heap on the ground.

Two flights from No. 4 Squadron again bombed Estaires and Merville in the afternoon of July 4th. Between 5 and 5.30 p.m. one of them flew low and machine-gunned balloon-grounds, roads, and billets, and, arriving at the town-square of Estaires, found two companies drilling there. They shot down a number of these men and pursued the others with a hot fire into surrounding houses. In the same evening six S.E.5's from No. 2 Squadron fell in with five Fokker biplanes flying at 18,000 feet just east of Armentières. Five of the Australians had a slight advantage of height over the enemy; one, F. R. Smith, was flying below. The top S.E.5's dived at the Fokkers and sent them down in a whirl past Smith; Smith picked out one, tumbled about in the air with it, firing several long bursts, and finally fired fifty rounds into it at close range. It fell and crashed to pieces on the main Lille road near Capinghem.

Both squadrons continued their bombing operations against

troops and railways on July 5th and 6th. Lieutenants A. T. Heller,[1] J. W. Milner,[2] O. B. Ramsay,[3] and Nelson, from No. 4 Squadron, flew in the early morning at very low heights—sometimes at no more than twenty feet—along a line of trenches and shell-holes from Merville to La Bassée, and fired over 2,000 rounds into German infantry. This, in a thick morning haze, was remarkably clever work, and the exposed troops were for the time utterly demoralized. The four Camels returned safely, though full of bullet-holes. A following patrol of six Camels at 9.45 a.m., under E. J. K. McCloughry, dropped 300 lbs. of bombs on Estaires, sank a barge at that place, and then flew along the German trenches between Merville and La Bassée and repeated the previous attack on the infantry garrisons. On July 6th both squadrons bombed dumps at Merville, Estaires, and Bac St. Maur, and also the railways around La Bassée and Steenwerck. These were all important points in the Germans' supply-system in the Lys salient.

"Train-strafing" was always high sport for airmen, and the constant visits to Lille suggested great possibilities in this way. No. 2 Squadron resolved to exploit them, and planned an early morning visit in the mist to Lille on July 7th. Ten machines, under the squadron-commander (Major Murray Jones), left the aerodrome at 4 a.m. on this adventure. Thick clouds at 2,000 feet made visibility very bad, and one pilot, having lost his way, took no part in the raid. The formation flew east towards Bethune by compass-bearing; there the clouds gave place to a white mist, through which sight of the ground was possible. The patrol picked up the La Bassée–Haubourdin Canal and flew along it to Haubourdin, where at 5.15 a.m. Murray Jones gave the signal to descend. The first target seen was a train leaving the station westward. Jones dropped two bombs close beside it from fifty feet, and set the train burning on each side. Cole lashed the same train with machine-gun fire and dropped his bombs in the goods-shed beside the railway. Copp followed Cole, and released two bombs clean into a stationary train at the station; he then

---

[1] Lieut. A. T. Heller; No. 4 Sqn. (previously Artillery). Jackeroo; of Hay, N.S.W.; b. Warrnambool, Vic., 19 July, 1896.
[2] Lieut. J. W. Milner; R.A.F. Attached No. 4 Sqn., 26 May to July, 1918.
[3] Lieut. O. B. Ramsay; No. 4 Sqn. (previously 1st Pioneer Bn.). Licensed surveyor; b. Tumbarumba, N.S.W., 12 Feb., 1892.

turned away and fired 200 rounds into a dump at Herlies, farther west. Lieutenant C. O. Stone[4] bombed Haubourdin station and silenced an anti-aircraft battery near by with his machine-guns. Forrest dived at the station at Wavrin, three miles south-west of Haubourdin, dropped two bombs in the middle of the railway track, flew on to meet a train coming from La Bassée, and fired 100 rounds into its windows. Lieutenant A. C. G. Cameron[5] bombed the railway behind Forrest and left more craters in the permanent way. Lieutenants F. Alberry,[6] J. J. Wellwood,[7] and Cox remained aloft to guard the raiders against any air-attack, but none came. Such was the matter-of-fact report of a raid which, made in a shrouding mist, blocked a main railway supply-line for some hours, and brought the camps of a whole countryside out like angry ants. So thick was the fog that most of the machines were unable to find their aerodrome on their return, and there were five forced landings away from home.

The bombing and machine-gunning of the enemy's forward trenches and villages in the Lys flats between Merville and La Bassée proceeded as a daily routine on the part of No. 4 Squadron. The enemy was beginning to take the air in stronger formations, and in the days after the bombing of Haubourdin great numbers of them were seen over Lille. In the evening of July 7th a flight from No. 4 Squadron, under Lieutenant N. C. Trescowthick,[8] escorting a bombing-patrol of D.H.9's, was suddenly attacked from above by fourteen Fokkers between La Bassée and Nieppe Forest. The Australians beat off the enemy after narrowly escaping disaster, several of the Camels being badly damaged. In marked distinction from the practice of the British airmen, the Germans, though numerous and active, seldom ventured across the lines except at great height. On such rare occasions they were prompt to turn away for home as soon as they were challenged.

---

[4] Lieut. C. O. Stone; No. 2 Sqn. Chauffeur; b. Chingford, Essex, Eng., Sept., 1893.

[5] Lieut. A. C. G. Cameron; No. 2 Sqn. (previously Artillery). Chemist; b. Maryborough, Q'land, Jan., 1898.

[6] Lieut. F. Alberry, D.C.M.; No. 2 Sqn. Labourer; b. Hobart, Sept., 1892. (He had lost a leg while serving in the infantry, but was none the less a daring and capable pilot.)

[7] Lieut. J. J. Wellwood, D.F.C.; No. 2 Sqn. (previously Artillery). Motor engineer; of Drouin, Vic.; b. Drouin, 15 Oct., 1892.

[8] Lieut. N. C. Trescowthick, D.F.C.; No. 4 Sqn. Boot manufacturer; b. Clifton Hill, Melbourne, Aug., 1895.

The enemy infantry activity around Merville and Estaires was pronounced, and Australian airmen made daily practice on transport, trenches, and gun-positions in this region, where the country had been so blasted by artillery bombardment that movement was almost impossible to hide. On one such patrol, in the morning of July 10th, Lieutenant R. Moore[9] was hit by a shell and crashed near Robecq, but escaped with his life; and Nelson, one of a bombing-patrol on July 14th, was shot down by ground-fire while machine-gunning transport near Estaires. He landed unhurt, and was taken prisoner.

That local defence measures in this flat, shell-torn country were easily discerned from the air has been stated above. For the same reason observation from the ground by the German gunners was almost impossible. Every house or other observer's vantage-point had been pounded to pieces by gun-fire. Hence German two-seater artillery aeroplanes became very busy in this region. Cobby destroyed one of them near La Bassée in the evening of July 9th; he caught it in a neat double burst of fire, first in a dive from above and behind, and then in a stalling attack from underneath its tail. E. J. K. McCloughry, out with Jones-Evans on a dawn hunt over Laventie on July 11th, crashed a Rumpler two-seater, and five minutes later, being attacked by several Pfalz scouts, shot down one out of control. Two more two-seaters were destroyed near Estaires, one by McCloughry in the afternoon of July 13th and one by Trescowthick next morning. Accompanying Trescowthick was Cobby. The sight of these machines in the vicinity had put the Estaires balloon-line into hasty motion earthward, and while Trescowthick chased the guardian two-seater, Cobby dashed at the nearest balloon and set it on fire.

A sharp fight in the afternoon of July 15th was an example of the daring of Cobby and another first-rate fighting pilot in No. 4 Squadron, Watson. They were flying in company over La Bassée at 6,000 feet, when they noticed five Pfalz scouts coming from Bailleul towards Armentières. The two immediately climbed over the clouds and flew towards the enemy. Diving through the clouds again with nice judgment, they found themselves just above and east of the Germans.

---

[9] Lieut. R. Moore; R.A.F. Attached No. 4 Sqn., 15 May to July, 1918.

Despite the presence of a formation of triplanes in the offing, the two Australians immediately attacked. Cobby shot one of the rearmost of the Pfalz formation into flames with his first burst at twenty-five yards' range. Simultaneously another fell from Watson's fire completely out of control. Cobby dived again at a third Pfalz, fought a sharp duel with it, and after the two machines had tumbled and rolled over each other for a minute or more, both wings of the Pfalz collapsed and the machine broke into pieces. By this time four triplanes had descended and were attacking the two Camels. Cobby and Watson escaped by diving away through clouds almost to the ground.

No. 4 Squadron was meeting with remarkable success from early-morning patrols. These were usually of six or eight machines, which would load up with bombs and leave the aerodrome before sunrise, timing their arrival over the Lys line of communications for the first light after dawn. On July 16th E. J. K. McCloughry and Jones-Evans, starting out ahead of six others, flew in the half-light straight for balloon-positions which they had marked down carefully by daylight. Arriving near the Lys, they dropped their bombs on Bac St. Maur and La Gorgue respectively, then stopped their engines and glided down on the unsuspecting balloons. Each shot down one of these in flames, and by the time they had zoomed up again and rejoined company, the other machines of the formation, under Trescowthick, had come up. These proceeded to deposit their loads of explosives on Laventie railway station, and then machine-gunned the enemy's trenches near Le Cornet Malo, between Bethune and Merville.

Next morning (July 17th), while three Camels bombed Armentières railway station at 4 o'clock, Lieutenants Smallwood and C. S. Scobie[10] attacked the Estaires end of the Lys line of supply, and Smallwood destroyed another balloon. Shortly afterwards Taplin, while roaming over the Pacaut area (north of Bethune) looking for his comrades, was attacked by four Pfalz scouts. Having the speed of these, he outclimbed them, counter-attacked at 17,000 feet, and put them to flight. Then near Merville he saw two Albatros two-seaters at 3,000 feet and dived on them. One

---

[10] Lieut. C. S. Scobie; R.A.F. Attached No. 4 Sqn., 12 May to July, 1918.

made immediately towards the ground, but the other stayed to fight. Taplin shot the observer, and then fired into the machine, till it fell and crashed south-west of Estaires. In the afternoon Cole, leading a formation of five from No. 2 Squadron, outmanœuvred near Armentières six Fokker triplanes which had refused combat, put his patrol in position east of them and slightly above, and himself dived on the leader. This triplane fell away on its back; Stone, following close behind Cole, took up the attack upon it, and, after another hundred rounds from him, the Fokker caught fire and dropped like a torch from 17,000 feet.

July 22nd broke a fine flying day, and British and German machines were alike out early over the Lys flats. No. 4 Squadron's dawn destroyer-patrol left in three sections— Moore and Ramsay at 3.30, Taplin and Lieutenant A. H. Lockley[11] at 4.30, and E. J. K. McCloughry, Lieutenants R. H. Youdale[12] and J. C. F. Wilkinson[13] at 5. They all flew straight for the region of Estaires. At 4 a.m. F. R. Smith led four S.E.5's from No. 2 Squadron into the higher air to cruise over Bethune and Lens, and at 6 a.m. Phillipps took out six more. Several German machines were flying low over the Lys. Moore sighted the first of them, a two-seater, near Pacaut Wood, at 1,500 feet, about 4.15 a.m. He had the height of this German by 500 feet, dived upon it, turned towards the ground, and pursued it earthward, firing heavily at close range. The German observer or his armament must have been crippled, for the enemy did not return the shooting. After Moore had fired some 500 rounds into it, the two-seater plunged into the earth in hopeless wreck. Ramsay amused himself meanwhile by firing into the Germans in Pacaut Wood trenches who were watching the incident. He and Moore then flew down the Lys, dropped their bombs on Bac St. Maur, and went home. The second section of the patrol, Taplin and Lockley, arrived soon afterwards, found no enemy over Pacaut Wood, and flew on to Estaires. Here they joined E. J. K. McCloughry, Youdale, and Wilkinson, who had

---

[11] Lieut. A. H. Lockley; No. 4 Sqn. Motor engineer; of Woolloomooloo, Sydney; b. Marrickville, Sydney, 8 May, 1898. Killed in action, 5 Sept., 1918.

[12] Lieut. R. H. Youdale; No. 4 Sqn. (previously A.A.S.C.). Clerk; of Burwood, Sydney; b. Burwood, 7 Sept., 1890.

[13] Lieut. J. C. F. Wilkinson, M.C.; R.A.F. Attached No. 4 Sqn., 12 June to Aug., 1918.

dropped bombs on Bac St. Maur, and attacked the balloon-line near Sailly. Against the balloons Youdale alone was successful. Wilkinson missed his intended victim, and McCloughry had just opened fire when he was attacked from behind by a Fokker biplane. This McCloughry dodged with a climbing turn, and counter-attacked side-on at point-blank range. The Fokker heeled over and crashed near Sailly. Meanwhile the first two offensive-patrols of No. 2 Squadron met no Germans, but a third formation of four machines under Manuel, cruising later in the morning east of Lens at 16,500 feet, came upon three Fokker biplanes about to attack a lower flight of S.E.5's. Manuel wheeled in a wide circle, dived on the Fokkers from behind, and shot down one in a slow wide spin. The S.E.5's then turned east and climbed to 17,000 feet over a scattered collection of fifteen Fokkers, triplanes, and Pfalz scouts. Manuel singled out the rearmost scout of a Pfalz formation, which fell away from the attack completely out of control. The remainder of the enemy prepared to fight, but the Australians, being short of petrol, avoided engagement.

Bad weather spoiled flying until three days later. The dawn of July 25th was marked by a heavy air attack on Armentières and the Lys by both Australian squadrons. Of a formation of seven from No. 4 Squadron, three pilots dropped their bombs on Bac St. Maur, two others heavily machine-gunned a train at Armentières station, and the remaining two, King and Watson, raided the river valley north-east of Armentières. Watson's objective was a balloon near Comines, whose position he had previously marked down. He found this balloon just leaving the ground to ascend, darted at it, and set it on fire from a range of 200 feet. Turning back, he and King sighted an L.V.G. two-seater north of Armentières. Watson, being the nearer, attacked it first, but without apparent effect; King then chased it from 3,000 feet to near the ground, firing into it repeatedly, and the German went straight into the earth nose-first. The two Australians then searched over Armentières for infantry billets, found and bombed several, and flew on up the Lys. They sprayed with their machine-guns a party of men at the Bac St. Maur dumps, and at Estaires shot a "flaming-onion" battery into panic with several hundred rounds. They had hardly left

25th-26th July, 1918] HARASSING THE ENEMY

this much-harassed scene, when five more Camels under Trescowthick bombed Bac St. Maur. The next two patrols from No. 4 Squadron—one of four machines (6.20 a.m.) and one of six (6.45 a.m.)—flew along the Lys from Merville, and aimed their bombs at reserve billets in Lestrem. At 8.15 four more machines, under King, bombed Bac St. Maur. This visitation coincided with the attack of fourteen S.E.5's from No. 2 Squadron on the Lille forts east of Armentières. No. 2's formation flew over in impressive array and dropped twenty-eight bombs at Le Corbeau, Fort Carnot, and Houplines. The bombs which fell into Houplines were not intended for that mark, but it happened that as Phillipps, with the escort section of the formation, was passing over the place at 17,000 feet, he saw seven Fokker biplanes some 2,000 feet below him. He and Cummings at once released their bombs to lighten weight for the attack. Phillipps selected what he believed to be the highest of the Fokkers, a red-tailed machine, and dived at it, but when half-way towards it he suddenly saw a green Fokker flitting from immediately underneath him. Phillipps put his machine straight on its nose in a dive at the green Fokker, and with one short burst from his double machine-guns shot its left wing away. The other Germans took alarm and flew eastward.

The dawn bombing-patrol of July 26th was chiefly remarkable for an accident on the Reclinghem aerodrome which the Australian pilots remember more readily than many flights. Taplin and Ramsay started at 4.20, each carrying a 40-lb. phosphorus and a 25-lb. high explosive bomb. The light was dim, and as Taplin rose under gathering speed, his undercarriage struck a bump on the ground, and the axle snapped. The pilot heard the snap and switched off his engine, in order to land again. His presence of mind in releasing his safety-belt at the same moment saved his life. As his machine touched earth again the under-carriage folded up, interfered with the bomb-release lever, and almost immediately the phosphorus-bomb exploded. The explosion threw Taplin clear of the wreckage and at the same instant set the machine on fire. There followed what the onlookers described as a first-class firework-display. The other bomb exploded, the tracer-bullets of the machine-gun belts spat out of the flames, and the Very lights soared up from the burning mass or fizzled furiously on the ground. Taplin ran for his life, and escaped, scorched and shaken. Meanwhile his comrade, Ramsay, had made height over the aerodrome, and seeing in the dim light the rockets, flares, the tracer-bullets, and the explosions, he believed that a German raid had arrived. For half-an-hour he circled over the aerodrome looking for the enemy. Thereafter he went off alone and dropped his bombs on a railway siding near La Bassée.

The enemy's hold of the Flanders front was gradually weakening, and from the end of July onward his position on the Lys flats grew steadily worse. The relentless bombing and machine-gunning of his forward areas contributed notably to his general demoralisation, and the time was in sight when a steady offensive would smash through his line at this point. Scottish infantry re-took Meteren village on July 19th. Ten days later two Australian companies advanced and captured with ease the battered ruins of Merris. The whole British front was waiting and ready for a spring; at last the German was at bay.

The design of the British High Command, in the air operations during the early summer so far described, was the breaking of the enemy's morale, while the army on the ground was being prepared for the final blow to come. What the Australian scout squadrons were doing in the Lys salient, other British squadrons were doing elsewhere. The long series of air-fights and bombing raids becomes meaningless if the object of these tactics is forgotten. On the other hand, to suppress the details of the daily effort of the airmen during this period would be to obscure the picture of their splendid endurance in the accomplishment of a great task. If the credit for the final defeat of the German belongs—as in the main it does—to the Allied infantry, the way was paved for that infantry all through the spring and early summer by the Allied airmen.

The dawn bombing raids had been thoroughly justified by the results, and on the principle that nothing succeeds like success, No. 4 Squadron continued them with increasing energy. On July 28th Ramsay, E. J. K. McCloughry, and

Jones-Evans left the aerodrome at 3.30 and made straight for the hunting-ground of the Lys. Ramsay dived on a train in Estaires station and hit it with a 25-lb. bomb from 500 feet. McCloughry hovered over the Estaires balloon-line at 6,000 feet until the light improved, dropped silently on a rising balloon, and set it on fire after following it down to within fifty feet of the ground. With the light of the burning fabric around the balloon-windlass in his eyes, the pilot climbed and flew northward along the Lys, and near Sailly he found eight horse-waggons on the march. He dropped two bombs in front of the leading waggon, which bolted immediately into the fields; then, diving a few hundred feet lower, he fired 300 rounds into the other seven. One capsized on the road. The drivers of the others jumped from the waggons and sprawled in the wayside ditches, and the maddened horses careered away over the surrounding fields. " This sort of stunt," as one Australian pilot had said of an earlier performance, " gives you a first-class appetite for breakfast and tones you up for the day." Jones-Evans dropped his bombs into a train leaving Armentières. A yellow L.V.G. two-seater interfered with him; he dived under its tail, zoomed up again, firing full into it at close range, and saw it crash into the ground. He then turned to come home; and being then attacked by a second L.V.G., he fought it by the same methods, and destroyed it also. By this time he had to climb to escape heavy ground-fire from all sides. He was hit in one foot by a bullet; but, though faint from loss of blood, he managed to steer his machine on a westerly course, and made St. Pol. There he crashed in trying to land. He had to crawl for a mile before he found assistance.

Meanwhile five more Camels under Weingarth, starting at 4 a.m., flew towards Bac St. Maur, and four of them bombed that place. The fifth pilot, Lieutenant A. F. G. McCulloch,[14] separated from the formation and dropped his bombs on the Estaires train which Ramsay had previously hit. Several enemy scouts and two-seaters, however, seized the advantage offered by the isolated Camel; McCulloch was attacked by superior numbers, forced to land near the Lys, and was taken prisoner.

---

[14] Lieut. A. F. G. McCulloch; No. 4 Sqn. (previously Infantry). Farm hand; b. Portsmouth, Eng., Sept., 1894.

Shortly after 5 a.m. Heller led a third patrol of five Camels in a raid on the Estaires dumps. They chased four German two-seaters east without decisive combat. Heller, flying home, passed five more machines going out from No. 4 Squadron under Trescowthick. Ahead of Trescowthick, Major W. A. McCloughry, the squadron-commander, scoured the Lys area at 7,000 feet, until he saw a grey L.V.G. two-seater, apparently unsuspicious, over Erquinghem, at 3,000. He flew east of this enemy, dived at it, and destroyed it with seventy rounds delivered from close under its tail. Trescowthick's patrol arrived about this time, and, passing Estaires, still smoking from Heller's visitation, dropped its load of bombs among the billets at Laventie. As Trescowthick's formation landed home again, Lieutenant M. T. G. Cottam[15] took off with another five to bomb Lestrem. Returning, his formation flew over Pacaut Wood and fired 1,400 rounds into the trenches there.

During this low-bombing by the Camels smaller patrols of two or three machines each from No. 2 Squadron were ranging the higher sky. They left the aerodrome at intervals of an hour or less. When in the forenoon heavy clouds obscured the ground at 2,000 feet, the S.E.5's also flew low and dropped bombs along the Lys villages. No enemy aeroplanes were seen over this region after 8 a.m., and the cloudy weather grew worse during the afternoon. Next morning, July 29th, it was still bad, but six machines from each of the Australian squadrons were out over the Lys flats between 4 and 6 a.m. Lieutenant R. F. McRae[16] in King's patrol at 5 o'clock met an L.V.G. in a thick mist near Armentières at 3,000 feet and saw it go down out of control after a protracted and half-blind duel. Cole's patrol, accompanied by Major Murray Jones (No. 2 squadron-commander), fought a duel with a Hannoveranner two-seater near Nieppe Forest, and shot its observer. While the Camels bombed the Lys villages, the S.E.5's scattered bombs along the Estaires–Le Bassée road.

Either this constant bombing had stung the enemy's air forces to action, or he was beginning important retiring

---

[15] Lieut. M. T. G. Cottam; No. 4 Sqn. (previously Infantry). Licensed surveyor; b. Alexandria, Sydney, 12 Oct., 1894.

[16] Lieut. R. F. McRae; R.A.F. Attached No. 4 Sqn., 26 May to July, 1918.

movements on the Lys flats, for about this time his battle-formations appeared on the Flanders front in great force, especially at daylight and dusk. On the British side also heavy bombing raids began in the evenings, at that hour of half-light when night movements of troops and transport would begin to get under way. About 7 p.m. King led six machines from No. 4 Squadron in escort of a raid by British D.H.9's on Armentières. This operation was a good example of cool and skilful air fighting. The escorting Camels picked up the bombers over Nieppe Forest at 12,000 feet and followed them towards Armentières, flying behind and slightly below them. As the formation approached the town, ten Fokker biplanes appeared and promptly dived to attack the D.H.9's. King, with the escort, at once gave the signal to engage. It was a trying situation, for the Australian scouts were below the Fokkers, and one of these attacked King from ahead. On the answering burst, the German half-rolled and fell away, followed immediately by Taplin, who engaged it till it fell on its back and then dropped like a stone into the lap of the mist below. King dived at another Fokker and fired 100 rounds into it at about thirty-feet range. This Fokker also went down completely out of control. Trescowthick defeated another, after dodging its attack, by shooting it in the belly from underneath. The other Fokkers dispersed discomfited, and, though in all nineteen of them were seen about this region, all the raiders, bombers, and escort were brought back without loss. The D.H.9's bombed Armentières during this fight, without hostile interference.

Enemy airmen were seen in numbers over the Aubers Ridge on July 31st. At 10 a.m. battle-patrols under Phillipps and King left the Reclinghem aerodrome. The Camels under King flew at about 8,000 feet, the S.E.5's under Phillipps at 19,000. Phillipps's formation, first on the scene, sighted, three miles east of Laventie, eight L.V.G. two-seaters escorted by nine Fokker scouts, flying at 18,000 feet. Phillipps and three others at once attacked the scouts, which dived away and left the two-seaters. Lieutenant F. W. Follett,[17] who had singled out the rearmost Fokker, fired sixty rounds into it at almost touching

---

[17] Lieut. F. W. Follett; No. 2 Sqn. (previously Engineers). Civil engineer; of Sydney; b. Marrickville, Sydney, 27 March, 1892.

distance and sent it down in a cloud of black smoke. Meanwhile Cummings made three successive attacks on a two-seater which had strayed from the formation, and at the third attempt the L.V.G. fell over on its side burning at the cockpit. The remaining L.V.G's fought off Cummings. Flying homewards near Merville, Cummings at 15,000 feet fell in with four more L.V.G's and began another fight. He dived at one German, so steeply that he nearly rammed it headlong; both machines fell out of control, the German plainly hit and the Australian from a too impetuous manœuvre. From the attentions of the remaining two-seaters Cummings again escaped.

Just as this fighting subsided seven Camels under Taplin and six S.E.5's under Cole crossed the lines near Nieppe Forest. Taplin's formation almost immediately met seven Fokker biplanes at 8,000 feet south-west of Estaires. The Australians secured a slight advantage in height, and the whole patrol dived at the Fokkers. Taplin, leading, fell on the nearest German like a fury, and from his fire the Fokker dropped disabled, and crashed at Lestrem. A few moments later a second Fokker, attacked by Lieutenant T. R. Edols,[18] fell in a heap close to the first. Taplin dived at another Fokker, which was manœuvring to escape the fire of some machine higher up, and that also fell out of control. Lieutenant T. C. R. Baker[19] pursued a fourth to near the ground. The patrols under Cole and King had meanwhile arrived, as also had some Bristol Fighters from a British squadron, and all were engaged with German scout formations east of Estaires. Cole had arrived just too late to join the Bristols in a combat south of Armentières, but flew on over Lille in chase of nine Fokkers. Of Cole's formation Stone fought a short indecisive combat with several triplanes north-east of Lille, and Wellwood at 19,000 feet chased a Rumpler two-seater all the way from Armentières to Lille; he shot the Rumpler's observer, but his guns jammed and he had to break off the pursuit. For the remainder of the day the British and Australian air-patrols were left in undisputed possession of the sky over the Aubers Ridge.

---

[18] Lieut. T. R. Edols; No. 4 Sqn. (previously Artillery). Of Burrawang, N.S.W.; b. Forbes, N.S.W., 4 Nov., 1897.

[19] Capt. T. C. R. Baker, D.F.C., M.M.; No. 4 Sqn. (previously Artillery). Bank clerk; of Adelaide; b. Smithfield, S. Aust., 25 April, 1897. Killed in action, 4 Nov., 1918.

CHAPTER XXII

THE BRITISH OFFENSIVE ON THE SOMME

ON the Somme the front of the Australian Corps remained for five weeks after the battle of Hamel more or less stationary, though in a state of repeated eruption. Till August 8th, when the British Army's grand offensive opened in this sector, there was no attack on a large scale; but the enemy was badly shaken, and his hold began gradually to loosen. The Australian infantry raided the enemy night and day with an audacity which was found to be completely justified by the nervous state of the German garrisons. This is not the place to record the many brilliant exploits of local initiative, particularly the cutting out of whole sections of trenches before Villers-Bretonneux and the recapture of the famous Monument Wood, or what was left of it. Viewed in the light of later events, this five weeks of raiding and harrying the German front-line garrisons was manifestly preparation for the victorious advance on what Ludendorff afterwards called Germany's "black days."

During July No. 3 Squadron photographed and bombarded new gun-positions as usual, and the spirit of the airmen rose with the success of the infantry. During this work the R.E.8's had several exciting encounters with enemy machines. On July 11th, when Francis and Sturgeon (observer) were attacked by a Fokker biplane, both the R.E.8's guns jammed at an early stage, and the Australians thus rendered helpless were compelled to twist and dodge while the German fired all its ammunition at them. Fortunately the enemy failed to shoot straight.[1] The weather at this time was frequently too stormy for flying, and thunder-storms and rain were specially heavy. At every interval of better weather the bombardment, directed by airmen's observation of enemy battery-positions, was resumed. On one such artillery patrol in the evening of July 15th, Lieutenants J. Gould-Taylor[2] and

---

[1] Francis's machine, No. A 4397, made a record in the British air forces on the Western Front by performing 440 hours 35 minutes' service-flying and making 147 trips across the line. The pilot and the squadron were specially congratulated by G.H.Q. The previous best record was 427½ hours' service-flying.

[2] Lieut. J. Gould-Taylor, D.F.C.; No. 3 Sqn. (previously Artillery). Student; of Upper Hawthorn, Melbourne; b. Young, N.S.W., 1897. Killed in action, 3 Oct., 1918.

B. G. Thomson[3] (observer) met a German two-seater flying over Méaulte at 4,000 feet, attacked it, and destroyed it in flames with one long burst of machine-gun fire. Thunderstorms more than once nearly caused disaster to the airmen, and the imagination is seized with the dramatic silencing of the guns in the roar of a mightier artillery. Four Australian R.E.8's, directing bombardment against German batteries at the end of a sultry day on July 17th, were caught in the full force of a storm of hail and lightning. They were unable to reach their aerodrome, and were forced to make for the edges of the storm and to land where best they could. This they managed to do inside the British lines, and luckily without injury. Again, on July 21st, another Australian R.E.8 was driven by a sharp thunder-storm to land under the shelter of a wood and narrowly avoided crashing.[4]

Looking backwards upon this time, the student of the campaign will note how the preparations leading up to the grand attack of August 8th overshadowed all minor events after the battle of Hamel on July 4th. The routine work done by No. 3 Squadron during the last two weeks of July was not consciously performed as part of the larger plans, although the daily bombardment of the enemy's batteries and the locating of his gun-positions were all part of the greater scheme. Only in the closing days of the month was the first inkling of the Army's intentions given by Australian Corps Headquarters to commanding officers of the flying squadron, the artillery, and the infantry divisions of the corps. Indeed, during the last week of July the airmen of No. 3 Squadron and the infantry on the Morlancourt Ridge were mainly busied in ensuring the success of another small attack above Sailly Laurette, which was made on the night of July 28th

---

[3] Lieut. B. G. Thomson; No. 3 Sqn. (previously A.A.M.C.). Accountant; of Kapunda, S. Aust.; b. Kapunda, 24 March, 1894. Killed in action, 3 Oct., 1918.

[4] To fly through a thunder-storm has been declared by many airmen to be a severe test of nerve. Richthofen has described how he once survived a terrific storm over the mountains of the Moselle near Metz. On this occasion he could not find the edge of the storm, and had to fly straight through it. He kept at lowest possible altitude in order to retain sight of earth and "was compelled absolutely to leap over houses and trees" with his machine as they came. Black cloud hid everything. "The gale seized the machine as if it had been a piece of paper, and beneath me I saw trees bent down by the wind. I had to jump trees, villages, spires, and steeples," he says, "for I had to keep within five yards of the ground. Otherwise I should have seen nothing at all. The lightning was playing around me. At that time I did not yet know that lightning cannot touch flying-machines. I shall never again fly through a thunder-storm unless the Fatherland should demand this." (*The Red Air Fighter*, p. 66.)

AN AIR SQUADRON'S CONTACT-PATROL ACCOMPANYING AN INFANTRY ADVANCE

(A composite photograph produced from several negatives in order to illustrate an infantry attack in the Third Battle of Ypres.)

Aust. War Museum Official Photo. No. E5988.

AEROPLANE VIEW OF THE COUNTRY SOUTH OF THE SOMME OVER WHICH THE AUSTRALIANS AND CANADIANS ATTACKED ON 8TH AUGUST, 1918

The photograph was taken from a machine of No. 3 Squadron above Morlancourt Ridge on 16th July, 1918

by the 8th and 14th Brigades. As soon as this was over, the
impending offensive was disclosed in secret conference. The
first steps were the withdrawal of Australian troops from the
Morlancourt Ridge and the extension of the right front of
the corps down to the north bank of the Luce. The
Australian Corps was now in position between the Somme
and the Luce, and No. 3 Squadron promptly sent out all pilots
and observers to learn the new front opposite the villages of
Cachy and Hangard. On the day of this change of area,
August 1st, the new front was thoroughly photographed. The
squadron further signalised the event by there putting out of
action six German batteries.

Some sharp air fighting occurred about 5 p.m. on that
day while the artillery work was in progress. Three R.E.8's
from No. 3 were at 4,000 feet over the lines observing shoots
on three separate batteries, when suddenly a grey Albatros
was seen at about 1,500 feet to be attacking a line of British
balloons near Blangy-Tronville. It was a neat attack, and
the German scout shot four balloons into flames in rapid
succession.[5] Three Australian artillery machines successively
engaged the Albatros for a few seconds as it flew eastward.
The pilot of the third R.E.8, Grigson, maintained fire until
his gun jammed; he then turned, and gave his observer,
H. B. James, the target. Both machines lost height in this
last chase, and were only 200 feet above the ground. After a
final burst of fire from James, the Albatros crashed between
Hamel and Cerisy just inside the German lines.

The next five days were marred by heavy rains, and
reconnaissance was possible only at intervals. Many of the
enemy's batteries were changing ground, dummies being left
in the old positions for the British to fire at. Most of these
moves were noted by the aeroplanes. The Australian Corps,
using every stratagem to hide its preparations, ordered
spasmodic firing to be continued upon the abandoned German

---

[5] The firing of these balloons was witnessed from the racecourse at Allonville, where the 4th Australian Division was holding a race-meeting, by a crowd of many thousands, including the commanders of the Fourth Army and the Australian Corps and most of the divisional and brigade commanders. Major Blake writes:—" I think this was the occasion of the first making of a bet from the air. One of the machines on its way to the line dropped a message bag in front of the judge's box in which many of the above-mentioned generals were located. It was addressed to me and handed to me by the army commander, who had visions of some urgent information being received from the line. On opening the bag it contained 150 francs and a message—' Put 150 francs on Major ———'s mare.' "

gun-positions in order to persuade the enemy that his deception was successful. Some machines of No. 3 Squadron were ordered to watch closely the activity of Australian artillery, infantry, and other traffic, in order that the corps staff might judge whether those movements might disclose anything to German observation. The airmen were also required to fly along roads over bodies of Allied troops, practising the rapid identification of units against the days when this identification would be of greatest importance. The excitement of all arms within the Australian area was rising to a high pitch, and, though none doubted of victory in the coming attack, the burden of all instructions was that assurance must be made doubly and trebly sure.

The penultimate day arrived. No work was done by any troops which could be rested, and, though a few machines flew over the lines on patrol, in the main the squadron spent the day in learning the intricate duties for the morrow. "A" Flight was to carry out artillery-patrols, "B" Flight counter-attack patrols, and "C" Flight contact-patrols with the assaulting infantry. Briefly, the artillery machines were to call down fire on every unengaged enemy battery observed to be in action. The counter-attack machines were to signal any and every enemy infantry concentration, and, after wirelessing such signals, to confirm the location by flying straight towards the centre of a threatened counter-attack, discharging a red flare for the guidance of the infantry. All enemy movements were to be recorded as far as possible, and messages were to be dropped at division and corps headquarters and at army report-centres. The contact-patrol airmen were required to memorise a special simple system of letter-code identifying all battalions; to recognise the positions reached by the advancing infantry from flares,[6] metal discs, and rifles laid parallel across tops of trenches—all these signs being given from the ground on the call of Klaxon horns from the pilots above—and to report in messages dropped at nearest brigade headquarters the position of the attacking line. "A" and "B" Flights were to carry phosphorus-bombs and drop them along an appointed line near Cerisy on the left flank of the advance, in order to obscure by the smoke German

---

[6] See note at end of chapter.

observation from the Morlancourt Ridge. A forward central wireless station was set up near Aubigny for the reception of any aeroplane-casualty signals, and for the constant testing of the wireless apparatus carried by all machines so fitted. The most careful recognition of the attacking units was demanded, so that, in the event of a "break through," no bombs might be dropped by mistake on Allied troops. The perusal of the battle-orders for the aeroplanes and every other arm engaged in the attack affords a fascinating insight into both the machinery of modern battle and its scientific employment.

In the event the airmen saw little of the opening of the attack. From the moment of "zero" (4.20 a.m.) till nearly 10 o'clock in the forenoon fog assisted the artifice of the smoke-screens on the Somme in hiding all the conflict in the valleys and copses between Cerisy and Warfusée–Abancourt and on the flat plateau of Bayonvillers. The fog was so thick that for a time six R.E.8's were deemed to be lost. They subsequently returned from forced landings at various villages near the aerodrome. The infantry attack, however, met with little or no difficulty. A lifting of the fog enabled contact-patrols to locate the line at 10 a.m. and 11.30. So swift and complete was the advance that the artillery and counter-attack machines had very little of their contemplated work to do. The German batteries were smashed or overrun. The German infantry delivered no counter-attack, for the simple reason that its reserves were rounded up and captured in great masses, while, by the wonderful work of the armoured cars, directing local staffs were either made prisoners or driven in hasty flight from headquarters.

The British air force secured as complete a control of the air over the battle as the infantry secured upon the ground. When the fog cleared, German airmen came out to fight, but were nearly everywhere subdued by British scouts, and few hostile machines attacked the low-flying R.E.8's. There were inevitable exceptions. Gould-Taylor and Thomson near Proyart, carried on three fleeting combats, twice with small scout formations, and once with two Hannoveranner two-seaters. British scouts were at hand, and the enemy attacked with no heart. Lieutenants H. S. Foale[7] and Sewell, on contact-patrol near La Flaque cross-roads about noon, attacked two enemy scouts seen to be engaging the Australian infantry, and shot down one in flames. Lieutenants McKenna and R. W. Kirkwood[8] shortly afterwards beat off a series of attacks by two Halberstadts at the same place. One contact-patrol machine—Lieutenants E. J. Bice[9] and J. E. Chapman[10] (observer)—was lost; it was attacked by nine Fokker biplanes near Méricourt about noon and shot down, both officers being killed. With the continuation of the attack next day—chiefly on the right flank—many more enemy airmen appeared over the battle area. No. 3 Squadron fought several indecisive combats with Fokker biplane scouts; McKenna and Kirkwood attacked and destroyed a German two-seater at Chipilly.

Every machine engaged the enemy on the ground with bombs and machine-gun fire as opportunity offered. The enemy was in desperate straits to reinforce his broken line south of the Somme, and that this line was spared further immediate smashing was due mainly to the fact that the British advance was arrested on the difficult ridge-position north of the river. From this quarter the Australian left flank —bent back along the river— was much worried by hostile artillery-fire. In the afternoon of August 9th, Gould-Taylor and Thomson specially reconnoitred that front; they located a number of batteries in action around and west of Bray, and directed upon them a fire which had the desired silencing effect. Next day the 4th Australian Division took over a sector on the northern bank of the Somme, thus putting the Australian Corps astride of the river valley, and adding the German artillery area about Bray to the sphere of activity of No. 3 Squadron.

Both flanks of the corps front had now to be cleared of obstinate German resistance, and there occurred some hot

---

[7] Lieut. H. S. Foale; No. 3 Sqn. (previously Infantry). Farmer; of Shackleton, W. Aust.; b. Adelaide, 24 Aug., 1898.

[8] Lieut. R. W. Kirkwood; No. 3 Sqn. Motor driver; b. Launceston, Tas., 1895.

[9] Lieut. E. J. Bice, M.C.; No. 3 Sqn. (previously Infantry). Marine engineer; of Canterbury, Melbourne; b. East Melbourne, 9 Nov., 1892. Killed in action, 8 Aug., 1918.

[10] Lieut. J. E. Chapman; No. 3 Sqn. (previously Light Horse). Blacksmith and wheelwright; of Bowenvale, Vic.; b. Bairnsdale, Vic., 3 Feb., 1895. Killed in action, 8 Aug., 1918.

Map No. 15

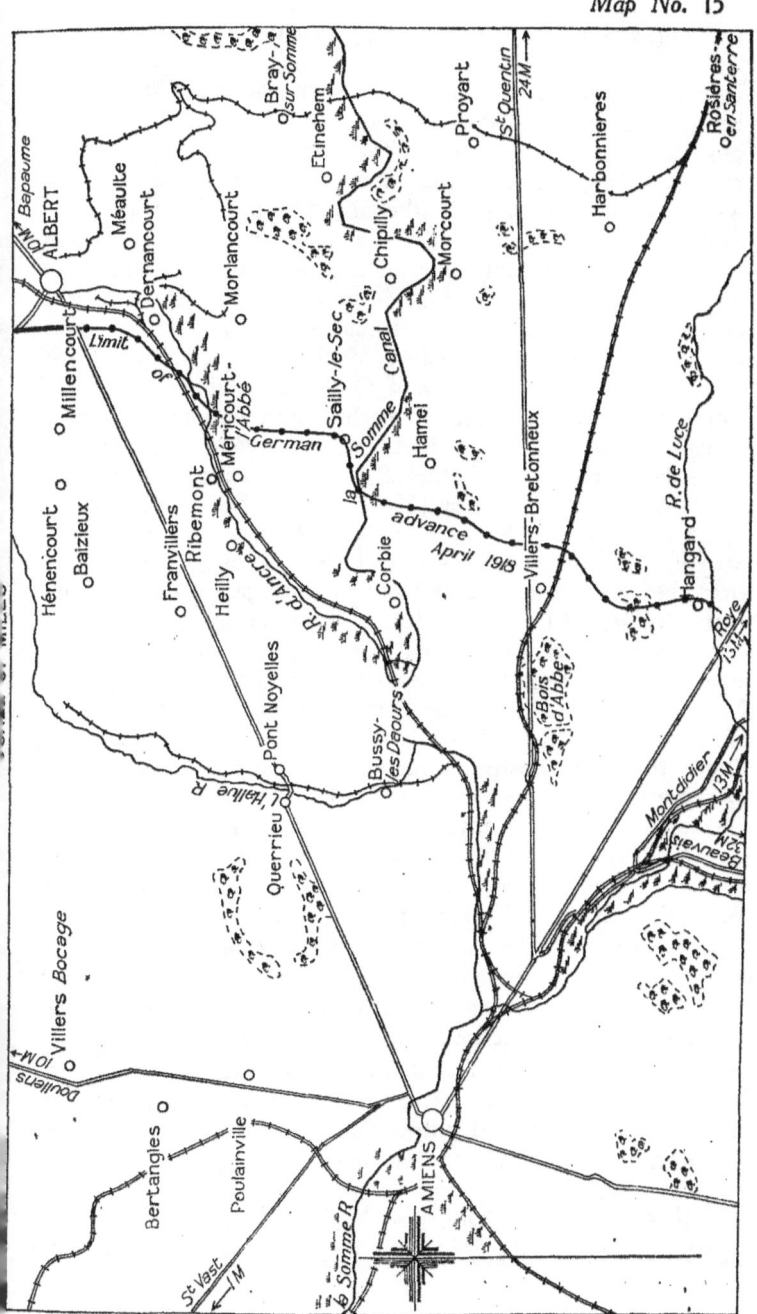

VILLERS-BRETONNEUX REGION, SHOWING AREA OF OPERATIONS OF No. 3 AUSTRALIAN SQUADRON, APRIL–AUGUST, 1918

fighting, particularly about Lihons on the right and in the bends of the river west of Bray on the left. While these flank positions were being secured, the line in general was resting and collecting for a further assault. These days, however, were strenuous enough in the air, and patrols from No. 3 Squadron were constantly on the watch for enemy counter-attacks, or for signs of a general retreat, which was also suspected. While scout formations opposed each other above, the lower-flying reconnaissance machines found ground-fire growing increasingly dangerous. On August 10th Lieutenants J. L. Smith[11] and O. G. Witcomb[12] (observer) were shot down by infantry machine-gun defence; the pilot, though wounded in the foot, made a good landing near Vauvillers. Next day another R.E.8 was damaged by ground-fire, and had to land near Morcourt. The strain on the squadron was very heavy, for, besides the duty of accompanying all advances, its services were required for artillery work before each attack and for photographing the line subsequently reached. Brigades and divisions, as well as corps, were coming to rely more and more upon the airmen for confirmation of all reports. The continuous demands made upon No. 3 Squadron during the first four days of the August offensive exhausted all hands—airmen and mechanics alike. Every threat of hostile counter-attack called forth patrols, carrying bombs, to judge the truth of the rumour and to locate the danger. Every " obscure " part of the line, where doubt of the position of outposts had to be cleared up, demanded a low air·reconnaissance of that sector. Batteries moving forward must be registered again on new targets. Fires and explosions behind the German lines might be the prelude to retirement at any moment. Any pronounced bombardment by the hostile guns prompted a fresh demand from the forward infantry for counter-action, and a patrol from No. 3 Squadron had then to go out to locate the enemy batteries concerned. The great part which the airmen played in securing the victory can be fully appreciated only by recognising the demand for their assistance from every unit on the ground below.

---

[11] Lieut. J. L. Smith, D.F.C.; No. 3 Sqn. (previously Signal Services). Electrician; of Sydney; b. Darlinghurst, Sydney, 24 Nov., 1893.

[12] Lieut. O. G. Witcomb; No. 3 Sqn. (previously A.A. Pay Corps). Bank clerk; of Port Wakefield, S. Aust.; b. Yacka, S. Aust., 28 Dec., 1893.

The important air-work on this front called in temporarily a strong force from the Australian No. 2 and No. 4 Squadrons from the northern front in Flanders to reinforce British fighting-scouts in the Fourth Army. On August 12th twelve machines from each squadron flew to Allonville to operate thence as a base. At 9.30 a.m. Phillipps and Cole (No. 2) and Cobby and King (No. 4) led their full force across the lines. The Camels found no Germans to fight, but the S.E.5's, flying in a circus with two flights of British Camels, encountered at 11 a.m. seven Fokker biplanes 15,000 feet over Licourt (east of Chaulnes). The British Camels attacked five Fokkers and started them downward. Cole's flight, remaining above, engaged the upper two Fokkers, of which Wellwood destroyed one, after chasing it down to 2,000 feet. Phillipps's flight joined the pursuit of the five engaged with the lower formations of the circus; Lieutenant F. C. M. Mills[18] shot down one out of control, and an opponent which Phillipps engaged in combat fell to pieces in the air. The hunting, however, was not so good as had been expected, and the enemy was plainly unwilling to come out and engage the force which the British airmen paraded. Next day the Australian scout squadrons repeated their sweep. The early patrol from No. 4 Squadron again saw no enemy in the sky; that of No. 2 met six Fokkers, of which Mills and Follett each shot down one out of control. In the afternoon the patrols were no luckier. King's flight found a solitary Albatros two-seater west of Péronne, and all six Camels fell on it like a hungry pack and destroyed it. The results obtained, however, were not worth the force expended, and by August 14th the two Australian scout squadrons were again confining their attentions to their allotted area on the Lys.

The advance on the Somme was to be resumed, and on August 16th the whole of the Australian Corps front was again photographed by No. 3 Squadron. The attack began on August 22nd, on the British front north of the Australians. Only the extreme left flank of the Australians participated, but that was enough to demand a heavy day's work from No. 3 Squadron. Contact-patrols were out early and

---

[18] Lieut. F. C. Markham Mills; No. 2 Sqn. (previously A.A.S.C.). Engineering student; of Parramatta, Sydney; b. Tuena. N.S.W., 20 Oct., 1893. Died of illness, 18 Dec., 1918.

established the new line by 9 o'clock. Matheson and C. T. Brown (observer) located twelve enemy batteries in action behind Bray and sent back zone-calls against all of them.[14] While directing the fire of British heavy guns on one of these positions, Matheson attacked a Halberstadt two-seater below him. The enemy dodged and withdrew, but soon afterwards returned, was again attacked, and was shot down east of Suzanne. Two other R.E.8's located sixteen active German batteries—eight about Maricourt, north of the Bray area, and eight around Dompierre, south of it. These also the British guns bombarded by wireless direction from the air. After the success of the first infantry advance, Grigson and H. B. James, returning from counter-attack patrol, and having seen no signs of hostile infantry concentration, observed another Halberstadt two-seater flying along the British line northward towards Bray and shooting off white rockets. Grigson pursued the German from Chuignolles across the river to "Ceylon Wood." Here a final burst of fire from James appeared to explode the German airman's supply of rockets; the Halberstadt gave forth a lively fireworks-display and then crashed near Ceylon Wood. Three other R.E.8's fought indecisive combats during the day, including a splendid running defence by Lieutenants L. P. Chase[15] and J. P. Jeffers[16] against six enemy two-seaters, from whom they escaped at length near the British balloon-line.

Next, morning, August 23rd, the British advance was extended south of the Somme, and at dawn the 1st Australian Division attacked the hilly and wooded position about Chuignes. The Germans were thrown out of strong natural defences on hills across a wide gully, and at the end of the day the enemy had suffered a loss of ground which made his further retreat certain. At the opening of the infantry assault machines from No. 3 Squadron dropped phosphorus-bombs to make a smoke-screen about the rise above Chuignes

---

[14] These wireless calls were sent back to C.I.B. (Central Information Bureau), a special forward field-station, which passed them on at once to units concerned—corps headquarters, infantry, artillery, flying corps, the tank headquarters, or all of them, as required. It was a nearly perfect parallel to the army's eyes registering to the army's brain.

[15] Lieut. L. P. Chase, A.F.C.; No. 3 Sqn. (previously Infantry). Station manager; of Skipton, Vic.; b. Fitzroy, Melbourne, 3 June, 1889.

[16] Lieut. J. P. Jeffers; No. 3 Sqn. Mechanic; of Brunswick, Melbourne; b. Cosgrove, Vic., 1892. Killed in action, 19 Sept., 1918.

village, and thereafter patrols re-enacted in their specially-defined duties the parts which they had learnt in the Villers-Bretonneux attack. The airmen worked from an advanced landing-ground at Glisy, between Corbie and Amiens. Gould-Taylor and Thomson, on the first artillery-patrol, between 5 and 8.15 a.m., ranged the whole front from Chaulnes on the south to Suzanne on the north, and signalled back the locations of ten active batteries and the presence in the offing of thirty hostile aircraft. Descending upon one German battery behind Ceylon Wood, they dropped six bombs, then continued on a low sweep and fired 900 machine-gun rounds into the enemy's trenches. At 8 a.m. T. L. Baillieu and Sewell, on contact-patrol, sketched the advancing line in the Chuignes valley. Lieutenants F. M. Lock[17] and Mart also reconnoitred the line at that hour, but were shot down by machine-gun fire from the ground and landed near Vauvillers. Meanwhile two British R.E.8's, as before, dropped ammunition-supplies for the attacking line. Matheson and C. T. Brown sent back wireless calls against six enemy batteries, bombed Foucaucourt village, fired 200 rounds into horse-transport on the road near by, and attacked and put to flight two Halberstadt two-seaters after a long fight. Lieutenants J. K. Robertson[18] and C. W. Gray,[19] on counter-attack patrol between 9.20 a.m. and 12.20 p.m., swept the enemy back areas for signs of German infantry reserves, but, finding none, flew back and machine-gunned the front-line garrisons resisting the attack on the right. McKenna and Heslop discovered significant easterly train- and road-transport traffic behind Foucaucourt and Estrées. They dropped bombs and fired 700 rounds into trains and horse-waggons. During the afternoon, while Australian infantry were climbing the Chuignes ridge, No. 3 Squadron sent out a formation of five machines to attack any hostile infantry or artillery retiring or assembling for counter-attack. Patrols in the evening noted burning supply-dumps and other symptoms of a possible

---

[17] Lieut. F. M. Lock; No. 3 Sqn. Postal assistant; of Port MacDonnell, S. Aust.; b. Allandale East, S. Aust., 17 March, 1895.

[18] Lieut. J. K. Robertson; No. 3 Sqn. Grazier; b. Essendon, Melbourne, 9 Nov., 1889.

[19] Lieut. C. W. Gray; No. 3 Sqn. Of North Carlton, Melbourne; b. Ararat, Vic., 6 June, 1891.

German retirement, and, at 6 o'clock Lieutenants S. K. Lavers[20] and G. S. Bell[21] attacked a German two-seater and shot it down to a forced landing at Soyécourt. During the next two days it seemed clear that the enemy was preparing for a general retreat and was firing off his remaining ammunition before pulling out his batteries. By the morning of August 25th some withdrawal was discovered north of the Somme, and Australian infantry were seen by the airmen to be leaving their trenches and moving forward across the open. Fires and explosions began to mark abandoned villages and dumps. Three machines late that afternoon reconnoitred the German rear areas as far back as the Somme bend at Péronne, and reported all that region apparently deserted and devoid of movement, though machine-gun fire from many places indicated that rear-guards at least were occupying the country. The enemy's retreat was skilfully conducted, and his concealment of it by day was masterly. On August 26th and 27th there was noted stray movement of traffic, all eastward. At 12.30 p.m. on the 27th a large collection of horse-waggons and horses was noticed in a valley north-west of Cléry, and Wackett and Lieutenant M. R. Shelley[22] (observer), who discovered this target, immediately called down artillery-fire on it. In addition a raid of five R.E.8's devastated the horse-lines in that valley under bombs and machine-gun fire. The unhappy fate of this transport park was probably due to disregard of orders for concealment of moving units, and was doubtless emphasised by the German staff as an object-lesson in the results of disobedience to instructions. To the enemy's credit it must be said that the airmen secured few such opportunities during the German retirement to the Hindenburg Line.

In the afternoon of the 27th, although the infantry still found resistance stubborn, the German withdrawal was beyond doubt. Coloured lights in the hostile lines on the right front made the airmen suspicious. Gould-Taylor and Thomson had seen several small bodies of horse-transport on various

---

[20] Lieut. S. K. Lavers; No. 3 Sqn. (previously A.A.M.C.). Audit clerk; of Hunter's Hill, Sydney; b. Kogarah, Sydney, 17 May, 1895.

[21] Lieut. G. S. Bell; No. 3 Sqn. (previously A.A.M.C.). Clerk; of Melbourne: b. Leith, Scotland, 2 July, 1890.

[22] Lieut. M. R. Shelley; No. 3 Sqn. (previously Infantry). Clerk; of Hunter's Hill, Sydney; b. Gladesville, Sydney, 6 Aug., 1895.

roads marching east, and the enemy's aeroplane scouts were out in some numbers to oppose British reconnaissance. Five Fokker biplanes swooped down upon Gould-Taylor's machine near Assevillers, but the Australians, after skilful manœuvring, defeated them and destroyed one, which crashed outside the village.

Of the general work of the squadron's patrols during the subsequent days Lieutenant-General Sir John Monash[23] writes: "Contact-patrols were maintained throughout every hour of daylight. Difficult as it was to identify the positions reached by our leading troops during an organised battle, where their approximate positions and ultimate objective lines were known beforehand, it was doubly so when no guide whatever existed as to the probable extent of each day's advance, or as to the amount of resistance likely to be encountered at different parts of the front. Yet it was under just these circumstances that rapid and reliable information as to the progress of the various elements of our front-line troops was more important than ever, and no means of obtaining such information was so expeditious as the contact aeroplane."[24]

On August 29th the whole Allied line advanced, with the German rear-guards retiring in front of it, and in the evening of that day the van of the Australian pursuit had come up against a stiffened defence of the enemy, standing to fight again, in the strong position at the Somme bend at Péronne and on the high ground about Bouchavesnes and Mont St. Quentin.

Note.—Writing of the flare system, General Monash in his book, *The Australian Victories in France in 1918*, says "these flares, on being lit, gave out a dense cloud of coloured smoke, easily distinguishable from a moderate height. The contact aeroplane, which would carry coloured streamers so that the infantry could identify it as flying on that particular duty, would, when ready to observe, blow its horn, and thereupon the foremost infantry would light their flares. It was a method of inter-communication between air and ground, which, after a little practice, came to be well understood and intelligently carried out." (pp. 171-172.)

[23] Lieut.-Gen. Sir John Monash, G.C.M.G., K.C.B., V.D. Commanded 3rd Aust. Div., 1916/18; Aust. Corps, 1918. Director-General, Repat. and Demob. Dept., London, 1918/19; subsequently Chairman of Commissioners and General Manager, State Electricity Commission of Victoria. Of Melbourne; b. Dudley-street, Flagstaff Hill, City of Melbourne, 27 June, 1865.

[24] *The Australian Victories in France in 1918*, p. 171.

Major Blake (commanding No. 3 Squadron) comments:—" The flare system, taking it generally, did not work well, and many and various devices were tried both experimentally and in practice as a substitute. The two alternatives mentioned were the most satisfactory. The infantry objected to the flares that the lighting of them disclosed the position not only to our own airmen but to the enemy's also, and that the result was to hasten hostile artillery-fire on the new line. Many infantrymen refused to light flares when called upon to do so, though the Australian infantry were generally better in this respect than others. In the later stages of the great advance, machines generally found it necessary to descend low enough to distinguish the cloth of the Australian uniform from the field-grey of the German. As this was often not possible at a greater height than 200 feet, contact-patrol work was very risky."

CHAPTER XXIII
THE BATTLES IN THE HINDENBURG LINE.

THE battle of Mont St. Quentin differed from all other Australian attacks in the last Somme campaign. It was perhaps largely a gamble. It was certainly a test of sheer morale as between Australian troops and the Germans. The enemy had retreated disconsolately from a series of smashing defeats; his whole line was going back; the Allies were at last plainly on the winning side. When, therefore, the Germans stood at Péronne and Mont St. Quentin, the Australians determined to assault immediately and without detailed preparation, in the attempt to keep the enemy on the run. The approach for the attack was difficult, and consisted solely of the narrow road north of the Somme running into Cléry village. This had to serve three divisions—in itself no light risk.

The Australians were outside Cléry at evening on August 29th with the hill-position of Mont St. Quentin looking down at them along an open gradual incline, cut obliquely by an awkward gully. A second and nearer natural bastion, also in German hands, the Bouchavesnes Spur, overshadowed the immediate left front. To assault this whole position an entire division had to make a crossing of the Somme from south to north in sight of the enemy. Local bridges were blown to pieces and only those some miles in rear could be guaranteed by the engineers. The leading portion of the 2nd Australian Division crossed the river on August 30th and with some difficulty reached Cléry, from which point the attack was to begin at dawn next morning.

During August 29th much attention was directed away from the coming battle area and rather to the south of Péronne, where the enemy was encouraged to believe that the crossing would be made. Visibility made reconnaissance difficult on August 30th, but patrols from No. 3 Squadron persisted devotedly in the location of enemy batteries and machine-gun positions on the hills north of Péronne. One counter-attack machine—Lieutenants J. J. Pengilley[1] and Witcomb (observer)

---
[1] Lieut. J. J. Pengilley; No. 3 Sqn. (previously Light Horse). Station manager: of Quirindi, N.S.W.; b. Yarraman Park, Quirindi, 31 Oct., 1894.

—flew as low as 300 feet east of the Somme between Brie and Halle with the object of drawing machine-gun fire in order both to locate the enemy's defences and to note down any passable bridge remaining. In the evening Francis and Sturgeon (observer) and Grigson and H. B. James marked down a large number of hostile batteries from flashes behind Mont St. Quentin, Péronne, and Le Mesnil. When the attack of the 5th Australian Infantry Brigade was launched on August 31st, contact- and artillery-patrols, handicapped by wet weather and low clouds, by a deficiency of close reconnaissance beforehand, and by the necessity of distinguishing the infantry with certainty, were obliged to fly very low on their work, and threw themselves valiantly into the gamble of the day. All had narrow escapes, and it is surprising that only one was shot down. The pilot of this machine, Lieutenant G. E. Kilburn,[2] was unhurt, and the observer, Lieutenant W. P. Moore,[3] only slightly wounded. This R.E.8 very gallantly fought thirteen attacking enemy scouts, and pilot and observer fired 200 rounds at them before their engine was hit and the machine was forced to descend—fortunately within the Australian lines.

That first day's fighting ended in the taking, and the losing again, of the coveted central position on Mont St. Quentin. It was, however, a case of *reculer pour mieux sauter* on the following day, and the artillery machines registered many more hostile batteries for the Australian guns against the second attempt. The R.E.8's were unable to accompany that second attack (on September 1st) owing to heavy rain, and no air observation was possible before 8 a.m. About that hour two contact-patrols reported the assaulting line (6th and 14th Brigades) along the western edge of Mont St. Quentin and in the western part of Péronne. The airmen had to fly very low owing to the bad light, and most machines came back riddled with bullet-holes. Other special patrols kept watch on the areas east of Péronne and the Somme and directed silencing fire on batteries south of Le Mesnil. Visibility improved in the afternoon, and, after Mont St. Quentin had been finally

---

[2] Lieut. G. E. Kilburn; No. 3 Sqn. (previously A.A.S.C.). Motor mechanic; b. East Melbourne, Apr., 1890.

[3] Lieut. W. P. Moore; No. 3 Sqn. (previously Engineers). Engineer; b. Mt. Shamrock, Q'land, May, 1891.

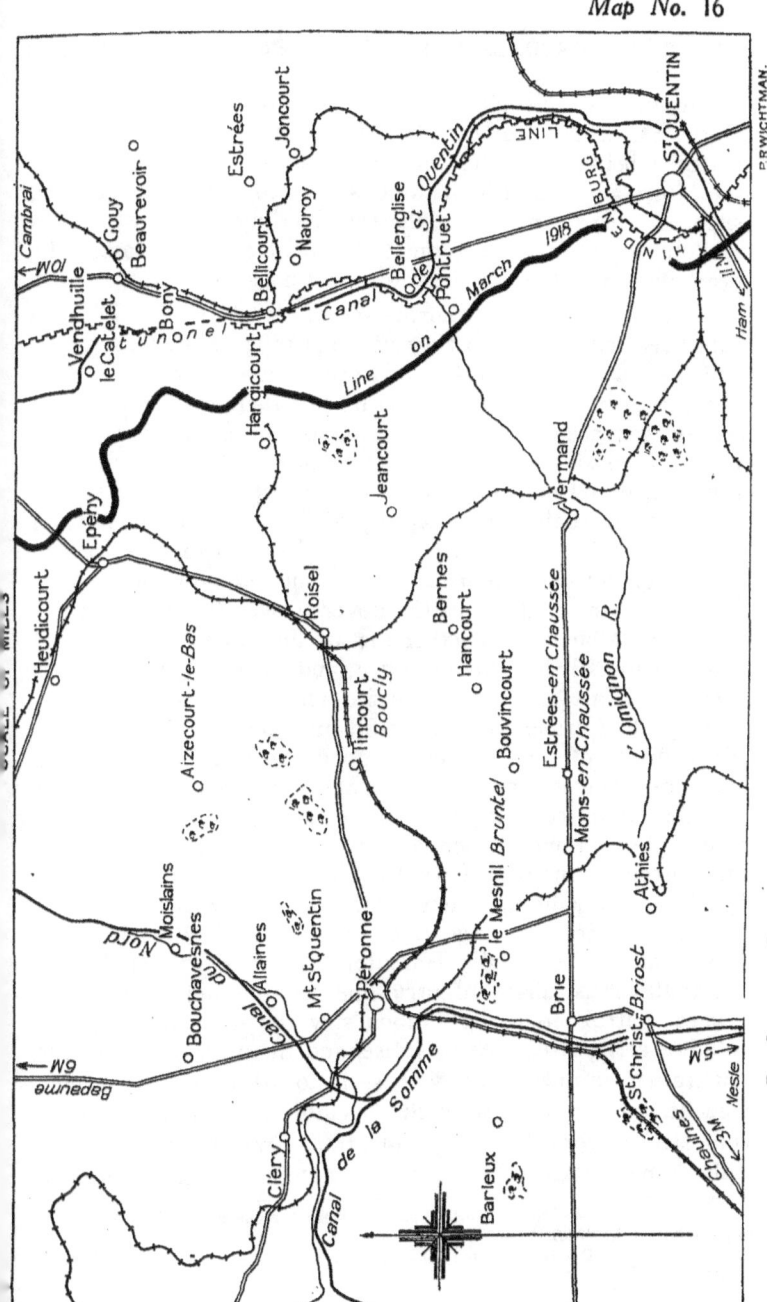

Map No. 16

St. Quentin Region, showing area of operations of No. 3 Australian Squadron, September and October, 1918

taken, two R.E.8's photographed the whole corps front line from St. Christ to Feuillaucourt. A number of enemy batteries behind Péronne were observed and bombarded during the afternoon, and at least three were seen to be damaged and silenced. Every machine, whatever its duty, bombed batteries or dumps, and machine-gunned forward trenches, to assist the heavy fight in which the infantry were engaged.

The battle on the north-eastern outskirts of Péronne continued with unabated fury next morning (September 2nd), and German airmen were out in great force. Doubtless their object was to prevent reconnaissance of their rear areas. The enemy was preparing to retreat again, since the loss of his defensive position at Péronne was now only a question of time. The first morning patrol from No. 3 Squadron returned with the report that great activity of the enemy in the air had hindered their work. Such a report deserves to be recorded, for rarely did No. 3 Squadron make such an admission. One large German scout formation hovered over the river-reaches south of Péronne and another east of Péronne over Buire and the Cologne River. Between 7.50 and 11 a.m. McKenna and Heslop, on artillery-patrol, carried on four separate engagements with German two-seaters about Doingt and Courcelles. They drove off one of these opponents twice in successive encounters and shot another down out of control. T. L. Baillieu and Sewell, on contact-patrol at the same time and place, had three fights; in one of them an attacking Fokker scout was hit and forced to land near Tincourt. The wireless calls sent back by these pilots brought out British scout formations, which cleared the air. At 12.30 p.m. Captain S. G. Brearley[4] and Lieutenant E. A. Devlin Hamilton[5] (observer) located from flares the Australian infantry line in the northern sector. Several patrols in the afternoon saw the dust of retreating columns along roads behind Roisel and Bussu, and at dusk the Australian infantry line was seen to be occupying enemy trenches well beyond Mont St. Quentin and in the stubbornly contested eastern Péronne ramparts. Francis and Sturgeon called down artillery-fire on eight active enemy batteries along

---

[4] Capt. S. G. Brearley, D.F.C.; No. 3 Sqn. (previously Artillery). Fitter apprentice; b. Geelong, Vic., Aug., 1894.

[5] Lieut. E. A. Devlin Hamilton, D.F.C.; No. 3 Sqn. (previously Light Horse). Student; b. Oct., 1894.

AN OBSERVATION BALLOON OVER BRITISH HEAVY ARTILLERY, MORCOURT, 25TH AUGUST, 1918

Aust. War Museum Official Photo. No. E3055.

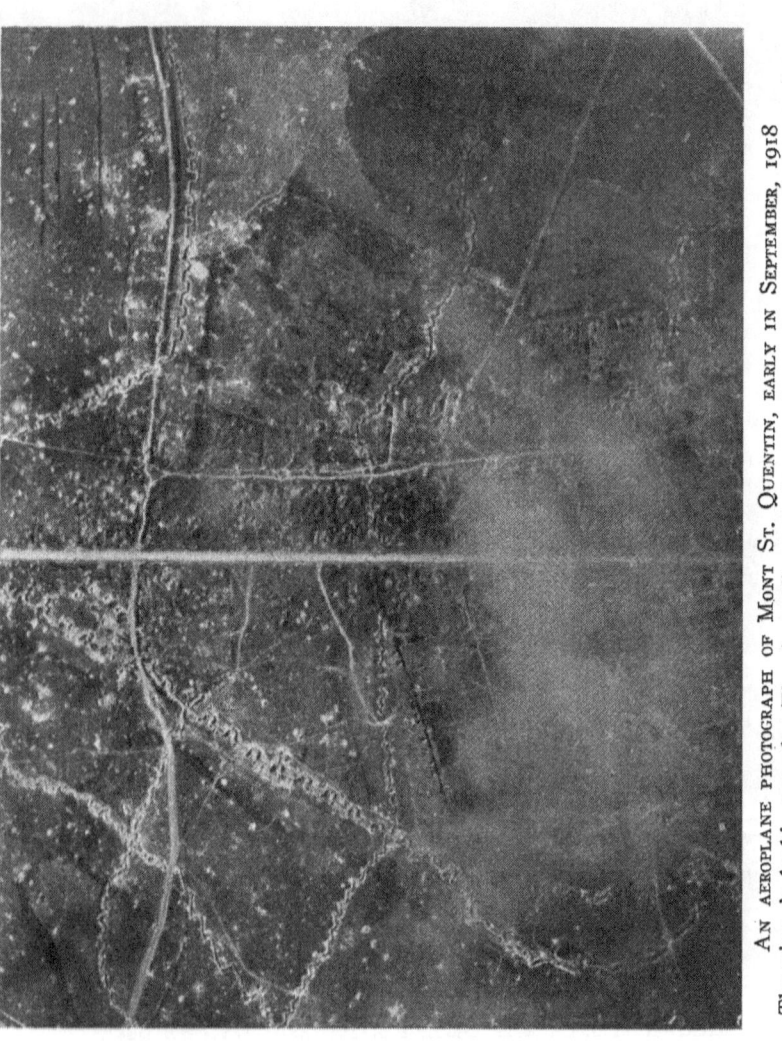

AN AEROPLANE PHOTOGRAPH OF MONT ST. QUENTIN, EARLY IN SEPTEMBER, 1918
The view is looking north. The Australian attack came from the west. The village can be seen through the haze to the right of the centre of the picture. The road from Péronne

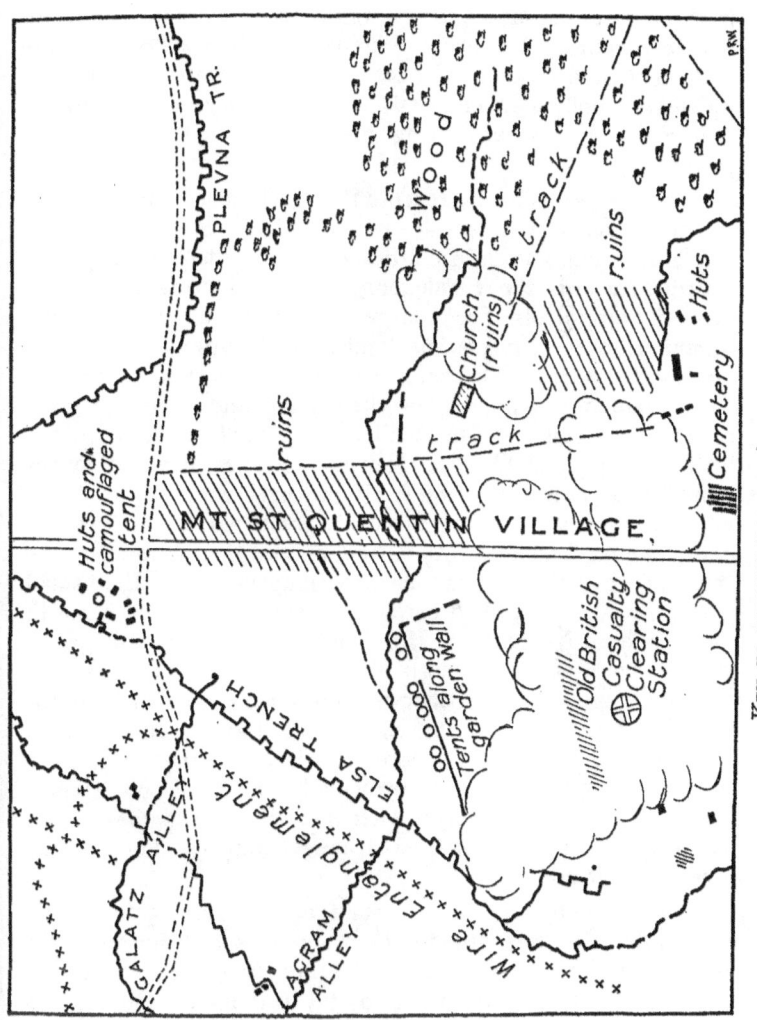

KEY TO PHOTOGRAPH ON OPPOSITE PAGE

the line Tincourt–Mons-en-Chaussée, which were covering the German infantry's retirement from the captured position. One battery at least was seen to be destroyed—explosions occurring in three gun-pits—and another was silenced by eight rounds in fifteen minutes. The evening landscape was pricked out here and there by fires about Cartigny and Le Mesnil, some caused by heavy shelling in emphasis of the victory, some showing where the enemy was firing his stores in preparation for retreat.

That retreat was hastened after further infantry attacks by the Australian Corps east of Mont St. Quentin on September 3rd, and on the 4th and 5th the enemy was plainly retiring towards the Hindenburg Line. During September 5th all air-patrols fired large quantities of machine-gun ammunition into retreating bodies of enemy infantry and transport. German batteries which had no time to fire off their ammunition pulled out their guns and exploded their remaining supplies. Every village was burning between the little Cologne and Omignon Rivers; the airmen no longer troubled to locate and count all the fires they saw. Along every road small "living targets" presented themselves for aeroplane machine-gun fire. The German Army's mainstay in retreat was always its machine-gunners, and the small rear-guard of this picked corps was often difficult to locate in the abandoned country. Here and there No. 3 Squadron's patrols were able to mark them down for the pursuing infantry's guidance. Otherwise the enemy was making for the Hindenburg Line as fast as he could, though, thanks to his machine-gunners, in good order. His aeroplanes, too, were active during the retreat, principally upon reconnaissance. They did not attempt to do what the British machines did in the way of heavy "ground-strafing" during the German advance in March.

That so many of the combats fought by No. 3 Squadron were indecisive was due to the want of speed for effective chasing on the part of the R.E.8's and to the reluctance of enemy two-seaters, as a rule, to stay and fight. During the enemy's retreat to the Hindenburg Line his reconnaissance two-seaters were numerous in the sky, but most of the engagements with them were short and distant affairs. On September

5th, however, Lieutenants A. R. Macdonald[6] and D. Ellis[7] (observer) fought a long duel with an obstinate Halberstadt over Tincourt, and after the Australian observer had fired 500 rounds the German was forced down to a landing near Roisel. On the following evening Lieutenants G. W. Hope[8] and G. E. Gamble,[9] while returning from artillery-reconnaissance, met a two-seater over Roisel, dived at it, and crashed it near that village.

The airmen on September 6th and 7th over the Roisel plains looked down on an inspiring spectacle. The whole army was moving forward in quick pursuit of the German rearguards—light horse and cyclists in advance; infantry in skirmishing waves and little columns of sections, and vast numbers of other columns in rear; the roads crowded with guns moving up, supply-transport, and engineers' repair-trains. Forward of this array of the pursuit wheeled the airmen, some already examining the Hindenburg Line defences, others flying lower to reconnoitre centres of resistance chosen by enemy rear-guards west of that line. No. 3 Squadron's machines were flying constantly forth and back over the front, and dropping messages regularly to the skirmishing line to acquaint it with the positions of German machine-gun pockets. There was little artillery shooting, for the guns of each side were in motion.

The squadron took advantage of the relief from fighting to move up from its now far-distant aerodrome north of Amiens to Proyart. It had hardly begun to lay out a new aerodrome there when the rapid advance placed Proyart also too far in rear, and a few days later preparations were begun for another forward move to Bouvincourt, south of Roisel. The aerodrome was set up in Proyart on September 6th, and at Bouvincourt on the 21st.

During September 8th and 9th the advance slowed down against the stiffening resistance of the enemy in the old British front-line trenches of March, 1918, and the so-called

---

[6] Lieut. A. R. Macdonald; No. 3 Sqn. (previously A.A.S.C.). Accountant; of Brisbane; b. New Farm, Brisbane, 15 June, 1890.

[7] Lieut. D. Ellis; No. 3 Sqn. (previously Light Horse). Student; of Geelong, Vic.; b. Hampdon, Terang, Vic., 3 March, 1894.

[8] Lieut. G. W. Hope; No. 3 Sqn. (previously Infantry). Merchant; of Melbourne; b. Perth, W. Aust., 4 May, 1890.

[9] Lieut. G. E. Gamble; No. 3 Sqn. (previously Machine Gun Corps). Fitter; b. Trentham, Vic., 5 Feb., 1893.

Hindenburg Outpost-Line. The outpost-line lay on that high ground over the St. Quentin Canal which forms the watershed between the Somme and the Scheldt (French l'Escaut). The British soldier always believed that the weather favoured the enemy, and it was curious that, as soon as the retreating Germans reached the ground on which they were to make their last stand, the fine weather changed to rain-storms and high winds. This stormy spell may not have greatly affected the immediate plans of the Allied Command, and the pursuit was in any case slowing down against another defensive position; but mud increased the labours of guns and supplies going up over the roads which the enemy had blown up in places as he left them behind. From September 10th to 13th hardly any flying was possible beyond a few patrols in one or two fairer intervals; on September 12th there was no flying at all. During one such hazardous patrol on September 11th, while flying low, T. L. Baillieu and Sewell were both wounded by ground machine-gun fire, but managed to land their machine near Bouvincourt.

The sun came out again on September 14th, and the R.E.8's resumed the old and ever-renewed business of photographing the corps fronts and locating the gun-positions, tracks, and dumps of the enemy's new defences against further infantry assault. British artillery-fire was directed at heavy traffic on the enemy's roads through Bellicourt and at points of considerable activity (diagnosed as the preparing of gun-positions) behind Le Verguier. Lieutenants H. R. Heathcote[10] and H. B. James (observer), on artillery-patrol at 6 p.m., were attacked by a formation of Fokker scouts over the lines west of Gricourt, but gallantly fought off the enemy and forced one of the attackers to land near St. Quentin. The German front was thickly defended by machine-guns, and the R.E.8's located many of them by flying low. On September 15th artillery machines signalled back to our guns the positions of seventeen hostile batteries. The same work was continued next day, and the heavy artillery was ranged on new German gun-positions, cross-roads, and various selected strong-points. A violent thunder-storm, accompanied by a cyclonic gale, swept over

---

[10] Lieut. H. R. Heathcote; No. 3 Sqn. (previously Engineers). Electrical engineer; of Parkville, Melbourne; b. West Melbourne, 11 Jan., 1895.

both armies in the dark hours of the morning on September 17th. No. 3 Squadron's hangars were torn to ribbons and many machines were severely damaged. The 18th was the day arranged for the attack on the Hindenburg Outpost-Line, and the squadron mechanics were compelled to work hard all day on the 17th to repair the damage against the morrow. It speaks volumes for the devotion of all hands that not only were all damaged machines repaired in the time allowed, but the squadron was able to maintain at least one machine in constant patrol of the line.[11]

Rain fell again with the opening of the attack by the 4th and 1st Australian Divisions on September 18th. The attack began at 5.20 a.m., but with the bad weather no air work was possible before 8 o'clock. Then six machines dropped smoke-bombs about the top of the ridge to reinforce the effect of the mist. About 10 a.m., when weather and visibility had improved, Lieutenants Dimsey and R. F. C. Machin[12] (observer) located without difficulty the attacking line near the top of the ridge; but Machin was shot in the back by ground machine-gun fire while on this duty, and died instantly. Half-an-hour later Brearley and Devlin Hamilton confirmed the line as having reached the objective on the crest at all points except on the extreme flanks, and by this hour the day's attack was an assured success. The enemy accepted his defeat without question; every Australian counter-attack patrol during the day reported no signs of hostile concentration to dispute it. The evening reconnaissances located a great number of batteries beyond the canal by their flashes, especially in the Nauroy and Beaurevoir Lines.[13]

During the late evening of September 18th, infantry of

---

[11] Major Blake comments:—" Out of eighteen machines, only three remained serviceable, and these were pegged down in the open during the storm. By nightfall—twelve hours later—fifteen machines were available for duty, a wonderful effort on the part of the squadron's equipment and technical department under Captain Ross, and of the mechanics."

[12] Lieut. R. F. C. Machin; No. 3 Sqn. (previously Infantry). Locomotive fitter; of Queenstown, Tas.; b. East Malvern, Melbourne, 6 July, 1896. Died of wounds, 18 Sept., 1918.

[13] The Hindenburg Main Line, Nauroy Line, and Beaurevoir Line faced the attackers in that order. All were part of the Hindenburg Line system, and their names were those of former prominent villages. The distances separating these lines were roughly—between the first and second 1,500 yards, and between the second and third 3,000 yards. Each was strongly fortified, as were numerous villages, farmhouses, ridges, and valleys between them. The canal line and the Nauroy Line were carried on September 29, 30, and October 1 and 2, and the Beaurevoir Line on October 3.

the 4th Australian Division made a further attack on the extreme right and secured the crest of the ridge at a point which they had failed to reach during daylight. Next morning, in its systematic fashion, No. 3 Squadron again photographed the ridge to show the line reached by the Australian Corps along its entire front. One of the machines engaged on this work did not return, and its crew, Lieutenants J. C. Peel[14] and Jeffers (observer), were never heard of again. Four machines registered no fewer than sixty-seven active hostile batteries during the afternoon and summoned counter-battery fire upon them. Thirty more gun-positions were located next day (September 20th), and, under close escort of scouts, patrols ranged for over three miles beyond the German lines photographing the Hindenburg defence system. This work completed a picture by air-photographs of both the Hindenburg and Nauroy Lines, a series which was of great value for the battle which followed. Again, on September 21st, Macdonald and Ellis flew over the rear slopes of the ridge, taking oblique photographs. That evening Francis and C. T. Brown located from flashes nineteen enemy batteries, and sent back calls for fire upon them. They repeated this performance in the evening of September 23rd.

In order to establish a required position for the coming grand attack, the British IX Corps made an advance on the right of the Australian front in the morning of September 24th, and in assistance of this operation eight R.E.8's from No. 3 Squadron dropped explosive bombs on an important enemy strong-post north of Gricourt. Lieutenants G. Pickering[15] and Shelley marked down all German bridges still intact along the canal between Bellicourt and Bellenglise. Artillery machines put out of action several German heavy batteries.

About this time No. 3 Squadron received two Bristol Fighters—two-seater fighting scouts—and in the afternoon of September 25th Wackett, with Shelley as observer, and escorted by a strong scouting formation, flew one of these machines nearly six miles beyond the enemy's front line to

---

[14] Lieut. J. C. Peel; No. 3 Sqn. Student; of Geelong, Vic.; b. Tower Hill, Inverleigh, Vic., 17 April, 1894. Killed in action, 19 Sept., 1918.

[15] Lieut. G. Pickering; No. 3 Sqn. (previously Infantry). Customs clerk; of Sydney; b. Musgrave Park, South Brisbane, 4 Dec., 1896. Died of illness, 21 Nov., 1918.

take photographs of the Joncourt defences.[16] The performance was particularly venturesome, for the airmen flew at only 1,500 feet over powerful defences and through a hail of anti-aircraft shrapnel and machine-gun fire. The Bristol Fighter came back hit in many places, including the radiator, but with highly important photographs.

Registering of the Australian field batteries was continued on September 26th, together with constant reconnaissance of the Hindenburg Main Line on the canal, the immediate obstacle in the coming attack. The Australian Corps had in the earlier fighting captured documents showing the whole defence system of this fortified zone, and the airmen scanned the ground for any sign of new earthworks. Apparently there were none, and the enemy must have had little time to make any. A great number of gun-flashes were again marked down to be compared with battery-positions shown on these plans. Three more German batteries were bombarded by the heavy artillery under direction from the air. That evening two R.E.8's fought a sharp engagement with several Pfalz scouts over Bellenglise. Lieutenants G. M. Deans[17] and T. H. Prince[18] (observer), on a counter-attack patrol, were first attacked by these scouts, and in a hot duel at eighty-yards' range Prince was wounded. Nevertheless he continued shooting until the arrival of another R.E.8 caused the enemy to break off the fight.

Next morning, September 27th, the battle began. The Hindenburg Line was deemed to require a preliminary bombardment in the old style of 1917 before the assault should be delivered, and for the next forty-eight hours massed artillery battered the defences of the canal, shot into every village behind it, and barraged every road. As the bombardment began, the 27th American Division, holding the left of the Australian corps front,[19] launched a minor preliminary attack to advance that section of the front over a thousand yards or so of stubbornly-held ground on the crest of the

---

[16] Part of the third line of the Hindenburg system at this point.

[17] Lieut. G. M. Deans; No. 3 Sqn. Solicitor; of Nhill, Vic.; b. Amherst, Talbot, Vic., 14 July, 1887.

[18] Lieut. T. H. Prince; No. 3 Sqn. (previously Engineers). Civil engineer; of Newcastle District, N.S.W.; b. Homebush, N.S.W., 11 Oct., 1891.

[19] The 30th and 27th American Divisions of the II American Corps (temporarily attached to the Australian Corps) were to open the attack on September 29, and the Australian Corps was then to pass through them on the first objective line and pursue the attack.

ridge, in order that the line might be formed up straight for the day of the grand assault. That minor attack was not successful. Lieutenants W. Palstra[20] and Devlin Hamilton, on an early contact-patrol to locate and assist the American infantry, could see nothing of the ground owing to the early morning fog and ground haze. The only thing they found was a German scout darting across in front of them soon after they had crossed the lines; the observer emptied a drum from his Lewis gun into this target and saw the enemy dive for the ground emitting much smoke. Later patrols identified some American troops on the desired line, but could get no flares in answer to signals, and German machine-gun fire directed at the airmen from the rear of these troops was not reassuring. The artillery bombardment was very heavy all day. Special bombardment-reconnaissances reported both Bellicourt and Bellenglise burning in a welter of shell-bursts. No. 3 Squadron's patrols contributed their mites to the fund of destruction by dropping bombs on Bony and other strongpoints, though in the general din and havoc these 25-lb. bombs could hardly have been distinguished. Towards evening, when it became clear that the American forward troops on the left front were in some places cut off, several machines were sent out to drop ammunition-supplies to them and messages urging them to hold on till reinforced.

The bombardment continued on September 28th with unabated fury. Till 3 p.m. heavy showers of rain fell over the front. As soon as the afternoon light improved, efforts were again made to locate the American left, but this could be done only at great risk in low flying, for the infantry apparently had no signal flares; at all events none were fired. The line was clearly broken and insecure in the left sector, but the general assault was imminent, orders for the artillery barrage programme could not be altered, and the bombardment roared on over the whole front. Beyond the zone of this fierce fire, several more enemy heavy batteries in the Nauroy Line were ranged by the airmen.

The great assault on the Hindenburg Line began at 5.50 a.m. on September 29th. The fighting of the Australian Corps was

---

[20] Lieut. W. Palstra, M.C.; No. 3 Sqn. (previously Infantry). Accountant; of Surrey Hills, Melbourne; b. Zwolle, Holland, 8 Oct., 1891.

part of an attack which involved practically the whole of the Western Front. No. 3 Squadron was prevented by heavy fog from accompanying the opening advance of the 30th and 27th American Divisions. No machine left the ground before 8 o'clock, and no airman could see anything till well after 10. Those machines which were detailed to drop smoke-bombs in certain places for the purpose of blinding enemy observation duly dropped them, rather out of a well-learned respect for orders than because they were necessary. Later in the forenoon, when the R.E.8's did manage to see something of the ground, the observation was only patchy. The Hindenburg Line was pierced here and there, but Bony village especially was holding out stoutly, and, broadly speaking, though the right front of the attack had driven through, the left was held up almost entirely. The infantry's reports revealed that the American attack had dissolved into lost fragments. The 5th and 3rd Australian Divisions, which were to pass through the American line beyond the canal—such was the scheme—and exploit the attack, found no American line at all, but only bewildered bunches of men, rather lost in the fog and dismayed by hostile machine-gun fire from almost every side. The reconnaissance machines of No. 3 Squadron flew daringly low to do their work as far as it could be done, and were all much shot about by this same ground-fire. By 5 p.m. rain fell again and blotted out their landscape. This air-work in a difficult situation and in abominable weather was very gallantly done, and the information it procured was as accurate as any the Australian staff received on that trying day.

The airmen's observation appears to have been assisted considerably by the ill-luck of another arm, the tanks. Many tanks exploded ground-mines and were wrecked or caught fire. The airmen could see these stranded across roads and trenches —in some places burning, in others providing a rallying point and cover for a collection of men fighting forward through a maze of hostile machine-gun nests. Lieutenants Pengilley and C. R. Fenwicke,[21] between 2.25 and 4 p.m., saw British transport moving up a road running north-east to Nauroy, tanks passing north-east out of Bellicourt under heavy shell-

---

[21] Lieut. C. R. Fenwicke; No. 3 Sqn. (previously Light Horse). Station overseer; b. Tamworth, N.S.W., 25 April, 1890.

fire, and fifteen other tanks in a sunken road just east of Bony, some stationary, others crawling north. But Bony was not taken yet, and the enemy were thickly garrisoning the Nauroy Line. The patrol of Palstra and Devlin Hamilton made this fact clear, and reported Bony and adjacent trenches strongly held by the enemy at 4 p.m. They also saw six tanks burning in front of the Hindenburg Line north of Bony. Lieutenants S. H. Deamer[22] and P. R. Fullerton[23] met just north of Bellicourt heavy machine-gun fire from a strong German defence position which was not dislodged that day, and Deamer was shot in the leg. Lieutenants K. A. Roberts[24] and Sturgeon, between 1.20 and 4.10 p.m., located and called down fire on five active hostile batteries and several small columns of transport, and had an indecisive engagement with a two-seater over Estrées. Shortly after 4 p.m. another contact machine—Lieutenants C. E. Frazer[25] and D. Ellis—reported the right front of the attack well out at Joncourt (the 5th Australian Division had pushed through in this region) and the battle-front swinging to face north and north-east. At 4.45, just as the rain began, Lieutenants J. B. Tait[26] and A. G. Barrett[27] observed a strong German counter-attack deploying south of Joncourt towards Nauroy, and four Halberstadts accompanying it at 2,000 feet. They signalled the news back to the artillery and, with three S.E.5 scouts, dived and drove off the Halberstadts, and then proceeded to fire into the advancing enemy column. The counter-attack was beaten off.

Heavy rain fell during the next day. The noon reconnaissance reported the Australian line in much the same position as on the previous night, but there were signs that pressure from the south was making the enemy in Bony uncomfortable. German flares from that village were so interpreted, and, as subsequently appeared, the interpretation

---

[22] Lieut. S. H. Deamer; No. 3 Sqn. Reporter; b. Hitchin, Herts., Eng., 1892.

[23] Lieut. P. R. Fullerton; No. 3 Sqn. (previously Light Horse). Grocer; of Rutherglen, Vic.; b. Rutherglen, 7 Sept., 1889.

[24] Lieut. K. A. Roberts; No. 3 Sqn. (previously Infantry). Hardware assistant; b. Bendigo, Vic., Nov., 1893.

[25] Lieut. C. E. Frazer; No. 3 Sqn. Civil servant; of Kew, Melbourne; b. Kew, 14 March, 1894.

[26] Lieut. J. B. Tait; No. 3 Sqn. Accountant; of Melbourne; b. Geelong, Vic., 15 Oct., 1890.

[27] Lieut. A. G. Barrett; No. 3 Sqn. (previously Artillery). Maltster; of Geelong, Vic.; b. Melbourne, 7 May, 1895.

was correct. The first contact-patrol on October 1st, a bright sunny day, reported Bony in Australian hands and the remainder of the Hindenburg Line clear of the enemy.

The attack stopped not for a moment, and the advance was now general all along the Australian front. The bright weather enabled the R.E.8's to locate a large number of enemy batteries and to photograph the front. German transport was seen retiring on most roads in rear of Beaurevoir and Montbrehain. The Australian machines recorded all such movement in wireless calls which, distributed to air squadrons and artillery, brought down shell-fire on the roads from the heavy guns, and sent low-flying scouts to the attack with bombs and machineguns. The forward German artillery was moving back to new positions and hostile shell-fire was slight. German airmen, though in strength, avoided fight; they were intent only on observing the Australian reserves and estimating the weight behind the thrust. The 5th and 3rd Australian Divisions stormed the whole Nauroy Line at dawn on October 2nd. Then, shortly afterwards, came an enemy counter-attack south of Joncourt. Palstra and Devlin Hamilton just as they had finished taking the flares of the advanced assaulting infantry, saw this movement developing on the right (on the British IX Corps front), and, sailing straight over the centre of it, fired a red light, the pre-arranged signal. The resulting artillery-barrage came down; with it the Australian machine and two British scouts dived upon the German infantry, firing all guns. They created great confusion, and this counterattack, like the former one, was smothered under the artillerybarrage before it could gather strength. The infantry battle died down towards noon, and the Australian infantry were photographed again as they dug in facing the Beaurevoir Line. Throughout the remainder of the day No. 3 Squadron's machines wirelessed back news of every group of transport on the enemy's rear roads, and kept strict watch on the railway station at Bohain. They fought several indecisive encounters with German scouts, but the British scouts allowed their opponents small chance of attacking the R.E.8's. Every now and then the Australian machines, finding no sign of counterattack, would swoop down and deliver long bursts of fire into Beaurevoir and Montbrehain villages.

By dawn next day only the 2nd Australian Division was left on the Australian front. The 3rd and 5th Divisions were relieved by British units, and sent back to rest areas, where the 1st and 4th had preceded them; the last obstacle, the Beaurevoir Line, was attacked that morning (October 3rd) by the 2nd Division with the British. Accompanying this assault, five machines from No. 3 Squadron at 6.30 dropped phosphorus smoke-bombs on the high ground at Beaurevoir Mill to screen the infantry from German observation. Among those assisting this attack were Gould-Taylor and Thomson on artillery-patrol; and to the intense regret of the squadron their machine did not return. It was reported that an R.E.8 had been hit by a shell. Three days later news was received that the grave of the two airmen had been found near Estrées.

Between 9.30 and 10 Lock and Barrett located Australian troops in the Beaurevoir Line. Only in the centre, on the main road, was the enemy still in possession, and the 5th Australian Infantry Brigade had to fight hard here all day before they drove him out. One strong counter-attack was seen preparing towards noon behind the Montbrehain rise, but was dispersed by artillery-fire, as before, while still assembling. The infantry pressed on slowly up this high ground between Beaurevoir and Montbrehain, and by the evening of October 4th were at the crest near the main road. That attack was rounded off next day by the capture of Montbrehain.

The duties of the airmen of No. 3 Squadron were considerably lighter on these last two days. The battle was practically won, and the last fighting was chiefly against resolute rear-guards. Great numbers of Fokkers patrolling the lines testified to the enemy's anxiety to safeguard the retreat of his main forces, which was plainly becoming general. The Fokkers showed no great desire to attack, except where reconnaissance machines tried to penetrate to the enemy's rear areas. The fires and explosions in those areas, the dust of retiring transport on all the roads, the dwindling of German gun-fire, all told the same story.

The 2nd Australian Division was relieved in the line on October 5th, and with it the Australian Corps Headquarters was also withdrawn to the rest area. Till October 19th No.

3 Squadron remained as corps squadron with the II American Corps, which took the place of the Australians in the pursuit to near Le Cateau. The aerodrome at Bouvincourt was moved on October 7th to better ground at Bernes, south of Roisel, but remained there for only eleven days. So rapidly was the German Army being chased out of France that by October 17th the squadron was required to move again to Prémont, a few miles south-west of Le Cateau.

On October 8th the British and Americans reached a line from Prémont to Fresnoy-le-Grand, and next day took Bohain and Busigny. On the 10th they reached the Selle River. No 3 Squadron's reports of these days were all of fires, explosions, blocks of traffic retreating on every road. In the afternoon of October 9th, four of its machines bombed this traffic at various places on the roads outside Le Cateau. The enemy was abandoning the whole country in front of the Selle River, and blowing up roads and railways and firing villages all over this area. His anti-aircraft batteries had gone. Occasionally there was an air duel. Grigson and Shelley on October 6th, and Robertson and Gray on the 8th, each drove down a Halberstadt two-seater to the ground—in the former instance apparently the enemy was wrecked. As a rule, however, the fighting, so far as No. 3 Squadron was concerned, amounted to little more than distant exchange of shots, for British scouts were out in great force against the enemy.

The squadron participated in the Americans' attack on October 17th around St. Benin and St. Souplet, south of Le Cateau, and photographed the new line next day. The Americans were relieved by British troops on October 19th; the front was shrinking as a result of the advance, and the British IX and XIII Corps now covered the Fourth Army front. This left the squadron, as its commander noted, " without a corps to work with." It was, therefore, ordered to stand by as a reserve squadron and to provide artillery-patrols when required. The squadron was at this time much interested in two improved Bristol Fighters, which were temporarily put on its strength for long-distance reconnaissance and artillery-shoots. With the two (later three) Bristol Fighters was formed temporarily a special flight (" O " Flight), under the command of Captain E. J. Jones.

" O " Flight accompanied the mobile columns which kept touch with the rapidly retreating enemy in the days leading up to the Armistice.

In this semi-attached rôle, the squadron carried out its last fighting service in the war. With artillery- and bombing-patrols, it accompanied the British attack at Le Cateau on October 22nd and 23rd and the greater battle of Landrecies on November 4th. Its participation in the bombing of the retreating enemy after that battle was the squadron's last offensive operation.

CHAPTER XXIV
THE LILLE AIR RAIDS

THE final three months of the war were a period of unceasing Allied offensive. Early in August the full wave of the restored British strength broke first over the enemy's retaining wall on the Somme and then gradually overwhelmed him all along the line. The present story of the Australian Flying Corps has sought to describe the mounting of that wave. Its culmination in the attack on the Somme of August 8th marked the end of all doubt and suspense in the Allied command. Henceforth the order was always for attack, attack, and again attack.

The work of the flying service, ever offensive, immediately expanded into still more audacious designs of aggression. Where British aeroplanes had previously dropped a dozen bombs, they now dropped fifty. They sought out the nerve centres of the German Army, not merely in its forward areas but far behind its front, and that too in great force. Offensive patrols by a squadron gave place to systematic sweeps of the sky by several squadrons combined, and by day and night the enemy on the ground was harassed and discomfited till his morale, under the general strain from all quarters, entirely broke. His airmen appeared in greater and ever greater formations as his defeat became definite and irreparable. The sweeps were the answer, and the Allied airmen vanquished and drove him out of the sky, as the army shattered his infantry-lines on the ground. The two Australian scouting squadrons worked in these sweeps with No. 88 Squadron, R.A.F. (Bristol Fighters). The machines would gain their height of rendezvous over a well-defined landmark (such as the Nieppe Forest), No. 4 Squadron (Camels) usually at 10,000 feet, No. 2 Squadron (S.E.5's) at 14,000, and the Bristol Fighters at 18,000. Sometimes the S.E.5's flew above the Bristols on the top level. Then, with the Camels leading and the other two formations flying above and slightly to the rear and flanks, the whole fleet would penetrate fifteen or twenty miles behind the enemy lines and search the sky from Ypres to Arras. Too often, as with the earlier circus on the Somme, the enemy gave this force a wide berth and avoided encounter; but at the end, when the German Army was threatened with a mightier Sedan, many German airmen came out to die fighting, and the ordinary familiar "dog-fight" grew to the proportions of a savage air-riot.

Before the beginning of the British offensive, No. 2 and No. 4 Australian Squadrons were already challenging the enemy with heavy combined patrols, which regularly scoured the air over Lille and surrounding aerodromes. These tactics were begun in July, and early in August were a regular custom. For the successful destruction of enemy machines such strong patrols at this stage were over-impressive. The Germans simply decamped on sight. A fleet of twenty-eight Australian machines, which visited Lille in the forenoon of August 1st, saw great numbers of hostile craft, but these promptly fled, and only one was caught and destroyed. This was a Rumpler two-seater going home alone at what it must have deemed the safe height of 19,000 feet. Lieutenants Wellwood, C. R. Ebeling,[1] and V. E. Knight[2] chased it as it dived away to escape, and after all three had fired bursts at it, Wellwood finally delivered fifty rounds at close range, and the Rumpler crashed south-east of Lille. Patrolling by roving couples or small formations was continued between the excursions of the combined sweeps. Taplin and King, out together on dawn-patrol over Merville on August 3rd, each drove down a two-seater—in Taplin's case after a particularly hot fight with an L.V.G., armoured on its underside and firing explosive bullets. On the evening of August 4th King and Watson destroyed another two-seater over Laventie in a joint attack.

Local bombing likewise continued a regular daily practice. Late in the afternoon of August 6th Cobby and Trescowthick found an ammunition train unloading shells at Vieille Chapelle dump. They dropped four bombs, blew up the dump, hit the train fairly in the centre, and set that also on fire. They then flew low and fired 800 rounds into the dump-workers and train-crew. Going out again in the evening with King,

---

[1] Lieut. C. R. Ebeling; No. 2 Sqn. Engineer and draughtsman; of Yarraville, Melbourne; b. Spotswood, Melbourne, 10 March, 1893. Died of injuries, 23 Aug., 1918.

[2] Lieut. V. E. Knight; No. 2 Sqn. (previously A.A.S.C.). Printer; of Westgarth, Melbourne; b. Christchurch, N.Z., 15 May, 1895.

Watson, and Major W. A. McCloughry, Cobby destroyed an
L.V.G. two-seater flying low over Bac St. Maur, while the
others bombed Lestrem and transport on the Sailly–Estaires
road. At dawn next morning both Australian squadrons were
out in force. One patrol from No. 4 Squadron bombed the Lys
Valley, while another of ten machines, protected by a formation
of eleven from No. 2, riding high, flew to south-west of Lille
and attacked the important field-railway loop round Sainghin
and Marquillies. Of eighteen 25-lb. bombs dropped on the
railway and Sainghin station, four were seen to hit the
permanent way and the station, while others exploded in and
around billets, from which soldiers hastily fled. Eight Fokker
biplanes appeared at 6.30 a.m. to counter-attack, but Cole
and F. R. Smith, from the watching S.E.5's above, dived down,
split up their formation, and shot two down out of control.
At noon a combined force of eleven Australian machines again
visited this region. While six Camels bombed Don railway
station, just south of Sainghin, five S.E.5's swooped upon
nine Fokkers (biplanes and triplanes) which came in from
the south. The enemy, diving away from the upper attack,
found the Camels below, and opened fire on these. The
Camels turned to face them, and a general engagement ensued
for several minutes at 8,000 feet. Heller and J. C. F.
Wilkinson, the first to be attacked, swerved aside and rolled
and tumbled around two of the triplanes. Each fired bursts
from his machine-guns at the two leading Fokkers, which
thereafter stood vertically on their noses and dropped down
into the mist. The remaining German machines, probably in
fear of the S.E.5's still above, broke away after a few hurried
exchanges, and disappeared.

Meanwhile Cobby and Trescowthick had crossed the lines
farther north. They descended to attack transport entering
Armentières from Lille, and bombed and machine-gunned
these vehicles from 200 feet with shattering results. Shortly
afterwards, having climbed again through clouds to 2,500
feet, they saw five Pfalz scouts flying north towards them
and slightly lower. The Australians attacked the two rearmost machines together; the mist was heavy, and they risked
the chance that any other enemy might be hovering above.
The two Pfalz victims selected were completely surprised

and received hot bursts of fire from just over their tails.
They fell simultaneously in flames. Overhauling the next
nearest Pfalz, Trescowthick, slightly ahead of Cobby, delivered
the closer attack, shattered the German's right wing, and that
machine collapsed in the air. As the two Camels returned
to the aerodrome, Taplin, Ramsay, and Baker took off with
a heavy load of bombs for Pont-du-Hem on the Estaires–La
Bassée road. They dropped their bombs around billets in
Pont-du-Hem from 3,500 feet, and at once flew on towards
two Albatros scouts observed near Laventie. The Camels
had the advantage of height by some 500 feet; they caught
up with the enemy, and, while Ramsay remained aloft on guard,
Taplin and Baker attacked. Taplin was a skilful pilot and
a dead shot. He reserved his fire till he reached almost
touching range, and then shot his Albatros into flames with
one short burst. Baker's fire severed the left lower wing
of the second Albatros, which then folded up in the air.
Throughout the evening a succession of small patrols from
No. 4 Squadron bombed the Lys villages, and Cobby, on one
of these excursions at 5.30 p.m., destroyed a German two-
seater in flames over Lestrem.

The news of the Australian victory on the Somme put the
squadrons in the highest spirits, and in the days after August
8th no pilot could rest on the aerodrome. The general
enthusiasm added sting to the bombing of the Lys villages.
The pilots themselves were in a mood to care nothing what
risks they took against enemy machines. Thus Taplin,
becoming separated from his patrol near La Bassée on August
9th, chased and destroyed a Hannoveranner, and immediately
afterwards was attacked by four Fokkers. He dodged them
in the clouds, flew on in pursuit of a second Hannoveranner,
and shot at it till he ran out of ammunition. Then, incapable
of offering or meeting further combat, he turned and flew
home from far over the German lines.

Early on August 10th Cobby, King, and Watson attacked
the Lys line of communications. They dropped ten bombs
at Lestrem, and then King saw a balloon on the ground near
Estaires. He dived from 2,000 down to 500 feet and set
it on fire. As he rose again, he perceived an S.E.5 chasing
an L.V.G. two-seater away from Merville. The German

was steering a course over Estaires, and, after watching the S.E.5 make two dives at it, King attacked it head-on. The L.V.G. slid away underneath him, but King turned again and fired at 50 feet, whereupon the enemy went down steeply, tried to land, and crashed. The patrol then roamed on towards Don and there at the station found a train; having no bombs left, they sprayed it with machine-gun fire. An hour later Smallwood, out with Taplin, destroyed a balloon at Sailly. Next day Lieutenant L. Wharton,[3] becoming isolated from one of these small patrols, attacked two L.V.G's over Armentières, and shot down one completely out of control, but was attacked in turn by six enemy scouts, whose fire perforated his petrol tank. The Australian escaped by diving through the clouds, but was then hit in the head by a piece of anti-aircraft shell, and in landing crashed into some barbed wire near Hazebrouck. He was taken to hospital, but insisted on delivering his report to the squadron-commander *en route*.

After two days' work in co-operation with the Allied advance on the Somme, regular joint offensive-patrols in Flanders were resumed by the Australian squadrons on August 14th and 15th. A combined formation of twelve machines visited the Lys area between 9.30 and 10.30 a.m. on the 14th, and, while the Camels bombed the dumps there, three S.E.5's under Captain E. L. Simonson[4] engaged over Nieppe (near Armentières) eight Fokkers which were fighting some British Camels. Mills destroyed one Fokker after a hot duel at close range. Combined operations were repeated at 5 p.m. Manuel, escorting a bomb-raid, attacked, with two other S.E.5's, six Fokker biplanes over Lompret (north of the Lomme aerodrome) and shot down one, which crashed near Pérenchies. Another formation at 6 o'clock escorted a flight of D.H.4's sent to bomb Tournai. One German two-seater was seen near Wavrin. It dropped hastily in a spin towards Haubourdin aerodrome as the S.E.5's approached, and then one of its wings suddenly collapsed and it fell like a stone through the remainder of the distance to earth. No shot had been fired at it.

---

[3] Lieut. L. Wharton, M.C.; No. 4 Sqn. (previously Infantry). Science master; of Armidale, N.S.W.; b. Parkes, N.S.W., 2 April, 1891.

[4] Capt. E. L. Simonson; No. 2 Sqn. (previously Infantry). Engineering student; of Melbourne; b. Brighton, Melbourne, 23 Jan., 1894.

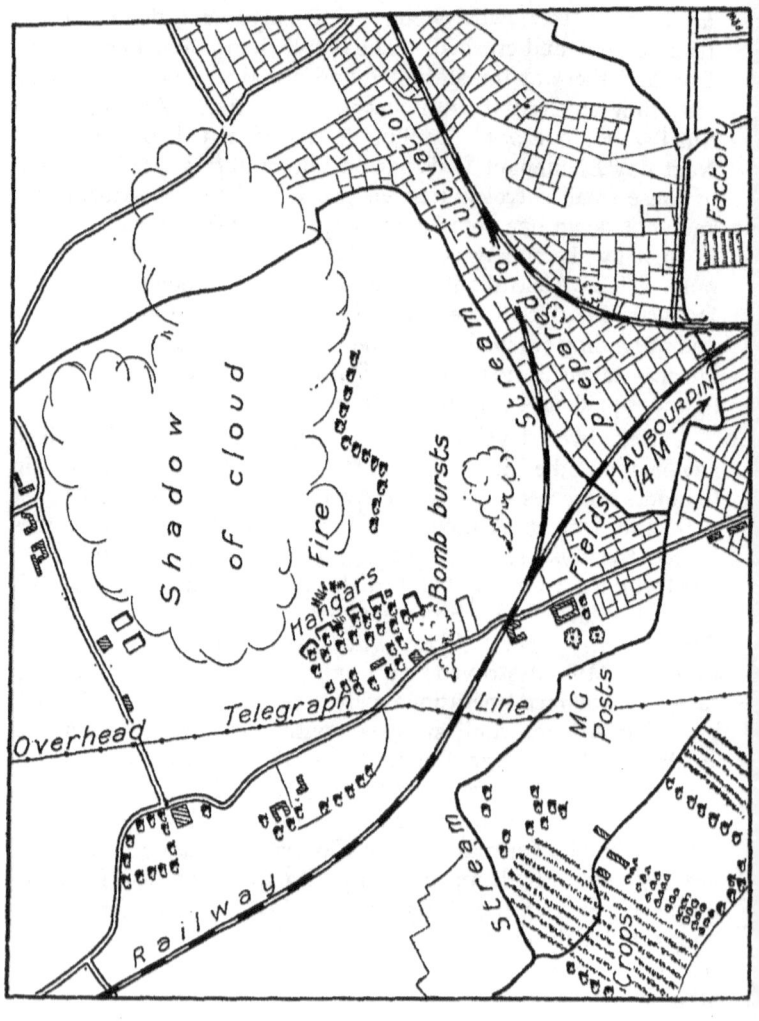

The opening of the bomb-raid by Nos. 2 and 4 Squadrons, A.F.C., on Haubourdin Aerodrome, Lille, 16th August, 1918

*British Air Force Photograph; taken by No. 88 Sqn.
Aust. War Museum Collection No. J389.*

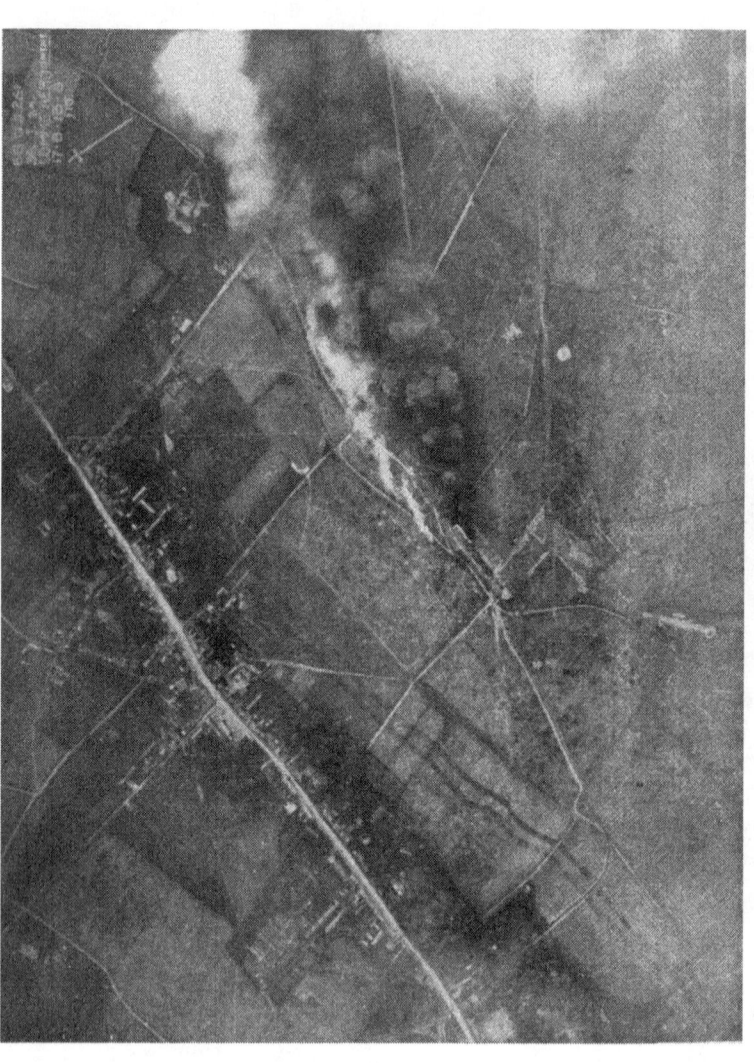

The bomb-raid by Nos. 2 and 4 Squadrons, A.F.C., on Lomme Aerodrome, Lille,

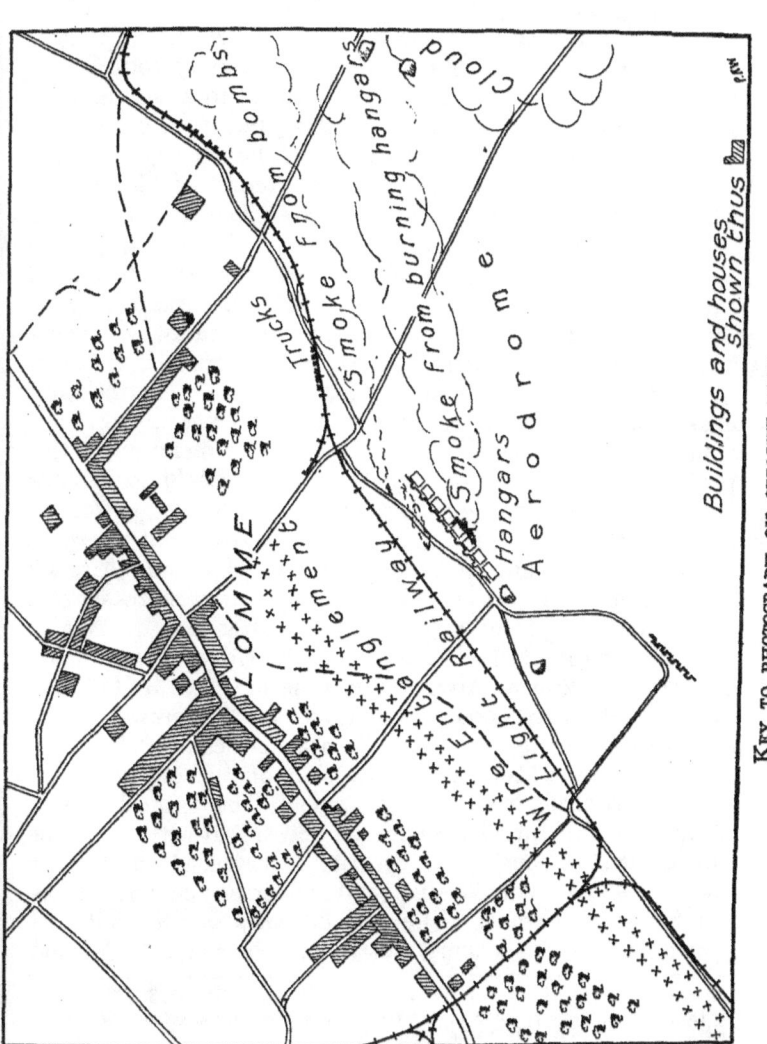

KEY TO PHOTOGRAPH ON OPPOSITE PAGE

On August 15th the weather was adverse to flying, with gusty westerly winds. The early morning bombing-patrol (five machines) from No. 4 Squadron met with bad luck over the Lys. Lieutenants S. Howard[5] and E. A. Cato[6] bombed Estaires, also a train at Armentières, drove away four L.V.G. two-seaters at Estaires, and then descended to attack an anti-aircraft battery at that place. At this juncture a bullet fired from the ground wounded Howard in the foot and another broke his control-stick. He regained control of his machine after some trouble, and landed at Hermaville, near Arras. Meanwhile Lieutenants Smallwood, M. H. Eddie,[7] and Edols bombed the Bac St. Maur dump and another anti-aircraft battery. Smallwood, too, came to grief. He was hit in the back by a piece of anti-aircraft shell, and turned away towards home, but became weak from his wound and crashed at Serny, near Aire. Cato, Eddie, and Edols also landed at the same place, and later flew home. The bad luck which seems to follow some men had not yet finished with the other members of this patrol; a few days later both Cato and Edols had narrow escapes in the same neighbourhood. Edols, on patrol on August 25th, was badly wounded in the right hand by a splinter of shell, and in landing he crashed on the Aire–La Bassée canal near Locon. Cato's mishap was more serious. While returning from a patrol in the afternoon of August 22nd in company with Lieutenant S. P. Keay,[8] a new pilot, the two collided over Aire. Keay's machine lost its tail, and the pilot fell from 3,000 feet and was fatally injured. The aileron of Cato's left wing was torn almost completely away, and his machine also fell. Cato shut off his engine to try to regain control, but without avail. The last desperate resource was to turn his engine on and try to get out of the spin in that manner. This partly succeeded, and after desperate efforts with joy-stick and rudder-bar he arrived low over Serny aerodrome. The next difficulty was to land. If he switched off his engine, he would spin again. To land

---

[5] Lieut. S. Howard; No. 4 Sqn. Student; b. Ballarat, Vic., 1898.

[6] Lieut. E. A. Cato; No. 4 Sqn. (previously Light Horse). Merchant; of Toorak, Melbourne; b. Malvern, Melbourne, 19 May, 1889.

[7] Lieut. M. H. Eddie; No. 4 Sqn. (previously A.A.M.C.). Clerk; of Launceston, Tas.; b. Launceston, 1 July, 1893. Killed in action, 5 Sept., 1918.

[8] Lieut. S. P. Keay; No. 4 Sqn. (previously Infantry). Clerk; of Melbourne; b. Williamstown, Melbourne, 7 June, 1895. Died as result of aeroplane accident, 22 Aug., 1918.

with his engine on meant doing so at highly dangerous speed. There was, however, no third course; and with his speed indicator showing 120 miles an hour he essayed to land. A crash was inevitable, and the machine was smashed to pieces as soon as it hit the ground. Cato escaped with bruises and a bad shaking.

The 80th Wing, to which both Australian scouting squadrons belonged, was now preparing a strong air attack on the railway communications and the aerodromes around Lille. The chief of these aerodromes were at Lomme and Haubourdin, the latter being also an important railway centre for the supply traffic on the whole Lys front. The main objectives of the attacks, however, were the aerodromes, for to destroy these ground-nests was the proper corollary to sweeping the sky of operating hostile aircraft. Though the sweeps were temporarily successful in clearing the sky, they failed to put the enemy airmen out of action. The tactics of the further scheme were simple: the wing was to take the air in full force, scare all German machines to the ground, and then go down after them and bomb them in their hangars.

All through the war Lille itself had been deliberately spared from bombardment by British artillery or aerial attack. This was owing mainly to French representations; the French were anxious that Lille should not be damaged; moreover in the earlier years of the war a tacit understanding seemed to be in vogue between British and Germans that Armentières (then on the British side of the line) should be spared so long as Lille was not shelled. This accounted for the comparative immunity from destructon (before 1918) of the Lys Valley above Armentières. The front here was regarded by each side as the nursery, or breaking-in ground, for new troops. Here newly-formed divisions, British and German alike, were sent to become accustomed gradually to trench warfare. Hither, too, divisions badly in need of rest were transferred for the recuperation of shattered nerves. Lille became the home of many German generals, and was never disturbed. When in 1917, before the Third Battle of Ypres, the Germans for the first time heavily shelled Armentières, Lille still went free, though Lomme and Haubourdin, western suburbs of the city, suffered from retaliatory shelling.[9] In 1918, the German northern offensive overran Armentières and the surrounding district, and put Lille almost out of reach of the British guns, but British airmen, in deference to French feeling, still forbore to drop bombs on the city. Under the 80th Wing's scheme of attack on the aerodromes at Lomme and Haubourdin, two great raids on those places took place on August 16th and 17th.

The first raid was against Haubourdin shortly after noon on the 16th. Sixty-five machines were concerned—every available aeroplane from No. 88 Squadron, R.A.F. (Bristol Fighters), No. 92 Squadron (S.E.5's), No. 2 Australian Squadron (S.E.5's), and No. 4 Australian Squadron (Sopwith Camels). This impressive fleet, loaded up with incendiary and explosive bombs and all the machine-gun ammunition it could carry, gained its positions of height over Reclinghem aerodrome at 12.30 p.m.—the Bristol Fighters at 13,000 feet, the British S.E.5's at 11,000, the Australian S.E.5's at 9,000, and the Camels at 7,000. Murray Jones led No. 2 Squadron's formation of nineteen and Cobby an equal number from No. 4 Squadron, with which also flew the wing-commander, Lieutenant-Colonel L. A. Strange.[10] The force flew straight for La Bassée, keeping appointed heights and order in wide-sweeping arcs. Over La Bassée each formation dipped to lose height. The plan was then for the two lower layers of the air-fleet to attack Haubourdin aerodrome in turn, while the Bristol Fighters and British S.E.5's ensured protection from possible attack. Thus, while the Camels dived first, No. 2 Squadron's formation, immediately above, flew in wide left-hand circuits, awaiting its turn.

Cobby led the attack at the head of his own flight. As the first six machines swooped down on the westernmost hangars of the aerodrome, one panic-stricken Fokker biplane, caught in the air under the descending avalanche, flew for the

---

[9] This shelling was due to other considerations also. The British Command wished, by artillery bombardment on a long front, to lead the enemy to believe that the opening attack in the Third Battle of Ypres would extend as far south as Armentières.

[10] Lt.-Col. L. A. Strange, D.S.O., M.C., D.F.C.; R.A.F. Aviator; of Blandford, Dorset, Eng.; b. Tarrant, Keynstone, Eng., 27 July, 1891. (Formerly a pilot, as lieutenant, with No 5 Sqn., R.F.C., when it went to France with the first British Expeditionary Force in August, 1914.)

ground and crashed into a tree near Wavrin. Cobby at 200 feet let fall two 25-lb. bombs at the outermost hangars and hit them fair; they did not catch fire, but the next two, on which his following bombs fell, were set ablaze. He then at 100 feet shot into flames a machine stationary on the ground. Dashing on, he turned his guns upon further hangars and a party of mechanics; then left those targets to overtake a party of 200 men running along the road from the aerodrome towards the hospital. Cobby fired 400 rounds—some from only fifty feet up—into this party, and numbers of them dropped. King followed his leader. His first three bombs fell as one into the nearest of the untouched hangars; from twenty feet up he fired 100 rounds into another large hangar plainly enclosing four or five machines, dropped his last bomb on the same target, and saw the hangar catch fire. The next thing in view was a two-horsed waggon on the road; King shot one horse, the vehicle capsized in a ditch, and two men fell out of it. Then he flew round the aerodrome, whipping bursts of fire into huts, billets, the aerodrome searchlight plant, anything that came into his line of sight. Lieutenants D. C. Carter,[11] Edols, Eddie, and Trescowthick pursued him close in a riot of destruction, and Edols with a 40-lb. phosphorus bomb set the mechanics' quarters on fire. Major W. A. McCloughry dived next, set burning a hangar and a machine on the ground outside it, and then engaged a party of mechanics running across the aerodrome. Both McCloughry and Colonel Strange (who followed him) fired heavily into a train on the line north of the aerodrome. Watson's flight, attacking next in succession, bombed a large group of officers' quarters and workshops in a wood beside some hangars. The western end of the aerodrome was now a mass of smoke and fire, and all its occupants were running wildly for the shelter of the railway embankment. Watson stampeded horse-transport from a dump. Baker chased a staff car on the road, till it ran up a bank and capsized; "No one," he reported, "left the car." Heller's flight followed Watson's and further fanned the flames; his machines also hotly attacked several

---

[11] Lieut. D. C. Carter; No. 4 Sqn. (previously Artillery) Clerk; of Prahran, Melbourne; b. Melbourne, 13 Nov., 1894. Killed in action, 5 Sept., 1918.

machine-gun defence posts.   With the last man of Heller's flight No. 4 Squadron had completed its effort.

No. 2 Squadron followed promptly. Murray Jones attacked first, fired a few bursts of machine-gun fire into the burning western group of hangars as he passed them, and dropped two bombs on the southern group. Dense black smoke rose up promptly and obscured them. Cole, leading his flight, pursued the same track—bombs on the southern group, machine-gun raking of the eastern. German mechanics had evidently rushed some machines out of the burning western group, for most of the pilots in Cole's flight saw damaged machines lying in front of these hangars, and ripped bursts of bullets into them in passing over to bomb the southern group. Cummings led the next six machines; all bombed the southern hangars, and some the smoking western ones as well. Follett, in this flight, following Cummings, was about to dive at the aerodrome when he noticed an Albatros two-seater in the air flying south-west at 2,500 feet. Whence this lone German appeared was never established; if from the wrecked aerodrome, he did not escape his fate, for Follett shot seventy rounds into him from behind and he crashed. The wreck which Cole's and Cummings's men had made of the southern group was completed by Manuel's flight, which dropped the last relay of bombs into a welter of smoke and flames. The German loss during this raid in machines alone was enormous. British estimates put the figure at thirty-seven aeroplanes destroyed.[12] That evening strong enemy aircraft formations appeared like angry ants from disturbed nests, and at 6.30 a small combined offensive-patrol from the Australian squadrons sighted twenty-eight Fokkers in two fleets cruising between La Bassée and Bailleul.

The 80th Wing carried out an identical attack next morning, August 17th, on Lomme aerodrome, about two miles north of that at Haubourdin. The strength of this raid was sixty, of which ground-attacking machines numbered thirty-

---

[12] It is to the raids from Lomme and Haubourdin that the following comment in the German Major Neumann's *The German Air Force in the Great War* appears to refer. "During July, 1918, large squadrons of seventy or eighty (British) machines would appear, and while two-thirds of their number remained at various heights to act as escort, the remainder would systematically attack our aerodromes one by one. Thus, for example, in the neighbourhood of Lille and Cortoyle, in the course of two days they succeeded in completely destroying three formations of fighting machines by bombs and machine-gun fire."

one—fourteen from No. 2 Squadron and seventeen from No. 4. The machines took up position over Reclinghem as before, and lost height over La Bassée. During the previous day's raid the S.E.5's, in the second attacking wave, found a difficulty in aiming their bombs, owing to the blurring of the targets by the smoke from the preceding attack. For the Lomme operation it was therefore arranged that each squadron should attend to precisely-defined objectives; and accordingly, when the Camels dived at a line of hangars on the north of the aerodrome, the S.E.5's dived simultaneously at a second line on the east. The hangars and workshops on both lines were badly damaged; most of them were hit direct and set on fire. The wind especially favoured the fire started on the north, carrying the flames from the westernmost shed along to the others. The German anti-aircraft machine-gunners stuck gamely to their work, despite furious attack from the raiders, and their fire hit Lieutenant E. P. E. McCleery's[13] machine in the Camel formation. It crashed heavily on the aerodrome floor, and McCleery was killed. Photographs disclosed that heavy damage was done to hangars and workshops during this raid, and prisoners subsequently taken stated that seventeen Fokker biplanes were destroyed in the wreckage.

At Reclinghem detailed instructions for all ranks were prepared against a return bomb-attack, but none followed. In the old days, or even a few months earlier, such a direct blow at their air force would have provoked the enemy to at least some effort in retaliation. But the Germans probably had their hands too full; their whole line was in danger farther south, and the northern flank was soon to be drawn into a general retreat.

Two days of quiet followed the Lomme attack, and then on August 19th the Australian scout-squadrons resumed their combined patrols. About 9 a.m. that day eight Camels, led by Baker and Heller, and eight S.E.5's under Cole and Manuel, set out to visit the old Lys haunts. The S.E.5's, riding high up, saw several formations of Fokkers, biplanes and triplanes, in the sky between Laventie and Haubourdin.

---
[13] Lieut. E. P. E. McCleery; No. 4 Sqn. Coachbuilder and engineer; of Berrima District, N.S.W.; b. Moss Vale, N.S.W., 1893. Killed in action, 17 Aug., 1918.

At 17,000 feet Cole and Wellwood, separated from their comrades, first sighted seven of the biplanes over Haubourdin, and dived to attack them. Cole shot down one out of control, and drove away another which was "sitting on the tail" of Wellwood's machine. Then the fight opened out over the sky. Cole followed one biplane from Lille south-eastward towards Douai, and dived several thousand feet after it, firing steadily. He had just fired a final burst which sent this Fokker down completely out of control, when, at 4,000 feet, he was attacked by five triplanes. This formation had been sighted by Manuel's flight from near Laventie, and was, when first observed, being engaged by several Bristol Fighters and S.E.5's and driven down towards Douai. Thus the triplanes, spinning away from a higher attack, found Cole below them. Cole was relieved from an awkward predicament only by the fact that the Bristols followed the Germans down.

For several days bad weather prevented useful flying. No. 4 Squadron's patrols continued harassing bomb attacks on Bac St. Maur and Estaires, and Baker on a solitary patrol in hazy weather on August 24th destroyed a balloon. The enemy as a rule either kept very high or did not appear in the sky at all. Following Baker's exploit on August 24th, King went out alone as far as Don railway station, bombed it, machine-gunned a train, and returned among the low clouds—all without seeing any enemy. Later the same morning (August 25th) Cole and Wellwood, patrolling east of Lens, drove down a Rumpler near Seclin, and then pursued a solitary D.F.W. from Givenchy (north of Arras) to Epinoy, outside Cambrai, where they finally destroyed it. The absence of hostile aircraft over the northern front was due to their withdrawing to the south, where the Allied offensive was steadily involving a wider front and was now threatening the region of Bapaume. No. 2 Squadron sought the Germans south of the Scarpe, and there two flights under Lieutenant E. E. Davies[14] and Manuel found them on August 27th. At 11 o'clock that morning Manuel's formation at 17,000 feet

---

[14] Capt. E. E. Davies, D.F.C.; No. 2 Sqn. (previously Light Horse). Barrister and solicitor; of Swan Hill, Vic.; b. Kerang, Vic., 16 March, 1890.

engaged twenty-eight Fokker and Pfalz scouts over Sains-les-Marquion, west of Cambrai. The fight was notable for the gallant performance of Cox, who singled out one Fokker, shot it into flames, and was then attacked by five other enemy scouts. By clever manœuvring he shot down out of control two of these in succession. Davies' patrol then appeared on the edge of the fight, and at 13,000 feet attacked four of the Fokkers. One of them was shot down by Davies and fell at Lécluse, in the Scarpe marshes south of Douai. The enemy thereafter abandoned the combat and retired.

At dawn on August 30th, King, Baker, and Ramsay found three D.F.W's together east of Laventie and destroyed two of them. Otherwise for days in succession every Australian patrol reported no German machines seen anywhere north of the Scarpe. The rare appearance of a few two-seaters only emphasised the fact that the enemy had left the air in this region. The Germans now lacked sufficient air force to meet the Allies on all fronts; and the signs were that the raids upon Lomme and Haubourdin, as well as other events, were compelling them to move their aerodromes to the eastward of Lille. His banishment from the air on the northern front was not the least serious of blows which the enemy suffered at this critical time.

CHAPTER XXV
FIGHTS OF THE SWEEP FORMATIONS

THE effect of the victorious Allied advance in the south had begun to affect the enemy's hold on Flanders during the latter part of August. First Merville was evacuated, and then, in the last days of August, Bailleul. The German salient in the area of the Lys—flat, wet, and exposed—was a position entirely without compensating strategic advantage to the enemy, save as a forward position for further attack. Since the intended prosecution of the offensive here in April had been abandoned, the retirement of the Germans in this sector had long been expected. That retirement had now begun. By September 6th the Lys salient had disappeared. Estaires, Steenwerck, Neuve Eglise, and Kemmel Hill were abandoned by the enemy, and the new line ran from Givenchy through Neuve Chapelle, Erquinghem, Nieppe, and Ploegsteert. Hitherto it had been no part of the Allied campaign of 1918 to attack in northern Flanders, but merely to harass the enemy's probable retreat. But during September plans were made for a general attack, from the Ypres side, by a British and Belgian army under the command of King Albert, and on September 28th this attack was launched, and overran in one day the whole Passchendaele Ridge and much beyond it. The advance continued steadily on the north, west, and south of Lille through early October. The whole German line fell back from Ostend to Douai. The Belgian coast was cleared by October 20th, Douai fell on October 17th, and early next day British troops had surrounded Lille, which had been evacuated by the enemy. By October 22nd the Allies were along the line of the Scheldt from Valenciennes to Avelghem (between Courtrai and Renaix).

This final period of the war was one of intense air fighting. The only stand made by the German troops after the piercing of the Hindenburg Line at the end of September was entirely temporary, and was designed to guard a general retreat into Germany. In the air the Germans fought hard, though spasmodically, against the Allied airmen's offensive. During the early part of September the enemy's air squadrons, still being drawn to other fronts, reappeared once or twice in the Armentières sector. The demand from the southern fighting fronts, the general strain, and the serious losses of the summer campaign were overtaxing the German Air Force; the enemy could not attempt to dispute the Allies' pressure in the air in all places at once, and accordingly he concentrated and exerted in big formations the strength in fighting scouts which remained to him. Fierce air battles were fought near Lille on September 5th, 16th, and 24th.

During October, as the retreat of the German Army became general and continuous, the length of the fighting front shrank considerably. This, and the fact that the only practicable line of retreat lay, like the original advance in 1914, through Belgium, drew the German air forces ultimately again to the northern front, and over Tournai and its vicinity the enemy airmen put forth their final effort. These last battles were more than encounters between patrols; they were aeroplane fleet-actions.

While his scouts were absent from the Flanders front in early September, the enemy was compelled to rely for air-observation almost entirely on balloons. King and Taplin in the early morning of September 1st destroyed two balloons on the Aubers Ridge behind Fromelles. While King and Taplin dropped bombs on Don railway station, Lieutenants Trescowthick and T. H. Barkell[1] attacked a "flaming-onion" battery near by, bombed it, raked it with machine-gun fire, and put it out of action. "Flaming-onions" were heartily detested by the airmen at all times, and to cripple an "onion" battery was sweet revenge. No enemy aeroplanes were seen in the sky at this time, but some hours later J. W. Wright's forenoon patrol of five machines from No. 4 Squadron sighted fifteen Fokkers attacking a solitary R.E.8 south-east of Bailleul, and forthwith flew to engage. Wright interrupted the foremost Fokker in the act of diving on the R.E.8, drove it away, and turned against a second Fokker close by. Into this machine he fired fifty rounds at forty-yards' range, and it fell into the clouds upside down. Next day (September 2nd) enemy airmen left the Armentières neighbourhood and concentrated on the Scarpe; the Australian squadrons found

---
[1] Lieut. T. H. Barkell, D.F.C.; No. 4 Sqn. Motor mechanic; b. Randwick, Sydney, 1892.

only a few solitary two-seaters on their front, of which Taplin in the evening destroyed one, a Halberstadt, near Aubers. The day passed chiefly in bombing the enemy's roads and transport.

No. 4 Squadron continued its bombing attacks throughout daylight on September 3rd. Patrols, flying in pairs, harried all the area west of Lille. Lieutenants Ramsay and H. W. Ross[2] bombed a train near Pérenchies; others dropped bombs on billets in Sainghin and Armentières; and Taplin set fire to a balloon behind Aubers. King and Lieutenant V. G. M. Sheppard,[3] each leading a patrol of four machines, bombed Don railway station and billets at Wez Macquart. Fournes, Armentières, and Sainghin were bombed by a big formation in the afternoon, and Taplin destroyed another balloon on the Aubers line. In the evening Cummings, leading a formation of thirteen S.E.5's from No. 2 Squadron, met seven Fokkers over Cambrai at 17,500 feet. The Australians manœuvred to the eastward and attacked. Stone and F. R. Smith each so badly damaged two opponents that these Fokkers fell completely out of control and emitting black smoke. The attack could not, however, be pursued, for the Australians in turn were assailed by a new force of twenty-five Fokkers from above, and had to break off the fight.

On the following morning, September 4th, both squadrons took the air with nearly full force. Two flights of S.E.5's again ranged the air over Cambrai and Douai, flying this time at 10,000 feet. They sighted a Fokker formation far out of reach at about 17,000 feet, but on turning homewards from a wide sweep beyond Douai they came upon eight Bristol Fighters engaged with fourteen Fokkers. The enemy fled before this reinforcement, but Knight caught one of them on the tail of a British machine and shot it down out of control into thick clouds. Meanwhile, beneath the clouds small formations from No. 4 Squadron hovered like hawks over all the Lys flats. Ramsay destroyed a balloon at La Bassée by dropping two bombs upon it from 1,000 feet; this balloon was directly alongside the gas-works, and under bombs from

---

[2] Lieut. H. W. Ross, D.F.C.; No. 4 Sqn. (previously Artillery). Printer; b. Darlington, Sydney, 1895.

[3] Lieut. V. G. M. Sheppard; No. 4 Sqn. Fruit-grower; of Emu Plains, N.S.W.; b. Emu Plains, 3 Sept., 1894.

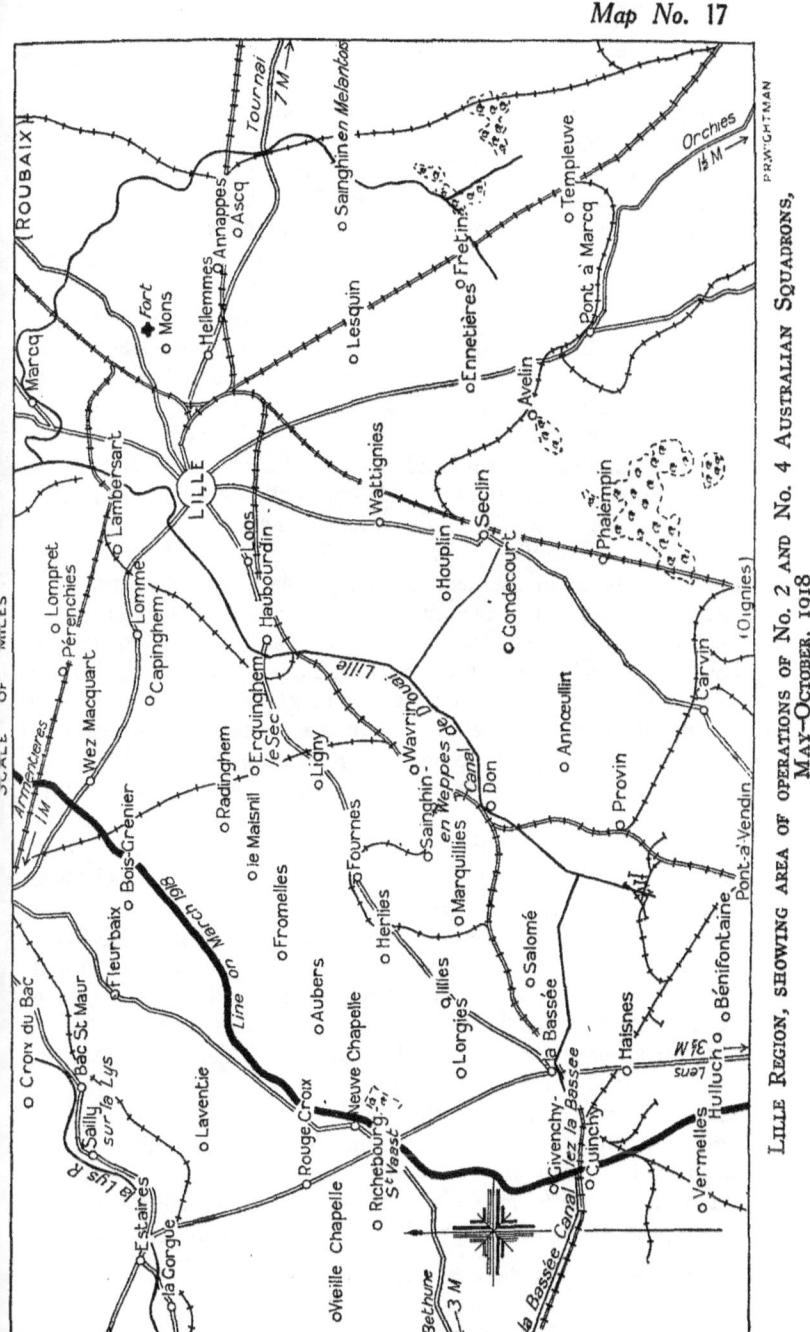

Map No. 17

LILLE REGION, SHOWING AREA OF OPERATIONS OF No. 2 AND No. 4 AUSTRALIAN SQUADRONS, MAY–OCTOBER, 1918

him and Lieutenant A. E. James,[4] who was patrolling with him, the gas chamber exploded as well as the balloon. While a third patrol of four bombed Sainghin railway station, Cobby and King attacked a train just south of Lille from 600 feet. They hit it with four bombs, blew a covered van off the rails, and raked the whole train with machine-gun fire. Returning home, King saw an L.V.G. two-seater at 2,000 feet making westward towards La Bassée. He shot two deadly bursts of fire into it; the two-seater toppled into a spin, its observer fell out, and the machine drifted down to a crash near Erquinghem-le-Sec, west of Haubourdin. Three Fokkers appeared and dived at King while thus engaged, but Cobby was waiting above, intercepted them, and at point-blank range shot their leader down out of control. He could not follow it, for he had to dodge the remaining two Fokkers, which finally left him at 700 feet. Another patrol under Trescowthick bombed Don station. By noon the weather threatened to break, and just before the rain fell James and Lockley set fire to two balloons, one south of Armentières and one at La Bassée. During the bombing attacks, repeated on the following morning, Taplin destroyed another balloon at Pérenchies. The complete absence of German machines from the vicinity of the balloon-lines, or indeed anywhere on the Armentières–La Bassée front, was sure evidence of the straits in which the Germans found themselves.

The afternoon of September 5th was marked by a very gallant fight by a patrol from No. 4 Squadron, which was defeated and almost destroyed. Five machines, under Trescowthick, had been ordered to co-operate with two formations from other squadrons in a sweep of the Douai area. Through some unfortunate misunderstanding the intended co-operation did not take place, and Trescowthick's patrol was attacked by three formations of Fokkers at 11,000 feet over Brebières, south-west of Douai. Trescowthick, leading his force in the orthodox "V"-formation, was flying, therefore, ahead of and below the others. The enemy vastly outnumbered and also had the height of the Australians, and attacked from two sides at once. Trescowthick, seeing no support at hand, and realising that to accept combat was

---
[4] Lieut. A. E. James; No. 4 Sqn. (previously Cyclist Corps). Bank clerk; b. Perth, W. Aust., 1896.

hopeless, gave the signal to avoid action and dived away, expecting his formation to follow suit. It did not. The four remaining—Taplin, Eddie, Carter, and Lockley—either did not see any signal to break off, or found themselves unable to do so. At any rate they stayed and met an attack of overwhelming numbers. Lockley was seen by Trescowthick to stall and meet his first oncoming opponent, fire into it from underneath, and send it down out of control. That was the last clear view of the engagement; the four were fighting at a hopeless disadvantage of position, and none of them returned. Subsequently news was received that all four were shot down, Taplin wounded and taken prisoner, the other three killed. The feelings of the leader, who had to return alone to report this disaster, may be easily imagined. The result was a clear proof of the soundness of his judgment; the Australians were denied from the outset any hope of success; and, after he had dived away, expecting his signal to be followed, to climb back again was beyond the range of possibility. Fighting airmen had always to make decisions on the instant, and such decisions at critical moments are quite beyond recall.

The best account of this fight is in the words of the only survivor of those Australians who took part in it, Lieutenant Taplin. His story of it runs thus:—" We *had* to fight. No signal to avoid action could have had any effect. The escape of one machine (Trescowthick) was due to the Germans' attention being centred upon us four. However, that is neither here nor there. The formation went over the line in " V "-formation—Trescowthick leading, Eddie and Carter above and behind him, and Lockley and myself above and behind them again. When a few miles over we turned north. We were flying at about 14,000 feet and our escort could not be seen; I did not like the situation, and climbed another 1,000 feet above the patrol. Soon after this, when in the region of Douai, we were attacked. There were three formations in the attacking enemy, all Fokker biplanes. Two formations of about twelve to fifteen machines attacked almost simultaneously, one from high up in the west, and one from the north. Later a very much larger formation came in from the east, which I at first thought was our escort coming to our rescue.

"Trescowthick dived away under the formation coming from the direction of our own lines, but the others were cut off. No German attempted to follow Trescowthick, so evidently he was unobserved. Meanwhile I was gaining all the height I could, and, as the formation from the north closed in, I dived into the middle of them. Apparently, by reason of my height, I had not been seen. The leader, a red-and-white-tailed Fokker, pulled up, and we went at it head-on. I got a good burst into his radiator, and he went down on a glide—not out of control, just engine out of action. Next moment I was right in the middle of them, and before I could do anything a German below me pulled his nose up and put a burst right through the bottom of my machine. One bullet went through my right hand, smashing it up and breaking the wrist. My Camel immediately stalled and half-rolled itself, and, to conform with poetic justice, came out of the stall right on the tail of my attacker, who was recovering from his own stall. I was now under control with my left hand and easily shot this German down. Just then I saw Lockley dropping past me completely out of control. I also saw during the fight two machines in flames, which I now suppose were Eddie and Carter.

"I was getting shot about and was firing at anything I saw, when a Fokker from somewhere (the sky seemed full of them) again got a burst into me. One bullet, an explosive, smashed the breech and crank-handle of one of my guns and sent a splinter through my nose. This dazed me and I fell out of control in an engine-spin. I spun down to about 1,000 feet and then recovered, to find two Fokkers had followed me down. I again had to fight, and luckily shot down one German easily; the other then left me alone. After this fight I was down to about 100 feet and started off towards home. My engine was just about done, from being shot about and from running full throttle through everything. I had only one hand and could not properly control the engine to gain height, so just staggered along. After running the gauntlet of ground-fire for several miles I was shot down from the ground when within a few hundred yards of the German front-line, and taken prisoner. I found out from the Germans that

Lockley was buried in Henin Liétard cemetery, but could get no news of the others."

The Australian squadrons avenged this defeat on the following evening at almost the same time and place. They were engaged in a circus sweep—this time in good cohesion—Bristol Fighters from No. 88 Squadron, R.A.F., in the top formation, six S.E.5's under Murray Jones below them, and six Camels below them again. At 14,000 feet seven Fokkers were sighted to the east over Douai, and the Camels flew on slightly below the enemy to decoy them. The Fokkers, evidently not having observed the upper escort, manœuvred to attack. The watching S.E.5's judged the moment well and fell on the Germans in irresistible fashion. F. R. Smith shot one down almost at once and it fell into the wood northeast of Douai. Wellwood drove down another, and followed it, as it tumbled like a leaf for 8,000 feet, firing furiously at every opportunity. The remaining Fokkers span away to escape. In doing so they dropped past the level of the Camels, which instantly fastened on to as many as possible. V. G. M. Sheppard, Wright, and G. Jones each shot down one out of control into the mist covering the ground.

Thereafter for some days air fighting in Flanders died down. There were simply no enemy machines to fight except occasional solitary two-seaters. The bombing of the enemy's discomfited ground-troops on the Aubers Ridge proceeded as usual, but a succession of stormy days checked air operations for nearly a week. The first sign of the return of the enemy's scouts to the Lille area was discerned on September 16th. At dawn that morning Watson and King—one of a number of raiding couples—encountered three black Fokker biplanes north-west of Lille at 4,000 feet. King destroyed one with two close-range bursts of fire; Watson shot down another, but, in the excitement of chasing after the third, did not stay to watch its fate. These machines appear to have been driven into the air by a bomb-attack by Ramsay and A. E. James a quarter of an hour earlier on the now nearly deserted Lomme aerodrome.

Meanwhile an offensive-patrol of eleven S.E.5's under Manuel and F. R. Smith, flying far above the flitting bombing couples of No. 4 Squadron, fell in with a fleet of fifteen Fokker biplanes and triplanes over Lille. The enemy were flying westward toward the lines. Smith led his flight to the east and dived at the enemy from behind; Manuel attacked from the south. Smith dived at the Fokkers' leader, who eluded him with a half-roll; up flew Smith again in a zoom, dived at another Fokker below him, and shot sixty rounds into it from over its tail at point-blank range. This Fokker fell completely out of control and badly damaged. The fight was now general. Smith sent down another Fokker, hit and spinning, from a close-range burst. Lieutenant G. E. Holroyde,[5] somewhere near him, attacked another enemy machine twice without result, but in his third dive separated it from the pack and followed it down, firing at every opportunity, to 8,000 feet. He was then compelled to abandon that combat because another Fokker was firing into him. Manuel, after repeatedly attacking without result, fastened on to a Fokker chasing either Holroyde or another (nothing could be certain in the *mêlée*) and shot it down, whirling and spinning, with a burst of 100 rounds. This Fokker also was followed down for 9,000 feet, still helpless, and then Manuel, too, was forced to turn and engage an enemy machine on his tail. Alberry, who attacked with Manuel's flight, cut out a Fokker early in the fight, and sent it down in flames. Then Alberry in turn was drawn into a fight with two Fokkers descending on him from behind. Copp, also in Manuel's flight, shot down his first opponent, which fell on its back and in this crippled fashion dropped through the air past Smith, lower down. After a few minutes of this savage mix-up, with five of the enemy shot down, one burning, the combatants were spread over a vast area of the sky, and, as they flew to regain formation, the fight ended. Manuel was leading his patrol home at 8 a.m. when he saw British anti-aircraft bursts over La Bassée at 9,000 feet. He made out a Fokker biplane crossing the lines, pursued it to St. Omer, and finally drove it down to a crash north-east of that town.

The defeated Fokker formation had not yet finished its adventures. Lieutenants Barkell, G. Jones, and A. J. Palliser,[6] from No. 4 Squadron, were on offensive-patrol at 7,000 feet

---

[5] Lieut. G. E. Holroyde; No. 2 Sqn. (previously Light Horse). Station hand; b. Brisbane, Oct., 1895.

[6] Lieut. A. J. Palliser; No. 4 Sqn. (previously A.A.S.C.). Motor mechanic; of Launceston, Tas.; b. Launceston, 2 March, 1890. Killed in action, 4 Nov., 1918.

near Armentières shortly after 8 a.m., and, when over Frélinghien, were attacked from above by this same mixed Fokker fleet, now consisting of eleven or twelve machines. Three of them dived at Barkell, four at Palliser, and two at Jones. Barkell and Palliser each rolled smartly and got the upper hand with an Immelmann turn; each then fired a devastating burst at a selected enemy from close range. These two Fokkers fell at once and crashed east of Armentières near the Lys. Jones was attacked a few seconds later than his comrades and just as he had seen a biplane—which had missed Palliser in its dive—swirl away below him. Dropping nose down to escape the enemy machines on his own tail, Jones caught up this lower Fokker, shot it into a spin, and saw it fall on its back to the ground south of Armentières. This enemy formation had by now lost interest in the morning's operations, and flew home.

From this time onward Lille again became a hunting-ground for seekers after hostile aircraft. The German airmen returned to the vicinity in great numbers, but always operated cautiously and at a great height. On September 16th five Fokkers were over Lille as high as 22,000 feet. The enemy, it was judged, was suspicious of preparations now being made for an attack by British and Belgians on this front. He had shortened and strengthened his Flanders front by abandoning the Lys salient; but he had withdrawn so many divisions from this sector in the endeavour to stop breaches in his defences farther south, that his garrisons from Ypres to Lens were still weak in numbers and doubtless shaken in morale. The consequent anxiety was sufficient to account for the renewed local activity of the enemy's airmen. The German machines as a rule avoided combat, thereby indicating that reconnaissance was their chief design; in this they were certainly persistent. For several days the battle-patrols of No. 2 Squadron sought the enemy unsuccessfully. During an otherwise uneventful sweep on September 21st, G. Cox's machine developed engine-defect and was forced to land near Armentières. He was later reported a prisoner of war.

Meanwhile No. 4 Squadron had been constantly and systematically bombing German billets and railway stations between Armentières and La Bassée, and for many days

without any interference from enemy airmen. Lieutenants
Barkell, P. J. Sims,[7] and T. C. Cox[8] were, however, surprised
and nearly overwhelmed on one of these bombing-patrols in
the morning of September 22nd. They were about to attack
Armentières station, when, at 6,000 feet, thirteen Fokker
biplanes came down upon them through the clouds. It was a
desperate situation, and each pilot had to look after himself.
Sims eluded the enemy and flew home; Cox escaped and
landed near Sailly; but Barkell came within an ace of
being lost. Four Fokkers attacked him from above; the
first and nearest Barkell avoided with a half-roll and then a
turn over his opponent's tail. He shot that Fokker down
out of control with a hot burst from his machine-guns at
twenty-five yards' range. Immediately, however, the three
others were upon him; Barkell turned again quickly and shot
another down with a short burst into its side, but then a
bullet pierced his own engine and he had to make for land.
He succeeded in reaching the British lines near Neuve Eglise.
One Fokker, still firing, followed him down to within 100 feet
of the ground. Barkell luckily escaped personal injury.

Early in the morning of September 24th a German two-
seater was reported as reconnoitring British rear areas behind
Ypres. The Fifth Army operations staff considered that
preparations for the coming Anglo-Belgian attack must have
been observed, and requested that this machine should, if
possible, be intercepted and destroyed. Two pairs of scouts
from No. 4 Squadron took off immediately. Lieutenants G.
Jones and V. H. Thornton[9] overhauled the enemy, a Halberstadt, near Lens at 3,000 feet. Jones cut it off from the
east, attacked from underneath, chased the enemy to near the
ground, and shot the observer, whose body fell hanging over
the side of the machine. He then attacked again from above,
both being then only 800 feet above the ground, and fired a
final burst into the Halberstadt at point-blank range. The
two-seater went vertically to the ground and crashed east of
Lens. The other pair—E. J. K. McCloughry and Youdale

---

[7] Lieut. P. J. Sims; No. 4 Sqn. (previously Artillery). Electrical-engineering student; of Springhurst, Vic.; b. Springhurst, 1 Jan., 1896. Killed in action, 29 Oct., 1918.

[8] Lieut. T. C. Cox; No. 4 Sqn. (previously Artillery). Station manager; of Singleton, N.S.W.; b. Quirindi, N.S.W., 4 June, 1895.

[9] Lieut. V. H. Thornton; No. 4 Sqn. (previously Light Horse). Farmer; b. Valparaiso, South America, 11 Dec., 1893.

—finding at first no enemy in the air, bombed a train near Lille and wrecked the rear part of it. McCloughry came in wounded in the foot and with his machine damaged, and landed in a half-conscious state near St. Venant.

After several days of long and fruitless patrols over the German lines in large formations at 12,000 feet, No. 2 Squadron met and severely defeated the enemy in force in the evening of September 24th. The S.E.5 formation was fifteen strong and was ranging west of Lille at 17,000 feet in three flights, the whole under the leadership of Cole. Over Haubourdin at 6.20 p.m. they encountered eleven Fokkers—five at their own level, and six 1,000 feet lower. Simonson's flight of four attacked the upper Fokkers, while the remainder dived on the six below. After a wild engagement of several minutes, Simonson manœuvred on to the tail of one Fokker, delivered a crushing fire, and the enemy fell and was wrecked. Mills also sank one, believed to have met the same fate. Meanwhile, below this combat, Lieutenant F. L. Roberts,[10] of Manuel's flight, shot one of the second Fokker formation down out of control; then suddenly F. R. Smith's flight dived from behind headlong into the whirling fray. Smith, leading, destroyed the nearest Fokker, which fell into a field south of Capinghem. Lieutenant L. Franks[11] followed another down through a long dive to 7,000 feet and saw it crash near Sequedin. At this juncture, just as both formations of Fokkers were more or less dispersed and demoralised, Simonson's formation (still flying higher than the others) was interrupted by the attack of three Pfalz scouts from above. The S.E.5's swirled away to join their comrades below. The Pfalzes, following, came down on Manuel's flight, and Simonson, turning, got on the tail of one and shot into it till it fell on its back and dropped. Smith's, following, had also rallied to the new engagement, and Smith himself dived on to this Pfalz just as Simonson zoomed up from it. He fired further bursts into it, and at 3,000 feet left it, still going down vertically. The other two Pfalz scouts were both destroyed; Wellwood set one in flames and saw it smash into the ground

---

[10] Lieut. F. L. Roberts; No. 2 Sqn. Engineer; of Bendigo, Vic.; b. Bendigo, 18 Aug., 1896.

[11] Lieut. L. Franks; No. 2 Sqn. (previously Artillery). b. Apollo Bay, Vic., 1888.

near Haubourdin areodrome; Cole crashed the other near Pérenchies.

In co-operation with the British, French, and Belgian attack on September 28th, No. 4 Squadron bombed villages and railway stations outside Lille. The Australian airmen were prepared for heavy air fighting, but the enemy attempted no such challenge. Six Camels chased nine Fokkers near Lille in the evening, and J. W. Wright caught up the rearmost Fokker and destroyed it, but the others escaped. The bombing was highly effective, and there were abundant signs from this day onwards of the enemy's preparations to evacuate Lille. The city was steadily becoming a salient in the German lines, and further Allied advance north and south would threaten to envelop it. In the afternoon of September 29th two patrols of three machines each from No. 4 Squadron bombed a small column of horse-transport near Aubers, and fired over 4,000 machine-gun rounds into parties of troops on the roads and village billets. Two others bombed and blew up a dump of ammunition and wrecked a light railway train at Fromelles. The change in the enemy's situation on this northern front led to a revival of low-bombing operations by No. 2 Squadron also, and in the events which led up to the capture of Lille the bombing of both squadrons played an important part.[12]

With the earliest light of dawn on October 1st the entire strength of each squadron was sent out to scour the Lille region, the Camels hunting in pairs low over the Aubers Ridge and the S.E.5's flying in a protecting cloud above them. The low-flying destroyers dropped bombs on railway stations, trains, anti-aircraft batteries, and moving troops and transport, and fired many thousands of rounds into them from a low height. Throughout that day and several days following small patrols were ceaselessly coming and going over the Wavrin-Armentières area, always bombing and shooting every ground target that offered. No German scouts were seen, and the enemy's whole northern front was crumbling away. Balloons were the Germans' chief resource for observation; these were attacked, and often set on fire, whenever they appeared. The Australian low-flying destroyer-patrols harassed and worried everything they saw—trains, motor-lorries, aerodromes, camps,

---
[12] See note at end of chapter.

here and there a battery in action or a barge on a canal; railway stations resounded with the clatter of bomb explosions; from villages invaded and occupied since 1914, the airmen now sped the departing enemy with a scourge like that of avenging angels. In a few days the whole country around Lille began burning. Armentières was re-occupied by British infantry, which swarmed across the Lys in a general advance.

The bombing of the railway stations around Lille became increasingly important during the preparations made by the Germans to evacuate the city, and between October 3rd and 5th the pilots of No. 4 Squadron devoted special attention to the stations on the south-west and south-east. A roving attack by Ramsay and A. E. James at dawn on October 4th began near Pérenchies, where they drove down a badly damaged Rumpler two-seater. They then made a tour of railway stations and aerodromes on the southern outskirts of Lille— Gondecourt, Phalempin, Seclin, Avelin, Merchin, and Houplin —and machine-gunned trains or hangars at all these places after their bombs were exhausted. A 40-lb. phosphorus bomb set fire to hangars at Merchin; two other bombs hit a train at Phalempin. In the early morning of October 5th nine machines from No. 4 Squadron dropped thirty-four bombs on collected railway and transport traffic at Avelin station, and fired over 3,000 rounds into the crowded confusion of the station yard. These were merely instances of the work in which all available British and Australian machines were engaged. The few solitary German two-seaters encountered were chased and shot down. The effect of these attacks on the demoralised enemy was enormous. He simply gave up attempting to save transport and stores in many scattered dépôts and either abandoned them or set them on fire. Scout formations of No. 2 Squadron roamed well beyond Lille into Belgium. Manuel's patrol in the morning of October 4th brought twelve Fokkers to action at 10,000 feet, and Blaxland shot down one. These distant reconnaissance-patrols brought in reports from Tournai and beyond, all confirming the enemy's rearward movement.

Elated with the success of the squadrons' operations on the western side of Lille, the 80th Wing organised for October 7th a grand combined raid on all roads and railway stations on the perimeter of the city. While patrols from No. 4 Australian Squadron ravaged the communications on the west and north of Lille, No. 2 Australian Squadron and No. 103 British Squadron (D.H.9's), protected above by No. 88 Squadron (Bristol Fighters), bore the utmost possible load of bombs for an attack on the entraining centres on the eastern side. That area was divided for the attack into three sections, each bounded by main railway lines. Cummings's flight of No. 2 Squadron was to range the section between the Roubaix and Tournai railways, F. R. Smith's flight that between the Tournai and Orchies lines, and Manuel's flight that between the lines to Orchies and Douai. The Australian formation crossed the lines at 7,000 feet in a tornado of anti-aircraft fire, and over Lille descended to 2,000 feet. Cole, leading, then fired a white light, and on this signal each flight turned off towards its allotted area. The arranged task of No. 2 Squadron was to search those areas for road-transport, while the D.H.9's bombed the big railway stations at Fives and Annappes. Just before the opening of the operations a German two-seater appeared out of the haze before the full array of the bombing fleet and flew for the ground in panic; without a shot fired at it, this German machine hit the earth nose first near Ennetières and was wrecked.

The S.E.5's spread out under flight-commanders' leadership to range the country towards Tournai, but found on the roads there none of the expected traffic. The only activity to be seen was at Annappes and Fives, where a number of trains were being loaded with troops and stores. Fives was especially busy, and a long troop-train was steaming into the station. Accordingly the Australian raiders joined the D.H.9's in attacking these centres. The flights under Cummings and Manuel made for Annappes, and Smith's flight for Fives. At Fives the D.H.9's dropped twenty bombs of a hundredweight each, and in their wake each machine of Smith's formation swept along the lines of trains with a shower of smaller bombs. Each pilot, having released his explosives, turned and again flew the length of the station, spraying the trains and buildings with machine-gun fire. The airmen flew in this attack so low that in several cases pilots' machines were damaged by fragments of their own bombs. A piece of one of Lieutenant A. L. Long's[13] bombs pierced his petrol tank. Long now had only his reserve tank, about ten minutes' supply. He flew straight for the British lines and just managed to reach them as he was forced to land. The losses of the enemy both at Fives and Annappes must have been considerable, for many bombs fell fairly among massed transport and on crowded railway carriages and buildings where troops from the trains fled for shelter. Near Annappes several machines attacked a farmhouse courtyard packed with motor cars and horse-transport, and the bombs hurtled into the midst of this collection.

The 80th Wing similarly raided Tournai on October 18th, the day on which Lille fell into British hands. No. 4 Squadron patrolled the area immediately east of Lille with a large formation of their new Sopwith Snipe[14] machines, while this raid was in progress. The Germans were falling back from Lille as fast as they could, and Tournai and the villages in its vicinity were found crowded with the impedimenta of the retreat. Just north-west of the town, at Froyennes, was an aerodrome still in active use. This and the railway station at Allain, on the south-eastern outskirts of Tournai, and the villages of Hertain and Marquain on the west, were the chief objectives of the raid. Cummings, leading the squadron formation, descended over Hertain on a train mounting an anti-aircraft battery and on much transport collected alongside it. One of his bombs fell directly upon one gun of this battery and another exploded a dump near by. Cole, Stone, Franks, and Davies all bombed Froyennes aerodrome and burned at least two hangars. Other pilots were attracted by trains at either Blandain or Allain. Simonson, Roberts, and Dibbs hit the train which Cummings had attacked, or the transport alongside it. Some of the escorting Bristol Fighters did the same. Transport was overturned, many horses fell, the locomotive was hit twice by bombs, trucks and carriages began to burn, and men scattered and dropped in all directions. Lieutenants Blaxland, Copp,

---

[13] Lieut. A. L. Long; No. 2 Sqn. (previously A.A.M.C.). Commercial traveller; of Hobart; b. Ringwood, Forcett, Tas., 15 Aug., 1896.

[14] See Chapter XXVI.

N. M. Heath,[15] J. A. Egan,[16] and Alberry attacked Allain and the siding at the main station north-east of Tournai. Their bombs wrecked trucks and set railway buildings on fire, and they had begun to pelt the confusion with machine-gun bullets, when a formation of Fokkers dived at them. The escort overhead promptly engaged them, but near Allain Blaxland and Alberry had to meet the attack of three Fokkers. Blaxland crashed one of them south-east of Tournai; Alberry chased down another, firing at it till his guns jammed, and left it in a spin only 800 feet above the ground. Lieutenants F. Howard[17] and Long bombed a château and military huts near Froyennes aerodrome; two bombs hit the château and others set the huts on fire. The only casualty suffered was that Davies had his oil-tank shot through by machine-gun fire, and owing to loss of oil, the pilot crashed, unhurt, within the British lines on the way home.

Note.—Extracts from operation orders of Major Murray Jones, commanding No. 2 Squadron, for the days of September 24th and 30th show the system of combined air operations at this time:—

(September 23rd.) " The following operations will be carried out to-morrow, the 24th instant. . . . Offensive Patrols: All offensive-patrols will work in the area bounded by the line Armentières–Pérenchies–Haubourdin–Provin–Pont-à-Vendin.   (*a*) 0900–1100. 'A' Flight, 10,000 feet; 'B' Flight, 9,000 feet. Rendezvous with No. 4 Squadron and No. 88 Squadron over E. edge of Forêt de Nieppe at above heights, 0935. When rendezvous is complete leader of No. 4 Squadron will fire a RED light which will be returned by the leader of our patrol and the formation will then move off. Care is to be taken that our patrols keep within striking distance of any enemy E.A. attacking the lower formation."

(September 29th.) " 1. Situation: Local Offensive Operations will be undertaken on the Fifth Army front to-morrow, 30th instant. All machines not actually working on offensive-patrols will stand by for bombing, and shooting-up favourable ground targets, and for low line work.

" 2. Low Line Patrols: The following pilots will, if necessary, carry out low line patrols:—Captains A. T. Cole, R. L. Manuel, E. D. Cummings, Lieutenants F. R. Smith, E. E. Davies, J. J. Wellwood. These patrols will work at 2,000 feet over the battle-front, paying extra attention to low-flying E.A. No bombs will be carried. Machines will work in pairs. It must be thoroughly understood that the responsibility of preventing the enemy from using low-bombing or

---

[15] Lieut. N. M. Heath; No. 2 Sqn. (previously Light Horse). Grazier; b. Malvern, Melbourne, 1895.

[16] Lieut. J. A. Egan; No. 2 Sqn. Bank clerk; b. Bendigo, Vic., Aug., 1891.

[17] Lieut. F. Howard; No. 2 Sqn. (previously Engineers). Railway engineering assistant; b. Clunes, Vic., 1894. Killed in action, 27 Oct., 1918.

shooting-up aircraft will rest on them; great damage can be done by the enemy in dispersing our reserves by use of his aircraft at low altitudes. This must be prevented at all costs.

"3. Low-bombing and Shooting-up Patrols: Machines will carry four 20-lb. bombs, and will shoot-up and bomb the enemy's convoys, troops, M.T., &c. No bombing or shooting-up will take place within 3,000 yards of our advanced troops and extending back to 15,000 yards. The chief rôle of these patrols is to disturb enemy in the back areas by dispersing troops, attacking M.T. convoys, &c., and harassing continually all active targets, of which many are bound to present themselves. Machines will fly low enough to distinguish between grey, blue, and khaki uniforms.

"4. Offensive Patrols: Offensive patrols will work in area bounded by Armentières–Pérenchies–Haubourdin–Provin–Pont-à-Vendin. They will on no account fly above 10,000 feet, and if all ammunition is not expended in combats machines will attack ground targets before leaving area.

0600–0800	..	'C' Flight	.. 10,000 feet.
		'A' Flight	.. 8,000 feet.
0800–1000	..	'B' Flight	.. 10,000 feet.
1500–1700	..	'A' Flight	.. 10,000 feet.
		'C' Flight	.. 8,000 feet."

CHAPTER XXVI

THE LAST GREAT AIR BATTLES

THE retreat of the Germans on the northern front left the Reclinghem aerodrome too far behind the lines, and at the end of September both No. 2 and No. 4 Squadrons moved a few miles farther east to Serny. From that date onwards a series of moves followed the rapid Allied advance. By October 30th the Australian aerodrome was at Auchel, just north of Bruay, the former home of No. 4 Squadron; six days later the squadrons were camped on the field which they had recently harried so pertinaciously south of Lille—No. 2 at Pont-à-Marcq, and No. 4 at Ennetières.

At Serny No. 4 Squadron acquired its Sopwith Snipe scouts, and during the second and third weeks of October it exchanged all its Camels for these machines. The Snipe was then the last word in scout design, and when, after the armistice, No. 4 Squadron took its Snipes with it to Cologne and showed their manœuvring powers in the air to some German airmen, these expressed their astonishment and also their gratification that personally they had had no occasion to meet it in action.[1] The appearance of the Snipes in the last strenuous air fighting was signally effective.

That period began in the second week of October. The circumstances which introduced it have already been explained. After the Hindenburg Line battles in early October the Germans realised that their only hope of preventing a mightier Sedan lay in withdrawal from France and Belgium. The rugged country of the Meuse behind them made such a general retreat no easy operation; the greater part of their still numerous forces had to retreat, as they had originally advanced, through Belgium and the bottle-neck of Liège. To protect this movement the enemy transferred the bulk of his air force to the northern front.

Lieutenants H. N. Kerr[2] and Thornton, from No. 4

---

[1] The Snipe, a single-seater fighting scout, 200 horse-power Bentley engine, carried two Vickers guns firing through the propeller. The interrupter-gear was of a different type from that used in the Camel, and the squadron mechanics had heavy work putting this gear into proper order.

[2] Lieut. H. N. Kerr; No. 4 Sqn. (previously Light Horse). Clerk; of Brisbane; b. Ithaca, Brisbane, 30 Sept., 1892.

Squadron, at dawn on October 9th were surprised to find a D.F.W. two-seater as far over the British lines as Nieppe, as low as 4,000 feet, and actually attacking them.[3] The two Australians shot it down to a forced landing near Nieppe and captured it intact, but Kerr, landing near it, crashed through striking some telephone wires, and was seriously injured. A few hours later Cole, leading a patrol of five S.E.5's west of Lille, found the sky in that region thick with enemy scouts, and counted forty or fifty in various formations. One of these formations, consisting of eight Fokkers, they engaged at 12,000 feet. F. R. Smith dived from 18,000 feet upon four of them and fired fifty rounds at close range into the topmost Fokker, which fell into a spin and then dropped like a stone. Franks, who dived with Smith, was counter-attacked by five other Fokkers, but the remaining S.E.5's fell on these from above. The enemy turned and flew for home; Lieutenant J. A. H. McKeown,[4] however, shot one down out of control, and Franks another, before the Germans escaped. Ten more Fokkers then appeared on the scene, but the Australians were too scattered to meet this challenge and, in their turn, withdrew. Just after this fight ended, four more S.E.5's, under Manuel, appeared at about 13,000 feet. These also observed a formation of twenty Fokkers flying high over Haubourdin, and some two-seaters still higher up. None of them, however, attacked Manuel. His patrol turned south and, after shooting down a solitary Halberstadt over Pont-à-Vendin, flew home.

After an interval of a few days of bad weather, both British and German machines again took the air in great force on October 14th. Cummings and Smith each led a flight of S.E.5's across the lines south of Lille in the forenoon, Smith's patrol on a bombing raid against Fretin railway station, and Cummings's to escort Smith. Of the escort-patrol Cummings, Simonson, Blaxland, and Dibbs were at 16,000 feet, with

---

[3] This was a sufficiently extraordinary event, in that, during the last twelve months or more of the war, air combats hardly ever occurred on the British side of the lines. Whenever the Australian airmen met German machines over Allied territory, the Germans were either at a great height—too high to be caught—or instantly turned home without accepting battle. British pilots always counted it a handicap against them that enemy machines, almost certainly destroyed, but without confirmation of the destruction by other witnesses, could so rarely be claimed by wreckage which could be visited on the ground.

[4] Lieut. J. A. H. McKeown; No. 2 Sqn. (previously Infantry). Baker; of Werribee, Vic.; b. Romsey, Vic., 23 Oct., 1894. Killed in action, 14 Oct., 1918.

Davies and Captain E. W. Cornish[5] in rear of them and about 1,000 feet higher. A few minutes after 10 o'clock Cummings perceived a formation of sixteen Fokkers some distance below and flying in a north-easterly direction. All four S.E.5's on the lower level dived to attack, while Davies and Cornish flew above the fight to safeguard their comrades from possible interference. Leading the attack, Cummings fired a short burst at 100-yards' range into one Fokker, which dived steeply away, but in his descent the German evidently saw the machines of Smith's bombing formation approaching, and zoomed up again eastward. Cummings was waiting for this, dived on the Fokker again, and shot it down to a crash near Cysoing. The Australians, much scattered, pursued the enemy in a running fight eastward for nearly a quarter of an hour, and Blaxland destroyed one Fokker in flames over Chereng. Dibbs, describing this fight, said:—"After a head-on encounter with one German, in which we liberally sprayed one another with tracer-bullets, I looked around and could see but one other S.E.5 in the fight. This machine, which I afterwards ascertained to be Blaxland's, was in the centre of a bunch of Fokkers, and tracer-ammunition seemed to be flying in all directions. As I turned towards Blaxland, he zoomed suddenly, and I followed him. Together we climbed above the German machines, which, apparently anticipating a renewed attack, dived away east. Both of Blaxland's and one of my guns were jammed and, while we were clearing the stoppages, seven Fokkers appeared from the south and passed a few hundred feet above us. They appeared not to see us, and flew unconcernedly on their way. However, being unable to resist the temptation to put a burst into one of them, I pulled up the nose of my S.E.5 and gave the rear left-hand machine twenty rounds with the remaining serviceable gun. The Germans were forthwith galvanised into activity, and, half-rolling, down they came. Blaxland and I dropped vertically, with stick well forward and a touch of the throttle, and left the German machines behind us. We did not see the remaining members of our own formation, from whom we had been separated in the fight, until we landed at the aerodrome."

---

[5] Capt. E. W. Cornish, M.C.; No. 2 Sqn. (previously Infantry). Clerk; b. Apr., 1897.

Meanwhile Smith's formation had appeared, flying lower, and was dropping bombs at Fretin, while Cummings's fight was proceeding. Some of the engaged Fokkers dived on Smith's patrol, but were avoided and beaten off. Smith's S.E.5's, having dropped their bombs, turned westward in a steady climb to reach the level of the fight. When they arrived at 16,000 feet, however, the sky was clear. They flew on in a left-hand sweep towards Tourcoing, as Cummings's patrol had done before them, and north of Lille saw, slightly below them, eight Fokkers manœuvring to attack some British machines lower down. Smith at once dived on the rearmost Fokker and destroyed it in flames. This counter-attack drove the enemy below the British machines, and the Fokkers immediately turned eastward to escape. Two of them, however, strayed from their formation, and Australian and British scouts together cut these off. Smith and Franks, leading, dived on the unfortunate Germans, then near Mouveaux, and each destroyed one.

Manuel's patrol at midday over this same area saw no hostile aircraft, but Smith led out ten machines again in the afternoon, and at 4 o'clock met twelve Fokkers at 16,000 feet over the Scheldt River, north-west of Tournai. A general "dog-fight" at once began, and extended for nearly twenty-five minutes over a wide spread of sky. As the opposing formations met almost head-on, Smith attacked the leader and, after a long burst of fire, ending at almost touching range, this Fokker fell and crashed near the little village of Havron, on the bank of the Scheldt. Stone and Roberts each shot down one German out of control at the first encounter. Smith turned to attack another Fokker on the tail of Stone's machine, fired 100 rounds into it, and that too went down steeply, turning very slowly. Meanwhile Stone, having put his first opponent out of action, found himself at 9,000 feet and in position to dive on another Fokker, which was climbing for the upper air. Into this he fired ninety rounds at deadly close range and saw it crash on the river bank. The fight had now broken up into a scattered series of duels. Three wrecked machines were seen to be lying on the river bank near Havron, but one of these may have been an Australian, for two of our pilots were shot down in the engagement—McKeown killed,

Map No. 18

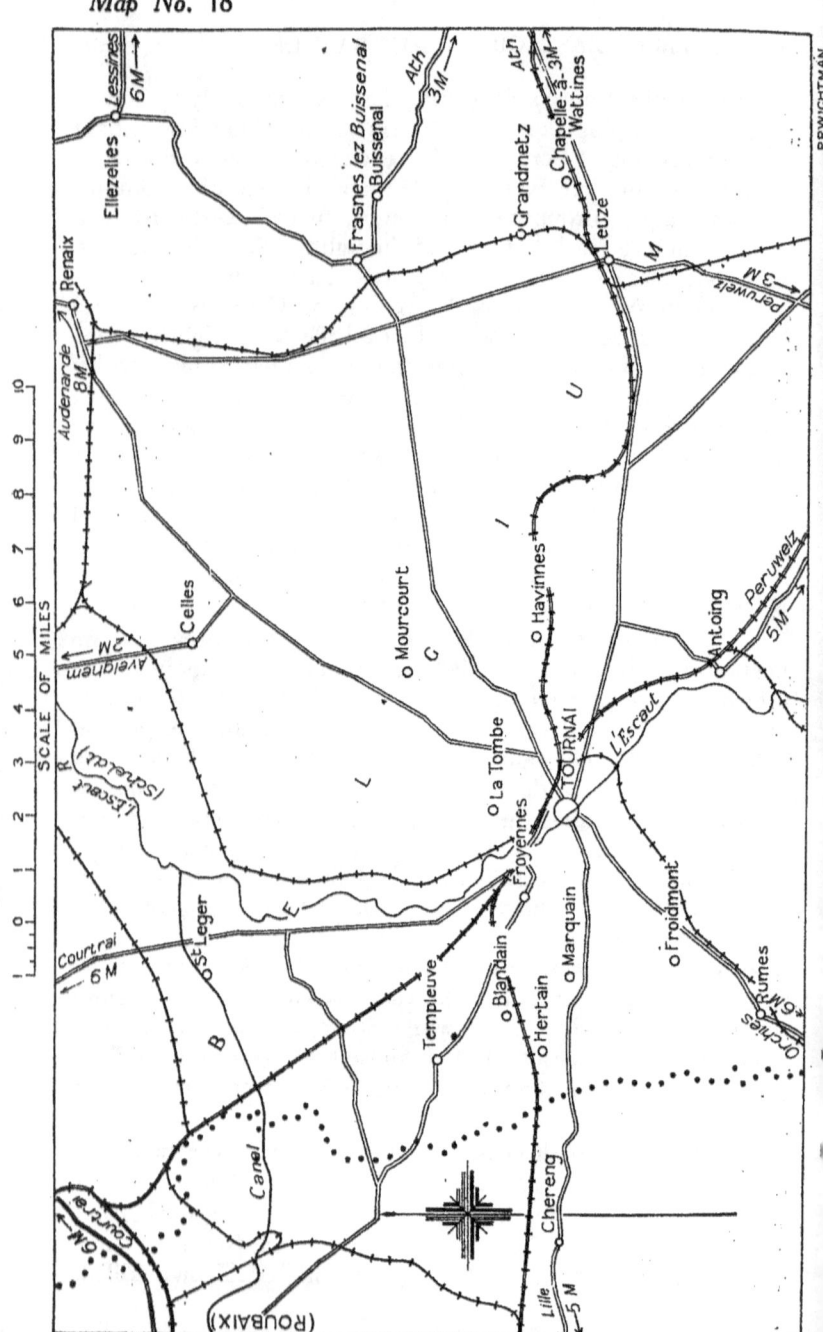

Composite photograph and drawing, showing an attack by a British scout-formation through a cloud upon a German formation

In the distance enemy machines are turning to counter-attack.

From the collection of the late Lieut.-Col. W. O. Watt, No. 2 Sqn., A.F.C.

To face p. 374.

AEROPLANE PHOTOGRAPH OF A POINT IN THE HINDENBURG LINE, SHOWING SYSTEMS OF TRENCHES AND WIRE

Lent by Capt. K. A. Goodland, 29th Bn., A.I.F.
Aust. War Museum Collection No. J205.

Cornish taken prisoner. Cornish was lost through his lack of experience in air fighting. He was a newly-joined pilot, and had won his captaincy in the infantry. He was a reckless fighter, and his comrades in the squadron were dismayed to see him during this engagement pursue one German, clinging hard upon its tail, through and below a bunch of other Fokkers, regardless of the danger to which he was thus exposing himself. Several of those other enemy machines promptly dived on him and shot him down.

During his withdrawal from Lille to the east of the Scheldt the enemy was favoured by bad flying weather—rain and clouds and haze—and took every advantage of it. The Australian airmen next met the German scouts far east of the Scheldt, which by October 22nd was the westernmost German line. The enemy held this broad and marshy river from Valenciennes northward as far as Avelghem with strong machine-gun rear-guards, while the remainder of his army made all haste across Belgium towards the Rhine. In this season of bad weather, No. 2 and No. 4 Squadrons moved their hangars to new grounds near Lille—Pont-à-Marcq and Ennetières. From Ennetières on October 26th Baker and Barkell led a double-patrol of nine of the new Snipe machines to the east of Tournai, and about 3.45 p.m. at 14,000 feet came upon fifteen Fokkers. The Snipes manœuvred into the afternoon sun and approached the Fokkers' level. As the two formations met, several of the enemy began to spin away, and when several Snipes dived at them a hot fight began. Barkell destroyed one Fokker in flames and sent down another out of control. Baker engaged the Fokker leader, but both the Snipe's guns jammed; a few seconds later Baker again attacked the German, then on the tail of another Snipe, and shot him down, badly damaged. Lieutenants E. J. Richards[6] and H. W. Ross likewise each drove down a Fokker out of control. The fight died out with the machines spread over a wide area. Barkell, wounded in one leg, landed as far away as Péronne, and a comrade machine with him.

During the next two days offensive-patrols from both Australian squadrons reconnoitred far into Belgium and

---

[6] Lieut. E. J. Richards; No. 4 Sqn. (previously Infantry). Journalist; b. Tyrendarra, Vic., 13 May, 1888.

half-way towards Brussels. Few enemy machines were met; the weather was cloudy, with high winds; and only a few fleeting engagements took place. From one such engagement on October 27th F. Howard, of No. 2 Squadron, was shot down and killed over Tournai. Next day the Germans took the air in great numbers, and Cole's forenoon patrol of fourteen machines from No. 2 Squadron, ranging as far east as Ath and Mons, found the sky strewn with ragged formations of scouts and two-seaters of all types. Many of these were too distant to engage, but about 11.15 a.m. twelve Fokkers were seen over Peruwelz attacking a bombing formation of D.H.9's at 15,000 feet.. Cole immediately led his formation to the attack. He himself intercepted the leading Fokker at the tail of the rearmost D.H.9, engaged it in a furious duel, and after firing 300 rounds into it, mostly at close range, set it on fire. The German pilot jumped from his machine with a parachute and "apparently descended safely."[7] He must have had an exciting journey earthwards, for, besides his own machine, several other Fokkers tumbled near him over the same distance—two in flames, shot down by Blaxland and Alberry; a fourth, shot down by Alberry and crashed near Peruwelz; and a fifth, shot down in a crippled spin by Stone. The S.E.5's, having dispersed this formation, chased six other Fokkers as far as Mons without overhauling them. Activity in the air was pronounced throughout the afternoon, when twelve S.E.5's under Murray Jones set out at 2 p.m. to bomb the town of Lessines, north of Ath, accompanied by an escort of ten Snipes under King. The sky over the Dendre River was thick with Fokkers; in the neighbourhood of Lessines alone there were one formation of fifteen at 10,000 feet and two more of seven and four respectively at 7,000. The S.E.5's dropped their cargo of bombs hastily on the town, and, without waiting to observe results, climbed to the combat. Meanwhile King and his Snipes had arrived over Ath, and at 12,000 feet attacked and annihilated a formation of six or seven Fokkers. The enemy was slightly higher, but did not seem to be aware of the Snipes, until King, finishing a climb, half-rolled on the leader

---

[7] This was the first instance recorded by the Australian Flying Corps of any airman leaving an aeroplane by parachute.

and fired his opening rounds into the enemy at fifty feet. The Fokker spun away under continual fire for 3,000 feet and then dropped on its back. Major W. A. McCloughry, in that part of the patrol which followed King, fastened on to another enemy and fired at him till he crashed outside Ath. Palliser shot down a third, which also fell near Ath, and, while climbing to rejoin formation, engaged and destroyed another Fokker. Baker led the other half of the Snipe formation to the attack from the sun and shot down the remaining two Fokkers—the first one completely out of control, and the second observed to crash near Ath. The S.E.5's were unable to reach the level of the fight before it was over, except one machine piloted by Simonson, who at 6,000 feet shot down one Fokker which was attacking a Snipe and followed it with a rattle of fire till it fell on the ground south of Lessines. Egan, of this formation, while climbing from the bombing, met an L.V.G. two-seater and destroyed it.

As King's formation of Snipes was returning home, it passed four other Snipes from No. 4 Squadron under H. W. Ross. These had hardly crossed the Scheldt over Tournai when twelve Fokkers dived at them. The Germans must have been astonished when the Snipes, instead of turning away with the usual tactics, put their noses up and climbed at wonderful speed to meet the attack. The manœuvre threw the Fokkers into confusion, and one of them, which got below Ross, received a shattering fire of 200 rounds from the double guns at fifty yards, and went down on its back.

These engagements were followed next day, October 29th, by one of the greatest air battles of the war. British machines were penetrating too far for his liking over the enemy's line of retreat, and his full available air force was now concentrated to thwart this reconnaissance. Early in the fine but hazy afternoon fifteen Snipes under King and Baker left the aerodrome for offensive-patrol of the area east of Tournai. This force towards the end of its patrol met about sixty Fokkers just east of Tournai flying at varying heights. Several British two-seaters were in the offing lower down. Five Fokkers promptly attacked King, who was flying lower than the others. King spun away to avoid them and at 3,000 feet ran across an L.V.G. two-seater in his path. Attacking this, he missed at the first dive, but returned a few minutes later, met the two-seater head-on, and destroyed it.

Meanwhile the others, at various levels between 14,000 and 11,000 feet, were fiercely engaged. Three machines led by G. Jones at 11,000 feet were the first in action, when, climbing to meet fifteen Fokkers just above them, they saw ten of this formation dive towards the British two-seaters. Jones's force at once attacked the ten, and at the same moment six Snipes under Ross entered the fight with a swarm of fresh Fokkers. Jones in his dive destroyed two of the enemy in quick succession; one crashed north-east of Tournai, and the other burst into flames. Almost simultaneously Palliser set another Fokker on fire. He turned at once to attack a second which whizzed past him on the tail of a Snipe, and destroyed that enemy also. Then four Fokkers in turn attacked him, and he was obliged to spin away to escape them. The air was so thick with German machines that, high or low, in every direction, a machine leaving the ruck of a fight could not fail to meet them. So Palliser, diving for safety, found another enemy lower down in his path, and this, too, he shot down out of control with a burst of eighty rounds ripped into the enemy as he dropped. Jones's patrol of three completely dispersed that particular body of Fokkers, but lost Sims. Sims was seen by Palliser to destroy one Fokker in flames, but shortly afterwards was himself shot down and killed.

Ross's formation of six had meanwhile taken up the combat at 11,000 feet. Ross himself picked off a Fokker from the tail of another Australian machine, fired one short burst into it at close range, and saw it crash at Mourcourt, north-east of Tournai. Lieutenants Thornton and O. Lamplough,[8] attacking with him, shot down two more Fokkers, one being seen to hit the ground in a wreck. Baker led his five machines to the attack from the sun, but the fight was at the moment so confused that for a few minutes none of these Snipes found an enemy. Then Baker attacked two Fokkers hard on the tail of another Snipe, and destroyed one of them between Mourcourt and Tournai. Several of the Snipes in this engagement were very badly shot about, and Cottam was forced to land, damaged, at Menin on the way home.

---

[8] Lieut. O. Lamplough, D.F.C.; No. 4 Sqn. (previously Infantry). Bank clerk; of Caulfield, Melbourne; b. Donald, Vic., 13 March, 1897.

In the following afternoon, October 30th, strong morning patrols from both Australian squadrons observed considerable activity at the German aerodrome at Rebaix, just north of Ath. It was resolved to attack this aerodrome in the afternoon. Twelve S.E.5's from No. 2 Squadron and a formation of D.H.9's with heavier bombs composed the raiding party, while eleven Snipes under King formed the escort. The wing-commander (Colonel Strange) took part in the bombing in a Sopwith Camel. The scouts dropped fifty-one bombs in the Rebaix aerodrome, and destroyed several hangars. In front of the hangars were seven or eight L.V.G. two-seaters lined up on the ground, and at least three of these were reported wrecked.

A cloud of Fokkers arrived during the bombing, and were met by the Snipes at 4,000 feet over Leuze. King and H. A. Wilkinson[9] opened the action by attacking two Fokkers which were diving at a D.H.9. Wilkinson shot his opponent into flames and King sent his down badly crippled, but could not follow it below 1,000 feet, as four Fokkers then set upon him from all sides at once. King, in his own words, " zoomed up through their formation and turned across in front of the highest enemy machine, which I had not previously seen. This machine fell over on its back in avoiding a collision, and, so doing, fell on a second Fokker which was zooming up at me below him. These two machines fell to pieces and crashed." Trescowthick destroyed another Fokker from a formation of eleven, and Baker at 8,000 feet shot down one so badly damaged that it dropped on its back, tail first, and when last seen was still falling in that attitude at 2,000 feet. The Australians lost Lieutenant M. J. Kilsby,[10] a newly-joined pilot, who was forced to land in enemy territory and was taken prisoner.

During these days all the British squadrons practically lived over the enemy's lines. With the whole German Army in rapid retreat eastward, the main roads and railways were crowded night and day with their troops and transport. All attempt to conceal the situation was abandoned. The morale of that once iron-disciplined army was abandoned also. Where appeals by the officers to German patriotism were still effective,

---

[9] Lieut. H. A. Wilkinson; No. 4 Sqn. Fitter and turner; b. 31 July, 1893.
[10] Lieut. M. J. Kilsby; No. 4 Sqn. Station hand; b. Mount Gambier, S. Aust., 1895.

the troops obeyed their leaders under the assurance that mutiny would involve them in a worse disaster. But often appeals to patriotism and discipline were of no effect; many of the German soldiers were already revolutionaries, after the pattern of the Russian Army. Only the best troops made any stand against the irresistible Allied advance. Among those who fought to the last were the German airmen, and the odds against them in the sky were overwhelming.

The four days after the air battles on October 29th and 30th were stormy and wet. The enemy kept out of the air and our own men flew little over the lines. In an interval of better weather on November 1st Cummings and Davies destroyed a solitary L.V.G. two-seater over Antoing. Then a bright day on November 4th brought on several severe air-fights east of Tournai. This was also the day of the last great British attack, at Landrecies, thirty miles to the south. All three flights of No. 2 Squadron left the aerodrome at 7 o'clock that morning, and while they were sweeping a few miles east of Renaix, Davies, flying at 15,000 feet, dived at an L.V.G. two-seater at 12,000 and destroyed it. Almost immediately afterwards, Stone and Wellwood, in Blaxland's flight, sighted seven Fokker scouts near Renaix, and, being closer than the other S.E.5's, promptly attacked. The Fokkers began circling and losing height. Wellwood fired several bursts before he overhauled and engaged one Fokker at close range, which then fell away and crashed near the village of Tombelle, south-east of Renaix. Stone also destroyed a selected opponent. By this time Davies' flight joined the combat and dived out of the sun upon the Fokker formation. Davies fired 120 rounds into one machine, saw it fall on its back and spin slowly down, but was then himself overturned in the air by a near anti-aircraft burst. Simonson, following Davies, shot another Fokker into a somersault and it also crashed near Tombelle.

A couple of hours later, Cato, leading four Snipes from No. 4 Squadron, saw seven Fokkers a little above him at 10,000 feet north-east of Tournai. Joining four British S.E.5's, he climbed towards the enemy. The S.E.5's manœuvred to the north, and the Snipes to the south, of the enemy, and, having made their height, dived at the Fokkers from 15,000 feet. Cato shot one down out of control, but two of the Snipes were lost in the scrimmage; Lieutenant E. J. Goodson,[11] hit by an anti-aircraft shell, crashed in the canal at Tournai, and Lieutenant C. W. Rhodes,[12] a newly-joined pilot, shot down in combat. Both were taken prisoner.

At noon the whole wing took the air to harass the German retreat on the Leuze–Ath road and to raid the aerodrome at Chapelle-à-Wattines just north of it, east of Leuze. The full squadron of Snipes formed the escort. Every machine of No. 2 Squadron was loaded up with bombs for the low-flying attack, as were also the heavier British bombers of the D.H.9 squadron. The S.E.5's were about to descend and bomb the aerodrome at Wattines, when the leading machines were attacked by five Fokkers at 4,000 feet from the north-east. A number of other Fokkers appeared above these five. The Australians released their bombs in a shower at the aerodrome and at once joined combat with the enemy. Colonel Strange (flying a Sopwith Camel) and the D.H.9's proceeded to a more leisurely bombing, and saw four hangars burning, one fired by No. 2 Squadron's bombs. Strange then flew in a northerly circle and with machine-gun fire stampeded horse-transport and troops at Grandmetz and at Leuze station. Meanwhile the first five Fokkers were all shot down after a furious encounter—two by Davies, and one each by Blaxland, Stone, and Simonson. The ground was hidden by a thick carpet of cloud, and into this the Fokkers fell spinning, one by one; beyond it they could not be watched. Of the upper Fokkers only three or four came down to fight, but these, on sighting the Snipes, sheered off.

King, leading the Snipes, escorted the bombers back across the lines and then, seeing twelve Fokkers following his formation, turned back, climbed, and dived on the enemy's leader. He fired 150 rounds into this machine, which stalled, fell on its side, and dropped earthward on its back. A general scrimmage ensued. King fastened on to another Fokker, which was shooting on the tail of a Snipe, and sent it down in flames after four rapid bursts of fire at 100-feet range. G. Jones attacked the rearmost German of the formation,

---

[11] Lieut. E. J. Goodson; No. 4 Sqn. (previously Infantry). Motor driver; b. Upton-on-Severn, Eng., 27 Apr., 1892.

[12] Lieut. C. W. Rhodes; No. 4 Sqn. Surveyor's assistant; of Sydney; b. Perth, W. Aust., 31 May, 1894.

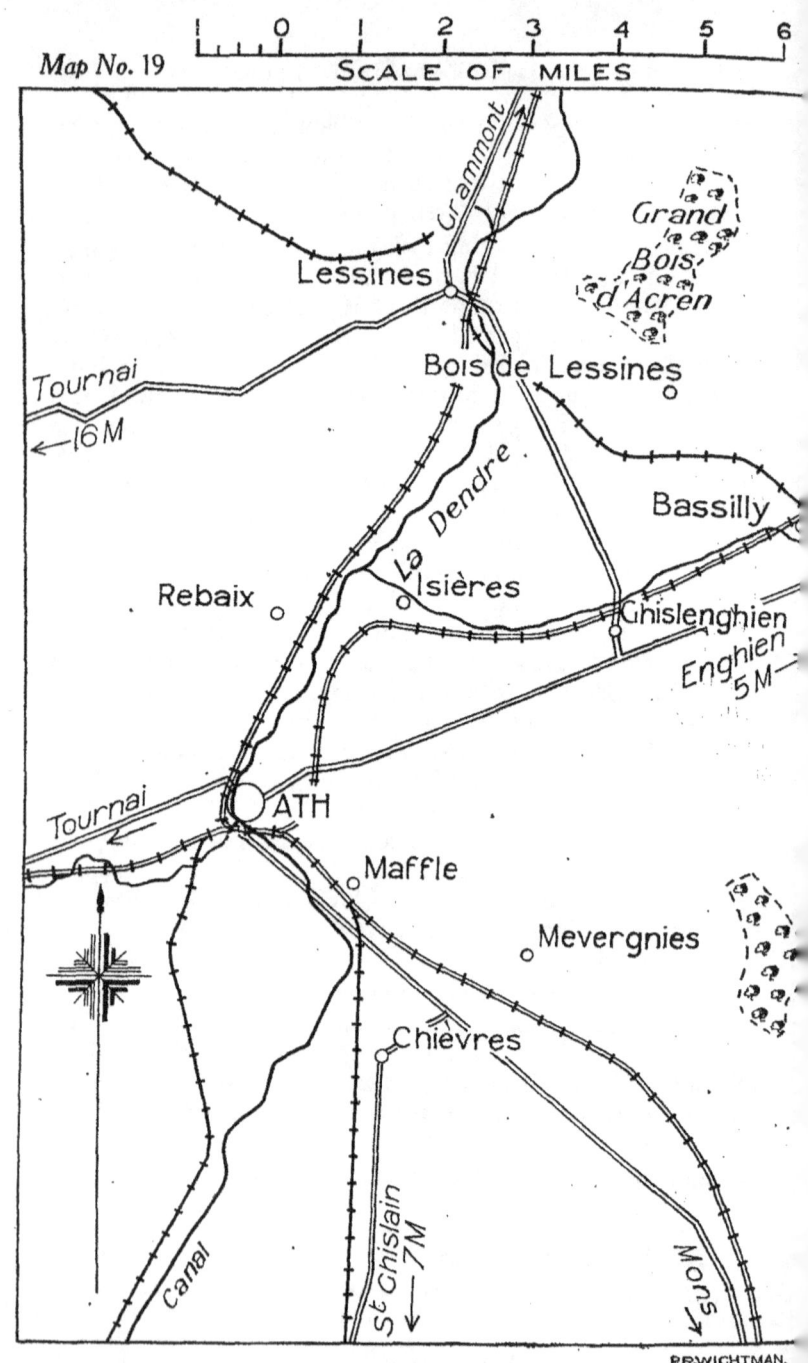

ATH REGION, SHOWING AREA OF OPERATIONS OF No. 2 AND No. 4 AUSTRALIAN SQUADRONS, OCTOBER AND NOVEMBER, 1918

A BIG HANDLEY-PAGE BOMBER, OF THE TYPE USED BY THE ROYAL AIR FORCE ON BOMBING RAIDS INTO GERMANY

Aust. War Museum Official Photo. No. E3733.

Skeleton of a large Gotha bomber, in the hands of No. 4 Squadron, A.F.C., at Cologne, Germany, December, 1918

Aust. War Museum Official Photo. No. E4147.

overran it during his opening fusillade, and sped on to another, which was attacking H. A. Wilkinson. This Fokker also fell in flames. Wilkinson, delivered from it, dropped with a quick turn on two more Fokkers behind and below him, fired a close-range burst into the nearer one, and saw it fall out of control. Such is the vignette of a short and willing encounter preserved in the laconic narratives of the Australian pilots. The fight lasted but two or three minutes, and died out in the usual way, with machines spread over a wide area and making to regain formation. When the Snipes had re-formed it was found that three splendid pilots had been lost in the action—Baker (a flight-commander), and Lieutenants Palliser and P. W. Symons.[13]

By November 8th the enemy rear-guards were in full retreat from the Scheldt, and the British and Belgians were pursuing them towards Mons and Brussels as fast as damaged roads and railways and destroyed bridges would permit. The morning patrol of No. 2 Squadron on November 9th reported explosions along the road and railway from Ath to Enghien, and in the afternoon another large bombing expedition, the full strength of the 80th Wing, attacked these communications and an aerodrome at Marcq, on the south side of Ath. A hangar and a Fokker on the ground outside it were destroyed by a few bombs dropped at Marcq aerodrome. The raiders then flew towards Enghien. From Ghislenghien onward great numbers of troops, transport, and trains were seen making east, and the bombers, swooping down on this crowded traffic, wrought terrible havoc. The D.H.9's dropped several 112-lb. bombs on troops and transport near Croisette aerodrome, demolished a hangar there with one heavy bomb, cut a train in two with another, and made three direct hits with other bombs on the road traffic. No. 2 Squadron released thirty-nine bombs on several trains at Enghien junction and station, of which twenty-one made full and direct hits. An ammunition-truck exploded, and all the trains began burning. Enghien railway station was also in flames. Several thousands of rounds were fired into the road traffic by all machines. The attacking force performed its work of destruction without any

---

[13] Lieut. P. W. Symons; No. 4 Sqn. (previously A.A.S.C.). Farmer; of Maitland, S. Aust.; b. Moonta, S. Aust., 4 Aug., 1893. Killed in action, 4 Nov., 1918.

interference from enemy aircraft. Motor-lorries were set on fire or wrecked; horses bolted over a confined area of ditches and farms and rising hilly ground on each side of the main road. The road itself was blocked with fallen waggons in a dozen places and littered with dead and dying men and animals. The raiders' only loss was F. R. Smith, leader of No. 2 Squadron's formation, who was shot down by ground-fire and taken prisoner, but returned through the enemy's lines three days after the Armistice.

The attack was repeated in this vicinity twice next day, the eve of the Armistice. Both Australian squadrons were out in full force—No. 2 bombing, No. 4 escorting. The morning raid between 8.30 and 10.30 found five trains in the blackened Enghien station and the town and roads crowded with troops and transport. The bombs from the S.E.5's damaged a railway bridge, destroyed an anti-aircraft battery, and hit the trains and the railway station in many places. Leaving the station enveloped in a cloud of smoke, the attackers dived upon the road transport, which was still very heavy, and spread panic along the route with their machine-guns. Five Fokkers endeavoured to interfere, but were beaten off or destroyed by Bristol Fighters, also escorting. The afternoon raid continued the same harrying work, with similar disastrous results, upon the retiring German columns at Enghien and on the Enghien–Hal road eastward.

This was the last aggressive operation of the Australian scouting squadrons in the war. After the Armistice machines from both No. 2 and No. 4 Squadrons maintained balloon-line patrols for some days, but these were mainly practice exercises. The enemy was beaten; his surrender, cautiously doubted by the army for some days, was final.

After the Armistice it was generally believed that the Australian Corps would advance with the Fourth Army to the Rhine, but eventually that army did not cross the German frontier, and only the Second Army moved on to occupy the Cologne bridgehead. No. 3 Australian Squadron remained in Belgium near Charleroi with the Australian Corps. No. 4 Squadron was the only Australian unit in the British Army of

Occupation, and that squadron entered Germany at 11.45 a.m. on December 7th, spent some days at Euskirchen, and arrived at the Bickendorf aerodrome, Cologne, on December 14th. No. 2 Squadron remained in the vicinity of Lille (Hellemmes) until demobilisation.

By the end of November No. 3 Squadron was running an aerial postal service between Fourth Army Headquarters at Namur and Australian Corps Headquarters at Ham-sur-Heure (south of Charleroi), and from Australian Corps to the divisions in the Hallencourt area near Abbeville.

The two and a half months spent by No. 4 Squadron at Cologne were uneventful. Soon after its arrival it took over 150 surrendered aeroplanes of all types from the German Air Force, and exhibited for the delectation of German pilots the flying qualities of the Snipe.

By the end of February each of the three Australian squadrons had handed over its machines and stores, and was preparing to depart from the war theatre for Le Havre, England, and home. March and April saw them on Salisbury Plain, and the members of all three squadrons embarked early in May on the transport *Kaiser-i-Hind* for Australia. No. 1 Squadron joined the same ship at Port Said. The disembarkation at Melbourne on June 16th was a general leave-taking among members of the Australian Flying Corps, and the airmen's sentiments have been fittingly expressed by one of them in a short account of the history of No. 4 Squadron. "Doubtless," he writes, "many of them will meet again, not only in every town and city of Australia, but right throughout the crowded highways and the wide, lone places of the whole world. Wherever two or more of them meet each other, one thing rests assured; their memories will go winging back to those happy times of splendid comradeship and strenuous endeavour among the pleasant fields of Britain, along the straight, tree-bordered roads and straggling villages of France, the wind-swept desolations of Belgium, and the final weeks with the Army of Occupation on the Rhine."

CHAPTER XXVII

FLIGHTS HOME TO AUSTRALIA

No narrative of the war service of the Australian Flying Corps can be quite complete without a recital of the flights, or attempted flights, home to Australia undertaken by some Australian airmen. During the demobilisation of the Australian Imperial Force in England after the Armistice, public interest in the preparations for the flight across the Atlantic[1] suggested to the Australian Government the offering of a prize for the first successful flight from Britain to Australia. The scheme was received enthusiastically by Australian airmen in England, and in March, 1919, the Commonwealth Government announced that it would award £10,000 to the first Australian airman who succeeded in flying from England to Australia. The principal conditions, announced in May, were:—

> The flight must be accomplished in an aeroplane or seaplane from Great Britain to Australia in 720 consecutive hours, that is, thirty days.
>
> The offer to remain open until midnight on 31st December, 1920.
>
> The aircraft competing, and all component parts, must have been constructed within the British Empire.
>
> The pilots and all the crew must be of Australian nationality.
>
> The entries must be through the Royal Aero Club, London. One machine only might be used throughout the flight, though replacement of parts and repairs to motors might be made *en route*.
>
> The starting-place must be Hounslow aerodrome or Calshot seaplane station, and the landing-place was to be " in the neighbourhood of Port Darwin."

---

[1] Capt. J. Alcock and Lieut. A. W. Brown flew the Atlantic in a Vickers-Vimy machine, from Newfoundland to Ireland, in a non-stop flight of 17 hours 27 minutes on 14th and 15th June, 1919. Both airmen were knighted. Sir John Alcock was killed in an aeroplane smash on 18 December, 1920, at Rouen, France.

The names of the airmen who essayed the flight to Australia, set out in the order in which they left England, were:—

1919.	Crew.	Machine.
Oct. 21.—	Captain G. C. Matthews, Sergeant T. D. Kay.[2]	Sopwith Wallaby (one 350-h.p. Rolls-Royce Eagle).

Crashed at Bali, in Java, 19th April, 1920, and further flight abandoned.

| Nov. 12.— | Captain Ross Smith, Lieutenant Keith Smith[3] (navigator), Sergeant J. M. Bennett,[4] Sergeant W. H. Shiers.[5] | Vickers-Vimy (two 360-h.p. Rolls-Royce). |

Arrived Port Darwin, Dec. 10th, and won the prize.

| Nov. 13.— | Lieutenant R. Douglas,[6] Lieutenant J. S. L. Ross.[7] | Alliance (one 450-h.p. Napier Lion). |

Crashed at Surbiton, England, on the same date, shortly after leaving Hounslow aerodrome; both officers killed.

| Nov. 21.— | Lieutenant V. Rendle,[8] Lieutenant D. R. Williams,[9] Captain G. H. Wilkins[10] (navigator), Lieutenant G. H. Potts.[11] | Blackburn Kangaroo (two 250-h.p. Rolls-Royce Falcon). |

Engine-defect discovered after leaving Suda Bay, Crete, on Dec. 8th. Delayed there with repairs. Flight abandoned.

---

[2] Sgt. T. D. Kay; No. 3 Sqn. Mechanical engineer; b. Spring Mount, Vic., 20 Sept., 1892.

[3] Lieut. Sir Keith Smith, K.B.E.; R.A.F. Aviator; b. Adelaide, 20 Dec., 1890.

[4] Lieut. J. M. Bennett, A.F.M.; No. 1 Sqn. Motor mechanic; b. St. Kilda, Melbourne, 1894. Killed in aeroplane accident, 14 April, 1922.

[5] Lieut. W. H. Shiers, A.F.M.; No. 1 Sqn. Electrical engineer; b. Norwood, Adelaide, 1890.

[6] Lieut. R. Douglas, M.C., D.C.M.; Aust. Flying Corps (previously Machine-Gun Corps). Printer; b. Charters Towers, Q'land, June, 1894. Killed in aeroplane accident, 13 Nov., 1919.

[7] Lieut. J. S. L. Ross; No. 2 Sqn. Telegraphist; b. Moruya, N.S.W., Aug., 1895. Killed in aeroplane accident, 13 Nov., 1919.

[8] Lieut. V. Rendle, R.A.F.

[9] Lieut. D. R. Williams; Aust. Flying Corps. Garage proprietor; b. Wodonga, Vic.

[10] Capt. G. H. Wilkins, M.C. Official Photographer to the A.I.F. Explorer; of Adelaide; b. Mount Bryan East, S. Aust., 31 Oct., 1888.

[11] Lieut. G. H. M. St. C. Potts; No. 3 Sqn. Electrical engineer; b. Euroa, Vic., 1897.

1919.	Crew.	Machine.
Dec. 4.—	Captain C. E. Howell,[12] Air-Mechanic G. H. Fraser.[13]	Martinsyde (one 275-h.p. Rolls-Royce Falcon).

Lost at sea off St. George's Bay, Corfu, on Dec. 9th. Captain Howell's body was recovered a fortnight later.

1920.		
Jan. 8.—	Lieutenant R. J. P. Parer,[14] Lieutenant J. C. McIntosh.[15]	D.H.9 (one 200-h.p. Siddeley-Puma).

Landed Port Darwin, August 2nd.

A Frenchman, Lieutenant Poulet, in a small Caudron machine started from France on 7th October, 1919, on a flight to Australia, and was overhauled by Ross Smith on November 29th, near Akyab, Burma. Poulet had many difficulties with his inadequately-powered craft and abandoned the flight at Rangoon.

Sir Ross Smith.

The story of the flight from England to Australia by Captain Sir Ross Smith is told in his own words, abridged from an account published after he reached Australia. He had with him his brother, Lieutenant Keith Smith (of the Royal Air Force), and two mechanics who had served in No. 1 Squadron of the Australian Flying Corps in Palestine, Sergeants Bennett and Shiers. The machine was a Vickers-Vimy (two 360-h.p. Rolls-Royce engines), of the same type as the craft in which Captain Alcock and Lieutenant Brown flew across the Atlantic from America to England. It carried 865 gallons of petrol and had a cruising range of 2,400 miles.

Sir Ross Smith had one advantage over all other competitors in the flight to Australia, in that he had a year previously flown over the route from Cairo to India with Generals Borton and Salmond in the giant Handley-Page machine used

---

[12] Capt. C. E. Howell, D.S.O., M.C., D.F.C.; R.A.F. (previously Australian Infantry). Draughtsman; b. Adelaide, 17 June, 1892. Drowned at sea, 9 Dec., 1919.

[13] Air-Mechanic G. H. Fraser; Aust. Flying Corps. Motor mechanic; b. Bendigo, Vic., 1886. Drowned at sea, 9 Dec., 1919.

[14] Lieut. R. J. P. Parer, A.F.C.; Aust. Flying Corps. Student; of Surrey Hills, Melbourne; b. St. Kilda-road, Melbourne, 18 Feb., 1894.

[15] Lieut. J. C. McIntosh, A.F.C.; Aust. Flying Corps (previously A.A.M.C.). Architect; b. Lumsden, Aberdeen, Scotland, 1892. Invented a type of aerial bomb. Killed in aeroplane accident, 28 March, 1921.

by No. 1 Squadron in Palestine during the final offensive. Sergeants Bennett and Shiers also accompanied him in this earlier adventure. From this flight and a further reconnaissance by sea of possible landing-places on a route through the Indies to Timor, Sir Ross Smith returned to England in September, 1919, and immediately negotiated with the Vickers-Vimy firm for assistance in the enterprise of the flight to Australia. Eventually the firm's approval was obtained, preparations were made with all speed, and the party was ready to begin the flight by the end of October. For a fortnight a start was delayed by exceedingly bad weather. Sir Ross Smith finally left England during a break in the autumn storms on November 12th.

"The day of our departure from England," says Sir Ross Smith, in the account referred to above, "broke with clear, frosty weather. Two hours later a ground haze drifted up, and the Air Ministry Weather Bureau forecasted bad weather, totally unfit for flying. But we had made up our minds, and decided to start. At 8.30 a.m. we started the engines, climbed into our seats, and took off from the snow-covered aerodrome. Shortly after reaching the French coast at Boulogne we ran into a big bank of snow clouds. We could not get underneath it, for it practically reached the ground. We therefore climbed above it, to a height of 8,000 feet. The cold was bitter, 25 degrees of frost, and for three hours our breath froze on our face-masks, and our sandwiches were frozen solid. It took us five days to cross Europe to Taranto in Italy. The circumstances were most trying, for the weather was execrable. The flight was made almost all the way through dense clouds, snow, and blinding rain. Only an occasional burst of sunshine cheered us on our way. The cloud belts were too thick to fly above them, and we were obliged to keep for the most part at dangerously low altitudes.

"We intended to fly from Rome to Athens, but at Rome we received certain information which made us doubtful as to whether it would be wise to adhere to our first route. So we flew to Crete, and stayed a night at Suda Bay. We met much rain, and clouds were troublesome, as we had to clear a high mountain range in the centre of the island, and feared we might crash. However, we escaped this peril and made a non-stop flight of seven and a half hours from Crete to Cairo, arriving at the Heliopolis aerodrome on November 18th.

"On November 19th we left Cairo for Damascus. Our route lay over the old battlefields, Romani, El Arish, Gaza, and Nazareth. It revived many memories for me, for this land over which we were passing was the arena of my war service. At Damascus we were welcomed by a squadron of the Royal Air Force. Next day we got off in a break of the bad weather at about 10 o'clock, and headed for Baghdad across the Syrian desert, viâ Abu Kemal to Ramadie, making our landing on the old Turkish battlefield. Here we were taken care of by the 10th (Indian) Lancers, and invaluable to us was their help. For that night a simoon swept down and nearly put an end to our efforts. We lashed the machine to the ground and, assisted by a great crowd of the Indian Lancers, hung on to it through that wild night of storm. By morning the wind died down, and after six hours spent in adjustments and clearing away the sand we made another start. This was the 21st November, and our objective was Basra. We flew over Kut el Amara, the scene of General Townshend's surrender, and over the legendary site of the Garden of Eden. This was the first good flying day we had had since we left England.

"Next day (November 22nd), we were all feeling very tired, and as the machine needed a certain amount of attention we decided to spend the day overhauling at Basra. On November 23rd we left Basra for Bandar Abbas, on the Persian Gulf, and landed there after a flight of eight hours over desert and mountainous country. Next day we reached Karachi, and on the following afternoon Delhi. From Basra to Delhi we had travelled 1,600 miles, and spent twenty-five and a half hours out of fifty-four in the air. Everything had gone remarkably well, both with the machine and the engines. We spent a day in Delhi working on the machine. On November 27th we reached Allahabad, and on the 28th Calcutta. We had expected to rest a day in Calcutta, but as the machine was going so well and we were feeling so fit we decided to go on. We made Rangoon in two days, staying the first night at Akyab. Between Akyab and Rangoon we passed in the air the French Lieutenant Poulet in his small

Caudron machine. He had left Europe twenty-eight days ahead of us. We had a most hospitable and popular welcome in Rangoon, which we left, on December 1st, for Bangkok, in Siam.

"We intended to fly direct from Bangkok to Singapore, but as we were informed that there was a good aerodrome at Singora, about half-way, we halted there. The Siamese notion of a good aerodrome nearly brought us all to an untimely end. A square patch had been hewn from the jungle, the trunks and upper portions of the trees had been removed, but the stumps were allowed to remain. We made a safe and miraculous landing, missing the stumps by inches. On December 3rd fell the heaviest rain I had ever experienced, and it kept us tied up at Singora. We reached Singapore on December 4th. The racecourse had been prepared for us to land on, and proved suitable, though small. Next day we left Singapore for Kalidjati, near Batavia in Java. This was a distance of nearly 700 miles and the worst stage of the journey as regards landing-grounds. We travelled 200 miles down the eastern coast of Sumatra, which was so densely wooded that it would have been impossible to make a landing. Then we turned seawards to Batavia.

"At Kalidjati we were received by the Governor-General of the Dutch East Indies. The Governor-General, learning that aeroplanes were flying from England to Australia, had ordered aerodromes to be constructed at different points in the Dutch islands. These greatly facilitated our flight. On December 6th we arrived at Sourabaya after passing over most glorious scenery, but we found the aerodrome had been placed on reclaimed land, hard apparently at the surface, but soft underneath, so that on landing our machine became deeply bogged.

"The thirty days of the competition were now closing in, and anxieties increased. We extricated the machine with the greatest difficulty, and at one time I feared it would be impossible ever to start off from that aerodrome again. I had a roadway of bamboo mats laid down, 350 yards long and 40 yards wide. The machine was hauled from the bog by a swarm of natives to this improvised pathway. We made a perilous take-off, with bamboo flying in all directions from our propellers, and late in the afternoon of December 8th we landed at Bima, in Soembawa. Next day we left Bima for Atamboea, in Timor, and flew east along the north coast of Flores and then south-east to Timor. It was only 350 (*sic*) miles from there to Darwin.

"Tired as we were, excitement kept us all from sleep that night. All going well we should land in Australia on the morrow. Before daybreak on December 10th we were down at the machine giving it the last test and overhaul before venturing on the wide stretch of sea. At 8.35 a.m. we taxied into a light breeze and took off with beautiful weather in our favour. As the hours rolled slowly by we strained our eyes towards Australia. A tiny speck upon the waters resolved itself into a warship, H.M.A.S. *Sydney*, in exactly the position we had asked her to be in case of need. The clouds and mist obscured all distant vision, and it was not until after 3 o'clock that I observed the first faint outline of land. We were then doing 83 miles an hour. The land speedily assumed more definite contour, and details became manifest. Darwin came into view. In a few minutes we were circling above the town. Then down, down, in a steep descending spiral—and we had touched Australian soil!

"The duration of the journey, with all stops, was just under twenty-eight days, but the actual flying time was 135 hours. The distance covered was 11,340 miles."

For this performance both officers were knighted, and the sergeant mechanics received the Air Force Medal and commissioned rank of lieutenants.[16]

LIEUTENANTS PARER AND MCINTOSH.

Travelling without mechanics, Parer and McIntosh flew from England to Australia after extraordinary adventures in a D.H.9 fitted with a 200-h.p. Siddeley-Puma engine. The Australian military authorities in London, being advised by the British Air Ministry that the power of the craft was inadequate, forbade the projected attempt, but the two airmen disregarded this notice. They reached Darwin after a seven-months' journey, during which their narrow escapes from

---

[16] Sir Ross Smith and Lieutenant Bennett were killed on 14 April, 1922, during a test flight in the Vickers-Viking (amphibian) in which Sir Ross Smith was preparing to essay a flight round the world.

disaster amply justified the warning they received in London.

They left Hounslow on 8th January, 1920, but were delayed in France by bad weather during the remainder of the month. Not till February 21st did they arrive at Cairo. In leaving Italy they flew over the crater of Vesuvius. The heat waves from the volcano caused the machine to fall out of control for 500 feet, and only skilful piloting saved them from disaster. Over Taranto they lost their maps in a gale.

From Cairo they reached Ramleh in Palestine, and on February 27th set out from Ramleh for Baghdad. After two forced landings in the desert—after the second of which they camped in the machine for the night and were in some danger from a force of badly-armed Arabs—they reached Baghdad on February 28th. Minor repairs delayed them for a few days, and then on March 7th they made Karachi. A week later they landed at Calcutta. Here they waited till March 24th, in order to fly in company with Captain Matthews. Engine trouble delayed their arrival at Akyab till April 1st. They flew on to Rangoon on April 2nd. At Moulmein, trying to avoid a crowd which had rushed on to the landing-ground, Parer crashed the machine; by great good fortune neither the airmen nor any of the crowd of natives were injured. Repairs to under-carriage and propeller occupied nearly two months. On May 28th the airmen reached Penang. Here engine-trouble again delayed them till June 15th. They crashed again on the flight to Singapore, but managed to make that town in spite of slight injury to the machine. At Singapore Parer was obliged to replace his propeller (for the fourth time), and was able to do so through the courtesy of the Dutch Government in Batavia.

Leaving Singapore on July 20th the adventurers ran into a thunder-storm, and were obliged to return with a damaged wing. They left again next morning and landed at Kalidjati on July 22nd. At Grisee on July 24th they again broke their propeller. They made Sourabaya on July 28th, and after a final overhaul of their much-worn machine they successfully crossed the Timor Sea and landed at Darwin in the evening of August 2nd. As they touched land their engine stopped. The final sea-flight of nearly nine hours had exhausted their last drop of petrol.

Captain Matthews and Sergeant Kay.

These airmen left London on 21st October, 1919, in their Sopwith Wallaby, and crossed Europe *viâ* France, Germany, and the Balkans. They made Mainz on the first day, but were here detained by snow and rain for nearly a month. At Vienna they were again delayed by bad weather for a week. After leaving that city they were obliged to land in open country, where, as Matthews relates, "we were surrounded by armed Jugo-Slavs, who took us prisoners and secured possession of our essential passports and identification papers. On the fourth day, taking advantage of the temporary absence of the guard, we grabbed our papers and bolted for the aeroplane, and got away easily, and in an hour located Belgrade. We landed at the Novisad aerodrome.

"The Serbian and French officers gave us a cordial welcome, but when we asked for petrol we were met with a look of blank consternation. After spending three weeks here, in the deepest despair, a French aviator arrived, and he was, with reluctance, induced to let us have sufficient petrol to take us to Bucharest, where we were compelled to land in a slushy field covered with two feet of snow. It was only possible to get away by rising before the snow thawed in the morning. We flew at an altitude averaging 13,000 feet while traversing portions of the Balkans in Serbia, Bulgaria, and Turkey, with the temperature 46 degrees below freezing point. In the afternoon we found ourselves in the vicinity of Adrianople. A temporary seizure in the petrol pump caused a forced landing in what from the air appeared to be a nice grass field, but as soon as the machine touched ground it sank to the axles in a quagmire.

"Sergeant Kay repaired the fault, but we could only get away by Kay hanging on the tail and making a flying jump for the fuselage at the take-off. It was then raining heavily —and almost dark, and in a few minutes we were enveloped in dense fog. Flying within fifty feet of the sea we were just able to distinguish the San Stefano lighthouse, and landed at Constantinople shortly before 5 o'clock, having been in the air almost ten hours, and the supply of petrol well-nigh exhausted.

"We spent three days in Constantinople and loaded up with petrol for the long jump across Asia Minor. But when giving the engine a final running trial we found a leak in the water jacket, and we spent ten days searching for an acetylene welder to make the repairs, but could not get one in all Constantinople. With the aid of chewing gum, powdered asbestos, and copper wire, we repaired the leak, and set off on the 1,700-mile flight to Baghdad. We were compelled to land in a ploughed field at Aleppo, where we were detained for a week. On the 550-mile stretch to Baghdad we were cheered by the first good weather of the trip. In Baghdad the damaged cylinder was replaced by a new one, and Bushire was reached in pleasant weather and without incident.

"Karachi, 1,200 miles distant, we hoped to reach in one flight, but after three hours we encountered a tremendous sand-storm, which we could not shake off. We fought it for twenty minutes, and were forced to land on the seashore, where the machine sank in the soft sand, the nose tilted, and the propeller, axle, and longeron were smashed. The wrecked machine was dragged up into a sheltered cove. I left Sergeant Kay in charge and set out to search for Bandar Abbas, which I thought I could reach on foot in about three hours. But I had to fight the burning sand and sun from 10.30 a.m. to 5.30 p.m., without either food or water, and reached Bandar Abbas exhausted. The British Consul headed a relief party to get Kay. He considered it would be impossible to reach the cove by land, so we went by boat. The launch left at 8 o'clock, but it, too, got caught in the storm, and was driven around the islands of the straits, where we were marooned for three days. When we got back to the wharf we found Sergeant Kay and others anxiously awaiting us. With some angle iron from a fence we repaired the longeron, and with an old iron bar spliced the broken axle. The rain and sun had warped the reserve propeller rather badly, and we were doubtful whether the shaken machine would stand the extra heavy drag. However, we decided to chance it, and it carried us safely through to the final crash at Bali.

"We were forced to land again at Jask, about three miles from Bandar Abbas, and in the take-off the spliced axle was bent, and one of the wings broken. We were then in the blazing desert under a scorching sun. We dragged it three miles to the shelter of an Englishman's verandah, and there repaired it up again. The machine was then dragged back three miles to the Bandar Abbas aerodrome, and from there we reached Karachi in a non-stop flight. Despite the heavy drag on the engine by the warped propeller the next stages to Delhi, Allahabad, Calcutta, Akyab, Rangoon, and Bangkok were safely accomplished. At Bangkok Sergeant Kay had a severe attack of dengue fever, and was rather bad for two or three days. We toiled for three days on the engine at Singora, and the first trouble after leaving there was in the landing at Kalidjati, where one of the engine's ball-races was smashed to pieces. The Dutch authorities got a motor-car ball-race, and, with some ingenuity, Sergeant Kay fitted this to the Rolls-Royce engine, and got it working again. We started cheerily on the penultimate stage of the journey to Australia. Sourabaya was safely reached, but soon afterwards the warped propeller caused trouble, and in a forced landing at Bali the wings were smashed. This was on 19th April, 1920. All hope of completing the final stage of the journey to Darwin was then abandoned."

APPENDIX No. 1.

TYPES OF FIGHTING AEROPLANES.

By Captain Andrew Lang
(late Australian Flying Corps).

In order to encourage aviation the German Government, some years before the outbreak of war, allotted £4,000,000 for prizes to aircraft and engine builders, the distribution to be spread over a period of five years. In 1914 an army law was brought into force allotting £400,000 for army aviation alone, which also benefited by a fair share of the four millions assigned for general aviation. At this period the air force, consisting of four battalions at seventeen army flying schools, was under the command of two inspectors-general, but in 1916 the whole of the flying service came under a commanding officer who held rank equivalent to that of the commander of an army corps. In 1913 orders for 240 aeroplanes—half monoplanes, half biplanes—were given on behalf of the air force. Among the monoplanes were Aviatik, Albatros, Bristol, Gotha, Jeannin, Fokker, and Rumpler, while the biplanes were Albatros, Aviatik, A.E.G.,[1] Bristol, Euler, D.F.W.,[2] L.V.G.,[3] and A.G.O.[4] machines. In 1914 every preparation was made for war, and new aeroplanes were purchased to replace the 1913 types. Altogether there were then 1,000 aeroplanes on the strength of the German Air Force, most of them of standard type, the monoplanes being built on Taube lines and the biplanes of the Arrow type. The Army Air-Law of 1914 laid down that all machines must be entirely of German manufacture, must have roomy seating accommodation for the pilot and passenger, and must include in the design fittings for bomb-dropping and a camera. The minimum speed was to be fifty-six miles an hour, the dimensions not to exceed a certain area, the horse-power of the engines not to be more than 100, and the minimum flying endurance to be four hours. It is worthy of note that, although speed, climb, and endurance all increased during the war, the proportionate horse-power showed but an infinitesimal advance. The Germans who laid down the conditions for 1914 possessed great foresight.

On the British side the Royal Flying Corps, formed in late 1911 with a naval wing and a military wing, could muster in 1914 four complete squadrons—Nos. 2, 3, 4, and 5 Squadrons, R.F.C. (all of the military wing), and the nucleus of several additional squadrons. No. 1 Squadron was of military airships. The naval wing was not organised in squadrons; it tended at this time (says General Sykes in his book, *Aviation in Peace and War*) "towards individualism rather than cohesion," and when war broke out was re-organised as the Royal Naval Air Service. The R.F.C. and the R.N.A.S. were not combined again until 1st April, 1918; then they became the Royal Air Force. The R.F.C. squadrons at the outbreak of war consisted each of three flights, each flight being of four machines with two in reserve—that is,

---

[1] A.E.G.—Allgemeine Elektrizitäts Gesellschaft.
[2] D.F.W.—Deutsche Flug-Werke.
[3] L.V.G.—Luft-Verkehrs Gesellschaft.
[4] A.G.O.—Aerowerke Gustav Otto.

eighteen machines to the squadron. In organisation the R.F.C. was ahead of both French and Germans; the unit of the squadron proved to be the best and most effectively handled, and concentration under the R.F.C.'s own headquarters staff was equally useful and far-sighted. Two of the four British squadrons in 1914 were equipped with B.E.2's throughout, and two with homogeneous flights of Farmans, Blériots, and Avros. By the time of the Armistice the R.A.F. had grown to a force of 300,000 officers and men, 201 squadrons, and 22,000 machines in use.

The French were in numbers far in advance of the British. In 1912 the French Army had taken delivery of nearly 500 machines, of which number 344 were looked upon as being serviceable in the event of war. During 1912 £880,000 was spent on military aviation, while the estimates for future years allowed for the spending of £1,000,000. In 1914 the total effectives, comprising pilots, observers, and mechanics, numbered 4,343, whereas at the signing of the Armistice the French air service included 6,000 serviceable machines, 6,417 pilots, 1,682 observers, and 80,000 men. The most efficient factory in France was that controlled by the Farmans, and one-third of the total number of machines in the French Flying Corps at the outbreak of war consisted of machines from this factory. The others were all of French makes.

The following details of various machines are based largely upon the results obtained from them when subjected to the testing system in use during the war. Probably ninety-nine per cent. of British pilots on the fighting front knew nothing of the work of test-pilots (which was carried out in England) in experimenting with new aero-engines—including carburettors, magnetos, plugs, oils, and propellers—and with new aircraft designs requiring modifications under tests, which often occupied many months of flying and involved many alterations, before they were pronounced fit to go into production. On some occasions, when a new British machine was almost passed for fighting work, the Germans would suddenly produce a type which would outclass it, and the designer would consequently be set a fresh task in the endeavour to beat the enemy. In instruments for this experimental work the French led the world. They possessed stations for experimental work only, where tests were carried out with bombs, cameras, guns, and all appliances appertaining to aircraft in warfare. The personnel of those stations consisted of specialists in their own departments. Not the least interesting department of the great war in the air was this study of types of machines used by the opposing armies, and the development of those types under the guidance of the test-pilots at the experimental stations. The British machines herein mentioned are those types with which Australian pilots became acquainted either in the field or in the training squadrons in England.

I.—British Types.

The British Experimental (B.E.).

The Royal Aircraft Factory at Farnborough, which later became known as the Royal Aircraft Establishment, was used before the war for the construction of airships and aeroplanes. The chief designer at that time was Captain Geoffrey de Havilland, who afterwards became famous as the designer of the Havilland machines. De Havilland was responsible also for the B.E. machines, and the B.E.2.c was well-known to every war pilot by the time he had secured his " wings " from the training schools.

B.E. were the initials of the Blériot Experimental, named after M. Louis Blériot, the inventor of the tractor-type of aeroplane. The tractor-type carries the propeller in front of the engine; the pusher-type carries it behind. By the time when war broke out the initials B.E. had come to represent the British Experimental. The first development from the B.E. was the B.E.2, and at the outbreak of war one of the early B.E.2's was to be found at the Point Cook School, near Melbourne. In progressive stages were developed by a series of improvements the B.E.2.b, B.E.2.c, B.E.2.d, and B.E.2.e. The two last-named types were eventually turned out in large quantities. In 1917 No. 1 Squadron, A.F.C., was flying the B.E.2.e. Then came further types of B.E. designated by a continuation of the numbering—B.E.3, B.E.4, B.E.5, and so on up to the B.E.12. These machines varied in that some were fitted with the 80-h.p. Gnome rotary engine, while others had the stationary 70 and 80-h.p. Renault, or the 90, 100, 140, and 200-h.p. R.A.F. (Royal Aircraft Factory) engines. The most sucessful of the rotary type was the B.E.8, commonly known as "the Bloater," but by the middle of 1915 these were practically out of existence. The B.E.12 proved the most successful of the series, and did good work in Egypt. During the early attacks on Zeppelins over London the B.E. machine was credited with some quite noteworthy performances. It was when mounted on one of the 2.c types that Lieutenant W. L. Robinson[5] brought down the first Zeppelin.

The Fighting Experimental (F.E.).

F.E. at first denoted Farman Experimental, M. Henri Farman having originated the pusher-type of aircraft, but since early in the war F.E. has stood for Fighting Experimental. The first of this type to fly as a successful war machine—about the end of 1915—was the F.E.2.b, fitted with a 120-h.p. Beardmore engine. Upon its first appearance over the lines it alarmed the Germans both on the ground and in the air. It suffered, however, from a disadvantage in its oleo-pneumatic under-carriage. This had fitted to it, and running forward of the nacelle, a V-shaped skid, to the end of which was attached a wheel to prevent the machine from turning over in the event of a bad landing on soft ground, but the apparatus was heavy and ungainly, and set up much air resistance. Subsequently a 160-h.p. Beardmore was fitted to the aeroplane and an alteration made to the under-carriage, eliminating a great deal of the head resistance. The machine passed through several stages of lettering, and eventually reached the F.E.2.d type, which was fitted with a 250-h.p. Rolls-Royce engine. Very slight modifications were necessary to fit the different-powered engines. The F.E. mounted with the 250-h.p. Rolls-Royce was used as a fighter; the F.E. mounted with the 160-h.p. Beardmore was an invaluable night-bomber right up to the day of the Armistice. Another F.E., which made its appearance towards the end of 1915, was the little single-seater scout, known as the F.E.8, mounted with a 100-h.p. Gnome-Monosoupape rotary engine. It was credited with a great turn of speed, and covered the speed course at Farnborough at about 100 miles an hour, but there were difficulties in the way of rapid production, and nothing more came of it.

[5] Capt. W. L. Robinson, V.C.; R.A.F.; b. Tollidetta, India, 14 July, 1895. Died 31 Dec., 1918.

The Reconnaissance Experimental (R.E.).

R.E. (Reconnaissance Experimental) machines were designated by successive numbers as their type progressed—such as R.E.2, R.E.3, R.E.4, up to R.E.7 and 8, the various classes fitted with different types of engines. One of the best of these to fly was the R.E.5. It was of considerable span and chord, mounted with a 120-h.p. Beardmore, and was produced in the middle of 1915. It had a large overhang on the top planes, but with the neat cowling over the engine it was of comely appearance, and glided very flat. This machine climbed well, and, like the B.E., was inherently stable, but its fast landing speed often made a forced landing dangerous, and therefore the R.E.5 did not see a large production. The first R.E. to be generally used was the R.E.8, with which type No. 3 Australian Squadron and many other corps squadrons were equipped. This R.E.8 was fitted with a 140-h.p. R.A.F. engine, and carried out good work in artillery-observation and night-bombing. In appearance it was very like the B.E.2.e, but its engine was of greater horse-power and it had less overhang on the top plane.

The Scouting Experimental (S.E.).

A number of Scouting Experimental machines—mostly with rotary engines, Gnome type—were turned out by the Royal Aircraft Factory before one was found suitable to meet the enemy. This was the S.E.5, and was fitted with a stationary 150-h.p. Hispano-Suiza engine. Having first gone into production in 1917, it was shortly afterwards installed with a 200-h.p. Hispano-Suiza engine, and was then known as the S.E.5.a. It was on this machine that the late Major McCudden was so successful, as was also No. 2 Australian Squadron. By this time, however, the Royal Aircraft Factory had become an experimental station—and not too soon. It had been largely in consequence of this Government establishment that Britain found herself so badly off for aircraft in comparison with France and Germany. So little encouragement was offered to British constructors that, had not the war intervened, most of them would have been forced to abandon business. Even after war broke out the Royal Aircraft Factory took the bulk of the early orders, and it was only after great agitation that drastic changes were made in the establishment.

The Avro.

The first machine built by A. V. Roe saw the light of day as far back as 1906. It was the first aeroplane built by a British subject which was able to leave the ground. In early 1909 A. V. Roe produced a triplane, mounted with an air-cooled 9-h.p. J.A.P. engine, and in this machine he left the ground at Lea Marshes, to the astonishment of the onlookers as well as of himself. Early in 1911 the firm of A. V. Roe sprang into existence. It was financed by a brother, H. V. Roe, head of a firm of webbing manufacturers in Manchester. H. V. Roe left the firm in 1917 to join the R.F.C., but was injured in an accident in France during night-flying operations, and since then has retired from the business, another brother, the Rev. E. V. Roe, taking his place. In 1911 the first " Avro " machine made its appearance in the capable hands of Howard Pixton, and one of this type was built for Mr. Duigan of Melbourne (subsequently captain in the Australian Flying Corps). At this date an extraordinary thing happened; the War Office actually gave an order to A. V. Roe & Co. for a series of machines to be built, fitted with 50-h.p. Gnome engines.

Those aeroplanes were the first to be designed and built by a British firm and delivered to the War Office. All other army machines were either of French or German make, or were turned out by the Royal Aircraft Factory. Not until early in 1913 did the Avro, well known to present-day pilots, make its appearance: fitted with an 80-h.p. Gnome, it was known as the "504 Model A biplane." It was on three of this type, starting from Belfort towards the end of 1914, that the big Zeppelin sheds at Friedrichshafen were successfully bombed.

In the middle of 1917 the 504A, unaltered aero-dynamically and in main dimensions, was fitted with the 100-h.p. Gnome-Monosoupape and given the designation of the "504K" model. Minor alterations to the engine-bearers now enable the fitting of either the Mono, the Le Rhone, the Clerget, or the 150-h.p. Bentley rotary. In consequence of this fact, and of its lightness on the controls, the 504K Avro is the standard training-machine for the army.

The De Havilland (D.H.).

During 1912 Mr. G. Holt Thomas organised the Aircraft Manufacturing Company, and secured the sole British rights for the building of the Henri and Maurice Farman biplanes. Later he obtained the rights for building the Gnome and Le Rhone aeroplane engines in England. For this company Captain Geoffrey de Havilland became the designer. De Havilland had chafed at the restrictions at the Royal Aircraft Factory, and, freed from the toils of red-tape, he produced a series of remarkably successful machines. The first of these was known as the D.H.1, and was a pusher, fitted with an 80-h.p. Renault, in tail-design not unlike the Henri Farman. She could be landed, in good hands, at 45 miles an hour, and with useful load could climb to 3,500 feet in 11¼ minutes, while her maximum speed low down was 78 miles an hour. The D.H.1.a, a single-seater, was a replica of the D.H.1, with the exception that she was braced up to carry a 120-h.p. Beardmore, giving her a climb to 3,500 feet in 6¾ minutes, with a low-down maximum speed of 89 miles an hour and a landing speed of 50. Most of these machines were sent out to Egypt, where they did good work. A few of them were turned out with all-metal wings for use in Africa. The D.H.1.a had no sooner taken the air, than the D.H.2 appeared. Like the F.E.8, it was mounted with a 100-h.p. Gnome-Monosoupape engine, but was far neater in general finish. The D.H.2 was brought out as a reply to the Fokker, which at that time was playing havoc among the B.E.2.c's, but it did not see the fighting zone until March, 1916.

One of the drawbacks to the D.H.2 was the propeller and engine torque. Until a pilot had considerable experience with the machine, he was greatly handicapped by the fear of getting into a spinning-nose-dive, the cure for which in those days was unknown. But with the fitting of a four-bladed propeller much of the trouble disappeared and the D.H.2 regained prestige.

The next development, the D.H.3, was never heard of at the front, although the experimental pilot knew all about it. It mounted two engines, and in 1915 was regarded by the authorities as a freak. Nevertheless, in 1917 a similar machine made its appearance, the actual difference being that in the 1915 model the two engines were 160-h.p. Beardmores fitted as pushers, while the 1917 model, the D.H.10, was fitted tractor-wise with two 360-h.p. Rolls-Royce engines.

The D.H.3 had a speed low down of 95 miles an hour, and with a disposable load of 711 lbs. could climb to 6,500 feet in 24 minutes and take the ground again at a speed of 55. The D.H.10 had a low-down speed of 117 miles, at 15,000 feet made 110 miles, landed at about 62, and carried a disposable load of 1,380 lbs. In appearance both machines were exactly alike; the difference was in propulsion. In the D.H.10.a it was decided to fit two 410-h.p. Liberty engines, but in this case the engine nacelles were placed on the bottom planes, while in the Rolls type they were mounted in the gap of the wings. These alterations resulted in a pronounced increase in the speed of the D.H.10.a, but added 140 lbs. to the empty weight of the machine. The speed was 128 miles low down, and at 15,000 feet 117 miles; with 1,250 lbs. of disposable load it landed at 65 miles. At the time of the Armistice the D.H.10.a was going into rapid production as a high-speed bomber.

To return to the earlier numbers. The D.H.4 (a two-seater) was the first high-speed, high-powered machine of medium weight built by the British. The first D.H.4 made its appearance in 1916, fitted with a 240-h.p. B.H.P. engine, and was credited with a speed and climb equal to the best of the rotary-engined single-seater scouts (at that period regarded as invincible for speed in all departments). The type was at once put into production for reconnaissance and photographic work. Its speed, with the B.H.P. engine, near the ground was 120 miles; it climbed to 15,000 feet in 29¼ minutes, and took the ground with a load of 580 lbs. at about 52 miles an hour. With the 365-h.p. Rolls-Royce engine the climb with the same load to 15,000 feet was reduced to 16¼ minutes; the low-down speed approached 135 miles. One of the remarkable features of this machine was the extensive use made of three-ply wood in the fuselage construction. From the radiator to the rear of the passenger's seat there was no wire bracing whatever. The engine-bearers, which hitherto had consisted of metal, were also wholly and solely made of three-ply. De Havilland's argument in favour of this method was that, in the usual girder system for rigging the fuselage, a chance shot in a vital spot weakened the structure at once, whereas with the three-ply that result would not occur. Such a departure from the orthodox showed de Havilland to be a man of unusual foresight.

The D.H.5 followed. The Air Ministry required a machine for "trench-strafing" and low flying, and instructions were issued to designers to produce a type which would give the pilot a good view overhead as well as below and in front. De Havilland designed a machine fitted with a 110-h.p. Le Rhone, with the pilot perched just behind it and under the leading edge of the top plane, which had considerable back stagger. With a disposable load of 260 lbs. the D.H.5 had a speed of 102 miles at 10,000 feet, but a fairly high landing speed of about 55. The D.H.6 (called "the Clutching Hand") was produced at the end of 1917 as an elementary training machine; it combined cheapness with strength and simplicity, and had a low landing speed. The D.H.7 and 8 never saw the light; the designer, after spending much time and money on them, abandoned them as bad cases from a military point of view.

The next type, the D.H.9, looked like a German, and the Germans, when they saw it, felt highly complimented by the British designers. The D.H.9 was a modification of the D.H.4, but was designed essentially for bombing work; the span, chord, and length were the same in each case. In this type the pilot's cockpit was removed from under the centre-section to aft of the trailing-edge of the top-plane; the under-carriage was shortened, the nose was built more on cigar lines, and the petrol-tank capacity was increased to 74 gallons from the 66 gallons of the D.H.4 The disposable load was 1,120 lbs. (580 lbs. in the D.H.4), an advantage secured with only slight loss of climb and speed. The type was greatly used by the Independent Air Force.

The Germans were, meanwhile, rapidly improving their bombers, and in response to a demand for improved British bombing-craft to keep pace with the enemy, de Havilland towards the end of 1917 designed a high-speed long-range bomber—an enlarged D.H.9—built to carry a Rolls-Royce engine and, later, a 410-h.p. Liberty. This machine he called the D.H.9.a. Its span was a little larger than that of the D.H.9's, but the overall length was less, though in the air it appeared greater. The empty weight was 2,656 lbs., and the tank capacity 112 gallons. With the Rolls-Royce engine she could climb to 10,000 feet in 20 minutes, carrying a load of approximately 1,200 lbs., while her speed at that height, with the same load, was 110 miles an hour. With reduced load the speed at 10,000 feet was 125, and at 15,000 feet 116, miles. A drawback was the flat gliding angle, which, to a pilot inexperienced with the tail-plane adjustment, was most deceptive. This fact accounted for so many of this type being crashed when they first went to France. Fitted with the 410-h.p. Liberty, the D.H.9.a climbed, without bomb-load, to 10,000 feet in 14 minutes, 15,000 in 25 minutes, and 20,000 in 49 minutes.

A few months prior to the Armistice an engine built by the Napier Company—the " Napier Lion "—after undergoing severe bench tests for about eighteen months, was fitted to a reinforced D.H.9, and made one of the most remarkable machines ever turned out. During October, 1918, this aeroplane carried a pilot, observer, two machine-guns, a full load of ammunition, full tanks, and two 112-lb. bombs, to 24,000 feet in 53 minutes, the speed at that height being about 95 miles an hour. Later, in January, 1919, the same machine, weighing, with pilot and observer, nearly a ton and a half, made a record by flying to a height of 30,500 feet in $66\frac{1}{4}$ minutes, taking only $19\frac{1}{2}$ minutes to climb to 20,000 feet.

The Martinsyde.

Martinsyde Ltd. were among the pioneers in British aircraft designing. Mr. Handasyde, a Scotch engineer, and Mr. Martin, a London financier, joined forces in the building of a monoplane as far back as 1908, this machine being known then as the Martin-and-Handasyde. It was not until the years 1912 and 1913 that success came their way with a large type of monoplane, which, in the hands of such capable pilots as Graham Gilmour and Edward Petre (a brother to Major H. A. Petre, late Australian Flying Corps), put up some remarkably good flights. Nevertheless, the fact that few, if any, pilots were trained or took certificates upon these machines prejudiced their chances of gaining approval from the War Office. Handasyde, however, in his bluff Scottish way, stuck to the job, and early in 1914 built to the order of the late Gustav Hamel an enormous monoplane, for an attempt at the trans-Atlantic flight. Hamel, unfortunately, was lost in a cross-channel flight, and never heard of again. This monoplane—called the " Martinsyde "—was one of the most ambitious things then attempted; it was designed to carry a ton of petrol, and was fitted with a 250-h.p. Sunbeam engine. Later in the same year the company produced a small, fast scout biplane, fitted with an 80-h.p. Gnome, which proved highly successful. Its performance was so good that, after the outbreak of war, the War Office ordered large numbers of it. The first of the type to be turned out had a peculiar under-carriage fitted with four wheels—two large wheels to take the bulk of the weight, and two small ones forward to prevent the machine from standing on its nose. In those days the Martinsyde assumed a flying position when standing idle on the ground, and it was not until nearly the end of 1915 that the ordinary " V " under-carriage was attached. The machine was very handy in the air, though in those days the pilot could not take many liberties with it, in consequence of the danger of spinning, which was in a great measure due to the torque of the propeller and engine. As a good example of the improvements made in aircraft, it is worthy of mention that the 1914 Martinsyde scout used fibre blocks in place of pulleys as guides for the lateral control-wires, and, if these were not kept well greased, the wear and stiffness of the controls were immense. At a later time pulleys in all aircraft were fitted with plain bearings, which in turn were replaced by ball-bearing pulleys.

Towards the end of 1915 a new Martinsyde appeared in the shape of a high-powered scout fitted with a 120-h.p. Beardmore. This machine vastly excelled the little machine with the rotary engine, and in the hands of the firm's test pilot (F. P. Raynham) performed some notable climbs. It was during a test on one of these that the tail broke, and Raynham fell for a couple of thousand feet with his machine upside down, landed in a ploughed field, and escaped with his life. Later the 120-h.p. engine was enlarged to 160-h.p., and with this the scout was known at the front as the " Tinsyde " or " Baby Elephant." No. 1 Australian Squadron did wonderfully good work with this Martinsyde in Egypt. In 1916 Handasyde designed one of the finest fighting scouts ever built by a British firm; it is, in fact, doubtful whether any firm in the world built anything to equal its performances. This machine was known as the F.3, and was fitted with a Rolls-Royce Falcon engine of 275-h.p.; but in consequence of the limited output of those engines the scout did not go into production. Not to be outdone, however, Handasyde adapted the same machine to take a 300-h.p. Hispano-Suiza engine, and, after exhaustive experimental tests, its production was put in progress six weeks before the Armistice. The impression gained by the experimental pilots who put this machine through its tests, was that it stood alone for ease of control, speed, and climb, and that it was absolutely " viceless." Low down its speed was 145 miles per hour, and at 20,000 feet it was 126. The climb to 10,000 feet occupied $6\frac{1}{2}$ minutes, to 20,000 feet $19\frac{1}{2}$ minutes, and to 27,000 feet 37 minutes. If the authorities had dealt more resolutely with some of the firms which produced engines, and had given others a chance, this scout would have been over the lines early in 1917. As things were, not a shot in defence of the country was fired through its propeller.

The Bristol.

The founder of the Bristol and Colonial Aeroplane Co., of Bristol, was the late Sir George White, the defender of Ladysmith, and one of the pioneers of electric tramways. This was the first firm in Great Britain to build large works with the intention of designing and producing aircraft only. The company was formed in 1910. From that time till the outbreak of war the firm went through trying financial experiences, although it trained a large number of pilots—some of whom eventually became famous—and built some high-class machines. To obtain an order from the War Office was like drawing blood from an aeroplane wing. Towards the end of 1912, during War Office trials for a prize of £5,000, the Bristol military monoplane, in the hands of Mr. Harry Busteed, the chief pilot to the firm (later Colonel, R.A.F.), put up a notably fine effort, though the late Colonel S. F. Cody, with a biplane mounting a 120-h.p. Austro-Daimler engine, carried off the prize. Towards the end of 1913, while Busteed was putting a seaplane of the monoplane-type through its tests for the Navy at Pembroke, he conceived the idea of a small biplane scout. He sketched it out roughly on the spot, and gradually modified it until he considered it good enough to submit to the chief designer of Bristols, Mr. F. S. Barnwell. The result was that, with very little alteration to the original drawing, this firm early in 1914 produced the famous scout, officially designated Type "D," but better known to aviation as the "Bristol Bullet." This machine not only made a world-record performance, and was delightful to handle, but also set the fashion in a new form of aeroplane, showing that, in order to obtain results, it was not necessary to design machines with large surface areas. At this time there was also produced a two-seater machine which, with an 80-h.p. Gnome engine, flew at 75 miles an hour low down, as against the 100-mile rate of the "Bullet." The two-seater was credited with having a minimum speed of 34 miles, which was remarkable for aeroplanes of that date; nevertheless, it was not popular with the War Office, though a considerable number of orders came through from Serbia, Roumania, Greece, and other foreign countries. With the war it acquired a much more favourable reception, and large orders for the small scout were placed at once. As time went on, and the German machines became faster, higher-powered engines were fitted into the Bristol, until such power plants as the 80-h.p. Gnome, 100-h.p. Mono-Gnome, 110-h.p. Le Rhone, and the 130-h.p. Clerget engines had been successively employed. By the time this last stage had been reached, the type had reached the limit of its development as a fighting unit, and the R.N.A.S. finally adopted it as a standard training-machine.

The next machine to be produced was the B.F.2.b, better known as the "Bristol Fighter," or "B.F." The fuselage was slung midway between the planes, giving a top and bottom centre section. A Rolls-Royce Falcon engine was carried as power plant, mounted on a set of special engine-bearers, built to absorb as much vibration as possible. Another feature of the machine was the adjustable tail-plane; here a wheel was fitted, as in the D.H.4, 9, and 10 types, so that the angle of incidence of the tail-planes could be altered by the pilot to offset the varying loads carried. The pilot was situated behind the trailing edge of the top plane, with the observer just behind him. The observer's cockpit was mounted with a scarf gun-ring, capable of carrying a pair of Lewis machine-guns. The forward armament was a fixed Vickers gun, mounted inside the cowling and firing through the propeller. Besides being almost as light as a scout to handle, this machine was one of the strongest turned out by any of the Powers, and whenever at British experimental stations extra severe propeller-tests and engine-destruction tests in the air were required, the machine used was always the Bristol Fighter. So far as performance was concerned, there was no machine built by any of the combatant nations more efficient for both reconnaissance and fighting. The Germans themselves admitted as much. With the Falcon Rolls-Royce engine its maximum speed low down was 125 miles, and at 10,000 feet 113 miles. With a load of 630 lbs. it could be landed comfortably at 50 miles an hour. The climb to 10,000 feet occupied 11 minutes, and to 15,000 feet 21 minutes. Some of these machines were fitted with the 200-h.p. Hispano-Suiza and 200-h.p. Sunbeam-Arab engines, and saw service with them, but the performances were not so good, especially in the case of the latter. Just prior to the Armistice the B.F. underwent some splendid tests when fitted with a 300-h.p. B.H.P. engine, climbing to 20,000 feet in 20 minutes.

In 1917 the same firm turned out a monoplane; but after exhaustive tests this did not pass into large production, owing greatly to the number of its "blind spots." The few that were turned out saw service in the East. Nevertheless, it made a capital performance, climbing to 15,000 feet with a load of 260 lbs. in 19 minutes, while its speed low down was 130 miles an hour, and at 10,000 feet 117 miles. It could be landed at 50 miles, a remarkably slow speed for a monoplane weighing, when loaded, 1,300 lbs. Its power plant was a 110-h.p. Le Rhone, and it carried one Vickers gun firing, as usual, through the propeller. It was a light and steady craft. After the Armistice one of these machines found its way out to South Australia, and was used for passenger carrying by Captain Harry Butler.

The Sopwith Types.

Mr. T. O. M. Sopwith took his pilot's ticket (No. 31) on a Howard-Wright biplane in 1910, afterwards building a machine which he called the "Sopwith-Wright Biplane," and later merged into the Sopwith aeroplane. One of his mechanics then broke the duration record on a Sopwith machine, which mounted a 40-h.p. A.B.C. motor. That mechanic was Mr. H. G. Hawker, of Melbourne, and his flight lasted 8 hours 23 minutes. In 1913 Hawker established a height record of 11,450 feet on a small Sopwith machine, mounted with an 80-h.p. Gnome. His machine was the "Tabloid," which he had flown in Australia. From this was evolved a very small, fast seaplane, known as the "Schneider" model, on account of its winning the Schneider Cup, at Monaco, against all comers. This little machine was fitted with the 100-h.p. Monosoupape-Gnome engine, and at the outbreak of war was ordered in large numbers by the Royal Naval Air Service, which knew it as the "Baby." The War Office authorities, however, considered it dangerous, on account of its risk of catching fire; but when there was evolved a similar machine, fitted with an 80-h.p. Gnome, carrying 3½ hours' fuel, and with a speed variation of from 40 to 90 miles, the War Office began to take notice. At this time Sopwiths were busy on another type of two-seater machine, which in 1915, fitted with an 80-h.p. Gnome, climbed to a height of 18,390 feet. This eventually developed into the "one-and-a-half-strutter,"[5] and in 1916 put up some magnificent performances.

In the meantime the little scout was undergoing tests, and finally emerged as the "Sopwith Pup," mounted for war purposes with an 80-h.p. Le Rhone engine, but for instructional work with an 80-h.p.

---

[5] The "one-and-a-half-strutter" designed by Sopwith contained a cabane with "V" struts for the centre section, the struts running upward and outward from the fuselage to the top-plane. These struts were about half the length of the outer strut (at the end of the wings) on each side, hence the name.

Gnome. With this small power the performance was surprisingly good, and no pilot flew anything more delightful than the Pup. With the 80-h.p. Le Rhone and two hours' fuel, the speed at 10,000 feet was 100 miles an hour, and the time occupied to climb to 10,000 feet was 15½ minutes. In course of time more power was put into the scout, until the whole machine was redesigned, but the puzzle which mystified airmen was the delay in fitting the 100-h.p. Monosoupape, seeing that the R.N.A.S. pilots were using that engine in practically the same machine in 1915.

Close on the heels of the Pup came the Sopwith triplane, vulgarly known as the "Tripe." This machine was mostly used, and with great success, by the R.N.A.S. over Dunkirk. An objection to the type was the ease with which the machine got out of alignment, especially after one or two steep dives; on the other hand, it was of great effect as a steep climber. About the time that this type made its appearance, the Germans produced something similar. The first two Sopwith triplanes which crossed the Channel landed by some mischance in the enemy's territory, and were taken by the Germans. Richthofen's Circus appeared with many of the triplane type, very similar to the British machine.

A new scout was produced by the Sopwith firm in 1917, under the name of the "Camel," type F.I. In appearance this machine was distinctive; the top plane was flat, while the bottom plane had considerable dihedral. Fitted with a 130-h.p. Clerget engine for fighting purposes—a 110-h.p. Clerget being generally used for training work—it could climb to 10,000 feet, with full military load, in 12 minutes, and at that height was capable of flying 113 miles an hour. During experimental work the Camel has climbed to 20,200 feet in 36 minutes. In the R.N.A.S. the Camel was fitted with the 150-h.p. Bentley rotary engine, mounted with two Vickers guns and one Lewis, and had a folding fuselage for stowing away on ships. It was with this type of aeroplane that No. 4 'Australian Squadron was equipped. That squadron was one of the first to use it, and excellent work it did. It was decidedly tricky to fly, but, when once a pilot mastered its eccentricities, he preferred it to any other. As was the case in all types, the machine was overloaded and expected to do the impossible; but in the history of the Sopwith productions there is no machine which accounted for itself better than the Camel. In the "Dolphin," type S.F.I, was fitted a water-cooled 200-h.p. stationary Hispano-Suiza engine. With a nose very like the D.H.9, and the radiators fitted to the side, this machine, when in the air, looked very business-like. Another feature was the back-staggering of the top plane and the position of the pilot, who was seated through the centre section, with his head well above the top plane. The armament was two Vickers guns firing through, and two Lewis firing over, the propeller. The climb to 10,000 feet, fully loaded, required 12 minutes, and the speed at that height was about 121 miles an hour.

Early in 1918 another Sopwith made its appearance, the "Snipe," type 7.F.I. It carried a 200-h.p. Bentley rotary engine. The fuselage was stream-lined in conformity with the cowling, which was of large diameter. Primarily designed for fighting high up, with full military load, it could climb to 10,000 feet in 9 minutes, and to 20,000 feet in about 27 minutes; the speed at 10,000 feet was 121 miles, and at 20,000 about 100 miles, an hour. Low down this machine was at first uncomfortable to handle—indeed, the higher it climbed the more controllable it became. To cure this fault at the lower altitudes, it was decided, after many tests had been carried out, to fit balanced ailerons. These at once overcame the difficulty. That this innovation was adopted so promptly was largely due to Lieutenant-Colonel T. O'B. Hubbard, who was exceptionally brilliant in experimental work, and had built his own machine and flown it. (In his youthful days Colonel Hubbard had worked his way round the world, and at one stage of his journey was boundary-riding on East Talgai Station, Southern Queensland. As a consequence, if ever he came in contact with Australians, he could not do too much for them, so long as they were " made of the right stuff.") No. 4 Australian Squadron was equipped with this type of machine in October, 1918.

The Vickers.

The famous firm of Vickers commenced aircraft operations as far back as 1911, placing them in the capable hands of the late Major H. F. Wood, who took his certificate (No. 37) on a Bristol biplane in 1910, and proved a great acquisition to the firm by attracting many army officers to the Vickers school at Brooklands. Besides turning out box-kite pushers for instructional work, the firm also produced an efficient monoplane, which did a great deal of work in pre-war days. A historic machine turned out by this firm was the famous " Gun Bus," a pusher mounting a 100-h.p. Gnome-Monosoupape engine. This was a two-seater, and at the outbreak of war the only practicable fighter in the possession of the British service. It was not unlike the F.E.2.b. The pilot sat in the back seat, and the observer in front, armed with a Lewis gun. In spite of its great weight for the horse-power—it weighed a ton without pilot, passenger, and equipment— the Gun Bus saved many a grave situation in 1914 and 1915, and brought down a number of German machines. It was in one of these craft that an early V.C. was won.

During the war Vickers turned out many experimental craft, probably one of the fastest being the "Bullet," which in 1915, fitted with the Monosoupape engine and in the hands of one of the greatest of pilots, the late Harold Barnwell, could be looped upwards, commencing at 100 feet, and would attain any height desired after a series of loops. The "stunt piloting" in those days was as good as it is to-day; but the pilots were mounted on vastly inferior machines, with unreliable engines, and no instruments to assist them in any way. Neither the cure for a "spin"[6] nor performances like the "roll"[7] and the "Immelmann turn"[8] were then known, but the pilot in those days was a natural pilot, and more artistic than many stars of the present day. Nevertheless, the Bullet was too blind for fighting purposes, and did not go into production. It was not till 1917 that "stunting" became part and parcel of a pilot's training. Although the experimental machines did not appeal to the authorities, Vickers were kept hard at work turning out orders to Government specifications. It was not until early in 1918 that the Vickers-Vimy made its appearance, fitted with two F.I.A.T. engines. The Vimy was not an attractive machine to look at; it had a very low under-carriage in proportion to the span, the bottom of the narrow fuselage being flush with the lower planes. With the F.I.A.T. engines its climb to 5,000 feet, with

---

[6] Spin—See Glossary.

[7] Roll—See Glossary.

[8] Immelmann Turn—See Glossary.

a load of 2,480 lbs., took 14 minutes; the speed at that height was 96 miles an hour. Fitted with two 200-h.p. Hispano-Suiza engines, the performance of the machine was not so good. Just as the Armistice was reached, another Vimy was brought out with two Rolls-Royce engines of 350-h.p. each. The disposable load on this machine was 2,000 lbs., and there was a very slight increase in the overall length, which did not increase the total surface area. The climb to 5,000 feet took 21 minutes with this load, while the speed at that height was 98 miles. The maximum speed low down was 103 miles. It was in machines of this type that the late Sir John Alcock and Sir Arthur Brown crossed the Atlantic, and the late Sir Ross Smith with his Australian crew flew from England to Australia.

The Handley-Page (H.P.).

In the middle of 1909 Mr. Handley Page formed a company to build his own machines and supply orders to specifications. The first successful machine to be built by the firm was a pretty monoplane which had swept-back wings, very much like a dove, and greatly resembled the inherently-stable German Taube. Following this type there was produced a biplane which at the outbreak of war was taken over by the Navy for instructional purposes. In 1916 Handley Page brought out a twin-engined machine fitted with two Rolls-Royce engines of 250-h.p. each, and during the same year the late Clifford B. Prodger piloted one of them to a height of 7,000 feet, with twenty passengers on board. This machine went into production, but one of the earliest to cross to France was presented to the Germans early in 1917. Two officers and three mechanics, its crew, landed by mistake near Laon, in territory occupied by the enemy. It is said that the capture of this machine set the example to the Gothas, but it is established that the Germans produced twin-engined machines long before the British.

After this incident the H.P. was considerably modified, and the power increased by the fitting of two 365-h.p. Rolls-Royce. These machines did great work in France and Egypt on long bombing-raids. One of them was used to bomb Constantinople, while another was the first to fly from England to India. Early in 1918 another machine made its appearance in the type V/1500, with four 365-h.p. Rolls-Royce carried tandem-wise. This type was designed principally for night bombing, and especially the intended bombing of Berlin. The first machine built crashed hopelessly during tests. Both crew and machine were destroyed through the wreck bursting into flames on the ground. When the second of the same type was produced, there was still a great deal of experimental work to be done. It was found, for instance, that the cowling over the engines affected stability. Then it was discovered that the machine was too short in overall length, and, in consequence, had to be altered. Finally, with a disposable load of 7,000 lbs., excluding fuel—the tank capacity being 1,000 gallons—the machine climbed to a height of 10,000 feet in 21 minutes, the speed at that height being 95 miles, while low down it was 103 miles an hour. Unlike the twin-engined type, this machine had both upper and lower planes of equal span, 126 feet, compared with a span of 100 feet in the top plane of the former. Three days before the Armistice this craft was being prepared for a raid on Berlin, and, when fully equipped, was a nest of machine-guns and bombs even to the tip of the tail, where an observer's cockpit was actually situated at the rudder.

The Armstrong-Whitworth (A.W.).

One of the most interesting firms building aircraft in Great Britain before and during the war was that of Sir W. G. Armstrong, Whitworth & Co., of Gosforth, Newcastle-on-Tyne, the great ship-builders. Their aviation department was opened early in 1913, and later, in 1915, they also contracted to build air-ships.

The first works-manager to be employed by this firm was Mr. F. Koolhoven, from the Deperdussin firm, in France. The famous A.W. two-seater was designed by Mr. Koolhoven. The first, the F.K.3 model, greatly resembled the B.E.2.c, with the difference that the observer sat behind the pilot. The engine was a 90-h.p. R.A.F., which developed a speed of 85 miles an hour. The landing speed was about 40, and the climb to 10,000 feet occupied 25 minutes.

The larger machine, the F.K.8, an improved F.K.3, was fitted with a 120-h.p. water-cooled Beardmore, and gave the impression of being a clumsy craft; but it carried out some wonderfully-fine work on all British fronts. It was used for bombing, photography, artillery-spotting, contact-patrol, and general reconnaissance work. The F.K.8 was considerably under-powered, and, in consequence, always overloaded; but even when the later type, fitted with a 160-h.p. Beardmore, was produced, the machine was invariably sent out with excessive loads. In the larger-engined type the lines of the cowling were modified, and the radiators made smaller and otherwise improved. Two guns were carried, one firing through the propeller, and the other attached to the observer's gun-ring. The landing speed was about 45 miles an hour, the maximum speed was 104 miles at 1,000 feet, and the climb to 10,000 feet occupied 18 minutes.

Among other early machines produced by the firm was a small scout fitted with a 50-h.p. Gnome, which had, for those days, a fine rate of speed of about 80 miles per hour. There were also a 250-h.p. triplane and a few 130-h.p. quadruplanes, none of which succeeded in meeting service requirements. Towards the end of 1918, however, a promising machine was produced in the 220-h.p. B.R.2 F.M. type, "Armadillo Scout," which incorporated some unique features of design. The fuselage was square, with the top plane resting on the top longerons. The round cowling had a box-like hump, part of the fuselage, under which were mounted two guns firing through the propeller. A V-type under-carriage was adopted, contrary to the usual A.W. practice, and there were two bays on each side of the fuselage. The landing speed of this machine was 55 miles an hour. At 1,000 feet it was credited with 140 miles, and the climb to 10,000 feet required only 4½ minutes.

The 320-h.p. A.B.C. F.M. type, "Ara," was not produced until after the Armistice, but this also made very creditable performances. The engine, a "Dragonfly," was of the fixed radial type characteristic of the A.B.C. products, and was capable of a speed of 150 miles an hour at 1,000 feet, landing at about 57, and climbing to 10,000 feet in 5½ minutes. Although these two machines were too late to participate in the war, the earlier A.W. machines played a conspicuous part.

The trend of design which followed the best efforts of different firms is worth a final note. The Sopwith and Avro products were essentially rotary-engine results, while the best results gained by Martinsyde, Bristol, and De Havilland were with the stationary water-

TYPES OF AEROPLANES

cooled machine. Vickers demonstrated what could be done with heavy low-powered aeroplanes. Monoplanes went out of existence as war machines in 1916. It proved difficult in designing them to overcome "blind spots." Their wing-surface spread being small, it was always necessary to land them at a fast rate of speed; in consequence they required a large landing-area.

II.—French Types.

The Blériot.

Among the pioneers of aviation who fought against public opinion and great financial odds was Louis Blériot. He startled the world by his flight across the English Channel on 9th July, 1909, in a small monoplane fitted with a 25-h.p. air-cooled engine of three cylinders, built by Anzani. This flight was in itself a record for duration for that type of engine. With the coming of the Gnome engine Blériot built larger machines, though similar in design to the cross-Channel type, and with these he won many important events. As a consequence he received large orders from foreign Governments. The late Maurice Guillaux used a Blériot when on his tour in Australia. Though the Blériot has been credited with being the first to loop, as a matter of fact the first aeroplane to perform this feat was a Caudron.

Just before the outbreak of the war Blériot produced a new type of monoplane, which he called the "Parasol." The difference between the original and this later type lay in the anchorage of the wings to the fuselage, the wings being attached to a cabane, or centre section, above the head of the pilot. This arrangement afforded a perfectly clear view below, which, in the ordinary type of monoplane, was rendered impossible by the obstruction of the wings. These machines remained in use until about the end of 1915, when they were abandoned as too slow. But it is remarkable that, though Blériot became one of the largest constructors in the world, and was at one time the leading designer and manufacturer—having commenced in 1906—he did not turn out one successful aeroplane after the advent of the Parasol. Though he made many attempts, they failed in performance; his factories were, consequently, used for the production of machines designed by other companies.

The Caudron.

Another interesting firm which began operations in the earliest days of aviation was that of Caudron, conducted by two brothers. One of them, Réné was killed.

The Caudron is one of the most efficient aeroplanes of its kind in the world, and has extraordinary capacity as a weight-lifter in proportion to surface and horse-power. The first of these machines was fitted with a three-cylinder 35-h.p. Anzani engine, and proved a wonderful success. It was remarkably safe, and no instance of fatal accident with a Caudron is known to the writer. Mr. A. W. Jones, who later joined the A.F.C., brought one such machine to Australia. Another Australian pilot who did good work before the war with a Caudron (45-h.p. Anzani) was Captain Delfosse Badgery. Later an 80-h.p. Gnome-engined Caudron, type G.2, was imported into Australia for private use; but at the outbreak of war the patriotic owner presented it to the Government, and the machine eventually found a resting-place at the Point Cook School. During active service the Caudron proved most useful. The original G.2, fitted with the 80-h.p.

Gnome, or the 80-h.p. Le Rhone, was at one time used all over the front by both French and British; it was adopted as a school machine by the British till the end of 1915, and by the French for instructional purposes until the completion of the war. Upon this type some of the world's greatest airmen were trained. The G.2 looks much like the Maurice-Farman Shorthorn, but, instead of the engine being situated at the rear of the nacelle, it is placed in the front, making a tractor of the machine. The under-carriage is the simplest of all aeroplane designs, and, when landed with even moderate skill, will run only a few yards after taking the ground, in consequence of the tailbooms acting as brakes. The G.2 was the first machine to be looped. A young French military pilot, Lieutenant Chanteloup, who was attached to the Caudron Escadrille, got it into his head that a machine should be able to loop, provided that there was sufficient speed behind it. He accordingly went up over Issy aerodrome, near Paris, and succeeded in the attempt, making about five good loops. Upon coming down he was informed that, if he repeated the performance, he would be placed under arrest and court-martialled. The following day he was sent off on a cross-country flight, and when over Buc, another French military aerodrome, he decided to show them the latest feat. Not content with about ten loops, he came down to observe the effect upon his brother pilots. The officer commanding this aerodrome was so excited about the exhibition put up by Chanteloup, that he telephoned the Issy aerodrome to congratulate them upon their magnificent pilot. Chanteloup was promptly placed under arrest by the orders of the commander at Issy. Pégoud, the chief Blériot pilot, happened to be on the Buc aerodrome at the time. He worked hard on his own machine, reinforced its tail, and thereafter performed a series of loops, from which he obtained the credit of being the first man in the world to loop. The army authorities then released Chanteloup, feeling that enough punishment had been meted out to him in the loss of that credit.

In 1915 Caudron produced a twin-engined machine built on the same lines as the G.2, but having two 80-h.p. rotary engines. It was on one of this type that Lieutenant Poulet in 1919 attempted the France-Australia flight. The great weight-lifting capacity of this machine, with its imperviousness to bad weather, commended it to the French for bomb-dropping. From 1915 onward Caudron specialised in twin-engined bomb-droppers. Among the most successful of these was the type C.23, fitted with two 250-h.p. Z.9 Salmson engines, and, in place of the old tail-boom system, built along the ordinary aeroplane lines with a beautifully stream-lined, cigar-shaped fuselage. The climb of this machine, fully loaded, to 3,000 feet, was 9 minutes, and to 9,000 feet 37½ minutes. The maximum speed at 3,000 feet was 143 kilometres, and the cruising speed 82; the maximum speed at 9,000 feet was 136.

The Farmans.

Farman Brothers was a pioneer firm with a romantic history. Of the three brothers, Henri and Maurice are the best known; the other, Dick, attends to the management of internal affairs, though he, too, is a brilliant pilot. These men are naturalised Englishmen, who at an earlier date had won many important bicycle-races. After the Wright brothers brought their biplane to France, the firm of Henri Farman Aeroplanes was established in 1908. Maurice also established works about the same time, and in 1912 they joined forces and built the

TYPES OF AEROPLANES

works which stand to-day at Billancourt, Paris. In 1912 they realised that war between France and Germany was inevitable, and that a great part would be played in the air. They therefore designed their factory so as to be able to turn out ten aeroplanes per diem. When the war eventually did break out, they were the only firm in the world who could turn out machines in quantity without having to revolutionise their works or add buildings. The factory is two miles long and employs 5,000 workers.

Two brothers named Séguin invented and built the Gnome engine, and after hawking this round to various "aircraft cranks," as they were called in those days, they lit upon Henri Farman. He at once gave them orders. He then set to and built an aeroplane around the engine, and with it put up record after record for speed, height, and duration. One of the most-controllable aeroplanes that ever took the air was the Henri-Farman, fitted with the 80-h.p. Gnome. Although this machine was put out of commission at the end of 1915, the "Maurice-Farman Shorthorn" was still in the lists at the time of the Armistice. Both the Henri and the Maurice were of the pusher type, the former with the rotary, and the latter with the stationary, engine. The first Henri was really a box-kite, and the Bristol and Grahame-White firms later adopted the same lines of design. Then the nacelle came into vogue, and Henri eliminated the front elevator and used one tail-plane with one rudder. Maurice meanwhile brought out a machine with the nacelle, retaining the front elevator with its ungainly booms. As the front booms looked like the horns of a bullock, the machine was christened the "M.F. Longhorn." This machine nearly won the War Office trials in 1912. Then followed another machine of the pusher type, which retained the nacelle and the fixed air-cooled engine, but eliminated the front elevator and the booms. Instead of the double tail-plane the single plane was adopted, with twin rudders placed on the upper surface of the after plane. This machine was known as the Maurice-Farman Shorthorn, and till the end of 1915 performed good work over the lines. The engine used in France in that year was the 80-h.p. Renault. All instructional work in the Royal Flying Corps was carried out with M.F. Longhorns and Shorthorns fitted with 70-h.p. and 80-h.p. Renaults. As Henri brought the Gnome engine to the fore, so did Maurice the Renault. The Farmans and the Renaults were boys together, and all through their lives the friendship has stood fast.

Maurice Farman further produced a machine which was largely used by the French for reconnaissance, bomb-dropping, contact-patrols, and artillery observation, and was fitted with a 135-h.p. Renault. From this was evolved another known as "The Horace," which had the old Henri tail and landing-gear, with the Maurice Shorthorn nacelle. The next step was a twin-engined type. From the outset the firm was successful with these productions, but the most successful in this line was the 50 B.N.2, fitted with two 275-h.p. Lorraine-De Dietrich engines. With full load at 1,000 metres this machine is capable of flying 147 kilometres an hour. Like the Caudron, it was a slow lander, and was therefore greatly in demand for night-bombing.

Before the outbreak of the war the Farmans also built seaplanes for the French Navy. One of this type was purchased in 1914 by Mr. Lebbeus Hordern, of Sydney. The owner had just taken delivery of it when war came, and the seaplane was presented to the Commonwealth Government. It found its way to New Guinea with the Australian Naval and Military Expeditionary Force, but was not used, and finally found a resting-place at the Point Cook School, where it was seldom, if ever, employed.

The Morane.

The firm of Morane is famous, and was in existence for years before the war. In the *Daily Mail* race round England in 1912, when Lieutenant Beaumont won on a Blériot, the 50-h.p. Gnome Morane, piloted by the late Jules Vedrines, was only a few minutes behind it. Later Morane produced a smaller monoplane, which, with an 80-h.p. Le Rhone, put up many notable performances. The Morane was a well-known fighting machine; though rather difficult to fly, it possessed a good climb, and was fast, especially the "Morane Bullet," but it had the gliding angle of a brick, and in forced landings was extremely dangerous. Another successful product was the "Parasol." Although Blériot produced the first monoplane Parasol, Morane was quick to perceive its advantages, especially for war purposes, and in designing his own Parasol he introduced a clever system of girders to support the planes. While the Bullet possessed a *monocoque* fuselage with balanced elevators and warping—with ailerons later—for lateral control, the first Parasol had a neat rectangular body, with balanced rudder and elevators, which made the machine very sensitive. Eventually a Parasol was produced with *monocoque* body, back-swept wings, ailerons, and a fixed tail-plane. This was fitted with a 160-h.p. Monosoupape-Gnome, had a good turn of speed, and was popular among the French fighting-scout squadrons. A few months prior to the Armistice, Morane died in Paris from influenza, after a few hours' illness, just as he was expecting final results from an experimental biplane of clever design, with back-swept wings and plenty of stagger, and fitted with a 420-h.p. Bugatti engine.

The Nieuport.

The Nieuport firm was established in 1910 by two brothers, both of whom died before the war. In the early days they specialised in the monoplane. One of the most successful of these was a small machine fitted with a horizontally-opposed twin-cylinder engine of 30-h.p., which was capable of 67 to 70 miles an hour. Unfortunately many fatal accidents occurred with this type, no doubt due to spinning when flying low down. In those days there was only one man known to have gone into a spin and to have got out of it alive—the late Lieutenant Wilfred Parke, R.N.—and he was in an early Avro. In 1915 there was produced a two-seater biplane which had a large upper plane with aileron control and a smaller lower plane connected by "V" inter-plane struts. The engine was a rotary; and the observer sat under the centre section, through which there was a man-hole to permit the gunner to stand up in order to use his *mitrailleuse* over the propeller. This gave him a great field of vision from above, but did not allow for attack from below. Later this machine was slightly altered in design, the pilot being placed under the centre section with the observer and the gun-mounting aft. Among British pilots this type was not popular, as, like the Morane, it had a poor gliding angle and was slightly underpowered at heights. From this was evolved the famous Nieuport "Biplan de Chasse," or destroyer, one of the successes of 1916-17. This little machine was built much on the lines of the two-seater, the upper and lower planes being connected by "V" inter-plane struts. The lower plane consisted of only one spar; this was designed to give girder formation to the wing bracing, but otherwise was of little aero-dynamic assistance.

TYPES OF AEROPLANES 415

There is probably no firm in France who spent more money upon experimental models than Nieuports. Machines were designed and fitted with Renault, De Dietrich, Hispano-Suiza, and Le Rhone engines, in all instances the "V" inter-plane strutting and smaller lower plane being adopted. Next to the little "Chaser," the Nieuport single-seater, type 28.c.1, was the most successful machine. It was fitted with a 160-h.p. Monosoupape engine and *monocoque* fuselage, but in place of the "V" inter-plane struts the usual pair of struts on each side was employed. From the front the machine looked like the Bristol Scout, except for the fact that the upper plane had a slightly larger span than the lower, and there was only about a third of the dihedral found in the Bristol.

The Spad.

The initials S.P.A.D. stand for "Société Pour Aviation et ses Dérives," though the firm was originally known as the "Société Pour les Appareils Deperdussin." Armand Deperdussin was the originator of the firm, and with his designer, M. Béchéreau, turned out many notable machines. It was on one of these that, before the war, Lieutenant Porte used to delight British spectators. His monoplane was fitted with a 100-h.p. Anzani, then regarded as a monster. There were smaller monoplanes built for school-work fitted with 35-h.p. Anzani engines, one or two of which found their way to the Point Cook School, but were there flown only once or twice. Deperdussin, as time went on, found himself in bad financial straits, but aviation had taken possession of him, and at all costs he was determined to carry on. He worked up a colossal swindle in silks which ran into millions of francs. In 1913 he was sentenced to imprisonment for a number of years. The aeroplane business was then carried on for the benefit of the creditors by M. Béchéreau, who had been appointed technical director and was fast becoming one of the world's foremost designers. As his assistant he had M. Koolhoven (who afterwards became designer to the B.A.T. Co. in England), and in 1913 they designed a monoplane which, flown by M. Prévost round a twenty-kilometre triangular-circuit, covered 124.8 miles in an hour. Soon after the outbreak of war the new company was formed, with M. Blériot at the head of the directorate and M. Béchéreau technical director. From the outset they built "aeroplanes de chasse," which probably held the French record for number of enemy machines destroyed.

There were four successful types turned out—type 7, fitted with a 150-h.p. Hispano-Suiza engine, and types 12, 13, and 17, with 220-h.p. engines of the same make. An outstanding feature of these machines was the neat design of the inter-plane struts, which appeared to be in keeping with the small gap. The same form of strutting is to be found on the small B.A.T. machines, and shows the trend of thought evolved in the Béchéreau-Koolhoven school. In all the above-mentioned types there is little difference in the measurements, the span and the length increasing very slightly with the increase of power. Their one drawback was their rapid forward stalling-speed, in consequence of which they had to be landed fast. Just prior to the Armistice a new Spad made its appearance, fitted with a 300-h.p. Hispano-Suiza, and credited with an extraordinary performance.

To sum up the French machines, the most marked points of difference from the British are the back-sweep of the planes, the *monocoque* fuselage, a tendency towards small lower-planes, "V" or single-girder strutting, and a small dihedral angle. The French Service, as the result of proper Government encouragement, was undoubtedly better equipped from the beginning than the British. Instead of purchasing foreign machines, as the British Government did, the French encouraged home industries and reaped the benefit when the war broke out.

III.—German Types.

The foresight with which the German Government laid the foundations of the German air service has been described. During the war there were about fifty firms in Germany designing and building aircraft, and many of them, thanks to Government encouragement, entered the business before war began. Time and again, in spite of the calls upon her air service, Germany held a limited superiority over the French and British on the Western Front. This was due to no other reason than her ability to change over rapidly to new types of machines which had proved successful in the experimental stage and could be rapidly turned out and placed in the air in large quantities.

The Fokker.

One of the most-respected machines employed by the Germans was the Fokker. In fact, in proportion to the horse-power it is very doubtful if there was any fighting aeroplane so efficient as the Fokker, especially the type D7 (160-h.p. Mercedes engine), which came out in 1918. One of these, captured intact, was pitted in practice against the latest British type, the Martinsyde F3 with 275-h.p. Rolls-Royce engine. Each machine was flown by a proved fighting-pilot. They fought, taking turn about in each machine, and the man in the Fokker won every time. Neither pilot had flown either of these two types before, so that no advantage lay with either on that score. To give away 115-h.p. is a great factor in itself, though, when it came to a matter of "ceiling," the Martinsyde was vastly superior. Nevertheless the manner in which the Fokker would "hang" on her propeller without stalling was itself worth considerable height.

Fokker, who is a Dutchman by birth, early became infatuated with flying, and in 1912 had a machine built by Goedecker to his own design on monoplane lines. It was inherently stable, was V-shaped, and used no lateral control. The machine was difficult to handle, and even Fokker himself, when flying with a German flying officer, came to grief, dived to earth, and killed the passenger. In 1912 the Fokker was offered to the British Government, but was turned down—and quite rightly, the machine not being at that time stoutly built. Under influential German encouragement Fokker improved his machine, until at the outbreak of war it had reached the stage at which it was considered sufficiently good to go into quantity-production. In 1915 it had still further improved, and during that year practically ruled the air in the hands of Immelmann, Boelcke, and others, who called the B.E. machines "Fokker fodder." The engine in this machine was an Oberursel rotary, as was also that used in 1916 in Fokker's fourth production, the D3. The fuselage of this machine was built on Morane *monocoque* lines with a balanced rudder of "comma" shape, characteristic of all Fokkers, and balanced elevators, while both the top and lower planes were of equal span and were warped in place of ailerons. The top planes were attached to a trestle-cabane on Nieuport lines, while the under-carriage was of Morane pattern.

As in the monoplane, the guns operated through the propeller. The machine on the whole proved very effective.

Then came the D4, with a fuselage built along whale-type lines, the nose running to a stream-lined taper, into which was fitted a stationary engine. The balanced rudder remained, with a balanced tail-plane, while ailerons were adopted in place of the warp. The D5 followed, and showed new departures in many details. It was probably produced after the British one-and-a-half-strutter had proved itself. The fuselage returned to the *monocoque* lines, but with greater diameter at the cowling, with the top plane sweeping back, much after the style of the pre-war machines, and reducing the stagger at the wing tips. The trestle-cabane was maintained, but, instead of two bays between the wings, only one pair of struts was adopted on each side. Following this came the D.R.1, or Fokker triplane, with fuselage of rectangular design. A *tail-plane of fish-tail shape* and balanced elevators took the place of the entirely balanced tail. The centre section consisted of four struts, two on each side, which sloped outwards from the bottom, but met at the top plane like an inverted "V" and were cross-braced by wires. The span of the three planes differed, the greatest being that of the top plane and the least that of the bottom plane. The under-carriage was decidedly after Morane, and the engine a rotary. This machine put up some great work during the war, and was responsible for the downfall of many of our best machines. It was one of the favourite machines of the late Baron von Richthofen.

But the most successful Fokker machine, and the one which evoked most interest among experts, was the type D.7, which came out in 1917. In this the fuselage was modified to carry the fixed 160-h.p. Mercedes, which also mounted, contrary to usual German method, a car-type radiator in front. The under-carriage was in design rather British. Both planes were in one piece, and almost square at the corners. There was no external wire-bracing, and the inter-plane struts were of three pieces in the shape of the letter "N." The climb to 3,000 feet took 4¼ minutes, to 10,000 feet 14 minutes, and to 16,000 feet 38 minutes. The speed at 3,000 feet was 116 miles, at 10,000 feet 103, and at 16,000 about 95—excellent performances for a machine of 160-h.p. A Parasol monoplane was evolved from it, with a rotary 200-h.p. Goebel engine installed in place of the fixed power-plant. This machine, however, came out only at the time of the Armistice.

The Albatros.

One of the principal aircraft-factories in Germany was that of the Albatros Werke, which commenced building machines in 1910 under licence to French constructors. In 1912 a graceful "Taube" (Dove) monoplane was produced, with enclosed cabin for a passenger and fitted with an Argus engine. The machine was exhibited later at the Paris Aero Salon and caused no little sensation by its good appearance. Aero-dynamically, however, it did not prove a success. When one Hirth, a prominent pilot, joined the firm as designer the monoplane came to the fore, fitted with a Benz engine. Hirth also devoted attention to seaplanes, with which in 1913 he was very successful. He further specialised in weight-lifting machines, and at different times established world's altitude-records for three and four passenger types. At the end of 1913 he produced a biplane which put up two world's duration-records of twenty-one and twenty-four hours' flights. This machine was fitted with a 150-h.p. Benz engine, and was one of the first tractor-biplanes built by the firm. At the outbreak of war the Albatros machines, fitted with 128-h.p. Mercedes engines, were not credited with an abundance of speed, but they had good lifting capacity, and at first were used as two-seater fighters and for general reconnaissance work. In 1916 a small scout, type D.1, made its appearance, fitted with a 160-h.p. Mercedes engine and capable of a speed of about 115 miles an hour. The outstanding feature was the undivided elevator; the fin and the rudder were carried forward of the elevator, and this arrangement eventually became characteristic of Albatros machines. At the beginning of 1917 appeared a new "Albatros Destroyer," type D.3, fitted with a Benz or Mercedes engine of 175-h.p. mounted in the nose of a cigar-shaped or *monocoque* fuselage. During 1917 this machine met with extraordinary success, due largely to some of the "aces" then predominant. Richthofen's Circus consisted of machines of this type, which were credited with speeds varying from 120 to 130 miles an hour. The latest scout was the type D.5, a modification in minor ways of the D.3. Fitted with a 225-h.p. engine, the type C.5 biplane became familiar to Australian pilots, and was really an enlarged D.1, except for a curious arrangement of the balancing of the ailerons.

Rolands.

Two firms in Germany which turned out successful machines were the L.F.G. Roland (Luft-Fahrzeug Gesellschaft Roland) and the L.V.G. (Luft-Verkehrs Gesellschaft). In the early pre-war days the Roland machines were known as the "L.F.G. Taube" (monoplane) and the "L.F.G. Arrow," a biplane which put up a duration record in 1914. Roland, like many of the early German firms, began building machines under licence to some established foreign firm, and the first types to be built by this company were Wrights. During 1914-15 the Arrow tractor-biplanes were greatly in use for reconnaissance work, and it was not until early in 1917 that a single-seat Roland scout made its appearance. The fuselage on this machine was built on *monocoque* lines of oval section, but finished up with a vertical knife-edge at the rudder post. There was an infinitesimal difference in the span of the planes, no stagger or dihedral, a slight back sweep with uniformity in chord and gap. The ailerons fitted to the top plane were of the unbalanced type and, unlike those in the majority of German machines, did not project. The engine was a 160-h.p. Mercedes. The latest "Roland Scout" at the time of the Armistice was fitted with a 190-h.p. B.M.W. engine.

Luft-Verkehrs Gesellschaft (L.V.G.).

The L.V.G. firm was one of the largest aircraft-manufacturers in Germany, and commenced business in 1910 by building machines under licence to the Farmans. In 1912 the L.V.G. procured the services of a Swiss engineer, who had been employed as a designer by the Nieuports. As was natural, one of the first machines turned out by the new designer followed very much the lines of the Nieuport monoplane. It proved a failure until the Gnome engine was built under licence in Germany; but the machine began to win prizes as soon as this power plant was fitted. At the same time was produced a biplane with a stationary engine, which proved so successful that in the great Prince Henry competition of 1914 three of these machines carried off the first, second, and third prizes, and at the conclusion it was taken as the standard for types of tractor biplane for German military purposes.

TYPES OF AEROPLANES

From the outset the L.V.G. has adopted a rectangular fuselage. The nose was flat on the keel surface, but otherwise rounded to cigar shape. The 1915-16-17 types of two-seaters were fitted with a 160-h.p. Benz motor, the observer sitting behind the pilot. The span of the upper plane was much in excess of the lower, and for a German machine there was considerable dihedral angle on both planes, especially in the 1916 model. As early as 1915 the firm adopted the system of building the radiator into the centre section, and this became more or less the standard throughout the German war machines. One of the most successful L.V.G. two-seaters was the type C.6, with a 230-h.p. Benz engine. A pronounced stagger of about ten inches contributed to make it appear on first sight much like the British D.H.9. The elevator was similar to that of the Albatros, being all in one piece, with the fin and rudder well forward. There were many features of design and workmanship in this aeroplane which caused much comment among Allied designers.

The Pfalz.

A machine which was little heard of until the beginning of 1917 was the Pfalz, though this firm was actually building before the war. One of its productions—a pusher—was at the outbreak of war in German South-West Africa, where it made some remarkably fine flights.

One of the first Pfalz war-machines was a monoplane, built somewhat on Fokker lines but not so comely, owing to the adoption of a fixed engine. Where the Fokker employed one gun firing through the propeller, the Pfalz used two. In 1917, however, the Pfalz firm produced a noteworthy machine in the shape of the single-seater type D.3, with a *monocoque* fuselage, which followed the cigar-shape to a greater extent than any other machine on the front, and mounted a 160-h.p. Mercedes. The wings were of decidedly Nieuport appearance, there being no dihedral on the upper plane, but a slight angle on the lower one. The upper plane was all in one piece, and fitted with ailerons. The radiator was carried on the starboard side of the upper plane. The tail-fin on this machine was built into the fuselage, and was extremely neat, while the tail-skid, of simple design, could be removed in a few minutes. The climb to 5,000 feet occupied 7 minutes, and to 10,000 feet $17\frac{1}{2}$ minutes. At 10,000 feet, flying level, it could make 102 miles an hour, and at 15,000 feet 91 miles. With two Spandau guns, and carrying $21\frac{1}{2}$ gallons of petrol, it was capable of staying in the air about $2\frac{1}{2}$ hours.

Another type of Pfalz, produced in 1918, was a complete departure from the D.3. This was the D.12, and was a single-seater fighter carrying a 180-h.p. Mercedes with a car-type radiator fitted, very much of the shape of the D.H.4. The fuselage was neatly streamlined oval-wise. There were two bays between the planes on each side of the fuselage; "N" struts were used, except in the centre section, which had "M"-shaped struts inclining outward. The tail-fin was a separate fitting, and the rudder ran down to the bottom of the stern post, necessitating the fitting of a pair of elevators.

The Halberstadts.

One of the crack German firms at the end of the war was that of Halberstadt. This firm in 1914 was manufacturing Taube machines under the name of Deutsche Bristol Werke, but it was changed to Halberstadt in 1915 and turned out biplanes which showed a marked relation to British and French designs. Its 1916 biplane was fitted with a 120-h.p. Argus engine, which had the sharp nose characteristic of the German, but a fuselage trailed off in Morane fashion. The petrol tank and radiator formed the centre section, while the upper and lower planes were of equal span, with a fair dihedral and considerable stagger. In 1917 was produced the type C.L.2, which at that time was quite the best of its kind in the German service. This also from a side view resembled the D.H.9. The tail-plane was whale-shaped, with a one-piece elevator, the rudder being well forward. The most notable features were the one-bay set of inter-plane struts on each side of the fuselage, a considerable set-back to the wings, and the pilot's and observer's cockpit in one. It had a splendid field of fire, and was easily manœuvred. It was on account of these two factors that the Halberstadt was a machine to be reckoned with. The climb to 5,000 feet required 9½ minutes, to 10,000 feet 24½ minutes, and to 14,000 feet 52 minutes. The service "ceiling," however, was not much over 13,000 feet. The speed at 10,000 feet was 97 miles an hour. In 1918 the type C.L.4 came into existence. The difference was largely in small measurements, such as the span of the upper plane.

The Gotha.

A company which did not pass through the initial "gruelling" stages of the pioneer was that of the Gotha. This firm was one of the wealthiest in Germany, and during the war financed many other firms of repute. It set out originally to manufacture in large quantities aeroplanes of proved design, and, by engaging the best pilots available, won many of the valuable prizes which were then to be picked up. In the early days much attention was paid to seaplanes, many of which were turned out for the Turks as well as for the German Navy. A small Falcon scout-biplane was developed, which greatly resembled the Morane in its fuselage; but the most famous of all the Gotha products was the twin-engined bomber. It has been already said that the landing of the big twin-engined Handley-Page bomber in Germany supplied the pattern from which to build twin-engine bombers, but that the Gotha firm was on the same track at the time Handley Page was experimenting. It began by building twin-engined seaplanes, its standard type being a pusher, whereas the H.P. was a tractor; there was also a considerable back-sweep on the German main planes, and not the overhang on the top plane noticeable in the H.P. machines. In the 1918 types the engines were neatly housed with the radiators facing the direction of motion or at the rear end of the power plants. A twin-engined tractor was evolved at the end of 1918, a likely-looking machine with decided modifications to the fuselage, under-carriage, and inter-plane strutting.

Other Types.

The Aviatik, A.G.O., A.E.G., D.F.W., Brandenburg, Hannoveranner, Kondor, Rumpler, and a host of others have all their historical interest. The main point worthy of note is that these German firms in the days before the war all built machines under licence to firms of established renown—a fact which shows the shrewdness of the German mind. As time went on they incorporated their own ideas with those of foreign makers, until finally aeroplanes appeared entirely characteristic of the German train of thought, which was purely and simply that of military utility.

APPENDIX No. 2.

CORRESPONDENCE RELATING TO FORMATION OF A.F.C.

Although the Australian Government did not of course attempt to prevent Australian civilians from enlisting in any British service, it came, mainly for national reasons, to set its face firmly against the policy, which for a short time had existed, of allowing privates or non-commissioned officers in Australian forces to apply for commissions in the British Army. Moreover, considerations of pay and administration induced both the British and Australian authorities to stop all transfers of men or officers between their respective forces. Such, however, was the importance of obtaining suitable men for the rapidly-expanding air service that the British authorities asked the Dominion Governments to allow the men of their respective forces to volunteer for promotion in the Royal Flying Corps. Although it had been made known to the British Government that this was contrary to the policy adopted by the Commonwealth, the request in this special case was urged in the following letter from the Secretary, War Office, to A.I.F. Headquarters, dated 11th July, 1916:—

> I am commanded by the Army Council to inform you that, owing to the expansion of the Royal Flying Corps, a large number of officer pilots will be required during the ensuing year.
>
> In view of the exceptionally good work which has been done in the Royal Flying Corps by Australian-born officers, and the fact that the Australian temperament is specially suited to the flying services, it has been decided to offer 200 commissions in the Special Reserve of the Royal Flying Corps to officers, non-commissioned officers, and men of the Australian Force.
>
> In the interests of the Service, it is recommended that the policy regarding commissions in the Imperial Service being offered to non-commissioned officers and men of the Australian Expeditionary Force should be relaxed in the case of the Royal Flying Corps, as it is considered that a large number of valuable men would thus be available as volunteers for this most important branch of the Service.
>
> I am to inquire whether there is any objection to this proposal; if not, the conditions of selection, appointment, etc., will be forwarded to you for communication to all concerned.
>
> (Sgd.) B. B. CUBITT.

The consent of Australia was obtained, and on September 12th General Birdwood called for applications from the A.I.F. as follows—181 (21 officers, 160 others) from A.I.F. in France and Great Britain, 19 (3 officers and 16 others) from A.I.F. in Egypt; totalling 200.

The appointment was, in each case, to be on probation. The applications of 197 candidates were shortly afterwards forwarded by the A.I.F. Fourteen of the applicants, for various reasons—defects of eyesight, unsuitability, etc.—were not eventually appointed officers in the flying corps. The number of those who became officers in the R.F.C. in consequence of this invitation appears to have been 183.

Many of these served with great distinction in the British forces, but their record, along with that of many other Australians, belongs to the magnificent history of those services and could not be touched upon in these pages, even if—as is not the case—there existed in Australia any means of collating them.

Although the Australian Government was thus induced to make, in the case of the British flying arm, a notable exception to its general rule against cross-enlistments, the proposal subsequently made by the British Government, that the Dominions should inaugurate their own air services, was completely in accord with its policy.

The correspondence between the Australian Government and the British and Indian Governments provides an interesting description of the manner in which the Australian Flying Corps came to be formed, and traces its gradual growth from the first small beginnings.

Australian (Mesopotamian) Half-Flight, A.F.C.

Cable message dated 8th February, 1915, from the Viceroy of India:—" Could you provide any trained aviators for service in Tigris Valley? All our trained officers are in Egypt and England. If officers available, can you also send machines complete with motor-transport, mechanism, personnel, spares, etc.? We should prefer biplanes. If available, we should like particulars of machines. Should you be unable to send machines, we can obtain Maurice-Farman or Blériot types from England. Have you any aviators who have handled either type?" The Australian Government replied on February 10th, offering two airmen and necessary mechanics, but stating that no aeroplanes were locally available. The airmen would prefer Maurice-Farman machines because accustomed to Army-type machines.

In response to a further message from the Viceroy of India, the Australian Government cabled on February 26th:—" We will send four flying officers, about twenty mechanics and drivers, one motor-bicycle, one motor-car, three motor-lorries for tools and stores, two motor-vehicles fitted with repair machinery and tools, six waggons to carry spares and portable hangars for which it is proposed to supply mules. This provides a half-flight complete, and extra transport will only be required to send petrol, oil, and supplies along line of communications. Suggest an adjutant or staff officer be detailed from your troops. Five aeroplanes should be provided, Maurice-Farman pattern with Renault engines, but if Gnome engines only available, Blériot pattern best. Renault engine much more suitable to local conditions."

The details of the half-flight were communicated to the Viceroy of India in a cable message dated March 23rd:—" Personnel consists 2 captains, 2 lieutenants, flying officers; 1 sergeant-major, 1 staff-sergeant, 1 sergeant, 3 corporals, 12 others, total 18, all air-mechanics; 1 quartermaster-sergeant, 1 farrier-sergeant, 15 mule-drivers, 2 cooks, 4 batmen, total 23, all soldiers; 3 riding horses, 4 teams six mules, 2 teams eight mules, and 30 spare in case of difficulty with mechanical-transport in sandy country."

The Viceroy of India early in April requested " Very early despatch " of the half-flight to Bombay. In response to another request, for information as to numbers of, and ranks of, each trade —carpenters, blacksmiths, riggers—included in the eighteen air-mechanics, the Australian Government cabled on April 21st:—
" Woodworker, 1 warrant-officer; woodworkers and riggers, 1 corporal,

FORMATION OF A.F.C.

5 privates; metal-workers, 1 staff-sergeant, 1 sergeant, 2 corporals, 6 privates; blacksmith, 1 private; total 18."

In May six more drivers and one wheeler were sent to the half-flight to complete revised establishment for the waggon section.

No. 1 Squadron, A.F.C.

Extract from despatch dated 20th September, 1915, from the Secretary of State for the Colonies:—" The conditions under which candidates from Dominions, who desire to serve in the Royal Flying Corps, can be accepted, are as follows:—

"(a) Officers must hold commissions in the forces of the Dominion, and must be recommmended by the Dominion military authorities as suitable for service in the R.F.C. Should any be specially commissioned they should be appointed second-lieutenants of infantry. On arrival in the United Kingdom they will undergo a course of instruction in aviation, and, if they graduate as pilots, will be posted to the R.F.C., but if not, they will become available for service with the contingents of their Dominion.

"(b) Other ranks should belong to one of the trades (shown in schedule) and should be enlisted as 2nd Air-Mechanics (2/A.M.).

"It is thought that Dominions might wish to raise complete aviation units. Such units would take their place in the general organisation as units of the R.F.C., but will be given distinguishing designations. The most convenient unit would be a squadron. The advanced training of pilots and the instruction of the rank and file would be carried out in the United Kingdom."

Cable message dated 24th November, 1915, from the Secretary of State:—" With reference to despatch dated September 20th, Army Council now states that, owing to completion of establishment of Royal Flying Corps, mechanics from Dominions cannot be accepted for enlistment. Above does not apply to men joining any complete aviation unit raised and paid for by your Government.".

The first response by the Australian Government, dated November 24th, read:—" Reference your despatch of September 20th, Commonwealth Government desires to co-operate, but considers impracticable to organise complete squadron either in Australia or in conjunction with other Dominions. Two complete flights, total 12 officers and 68 other ranks of trained personnel, could be organised and despatched if acceptable, to be equipped and paid by this Government."

The Secretary of State replied on December 14th:—" Army Council suggest that if there are difficulties in forming complete squadron due to lack of suitable personnel, officers and men of Australian Expeditionary Force, many of whom have asked for employment in flying corps, could be used, and also some of personnel now in Mesopotamia. In this way Australian unit would be made identical with other units of Royal Flying Corps and could be probably kept wholly Australian."

This was approved by the Australian General Staff, and the Australian Government replied on December 27th:—" Commonwealth Government will organise a squadron, flying corps, 28 officers and 181 other ranks, for despatch in February."

Cable message, dated 12th January, 1916, from the Secretary of State:—" Army Council appreciate highly action of your Government in raising aviation unit. As personnel presumably will require further instruction before they can take the field, Army Council suggest that it would be most convenient if unit were despatched to Egypt, where training can commence at an earlier date than in England, and where also it may be possible to employ unit in same area as other Australian troops, though it is impossible to guarantee latter. Please telegraph when squadron will reach Egypt."

Cable message dated February 3rd, from Australian Government:—" Squadron, flying corps, with first reinforcements numbering twenty, will leave Melbourne about March 14th. Unit can disembark Egypt if so desired."

Cable message dated February 9th, from Secretary of State:—" Squadron should disembark at Egypt. Necessary equipment will be despatched to officer commanding 5th Wing, Royal Flying Corps, under whom squadron will be placed."

No. 2 Squadron, A.F.C.

Cable message from Australian Government dated 29th July, 1916:—" Australian Government offer personnel for a second flying squadron complete except seven observers and six pilots. Suggest deficiency be supplied by attaching officers Royal Flying Corps. Squadron could embark November. If accepted, please notify destination."

Reply from Secretary of State dated 15th August, 1916:—" Army Council grateful for personnel offered, but, in view of difficulty of training in Australia and urgent need of their services, consider very desirable that whole personnel should be despatched immediately to England to be trained. They recommend officers should be appointed to second-lieutenants only and non-commissioned officers for voyage only, and would propose to appoint Australian-born officer of R.F.C. to train and command squadron and select flight-commanders for winter training. War establishment of squadron is officers 36, warrant-officers 2, sergeants 18, rank and file 196."

Cable message from Australian Government dated August 22nd:—" Concur with proposal, but can send only some twenty-four officers. Personnel will be despatched October. Should first reinforcements accompany squadron, and are subsequent monthly reinforcements required for the two squadrons? If so, at what rate?"

Reply from Secretary of State dated September 2nd:—" Army Council would like flying squadron to be sent to England in September if transport can be arranged, and carry out whole training here. First reinforcements should accompany squadron, and these, with monthly reinforcements—two selected candidates for flying officers and twenty mechanics—should form reserve training squadron to fill wastage in two squadrons. Strength of reserve squadron might be kept up by volunteers from Expeditionary Force in England and France. Establishment of reserve squadron is 21 officers, 2 warrant-officers, 17 sergeants, 136 other ranks."

No. 3 Squadron, A.F.C.

This squadron was raised in Egypt and sent to England for training at the end of 1916.

FORMATION OF A.F.C.

No. 4 Squadron, A.F.C.

Cable message from A.I.F. Headquarters, London, to Australian Government, dated 22nd September, 1916:—" War Office desires to be informed total number of flying corps squadrons (service and reserve) which you might be able and willing to raise, and that for each two service squadrons one reserve squadron should be provided for training purposes and for replacement of wastage of personnel. Service squadrons, when ready, to be stationed on the various fronts to co-operate with their own troops. Mobilisation equipment of service squadrons to be provided by War Office, and resources of Royal Flying Corps will be made available for this purpose for training of personnel when training undertaken in Egypt and United Kingdom."

Reply of Australian Government dated October 2nd:—" Second Flying Squadron leaving October per *Ulysses*. Fourth Flying Squadron can be raised and despatched December, and monthly reinforcements at ten per cent. sent to build up two reserve squadrons for the four squadrons which will then exist, including Third Squadron already raised in Egypt. Is percentage of reinforcements sufficient? Squadrons and reinforcements will be incomplete as regards officers, majority of whom can receive only brief training aviation before embarkation."

Extract from cable message dated 2nd January, 1917, to A.I.F. Headquarters, London:—" Fourth squadron embarks *Omrah* 17th January, 1917."

APPENDIX No. 3.

WAR FLYING INSTRUCTION IN AUSTRALIA.

Pilots and mechanics for the Australian Flying Corps were drawn from all military districts of the Commonwealth. While in training at Point Cook, they were regarded as on probation, and any who were found to be technically unsuitable for the work were transferred. At Point Cook all ranks received as much training as the time prior to embarkation would permit.

Eight courses of flying instruction were held there:—

First course, August–November, 1914—four officers attended; all qualified as pilots.

Second course, March–June, 1915—eight officers attended; all qualified.

Third course, began August, 1915—eight officers attended; included also advanced course of two months for four officers who had previously qualified.

Fourth course, began March, 1916—eight officers attended; all qualified.

Fifth course, began August, 1916—sixteen officers attended; four sent away as unsuitable, twelve sent to No. 2 Squadron (then being formed) before completion of course.

Sixth course, began November, 1916—twenty-four officers attended and were transferred to No. 4 Squadron (then being formed) before completion of course.

Seventh course, began February, 1917—twenty-four officers and seven non-commissioned officers (A.F.C.) attended; thirteen qualified. Owing to bad weather and lack of instructional machines, work was seriously handicapped.

Eighth course, began June, 1917—eight officers and nine non-commissioned officers (A.F.C.) attended.

APPENDIX No. 4.

AIRCRAFT WIRELESS.

Eastern Front.—Not until the end of 1916 did aircraft wireless come into general use on the Eastern Front. Till then work in that direction had been experimental. Early in 1917 began the serious business of co-operation with the artillery. No. 1 Australian Squadron was at this time a corps reconnaissance squadron, and all its machines were fitted to take the Sterling No. 1 transmitter set, at that time the regulation apparatus for co-operation with artillery. These sets were small and light, and were in the B.E. machines fitted immediately in rear of the pilot's seat. The aerial on the machine consisted of 120 feet of stranded copper-wire, with a 3-lb. lead weight at the free end in order to keep the wire hanging as perpendicular as possible. It was wound on a drum placed in the cockpit of the observer and convenient to his right hand, and from the drum the aerial was led through the bottom of the fuselage by means of an insulated gland. To run out the aerial the observer released a brake on this drum. At the conclusion of transmission the aerial was wound in, and the brake held the drum secure with the lead weight home against the bottom of the gland through the fuselage.

As Bristol Fighter machines were used by the squadron when it became an army squadron, a different method of installation had to be adopted. The observer's cockpit in this machine was larger than that of a B.E., and the instruments, suspended by rubber shock-absorber, were usually placed in front of the observer. The wind-driven generator, in the case of a wireless set employing one, was clamped to the under-carriage of the machine in such a position that its propeller was in the slip stream of the aeroplane's propeller.

The aerial arrangement was similar to that of the B.E., except that the drum was fitted with a quick-release device, by means of which, should the aeroplane be attacked while wireless work was proceeding, the aerial could instantly be freed from the machine, thus permitting of sudden manœuvres being carried out without the danger of the aerial fouling the wings or the tail.

The Sterling No. 1 sets had a range of approximately eight to ten miles, and in No. 1 Squadron operated on a wave-length of 180 metres. Different wave-lengths were adopted by different R.F.C. squadrons, in order to obviate interference.

The battery wireless-stations were, for obvious reasons, made as inconspicuous as possible. The usual arrangement was a single aerial about 100 feet long, supported by two light poles twelve feet high, with one end of the aerial wire led down into the operator's dugout. The receiving instrument used throughout at the batteries was the Short Wave Mark III. Tuner, a piece of apparatus remarkable for simplicity of adjustment, robustness, and reliability. The earth system normally consisted of two copper-gauze nets, either spread on the bottom of the dugout, or on the ground near the receiver.

Two flying corps operators were allotted to each battery wireless-station, and it was their duty to maintain a continuous watch during the hours of daylight for aeroplane wireless-calls to their battery, each of which had its own call letters. Signals from the machine were passed on to the battery-commander usually by telephone. Signals from ground to aircraft were made by means of white strips placed on the ground, the arrangement of the code being such that four strips were the maximum necessary to convey any message. In addition to the battery stations it was usual to establish a wireless receiving-station at artillery brigade headquarters. The function of this station was to check aeroplane "shoots" of various batteries, and, in response to wireless requests from the air, to detail batteries to fire on any particular target. Throughout its period of service No. 1 Squadron maintained an average of twelve battery wireless-stations.

In 1917, when No. 1 Squadron became an army squadron, the system of wireless necessarily changed, as the work now being done comprised long strategical reconnaissances, and made the use of long-range apparatus necessary. The sets then employed were the type 54A (200-watts power, worked from accumulators), the type 52A (150-watts power, worked from a wind-driven alternater fitted to the machine), and, towards the end of the war, the type "W" Continuous Wave transmitter, worked by a 600-volt wind-driven generator. These sets had a range of about 70-80 miles, the two former operating on a 200-metre and the latter on a 1,200-metre wave-length. Reconnaissance machines telegraphed back to the aerodrome any bombing targets which they saw during flight, and these targets were then attacked by machines held in readiness. Principally from considerations of space and weight, it was not usual to fit receiving instruments in machines. But towards the end of the war reception in the air was practised at the aerodrome. It was about this time that the latest wireless-telegraph (aircraft) sets began to arrive in Palestine, but wireless-telephone sets, such as were being used on the Western Front, never made their appearance in this war-theatre.

Experiments in wireless telephony with apparatus made up in the field were undertaken by No. 1 Squadron about the middle of 1918, and although the results obtained were satisfactory from an experimental point of view, the lack of apparatus and renewed activity on the front prevented their development. Greater success was achieved in the adaptation of captured German aircraft wireless-gear, particularly as ground transmitters for inter-squadron work. Some consternation was caused at G.H.Q. when work with these Telefunken transmitters was first undertaken, but upon identity being established, the use of these extemporised transmitting-sets was permitted.

Western Front.—On the Western Front, when No. 3 Australian Squadron arrived in England (December, 1916), a wireless section, consisting of a wireless officer and thirty other ranks, was attached to the squadron, and when training operations commenced, the wireless section was sent to the R.F.C. Wireless Training School at Farnborough (Hants.). The wireless operators, without their officer, were sent to Belgium in July, 1917, and were temporarily attached to various R.F.C. squadrons for artillery co-operation; shortly after their arrival they were in the Passchendaele action, during which they suffered a number of casualties. In August of the same year another detachment of thirty operators proceeded to France, and these were similarly attached to R.F.C. units, while No. 3 Squadron was undergoing final training. When this squadron was attached for work with the Australian Corps, all A.F.C. wireless operators were collected again under their own wireless officer.

AIRCRAFT WIRELESS

Thenceforward the wireless section assisted in aircraft co-operation with all classes of artillery, from heavy batteries to trench-mortars. The maximum number of battery stations under the control of No. 3 Squadron was ninety-six. These stations were not entirely manned by A.F.C. wireless operators, whose total strength was 108.

Artillery co-operation was carried out by means of the Standard Sterling Transmitter in the R.E.8 machines, and Mark III. crystal receivers on the ground. At the squadron station and the central wireless station, amplifiers were used for reception, and, as it frequently happened that six machines were carrying out "shoots" at the same time, these two stations were called on to intercept the signals from all six machines simultaneously, with remarkably good results. The crowding on the fighting front of machines fitted with transmitters called for special skill by mechanics in correctly tuning transmitters and in the reception of the correct signals. "Wireless-failure" reports were very few.

Shortly before the Armistice, when a few Bristol Fighters were supplied to No. 3 Squadron, special continuous wave-receivers (C.W. Mark III) and 52A type C.W. transmitters were fitted in these machines for communication to and from the ground. Owing to the Armistice, however, only a small portion of the work intended for these machines—i.e., long-distance "shoots"—was carried out.

No. 2 and No. 4 Australian Squadrons did not possess machines fitted with wireless, and were not supplied with wireless personnel until August, 1918, when two operators were supplied to each squadron, so as to equip stations at squadron headquarters for the interception of reports and instructions from the wing, sent by wireless.

For the improved communication of intelligence from machines to the ground there was brought into operation in August, 1918, the "Central Information Bureau" (C.I.B.) system. All machines, especially corps counter-attack patrols, reported all enemy movements, transport, tanks, aircraft, or information about our own troops, by wireless to a station in an advanced position, which was constantly moved forward, as the fighting front advanced, to keep in touch with aeroplanes on the line. The station collected all "C.I.B. calls" from the air and sent them, by telephone or by wireless, to the various units concerned. Most of these calls were sent on to the army wing, which kept scout machines standing by ready to take the air at any moment. The C.I.B. system of collecting and distributing information allowed machines to carry a weaker and less cumbersome wireless set than would have been necessary if they had had to transmit messages direct to more-distant stations in the back areas.

Each corps squadron also had its own central wireless station (C.W.S.) some distance in advance of the aerodrome and situated in a central position as regards the heavy artillery. It was connected by telephone with squadron and artillery headquarters. It kept a running record of all "shoots" and zone calls, in order to assist in any difficulty which might arise between pilots in the air and batteries.

APPENDIX No. 5.

A.F.C. TRAINING IN ENGLAND.

The system of training pilots of the Australian squadrons in England during the first eight months of 1917 is described by Captain E. G. Knox,[1] Recording Officer of No. 3 Squadron. In the main, what he says of No. 3 Squadron holds good also for the others.

Flying Officers.—Selected candidates, after medical tests, were despatched to either No. 1 School of Military Aeronautics, Reading, or to No. 2 School of Military Aeronautics, Oxford, for a six weeks' course, which included lectures on the theory of flight, aerial navigation, aero-engines, and construction of aeroplanes. In addition, practical experience was gained in aero-engines and in rigging, as well as in Morse-code buzzing, elementary artillery-observation, bombing, compass, map-reading, &c. At the conclusion of the course the candidates were subjected to a written examination and, if successful, were sent to an elementary training squadron for instruction in aviation.

Two types of machine were then in use in these elementary training squadrons—the Maurice-Farman (Shorthorn or Longhorn), and the Grahame-White. From 1917 onwards pilot-pupils began their training on Avros.

The average pupil after three-hours' dual instruction, split up into breaks of fifteen minutes, was considered ready for a first solo-flight. This successfully accomplished, the pupil was required to complete a total of five hours' solo in the elementary machine, including as many landings as possible, or until the instructor was satisfied that the pupil could land the machine. The solo time on "Rumpitees" (as the M.F. Shorthorns were generally called) was varied from time to time. In 1916, for example, pupils were required to do only two hours' solo before being sent on for higher training. The time was increased to five hours, and later, in 1917, reduced to four hours.

Some little idea was gained in these elementary squadrons of the capabilities which the pupils exhibited, and an indication was obtained of the aptitude for one or other of the types used on service. Pupils who did best in elementary machines were usually selected for higher training in a scout squadron, while those not considered suitable for fast and light machines were sent to two-seaters. Mistakes in selection were sometimes made. Many pilots of the two-seater squadrons were quite as good as the so-called scout-pilots. Pilots in fighting two-seaters, e.g., Bristol Fighters, were required to be just as efficient pilots as those in scouts.

Since No. 3 Squadron was destined for service in France as a two-seater corps squadron, training of pilots for this class of work was allotted to it. Here the pupil recommenced dual flying, but this time in a more difficult machine. About this period the Avro (80-h.p. Gnome) was used in the majority of higher-training squadrons for preliminary instruction. About two and a half to three hours' dual

[1] Maj. E. G. Knox, M.B.E.; No. 3 Sqn. (previously Infantry). Journalist; b. Glebe, Sydney, 25 June, 1889.

TRAINING IN ENGLAND

was necessary before the pupil was sent off solo. After doing about five hours' solo on an Avro, the pupil was given a few landings in a service machine and then sent solo in that.

A sum total of twenty-hours' solo (including the time in elementary machines) was necessary before a pupil could graduate as a pilot. But several further tests were introduced. He must perform a cross-country flight of at least forty miles and make two landings away from his own aerodrome. He had to climb to a height of 8,000 feet, shut off his engine, and land on his own aerodrome without assistance from the engine. He had to make two landings by night guided by flares. Among special tests were:—

Bomb dropping: to fly three times over a Bachelor mirror, an instrument for judging the exactitude with which bombs could be dropped.

Photography: to photograph from a height of from 1,500 to 5,000 feet six out of eighteen points given by map-reference.

Buzzing: to send and receive eight words a minute on a buzzer.

Artillery Observation: to conduct at least one successful shoot on a picture-target on the ground and one successful shoot from the air, with a puff-target, observations being sent down by wireless.

Formation Flying: to take part in at least one formation flight.

Fighting Practice: to carry out elementary fighting practice in the air.

Machine-gunnery: to satisfy examiners in knowledge of Vickers and Lewis guns, stripping and assembling, and shooting on ground range. The camera-gun generally used in practice was of the Lewis type. It was used both on the ground—for firing at machines in the air round the aerodrome—and on machines in fighting practice. They were of such great value that the fighting squadrons in France each had two allotted. Thus in the service squadrons pilots could, when opportunity offered, get further practice.

Having completed these tests and the twenty-hours' solo, the pupil was considered a graduated pilot, and was given permission to wear his "wings."

During the early months of 1917, the B.E.2.e was still the principal machine used for corps work in France, and it was in this type that pupils in No. 3 Squadron graduated; but towards April and May, in consequence of the changing over in France to R.E.8's and A.W's, pupils were frequently sent to other training squadrons after graduation, in order to fly types of machines which they would eventually fly oversea. Frequently a pupil who, during his elementary training, was not regarded by his instructor as a likely scout-pilot, showed during later training for a corps squadron signs of playing that part with success. Such pupils were graduated in No. 3 Squadron, and were recommended for further training with scouts.

Mechanics.—The training of the mechanics of the squadrons was a highly important work. A mechanic could make or mar the efficiency of a machine in air fighting, and every successful pilot during the war learned the importance of having his machine well kept. The tradesmen of whom air-mechanics are composed are:—Acetylene-welders, blacksmiths, coppersmiths, fitters (engine), riggers, electricians, magneto-repairers, fitters (general), and machinists. The school at

Halton Camp, where the Australian air-mechanics were trained, was divided into eight technical sections, numbered 1 to 8, each of which, to facilitate records, technical returns, and administration, was allotted a distinctive colour.

Acetylene welders (Section 1) were instructed in all branches of acetylene-welding, and their course was of eight-weeks' duration. Blacksmiths' work (Section 1) consisted of making forgings of engine parts, preparing blacksmiths' tools, and all ordinary blacksmiths' work, in which they received twelve-weeks' instruction. Coppersmiths (Section 1) received eight weeks' instruction in all coppersmiths' work, and especially in the making of induction pipes and in tube bending. Included in this branch were also sheet-metal workers and tinsmiths, who instructed fitters (engine) in the making of engine-cowlings, sweating of joints, and metal-work repairs.

Fitters (engine) proceeded through three technical sections before they were ready for posting away for duty. On arrival at the school they entered Section 7, where they had five-weeks' instruction in bench-fitting to make them proficient in the use of tools and to teach them accuracy in, e.g., the making of simple engine-parts. For the more advanced work on aero-engines they were passed on to Section 2. Here pupils remained for eight weeks. They were first taught the principles of the internal-combustion engine, and later received advanced and specialising instruction in one engine only, so that each fitter (engine) was passed out classed as "Fitter (engine) Clerget," or otherwise, according to whatever engine he had been trained upon. In this section pupils had to pass a written as well as a practical examination at the end of their course, after which they proceeded to Section 5, for three weeks' instruction, which embraced erecting, i.e., mounting the engine into the aeroplane; squadron-routine, i.e., the marking of the aerodrome with wind-cones and flares, keeping the aerodrome clear of obstruction, &c.; engine-running and adjustments, i.e., swinging the propeller and methods of obtaining the best running-results out of an engine; handling the machine; how to start up a machine; the proper place available on the machine for holding and method of chocking it for the "get away"; how to receive a machine on landing; and gun-gears. During their course in Section 5 pupils attended classes in Section 1 for two-days' instruction in copper-smithing for simple repairs, and then finished training in Section 5 with one week on the workshop lorries—fitting, turning, and general repairs.

Riggers on arrival entered Section 3, and for seven weeks they received instruction in the rigging of a machine, splicing, sailmaking, instrument repairing, and general repairs to aeroplane. They then had a written examination and proceeded to Section 5 for a further week's instruction, which consisted of squadron-routine, engine-running and adjustment, and handling the machine.

Electricians and magneto-repairers were trained in Section 4. The electricians' course comprised elementary theory, internal and external wiring, accumulator charging and discharging, repairing and making, repair of instruments, car-lighting sets, handling, running and repair of motor and generators, telephone- and bell-wiring—twelve-weeks' instruction in all. Magneto-repairers received ten-weeks' training in elementary theory, working, repair, and testing of all makes and types of magnetos. They also received instruction in car-lighting sets.

Fitters (general) performed work entirely different from that of fitters (engine). They were employed in repair-parks and dépôts, working with machinists. Fitters (general) entered Section 7, for eight-weeks' instruction, and then passed on to Section 8. In this section machinists were trained for sixteen weeks in the use of machine tools, and fitters (general) remained for eight-weeks' instruction, working in conjunction with the machinists. This training was to enable them to carry out work on machine-tools which did not require specialists, such as drilling, plain turning, shaping.

APPENDIX No. 6.

ORGANISATION OF R.A.F. IN FRANCE.

The Royal Flying Corps (later Royal Air Force) was divided into brigades, wings, and squadrons.

A brigade, R.A.F., consisted normally of three wings—the army wing, the corps wing, and the balloon wing (consisting of a balloon-company for each corps in the line). One R.A.F. brigade was attached to each army.

The army wing usually included about six squadrons. There were one or two long-distance bombing-squadrons (usually D.H.4 or D.H.9 machines), one or two long-distance reconnaissance-squadrons (usually Bristol Fighters), and two or more squadrons of fast single-seater fighting-machines (fighting scouts). Towards the end of the war an extra army wing, consisting solely of fighting scouts, was added to the brigade. The types of scouts varied, for new machines were continually being introduced. No. 2 and No. 4 Australian Squadrons were army scout-squadrons. No. 2 Squadron flew, first D.H.5's, and then (December, 1917) S.E.5.a's. No. 4 Squadron used Sopwith Camels until October, 1918, when it was equipped with the new Sopwith Snipes. The principal work of the scout squadrons was offensive-patrols and low-flying bombing-patrols over the enemy's forward areas, these patrols being always carried out in formation. Offensive-patrols were designed to attack and destroy as many enemy machines as possible. The objective of the fighting scouts was to keep the air clear of the enemy, in order to make possible the utmost opportunity for uninterrupted reconnaissance by the corps squadrons. Machine-gun attacks and bombing-raids on enemy positions became in emergency the duty of all classes of machines. Such raids might be great or small. Sometimes as many as sixty or seventy machines were employed on this duty, as in the great bomb-raids on Lille towards the end of the war. Or, again, there was the form of low-flying harassing attack like that employed by No. 4 Squadron on the Lys before the German retreat, when small patrols of two or three machines would fly continually over the enemy's rear lines to disturb work at his supply-dumps and on his lines of communication, and to worry his infantry in village rest-billets. At times corps machines also performed bombing-raids, individually or in small formations, and sometimes on this work they carried, instead of an observer, 150-lbs. weight of sandbag-ballast (flying ballast) in the rear cockpit or two iron bars on the tail-plane, one on each side of the rudder (flying tail-weight).

Long-distance bombing, e.g., into Germany, was the duty of special bombing-squadrons, and even of a specially organised service of the R.A.F., the "Independent Air Force."

The duties of the scouts were fairly constant; those of the machines in the corps wing covered a much wider range, though more confined as regards locality. The scouts, being in an army wing, ranged the entire army front; at times they searched beyond it in liberal interpretation of their duty to seek out and destroy the enemy air forces. Each British army had generally two, sometimes more, corps in line on its battle-front. Each corps had a squadron of two-seater machines attached to it for work detailed by corps headquarters. Such a squadron used either R.E.8 or A.W. machines, often in the latter part of the war with one or two Bristol Fighters attached for long-distance reconnaissance. No. 3 Australian Squadron was a corps squadron attached to the Australian Corps, and flew R.E.8's.

The work of a corps squadron included detailed reconnaissance of its corps front, artillery observation, photography, and emergency low-flying patrols. The squadron was a vital part of the corps intelligence-service. Whenever the weather was fit for flying—and often when it was not—at least one machine was kept out on artillery-patrol. Its duty was to watch for enemy batteries firing, enemy transport, and other good targets for the corps artillery, and to report them to that artillery by wireless. These wireless messages were known as "zone calls." The enemy area opposite was divided into zones of fire (of about 3,000 yards square), and in trench-warfare each British battery had its allotted fire-zone.

Artillery observation was the most important branch of the corps squadron's offensive-work in stationary warfare. It entailed the current recording from the air of "counter-battery shoots" (bombardments of enemy batteries) or bombardments of other targets. Generally there were attached to the squadron one or two officers on loan from heavy-artillery batteries, called "artillery liaison officers" (A.L.O.). A counter-battery programme was issued each evening by the "counter-battery staff-officer" (C.B.S.O.) to battery commanders and the A.L.O. The A.L.O. kept a file of aeroplane-photographs of all known enemy batteries on the corps front, and prepared for each pilot a photograph of his target, marked with circles around the ranging-point to aid him in making corrections. The pilot also obtained from the battery, or the A.L.O., the number of guns to be used, the time of flight of the shell, positions of ground-strips, and any other information required. "Shoots" were practically always recorded ·by the pilot, and not by the observer, as were also photography- and artillery-patrol reports. The observer's time was fully occupied in looking out against attacks from enemy aircraft, against which his machine-gun was the machine's main defence. Thus of 515 bombardments carried out by No. 3 Squadron in 1917-1918, only six were conducted by observers.

In artillery "shoots" observation of the fall of each round fired by his battery was signalled back by the pilot by means of the "clock-face"

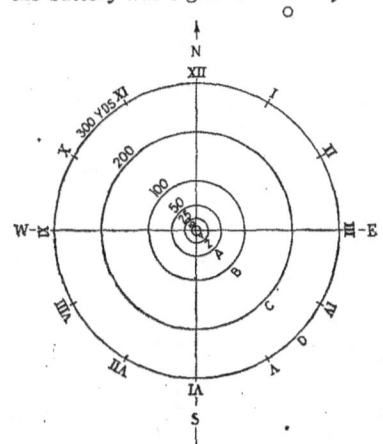

Sketch illustrating "clock-face" method of checking artillery fire upon enemy batteries. In observing artillery fire, the fall of the rounds was noted with reference first to the smallest circle within which they were contained, and secondly to clock hour to which they were nearest. Thus a shot which fell 90 yards east of the target would, according to this code, fall at B 3, that is, within the B or 100 yards circle and towards 3 o'clock.

system. That is to say, the target was regarded as a clock-face, with due north taken as 12 o'clock. Distance of shots from the centre of the target was then reported by code, thus:—

O.K.—Exact centre.	A.—50 yards out.	D.—300 yards out.
Y.—10 yards out.	B.—100 yards out.	E.—400 yards out.
Z.—25 yards out.	C.—200 yards out.	F.—500 yards out.

Aeroplanes were fitted with wireless instruments for sending, but not for receiving, and all signalling from guns to the machine was, therefore, done by means of ground-strips—large white strips of cloth laid out beside the battery wireless-station. In winter, at such times as the ground was covered with snow, the strips were of red or black cloth.

For photography the camera, a long sheath-box arrangement, was, in early types of aeroplane, carried at the side of the machine, handy for the pilot's use. From 1916 onwards the camera was carried in a camera-fitting built in behind the observer's cockpit. It was operated by various mechanical devices from the pilot's seat. The observer changed the plates. Photographs were of two sorts—oblique and vertical. Oblique (bird's-eye-view) photographs were taken by corps squadrons from a height of 1,000 to 1,500 feet. They provided an excellent picture of a large area of country. Vertical photographs were taken from a height of 5,000 to 8,000 feet and as far as 4,000 yards behind the enemy's front-line. Photographs of areas farther in the rear were made by army machines (Bristol Fighters and D.H's) from heights up to 20,000 feet. Vertical photographs for mapping purposes were normally taken with a wide-angle lens at from 8,000 to 10,000 feet, in order to include as wide an area, and as many "fixed points," as possible. Photographic distortion was found to be less pronounced from the higher altitudes. Both kinds of photograph were of great value in acquainting the infantry with features of the enemy's front-line defences, and in confirming locations, obtained by ground-observation and sound-ranging instruments, of hostile batteries.

Low-flying patrols, a regular duty of a corps squadron, included:—

(1) Close special reconnaissance of the enemy's trenches, performed by the "infantry flight" or "trench flight" of the squadron.

(2) Contact-patrols during an infantry attack upon the enemy, keeping in touch with the infantry advance and notifying distant command-posts of the positions reached. A contact-patrol machine could fly over the attacking troops and sound a series of "A's" (in Morse code) on a Klaxon horn. The arranged response of the infantry was to light flares in trenches or shell-holes (so as to hide the signals from the enemy); or to show bright tin-discs or white cloths. Another ground-signal was the laying of rifles, muzzles outward, on the parados (opposite side from the parapet) of a captured trench.

(3) Counter-attack patrols, patrols maintained over the line during and after an infantry attack on the enemy in order to watch for signs of any infantry counter-attack. If any massing of the enemy was observed, the counter-attack machine would send back an S.O.S. signal for a general bombardment by all supporting artillery within reach. Besides the S.O.S., there were other calls arranged for minor emergencies.

In No. 3 Squadron "A" Flight was known as the artillery-flight, and "B" Flight as the counter-attack flight. During stationary warfare both these flights were engaged in artillery-patrols and artillery-observation, and "B" Flight in counter-attack patrols. "C" Flight was the infantry-flight or trench-flight. All flights were available for photography, though photography was usually undertaken by pilots who showed a special aptitude for that work.

APPENDIX No. 7.

AEROPLANE COUNTER-ATTACKS ON THE GERMAN ARMY, MARCH, 1918.

To assist the reader's mental picture of the dangers risked and the damage wrought in the low-flying aeroplane attacks on the enemy's ground forces during the March offensive, it is worth while to quote some detail of No. 4 Squadron's performances from the pilots' own reports as made at the aerodrome on their return from each attack. The following extract from the squadron record-book describes part of the day's work of March 26th:—

"Lieutenant Schafer: Dropped two 25-lb. bombs on road running from Bapaume to Ervillers from 2,000 feet (8.30 a.m.). Was attacked by Albatros scout and two triplanes, which drove me practically on to the ground and damaged my machine. Fired 250 rounds on Bapaume–Albert road at troops and transport from about fifteen feet.

"Lieutenant F. J. Scott: Dropped two bombs, one on village of Gommecourt and one on village of Achiet-le-Grand from 1,000 feet (11.25 a.m.). Fired 600 rounds at troops and transport on road Bihucourt–Sapignies from 800 feet. Observed number fall and remainder seek cover. Bomb dropped on Gommecourt exploded amongst vehicles and guns.

"Lieutenant Barry: Dropped two bombs on 'flaming-onion' battery on Cambrai–Bapaume road from 3,000 feet (8.45 a.m.). Fired 450 rounds at troops in village of Velu from 1,000 feet.

"Captain Malley: Dropped one bomb on motor-transport and troops on road Bapaume–Ervillers (8.30 a.m.) from 2,000 feet. Observed fire start. Was attacked by Albatros scout and two triplanes, which drove me practically on to the ground and damaged my machine. Fired about 400 rounds at troops in fields and in trenches north-west of Bapaume from about 15 feet. Saw many fall apparently hit and the remainder scatter in all directions.

"Lieutenant Trescowthick: Dropped one bomb on troops on Bullecourt–Ecoust road from 1,500 feet (11.30 a.m.). Dropped one bomb on Ecoust from 1,500 feet (11.35 a.m.). Fired 400 rounds at troops on Bullecourt–Ecoust road from 1,000 feet.

"Lieutenant Elwyn: Dropped two bombs on troops and transport on St. Leger–Vaulx road from 1,500 feet (11.30 a.m.). Observed one bomb explode among troops. Fired 350 rounds at troops and transport on St. Leger–Vaulx road from 1,000 feet.

"Lieutenant Courtney: Dropped two bombs on park of transport at Achiet-le-Grand (11.20 a.m.) from 1,500 feet. Observed one of these bombs get a direct hit among this transport. Fired 350 rounds at troops and transport at Achiet-le-Grand from 1,000 feet. Shooting caused troops to scatter and seek cover.

"Lieutenant A. W. Adams: Dropped one bomb on park of transport and one bomb on village of Villers-au-Flos from 1,500 feet (11.20 a.m.). Fired 450 rounds at troops at Achiet-le-Grand from 1,000 feet. Caused many casualties, and the remainder dived for cover.

"Lieutenant Watson: Dropped two bombs from 1,000 feet (11.30 a.m.) on billets at Achiet-le-Grand. Fired 500 rounds at troops and transport in Achiet-le-Grand from 600 feet. Observed a number of casualties and remainder scatter for cover.

"Lieutenant Cobby: Dropped two bombs on column of troops on Bullecourt–Ecoust road from 1,500 feet (11.30 a.m.). One bomb exploded among this column, causing numerous casualties. Fired 400 rounds into the troops from 1,200 feet.

"Captain W. B. Tunbridge: Dropped one bomb on troops and transport at Bihucourt and obtained direct hit. Dropped one Cooper-bomb on transport and troops at Vaulx and obtained another direct hit. Fired 200 rounds into troops and transport at Bihucourt from 800 feet and 200 rounds at troops and transport at Vaulx from 800 feet. Shooting caused many casualties and column to break and seek cover.

"Lieutenant A. E. Robertson: Dropped two bombs on Bullecourt (11.25 a.m.) from 1,000 feet. Observed both bombs explode. Fired 500 rounds at column of troops on Bullecourt–Ecoust road from 1,500 feet. Saw a number fall and the remainder scatter in all directions.

"Lieutenant J. W. Wright: Dropped two bombs on troops and transport at Bihucourt from 1,500 feet (11.30 a.m.). Fired 200 rounds into troops and transport at Bihucourt from 1,000 feet. Fired 200 rounds at troops and transport on road at Vaulx from 1,000 feet.

"Lieutenant Schafer: Dropped two bombs on troops on side of road Miraumont–Pys from 1,500 feet (12.30 p.m.). Fired 600 rounds at troops and transport collected on same road from 1,000 to 800 feet.

"Captain Malley: Dropped two bombs on troops on side of road Miraumont–Pys from 1,500 feet (12.30 p.m.). Fired 500 rounds at troops and moving vehicles on road from about 800 feet.

"Lieutenant Wright: Dropped two bombs on infantry on road N.E. of Bapaume from 200 feet (3.20 p.m.). Fired 500 rounds into the same infantry from 200 feet. Was hit in back with a bullet passing through petrol tank, so switched on to gravity-tank and came back to aerodrome.

"Lieutenant Trescowthick: Dropped two bombs on troops and transport on Bapaume–Bihucourt road from 1,000 feet (3.15 p.m.). Fired 450 rounds at the same troops and transport.

"Lieutenant Elwyn: Dropped two bombs into village of Vaulx at troops and transport from 1,200 feet (3.25 p.m.). Fired 100 rounds at troops along Vaulx–Beugny road from 1,500 feet.

"Lieutenant Barry: Dropped two bombs on cavalry on Vaulx-Beugnâtre road from 1,800 feet (3.40 p.m.). Fired 450 rounds at troops and transport on Vaulx–Lagnicourt road from 1,000 feet.

"Lieutenant Adams: Dropped two bombs on troops and transport on Bapaume–Bihucourt road from 1,500 feet (3.30 p.m.). Fired 400 rounds into these troops and transport.

"Lieutenant Courtney: Dropped two bombs on road Gommecourt-Sapignies from 1,500 feet (3.20 p.m.). Observed one direct hit on motor-transport. Fired 600 rounds on road Bihucourt–Bapaume and behind railway near Achiet-le-Grand from 800 feet.

"Lieutenant Scott: Dropped two bombs on park of transport at Gueudecourt from 1,000 feet (3.45 p.m.). Fired 550 rounds at troops and billets along road Le Sars–Gueudecourt from 800 feet.

"Captain Tunbridge: Dropped two bombs on transport and troops on Bapaume–Bihucourt road from 1,000 feet (3.20 p.m.). Fired 450 rounds into transport and troops on same road from 800 feet. One bomb exploded among the troops.

"Lieutenant Jeffree: Dropped two bombs on gun-limbers in wood at Ligny from 1,000 feet (3.30 p.m.). Fired 500 rounds on transport and troops on Bapaume–Albert road at Ligny.

"Lieutenant Robertson: Dropped two bombs on transport and troops on Bapaume–Bihucourt road from 1,200 feet (3.20 p.m.). Both bombs exploded among this column. Fired 300 rounds into transport and troops on same road from 1,000 to 800 feet. Fired 100 rounds into cavalry from 900 feet on Ervillers–Bapaume road. Observed number of horses and men lying on road and remainder scatter for cover."

APPENDIX No. 8.

AERODROME WORK IN THE SQUADRON.

The daily work at the aerodrome in the squadron repair-shops was enormous, and the effect of rapid and skilful work by mechanics in all branches was an important factor in the efficiency of a squadron for fighting. A brief outline of that work—in the form of squadron reports—will show the interior domestic economy of an air squadron.

Equipment Officer's Work.

"*Accountancy of Stores.*—Stores are accounted for by means of Receipts and Issues Ledger. To save too much handling of ledger, an issue book is kept on stores counter, and every article issued during the day is entered in ledger after the day's issues have finished.

"*Replacement of Stores.*—Urgent stores are those required for immediate minor repairs upon unserviceable aeroplanes, engines, or motor-transport. These are indented for on Aircraft Parks *viâ* Wing by telegram, and have priority over anything else. Crash reports are rendered to equipment officer by flight concerned, and all parts not in store are wired for to the Park immediately. Park advises when parts are ready and squadrons collect. Some parks deliver spares to make machines and motor-transport serviceable directly they are ready for issue. Ordinary stores and spare parts to complete squadron to mobilisation equipment are indented for fortnightly in triplicate, *viâ* Wing.

"*Organisation of Headquarters' Workshops.*—The engine-repairing and overhaul department consists of one engine-sergeant and one engine-fitter from headquarters. The remainder of the engine-fitters (six in number) are drawn from flights, and work on engines in pairs. All engines are received into workshops with their log-books correctly entered up. On arrival for repair or overhaul, the engine is dismantled and indent is placed at technical stores for spare parts necessary to make the engine serviceable. Apart from the log-book a report is kept of the history of each engine dealt with in workshops. Attached herewith is a specimen of form for recording engine details for the engine-sergeant's use. In the event of cylinders being removed from the crank-case they are placed in a bath of caustic soda, which facilitates cleaning. In order to keep parts of a dismantled engine together, a tray is used, suitably divided.

"The maintenance of all magnetos and testing of spark plugs is carried out by the electrician."

Armament Officer's Work.

"*Organisation of Armoury.*—The armoury is an important branch of a squadron and entails a lot of work, particularly with a squadron of twenty-five machines, each machine carrying a Vickers gun. The average personnel of armourers and gear-men to a squadron is one armament-officer, one sergeant-armourer, one gear-armourer, one armourer-corporal, nine other armourers, and six gear-men. The work was distributed as follows:—

"The armament officer is responsible to the squadron-commander for the care, cleaning, and upkeep of all guns on machines, for the

AERODROME WORK

fitting and correct alignment of sights, and for the training of pilots in gunnery.

"The armourer-sergeant is responsible to the armament officer. He supervises the work of armourers, and reports when machines are serviceable.

"The armourer-corporal is usually a first-class mechanic, and all special fittings and improvements he carries out.

"Two armourers are attached to each flight, and have four machines allotted to them. They are responsible for the guns on these machines, that they are cleaned and kept serviceable, and that ammunition boxes are kept filled with small arms ammunition.

"*Belt-Filling and Testing S.A.A.*—Two men are kept at belt-filling and testing S.A.A. S.A.A. must be filled in right sequence, and belt ammunition must be stored in dry place.

"*Gears.*—The gear-sergeant is in charge of gears, and has under him six gear-men, two of whom are attached to each flight. Gears require constant attention and to be checked before and after each flight.

"*Replacements.*—When a gun is damaged on a machine during combat or in a crash, and the machine is repaired in the squadron, if the gun cannot be repaired, a spare gun (four of which are carried) is fitted and the damaged one returned to the Aircraft Dépôt and a new gun is drawn. When a machine is lost or struck off strength, the new machine to replace arrives fitted with gears and guns. These generally require much attention, new pins and springs fitted to gear, guns eased and tested, and sights fitted and aligned.

"*Stores.*—Ammunition and all stores required for armoury or gears are indented for through the squadron equipment officer. It is necessary to keep a good supply of ammunition in hand (say, 50,000 rounds), for if the squadron is active this is about a three days' supply. Under normal conditions the average amount of S.A.A. used daily is 3,000 rounds. All stores that arrive are entered up in a special book, showing ammunition used and in hand daily, and also total amount of all gunnery stores held in the squadron. A log-book is also kept showing number of machine, number of guns on machine, ammunition fired from these guns, stoppages, cause, breakages, etc., and when new barrels are fitted. It is important to record the performance of the gun, as it assists to rectify any trouble that occurs.

"*Workshop Lorries.*—Each workshop lorry has one mechanic in charge of plant whose duty it is to carry out any machine-work required by the squadron. The squadron electric supply is obtained from these lorries.

"*Blacksmiths' Shops and Oxy-Welding Plant.*—These are accommodated in a separate building. This section consists of two blacksmiths and one oxy-welder.

"*Coppersmiths' Shop.*—When possible, a separate building should be erected for coppersmiths. There are four coppersmiths—one in headquarters and one in each flight.

"*Vulcanisers.*—One vulcaniser is employed entirely on motor-transport work and another on aero work. They have their plant in a separate building. This is necessary to minimise fire risk.

"*Fabric Workers.*—Two fabric workers are on the strength of headquarters. They are chiefly employed repairing fabric on machines and doping it. All sewing-machine work is carried out in the squadron workshops.

"*Carpenters.*—The woodwork is carried out by a corporal and two mechanics."

SPECIMEN WORKSHOP ORDER.

Date sent in............   Workshop No............
WORKSHOP ORDER.
........Flight ....F./Sgt. Authority............

Description of Job.	Material Used.
(This side for use of person requesting work to be done.)	(This side for workshop use only.)

Signature of Mechanic on Job.:..................
Date finished......................................
Received satisfactory by..........................

APPENDIX No. 9.

USE OF INCENDIARY BULLETS.

(See also Glossary.)

The increasing numbers of aircraft which were shot down in flames on both sides during 1918 must be given its proper significance. Neither aeroplanes nor airships could be so destroyed in air fighting by the use of ordinary bullets, or even of tracer bullets, which latter merely contained at the base of the ball sufficient phosphorus to mark to the gunner's eye the track of the bullet through the air. The use of poison-gas and other abuses of the rules of the Hague Convention were licences in the conduct of war which would earlier have been denounced as barbarous, and which were in fact so denounced by one side or the other when first introduced during the War of 1914-1918. The Zeppelin attacks on civilians and unfortified towns were protested against by the British; when mere protest produced no results, they themselves used explosive bullets against Zeppelins, and the deadly effect of the Brock bullet and the Pomeroy bullet made airship attacks too hazardous to be continued. Though during the war the official orders were that the Pomeroy might be used against Zeppelins or balloons, but not against aeroplanes in air fighting over the lines, there is no doubt that explosive bullets were used at times by both German and British airmen against each other. Captured German aeroplanes were found to have their machine-gun belts loaded with incendiary ammunition. This was the case, for example, with the L.V.G. captured after it had shot down Lieutenant Walker in flames (Chapter XI.), and with the Halberstadt driven in by No. 3 Squadron in June, 1918 (Chapter XIX.); and British (including of course Australian) airmen loaded their belts and drums with incendiary and tracer bullets as well as with the ordinary kind. The methods of loading belts and drums was in the various squadrons officially recorded as follow:—

> No. 1 Squadron—3 ordinary, 1 tracer, 1 armour-piercing, 1 Buckingham.
> No. 2 Squadron—Vickers: 3 ordinary, 1 tracer, 1 armour-piercing.
> Lewis: 3 ordinary, 1 tracer, 1 armour-piercing, 1 Buckingham.
> No. 3 Squadron—3 ordinary, 1 tracer, 1 armour-piercing, 1 Buckingham.
> No. 4 Squadron—3 ordinary, 1 tracer, 3 ordinary, 1 armour-piercing, 3 ordinary, 1 Buckingham.

The armour-piercing bullets were inserted for effect against the engine of an opponent's machine. The Buckingham (incendiary) bullet was highly effective, and was used by British aeroplanes in everyday air fighting. The Pomeroy (explosive) bullet was deadly enough to smash the strut of a machine's wings where an ordinary bullet would merely pierce it; it was, in fact, so deadly that it had to be packed in cotton-wool in the ammunition cases. It was never used in machine-guns firing through the propeller on account of the danger of its striking a blade. It could, however, be used from a forward gun mounted above the centre section, or from the Lewis gun of an observer. British pilots were convinced, from the loss of British machines in flames in duels with the Germans, that the enemy was using the best explosive bullet he could manufacture; hence the Buckingham, and more rarely the Pomeroy, bullet was employed against German aircraft by way of reprisal. Towards the close of the war British inventors' evolved a bullet even more destructive, which would explode upon striking even a sheet of brown paper. This bullet was never used against the enemy.

From headquarters of the Royal Australian Air Force it is stated officially:—" The explosive bullet generally was not so effective for incendiary purposes (that is, for setting the aeroplane on fire) as the purely incendiary bullet, non-explosive, but with a phosphorus base to the incendiary mixture. The most effective German incendiary bullet contained an armour-piercing point and an explosive pellet in addition to the purely incendiary portion. The British air force never use a combined bullet of this nature, but achieved the same effect by mixing bullets of different types, each type intended primarily to fulfil one function only. The British pilot aimed at setting the enemy machine on fire and thus making sure of its complete destruction. When a machine was definitely reported to have been seen in flames, there was never any need to obtain further confirmation of its fate. Although it was possible to set a machine on fire with a Pomeroy, Brock, or other explosive bullet, these bullets were more effective for bursting petrol-tanks, the streaming petrol to be subsequently set alight by incendiary bullets. Explosive bullets are not nearly so effective as are incendiary bullets for the purpose of setting petrol tanks alight. It was the reverse when dealing with Zeppelin airships, as the explosion of a Pomeroy bullet against part of the metal framework was almost certain to ignite the gas, whereas the incendiary bullet often passed through the envelope without setting the gas on fire. The British incendiary bullet was the Buckingham, and the composition had a phosphorus base and was almost identical in this respect with German incendiary bullets."

GLOSSARY

ACE (French *As*): The title given in the French Army to every pilot who was officially recognised as having destroyed five enemy machines or more. Their destruction must be confirmed by at least one witness, or by other good evidence.

ADVANCED LANDING-GROUND: A landing-ground in the forward area of a region of active operations where machines of one or more squadrons may, more conveniently than at a distant aerodrome, be refilled with petrol, oil, and ammunition, or be attended to for minor repairs.

A.E.G. (ALLGEMEINE ELEKTRIZITÄTS GESELLSCHAFT): *See* Appendix No. 1.

AERIAL AND WEIGHT: A length of copper-wire used for sending wireless. It is weighted at the end and carried on a drum in the cockpit, being unwound for use after taking-off.

A.G.O. (AEROWERKE GUSTAV OTTO): *See* Appendix No. 1.

AILERONS: Hinged portions on the outer trailing edge of the wing, by which lateral stability is maintained, and which are manipulated by the pilot's control-lever.

ALBATROS: *See* Appendix No. 1.

ALDIS SIGHT: A telescopic sight fitted to aeroplanes and enabling the pilot to align his machine-gun correctly at the target.

ALTIMETER: An aneroid barometer graduated to show height (usually in hundreds of feet) instead of air-pressure.

"ARCHIE": The name universally employed by British airmen to designate the anti-aircraft gun on either side. It was given in Flanders in early 1915, and followed a habit which has existed among gunners in the navies and armies of all nations since cannon were first used in battle. "Grandma" (the first British 15-inch howitzer behind Ypres), "Quick Dick" (for a high-velocity gun), "Percy" (an early name for a 4.7-inch naval gun in the field), are other examples. Why an anti-aircraft gun was named "Archibald" is a matter of mystery, though it is said that our own "archies"—since for a long time they could never hit the air anywhere near a German machine—owed the title to the music-hall song "Archibald, Certainly Not."

ARMADILLO SCOUT: *See* Appendix No. 1.

ARMOUR-PIERCING BULLETS: *See* Incendiary Bullets.

ARMSTRONG-WHITWORTH (A. W. and F. K.): *See* Appendix No. 1.

ARTILLERY OBSERVATION: *See* Chapter XV, pp. 199-202, and Appendix No. 6.

AVIATIK: *See* Appendix No. 1.

AVRO: *See* Appendix No. 1.

"BABY ELEPHANT" (MARTINSYDE): *See* Appendix No. 1.

BANK, To: To incline the machine, in flight, at an angle laterally from the horizontal, in order to turn without slipping sideways through the air.

B.E. (BRITISH EXPERIMENTAL): *See* Appendix No. 1.

B.F. (BRISTOL FIGHTER): *See* Appendix No. 1.

BLÉRIOT: *See* Appendix No. 1.

GLOSSARY

BLIND SPOT: A point (below the tail of an aeroplane) at which an approaching adversary was hidden from the sights of the observer's guns. It was therefore the position usually taken up, if possible, by an adversary attacking a two-seater.

BOMB-RACKS: Gear by which bombs are attached to the machine so that they may be instantaneously released.

BRANDENBURG: *See* Appendix No. 1.

BRISTOL: *See* Appendix No. 1.

"BULLET"(BRISTOL, MORANE, VICKERS): *See* Appendix No. 1.

CAMBER: The convexity of an aeroplane wing in section.

CAMEL (SOPWITH): *See* Appendix No. 1.

CAMERA: Photographic cameras used in aircraft were of various kinds, but may be divided into two classes:—(1) Those fixed to the machine and intended for taking photographs vertically downwards; (2) those not fixed to the machine but held by the operator and intended for taking photographs at any angle. The latter were fitted with a sight to enable the operator to align his instrument on the object.

The fixed cameras could be operated by either the pilot or the observer by hand, if situated conveniently, or by either of them by means of a Bowden wire control if the camera was placed out of hand's reach. As a rule the pilot took the photographs and the observer changed the plates. Changing of plates could not be done by the pilot. The hand camera was almost entirely operated by the observer.

CAUDRON: *See* Appendix No. 1.

CEILING: The extreme height of an aeroplane's efficient flying capacity. Technically this is fixed at the height at which a machine requires a full minute by the test-pilot's watch to climb 100 feet.

CENTRE SECTION: A short section of plane situated immediately above or below the fuselage (or body) of the machine. It is on either side of this section that the main planes, which are usually not continuous, are attached.

CIRCUS: A roving formation of fighting machines, whose primary duty was to seek out and destroy hostile aircraft. It originated in the German flying service with Boelcke's (afterwards Richthofen's) Circus. The British for a while adopted the same plan. With the Germans a circus was an assemblage of crack fighting airmen from different squadrons; with the British, it was composed generally of one or more selected squadrons.

CLOSE OFFENSIVE-PATROL: A number of fighting scouts in close "formation," whose duty it is to pursue a vigorous offensive. The close formation was adopted because, where the enemy was met in numbers, the utmost concentration of the attack was necessary.

COCKPIT: Seating compartment for pilot. The observer also had his cockpit. In all fighting two-seaters the observer was seated behind the pilot. Among airmen the cockpit was commonly known as "the office."

CONTACT-PATROL: A patrol charged with the duty of maintaining communication with advancing infantry in attack on the enemy. This was accomplished by low-flying machines fitted with means for sound and visual signalling.

CONTROL-LEVER (or CONTROL-STICK): Commonly called the "Joystick." It was situated between the knees of the pilot. Operated sideways it controls the ailerons and banks the machine; worked backward or forward it acts on the elevators and causes the

GLOSSARY

machine to climb or dive. In some machines the process of diving and climbing is further regulated by alterations in the tail plane, which in that case is made movable and is controlled by a small wheel in the pilot's compartment. The act of operating this is called "Trimming the Tail." As a rule the pilot fired the forward gun (or guns) by means of a Bowden wire acting on the trigger and controlled by means of a lever attached to the control-stick.

COUNTER-ATTACK PATROL: A detailed reconnaissance of the forward areas of the enemy's territory carried out by low-flying machines, during or immediately after an advance by the infantry or other ground-troops, in order to discover any signs of concentration for, or launching of, a counter-attack.

COWLING A sheet-metal covering for an engine.

D.F.W. (DEUTSCHE FLUG-WERKE): *See* Appendix No. 1.

D.H. (DE HAVILLAND): *See* Appendix No. 1.

DIHEDRAL: An angle at which the wings of some aeroplanes are set. When viewed in front elevation the wings of many machines are not in a straight line from tip to tip, but are set with a slight slope upwards and outwards. This slope is known as Dihedral, and improves the lateral stability of the machine.

"DOLPHIN" (SOPWITH): *See* Appendix No. 1.

DOUBLE GUNS: When an observer carried two guns, either he had one gun on his scarfe-mounting and one in reserve in the cockpit—in which case he was not said to be using double guns—or he had both guns on the mounting which fixed them jointly. When in position on the mounting, double guns were so clamped that their lines of fire converged at a certain short range and one sight only was used for both.

ECHELON: Aircraft flying in battle-formation fly in echelon both in height and in plan. Echelon in height is the formation of machines flying in rear of, and above or below, one another. Echelon in plan is the formation of machines flying in rear, and to the flank, of one another.

ELEVATORS: Hinged planes attached behind the tail plane, so controlled by the pilot as to cause the machine to dive or climb.

EXPLOSIVE BULLETS: *See* Incendiary Bullets.

FALCON BIPLANE SCOUT: *See* Appendix No. 1.

FARMANS: *See* Appendix No. 1.

F.E. (FIGHTING EXPERIMENTAL): *See* Appendix No. 1.

"FLAMING-ONIONS": A form of incendiary and illuminating shell much used by the Germans. In appearance it was a string of fireballs. This shell was used both in order to point out the location of a machine to German anti-aircraft batteries and also against the machines themselves as a means of setting them on fire.

FLARES, GROUND: Waste soaked in petrol, or petrol in buckets, set on fire and used as a landing light for night-flying.

FLARES, PARACHUTE: Magnesium light attached to a parachute and electrically fired; released from an aeroplane when near the ground to facilitate landing at night, and for other purposes.

FLARES, WING-TIP: Magnesium lights attached to the tips of the wings and electrically fired. Used to facilitate landing at night.

FLASH-SPOTTING: Marking down the map-position of hostile guns from observation of their flashes in action. From intimate knowledge of country patrolled, aeroplane pilots and observers would

GLOSSARY

report probable situations of hostile batteries thus observed, and these reports would be checked from the study of aeroplane-photographs. Strictly speaking, flash-spotting was the unceasing work of balloon observers and special detachments of Royal Engineers, who would calculate the position of all hostile gun-flashes by timed observation from two or more stations, and by triangulation of the points from compass bearings.

FLATTENING OUT: The gradual decrease of a gliding or diving angle of an aeroplane in flight until the machine resumes the horizontal, either from a manœuvre in the air or preparatory to landing.

FLYING WIRES: Wires which, running outwards and upwards, take the strain from the wings and prevent them from folding up while the machine is in normal flight.

FOKKER: *See* Appendix No. 1.

FORMATION FLYING: The adoption and maintenance of the same relative position among a number of aeroplanes flying in company. The commonest formation was the "V," which was really a double-echelon. Echelon was maintained in height as well as in plan.

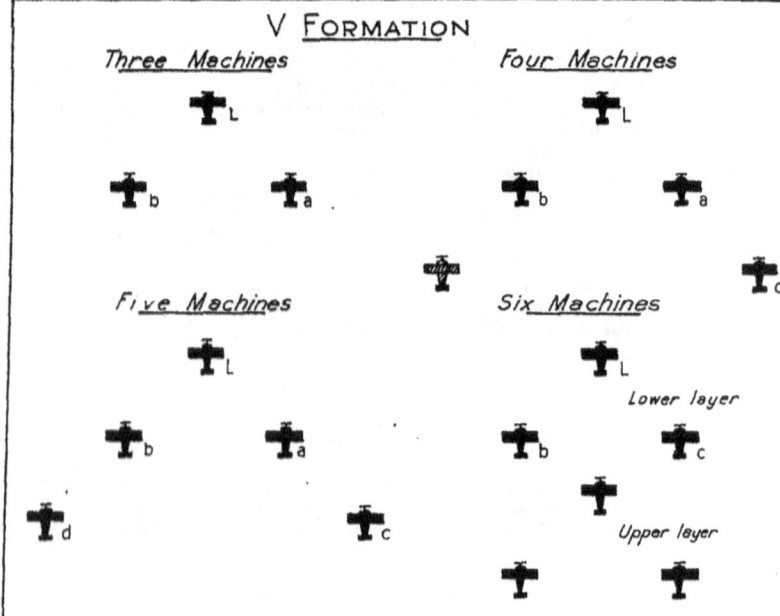

In the V, *a* and *b*, the machines just in rear and on the flanks of the patrol-leader (L), flew slightly higher than L. Again, *c* and *d*, prolonging the wings of the V, flew slightly higher then *a* and *b*. This was for mutual protection and to facilitate manœuvre.

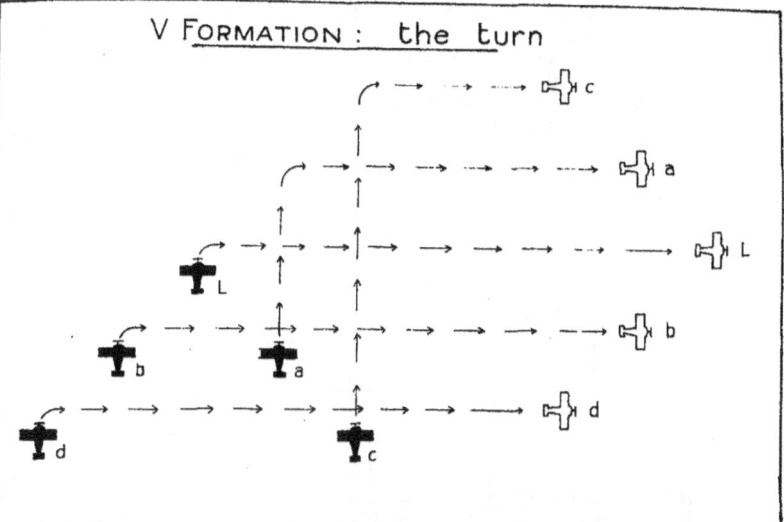

L (flying lowest) turns at once in desired direction. Machines on wing of V on opposite side to L's turn conform at once with L. Here b and d turn sharp to right with L.

Machines on wing of V on side on which L has turned maintain their courses until each machine in turn sees over his tail his next ahead on the new course, then turns to conform. Here a flies on straight ahead till he sees L to his right rear, then turns to conform; c flies on till he sees a in like position, then c also turns.

FUSELAGE: That part of an aeroplane which usually contains the engine, tanks, crew, etc., and to which the wings, under-carriage, and other members are attached.

GOTHA: *See* Appendix No. 1.
HALBERSTADT: *See* Appendix No. 1.
HANNOVERANNER: *See* Appendix No. 1.
HENRI-FARMAN: *See* Appendix No. 1.
H.P. (HANDLEY-PAGE): *See* Appendix No. 1.

IMMELMANN TURN: A manœuvre named after the famous German fighting-pilot who first devised it. Suppose one machine at high speed meeting another from an opposite direction. The control-stick is pulled straight back and the rudder kicked hard on. This movement is partly a loop; at its close, the machine, after a banking turn, comes into a dive and travels in the same direction as the opposing machine; if the time and distance are rightly judged, it will be close on the tail of its adversary. It was by this manœuvre that Immelmann accounted for many opponents.

INCENDIARY BULLETS: Bullets devised to set fire to the object struck. Bullets used by aircraft may be divided into—(1) ordinary small-arms ammunition, (2) armour piercing, (3) tracer, (4) incendiary, and (5) explosive. Since (1), ordinary S.A.A., lacked sufficient destructive power against the engines of aircraft, (2), armour-piercing bullets, were introduced. These consisted of S.S.A. bullets in which a hard steel core was incorporated. They were particularly effective against the steel portions of aircraft engines and also against the light armour sometimes used to protect the personnel. (3) The original tracer bullet was filled with a magnesium compound, which left a trail of light or smoke and was intended solely as a guide in aiming the gun. It was very effective for igniting petrol tanks. Later was introduced (4), the Buckingham incendiary bullet, which contained phosphorus. This would not only "trace" satisfactorily but was particularly effective as an incendiary bullet against Zeppelins, kite-balloons, and aircraft petrol-tanks. (5) Explosive bullets were the Pomeroy and the Brock. There were used chiefly against Zeppelins. The R.T.T. bullet, designed at the end of the war, was a very sensitive explosive bullet and would detonate against a single layer of fabric. It was not brought into use at the front.

German bullets were more or less similar to those in the categories mentioned above. *See also* Appendix No. 9.

INTERRUPTER-GEAR: A device by which a machine-gun can be fired so that its bullets pass between the blades of a propeller in motion. The Constantinesco Gear (invented by M. Constantinesco, a Roumanian) came into general use towards the end of the war. Its action is hydraulic. A pump attached to the engine transmits impulses to a pipe-line filled with oil under pressure. A similar pump fitted to the gun responds to these impulses and fires the gun at the desired moment, so that the bullet will pass between the blades of the propeller. The Kauper Gear, which achieves the same purpose by purely mechanical action, was invented by Mr. H. A. Kauper, an Australian motoring-pioneer and later works manager to the Sopwith Aviation Company. It was adopted in some Sopwith machines.

JOY-STICK: *See* Control-lever.

LANDING TEE: A ground-sign indicating the direction of the wind. Originally an arrow-shaped sign was employed, but in order that air men might better distinguish it from the air the tip of the arrow was widened to a "T." With the "T" was generally used the "sausage," a wind-indicator which consists of a white conical-shaped open bag suspended from a pole. The landing-T was frequently made automatic by arranging it on a pivot and fitting it with a vane; so that it turned into the wind like a weathercock.

LANDING WIRES: Wires, running outwards and downwards from the centre-section above, which support the weight of the wings while the machine is on the ground.

LEADING EDGE: The front edge of the wings.

L.F.G. (LUFT-FAHRZEUG GESELLSCHAFT): *See* Appendix No. 1.

LONGERONS: Main wooden rails running longitudinally through the fuselage or body of the machine.

L.V.G. (LUFT-VERKEHRS GESELLSCHAFT): *See* Appendix No. 1.

MARTINSYDE: *See* Appendix No. 1.

MAURICE-FARMAN: *See* Appendix No. 1.

MORANE: *See* Appendix No. 1.

NACELLE: A very short body containing the engine and built into "pusher" machines and into those large aeroplanes which have engines mounted in the wings.

GLOSSARY

NAVIGATION LIGHTS: Electric lights carried by night-flying machines. They are four in number; a red and green on the port and starboard wing-tips respectively, and two white, one under the nose and one under the tail.

NIEUPORT: *See* Appendix No. 1.

NORMAN COMPENSATING WINDVANE SIGHT: A sight invented by Major G. H. Norman, R.A.F., for movable machine-guns fitted in aircraft. By means of a windvane an automatic allowance is made for the speed and direction of flight of the gunner's aeroplane.

OUT OF CONTROL: The condition of a descending aeroplane when for some reason the pilot ceases to control it. The movement of a machine so situated is generally erratic as compared with a controlled descent.

PARASOL (BLÉRIOT, FOKKER, MORANE): *See* Appendix No. 1.

PFALZ: *See* Appendix No. 1.

R.E. (RECONNAISSANCE EXPERIMENTAL): *See* Appendix No. 1.

RIGGING: The whole of the wiring and struts of the machine.

ROLAND: *See* Appendix No. 1.

ROLL: A manœuvre used in air fighting. In the roll the speed of the machine has to be kept high; at the critical moment the control-lever is pulled completely back and to the right or the left according to the direction in which the pilot wishes to roll, the rudder being kicked hard-on to correspond. The result of the lever movement alone would make the machine loop, but as it is at the same time also pulled hard over to the one side, the combined effect is to cause a steep banking motion. The rudder hard-on and the speed of the machine overcome the looping tendency, and the machine rolls completely over sideways.

RUDDER: The steering device, controlled by a bar operated by the feet.

RUMPLER: *See* Appendix No. 1.

SCARFE-MOUNTING: Circular Lewis gun mounting fixed to the observer's cockpit.

S.E. (SCOUTING EXPERIMENTAL): *See* Appendix No. 1.

SLIP-STREAM: The current of air which is in motion owing to the action of an airscrew during rotation.

"SNIPE" (SOPWITH): *See* Appendix No. 1.

SOPWITH: *See* Appendix No. 1.

SPAD: *See* Appendix No. 1.

SPIN: The rotation (nose downwards and spirally about a vertical axis) into which an aeroplane commonly falls after stalling. A pilot would often "put his machine into a spin" to escape from attack. In order to spin with the engine off, the control-lever would be brought back into the stomach, and the right or the left rudder kicked hard on, according to the direction in which the pilot wished to spin. To get out of a spin, the control-lever and the rudder would generally be put into a neutral position, and, as the spin stopped, the downward speed of the machine would increase sufficiently to allow the pilot to assume control again in a gliding angle or the horizontal.

STAGGER: The position of the wings of a biplane or multiplane when they are so designed that the upper wing is not superimposed in a direct vertical line over the lower, but is either ahead of or behind it.

GLOSSARY

STALLING: A machine is said to be stalled when its air speed is so reduced in the course of climbing that it ceases to be under control. The nose of the machine then naturally drops, and in order to recover forward speed the machine must dive.

STREAMERS: Pennants attached to the rear struts, or to the trailing edges, to identify machines on special duty, e.g., contact-patrol machines.

STRUTS: Vertical members between the wings or between the body and the centre section (*q.v.*).

TAIL-PLANE: Small horizontal plane at the rear of the machine for the maintenance of fore and aft stability.

TAKING-OFF: Leaving the ground.

TAUBE: *See* Appendix No. 1.

"TAXI," To: To run on wheels over the ground, or to move on floats over the surface of the water, with the engine running at a number of revolutions insufficient to produce flying-speed.

TRACER BULLETS: *See* Incendiary Bullets.

TRAILING EDGE: The rear edge of the wings.

TRIPLANE: *See* Appendix No. 1.

VICKERS: *See* Appendix No. 1.

VICKERS-VIMY: *See* Appendix No. 1.

ZOOM: To ascend very steeply after flying level at full speed.

INDEX

Ranks shown after the surnames of officers and men are the highest attained by each during the war.

Plates, Maps, and Sketches referred to after names of places are those which best indicate their positions.

Page-numbers followed by *n* indicate that the reference is to a footnote on the page specified.

ABBASSIA, 35
ABBEVILLE (Sk. p. 241), 237, 385
ABD, BIR EL (Map p. 42), 37, 38, 40, 75
ABEELE, 211, 212
ABU AWEIGILA (Map p. 42), 46, 49
ABU KEMAL, 390
ABU LESAL, 124
ABU SALIBIQ (Map p. 4), 10
ABU TELLUL, 121
ACCROCHE WOOD, 274
ACHIET-LE-GRAND, 237, 437, 438
ACRE, 162
ADAIR, Lt. R. S. (b. Maryborough, Q'land), 113-4, 131-2, 135, 142
ADAM, Lt. J. A., 254
ADAMS, Lt. A. G. (b. South Yarra, Vic.), 37
ADAMS, Lt. A. W. (b. Woodend, Vic.), 219, 225, 239, 438
ADAMS, 44 Air-Mechanic F. L. (of Spreydon, N.Z.; b. Sydenham, N.Z.), 26
ADAMS, Lt. W. Q., 218, 256, 258
ADDISON, Maj. S. W. (b. Huon, Tas.), *quoted*, 97, 168*n*; mentioned, 94, 100, 109, 127, 133, 171
ADRIANOPLE, 394
Aerial, 28
AFION KARA HISSAR, 27
AFULE, EL (Map p. 137), 85, 86, 95, 142, 154, 155, 157, 158; German aerodrome at, bombed, 3 *Jan.* 1918, 96; town bombed, 19 *Sep.,* 152
AGNEW, Lt. I. C. F. (of Epping Forest, Tas.; b. Oatlands, Tas.), 180

AHWAZ (Map p. 4), 7
AINSWORTH, Lt. P., 44
AIRCRAFT, increasing importance of, in warfare, xvi-xvii; types and development of: xx-xxv, xxvii, in 1916-17, 33, 38, 47, in 1917-18, 87-8, British, 398-411, French, 411-6, German, 416-20; unsuitability of, in Mesopotamia, 5-6, 9, 12, 18-9; German superiority in, 1916-17, 38, 46-7, 71-3; Bristol Fighters arrive in Palestine, *July* 1917, 74, issued to No. 1 Sqn., *Jan.-Mar.* 1918, 88; British superiority in, 1917-18, 81, 87-8, 97, 111-2; No. 2 Sqn. equipped with S.E.5's, 197*n*, No. 4 Sqn. with Sopwith Snipes, 370; repair work in a squadron, 440-2
AIRCRAFT DESTROYED, methods of reckoning up, xviii-xix. ALLIED, 21-25 *Mar.* 1918, 238. AUSTRALIAN: *Half-Flight,* 10; *No. 1 Squadron,* 96, 108, 116, 118, 131, 144; *No. 2 Squadron,* 180, 184, 185, 186, 188, 258, 376; *No. 3 Squadron,* 209, 210, 272, 310, 334; *No. 4 Squadron,* 217, 242, 278, 287, 349, 357-8, 378. BRITISH, 12, 63, 96, 108, 150. GERMAN: in Sinai and Palestine, 1917, 56, 66, 80; 1918, 96, 111, 119, 122, 123, 127, 132, 134, 139-40, 142, 144-7, 164, 165, 169; in France and Belgium, 1917, 190, 194, 195, 196, 202, 210; 1918, 209, 212, 214, 219, 222, 224, 225, 226, 230, 231, 232, 235, 236, 238, 239, 240, 244, 249, 254 *et seq.,*

453

454　INDEX

AIRCRAFT DESTROYED—continued.
267, 268, 274, 277, 278, 282 et seq., 295 et seq., 310, 313, 317, 338, 339, 340, 341, 346-8, 350, 351, 354, 359, 360, 363, 364, 366, 371 et seq.

AIRE (Map p. 179), 259, 291, 344

AIRE-LA BASSÉE CANAL, 344

AIR FIGHTING, 61, 75-6, 87, 90-1, 96-7, 106-7, 114, 122, 131-2; development and tactics of, xv-xviii, 64-5, 122*n*, 337; battles: No. 4 Sqn. and No. 110 British Sqn., 11 *May* 1918, 278-80, No. 4 Sqn., over Tournai, 29 *Oct.*, 377-8, over Ath, 30 *Oct.*, 379. *No. 1 Squadron*, over Beersheba, 45, 72; at First Gaza, 60; *July* 1917, 71-2; at Third Gaza, 79-80; at Amman, *Mar.* 1918, 110-1; in second action of Es Salt, 116-8; *May* 1918, 123; *June*, 124-8, 131-2; *July*, 138-9; *Aug.*, 142, 144-5. *No. 2 Squadron, Oct.* 1917, 178-81; *Nov.*, 190, 192-4; *Dec.*, 195-7; *Feb.* 1918, 217-9; *Mar.*, 222-4, 229-30, 232, 235, 240; *June*, 256-9; over the Lys, *July-Aug.*, 292, 297, 298, 339-40, Lille, *July-Oct.*, 299, 359-60, 363-4, 371-5, Aubers Ridge, 31 *July*, 303-4, the Somme, 12-14 *Aug.*, 313, Cambrai, 3 *Sep.*, 354, Tournai, *Oct.-Nov.*, 373-5, 380, Ath, *Oct.-Nov.*, 376-7, 381-3. *No. 3 Squadron, Oct.* 1917, 181; *Dec.*, 203-4; *Apr.* 1918, 212, 260, 261; with Richthofen's Circus, 21 *Apr.* 1918, 249-52; *May*, 265; *June*, 268-9; *July*, 305; *Sep.*, 322, 325, 329. *No. 4 Squadron, Feb.* 1918, 217, 219; *Mar.*, 222-3, 231, 232, 236, 239; with Richthofen's Circus, 16 *Mar.* 1918, 225, 21 *Mar.* 1918, 226-7; over Armentières, 11 *May*, 278-80, *May*, 283; *June*, 287-8; over the Lys, *July-Aug.*, 291, 295-6, 303, 339-40, Aubers Ridge, 31 *July*, 303-4, the Somme, 12-14 *Aug.*, 313, Brebières, 5-6 *Sep.*, 356-9, Lille, *Sep.*, 359-63, Ath, *Oct.-Nov.*, 376-7, 379, 381-3. Tournai, *Oct.-Nov.*, 375, 377-8, 380-3.

AIR FIGHTING—continued.
See also AUSTRALIAN FLYING CORPS, BOMBING RAIDS, BRITISH AIR FORCE, GERMAN AIR FORCE

AIR RECONNAISSANCE, *see* ARTILLERY RANGING, PATROLS, RECONNAISSANCES

AIR SURVEY, xvi; methods of, 70-1, 436; compilation of maps from air-photos., 64, 93-5; importance and growth of, 205-7; in Mesopotamia, 20-1, of Turkish position at Es-Sinn, 13; in Sinai and Palestine: of El Arish and Magdhaba, 43, 44, 45-6, Beersheba area, 72-3, 77, Es Salt, 113, Damieh region, 122-3, Samaria–Nablus area, 126, 141, Et Tire, 136; on Western Front: of Messines Ridge, 205-7, Ville-sur-Ancre, 267, Ancre–Somme sector, 271, German position at Hamel, 272-4, Cachy and Hangard, 307, Somme area, 313, Mont St. Quentin, 322, Hindenburg Line, 326, 328, Joncourt defences, 328-9, Beaurevoir Line, 333; *see also* MAPS

AJJEH, 157

AKABA (Map p. 42), 53*n*, 148, 163

AKYAB, 388, 390, 393, 396

ALBERRY, Lt. F. (b. Hobart), 294, 360, 368, 376

ALBERT (Maps pp. 179, 311), 234, 239, 240, 249, 255, 258, 261, 267, 271

ALCOCK, Capt. Sir J. W., 386*n*, 388, 409

ALEPPO (Map p. 170), 169, 395; captured, 171

ALEXANDRETTA (Map p. 170), 169, 171

ALLAHABAD, 390, 396

ALLAIN, 367, 368

ALLENBY, Field-Marshal Lord (of Felixstowe, Eng.; b. Brackenhurst, Notts., Eng.), succeeds Murray, 63; his plans for Palestine campaign, 92, for final overthrow of Turkish forces, 151; *quoted*, 133, 171; mentioned, 105, 134, 135, 146, 148, 149, 161, 168

ALLONVILLE, 307*n*, 313

INDEX

AMARA (Map p. 4), 9, 12, 15, 16, 28; occupied by British, 7

AMERICA, 31

AMERICAN EXPEDITIONARY FORCES, 264. *II Corps*, 329n, 335. *27th Division*, attacks Hindenburg Line, 329, 330-1. *30th Division*, 329n; attacks Hindenburg Line, 331

AMIENS (Maps pp. 179, 311; Sk. p. 241), 174, 211, 237, 240, 241, 248, 249, 250, 253, 263, 315, 325; strategical importance of, 276; Battle of: British preparations for, 306-9, opening phase of, 309-10, No. 3 Sqn. at, 310-2

AMMAN (Plate p. 123; Map p. 101; Sk. p. 89), 92, 93, 95, 98, 99, 105, 113, 116, 117, 118, 123, 124, 126, 131, 132, 135, 138, 140, 141, 142, 148, 151, 158, 162, 165, 166, 167, 168; airmen raid aerodrome at, 100, 125, 147; unsuccessful mounted raid on, 21 *Mar.*-2 *Apr.* 1918, 108-12

AMMAN RAILWAY STATION (Plate p. 126), 114, 119, 142, 162; airmen raid, 110, 113

AMMAN ROAD, 118

ANATOLIA, 26

ANCRE, RIVER (Map p. 311; Sk. p. 266), 234, 264, 271

ANDERSON, Lt. A. M. (b. Melbourne), 213

ANDERSON, Maj. W. H. (of Melbourne; b. Kew, Vic.), 35, 181, 200

ANEBTA (Map p. 137; Sks. pp. 130, 154), 126, 154, 157

ANNAPPES (Map p. 355), 366, 367

ANTI-AIRCRAFT GUNS, 45, 56, 63, 66, 190-1, 290; accuracy of German and Austrian shooting with, 97-8; British airmen's method of silencing, 142; increased activity of German, *Jan.* 1918, 209-10

ANTOING (Map p. 374), 380

ANZAC MOUNTED DIVISION, *see* AUSTRALIAN IMPERIAL FORCE

ARAB NORTHERN ARMY, 162-5; *see also* HEJAZ

ARABS, their treatment of prisoners, 10-11, 12, 19; of Beni Sakr tribe, fail in Es Salt raid, 112,

ARABS—*continued*.
115, 116; *see also* BEDOUINS, HEJAZ

ARAR, TEL, 162

ARISH, EL (Map p. 42), 31, 36, 38, 40, 41, 43, 44, 45, 49, 52, 54, 58, 390; occupied by Light Horse, 48; British concentrate at, *Feb.* 1917, 56

ARISH, WADY EL (Map p. 42), 41, 45, 48

ARMAGEDDON, PLAIN OF, 121, 148, 156; *see also* MEGIDDO

ARMENTIÈRES (Map p. 279), 233, 242, 254, 255, 283, 285, 287, 289, 292, 295, 296, 298, 301, 302, 303, 304, 339, 341, 344, 345, 346, 353, 354, 356, 361, 368, 369; airmen raid, 11 *May* 1918, 278; Germans refrain from shelling, 345; British re-occupy, 365

ARMISTICE, with Turkey, 171

ARMS, *see* BAYONET

ARMSTRONG, Lt. R. C. (b. Footscray, Vic.), 268, 269-70

ARMSTRONG, Sir W. G., 410

ARRABE (Map p. 137), 138, 156, 157

ARRAS (Maps pp. 179, 220; Sk. p. 241), 173, 174, 177, 181, 216, 219, 222, 230, 233, 237, 239, 240, 241, 291, 337, 344, 350; strategical importance of, 276

ARTILLERY (BRITISH), at Battle of Nablus, 152; intensity of its fire at Ypres, 183; at Hamel, 274; bombards Hindenburg Line, 329, 330

ARTILLERY (GERMAN), intensity of its fire at Ypres, 183; shells Bailleul at long range, *Mar.* 1918, 210-1; at opening of German offensive, *Mar.* 1918, 228; captured, 262; at Hamel, 274; dummy batteries of, *Aug.* 1918, 307; *see also* ANTI-AIRCRAFT GUNS

ARTILLERY (TURKISH), 62; captured at Kurna, 7, Kut, 14, Ctesiphon, 24, Third Gaza, 77; destroyed by airmen in Wady Fara, 161

ARTILLERY OBSERVATION, *see* RECONNAISSANCE

INDEX

ARTILLERY RANGING, duties of aeroplanes in, 199-202, 435-6; No. 3 Sqn., 21-23 *Apr.* 1918, 261-2, at Ville-sur-Ancre, 18-21 *May*, 266-7, 268, over Somme, 314, Hindenburg Line, 320, 328-9

ASLUJ (Map p. 78), demolitions on Turkish railway at, 65

ASSEVILLERS, 317

ASWAD, JEBEL, 168

ATAMBOEA, 392

ATH (Maps pp. 179, 382), airfights over, 1918, 376-7, 379, 381-3

ATHENS, 389

ATKINS, Capt. B. S. (of Lowestoft, Eng.; b. Kimberley, Eng.), 27; captured, 12

ATLANTIC, flight across, 386, 388

ATTACKS AND COUNTER-ATTACKS—
—AUSTRALIAN, at Sailly-Laurette, 28-29 *July* 1918, 306-7
—GERMAN, counter-attack at First Battle of Cambrai, 192-7, at Nauroy, 332, at Joncourt, 333
—TURKISH, after Second Gaza, 63; in attempt to re-capture Jerusalem, 90; in second action of Es Salt (Damieh), 115; at Abu Tellul, 121
—*See also* BATTLES

AUBERS (Maps pp. 279, 355), 354, 364

AUBERS RIDGE, 353, 359, 364; airfights over, 31 *July* 1918, 303-4

AUBIGNY (Map p. 179), 309

AUCHEL (Map p. 179), 213, 370

AUJA, EL (Maps pp. 42, 137), 46, 49, 50, 51; Turks evacuate, 56; ford at, 115

AUJA, WADY EL (Sk. p. 89), 90, 102, 139

AUSTIN, Capt. R. A. (of Lake Bolac, Vic.; b. Eilyer Vic.), 66, 87, 96, 106, 107

AUSTRALIA, only British dominion to form a flying corps, 31; flights from England to, 386-96

AUSTRALIAN FLYING CORPS, development of, 31; arrangement with Britain for equipping, 32; formation and composition, 421-5; training in Australia, 426, in England, 430-3. *Half-Flight*, 7; formation and com-

AUSTRALIAN FLYING CORPS—*contd.* position, xxv, 1-3, 422-3; embarks, 3; arrives at Basra, 3; becomes part of No. 30 Sqn., R.F.C., 11; at Battle of Kut, 1915, 15; service career ends, 25; *see also* BRITISH AIR FORCE (*No.* 30 *Squadron*). *No.* 1 *Squadron*, xxiv, xxvii, 44, 47, 52, 56, 66, 68, 86, 87, 97, 133, 139*n*, 162, 168, 175, 176, 388, 399, 404, 427, 428, 443; formation and composition, xxvi, 32, 423-4; embarks, 32; command, 32, 35, 64; receives technical equipment in Egypt, 32; training in Australia, 32-3; arrives in Egypt, 33; training in Egypt, 35, 42; operations, *June-Dec.* 1916, 36-41; co-operates with mounted troops at Maghara, 43, and at Nekhl, 54-5; its air-photography, over Sinai, 44, *Jan.* 1918, 93-5, for second action of Es Salt, 113; reconnoitres Maghara, Gaza, and Rafa, 48-50; at Magdhaba, 49, Rafa, 50, First Gaza, 60; transfers pilots and mechanics to other Australian squadrons, 69-70; light horsemen transfer to, 69-70; its duties from *July* 1917, 74; equipped with R.E.8's, *Oct.* 1917, 76; at Third Gaza, 79-80; its work during 1918, 88-9, 134*n*; in advance to Jericho, 103; in second action of Es Salt, 115-9; total enemy aircraft destroyed by, *July-Aug.* 1918, 134; efficiency of, 146*n*, 171; co-operates with Hejaz, 1918, 148-9; opens offensive in final advance, 152, duties, 151-2; at Battles of Megiddo, 152-61; destructive work of, at Wady Fara, 159-61; returns to Australia, 385. *No.* 2 *Squadron*, xxiv, xxvii, 174, 176, 181-2, 213, 216, 221, 241, 252*n*, 261, 276, 337, 338, 361, 370, 400, 426, 429, 434, 443; formation and composition, xxvi, 41, 424; command, 41, 69, 175; arrives in England, 175, in France, 178; training in England, 175; at First Battle of Cambrai, 184-97; casualties, 184, 188; General

AUSTRALIAN FLYING CORPS—*contd.*
Trenchard's estimate of, 188;
equipped with S.E.5's, *Dec.*
1917, 197; during German offensive, *Mar.* 1918, 229-30, 232,
235, 239-40; at Second Battles
of the Somme, 248-9; circus
fighting, *May-July*, 252-9;
rivalry between No. 4 Sqn. and,
253, 291; over the Somme, 12-14
Aug. 1918, 313, the Lys, *Aug.*
350-1, Cambrai and Douai, 3-4
Sep., 354; Brebières, 6 *Sep.*,
359; returns to Australia, 385.
No. 3 Squadron, xxvi, 47n, 174,
182, 198, 213, 217, 241, 270,
272n, 384, 400, 428, 430, 431,
436, 443; formation, xxvii, 424;
command, 175; arrives in England, 175, in France, 177-8;
training in England, 175; casualties in England, 177; artillery
observation of, *Dec.* 1917, 199-
202; its air-photography, over
Messines Ridge, *Jan.* 1918,
205-7; moves from Bailleul to
Abeele, 22 *Mar.* 1918, 211, to
Somme, *Apr.,* 211-2; operations
over the Somme, *Apr.-July*,
260-74, 305-6; its duties, *May-
July*, 264; at Ville-sur-Ancre, 19
May, 266-8, Hamel, 4 *July*,
273-4; its duties for Battle of
Amiens, 308-12; at Second
Battles of the Somme, 313-7,
Mont St. Quentin, 319-20,
Péronne, 322, during German
retreat to Hindenburg Line,
324-5, in Battles of Hindenburg
Line, 327-34, Battle of Beaurevoir Line, 334; with II American Corps, *Oct.* 1918, 335; conducts aerial postal service, *Nov.*
1918, 385; returns to Australia,
385. *No. 4 Squadron*, xxiv,
xxvii, 174, 216, 221 *et seq.*, 230,
241, 259, 294, 337, 344, 353, 368,
384, 407, 408, 426, 429, 434, 443;
formation, xxvi, 425; command,
175, 213; arrives in England,
175, in France, 213; training in
England, 175; during German
offensive, *Mar.* 1918, 231-7,
239-40, in counter-attack patrols,
437-0; at Battle of the Lys,
242-6; rivalry between No. 2

AUSTRALIAN FLYING CORPS—*contd.*
Sqn. and, 253, 291; over the
Lys, *May-Aug.* 1918, 277-90,
350-1, the Somme, 12-14 *Aug.*,
313, Brebières, 5-6 *Sep.*, 356-9;
equipped with Sopwith Snipes,
Oct., 370; at Cologne, *Dec.*, 385;
returns to Australia, 385. *See
also* AIRCRAFT DESTROYED, AIR
FIGHTING, AUSTRALIAN MILITARY FORCES, BOMBING RAIDS
AUSTRALIAN GOVERNMENT, offers
£10,000 for first flight from
England to Australia, 386; policy
regarding transfers from A.I.F.
to British Army, 421
AUSTRALIAN IMPERIAL FORCE, arrangement with Britain for upkeep of, 32
—I ANZAC CORPS, 181
—AUSTRALIAN CORPS, 211, 212,
240, 241, 260, 264, 268, 305, 307,
310, 324, 328, 329, 330, 334, 384,
385, 428, 435
—DESERT MOUNTED CORPS, *see*
BRITISH ARMY
—1ST DIVISION, 243, 245, 254,
264, 289, 334; at Chuignes, 314;
in Battles of Hindenburg Line,
327
—2ND DIVISION, 319, 334
—3RD DIVISION, 334; in Battles
of Hindenburg Line, 331, 333
—4TH DIVISION, 239, 307n, 310,
334; in Battles of Hindenburg
Line, 327, 328
—5TH DIVISION, 271, 334; in
Battles of Hindenburg Line, 331,
332, 333
—ANZAC MOUNTED DIVISION, 39,
64, 67; captures Magdhaba, 49;
at Third Gaza, 77, 79; captures
Jericho, 102-3; in Amman raid,
108; in second action of Es Salt,
115; advances from Jordan
Valley, *Sep.* 1918, 166
—AUSTRALIAN MOUNTED DIVISION, 64, 67; in Battles of
Megiddo, 152
—ARTILLERY: 12*th* (*Army*) *Brigade*, 243. 53*rd Battery*, 251
—CAMEL CORPS, *see* BRITISH
ARMY
—ENGINEERS, at Hajla, 108
—FLYING CORPS, *see* AUSTRALIAN FLYING CORPS

INDEX

AUSTRALIAN IMPERIAL FORCE—*con.*
—INFANTRY, transfers to flying service from, xxvi; re-organised and despatched to France, 1916, 31. *5th Brigade* (*N.S.W.*), at Mont St. Quentin, 320, Battle of Beaurevoir Line, 334. *6th Brigade* (*Vic.*), captures Ville-sur-Ancre, 19 *May* 1918, 266, 267; at Mont St. Quentin, 320. *7th Brigade* (*Q'land, S. Aust., W. Aust.*), 269; attacks Morlancourt Ridge, 10-11 *June* 1918, 270-1. *8th Brigade* (*N.S.W., Vic., Q'land, S. Aust.*), 271, 307. *9th Brigade* (*N.S.W.*), 249. *14th Brigade* (*N.S.W.*), 307; at Mont St. Quentin, 320. *15th Brigade* (*Vic.*), 271. *21st Battalion* (*Vic.*), 204
—LIGHT HORSE, 40; aptitude of light horsemen for air work, xvii-xviii, 69-70; transfers to flying service from, xxvi, xxvii; remains in Egypt, 1916, 31; at Rafa, 50, First Gaza, 60, Battles of Megiddo, 161. *1st Brigade* (*N.S.W., Q'land, S. Aust., Tas.*), at Romani, 39-40, Third Gaza, 77. *2nd Brigade* (*N.S.W., Q'land*), at Romani, 39-40, First Gaza, 59, Third Gaza, 77. *4th Brigade* (*N.S.W., Q'land, S. Aust.*), in second action of Es Salt (Damieh), 115. *5th Brigade* (*all States*), in Battle of Nablus, 157. *11th Regiment* (*Q'land, S. Aust.*), reconnoitres Nekhl, 13-18 *Feb.* 1917, 54
AUSTRALIAN MILITARY FORCES: *Central Flying School*, 32-3, formation, 1
AUSTRALIAN NAVY, *Sydney*, 392
AVELGHEM (Map p. 179), 375; position of, 352
AVELIN (Map p. 355), 365
AWOIGNT, 196
AYERS, Lt. S. W. (b. Cootamundra, N.S.W.), 191
AZIZIYEH (Map p. 17), 19, 20, 23, 25; British use for concentration, 15-18
AZRAK (Sk. p. 163), 124, 148, 162, 163
AZZUN-FUNDUK ROAD, 157

BAC ST. MAUR (Maps pp. 279, 355; Sk. p. 280), 284 *et seq.*, 293, 296 *et seq.*, 339, 344, 350
BADGERY, Capt. A. D. (b. Sutton Forest, N.S.W.), 43, 411
BADRAH, 18
BAGHDAD (Map p. 17), xxv, 12, 15, 16, 27, 28, 29, 31, 390, 393, 395; advance on, 1915, 21-5; *see also* CTESIPHON KUT
BAGHDAD RAILWAY, 169
BAHARIA (Map p. 34), 36, 37
BAHR, RUJM EL (Maps pp. 101, 137), 89, 99, 102
BAILLEUL (Maps pp. 179, 279), 181, 199, 253, 277, 282, 283, 295, 348, 352, 353; German airmen raid, 210-1
BAILLEUL-ARMENTIÈRES ROAD, 277
BAILLIEU, Capt. R. F. (of Melbourne; b. Queenscliff, Vic.), 56, 59, 69, 72
BAILLIEU, Lt. T. L. (of Toorak, Vic.; b. Canterbury, Vic.), 265, 268, 315, 322, 326
BAIZIEUX (Maps pp. 179, 311), 178, 213
BAKA (Map p. 137), 154
BAKER, Capt. T. C. R. (of Adelaide; b. Smithfield, S. Aust.), 304, 340, 347, 349, 350, 351, 375, 377, 378, 379, 383
BALATA (Map p. 137), 136, 138, 139, 158, 159
BALI, 387, 395
BALL, Capt. A., V.C., xxiv
BALLOONS (Plate p. 322), xxi; No. 4 Squadron's attacks on, 284-7
BALLOONS DESTROYED: Allied, 21-25 *Mar.* 1918, 238; British, *Aug.* 1918, 307; German, *Mar.* 1918, 238, *May*, 284, 285, *June*, 286, 287, 288, *July*, 292, 295, 296, 298, 301, *Aug.*, 340, 341, 350, *Sept.*, 353, 354-6
BANDAR ABBAS, 390, 395, 396
BANG FARM (MESSINES), 203
BANGKOK, 391, 396
BANKS, Lt. E. C. (of Mosman, N.S.W.; b. Paddington, N.S.W.), 249, 250
BANTOUZELLE, 194, 196
BAPAUME (Map p. 189), 173, 193, 226, 227, 230, 233 *et seq.*, 254, 255, 350, 438; Germans capture, 231-2

INDEX

BAPAUME–ALBERT ROAD, 261, 437, 439
BAPAUME–BIHUCOURT ROAD, 438, 439
BAPAUME–CAMBRAI ROAD, 231, 233, 236, 437
BAPAUME–ERVILLERS ROAD, 437, 439
BARBAT, Lt. V. P. (of Newtown, N.S.W.; b. Ipswich, Q'land), 182
BARBE, Lt. A. E., 72
BARKELL, Lt. T. H. (b. Randwick, N.S.W.), 353, 360-1, 362, 375
BARRETT, Gen. Sir A. A., 6
BARRETT, Lt. A. G. (of Geelong, Vic.; b. Melbourne), 332, 334
BARROW, Lt. A. V. (b. Harrogate, Eng.), 249, 250
BARRY, Lt. O. C. (b. Harwood Island, N.S.W.), 278, 437, 438
BASRA (Map p. 4), 6 *et seq.*, 18, 22, 25, 390; Australian Half-Flight arrives at, 3; aerodrome constructed at, 3; captured, 6; aircraft park at, 8, 11
BASSÉE, LA (Map p. 355), 181, 211, 214, 224, 225, 242, 277, 292, 293, 294, 295, 300, 340, 346, 348, 349, 354, 356, 360, 361
BASSÉE–HAUBOURDIN CANAL, LA, 293
BATAVIA, 391, 393
BATTLES, ENGAGEMENTS, ETC., *see* AIR FIGHTING, AMIENS, AMMAN, BAGHDAD, BEAUREVOIR LINE, BEERSHEBA, BOMBING RAIDS, CAMBRAI, CTESIPHON, DAMASCUS, GAZA, HAMEL, HINDENBURG LINE, JERICHO, JERUSALEM, KURNA, KUT, LANDRECIES, LYS, MAGDHABA, MEGIDDO, MERRIS, MESSINES, MONTBREHAIN, MORLANCOURT RIDGE, NABLUS, NASIRIYEH, PASSCHENDAELE, PÉRONNE, RAFA, ROMANI, ST. QUENTIN (MONT), SALT (ES), SHAIBA, SHARON, SOMME, SUEZ CANAL, VILLERS-BRETONNEUX, VILLE-SUR-ANCRE, YPRES
BAYONET, Indian infantry charge with, at Kut, 14
BAYONVILLERS, 309
BAYUD, BIR EL (Map p. 42), 53

BEATON, Lt. E. B. S. (b. Durban, S. Africa), 106, 116, 117, 139
BEAUREVOIR (Map p. 321), 333, 334
BEAUREVOIR LINE, 327, 333; Battle of the, 334
BEAUREVOIR MILL, 334
BEDOUINS, 105, 114, 120; respect British aeroplanes, 149; *see also* ARABS
BEE FARM (MESSINES), 203
BEERSHEBA (Maps pp. 42, 78), 47, 48, 52, 56, 58, 60, 66, 70 *et seq.*, 135, 149; airmen raid, 45, 51, 61-2; Turkish H.Q. withdraws from, 50; captured, 77; *see also* GAZA (THIRD BATTLE)
BEERSHEBA ROAD, 73
BEIDAN, WADY, 159
BEIRUT (Map p. 170), 168, 169
BEISAN (Map p. 137), 141, 155, 157, 158, 159
BEIT JIBRIN (Map p. 78), 51
BEIT LAHM, 141
BEIT LID (Sk. p. 130), 157
BELAH, DEIR EL (Map p. 42), 59, 75
BELGIAN ARMY, 352, 361, 362, 364, 383
BELGRADE, 394
BELL, Lt. G. S. (of Melbourne; b. Leith, Scotland), 316
BELL, Capt. J. (of Rokewood, Vic.; b. Melbourne), 43, 184, 185, 187
BELL, Lt. J. R. (of Devonport West, Tas.; b. Scottsdale, Tas.), 181, 200, 202
BELLENGLISE (Map p. 321), 328, 329, 330
BELLEVUE (Map p. 179), 241, 248
BELLICOURT (Map p. 321), 326, 328, 330, 331
BELLUMS, 28*n*
BENAT YAKUB, JISR, position of, 167
BENJAMIN, Lt. L. (of St. Kilda, Vic.; b. St. Kilda), 195, 218, 219, 240
BENNETT, Lt. J. M. (b. St. Kilda, Vic.), accompanies Ross Smith in flight to Australia, 387, 388-92; killed, 392*n*
BERLIN, 409
BERNES (Map p. 179), 335
BERTANGLES (Map p. 311), 212

BERTHOLD, Lt., 84
BEST, Lt. G. W. (of Hobart; b. Hobart), 260
BETHLEHEM, 51
BETHUNE (Map p. 179), 241 et seq., 293, 296, 297
BICE, Lt. E. J. (of Canterbury, Vic.; b. East Melbourne), 310
BICKENDORF, 385
BIHUCOURT, 438
BIHUCOURT-SAPIGNIES ROAD, 437
BILL, Lt. A. G. (of Melbourne; b. Armadale, Vic.), 182
BIMA, 392
BIRDWOOD, Gen. Sir W. R., 188, 276, 421
BIREH (Maps pp. 78, 137; Sk. p. 89), 86, 126, 127, 138
BISHOP, Lt.-Col. W. A., V.C., xxiv, xxv; *quoted*, xxii, 199, 250-1
BLACKETT, Lt. B. J. (b. Potter's Bar, Eng.), 182
BLAIR, Lt. J. R. (b. Rockhampton, Q'land), 209
BLAKE, Maj. D. V. J. (of Parramatta, N.S.W.; b. Parramatta), *quoted*, 274-5, 307n, 318, 327n; mentioned, vii, 35, 175, 177, 182, 272n
BLAKE, Lt. H. A. (of West Perth, W. Aust.; b. Brisbane), 135, 150
BLANDAIN (Map p. 374), 367
BLANGY-TRONVILLE, 307
BLAXLAND, Capt. G. H. (of Fremantle, W. Aust.; b. Broken Hill, N.S.W.), 248, 255, 365, 367, 368, 371, 372, 376, 380, 381
BLÉRIOT, M. LOUIS, 399, 411, 415
BOELCKE, Lt., xxiii, 215, 248, 416
BOHAIN (Map p. 179), 333, 335
BOMBAY, 3, 16, 422
BOMBING RAIDS—
—AUSTRALIAN: *Half-Flight,* at Battle of Kut, 15; on Arab camp at Badrah, 18. *No. 1 Squadron,* on Mazar, 4-7 *Sep.* 1916, 40, Masaid, 5 *Oct.,* 43, Maghara, 15 *Oct.,* 43, Beersheba, 11 *Nov.,* 45, and 14-19 *Jan.* 1917, 51, and 12 *Apr.,* 62, Magdhaba and Irgeig, 22 *Dec.* 1916, 48-9, Sheria and Junction Station, *Mar.* 1917, 58-9, and 10 *Nov.,* 82, Hareira, *Aug.,* 75; at

BOMBING RAIDS—*continued.*
Third Gaza, 79-80; on Rujm el Bahr, *Dec.,* 89, Huwara, 25 *Jan.* 1918, 98-9, Messudie, 18-22 *Jan.,* 99, Amman, *Jan.-Apr.,* 100, 110, 113, Miske, 2-3 *Feb.,* 100-2, Kutrani, *Feb.-Mar.,* 102, 107-8, Kerak, 25 *Feb.,* 102, Shunet Nimrin, *Feb.-Mar.,* 103, 106, 108, Lubban-Nablus road, 9-10 *Mar.,* 107, Damieh Bridge, *Mar.,* 107, Kastal, 27 *Mar.,* 110, Es Salt and Amman, 4 *May,* 119, Jenin, 9 *May,* 122, Deraa, *Sep.,* 149-50, 164-5, Afule, 19 *Sep.,* 152, Mafrak, 25 *Sep.,* 166-7, Rayak, 2 *Oct.,* 169, Muslimie, 23 *Oct.,* 169. *No. 2 Squadron,* near Lille, *July-Oct.* 1918, 293-4, 364-7, 371, 373; on the Lys Valley, *July-Aug.,* 302, 339, Haubourdin aerodrome, 16 *Aug.,* 346, 348, Lomme aerodrome, 17 *Aug.,* 349, Tournai, 18 *Oct.,* 367-8, Rebaix, 30 *Oct.,* 379, Wattines, 4 *Nov.,* 381, Ath, 9-10 *Nov.,* 383-4. *No. 3 Squadron,* about Oppy and Neuvireuil, 31 *Oct.* 1917, 181; on Gricourt, 24 *Sep.* 1918, 328. *No. 4 Squadron,* on Douai, 16 *Mar.* 1918, 224-5, Bapaume, 24 *Mar.,* 231-2, 233, Armentières, 11 *May,* 278; on artillery near Bailleul, 15 *May,* 282; on La Gorgue, 16-21 *May,* 283, 284; the Lys Valley, *May-Aug.,* 285n, 302-3, 339, 340-1, Estaires, 1-6 *July,* 291, 292, 293, Bac St. Maur, 25-28 *July,* 299, 301; on ammunition train at Vielle Chapelle, 6 *Aug.,* 338; on Haubourdin aerodrome, 16 *Aug.,* 346-8, Lomme aerodrome, 17 *Aug.,* 349; near Lille, *Sep.-Oct.,* 354-6, 364-7; on Rebaix, 30 *Oct.,* 379
—BRITISH, 38; on El Arish, *Sep.-Oct.* 1916, 43, Irgeig, 22 *Dec.,* 48, Sheria, 5-7 *Mar.* 1917, 56-8, Junction Station, 8 *Mar.,* 58, Ramleh, *Apr.-June,* 61, 66, Beersheba, 12 *Apr.,* 61-2; on Turkish Fourth Army H.Q. at Jerusalem, 26 *June,* 66; on Afule, 3 *Jan.* 1918, 96, Jenin,

INDEX

BOMBING RAIDS—continued.
4 Jan., 96, and 19 Sep., 155, Kutrani, 4 Mar., 106, Kalat el Hesa, 5 Mar., 106, Damieh Bridge, 26-27 Mar., 110, Amman, June-Aug., 125, 147; on harvesting operations near Kutrani, 16 June, 125; on Jauf ed Derwish, 8 July, 135; during German offensive, Mar. 1918, 228, 235-6; on Armentières, May-July, 278, 302-3, Haubourdin aerodrome, 16 Aug., 346-8, Lomme aerodrome, 17 Aug., 348-9; near Ath, 9-10 Nov., 383-4
—GERMAN, near Romani, 31 July 1916, 38; on Port Said, 1 Sep., 40, El Arish, 7 Jan. 1917, 50, Rafa, 12 Apr., 61; on yeomanry, Aug., 75; on Shunet Nimrin, 28 Mar. 1918, 110, Bailleul, 1917-18, 210-1, Bethune and Bruay, Apr. 1918, 245-6, Clairmarais, 18 and 30 May, 283
BOMBS (Plate p. 194), used in Mesopotamia, 5
BONY (Map p. 321), 330, 331, 332; captured, 333
BORTON, Brig.-Gen. A. E., 95, 123, 146, 388
BOTT, Capt. A. J. (b. Stoke-on-Trent, Eng.), escapes from captivity, 27-8
BOUCHAVESNES (Map p. 321), 317
BOUCHAVESNES SPUR, 319
BOULOGNE (Sk. p. 241), 389
BOURLON (Map p. 189), 191
BOURLON WOOD, 190 et seq., 230
BOUVINCOURT (Map p. 321), 325, 326, 335
BRASELL, Lt. J. S. (of Melbourne; b. Wanstead, Eng.), 66
BRAY (Map p. 311), 239, 257, 271, 310, 314
BREARLEY, Capt. S. G. (b. Geelong, Vic.), 322, 327
BREBIÈRES (Map p. 220), 218, 230; position of, 216, 356; No. 4 Sqn.'s disastrous fight over, 5 Sep. 1918, 356-9
BRETTINGHAM-MOORE, Lt. G. R. (of Hobart; b. St. Servan, France), 249
BRIE (Map p. 321), 320
BRIDGES, across Jordan, 108

BRIGADES, see AUSTRALIAN IMPERIAL FORCE, BRITISH AIR FORCE, BRITISH ARMY, INDIAN ARMY, NEW ZEALAND EXPEDITIONARY FORCE
BRISTOL FIGHTER, arrives in Palestine. July 1917, 74; Germans fear, 111-2; Turks fear, 151
BRITISH AIR FORCE, 214n, 231; treats captured airmen chivalrously, xviii; Balloon Cov., R.E., becomes Air Bn., R.E., xx; Air Bn., R.E., becomes R.F.C., xx; R.F.C.: formation, xx, 397, strength, 1914, xxiin, dominion airmen in, xxv, merged into R.A.F., 178n, 397; R.N.A.S.: 66, formation, xx, 397, dominion airmen in, xxv, merged into R.A.F., 178n, 397; history and development of, xix-xxii, xxiv-xxv; strength, 1918, xxiin; formation, 178n, 397-8; re-organisation in Palestine, Apr.-Oct. 1917, 64, 74; air supremacy of, 1918, 133; destructive work of, in Wady Fara, 161; Australians in, 182; superiority over German airmen, Battle of Amiens, 309; transfer of A.I.F. personnel to, 421-2; organisation and duties of, 434-6. *Independent Air Force*, 403. *2nd Brigade*, 209. *9th Brigade*, 259. *10th Brigade*, 259. *Palestine Brigade*, 64; composition, 1917 and 1918, 68. *1st Wing*, 177. *2nd Wing*, 211. *5th Wing*, 33, 88, 424; composition, 68. *10th Wing*, 213. *13th Wing*, 178. *40th Wing*, 64, 133n; composition, 68; duties in Allenby's final advance, 151. *80th Wing*, 259, 345, 381; bombing raids: on Lomme and Haubourdin, Aug. 1918, 346-9, near Lille, 7 Oct., 365-6, on Tournai, 18 Oct., 367-8, Ath, 9-10 Nov., 383-4. *No. 1 Squadron*, 397. *No. 2 Squadron*, 397. *No. 3 Squadron*, 397. *No. 4 Squadron*, 397. *No. 5 Squadron*, xxii, 178, 397. *No. 9 Squadron*, 274. *No. 14 Squadron*, 35 et seq., 52, 56, 58, 61, 66, 68, 70, 72, 77; at Romani, 40;

BRITISH AIR FORCE—*continued*.
bombs El Arish, 43. *No.* 16 *Squadron*, 178. *No.* 17 *Squadron*, 35. *No.* 29 *Squadron*, 177. *No.* 30 *Squadron*, 11, 12, 22; at Battle of Kut, 1915, 14-5. *No.* 32 *Squadron*, 177. *No.* 43 *Squadron*, 248, 252. *No.* 46 *Squadron*, 259. *No.* 57 *Squadron*, 54. *No.* 67 *Squadron*, xxvi; *see also* AUSTRALIAN FLYING CORPS (*No.* 1 *Squadron*). *No.* 68 *Squadron*, xxvi, 174*n*; *see also* AUSTRALIAN FLYING CORPS (*No.* 2 *Squadron*). *No.* 69 *Squadron*, xxvii, 174*n*; *see also* AUSTRALIAN FLYING CORPS (*No.* 3 *Squadron*). *No.* 71 *Squadron*, xxvi, 174*n*; *see also* AUSTRALIAN FLYING CORPS (*No.* 4 *Squadron*). *No.* 80 *Squadron*, 248, 252. *No.* 88 *Squadron*, 337, 346, 359, 366, 368. *No.* 92 *Squadron*, 346. *No.* 103 *Squadron*, 259, 366. *No.* 110 *Squadron*, 278, 280. *No.* 111 *Squadron*, 68, 74, 75, 77, 86, 87, 88, 89, 94, 111, 147; its duties in second action of Es Salt, 113, and in Allenby's final advance, 151. *No.* 113 *Squadron*, 68, 74, 75, 87, 96. *No.* 142 *Squadron*, 68, 88, 106, 107, 110, 116, 125; its duties in second action of Es Salt, 113. *No.* 144 *Squadron*, 68, 149, 167; its duties in Allenby's final advance, 151. *No.* 145 *Squadron*, 68; its duties in Allenby's final advance, 151. "*X*" *Squadron*, 77. "*X*" *Aircraft Park*, 35. "*X*" *Flight*, co-operates with Hejaz, 1918, 148. *No.* 21 *Balloon Company*, composition, 68. *No.* 49 *Balloon Section*, 68. *No.* 50 *Balloon Section*, 68. *No.* 57 *Balloon Section*, 68

BRITISH ARMY, *see also* EGYPTIAN EXPEDITIONARY FORCE
—FIRST ARMY, 213, 216, 241
—SECOND ARMY, 280, 384
—THIRD ARMY, 178, 183, 227, 230, 232, 233, 237, 239, 240
—FOURTH ARMY, 313, 335, 384, 385

BRITISH ARMY—*continued*.
—FIFTH ARMY, 228, 230, 232, 237, 362, 368
—EASTERN FORCE, disbanded, 63; *see also* XX CORPS below
—DESERT COLUMN, becomes Desert Mounted Corps, 63-4
—DESERT MOUNTED CORPS, formation, composition, and command, 64, 67; at Third Gaza, 77, 79, in Battles of Megiddo, 157
—IX CORPS, 328, 333, 335
—XIII CORPS, 178, 335
—XX CORPS, 89; formation, composition, and command, 63, 68; in Battle of Nablus, 157
—XXI CORPS, 89-90, 121; formation, composition, and command, 63, 68; at Battle of Sharon, 152
—5TH DIVISION, 289
—10TH (IRISH) DIVISION, 68; at Third Gaza, 79; in Battle of Nablus, 157
—24TH DIVISION, 229
—29TH DIVISION, 243
—31ST DIVISION, 243
—35TH DIVISION, 232
—42ND (E. LANCS.) DIVISION, 68
—51ST (HIGHLAND) DIVISION, 243
—52ND (LOWLAND) DIVISION, 67, 68; at Third Gaza, 79; sent to France, 121
—53RD (WELSH) DIVISION, 67, 68; arrives in Palestine, 46; in advance to Jericho, 102
—54TH (E. ANGLIAN) DIVISION, 67, 68; at Third Gaza, 79
—60TH (LONDON) DIVISION, 68; at Third Gaza, 77, 79; in advance to Jericho, 102, Amman raid, 108, second action of Es Salt, 115, Battle of Sharon, 157
—74TH (YEOMANRY) DIVISION, 68; at Third Gaza, 77, 79; sent to France, 121
—75TH (TERRITORIAL AND INDIAN) DIVISION, 68
—IMPERIAL MOUNTED DIVISION, 67
—4TH CAVALRY DIVISION, 67; in Battles of Megiddo, 152
—5TH CAVALRY DIVISION, 67; in Battles of Megiddo, 152, 161

INDEX

BRITISH ARMY—*continued.*
—CHAYTOR'S FORCE, composition, 166; advances from Jordan Valley, 24 *Sep*. 1918, 166, 168
—CAMEL CORPS, 31. *I.C.C. Brigade*, 60, 67; at Third Gaza, 77
—CAVALRY, 54, 249; yeomanry at First Gaza, 59; nine yeomanry regiments of, sent to France, *Apr*. 1918, 121. *5th Yeomanry Brigade*, 67; overwhelmed by Turks at Romani, 39. *6th Yeomanry Brigade*, 67. *22nd Yeomanry Brigade*, 67. *King Edward's Horse*, 243
—ENGINEERS, work of survey companies, 64
—INFANTRY, 39, 161; at First Gaza, 59. *13th London Regiment*, 180. *British West Indies Regiment*, 66
—MACHINE GUNS, *see* MACHINE GUNS
—ROYAL FLYING CORPS, *see* BRITISH AIR FORCE
BRITISH GOVERNMENT, arranges with Australia regarding upkeep of A.I.F., 32; asks for A.I.F. personnel for R.F.C., 421
BRITISH NAVY, monitors of, co-operate with airmen, 37, 38; *Comet*, 7, 18; *Espiègle*, 6; *Shirin*, 22-3; Launch *L6*, 23; Tug *T3*, 22-3
BROADMEADOWS, 2
BROKE-SMITH, Lt.-Col. P. W. L. (of Cheltenham, Eng.; b. Plymouth, Eng.), 3, 7, 8, 16
BROOK, Lt. A. O'C. (of Tallangatta and Benalla, Vic.; b. Dederang, Vic.,) 272
BROOKES, Capt. C. A. (of Bradford-on-Avon, Eng.; b. Winsley, Eng.), 71
BROUN, Maj. A. A. J. (of Spreyton, Tas.; b. Orchard, Scotland), 35
BROWN, Capt. A. R. (of Launceston, Tas.; b. Launceston), 93, 95, 96, 98, 109, 113, 118, 125, 131, 135, 138, 140, 142, 143, 144, 153, 155, 156, 159, 165, 167
BROWN, Lt. Sir A. W., 386*n*, 388, 409
BROWN, Lt. C. le B. (of Inverell, N.S.W.; b. Paterson, N.S.W.), 66

BROWN, Lt. C. T. (b. Charters Towers, Q'land), 209, 314, 315, 328
BRUAY (Map p. 179), 213, 222, 225, 226, 234, 242, 246, 370
BRUSSELS, 376, 383
BUCHAREST, 394
BUCKLAND, Lt. W. A. J. (of Mirboo North, Vic.; b. Moe, Vic.), 264
BUIRE (Sk. p. 266), 322
BUKSASE, SEIL EL, 100
BULFIN, Lt.-Gen. Sir E. S., commands XXI Corps, 63
BULGARIA, 28
BULLECOURT, 230, 438
BULLECOURT-ECOUST ROAD, 437, 438
BURKA (Sk. p. 130), 155, 156; position of, 129
BURN, Lt. W. W. A. (of Christchurch, N.Z.; b. Gippsland, Vic.), 3, 7, 9, 19; killed by Arabs, 10
BURTON, Lt. R. (of Kalgoorlie, W. Aust.; b. Payneham, S. Aust.), 118
BUSHIRE, 395
BUSIGNY (Map p. 179), 335
BUSSU, 322
BUSTEED, Lt.-Col. H. R., 405
BUTLER, Capt. H., 406
BUTLER, Lt. J. H. (of Hobart; b. Bellerive, Tas.), 67
BYNG, Gen. Lord, 174, 183, 184, 188, 191, 192

CACHY, 265, 307
CAIRO (Map p. 34), 37, 38, 148, 388, 390, 393; German airman bombs, 45
CALCUTTA, 390, 393, 396
CALONNE (Map p. 279), 245
CALSHOT, 386
CAMBRAI (Maps pp. 179, 189), 183, 229, 350, 351, 354; Battle of, 174, 184-92, German counter-attack, 192-7
CAMEL CORPS, *see* BRITISH ARMY
CAMERON, Lt. A. C. G. (b. Maryborough, Q'land), 294
CAMERON, Lt. C. C. (of Jamestown, S. Aust.; b. Jamestown), 110, 143, 152

CAMM, Lt. R. A. (of Scottsdale, Tas.,; b. Zeehan, Tas.), 113, 117-8, 122, 123, 124-5
CAMPAIGNS, *see* DARDANELLES, MESOPOTAMIA, PALESTINE, WESTERN FRONT
CAMPS (TURKISH), at Amman, 109, Mukhalid, 113, 147, Shunet Nimrin, 114; airmen attack, *Aug.-Sep.* 1918, 147-8
CANADIAN EXPEDITIONARY FORCE, 178
CANALS, *see* SUEZ CANAL
CANDLER, E., *quoted*, 9-10, 24, 28
CAPINGHEM (Maps pp. 279, 355), 292, 363
CAPPY, 256
CARNOT, FORT, 299
CARTER, Lt. D. C. (of Prahran, Vic.; b. Melbourne), 347, 357, 358
CARTIGNY, 324
CASH, Lt. J. N. (b. Newcastle, Eng.), 214
CASSEL (Map p. 179), 277
CASUALTIES (*see also* AIRCRAFT DESTROYED)—
—AUSTRALIAN: *Half-Flight*, 10-11; *No. 1 Squadron*, 66, 71, 72, 96, 118, 128, 131; *No. 2 Squadron*, 180, 184, 188, 190-1, 230, 239, 258, 373, 376; *No. 3 Squadron*, 177, 199, 209, 210, 211, 260, 264, 265, 272, 310, 312, 320, 327, 328, 334; *No. 4 Squadron*, 213-4, 217, 239, 242, 244, 278, 285, 287, 295, 341, 344, 349, 357-9, 378, 383
—BRITISH: *6th Indian Division*, 24. *No. 110 Squadron*, 280
—GERMAN, 145
—INDIAN: *6th Indian Division*, 24
—NEW ZEALAND, 10-11
—TURKISH, 77, 92, 96, 99
CATEAU, LE (Map. p. 179), 335, 336
CATO, Lt. E. A. (of Toorak, Vic.; b. Malvern, Vic.), 344-5, 380
CAVALRY, *see* AUSTRALIAN IMPERIAL FORCE (LIGHT HORSE), BRITISH ARMY, INDIAN ARMY, TURKISH ARMY
CERISY (Sk. 266), 272, 307, 308
CEYLON WOOD (SOMME), 314, 315

CHALLINOR, Lt. R. T. (of Brisbane; b. Beenleigh, Q'land), 116
CHAMPAGNE, 172, 173, 174, 175, 221, 252
CHAPELLE-À-WATTINES (Map p. 374), 381
CHAPMAN, Lt. J. E. (of Bowenvale, Vic.; b. Bairnsdale, Vic.), 310
CHARLEROI, 384, 385
CHASE, Lt. L. P. (of Skipton, Vic.; b. Fitzroy, Vic.,) 314
CHATEAU-THIERRY, 264
CHAULNES (Map p. 179), 313, 315
CHAUNY, 238
CHAUVEL, Lt.-Gen. Sir H. G. (of Clarence River District, N.S.W.; b. Tabulam, N.S.W.), 39, 52; commands Desert Mounted Corps, 64
CHAYTOR, Maj.-Gen. Sir E. W. C., 166
CHAYTOR'S FORCE, *see* BRITISH ARMY
CHEMIN-DES-DAMES, 241
CHERENG (Map p. 374), 372
CHETWODE, Lt.-Gen. Sir Philip W., commands XX Corps, 63
CHIPILLY (Map p. 311), 310
CHUIGNES, 257, 314, 315
CHUIGNOLLES, 314
"CIRCUS," definition and functions of a, 247-8; *see also* GERMAN AIR FORCE and Glossary
CLAIRMARAIS, NORTH (Map. p. 179), 283n; position of, 246
CLAIRMARAIS WOOD, 283
CLARK, Lt. A. G. (b. Ashfield, N.S.W.), 218, 219, 235, 248, 249
CLARK, Lt. D. G. (of Killara, N.S.W.; b. Picton, N.S.W.), 191
CLARK, Lt. R. L. (of Annandale, N.S.W.; b. Glebe, N.S.W.), 185
CLÉRY (Map p. 321), 316, 319
CLIMATE, *see* WEATHER
CLIMIE, Lt. L. S. (b. Albany, W. Aust.,), 154
COBBY, Capt. A. H. (of Glenhuntly, Vic.; b. Prahran, Vic.), estimate of, 292; in raid on Haubourdin, 346-7; mentioned, vii, 216, 226, 232, 244, 282 *et seq.*, 295, 296, 313, 338, 339, 340, 356, 438
CODY, Col. S. F., xx, 405
COLE, Capt. A. T. (of Melbourne; b. Malvern, Vic.), 52, 54, 56, 63,

INDEX

COLE, Capt. A. T.—*continued.*
65, 66-7, 69, 257, 293, 297, 302, 304, 313, 339, 348, 349-50, 363 *et seq.*, 371, 376

COLOGNE, 370, 384, 385

COLOGNE RIVER, 322, 324

COMINES (Map p. 279), 290, 298

CONRICK, Lt. F. C. (b. Cooper's Creek, Vic.), 142, 146, 159, 168

CONSCRIPTION, Britain enforces, 30

CONSTANTINOPLE, 21, 27, 394, 395, 409

CONTACT-PATROLS, *see* PATROLS

COPP, Capt. C. H. (of Middle Park, Vic.; b. Middle Park), 258, 293, 360, 367

CORBEAU, LE, 299

CORBIE (Map p. 311), 240, 248, 262, 272, 315

CORNELL, Lt. H. G. (of Ballarat, Vic.; b. Richmond, Vic.), 193

CORNET MALO, LE (Map p. 279), 296

CORNISH, Capt. E. W., 372, 375

CORTOYLE, 348*n*

COSTIGAN, POINT (Map p. 101), 99

COTTAM, Lt. M. T. G. (b. Alexandria, N.S.W.), 302, 378

COURCELLES, 322

COURTNEY, Lt. J. C. (of Manly, N.S.W.; b. Auckland, N.Z.), 219, 224, 226, 231, 232, 236, 242, 437, 438

COUTRAI (Map p. 179), 352

COUSTON, Lt. A. (b. Launceston, Tas.), 219

COX, Lt. G. (b. Carlton, Vic.), 255, 257, 294, 351, 361

COX, Lt. T. C. (of Singleton, N.S.W.; b. Quirindi, N.S.W.), 362

CRETE, 389, 390

CROISETTE, 383

CTESIPHON (Map p. 17), 16, 27, 28; Turkish positions at, 18; Battle of: 21-5, preparations for, 20-1, British and Indian casualties at, 24, British retreat from, 24-5

CUMMINGS, Capt. E. D. (b. Franklin, Tas.), 254, 257, 299, 304, 348, 354, 366, 367, 368 371-2, 373, 380

CURRAN, 45 Air-Mechanic D. (b. Ireland), 26

CURTIS, Lt. R. H. (of Glen Innes, N.S.W.; b. Glen Innes), 214

CURWEN-WALKER, Lt. J. K. (of Prahran, Vic.; b. Windsor, Vic.), 118

CUVILLY, 258

CYSOING, 372

DAKHLA (Map p. 34), 36, 37

DAMASCUS (Map p. 170; Sk. p. 167), 65*n*, 92, 161, 167, 390; mounted troops enter, 168

DAMIEH, JISR ED (Plate p. 107; Maps pp. 101, 137), 95, 106, 109, 116, 119, 124, 127, 155, 158, 161, 162; airmen raid, *Mar.* 1918, 107, 110; Turks counter-attack 4 L.H. Bde. at, 115; air-photography of country surrounding, 122-3

DAMIEH-BEISAN ROAD, 155, 159

DAMIEH-ES SALT ROAD, 117

DARDANELLES CAMPAIGN, 29, 30

DARWIN, PORT, 386, 387, 388, 392, 393, 396

DAVIES, Capt. E. E. (of Swan Hill, Vic.; b. Kerang, Vic.), 350, 351, 367, 368, 372, 380, 381

DEAD SEA (Map p. 101), 44, 47, 89, 90, 92, 102, 106, 123, 124, 135; air reconnaissance of, *Jan.* 1918, 99-100

DEAMER, Lt. S. H. (b. Hitchin, Eng.), 332

DEANS, Lt. G. M. (of Nhill, Vic.; b. Amherst, Talbot, Vic.), 329

DEFENCES, *see* FORTIFICATIONS

DE HAVILLAND, Capt. G., 398, 401, 402, 403

DELAMAINE, Maj.-Gen. Sir W. S., 14

DELHI, 390, 396

DELVILLE WOOD, 232

DEMOBILISATION, of A.F.C., 385

DEMOLITIONS, on Turkish railway, 1917, 65

DÉMUIN, 240, 248

DENDRE, RIVER, 376

DERAA (Plate p. 146; Sk. p. 163), 148, 149, 151, 161, 162, 164, 165, 167, 169; airmen raid, 149-50, 164-5

DERWISH, JAUF ED, airmen raid, 135

DESERT, difficulty of fighting in, 53

INDEX

DESERT MOUNTED CORPS, *see* BRITISH ARMY

DESERTION, British propaganda among Germans to induce, 208-9

DIALA, RIVER, 21, 25

DIBBS, Lt. E. R. (of Mosman, N.S.W.; b. North Sydney), vii, 181, 182, 367, 371, 372

DIMSEY, Lt. D. F. (of Albert Park and Mildura, Vic.; b. Dimboola, Vic.), 274, 327

DISEASES, malaria, 8; of prisoners at Kut, 26

DJEMAL PASHA, 53n

DOINGT, 322

DOMPIERRE, 314

DON RAILWAY STATION (Map p. 355), 339, 341, 350, 353, 354, 356

DONAHAY, Lt. C. (of Hawthorn, Vic.; b. Camberwell, Vic.), 209

DOUAI (Maps pp. 179, 220), 214 *et seq.*, 222, 224, 225, 350, 351, 352, 354, 356, 357, 359, 366

DOUGLAS, Lt. R. (b. Charters Towers, Q'land), attempts flight to Australia, 387

DOULLENS (Map p. 179), 211, 241

DOWLING, Lt. D. R. (b. Murwillumbah, N.S.W.), 102, 135, 138, 146-7, 150, 153

DRANOUTRE (Map. p. 279), 209

DROCOURT (Map p. 220), 242

DRUMMOND, Capt. R. M. (of Cottesloe, W. Aust.; b. Perth), 43, 54, 56, 61, 65, 87, 90

DUIGAN, Capt. J. R. (of Melbourne; b. Terang, Vic.), 262, 265, 400

DUMM, TALAT ED, 103

EASTERN FORCE, *see* BRITISH ARMY

EBELING, Lt. C. R. (of Yarraville, Vic.; b. Spotswood, Vic.), 338

ECOUST, 437

EDDIE, Lt. M. H. (of Launceston, Tas.; b. Launceston), 344, 347, 357, 358

EDOLS, Lt. T. R. (of Burrawang, N.S.W.; b. Forbes, N.S.W.), 304, 344, 347

EDSON, Lt. C. R. (of Port Adelaide; b. York, S. Aust.), 182

EDWARDS, Lt., 39

EGAN, Lt. J. A. (b. Bendigo, Vic.), 368, 377

EGYPT, 31, 33; boundary between Turkey and, 51

EGYPTIAN EXPEDITIONARY FORCE, re-organisation of, *Apr.-Oct.* 1917, 63-4, *Apr.-June* 1918, 121; composition, 1917 and 1918, 67-8; *see also* AUSTRALIAN FLYING CORPS, AUSTRALIAN IMPERIAL FORCE, BRITISH AIR FORCE, BRITISH ARMY, INDIAN ARMY, NEW ZEALAND EXPEDITIONARY FORCE

EGYPTIAN LABOUR CORPS, German airmen demoralise, 52

ELLIS, Maj. A. W. L. (of Malvern, Vic.; b. Steiglitz, Vic.), 38-9, 40, 51, 61, 69, 75

ELLIS, Lt. D. (of Geelong, Vic.; b. Terang, Vic.), 325, 328, 332

ELWYN, Lt. G. M. (b. Texas, Q'land), 227, 437, 438

ENGHIEN, 383

ENGHIEN–HAL ROAD, 384

ENNETIÈRES (Maps pp. 179, 355), 366, 370, 375

EPEHY (Map p. 321), 230

EPINOY (Map p. 189), 350

EQUIPMENT, arrangement between Britain and Australia regarding, 32

ERQUINGHEM (Sk. p. 286), 302, 352

ERQUINGHEM-LE-SEC (Maps pp. 279, 355), 356

ERVILLERS (Map p. 189), 237, 254, 437

ESAL, WADY, 135

ESANI, BIR EL (Map p. 78), 72, 74, 75

ESDRAELON PLAIN, 71, 92, 140, 155

ESQUERCHIN (Map p. 220), 219

ES SALT, *see* SALT, ES

ESTAIRES (Maps pp. 279, 355; Sk. p. 286), 243, 244, 245, 283 *et seq.*, 292, 295, 296, 297, 298, 301, 304, 340, 341, 344, 350, 352; No. 4 Sqn. raids, 285n, 291, 293

ESTAIRES–LA BASSÉE ROAD, 302, 340

ESTAIRES–MERVILLE ROAD, 244

ESTRÉES (Maps pp. 220, 321), 315, 332, 334

ESTRÉES-EN-CHAUSSÉE (Map p. 321), 257

ETINEHEM (Map p. 311), 261, 269

INDEX

EUPHRATES, RIVER (Maps pp. 4, 17), 16, 21; Turks concentrate on, 6; British advance up, 9, *see also* NASIRIYEH
EUSKIRCHEN, 385
EVANS, Maj. A. J., 107, 108*n*

FAGEIRA, 49
FAO (Map p. 4), captured, 6
FARA (JERICHO), WADY, 95, 103
FARA (NABLUS). WADY (Plates pp. 159, 166; Map p. 160; Sk. p. 89), 95*n*, 106, 107, 109, 117, 119, 124, 138, 140, 141, 142, 143, 147, 153, 156, 158, 162; destructive work of British and Australian airmen at, 159-61
FARMAN, HENRI, xxii, 399, 412, 413
FARMAN, MAURICE, xxii, 412, 413
FARQUHAR, Lt. A. W. K. (of Sydney; b. Ingham, Q'land), 128
FEEZ, Lt. C. M. (of Yeronga, Q'land; b. Brisbane), 225, 239
FEISAL, EMIR, 123, 148
FELMY, Capt., 65*n*
FELMY, Lt. G., 71-2, 73, 82, 83, 91, 128; biography and estimate of, 65, 66
FENWICKE, Lt. C. R. (b. Tamworth, N.S.W.), 331
FERWEH, KHURBET (Maps pp. 137, 160), 109, 156, 157, 158, 159
FESTUBERT, 218
FEUILLACOURT, 322
FINANCE: Arrangement between Britain and Australia regarding upkeep of A.I.F., 32
FINLAY, Lt. G. (b. Sydney), 87, 98, 106, 111, 113, 118, 122, 131, 135, 138, 140, 142, 143, 144, 153, 155, 159, 165, 167
FINNIE, Lt. A. (b. Botany, N.S.W.), 285
FIVES, 366, 367
FLAQUE, LA, 310
FLARES, *see* SIGNALLING
FLESQUIÈRES (Map p. 189), 184
FLESSELLES, 269
FLETCHER, Lt. H. B. (of Stanthorpe, Q'land; b. Newcastle, N.S.W.), 114, 118, 141, 143, 144-5, 153
FLEURBAIX (Maps pp. 279, 355; Sk. p. 286), 242

FLIGHT, Lt. O. T. (b. Bendigo, Vic.), 239
FLOCKART, Capt. D. P. (of Melbourne; b. Casterton, Vic.), 216, 217, 222
FLORES, 392
FLY BUILDINGS (MESSINES), 203
FOALE, Lt. H. S. (of Shackleton, S. Aust.; b. Adelaide), 310
FOCH, Marshal, 174, 264, 276
FOGS, *see* WEATHER
FOKKER, development and fighting tactics of, xxiii-xxiv
FOLLETT, Lt. F. W. (of Sydney; b. Marrickville, N.S.W.), 303, 313, 348
FONTAINE (Map p. 189), 191, 192, 194, 196
FOQUOROLLES, 258
FORREST, Capt. H. G. (b. Brunswick, Vic.), 177, 195, 216-7, 229, 230, 232, 240, 248, 253, 254, 257, 258, 294
FORTIFICATIONS, Turkish: at Ctesiphon, 18, Rafa, 50; British line at Romani, 39; German line in Flanders, 6 *Sep.* 1918, 352, in Belgium, 22 *Oct.*, 375
FOUCAUCOURT, 315
FOURNES (Maps pp. 279, 355), 242, 354
FRANCE, development of aviation in, 1912-14, 398; *see also* WESTERN FRONT
FRANCIS, Capt. R. G. D. (of Kew, Vic.; b. Corio, Vic.), 212, 272, 305, 320, 322, 328
FRANKS, Lt. L. (b. Apollo Bay, Vic.), 363, 367, 371, 373
FRASER, Air-Mechanic G. H. (b. Bendigo, Vic.), attempts flight to Australia, 388
FRASER, Lt. H. L. (b. Rockhampton, Q'land), 93, 94, 98
FRAZER, Lt. C. E. (of Kew, Vic.; b. Kew), 332
FREEMAN, Maj. R. H., 47
FRÉLINGHIEN (Map p. 279), 361
FRENCH FLYING CORPS, history of, xxi, xxiv; composition, 1914 and 1918, 398; during German offensive, *Mar.* 1918, 238
FRENCH NAVY, 56
FRESNOY-LE-GRAND (Map p. 220), 335
FRETIN (Map p. 279), 371, 373

468   INDEX

FROMELLES (Maps pp. 279, 355), 353, 364
FROYENNES (Map p. 374), 367, 368
FRYBERG, Lt. L. (b. Bendigo, Vic.), 260
FULLERTON, Lt. P. R. (of Rutherglen, Vic.; b. Rutherglen), 332
FULTON, Capt. E. J., 14, 18, 25, 27
FYSH, Lt. H. (of St. Leonards, Tas.; b. Launceston, Tas.), 94, 109, 117, 124, 127, 135, 141, 142, 143, 146, 147, 152

GAMBLE, Lt. G. E. (b. Trentham, Vic.), 325
GANADIL (Map p. 42), 40
GARRETT, Lt. S. G. (of Box Hill, Vic.; b. Bendigo, Vic.), 249, 250
GAZA (Maps pp. 42, 78), 47, 48, 51, 52, 58, 59, 61, 62, 63, 71, 90, 93, 390; First Battle of: 57, 59-60, plans, 59, withdrawal, 60; Second Battle of: 62-3, preparations, 62, Turks counter-attack, 63; Third Battle of, 69, 70, 77-80
GAZA-BEERSHEBA LINE, 52, 56, 57n, 61, 62; Turks retire to, 49
GAZA-HAREIRA ROAD, 60
GERMAN AIR FORCE, 33, 37-8, 40, 45, 48, 61, 169, 278, 337; treats captured airmen chivalrously, xviii, 71-2; history of, xxi, xxiii-xxv; at Kut, 26; airmen of, raid Romani area, 38; lacks aggressiveness in Palestine, 1916, 46-7; demoralises Egyptian Labour Corps, 52, Arabs, 162, 163, 164; at Second Gaza, 63; airmen of, raid British communications, *May-June* 1917, 65-6; its decline in Palestine, 1918, 112, 128-9, 133, 147; at First Battle of Cambrai, 192-7; during German offensive, *Mar.* 1918, 235; airmen of, raid Clairmarais, 283n; at Battles of Cambrai, 1918, 333; inability of, to retaliate on British, *Aug.,* 349, 351; tactics of, *Sep.* 1918, 353; bravery of airmen, 380; surrenders aeroplanes after Armistice, 385; composition of, 1913-14, 397. *Richthofen's Circus,* 225, 226, 248, 407; tactics of, 215n-6; fights No. 3 Sqn., 21 *Apr.* 1918, 249-52. *No.* 300 *Squadron,* 81.

GERMAN AIR FORCE—*continued.*
No. 301 *Squadron,* 81, 82, 84, 134. *No.* 302 *Squadron,* 81, 82, 111. *No.* 303 *Squadron,* 81, 83, 85. *No.* 304 *Squadron,* 81; disorderly retreat of, from Arak el Menshiye, 82-6. *No.* 305 *Squadron,* 122
GERMAN ARMY, its plans for *June-July* 1918, 276; retreats to Hindenburg Line, 324-5, and farther, 334-6; morale of troops, *Oct.* 1918, 379-80
GERMANS, at variance with Turks, 128
GERMANY, development of aviation in, before War, 397
GHANEIM, BIR (Map p. 137), 152
GHARBI, ALI (Map p. 17), 12, 26; transport delays at, 15, 18; British retire to, 24
GHAZALE (Sk. p. 163), 162, 163
GHISLENGHIEN (Map p. 382), 383
GHORANIYE (Maps pp. 101, 137), 92, 108, 109, 115; bridge-head at, 95, 103, 106, 108, 112, 115, 121
GHUZZE, WADY, 60
GIDDI, BIR EL (Map p. 42), 54
GILMOUR, GRAHAM, 403
GIVENCHY (Map p. 355), 352; position of, 350
GLEN, Lt. J. M., 52, 56
GLISY, position of, 315
GOMMECOURT, 437
GOMMECOURT-SAPIGNIES ROAD, 438
GONDECOURT (Map p. 355), 365
GONNELIEU (Map p. 189), 193
GOODSON, Lt. E. J. (b. Upton-on-Severn, Eng.), 381
GORDON, Maj. R., 11, 16, 18, 19, 20
GORGUE, LA (Maps pp. 279, 355; Sk. p. 286), 245, 284, 296; bombing raids on, 16-18 *May* 1918, 283
GORRINGE, Maj-Gen. Sir G. F., 9; commands 12 Indian Div., 7
GOUGH, Gen. Sir Hubert, 237
GOULD-TAYLOR, Lt. J. (of Upper Hawthorn, Vic.; b. Young, N.S.W.), 305, 309, 310, 315, 316-7, 334
GOUZEAUCOURT (Map p. 189), 192, 194, 195
GRAHAME-WHITE, C., 413
GRANDMETZ (Map p. 374), 381

INDEX

GRAY, Lt. C. W. (of North Carlton, Vic.; b. Ararat, Vic.), 315, 335
GREGORY, Lt. L. W. (b. Kogarah, N.S.W.), 155
GRICOURT, 326, 328
GRIGGS, Lt. A. (b. Meridian, Miss., U.S.A.), 191
GRIGSON, Lt. A. E. (of Sydney; b. Sydney), 274, 307, 314, 320, 335
GRISÉE, 393
GUEUDECOURT (Map. p. 189), 438
GUFARS, 28
GUILFOYLE, Lt. W. J. Y., 43, 44, 45, 46
GUILLAUX, MAURICE, 411
GUNS, *see* ANTI-AIRCRAFT, ARTILLERY
GURY, 259
GUYNEMER, Capt. G. M. L. J., xvii, xxiv

HADITE, GHOR EL (Map p. 101), 99
HAGUE PEACE CONFERENCE, 1907, xv, 443
HAIFA (Maps pp. 137, 170), 126, 140, 162, 168, 171
HAIG, Lt. F. W. (of Kew, Vic.; b. South Melbourne), 97, 102, 107, 116
HAINSWORTH, Lt. R. (b. Willoughby, N.S.W.), 212, 265
HAJLA, MAKHADET (Maps pp. 101, 137), 108, 109, 115
HALLE, 320
HALLENCOURT, 385
HAM, 238
HAMA (Map p. 170), 168, 169
HAM-SUR-HEURE, 385
HAMEL (Map p. 311; Sk. p. 266), 249, 261, 266 *et seq.*, 307; captured by Australians, 4 *July* 1918, 273-4, 305, 306
HAMEL, GUSTAV, 403
HAMILTON, Lt. E. A. D., 322, 327, 330, 332, 333
HAMMOND, Lt. T. J. (b. Sydney), 258
HANCOCK, Lt. F. (b. Prahran, Vic.), 97, 98
HANDLEY-PAGE BOMBER (Plate p. 382), arrives in Palestine, 146
HANGARD (Map p. 311), 263, 307
HANUTA, BIR EL (Map p. 137), 145, 152

HARBONNIÈRES, 262
HAREIRA (Map p. 78), 63, 65, 75, 76
HARPER, Lt. S. H. (b. Armidale, N.S.W.), 169
HARRISON, Maj. E. (b. Castlemaine, Vic.), 1
HASSANA, BIR EL (Map p. 42), position of, 53
HAUBOURDIN (Plate p. 342; Maps pp. 279, 355), 219, 293, 294, 341, 345, 349, 350, 351, 356, 363, 364, 368, 369, 371; destructive raid on German aerodrome at, 16 *Aug.* 1918, 346-8
HAURAN HILLS, 165
HAVRE, LE, 385
HAVRINCOURT WOOD (Map p. 189), 185
HAVRON, 373
HAWKER, H. G., 406
HAWLEY, Lt. F. C. (of Sydney; b. Wellington, N.Z.), 114, 116, 148, 149, 163*n*
HAZEBROUCK (Maps pp. 179, 279), 174, 211, 242, 243, 245, 276, 341
HEADLAM, Lt. E. S. (b. Bothwell, Tas.), 63, 106, 110-1, 143, 144, 152, 164, 169
HEATH, Lt. N. M. (b. Malvern, Vic.), 368
HEATHCOTE, Lt. H. R. (of Parkville, Vic.; b. West Melbourne), 326
HEATHCOTE, Lt. L. W. (b. Collingwood, Vic.), 51, 58
HEBRON ROAD, 77
HEITAN, GEBEL EL, 53
HEJAZ, 99, 102; hostile to Turks, 1916, 53-4; its army operates against Turks, 1918, 92, 148-9; raids communications, 105, 123-4, occupies Aleppo, 171; organisation of its army, 148; Northern Army, plans, 1918, 148; command, 149, operations, *Sep.* 1918, 162-5; Southern Army, plans, 1918, 148
HEJAZ RAILWAY, 47, 121; Arabs raid, 105; Australian airmen raid, 135
HELAL, GEBEL, 53
HELIOPOLIS, 33, 35, 36, 42, 390
HELLEMMES (Maps pp. 179, 355), 385

INDEX

HELLER, Lt. A. T. (of Hay, N.S.W.; b. Warrnambool, Vic.), 293, 302, 339, 347, 348, 349
HENAIK (Map p. 42), 54
HÉNENCOURT (Map p. 311), 260
HENIN-LIÈTARD (Map p. 220), 222, 359
HENU, EL, 121
HERBERT, Capt. W. V. (b. Ocean Grove, Vic.), 203, 261, 262, 263
HERLIES (Maps pp. 279, 355), 294
HERMAVILLE, 344
HERTAIN (Map p. 374), 367
HESA, KALAT EL (Map p. 101), 135; airmen raid, 5 *Mar.* 1918, 106
HESI, WADY (Map p. 78), 79, 83
HESLOP, Lt. W. S. J. P. (b. Preston, Vic.), 272, 315, 322
HILL, Lt. C. W., 27*n*
HINDENBURG LINE (Plate p. 375), 173, 183, 184, 242, 316, 352, 370; Germans retreat to, 324-5; description of, 327*n*; Battles of the, 327-34; Germans retreat from, 334-6
HODS, description of, 37*n*
HODGSON, Lt. K. C. (b. Camberwell, Vic.), 181, 204, 261
HOLDEN, Capt. L. H. (of Turramurra, N.S.W.; b. East Adelaide), 178, 185, 191, 218, 219, 223, 230, 240
HOLMES, Lt. K. W. (b. Prahran, Vic.), 182
HOLROYDE, Lt. G. E. (b. Brisbane), 360
HOMS (Map p. 170), 168, 169
HOPE, Lt. G. W. (of Melbourne; b. Perth, W. Aust.), 325
HOSKING, Lt. T. (b. Brockley, Eng.), 239
HOUNSLOW, 386, 393
HOUPLIN (Map p. 355), 365
HOUPLINES (Map p. 279), 299
HOWARD, Lt. F. (b. Clunes, Vic.), 368, 376
HOWARD, Capt. R. W. (of Hamilton, N.S.W.; b. Sydney), 178, 190, 192, 196, 217, 218, 222-3, 225, 230
HOWARD, Lt. S. (b. Ballarat, Vic.), 344
HOWEIJ, EL, 148
HOWELL, Capt. C. E. (b. Adelaide), attempts flight to Australia, 388

HUBBARD, Lt.-Col. T. O'B., 408
HUDSON, 12 Air-Mechanic K. L. (b. Launceston, Tas.), 26
HUGHES, Sgt. H. F. (b. Prahran, Vic.), 203-5
HUGHES-CHAMBERLAIN, Maj. R. E. A. W., 213, 221
HUJ (Map p. 78), 57*n*, 60, 72, 79, 81
HULEIKAT, 81
HUSSEIN, SHERIF ALI IBN, 123*n*
HUWARA (Map p. 137), 109, 123, 156, 157; position of, 98
HUXLEY, Lt. F. G. (b. King Island, Tas.), 185, 190, 191, 195, 196-7, 217-8
HYAM, Lt. W. R. (of Bairnsdale, Vic.; b. Thirsk, Yorks., Eng.), 60

IMMELMANN, Lt., xxiii, 215, 416, 449; killed, xxiv
INCENDIARY BULLETS, 96*n*, 443-4, 449-50
INDIA, 2, 15
INDIAN ARMY; *see also* BRITISH ARMY (75TH DIVISION, 4TH AND 5TH CAVALRY DIVISIONS)—
—INDIAN EXPEDITIONARY FORCE "D," 12; name of, 6; composition and command, 6-7; retreats from Ctesiphon, 24-5
—3RD (LAHORE) DIVISION, 68; at Battle of Sharon, 157
—6TH (POONA) DIVISION, 6, 9, 21, 24; command, 7; at Battle of Kut, 1915, 14; casualties at Ctesiphon, 24; invested in Kut, 24
—7TH (MEERUT) DIVISION, 68; at Battle of Sharon, 157
—12TH DIVISION, 9; command, 7
—ARTILLERY, 163
—CAVALRY, 14, 121. 10*th Lancers*, 390
—INFANTRY, 54, 149, 163. 16*th Brigade*, 6, 14. 17*th Brigade*, 14. 30*th Brigade*, 7
INFANTRY, *see* AUSTRALIAN IMPERIAL FORCE, BRITISH ARMY, INDIAN ARMY
INTELLIGENCE: Germans' and Turks' ignorance of situation in Palestine, *July-Aug.* 1918, 133-4, 19 *Sep.*, 154, 20 *Sep.*, 157-8; value of air-photographs, 205-7;

INDEX

INTELLIGENCE—*continued*.
British knowledge of plans for German offensive, *Mar.* 1918, 211, 221, 222, 226
IRGEIG (Maps pp. 42, 78), 48, 73, 75
ISKANDERUNEH, NAHR, 140, 152
ISMAILIA (Map p. 42), 33, 35, 40, 43, 54, 55

JAFFA (Maps pp. 34, 137; Sk. p. 89), 56, 82, 86, 90, 126, 134, 147
JAMES, Lt. A. E. (b. Perth, W. Aust.), 356, 359, 365
JAMES, Lt. H. B. (b. Harden, N.S.W.), 274, 307, 314, 320, 326
JASK, 395
JEFFERS, Lt. J. P. (of Brunswick, Vic.; b. Cosgrove, Vic.), 314, 328
JEFFERY, Lt. J. H. (b. Armadale, Vic.), 268, 269
JEFFREE, Lt. E. R. (of Sydney; b. Sydney), 239, 277, 439
JELIL, 144
JENSEN, 506 Cpl. N. P. B., No. 1 Sqn. (b. Bornholm, Denmark), 118
JENIN (Plate p. 139; Map p. 137), 92, 94, 96, 105, 113, 126, 129, 130, 134, 136, 138, 141, 143, 146, 147, 151, 153, 156, 157, 158; airmen raid, 122, 155
JERICHO (Maps pp. 101, 137; Sk. p. 89), 51, 90, 92, 95*n*, 98, 99, 100, 105, 106, 124, 127, 140; advance to, 102-4; light horse enter, 103
JERICHO ROAD, 103
JERUSALEM (Plate p. 87; Maps pp. 78, 137; Sk. p. 89), 51, 66, 82, 86, 92, 124, 140; captured, 89; Turks attempt re-capture of, 90
JERUSALEM–NABLUS ROAD, 89
JILJULIEH (Map p. 137), 106
JONCOURT (Map p. 321), 332, 333; defences of, 329
JONES, Maj. A. MURRAY (b. Caulfield, Vic.), vii, 36-7, 51, 56, 60, 61, 62, 65, 72, 73, 255, 293, 302, 346, 348, 359, 368, 376; commands No. 2 Sqn., 69, 252
JONES, Lt. A. W., 411
JONES, Lt. E. H., 27*n*
JONES, Capt. E. J. (of South Yarra, Vic.; b. Abbotsford, Vic.), 181, 204, 261, 265, 335

JONES, Capt. G. (b. Rushworth, Vic.), 219, 235, 239, 359, 360-1, 362, 378, 381
JONES-EVANS, Lt. G. S., 290, 295, 296, 301
JOHNSTON, Lt. H., vii
JORDAN RIVER (Map p. 137; Sk. p. 89), 92, 95, 99, 100, 103, 105, 106, 108, 109, 112, 115, 117, 121, 124, 133, 139, 151, 153, 157, 158, 159, 161, 163, 167
JORDAN VALLEY, 90, 93, 99, 100, 102, 112, 124, 126, 127, 144, 155; Chaytor's Force advances from, 166, 168
JUDÆA, 90
JULIS (Map p. 78), 80, 89; German airmen bomb, 87
JUNCTION STATION (Maps pp. 78, 137), 52; airmen raid, 58-9; captured, 82

KAKON, 113, 123, 126, 140, 153, 154
KALIDJATI, 391, 393, 396
KALKILIEH (Map p. 137), 114, 144, 146; position of, 98
KANEITERAH, TUBK EL (Map p. 101), 102
KANTARA (Plate p. 36; Maps pp. 34, 42), 33, 35, 36, 37, 40, 44, 45, 46, 65*n*, 66, 76, 171
KARACHI, 390, 393, 395, 396
KARM (Map p. 78), 75, 76, 79
KARUN, RIVER, 6, 7
KASTAL, EL (Map p. 101), 124; airmen raid, 110
KATIA (Map p. 42), 38, 39, 40
KAY, Sgt. T. D. (b. Spring Mount, Vic.), attempts flight to Australia, 387, 394-6
KEAY, Lt. S. P. (of Melbourne; b. Williamstown, Vic.), 344
KELT, WADY EL, 95*n*
KEMBALL, Maj.-Gen. Sir G. V., 19, 20
KEMMEL, 284
KEMMEL HILL (Map p. 279), 277, 352
KENNY, Lt. E. P. (b. Trafalgar, Vic.), 93, 114, 123, 135, 140, 142, 164, 165
KERAHI, SEIL EL, 99
KERAK (Plate p. 122; Map p. 101), 99, 100, 105, 107, 109, 131; position of, 92; airmen raid, 102

INDEX

KERAK ROAD, 124
KERR, Lt. H. N. (of Brisbane; b. Ithaca, Q'land), 370-1
KERR, Lt. P. H. (b. Melbourne), 272
KHALASA (Maps pp. 42, 78), 67, 77
KHARGA (Map p. 34), 36
KHASM ZANNA (Map p. 78), 77
KIFRI, 21
KILBURN, Lt. G. E. (b. East Melbourne), 320
KILLIS, 169
KILSBY, Lt. M. J. (b. Mount Gambier, S. Aust.), 379
KING, Capt. R. (of Forbes, N.S.W.; b. Bathurst, N.S.W.), 282, 288, 290, 298, 299, 302, 303, 304, 313, 338, 340, 341, 347, 350, 351, 353, 354, 356, 359, 376, 377-8, 379, 381
KIRK, Lt. W. A. (of Lismore, N.S.W.; b. Belfast, Ireland), 99, 109, 110, 123, 126, 127, 129, 135, 136, 139
KIRKWOOD, Lt. R. W. (b. Launceston, Tas.), 310
KISSIR (Map p. 101), 100, 111, 113, 135, 147
KISWE (Map p. 170; Sk. p. 167), 168
KITCHENER, Field-Marshal Earl, 276; on Suez Canal Defence Scheme, *quoted*, 33
KNIGHT, Lt. V. E. (of Westgarth, Vic.; b. Christchurch, N.Z.), 338, 354
KNOX, Maj. E. G. (b. Glebe, N.S.W.), 430
KOOLHOVEN, F., 410, 415
KOSSAIMA, EL (Map p. 42), 46, 49, 50, 51, 53
KREIG, Lt. L. P. (of Toowoomba, Q'land; b. Dimboola, Vic.), 126, 135, 138, 141
KRESSENSTEIN, Gen. von, 80
KULUNSAWE (Map p. 137), 123, 130, 153
KURNA, 5, 10*n*; first action of, 6; second action of, 7-8, 28
KUS KUS (Map p. 137), 142; position of, 140
KUT (Map p. 17), xxv, 9, 11, 12, 13, 16, 18, 20, 22, 23, 30, 390;

KUT—*continued*.
Battle of, 14-5; 6th Indian Division invested in, 24; surrendered to Turks, 24-6
KUTANIYEH (Map p. 17), 18, 19
KUTRANI, EL (Plate p. 138; Map p. 101), 81, 93, 100, 105, 109, 123, 124, 126, 130, 131, 135, 148; airmen raid, 102, 106, 107-8, 125

LACOUTURE, 242
LAGNICOURT, 231
LAHFAN (Map p. 42), 41
LAJJ (Map p. 17), 24
LAMPLOUGH, Lt. O. (of Caulfield, Vic.; b. Donald, Vic.), 378
LANDRECIES, BATTLE OF, 336, 380
LANG, Capt. A. (of Melbourne, Vic.; b. Corowa, N.S.W.), vii, xxvii, 175, 397
LANG, Lt. R., 218, 219
LATEAU WOOD, 196
LAVENTIE (Maps pp. 279, 355; Sk. p. 286), 241, 242, 243, 244, 288, 295, 296, 302, 303, 338, 340, 349, 350, 351
LAVERS, Lt. S. K. (of Hunter's Hill, N.S.W.; b. Kogarah, N.S.W.), 316
LAWRENCE, Lt.-Col. T. E. (b. Wales), 124, 148, 149, 162, 163, 164
LEBAN, 109
LÉCLUSE, 351
LEE, Lt. O. M. (b. Mole Creek, Tas.), 95, 96, 107
LEES, Lt. M. D. (of Goulburn, N.S.W.; b. Goulburn), 143, 152
LEJJUN (Map p. 137), 142, 155; *see also* MEGIDDO
LENS (Maps pp. 179, 220), 173, 181, 218, 219, 222, 223, 224, 225, 233, 241, 297, 298, 350, 361, 362
LESSINES (Map. p. 382), 376, 377
LESTREM (Map p. 279), 245, 299, 302, 304, 339, 340
LETCH, Lt. H. A. (of Hampton, Vic.; b. Donnybrook, Vic.), 118, 125, 139, 142, 144
LEUZE (Map p. 374), 379, 381
LEUZE-ATH ROAD, 381
LEWIS, Lt. O. G. (of Armadale, Vic.; b. Elsternwick, Vic.), 260
LICOURT, position of, 313
LIÉGE, 370
LIETTRES (Map p. 179), 259

INDEX

LIGHT HORSE, see AUSTRALIAN IMPERIAL FORCE
LIGNY (Maps pp. 279, 355), 439
LIHONS, 312
LIKTERA, 153
LILLE (Map p. 179), 214, 216, 217, 218, 225, 289, 291, 292, 299, 304, 338, 339, 348n, 350 et seq., 359, 361, 363, 370, 385, 434; British refrain from shelling, 345; Germans prepare to retire from, 364; air raids round, 293-4, 346-9, 354-6, 364-7, 371, 373; captured, 367; air-fights over, 371-5
LILLE–LA BASSÉE ROAD, 242
LILLERS (Map p. 179), 211, 245
LILLY, Lt. W. H. (of Kalgoorlie, W. Aust.; b. North Melbourne), 143, 144, 152, 164, 169
LOCK, Lt. F. M. (of Port MacDonnell, S. Aust.; b. Allandale East, S. Aust.), 315, 334
LOCKLEY, Lt. A. H. (of Woolloomooloo, N.S.W.; b. Marrickville, N.S.W.), 297, 356, 357, 358, 359
LOCON, 344
LOCRE, 277
LOGAN, Lt. G. C., 221
LOISNE, RIVER, 242, 243, 244
LOMME (Plate p. 343; Maps pp. 279, 355), 341, 345, 351, 359; German aerodrome at, raided, 17 Aug. 1918, 348-9
LOMPRET (Maps pp. 279, 355), 341
LONG, Lt. A. L. (of Hobart; b. Ringwood, Tas.), 367, 368
LOOS (Maps pp. 279, 355), 172, 217
LORD, 23 Air-Mechanic W. H. (b. Fitzroy, Vic.), 26
LOVE, Lt. H. K. (of East Malvern, Vic.; b. Brighton, Vic.), 244
LUBBAN, EL (Plate p. 86; Map p. 137), 86, 113, 135, 139, 158
LUBBAN ROAD, 107, 126, 127, 129, 138
LUCE, RIVER (Map p. 311), 307
LUDD (Maps pp. 78, 137), 82, 90, 134
LUDENDORFF, Gen., 223, 226, 228, 241, 263, 305; quoted, 276n
LUKIS, Capt. F. W. F. (b. Balingup, W. Aust.), 71, 116, 117, 139
LYS, RIVER (Sk. p. 286), 241, 259, 276, 277, 284, 285, 287, 288, 292

LYS, RIVER—continued.
et seq., 313, 339, 340, 341, 344, 345, 349, 352, 354, 361, 365, 434; Battle of, 242-6
LYS VALLEY, 345

MAAN, 53n, 123-4, 135, 148, 149, 165, 168; Hejaz raid on, Jan. 1918, 92
MACARTNEY, Lt.-Col. H. D. K. (of Brisbane; b. Waverley Station, Q'land), 35
MACAULAY, Capt. T. C., 106
MCCANN, Lt. A. V. (b. Yea, Vic.), 138, 139, 152, 165, 169
MCCLEERY, Lt. E. P. E. (of Berrima District, N.S.W.; b. Moss Vale, N.S.W.), 349
MCCLOUGHRY, Capt. E. J. K. (of North Adelaide; b. Hindmarsh, S. Aust.), 287, 288, 291, 293, 295, 296, 297, 298, 300-1, 362-3
MCCLOUGHRY, Maj. W. A. (of Adelaide; b. Knightsbridge, S. Aust.), commands No. 4 Sqn., 213; mentioned, 178, 283, 302, 339, 347, 377
MCCUBBIN, Capt. G. R., xxiv
MCCUDDEN, Maj. J. T., V.C., xxiv, 400; quoted, xxii, xxiii-xxiv, 176
MCCULLOCH, Lt. A. F. G. (b. Portsmouth, Eng.), 301
MACDONALD, Lt. A. R. (of Brisbane; b. New Farm, Q'land), 325, 328
MCELLIGOTT, Lt. J. (b. Bundaberg, Q'land), 111, 116
MCGINNESS, Lt. P. J. (b. Framlingham East, Vic.), 116-7, 124, 135, 141 et seq., 152
MACHIN, Lt. R. F. C. (of Queenstown, Tas.; b. East Malvern, Vic.), 327
MACHINE-GUNS — Australian: at Leban, 109, in second action of Es Salt, 116, increased use of, from aeroplanes, 136-8, No. 4 Sqn., during German offensive, Mar. 1918, 231, 232, 233, 234; British: at Damieh, 107, Mar.-June 1918, 128-9; German, during retreat to Hindenburg Line, 324

INDEX

McINTOSH, Lt. J. C. (b. Lumsden, Scotland), in flight to Australia, 388, 392-3

McKENNA, Lt. F. N. (of Taradale, Vic.; b. Bendigo, Vic.), 272, 310, 315, 322

McKENZIE, Lt. R. W. (b. Adelaide), 180, 184, 195, 196, 218, 224, 230

McKEOWN, Lt. J. A. H. (of Werribee, Vic.; b. Romsey, Vic.), 371, 373

MACKINOLTY, Lt. G. J. W. (of Korumburra, Vic.; b. Leongatha, Vic.), 25

McNAMARA, Capt. F. H., V.C. (b. Rushworth, Vic.), 51, 59

MACNAUGHTON, Capt. A. L. (of Brisbane; b. Townsville, Q'land), 69

McRAE, Lt. R. F., 302

MADEBA, 105, 114

MAFRAK (Sk. p. 163), 162, 163, 164; airmen raid, 166-7

MAGDHABA (Map p. 42), 41, 44, 45, 46, 50, 59; Turks concentrate at, 48; Anzac Mtd. Div. captures, 49, 50

MAGEIBRA (Map p. 42), 37

MAGHARA, 40, 48; mounted reconnaissance to, 43, 53

MAHEMDIA (Map p. 42), 36, 38, 40, 45

MAINZ, 394

MALLEY, Capt. G. F. (b. Mosman, N.S.W.), *quoted*, 233-5, 280; mentioned, vii, 224, 225, 231, 277, 278, 282, 283, 285, 286, 290, 437, 438

MALONE, Lt. J. J., vii

MANUEL, Capt. R. L. (of Kerang, Vic.; b. Kerang), 222, 240, 248, 257, 258, 298, 341, 348, 349, 350, 359-60, 363, 365, 366, 368, 371, 373

MANWELL, Capt. D. T. W. (b. Queenscliff, Vic.), 1, 32

MAPS, compilation of, from air-photographs—
—MESOPOTAMIA, 20-1
—PALESTINE, 46; of Gaza-Beersheba area, 70-1; of Turkish front-line region, *Jan.* 1918, 93-5; for second action of Es Salt, 113; of Damieh region, 122-3; of Es Salt and Samaria-

MAPS—*continued*.
Nablus areas, 126, 141; of Et Tire area, 136
—WESTERN FRONT, of Messines Ridge, 205-7
—*See also* AIR SURVEY

MARCOING (Map p. 189), 190, 254

MARCQ (Map p. 355), position of, 383

MARICOURT, 314

MARNE, RIVER, 175, 263, 264, 276

MARQUAIN (Map p. 374), 367

MARQUÉGLISE, 259

MARQUILLIES, 339

MART, Lt. F. J. (b. Semaphore, S. Aust.), 269-70, 274, 315

MARTIN, Lt. C. H. (of Port Melbourne; b. Port Melbourne), 217

MARTIN, Lt. W. S. (of Geelong, Vic.; b. Geelong), 283, 287

MASAID, 43, 44, 47, 49

MATHESON, Capt. C. C. (b. Trafalgar, Vic.), 209, 314, 315

MATTHEWS, Capt. G. C. (b. Stranraer, Scotland), attempts flight to Australia, 387, 394-6; mentioned, 177, 213, 393

MATULICH, Lt. C. de C. (of Adelaide; b. Peterborough, S. Aust.), 61

MAUBEUGE (Map p. 179), xxii

MAUDE, Lt.-Gen. Sir F. S., 31

MAUGHAN, Lt. H. S. R. (of Ipswich, Q'land; b. Brisbane), 117, 118, 126, 142, 152, 155, 157, 164, 165, 168

MAZAR, BIR EL. (Map p. 42), 37, 38, 44, 45, 47, 61; light horse reconnoitre, 40-1; position of, 43

MÉAULTE (Map p. 311), 240, 306

MECCA, 53

MECHANICS, AIR-, for Aust. Half-Flight, 2; Allenby on efficiency of, 171; duties, 440-2

MEGIDDO, BATTLES OF, 152-62; *see also* NABLUS, SHARON

MEJDEL, EL (Plate p. 95; Map p. 78), 60, 79, 80, 89, 122

MEJDEL, BENI FADL, 117

MEJDEL YABA (Map p. 137), 139

MENIN (Map p. 179), 378

MENSHIYE, ARAK EL (Map p. 78), 57, 58, 79, 82, 83, 84, 85; German aerodrome at, bombed and destroyed, 80

INDEX

MERCHIN, 365
MERICOURT (Map p. 220), 310
MERRIS (Map p. 279), 264, 283, 289; Australians capture, 300
MERVILLE (Map p. 279), 243, 244, 245, 284, 286, 287, 288, 290 *et seq.*, 299, 304, 338, 340, 352
MERVILLE–ARMENTIÈRES ROAD, 277
MERZ, Lt. G. P. (of Melbourne; b. Prahran, Vic.), 1, 2, 3, 8, 9, 19; killed by Arabs, 10
MESNIL, LE (Map p. 321), 320, 324
MESOPOTAMIA, 2, 9, 10; unsuitable aeroplanes in, 5-6
MESOPOTAMIAN CAMPAIGN, 29; *see also* BAGHDAD, CTESIPHON, KURNA, KUT, NASIRIYEH, SHAIBA, TIGRIS
MESSINES (Map p. 279), 181, 198, 264, 290; Battle of, 183; *see also* WYTSCHAETE
MESSINES RIDGE, 198, 202, 217, 290
MESSUDIE (Sk. p. 130), 98, 126, 157; airmen raid, 99
MESSUDIE RAILWAY STATION, 129, 130, 155
METEREN (Map p. 279), 254, 287; captured, 300
MEUSE, RIVER, 370
MEZERIB JUNCTION (Sk. p. 163), 149, 163
MIDDLETON, Lt. E., *quoted*, 238
MILLS, Lt. (R.A.F.), 99
MILLS, Lt. F. C. M. (of Parramatta, N.S.W.; b. Tuena, N.S.W.), 313, 341, 363
MILNER, Lt. J. W., 293
MINCHIN, Lt.-Col. F. F., 47
MIRAUMONT, 237
MIRAUMONT–PYS ROAD, 438
MISKE, airmen raid, 100-2
MOAB, description of, 99-100
MŒUVRES (Map p. 189), 195
MOIR, Lt. S. J. (b. Paddington, N.S.W.), 182
MONASH, Lt.-Gen. Sir J. (of Melbourne; b. Melbourne), 317
MONS (Map p. 179), 376, 383
MONS-EN-CHAUSSÉE (Map p. 321), 324
MONTBREHAIN (Map p. 179), 333; captured, 334
MONT-DES-CATS, 277
MONTDIDIER (Map p. 179), 248, 256, 259, 269, 277

MONT ST. QUENTIN, *see* ST. QUENTIN, MONT
MONUMENT WOOD, 305
MOORE, Lt. R., 295, 297
MOORE, Lt. W. P. (b. Mt. Shamrock, Q'land), 320
MORCOURT (Map p. 311), 312
MORGAN, Lt. A. J., 54, 57, 63
MORLANCOURT (Map p. 311; Sk. p. 266), 265 *et seq.*
MORLANCOURT RIDGE, 250, 264, 270, 271, 309; Australians attack, at Sailly-Laurette, 306-7
MORRISON, Lt. D. G. (b. Kilmore, Vic.), 180
MORY (Map p. 189), 233
MOSQUITOES, 8
MOSUL, 27
MOTTE, LA, 249
MOULMEIN, 393
MOURCOURT (Map p. 374), 378
MOUVEAUX, 373
MUHAMMERAH (Map p. 4), 6
MUIR, Capt. S. K. (of Mathoura, N.S.W.; b. Elsternwick, Vic.), 40, 43, 44, 47, 48, 50, 51
MUKHALID (Map p. 137), 113, 123, 126, 143, 147
MULEBBIS (Map p. 137), 91, 146
MULFORD, Lt. E. A. (b. Sydney), 135, 138, 142, 146, 147, 150, 152, 153
MUNRO, 47 Air-Mechanic J. (b. Darlinghurst, N.S.W.), 26
MURPHY, Lt. A. W. (b. Kew, Vic.), 117-8, 128, 148, 149, 163
MURRAY, Capt., 23
MURRAY, Gen. Sir A. J. (b. Sutton, Eng.), 46, 50, 52, 53, 56, 59, 60, 62; Allenby takes over from, 63
MUSLIMIE (Map p. 170), position of, 169; airmen raid, 169
MUSTABIG, 45, 47, 49
MUSTARD, Lt. E. A. (of North Fitzroy, Vic.; b. Oakleigh, Vic.), 94, 98, 106, 113, 122, 164

NABLUS (Plate p. 167; Map p. 137; Sk. p. 89), 86, 90, 92, 97, 98, 105, 107, 109, 111, 113, 114, 117, 122, 123, 126, 129, 136, 138, 140, 141, 143, 146, 151 *et seq.*, 163, 165; Battle of, 148, 152-5, 158
NABLUS HILLS, 71, 94; Turks retreat to, after Third Gaza, 82

INDEX

Nablus Road, 121, 139
Nablus-Khurbet Ferweh Road, 157
Nablus-Messudie Road, 145
Nablus-Tul Keram Road, 95
Nakhailat (Map p. 17), 13, 15
Nakurah, En (Sk. p. 130), 130; position of, 129
Namur, 385
Nasib, 163
Nasiriyeh (Map p. 4), 6, 11, 16; captured, 9
Nauroy (Map. p. 321), 331, 332
Nauroy Line, 327, 330, 332, 333
Nazareth (Map p. 137), 80, 133, 140, 151, 157, 390
Nazir, Sherif, 124
Nekhl (Plate p. 37; Map p. 42), 53; mounted reconnaissance to, 54-5
Nelson, Lt. E. B. (of North Sydney; b. St. Leonard's, N.S.W.), 214
Nelson, Lt. R. C. (of Jamberoo, N.S.W.; b. Jamberoo), 283, 293, 295
Neuf Berquin (Map p. 279), 277, 282, 285
Neumann, Maj. G. P., *quoted*, 348*n*
Neuve Chapelle (Maps pp. 279, 355), 172, 243, 352
Neuve Eglise (Map p. 279), 284, 352, 362
Neuville St. Vaast (Map p. 220), 181
Neuvireuil, 181
New Zealand Expeditionary Force: *N.Z.M.R. Brigade*, 31, 39; at First Gaza, 59, Third Gaza, 77, 79; enters Amman, 30 *Mar.* 1918, 109. See also Australian Imperial Force (Anzac Mounted Division)
Nicholls, Lt. W. H. (b. Adelaide), 225
Nicholson, Sgt. W. H. (b. Parramatta, N.S.W.), 272*n*
Nieppe (Map p. 279), 341, 352, 371
Nieppe Forest, 280, 288, 289, 294, 302, 303, 304, 337, 368
Nile, River, 36
Nisibin, 26
Nixon, Gen. Sir J. E., 5, 9; commands Indian Exped. Force "D," 7; *quoted*, 24

Norvill, Lt. V. A. (b. Melbourne), 177
Nowland, Lt. G. (of Clifton Hill and North Fitzroy, Vic.; b. Fitzroy), 222, 285
Noyon (Map p. 179), 174, 252, 256, 258, 259, 263, 270, 276, 277
Nunan, Lt. S. A. (of Parkville, Vic.; b. Malvern, Vic.), 131, 132, 138, 142, 146, 155, 159, 168
Nunn, Capt. W., 7

Observation, *see* Reconnaissances
Observers, Air, training of, in England, 175-6
Odessa, 28
Oghratina (Map p. 42), 37, 38
Olives, Mount of, 66
Omignon, River (Map p. 321), 324
Oppy (Map p. 220), 181, 242
Orchies (Map p. 179), 366
Oshir, Rujm el (Map p. 101), 108, 162
Ostend, 352
Oultersteene, 290
Oxenham. Lt. G. V. (of Boggabri, N.S.W.; b. Randwick, N.S.W.), 118, 131

Pacaut (Map p. 279), 245, 296
Pacaut Wood, 297, 302
Page, F. Handley, 409
Paget, Lt. G. L., 72
Palestine Campaign, attitude of British Government towards, 29-30; British and Turkish preparations for, after Second Gaza, 64; Allenby's plans for, *Jan.* 1918, 92, *Sept.* 1918, 151; *see also* Amman, Beersheba, Damascus, Gaza, Jericho, Jerusalem, Megiddo, Nablus, Salt, Sharon
Palliser, Lt. A. J. (of Launceston, Tas.; b. Launceston), 360-1, 377, 378, 383
Palstra, Lt. W. (of Surrey Hills, Vic.; b. Zwolle, Holland), 330, 332, 333
Parachutes, 284-5, 376
Paradis (Map p. 279), 245
Parer, Lt. R. J. P. (of Surrey Hills, Vic.; b. Melbourne), flies to Australia, 388, 392-3
Paris, 263

INDEX

PARKE, Lt. W., 414
PARKINSON, Lt. V. J. (of Sydney; b. Auckland, N.Z.), 96
PASSCHENDAELE RIDGE (Plate p. 206), 174, 198, 352, 428; British capture, 183
PATE, Lt. A. D., 285
PATROLS, of No. 4 Sqn. over the Lys, *July* 1918, 296-9; contact, functions of, xvii, over Ville-sur-Ancre, 267; counter-attack, functions of, xvii, during German offensive, *Mar.* 1918, 211, 437-9; retaliation and offensive, definition, 198-9; reconnaissance, example of, 202-3; *see also* RECONNAISSANCES
PATTERSON, Lt. A. S., 262, 265
PAUL, Lt. C. S. (b. Thanis, N.Z.), 123, 126-7, 129, 130, 136, 138, 140, 143, 144, 155, 157, 158
PAUL, Lt. G. A. (of North Adelaide; b. Beechworth, Vic.), 260
PAXTON, Lt. A. L., 217-8
PEEL, Lt. J. C. (of Geelong, Vic.; b. Inverleigh, Vic.), 328
PENANG, 393
PENGILLEY, Lt. J. J. (of Quirindi, N.S.W.; b. Quirindi), 319, 331
PÉRENCHIES (Maps pp. 279, 355), 341, 354, 356, 364, 365, 368, 369
PÉRONNE (Map p. 321), 173, 313, 316, 317, 375; captured, 319-22
PERSIA, 6, 16
PERSIAN GULF, 390
PERUWELZ, 376
PÉTAIN, Marshal, 238, 240
PETERS, Capt. G. C. (b. Adelaide), 114, 122, 123, 124, 126, 138, 139, 144-5, 153, 163, 164
PETRE, E., 403
PETRE, Maj. H. A. (of South Yarra, Vic.; b. Ingatestone, Eng.), commands Aust. Half-Flight, 2; at Battle of Ctesiphon, 25; mentioned, 1, 3, 7, 9, 12, 13, 16, 21, 22, 26, 403
PETSCHLER, Capt. N. L. (of St. George district, N.S.W.; b. Rockdale, N.S.W.), 224, 278
PFALZ SCOUTS, arrive in Palestine, 143
PFLAUM, Capt. E. F. (of Loxton, S. Aust.; b. Birdwood, S. Aust.), 216, 226
PHALEMPIN (Map p. 355), 365

PHILLIPPS, Maj. R. C. (of Perth, W. Aust.; b. North Sydney), 177, 181-2, 184, 190, 219, 229, 230, 232, 235, 240, 253, 255, 256, 257, 259, 297, 299, 303, 313
PHOTOGRAPHS, *see* AIR SURVEY, MAPS
PICKERING, Lt. G. (of Sydney; b. South Brisbane), 328
PILOTS, essential qualification of, xvii; scarcity of, in German Air Force in Palestine, *July-Aug.* 1918, 134; training of, in England, 175-6
PIXTON, Howard, 400
PLOEGSTEERT (Map p. 279), 352
POINT COOK, 426; *see also* AUSTRALIAN MILITARY FORCES
PONT-A-MARCQ (Maps pp. 179, 355), 370, 375
PONT-A-VENDIN (Map p. 355), 218, 368, 369, 371
PONT-DU-HEM, position of, 340
PONT NOYELLES (Map p. 311), 272
POOLE, Lt. A. A. (b. Surry Hills, N.S.W.), 98
PORT MELBOURNE, 32
PORT SAID (Maps pp. 34, 42), 36, 37, 40, 385
PORTUGUESE ARMY, 241, 242
POSTAL SERVICES, No. 3 Sqn. conducts aerial service for, *Nov.* 1918, 385
POTTS, Lt. G. H. M. St. C. (b. Euroa, Vic.), attempts flight to Australia, 387
POTTS, Lt. J. D. S. (of Sydney; b. Malden, London), 96
POTTS, Lt. L. M. (b. Karori, N.Z.), 67, 97
POULAINVILLE (Map p. 311), 212
POULET, Lt., attempts flight from France to Australia, 388, 390-1, 412
POZIÈRES, 234, 240, 256
PRATT, Lt. A. J. (b. Ascot Vale, Vic.), 185, 190-1
PRÉMONT (Map p. 179), 335
PRIMROSE, Lt. L. J. (of Ballarat, Vic.; b. Ballarat), 249, 257
PRINCE, Lt. T. H. (of Newcastle district, N.S.W.; b. Homebush, N.S.W.), 329

PRISONERS (AUSTRALIAN), chivalrous treatment of, by German airmen, 71-2; *Half-Flight*, 12, 22, experiences of those captured at Kut, 25-8, mortality among, 26; *No. 1 Squadron*, 71, 96, 108, 116, 131, 153, 154; *No. 2 Squadron*, 180, 185, 221, 239, 257, 361, 375, 384; *No. 4 Squadron*, 214, 219, 221, 225, 239, 244, 282, 286, 295, 301, 357, 358, 379, 381

PRISONERS (BRITISH), 12, 22, 25, 56, 108; chivalrous treatment of, by German airmen, xviii; captured at Kut, 26, 27

PRISONERS (GERMAN), 76, 144, 158; chivalrous treatment of, by British airmen, xviii

PRISONERS (INDIAN), captured at Kut, 26

PRISONERS (TURKISH), captured at Kurna, 7, Ctesiphon, 24, Mazar, 41, Magdhaba, 49, Rafa, 50, near Gaza, 59*n*, at Third Gaza, 77, by Hejaz, *Jan.* 1918, 92

PRODGER, C. B., 409

PROPAGANDA, British method of distributing among Germans, 208-9

PROVIN (Map p. 355), 368, 369

PROYART (Map p. 311), 309, 324, 325

QUÉANT, 180
QUERRIEU (Map p. 311), 269

RACKETT, Lt. A. R. (b. Port Adelaide), 223, 230, 257
RAE, Lt. F. J. (of Yea, Vic.; b. Blackwood, Vic.), 203
RAFA (Map p. 42), 44, 45, 47, 48, 52, 57, 59, 61, 75; engagement at, 50; German airmen bomb aerodrome at, 61
RAIDS, of Aust. infy., along Morlancourt Ridge, 264, 271, at Villers-Bretonneux, 305; *see also* AMMAN, MERRIS, SALT
RAILLENCOURT, 190
RAILWAYS: DESERT LINE, reaches Salmana, *Oct.* 1916, 44, progress, *Dec.*, 46, reaches Mazar, *Dec.*, 47, El Arish, *Jan.* 1917, 49, El

RAILWAYS—*continued*.
Burj, *Feb.*, 52, near Karm, *Sep.*, 75. TURKISH, 52; demolitions on, 23 *May*, 1917, 65; *see also* HEJAZ, TRAINS
RALFE, Capt. H. D. E. (of Brisbane; b. Sydney), 264
RAMADIE, 390
RAMIN (Map p. 137; Sk. p. 130), 138
RAMLEH (Maps pp. 78, 137), 52, 73, 84, 85, 86, 122, 128, 134, 144, 146, 148, 149, 157, 163, 164, 165, 168, 171, 393; German aerodrome at, 51, bombed, 56, 61, 66; captured, 82
RAMSAY, Lt. O. B. (b. Tumbarumba, N.S.W.), 293, 297, 299, 300, 301, 340, 351, 354, 359, 365
RANDELL, Lt. W. B. (b. Mt. Pleasant, S. Aust.), 221
RANGOON, 390, 393, 396
RAWLINSON, Gen. Lord, 272*n*
RAYAK (Map p. 170), German aerodrome at, bombed, 169
RAYMENT, 49 Air-Mechanic W. C. (of Surrey Hills, Vic.; b. Jan Juc, Vic.), 26
RAYNHAM, F. P., 404
R.E.8's (Plates pp. 179, 194), 47, 400; No. 1 Sqn. equipped with, 76
REBAIX (Map p. 382), German aerodrome at, bombed, 379
RECLINGHEM (Map p. 179), 259, 299, 303, 340, 349, 370; position of, 291
RECONNAISSANCES, defined, 70*n*; mounted, of Maghara, 43, Nekhl, 54-5; air: functions of, xvi-xvii; in Mesopotamia, at second action of Kurna, 7, at Nasiriyeh, 10, of Turkish position at Es-Sinn, 13, at Battle of Kut, 1915, 14-5, and after, 16-8, round Ctesiphon, 18; in Egypt, of Senussi district, 36-7; in Sinai and Palestine, 64-5, 92-3, 106, of Maghara and El Arish, 43-4, 48, Gaza and Rafa, 48, 50, Bethlehem, Jerusalem, and Jericho, 51-2, at First Gaza, 60, prior to Second Gaza, 62, *July-Oct.* 1917, 70-1,

INDEX

RECONNAISSANCES—continued.
77, of Dead Sea, 99-100, during Amman raid, 109-11, at second action of Es Salt, 116-7, of Haifa, 126, Nablus and Amman, 140-1, after capture of Damascus, 168-9; on Western Front, of German preparations for, *Mar.* 1918, 221-2, 226, of Morlancourt Ridge, 266-7, Hamel, 271-2, Hindenburg Line, 329-32; artillery-observation, duties in, 199-200, of No. 3 Sqn., at Ville-sur-Ancre, 267, 9 *June* 1918, 269, *Aug.*, 308, over Somme, 315, at Mont St. Quentin, 319-20, over Hindenburg Line, 327, 329; *see also* ARTILLERY RANGING, PATROLS

RED SEA, 148

REES, Lt. A. W. (b. Junee, N.S.W.), 260

REGIMENTS, *see* AUSTRALIAN IMPERIAL FORCE, BRITISH ARMY, INDIAN ARMY

RENAIX (Map p. 374), 352, 380

RENDLE, Lt. V., attempts flight to Australia, 387

REILLY, Maj. H. L., captured, 22; mentioned, 3, 7, 8, 9, 10, 14, 16, 18, 27

REYNOLDS, Lt.-Col. E. H. (b. Paddington, N.S.W.); 35; commands No. 1 Sqn., 32

RHEIMS (Sk. p. 241), 252, 276n

RHINE, RIVER, 384, 385

RHODES, Lt. C. W. (of Sydney; b. Perth, W. Aust.), 381

RIBECOURT, 259

RICHARDS, Lt. E. J. (b. Tyrendarra, Vic.), 375

RICHEBOURG–ST. VAAST (Map p. 355), 243

RICHTHOFEN, Baron von, tactics of, 215-6; killed, 249-52; *quoted*, 306n; mentioned, xviii, xxiii, xxiv, 225, 260, 417

RIDGE FARM (MESSINES), 203

RINTOUL, Lt. A. (b. Melbourne), 286

ROADS, wire-netting used for, 46, 52

ROBECQ (Map p. 279), 245, 295

ROBERTS, Lt. E. G. (of Canterbury, Vic.; b. Camberwell, Vic.), 43, 51, 52

ROBERTS, Lt. F. L. (of Bendigo, Vic.; b. Bendigo), 363, 367, 373

ROBERTS, Lt. K. A. (b. Bendigo), 332

ROBERTSON, Lt. A. E. (b. Prahran, Vic.), 226, 232, 236, 438, 439

ROBERTSON, Lt. J. K. (b. Essendon, Vic.), 315, 335

ROBERTSON, Capt. W. A. (b. Albert Park, Vic.), 195, 196

ROBINSON, Capt. W. L., V.C. (b. Tollidetta, India), 399

ROE BROS., 400

ROGERS, Lt. L. W., 93

ROISEL (Map p. 321), 322, 325, 335

ROMANI (Map p. 42), 37, 38, 39, 390; Turks overwhelm yeomanry at, 39; Battle of, 39-40

ROME, 389

Ross, Lt. H. W. (b. Darlington, N.S.W.), 354, 375, 377, 378

Ross, Lt. J. S. L. (b. Moruya, N.S.W.), attempts flight to Australia, 387

Ross, Capt. R. (of Toorak, Vic.; b. Carnegie, Vic.), 35, 327n

ROUBAIX (Map p. 179), 366

ROUEN (Sk. p. 241), 263

ROUGE CROIS CROSS-ROADS, 243

ROUMANIA, enters war, 30

ROWNTREE, Lt. E. F. (of Hobart; b. Hobart), 265

ROYAL AIR FORCE, *see* BRITISH AIR FORCE

ROYAL NAVY, *see* BRITISH NAVY

ROYE (Map p. 179), 263

RUAFA, EL (Map p. 42), 49

RUTHERFORD, Capt. D. W. (of Rockhampton, Q'land; b. Rockhampton), 59, 60, 111, 116

RUTLEDGE, Maj. T. F. (of Melbourne; b. Warrnambool, Vic.), vii, 35, 64

RYRIE, Maj.-Gen. Sir G. de L., 59

SABA, TEL EL (Map p. 78), 77

SABA, WADY, 77

SAHIL, 6

SAID, Brig.-Gen. Nuri, commands Arab Northern Army, 149

SAILLY–ESTAIRES ROAD, 339

SAILLY–LAURETTE (Sk. p. 266), 267, 269, 270, 306-7

INDEX

SAILLY-SUR-LA-LYS (Maps pp. 279, 355; Sk. p. 286), 242, 270, 287, 298, 301, 341, 362
SAINGHIN (Map p. 355), 339, 354, 356
SAINS-LE-MARQUION (Map p. 189), 351
ST. BENIN, 335
ST. CHRIST (Map p. 321), 322
ST. GEORGE'S BAY (CORFU), 388
ST. LEGER–VAULX ROAD, 437
ST. OMER (Map p. 179), 177, 178, 213, 246, 360
ST. POL (Map p. 179), 177, 204, 211, 301
ST. QUENTIN (Maps pp. 179, 321; Sk. p. 241), 174, 178, 211, 226, 228, 229, 230, 326
ST. QUENTIN CANAL (Map p. 321), 326
ST. QUENTIN, MONT (Plate p. 323; Map p. 321), 317, 324; captured, 319-22
ST. SOUPLET, 335
ST. VENANT (Map p. 279), 245, 286, 363
SAKATI (Map p. 78), 77
SALISBURY PLAIN, 385
SALMANA (Map p. 42), 37, 38, 40, 43, 44, 53, 66
SALMOND, Air Vice-Marshal Sir W. G. H., 388; *quoted*, 42; his admiration for No. 1 Sqn., 146*n*
SALONICA, 28, 35
SALT, Es (Plate p. 106; Map p. 101; Sk. p. 89), 93, 95, 105, 107, 109, 124, 126, 147, 155, 162, 165, 167; light horse capture, in first action, 108; second action of: 112, 113, 114, mounted troops enter, 115; No. 1 Sqn. co-operates in general withdrawal from, 115-9
SALT–AMMAN ROAD, Es, 108, 110, 114, 165
SALT–NIMRIN ROAD, Es, 148
SAMARIA (Sk. p. 130), 129
SAMARIA–EL AFULE ROAD, 156
SANDY, Lt. J. L. (of Burwood, N.S.W.; b. Ashfield, N.S.W.), 203-5, 209
SANIYEH (Map p. 4), 6
SANNIYAT (Map p. 17), 12, 13
SAVY (Map p. 179), 177, 181, 182, 213, 222

SCARPE, RIVER (Map p. 220), 214, 222, 224, 225, 226, 230, 241, 350, 351, 353
SCHAFER, Lt. P. K. (b. Ascot Vale, Vic.), 225, 437, 438
SCHELDT RIVER, 174, 326, 352, 373, 375, 377, 383
SCHMARJE, Lt., 75
SCOBIE, Lt. C. S., 296
SCOTT, Lt. F. J. (b. Korumburra, Vic.), 222, 231, 236, 239, 437, 438
SCOTT, Lt. W. N. E. (of Elsternwick, Vic.; b. Elsternwick), 199
SCOUTING, methods of, 253
S.E.5's (Plates pp. 215, 234), 400; No. 2 Sqn. equipped with, 197*n*
SEARLE, Lt. A. H. (of Hampton, Vic.; b. Bendigo, Vic.), 72, 73
SEA TRANSPORT, *see* TRANSPORTS
SEBUSTIE (Map p. 137; Sk. p. 89), 98
SECLIN (Map p. 355), 350, 365
SELEUCIA (Map p. 17), 18, 22
SELLE, RIVER, 335
SEMAKH (Map p. 137), 141, 165
SENUSSI, 33, 36, 37
SEQUEDIN, 363
SARS–GUEUDECOURT ROAD, LE, 438
SERAPEUM, 54
SERNY (Map p. 179), 344, 370
SEWELL, Lt. F. A. (of Kew, Vic.; b. Caulfield, Vic.), 261, 262, 263, 268, 310, 315, 322, 326
SHAIBA (Map p. 4), 6; Battle of, 7
SHAMAL, THE, 9, 11
SHAPIRA, Lt. F. C. (of Sydney; b. Stepney, London), 177
SHARON, BATTLE OF, 155, 156-8, 159-62
SHATT-EL-ARAB (Map p. 4), 3, 6
SHATT-EL-HAI (Maps pp. 4, 17), 16
SHEBAB, TEL ESH, 163
SHEIKH ABBAS RIDGE, 60, 62
SHEIKH HASAN, 79
SHEIKH NURAN, WELI (Maps pp. 42, 78), 50, 51, 52, 56, 57, 61, 75, 77, 89
SHEIKH SAAD (Map p. 17), 15, 28
SHEIKH ZOWAIID (Map p. 42), 50, 52

INDEX

SHELDON, Maj. W. (of Melbourne; b. Singapore), commands No. 2 Sqn., 69; mentioned, 32, 35, 36, 175
SHELLAL (Map p. 78), 52, 56
SHELLEY, Lt. M. R. (of Hunter's Hill, N.S.W.; b. Gladesville, N.S.W.), 316, 328, 335
SHEPPARD, Lt. G. W. (b. Murrumbeena, Vic.), 135, 138, 141
SHEPPARD, Lt. V. G. M. (of Emu Plains, N.S.W.; b. Emu Plains), 354, 359
SHERAF, DEIR (Map p. 137; Sk. p. 130), 155, 157
SHERIA, TEL EL (Map p. 78), 52, 58, 60, 61, 63, 66, 79, 83; airmen raid, 56-8; see also GAZA (THIRD BATTLE)
SHERIKA (Map p. 34), 36
SHERT, UMM ESH (Maps pp. 101, 137), 115, 119
SHIBLEH, AIN (Maps pp. 137, 160), 159
SHIBLEH–BEISAN ROAD, 161
SHIERS, Lt. W. H. (b. Norwood, S. Aust.), accompanies Ross Smith in flight to Australia, 387, 388-92
SHOBEK, EL, 149
SHUNET NIMRIN (Map p. 101), 100, 105, 112, 114, 115, 119, 162; British and Australian airmen raid, 103, 106; Turkish camp at, bombed, 108; German airmen bomb troops at, 110
SHUSHA (Map p. 34), 37
SIGNALLING, during artillery-ranging, 435-6; by flares, 94, 308, 317, 318; by klaxon horns, 139n, 308; by wireless on aeroplanes, 280-2, 308, 314, 427-9
SIMONSON, Capt. E. L. (of Melbourne; b. Brighton, Vic.), 341, 363, 367, 371, 377, 380, 381
SIMPSON, Lt. T. L. (of Hamilton, Vic.; b. Hamilton), 249, 250
SIMS, Lt. P. J. (of Springhurst, Vic.; b. Springhurst), 362, 378
SINAI CAMPAIGN, see MAGDHABA, RAFA, SUEZ CANAL
SINCLAIR, Lt. K. L., 282
SINGAPORE, 391, 393
SINGORA, 391, 396
SINN, Es (Map p. 17), 12, 13, 14, 15, 24

SIR, AIN ES, 117, 119, 142, 147, 153, 162, 166
SIR, WADY ES, 112
SIWA (Map p. 34), 37
SLOANE, Air-Mechanic W. D. (b. Mulwala, N.S.W.), 177
SLOSS, 11 Flight-Sgt. J. McK. (of Malvern, Vic.; b. Naring, Vic.), 25-6; attempts escape from captivity, 26-7
SMALLWOOD, Lt. R. G. (b. Ballina, N.S.W.), 282, 296, 341, 344
SMITH, Capt. F. R. (b. Brisbane), 254, 292, 297, 339, 354, 359-60, 363, 366, 368, 371, 372, 373, 384
SMITH, Lt. J. L. (of Sydney; b. Darlinghurst, N.S.W.), 312
SMITH, Lt. Sir K. (b. Adelaide), flies to Australia, 387, 388-92
SMITH, Lt. L. H. (of Hurstville, N.S.W.; b. Cardiff, Wales), 131, 155
SMITH, Laurence Yard, quoted, xxi
SMITH, Capt. Sir Ross M. (b. Adelaide), quoted, 129-30; flies to Australia, 387, 388-92; killed, 392n; mentioned, 51, 54, 59, 75, 94, 98, 106, 113, 122 et seq., 135, 136, 139, 148, 152, 155, 158n, 164, 169, 409
SMITH, Capt. Winfield, 26
SMOKE SCREENS, 314, 331
SNELL, Lt. P. W., 57, 58
SOISSONS (Sk. p. 241), xxvii, 174, 241, 258, 264n, 276
SOLEY, 10 Cpl. T. (b. Eltham, Eng.), 26
SOMME RIVER (Map p. 311), 30, 211, 243, 248, 249, 255, 256, 260 et seq., 268, 269, 270, 271, 305, 307, 309, 310, 326, 337, 338, 340, 341; Battles of the, 1916, 173; First Battles of the, 1918, 228-42, German objectives, 237, German advance arrested, 240-2; Second Battles of the, 1918, 313-7, 319-24, see also PÉRONNE, ST. QUENTIN (MONT)
SOPWITH SNIPES (Plate p. 214), No. 4 Sqn. equipped with, 370, 408
SOPWITH, T. O. M., 406
SOURABAYA, 391, 393, 396

SOYÉCOURT, 316
SPRAGG, Lt. E. L. (of Morven, Q'land; b. Sydney), 117
STEELE, Lt. N. L. (b. Kew, Vic.), 61, 62, 63, 73
STEELE, Capt. R. C., 76
STEENWERCK (Map p. 279), 293, 352
STONE, Lt. C. O. (b. Chingford, Eng.), 294, 297, 304, 354, 367, 373, 376, 380, 381
STONES, Lt. G. C. (of Matlock, Eng.; b. Wisbech, Eng.), 63
STOOKE, Lt. E. C. (b. Hawthorn, Vic.), 114, 123, 126, 127
STORES, in sqn. repair shops, 440; *see also* EQUIPMENT, SUPPLIES
STORRER, Capt. H. H. (of Geelong, Vic.; b. Geelong), 199
STRANGE, Lt.-Col. L. A. (of Blandford, Eng.; b. Tarrant, Eng.), 346, 347, 379, 381
STREETER, Lt. H. (b. Brunswick, Vic.), 210
STURGEON, Lt. H. A. J. (b. Brighton, Eng.), 272, 305, 320, 322, 332
SUDA BAY, 387, 389
SUDR, AIN (Map p. 42), 54
SUESS, Lt. O. H. (b. Brisbane), 260
SUEZ (Map p. 42), 33, 36, 40, 42, 52, 53, 54
SUEZ CANAL (Map p. 42), 31, 33, 36, 38; Turkish attack on, 1915, 52, 53n; defences of, 54, 63
SUK-ESH-SHEYUKH (Map p. 4), 10; captured, 9
SULLIVAN, Lt. E. (b. Carlton, Vic.), 150
SULTANE, WADY ES, 135
SUMATRA, 391
SUMRAH, 154
SURAB, UM ES (Sk. p. 163), 162, 164, 165
SURAR, WADY ES (Map p. 78), 82, 83, 84, 85
SUTHERLAND, Lt. L. W. (of Murrumbeena, Vic.; b. Murrumbeena), 96, 127, 135, 140, 142, 152, 165
SUWEILE, 118, 119, 162
SUZANNE, 240, 314, 315
SYKES, Maj.-Gen. Sir F. H., 397; *quoted*, xx, xxii$n$

SYMONS, Lt. P. W. (of Maitland, S. Aust.; b. Moonta, S. Aust.), 383
SYRIA, 162, 169

TACTICS, air fighting, xvi-xvii, comparison of, with naval, xix, of two-seater and single-seater machines, 122n; in formations, 223, 224, 448-9; on eve of offensive, 255-6
TAFILE, ET (Map p. 101), 105, 106, 124; Hejaz capture, 92
TAIT, Lt. J. B. (of Melbourne; b. Geelong, Vic.), 332
TAIYIBEH, ET (Map p. 137), 114
TAMMUN, JEBEL, 159
TANKS, 61, 191, 274; at First Battle of Cambrai, 183, 184; attack Hindenburg Line, 331-2
TANNER, Maj. F. I., 288
TAPLIN, Lt. L. T. E. (of Parramatta, N.S.W.; b. Unley, S. Aust.), *quoted*, 357-9; mentioned, 93, 94, 296, 297, 299-300, 303, 304, 338, 340, 341, 353, 354, 356
TARANTO, 389, 393
TARBANE, 140
TARRANT, Lt. F. J. (of Clifton Hill, Vic.; b. Carlton, Vic.), 210
TAURUS MOUNTAINS, prisoners work on railway through, 26
TAYLOR, Lt. A. L. D. (b. Williamstown, Vic.), 261, 265
TAYLOR, Lt. H. (b. Birmingham, Eng.), at First Battle of Cambrai, 185-8; mentioned, 191-2, 193, 195
TAYLOR, Lt. T. (b. Lucknow, Vic.), 71
TEKRIT, 28
THEMADA, BIR EL (Map p. 42), 54, 55
THÉROUANNE, 259
THIEPVAL, 261
THOMPSON, Lt. W. C. (of Abbotsford, Vic.; b. Abbotsford), 143
THOMSON, Lt. B. G. (of Kapunda, S. Aust.; b. Kapunda), 306, 309, 310, 315, 316, 334
THORNTON, Lt. V. H. (b. Valparaiso, S. America), 362, 370-1, 378
TIBERIAS, LAKE (Maps pp. 137, 170), 141, 143, 159, 162, 167

INDEX

TIGRIS EXPEDITIONARY FORCE, command, 5

TIGRIS, RIVER (Maps pp. 4, 17), xxv, 6, 7, 10n, 16, 18, 21, 30; difficulties of navigation on, 28

TIMOR, 389, 392

TIMOR SEA, 393

TINCOURT (Map p. 321), 322, 324, 325

TINE, ET (Map p. 78), 83, 84, 85; German aerodrome at, destroyed, 80

TIRE, ET, 136, 153

TOMBELLE, 380

TONKIN, Lt. A. V. (of Glenferrie, Vic.; b. Avenel, Vic.), 98, 120, 122, 123, 124-5, 138, 139, 143, 149, 154

TOURCOING (Map p. 179), 373

TOURNAI (Map p. 374), 341, 353, 365, 366, 376, 377, 380, 381; airmen raid, 367-8; air-fights over, 373-5, 377-8

TOWNSHEND, Maj.-Gen. Sir C. V. F., commands 6 Indian Div., 7; invested in Kut, 24; mentioned, xxv, 12, 13, 14, 18, 21, 29, 390

TRAILL, Lt. J. H. (b. Bligh, N.S.W.), 114, 123, 124, 138, 139, 144-5, 153, 163, 164

TRAINING, of A.F.C., in Australia, 1, 32-3, 426, Egypt, 35, 42, England, 175, 176, 430-3

TRAINS, raided by British and Australian airmen, 293-4, 356, 363, 383, 384; see also RAILWAYS

TRANSPORT, difficulties of, on Tigris, 28; German, destroyed, 236, 301; Turkish, destroyed, 161; see also RAILWAYS

TRANSPORTS: *Bankura*, 3; *Kaisar-i-Hind*, 385; *Morea*, 3; *Omrah*, 425; *Orsova*, 32; *Ulysses*, 3

TRELOAR, Lt. W. H. (of Albert Park, Vic.; b. Fairfield Park, Vic.), captured, 12; mentioned, 2, 3, 9, 27

TRENCHARD, Air-Marshal Sir H. M., his admiration for No. 2 Sqn., 188

TRENCHES, see FORTIFICATIONS

TRESCOWTHICK, Lt. N. C. (b. Clifton Hill, Vic.), 294, 295, 296,

TRESCOWTHICK, Lt. N. C.—*contd*. 299, 302, 303, 338, 339-40, 347, 353, 356, 357, 358, 379, 437, 438

TRIPOLI (Map p. 170), 169

TROUVILLE, 263

TUBAS (Map p. 160), 156

TUL KERAM (Plate p. 155; Map p. 137; Sks. pp. 89, 154), 66, 90, 96, 98, 113, 114, 122, 126, 130, 138, 140, 141, 144, 152, 153; airmen raid, 86-7; captured, 154

TUNBRIDGE, Lt. J. V. (b. Ballarat, Vic.), 57, 63, 65

TUNBRIDGE, Capt. W. B. (b. Ballarat, Vic.), 233, 236, 277, 278, 438, 439

TURKEY, enters war, 6; boundary between Egypt and, 51

TURKISH ARMY, strength of, at Kutaniyeh, 18; dispositions of corps in Palestine, *Dec.* 1917, 90; final retreat of, *Sep.-Oct.* 1918, 152-71
—YILDERIM ARMY GROUP, 80
—FOURTH ARMY, 81, 115, 151; airmen bomb H.Q. of, 66; its ignorance of situation, 20 *Sep.* 1918, 158; in retreat, 22-24 *Sep.*, 162, 165-8
—SEVENTH ARMY, 151, 168; its ignorance of situation, 19-20 *Sep.* 1918, 154, 157-8; its lines of retreat closed, 20 *Sep.*, 157, 158; destroyed as a fighting force, 21 *Sep.*, 158-61
—EIGHTH ARMY, 84, 134, 151, 168; retreat of, *Sep.-Oct.* 1918, 153-6
—II CORPS, surrenders, 168
—III CORPS, 90
—XX CORPS, 90
—XXII CORPS, 90
—45TH DIVISION, at Battle of Ctesiphon, 24
—53RD DIVISION, commander of, captured, 59n
—ARTILLERY, see ARTILLERY (TURKISH)
—CAVALRY, 24; at First Gaza, 60, Second Gaza, 63

TURKISH FLYING CORPS, *No.* 14 *Squadron*, 81; see also GERMAN AIR FORCE

INDEX

TURKS, at variance with Germans, 128
TURNER, Lt. V. P. (b. Digby, N.S.W.), 37, 44, 45, 46, 54, 61
TWINS (MESSINES), THE, 203

UMBRELLA HILL (GAZA), 79
UMTAIYE, EL, 162, 163
UNITED STATES, see AMERICA

VAIRE WOOD, 262, 268
VALENCIENNES (Map p. 179), 352, 375
VARNA, 28
VAULX-BEUGNÂTRE ROAD, 438
VAULX-BEUGNY ROAD, 438
VAULX-LAGNICOURT ROAD, 438
VAULX-VRAUCOURT (Plate p. 231; Map p. 189), 231, 233, 234, 236, 438
VAUTIN, Lt. C. H., (of Perth, W. Aust.; b. Warracknabeal, Vic.), 71-2, 73
VAUVILLERS, 312, 315
VELU, 437
VERDUN, 30, 172, 173
VERGUIER, LE, 229, 326
VICTORIA CROSS, awarded to Capt. McNamara, 59n
VIEILLE CHAPELLE (Maps pp. 279, 355), 242, 244, 338
VIEUX BERQUIN (Map p. 279), 277, 289
VILLERS-AU-FLOS (Map p. 189), 437
VILLERS-BRETONNEUX (Maps pp. 179, 311), 241, 248, 249, 262, 265, 276, 305, 315; re-captured by Australians, 263
VILLERS-GUISLAIN, 195
VILLE-SUR-ANCRE, 6 Inf. Bde. attacks and captures, 267
VIMY RIDGE (Map. p. 220), 174, 232, 243
Voss, Lt., 215, 248
VYNER, Lt. C. J. (of Walcha, N.S.W.; b. Harrogate, Eng.), 97, 117, 120, 131-2, 143, 149

WACKETT, Maj. L. J. (of Townsville, Q'land; b. Townsville), 37, 38-9, 43, 44, 45, 48, 272n, 316, 328
WALKER, Lt. J. M. (b. Grenville, Vic.), 111, 139, 141, 144, 443

WARD, Lt. L. N. (b. Walkerville, S. Aust.), 185
WARFUSÉE-ABANCOURT (Map p. 189), 309
WARLOY, 178
WARNETON (Map p. 279), 202
WATER-SUPPLY, lack of, its effect on Magdhaba and Rafa engagements, 50; at Beersheba, 79
WATSON, Capt. H. G. (of Sydney; b. Caversham, N.Z.), 278, 282, 284 et seq., 295-6, 298, 338, 340, 347, 359, 438
WATT, Lt. C. N. (of St. Kilda, Vic.; b. Melbourne), 106
WATT, Lt.-Col. W. O. (of Sydney; b. Bournemouth, Eng.), commands No. 2 Sqn., 69; estimate and biography of, 41-2; quoted, 176n; mentioned, vii, 35, 175, 178
WAVRIN (Maps pp. 279, 355), 294, 341, 347, 364
WEATHER, in Mesopotamia, 8-9; in Palestine, Jan. 1918, 96, Mar.-Apr., 110; on Western Front, Nov. 1917, 198, winter, 1917-18, 205, Jan.-Feb. 1918, 214, Apr., 249, 261, May, 255, June, 259, 288, July-Aug., 291, 302, 307, 350, Sep., 326, 359, Oct.-Nov., 371, 375, 380; dust, 49, prevents flying, Mar. 1917, 58; fog: at First Gaza, 59, First Battle of Cambrai, 184, 192, 193, 194-5, at opening of German offensive, 1918, 225-6, over the Somme, 24 Apr., 262-3, at Armentières, 11 May, 280, over the Lys, 7 July, 294, at opening of Battle of Amiens, 309, in Battles of Hindenburg Line, 29 Sep., 331; rain: in Palestine, Jan. 1917, 49, prevents flying, Dec., 89, on Western Front, July 1918, 305, 306, Sep., 326-7, 330, 332
WEBSTER, Lt. F. W., 280
WEINGARTH, Lt. J. H. (of Darling Point, Sydney; b. Marrickville, N.S.W.), 278, 301
WEIR, Lt. W. J. A. (b. Leichhardt, N.S.W.), 123, 126, 129, 130, 136, 138, 140, 143, 144, 155, 168

INDEX

WELLWOOD, Lt. J. J. (of Drouin, Vic.; b. Drouin), 294, 304, 313, 338, 350, 359, 363, 368, 380

WESTERN FRONT, 92, 121; the decisive theatre of the war, 29; situation on, in 1916, 30, in spring, 1918, 276; *résumé* of operations on, 1914-18, 172-5; German offensive on, *Mar.* 1918: 211, 228-46, German preparations, 221-2, 223, British preparations, 226, German objective, 237, arrested, 240-2

WEZ MACQUART (Maps pp. 279, 355), 354

WHARTON, Lt. L. (of Armidale, N.S.W.; b. Parkes, N.S.W.), 341

WHITE, Field-Marshal Sir George S., V.C., 404

WHITE, Capt. T. W. (of Melbourne; b. North Melbourne), *quoted*, 3-5, 8n, 25-7; narrowly escapes capture, 19; captured, 21-2; escapes from captivity, 27-8; mentioned, vii, 1, 2, 7, 10, 12, 16, 18, 20

WHIZZ FARM (MESSINES), 203

WILKINS, Capt. G. H. (of Adelaide; b. Mount Bryan East, S. Aust.), attempts flight to Australia, 387

WILKINSON, Lt. H. A., 379, 383

WILKINSON, Lt. J. C. F., 297, 298, 339

WILLIAMS, Lt. D. R. (b. Wodonga, Vic.), attempts flight to Australia, 387

WILLIAMS, 16 Air-Mechanic L. T. (b. Fitzroy, Vic.), 26

WILLIAMS, Lt.-Col. R. (of Moonta, S. Aust.; b. Moonta), *quoted*, 33, 71-2, 158n; at Nekhl, 54-5, Sheria, 56-7; mentioned, vii, 1, 32, 35, 36, 37, 38, 44, 46, 50, 52, 56, 63, 64, 65n, 79, 133n

WILLMOTT, Lt. F. B. (b. Adelaide), 214

WILSON, Capt. G. C. (b. Minnie, Eng.), *quoted*, 186-8; mentioned, 177, 184, 192, 193, 194, 196

WINGLES, 223, 224

WINTER-IRVING, Capt. S. I. (b. Melbourne), 69

WIRELESS TELEGRAPHY, *see* SIGNALLING

WITCOMB, Lt. O. G. (of Port Wakefield, S. Aust.; b. Yacka, S. Aust.), 312, 319

WOLFF, Lt., 215

WOOD, Capt. A. H. O'Hara, 213, 214, 216, 217, 221

WOOD, Maj. H. F., 408

WOOLHOUSE, Lt. F. S. (of Perth, W. Aust.; b. Roebourne, W. Aust.), 217, 222, 244

WOUNDED, *see* CASUALTIES

WRIGHT BROS., xxi, 412

WRIGHT, Lt. B. W., 278

WRIGHT, Capt. J. W. (of Wahroonga, N.S.W.; b. Quirindi, N.S.W), 239, 353, 359, 364, 438

WYTSCHAETE (Map p. 179), 183, 210, 278, 285, 290

WYTSCHAETE RIDGE, 203

YEATS-BROWN, Capt. F. C. C. (b. Genoa, Italy), narrowly escapes capture, 19; captured, 21-2; mentioned, 20, 27

YELLEG, GEBEL, 53

YEOMANRY, *see* BRITISH ARMY

YILDERIM ARMY GROUP, *see* TURKISH ARMY

YOUDALE, Lt. R. H. (of Burwood, N.S.W.; b. Burwood), 297, 298, 362

YPRES (Plate p. 195; Map p. 179; Sk. p. 241), 172, 177, 198, 211, 233, 241, 277, 280, 282, 337, 361, 362; Third Battle of, 174, 177, 183-4, 345, 346n; Battle of, 1918, 352, No. 4 Sqn. at, 364-5

YPRES SALIENT, 277

YUNIS, KHAN, 45, 59

ZABIRANI, WADY, 168

ZEIMER, WADY (Sk. p. 154), 154

ZERKA, KALAAT EZ (Sk. p. 163), 113

ZERKA, NAHR EZ, 109, 110, 132

ZEPPELINS, xxi

ZEUR (Map p. 17), 22; Turkish advanced positions at, 16, 18, 19

ZILLEBEKE, 282

By Authority: Albert J. Mullett, Government Printer, Melbourne.

www.ingramcontent.com/pod-product-compliance
Lightning Source LLC
Chambersburg PA
CBHW021823220426
43663CB00005B/111